The Political Economy of
Development and Underdevelopment

The Political Economy of Development and Underdevelopment

Second Edition

Edited by

Charles K. Wilber

University of Notre Dame

Random House New York

For my parents, who helped me to see
  and to understand . . .
For my wife, who hasn't let me forget . . .
For my children, who in turn, I hope,
  will see and understand. . . .

I have a dream that one day every valley shall be exalted,
every hill and mountain shall be made low, the rough
places will be made plain, and the crooked places will
be made straight, and the glory of the Lord shall be
revealed, and all flesh shall see it together.

Martin Luther King, Jr.
The March on Washington
August 1963

Second Edition
98765432
Copyright © 1973, 1979 by Random House, Inc.

Library of Congress Cataloging in Publication Data

Wilber, Charles K.   comp.
  The political economy of development and underdevelopment.
  Bibliography: p.
  1. Economic development—Addresses, essays,
lectures. I. Title.
HD82.W525 1978   330.9′172′4   78–16805

ISBN: 0-394-32230-4

Manufactured in the United States of America
Cover design by Ira Hechtlinger

preface to the
second edition

During the late 1960s and early 1970s the economic growth approach to economic development was being attacked. In addition, political economy was emerging with an alternative critique of underdevelopment. The first edition emphasized and promoted these two trends in the selection of articles reprinted and particularly in the new articles written expressly for the collection by Celso Furtado, Ronald Müller, and James Weaver.

By the last half of the 1970s the battle began to shift grounds. Almost everyone has conceded the validity of the attack upon the economic growth approach. Now the problem is to create alternative approaches. Both traditional economics and political economy have begun to do so. Many economists of traditional orientation, for instance Irma Adelman, have been constructing a variety of development strategies that can be grouped under the general heading of "growth with equity." Political economists have been building alternative strategies also. Just as the growth-with-equity people draw upon the experiences of Taiwan, South Korea, Singapore, Hong Kong, and Israel, the political economists have tended to generalize from the experience of countries such as China and Tanzania. The readings in the second edition, therefore, show less emphasis on criticism of the growth approach, and instead focus on these emerging alternatives.

Many people have given me valuable help in preparing this second edition. They provided critiques of the first edition, suggested new readings, and encouraged me to go ahead. I particularly want to thank James H. Weaver, The American University; Kenneth P. Jameson and Michael Francis, University of Notre Dame; Thomas E. Weisskopf, University of Michigan; Richard Du Boff, Bryn Mawr College; Michael Conroy, University of Texas; and Alain de Janvry, University of California, Berkeley. My graduate assistant, Robert Harrison, helped me prepare the introductions. My daughter, Alice Wilber, provided invaluable assistance in editing and typing. Her cheerfulness made the work seem much easier. Finally, I want to thank Paul Shensa of Random House for his continued support.

Charles K. Wilber
University of Notre Dame
June 1978

preface to the
first edition

Economists assume that the problem of a more human society is solved
by expertise, by know-how. Since they assume that the question of the
nature of a good society is already answered, the issue becomes one of
solving certain practical problems. The good society is simply assumed to
be an idealized version of the United States economy, that is, a consumer
society. The key to a consumer society is growth of per capita income.
Thus the vast bulk of the development literature has focused on growth
rates as the *deus ex machina* to solve all problems. Even much of the
socialist writing on development argues that the superiority of socialism
over capitalism lies in faster growth rates.

There is much to be said for this approach because some minimum
level of food, clothing, shelter, recreation, etc., is necessary before a person
can be free to be human. However, the emphasis on consumption and
growth of per capita income has not led to a decrease of poverty in the
underdeveloped world. If anything it has increased. A thin layer has
prospered while the vast majority of the population sinks ever deeper into
the backwater of underdevelopment. Therefore, during the past several
years a new look has been taken at the meaning of development. Dudley
Seers, Mahbub ul Haq, Ivan Illich, and others have questioned the emphasis
on chasing the consumption standards of the developed countries via
economic growth. Instead they argue for a direct attack on poverty
through employment and income redistribution policies. Denis Goulet and
Paulo Freire argue that development must include "liberation" from
oppression, cultural as well as political and economic.

Both of these positions have merit, and they are not necessarily
mutually exclusive. That is, the study of political economy should lead one
to ask whether stressing the importance of rapid economic growth has to
mean that the growth will consist of movies, bikinis, deodorants, key clubs,
and pollution. An analysis of political economic systems should lead one to
see why growth has meant luxuries being produced for some while others
go hungry.

This book is about economic development and underdevelopment, and
is designed to be used with a standard textbook in advanced undergraduate
and beginning graduate courses. The readings emphasize the *political
economy* rather than the narrowly *economic* approach and issues.

Many of the readings are excellent examples of radical political economy. Political economy recognizes that man is a social being whose arrangements for the production and distribution of economic goods must be, if society is to be livable, consistent with congruent institutions of family, political, and cultural life. As a result, a political economy analysis must incorporate such noneconomic influences as social structures, political systems, and cultural values as well as such factors as technological change and the distribution of income and wealth. The readings are radical in the sense that they are willing to question and evaluate the most basic institutions and values of society.

While I hope that the work presented here is objective, there is no artificial stance of neutrality. I am committed to certain values that undoubtedly influence the choice of questions asked and the range of variables considered for selection. In general, my system of values posits material progress (at least up to some minimum level), equality, cooperation, democratic control of economic as well as political institutions, and individual freedom as positive goods. It should be noted that there may be contradictions among these criteria, and thus society is faced with choices. With these values in mind the reader can judge the degree of objectivity attained.

It is a pleasure to acknowledge my indebtedness to those who have helped me shape my ideas on economic development and underdevelopment. First of all I want to thank Professors W. Michael Bailey, James H. Weaver, Celso Furtado, Branko Horvat, E. J. Mishan, Ronald Müller, Brady Tyson, Albert Waterston, and Irving Louis Horowitz—critics, colleagues, and friends. Some of my greatest debts are to those whom I know only through their writings—Karl Polanyi and R. H. Tawney. Their example of scholarship and social commitment has been a guide and inspiration. I want to thank Sandy Kelly for her invaluable help in editing and typing, and Bob Devlin for his assistance in research and editing. Barbara Conover and Nancy Perry, editors at Random House, have been invaluable in seeing the book through to publication.

My greatest debt, however, in this as in all my endeavors, is to my wife, Mary Ellen, and our children: Kenneth, Teresa, Matthew, Alice, Mary, Angela, and Louie. I owe all to their love and encouragement.

Charles K. Wilber
Washington, D.C.
September 1973

contents

part one

Methodological Problems of Economic Development

economists have traditionally measured the level of "economic development" in terms of per capita Gross National Product (GNP). In the past few years serious doubt has been cast upon the validity of this measuring rod. Many countries—Brazil, Pakistan, and even Mexico—have had rapid growth rates in per capita GNP while unemployment and the level of poverty of the mass of the population have remained unchanged or even increased. The underlying thesis of this book is that economists have misconceived the nature of the main challenge of the last quarter of the twentieth century. The challenge is not to achieve high growth rates of per capita GNP but to reduce poverty, unemployment, and inequality.

In the first article Peter Henriot summarizes the old economic growth strategy and explores alternative approaches to the topic of development. He focuses on three questions: (1) What are the alternatives to defining the *problems* faced in development? (2) What are the alternatives to proposing the *strategies* to be followed in development? (3) What are the alternatives to specifying the *values* guiding development?

While the first article in this section focuses on the problems and implications of adopting a particular meaning of development, the next three articles all confront, though from different angles, the problem of using traditional economic theory as the main tool for analyzing the process of development. A distinction should be made between economic growth, which is analyzed in terms of changes in the value of economic parameters in given institutional conditions, and economic development, in which changes in the value of economic parameters are accompanied or even preceded by institutional changes. Traditional economic theory is a more efficient instrument for analysis of economic growth since long-run factors of a sociopolitical nature may be held constant. Economic development, however, is a process that affects not only economic relations but also the entire social, political, and cultural fabric of society. In the dynamic world of economic development, the variables usually impounded in *ceteris paribus* are in constant motion as factors making for change.

Keith Griffin points out that most of the theorizing on economic development has been done by economists who live in and were trained in the developed countries of the West. Most have suffered from two serious handicaps—"lack of knowledge about the broad historical forces associated with underdevelopment and ignorance of the institutions, behavior responses and ways of life of the largest sector within the underdeveloped countries, the rural areas." Griffin maintains that this ignorance coupled with traditional economic theory has produced theories of development that are inappropriate to the realities of underdevelopment. His article focuses on the theories of the dual economy developed by W. Arthur Lewis, Ranis and Fei, and others, and questions the reality of their assumptions and the empirical validity of their conclusions.

Warren Ilchman and Ravindra Bhargava argue that the major development strategies—"Big Push" balanced growth, unbalanced growth, and capital formation through unlimited supplies of labor—advanced by Ragnar Nurkse, Albert Hirschman, and W. Arthur Lewis are relevant operationally only in highly specific situations. These situations are defined by crucial political, sociological, and administrative factors, as well as economic ones. Ilchman and Bhargava analyze these development strategies in terms of the major social problems that might arise from undertaking them and the political regime and administrative systems they presuppose.

The last article in this part utilizes the issue of population control to illustrate the value-laden nature of economic theory. Most hypotheses in economics are incapable of rigorous falsification because of data problems and the use of *ceteris paribus* clauses. As a result, hypotheses congenial to the prevalent ideological biases (for example, Malthusian population theory) maintain their standing in economic development theory despite their lack of empirical support.

It is preferable to think of the concepts of economic theory (whether traditional or Marxian) as ways to organize chaotic material into coherent patterns rather than as formal scientific laws of empirical reality. The real test, therefore, of an economic concept or theory is its usefulness in illuminating the process of development and underdevelopment; its ability to survive some formal verification procedure is of much less importance.

Many of the readings in this book utilize, explicitly or implicitly, the concept of the economic or social surplus as a means of highlighting certain aspects of the development process. The concept of the social surplus was widely used by the classical writers. Adam Smith labeled it the "surplus part of the produce" and David Ricardo as the "net produce." John Stuart Mill defined it as the "surplus of the produce of labour . . . the fund from which the enjoyments, as distinguished from the necessities, of the producers are provided . . . from which all are subsisted, who are not themselves engaged in production; and from which all additions are made to capital."[1] In view of the value connotation associated with Karl Marx's use of the concept of "surplus value" and the attendant concept of "rate of exploitation," later economists discarded it completely. The social product was viewed in terms of "cost of factors," savings being no longer conceived as the result of an existing social surplus but as the result of an act of "abstinence" or "waiting." But as the contemporary developmental economist Celso Furtado points out, "from the point of view of the theory of development, in which the accumulation process acquires great importance, there is some convenience in coming back to the classic concept of the surplus, leaving aside . . . any intimation of moral values."[2]

The social surplus may be viewed as a residual factor—that which remains from total output after necessary consumption has been subtracted. In every organization of society, past or present, the total annual production of goods and services may be divided into two parts—the necessary subsistence of the population and a surplus that may be either consumed or saved in the form of additions to the country's stock of capital. Of course, the level of necessary consumption may be expected to vary from country to country and from time to time. However, for studying the process of development, this variation should cause no serious difficulties.

It is essential to differentiate between the two variants of the concept of social surplus.[3] The first variant is the *actual social surplus*—the difference between a country's *actual* current production and its *actual* current consumption. The second variant is the *potential social surplus*—the difference between the output that *could* be produced in a given natural and technological environment and what might be regarded as necessary consumption.

In the context of economic development, the realization of the potential social surplus would presuppose a somewhat drastic reorganization of the production and distribution of output and probably involve extensive changes in the social structure of a country. There are three factors that affect difference between the potential and the actual social surplus. First, part of the potential surplus is used to support the excess consumption of the upper-income groups in the society. Second, development-conducive output is lost to society because there are many unproductive workers. Third, output is lost because of irrationality and wastefulness of the prevailing economic and social organization.

The main factors of economic development have to do with the size and distribution of the social surplus. Thus, a development strategy must be examined in terms of its impact on the size and utilization of the surplus. In each of the succeeding parts of this book, the concept of social surplus is utilized by various authors as a tool (in combination with other concepts) in their analysis of underdevelopment and development.

1. ADAM SMITH, *The Wealth of Nations* (New York: The Modern Library, 1937), p. 17; DAVID RICARDO, *On the Principles of Political Economy and Taxation*, Vol. I, *The Works and Correspondence of David Ricardo*, ed. Piero Sraffa (Cambridge: Cambridge University Press, 1951), p. 391; JOHN STUART MILL, *Principles of Political Economy*, ed. Sir W. J. Ashley (London: Longmans, Green and Company, 1929), pp. 163-164.

2. CELSO FURTADO, *Development and Underdevelopment* (Berkeley: University of California Press, 1964), p. 79.

3. PAUL A. BARAN, "Economic Progress and Economic Surplus," *Science and Society*, Vol. XVII, No. 4 (Fall 1953), pp. 289-317. See also his *The Political Economy of Growth* (New York: Monthly Review Press), pp. 22-43. Baran differentiates a third meaning of surplus—planned surplus—that is unimportant for our purposes.

1

Development Alternatives: Problems, Strategies, Values

Peter J. Henriot

INTRODUCTION

To speak of "development" today is to undertake an especially difficult task. In recent years, the entire field of development has been in considerable disarray, both theoretical and practical. The "conventional wisdom" of the 1960s has by and large been discredited, as theories which were expected to guide dramatic improvements in the lot of the world's poor have proved ineffective or even counter-productive. The "success stories" of several developing countries have turned out, over a longer period of time and under more stringent analysis, to be less than successful in human terms. And the nations of Latin America, Asia, and Africa—the so-called "Third World"— have posed increasingly serious challenges to the industrialized nations. The "North/South" confrontation has replaced the "East/West" confrontation as the most dangerous threat to world peace. The meaning and implications of development is a major key to that confrontation.

. . .

[I]t is . . . critical that we have a better understanding of precisely what we mean when we speak of "development." It is to this task that the current paper addresses itself.

Because the author of this paper is a political scientist and not an economist, the emphasis here will be more on a policy analysis of the meaning of development than on a strictly economic analysis of models and theories. The approach taken here will be to explore a series of alternative ways of approaching the topic. "Alternatives" must be spoken of because there is no "one way" of explaining what is meant by development. The focus of this paper, then, will be on three questions:

1. What are the alternatives to defining the *problems* of development?
2. What are the alternatives to proposing *strategies* faced in development?
3. What are the alternatives to specifying the *values* guiding development?

No effort is made to be exhaustive in examining alternatives, but simply to offer a few approaches in hopes of clarifying the overall topic.

Reprinted by permission from the *Occasional Population Papers* series of the Cultural Values and Population Policy Project, January 1976, © Institute of Society, Ethics and the Life Sciences, Hastings-on-Hudson, New York, 10706.

I
ALTERNATIVES: THE PROBLEMS FACED

It is clear that the manner in which a problem is defined has much to do with the possible solutions which can be suggested. In the alternative definitions suggested in what follows, it is not possible to make any completely exclusive distinctions since the various definitions overlap. Rather what is being pointed to is the *emphasis* made in each way of defining the problem. This emphasis—whether on what will be called here "capitalization," "marginality," or "dependency"—determines the priorities given certain programs and policies over others, the measurements of success employed, and the relationship of individual nations to the international order among nations.

A. "Capitalization" and the First Development Decade

In the first alternative definition of the problem faced in development, focus is upon the standard measurement of gross national product per capita (GNP/capita). This represents the total economic worth of goods and services produced, divided by the number of people in the country. The standard measurement utilized by the World Bank for dividing the world into sectors is GNP/capita. In general, those nations with a GNP/capita of more than $1,000 are considered "developed" countries, while those below that figure are "less developed" countries (LDCs). Some exceptions to this division do occur, however, notably in the instance of several of the nations which make up the OPEC bloc (Organization of Petroleum Exporting Countries).

When the degree of development is measured primarily in terms of GNP/capita, then the goal of increasing development—i.e., moving from a "less developed" to a "developed" stage—must be stimulation of the growth in GNP. The traditional theories of economic development relate increases in GNP growth to four major factors: capital accumulation, new resources (and/or new "frontiers"), technological progress, and population growth. The primary key to growth is seen to be capital accumulation, which permits increasing production through facilitating patterns of investment. In fact a cyclic pattern is used to describe the development process:

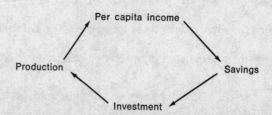

Essential to a healthy "development cycle" is the level of net savings and investment. Higgins describes the phenomenon as follows:

In the now advanced countries, net savings and investment during the periods of rapid growth averaged between 10 and 20 per cent of national income. In most, but not all of the now underdeveloped countries net savings and investment run between 5 and 10 per cent of the national income. Here is one of the many vicious circles encountered in any study of the problem of economic development. A high level of national income results in a high level of savings and investment, and consequently, in a rapid rate of economic growth. Underdeveloped countries in general have such low incomes that any substantial volume of savings and investment out of existing income is extremely difficult. To a large degree, the problem of economic growth is a problem of "getting over the hump" to the point where levels of per capita income are high enough to permit sufficient net savings and investment to guarantee continued expansion.[1]

Another way of describing the development process according to this strictly "economic model" has been offered by Rostow in his historical account of development in the industrialized West.[2] When *The Stages of Economic Growth* appeared in 1960, it presented an interpretation of the stages through which modern societies have evolved to their present levels. Rostow outlined five stages:

1. *Traditional society*—productivity limited because of insufficiently developed economic techniques.
2. *The preconditions for take-off*—development of a "leading sector" in the economy which positively influences other sectors; increase in agricultural productivity to support leading sector activities; improvements in transportation and other forms of social overhead capital.
3. *The take-off*—interval when the old blocks and resistances to steady growth are finally overcome and growth becomes normal condition for all sectors of society; main feature is increase in ratio of savings and investment to national income of 5 percent or less to 10 percent or more; also emergence of political, social, and institutional framework to facilitate impulses toward expansion.
4. *The drive to maturity*—long interval of sustained if fluctuating progress, with 10 to 20 percent of the national income steadily invested; new leading sectors supporting older ones.
5. *Age of high mass-consumption*—structural change no longer takes place at a rapid rate; leading sectors shift toward consumer goods and services.

Central to Rostow's "take-off" theory is the capital accumulation made possible by an increasing level of savings and investment.

Guided by the "conventional wisdom" underlying this economic model of development, great efforts were made in the 1960s to meet the problem of insufficient capitalization. The United Nations' First Development Decade (1960–1970) set a quantitative target of a 5 percent annual increase of GNP in the developing countries. Heavy industrialization was the instrument for achieving this growth rate, and large hydroelectric dams, steel mills, factories, etc., were promoted on a grand scale. In order to mount this effort, capital assistance from the rich countries was a necessity. Foreign aid was expected to fill the gap between the capital requirements for a take-off into sustained growth and the domestic capabilities for savings and investment. Hence, bi-lateral and multi-lateral programs and institutions for transfer of capital were strongly pushed during the 1960s, such as the U.S. Agency for International Development, the Alliance for Progress, the International Bank for Reconstruction and Development (World Bank), and the United Nations Development Program.

During the First Development Decade, a target was set for a transfer of public and private capital to developing countries equal to 1 percent of the GNP of the developed countries. Such a target was not met during the 1960s. In fact, the net flow of official development assistance from the industrialized countries declined from a total of 0.52 percent of GNP in 1960 to 0.34 percent in 1970, and continued slipping to 0.29 percent in 1975. (The comparable figures for the United States are 0.53, 0.31, and 0.20.)[3] Nevertheless, significant infusions of capital into the developing countries did take place.

It is important to note that in describing this particular definition of the problem of development which emphasizes capitalization, the nations which are developing are viewed more or less in isolation. Their difficulties are seen to be primarily internal, the results of local structures inadequate to the task of increasing GNP/capita. In a sense, their history of relationships—primarily colonial—with the industrialized Western nations is forgotten and the present-day implications of that history neglected.

B. "Marginality" and the Second Development Decade

Seen in historical perspective, the overall economic growth rate which has been experienced in the developing nations has been truly remarkable. "The 5 percent annual increase in gross national product achieved as a Third World average during the 1960s, and which was the quantitative target for the United Nations' First Development Decade, is roughly double the rate of economic growth achieved in nineteenth century Western Europe and North America."[4] In classical economic terms, such an outstanding increase could not help but be seen as an indication of significant "development." Yet by the end of the 1960s, it became more and more obvious that the "development" measured by per capita increase in GNP was not reaching the lives of ordinary people in terms of jobs, income distribution and basic alleviation of critical poverty.

One development economist put the issue in the following way:

> The questions to ask about a country's development are therefore: What has been happening to poverty? What has been happening to unemployment? What has been happening to inequality? If all three of these have declined from high levels, then beyond doubt this has been a period of development for the country concerned. If one or two of these central problems have been growing worse, especially if all three have, it would be strange to call the result "development," even if per capita income doubled.[5]

Stirred by questions such as these, another view of how to define the problem of development began to emerge. According to this view, the problem of development was not the degree of capitalization but the relationship any increase of GNP had to the poor—especially those poorest 40 percent of the population in the developing countries. These poorest 40 percent are the "marginals," people who neither contribute to the productivity of the nation nor share in the benefits of increased productivity. The arguments traditionally advanced to counter objections to growth models of development which do not directly benefit the poor have concentrated on the "trickle down" theory. Given sufficient prosperity in the upper sectors of society— in particular, among those who directly benefit from increased GNP growth —it is to be expected that benefits will flow to the lower classes because of increased employment, some redistributive tax measures, and the general health and stability of the economy. But as a matter of fact this benefit flow was not occurring in the developing countries during the 1960s. Quite the contrary was occurring, especially in the so-called "success stories" of Brazil, Mexico, and India, which had experienced very high rates of GNP growth during the 1960s. As Adelman notes, "Not only is there no automatic trickle-down of the benefits of development; on the contrary, the development process leads typically to a trickle-up in favor of the middle classes and the rich."[6]

The problem of the "marginals," exacerbated by development models which aimed chiefly at GNP/capita increase and which ignored distributive characteristics, was addressed directly by Robert McNamara before the Board of Governors of the World Bank Group meeting in Nairobi in 1973:

> The basic problem of poverty and growth in the developing world can be stated very simply. The growth is not equitably reaching the poor. And the poor are not significantly contributing to growth.
>
> Despite a decade of unprecedented increase in the gross national product of the developing countries, the poorest segments of their population have received relatively little benefit. Nearly 800 million individuals— 40% out of a total of two billion—survive on incomes estimated (in U.S. purchasing power) at 30 cents per day in conditions of malnutrition, illiteracy, and squalor. They are suffering poverty in the absolute sense.
>
> Although the collection of statistics on income distribution in the developing world is a relatively recent effort, and is still quite incomplete, the data point to what is happening. Among 40 developing countries for which data are available, the upper 20% of the population receives 55% of national income in the typical country, while the lowest 20% of the population receives 5%. That is a very severe degree of inequality—considerably greater than in most of the advanced countries.
>
> The data suggest that the decade of rapid growth has been accompanied by greater maldistribution of income in many developing countries, and that the problem is most severe in the countryside. There has been an increase in the output of mining, industry, and government—and in the incomes of the people dependent on these sectors—but the productivity and income of the small farmer have stagnated.
>
> One can conclude that policies aimed primarily at accelerating economic growth, in most developing countries, have benefitted mainly the upper 40% of the population and the allocation of public services and investment funds has tended to strengthen rather than to offset this trend.[7]

Recognition of the need to attend more closely to the social consequences of development has been assisted in recent years by what is called the "social indicators movement." This comprises efforts to devise non-economic measurements of the quality of life—such as education, health, housing, crime, social mobility, etc., as well as the utilization of economic measurements which indicate more distributive characteristics—such as income distribution, employment ratios, etc. The United Nations had devoted considerable research to these "social indicators" in recent years in comparative studies of developed and developing countries.[8]

When the strategy for the Second Development Decade of the United Nations (1970–1980) was devised, therefore, social goals were given explicit attention. These goals focused on the infrastructures of education, medical care, nutrition, and housing, as well as income distribution, land reform, and community organization. The repeated emphasis of the speeches of World Bank President McNamara has been on the social goals, and a "rethinking" of development has also influenced the direction of the U.S. Agency for International Development. The latter, for example, has been mandated, under the Foreign Assistance Act of 1973, to concentrate on assistance for agriculture, rural development, nutrition, health and population planning, education, and human resource development.[9]

This second definition of the problem of development, emphasizing "marginality," is similar to the first definition which emphasizes "capitalization," in that it also locates the problem primarily as *internal* to the developing countries. No effort is made in the analysis—or in the consequent policy response recommended—to place the problem in any kind of international context.

C. "Dependency" and the New International Economic Order

The first two alternatives in defining the problem of development look at the less developed country primarily in terms of its own internal structures. A growing number of analysts, however, particularly those from developing countries, prefer a definition of the problem which is more historical in its emphasis upon the evolving relationships between developed and developing countries. They see the focus of the problem not located principally within the developing world. For this group of development analysts, at issue is not so much the *quantity of economic growth* (according to the first alternative), or even the *quantity of social growth* (according to the second alternative), but the *quality of the process* by which the growth is achieved.[10]

Economic and social development is important, but the key question to be asked, according to the third alternative is: Who is controlling the development? To apply Paulo Freire's terminology of the educational process[11] to the international economic process, are the countries *objects* of development—at someone else's hands, or are they *subjects* of development—in control of their own destiny? Answers to this basic question give rise to the theories of "dependency" and of "underdevelopment." In one form or another these theories have become increasingly influential in Latin America and other Third World areas.

"Dependency" means that the major decisions which affect socioeconomic progress within less developed areas—decisions, for example, about commodity prices, investment patterns, monetary relationships—are made by individuals and institutions outside those countries. It is a situation "in which the economy of certain countries is conditioned by the development and expansion of another economy to which the former is subjected. . . . The concept of dependence permits us to see the internal situation of these countries as part of world economy."[12]

"Underdevelopment" is seen as the flip-side of the coin of "development."[13] It refers to the process whereby a country, characterized by subsistence agriculture and domestic production, progressively becomes integrated as a dependency into the world market through patterns of trade and/or investment. The production of that country thus becomes geared primarily to the demands of the world market, in particular the demands dictated by the industrialized nations, with a consequent lack of integration within the country between the various parts of its own domestic economy.

These theories of dependency and underdevelopment have been sketched in studies by Celso Furtado, Andre Gunder Frank, Theotonio Dos Santos, Fernando Henrique Cardoso, and others. All of them take seriously the colonial relationships which have historically marked the growth of the countries of Latin America, Africa, and Asia. They argue that outside of an explicit recognition of the consequences of that relationship no accurate understanding of the present situation of these countries is possible. For example, Furtado suggests three historical stages in the process of underdevelopment,[14] which can be summarized as follows:

1. **Comparative advantages.** During the period following the industrial revolution, when the system of the international division of labor was being created and a world economy was being structured, the industrialized countries by and large specialized in activities marked by a high degree of widespread technical progress. In other countries, however, domestic and international investment was either in sectors with minimum technology in the productive process (e.g., agricultural plantations oriented toward "cash crops") or in sectors wherein technical progress was isolated (e.g., in the "enclaves" controlled from outside which operated the mineral extractive industries). In both instances, there was little or no technological advance throughout the nation and the income benefits went mainly to a tiny minority. What resulted was the creation of a primary commodity exporting economy.

2. **Import substitution.** The formation of a small privileged social group within the underdeveloped nation gives rise to the necessity of importing numerous goods to meet the patterns of consumption which this group has adopted in imitation of the rich nations. But poor balance of payments and restrictive trade policies then in turn give rise to local manufacture of the same goods previously imported for consumption. Thus the production of consumer goods becomes strongly skewed toward the needs of the rich minority, income distribution patterns are affected because of the needs for heavy capital accumulation, and there evolves a dependency on imports for the means of production (technology, parts, etc.). In this way the ability of certain rich countries to control technical progress and to impose consump-

tion patterns becomes the decisive factor in structuring the productive apparatus of other countries—those which have become "dependent."

3. Multinational corporations. The rise of the multinational corporation (MNC) has become the most important phenomenon in the international economic order, as internal transactions of MNCs have replaced ordinary market operations. Investment in the manufacturing sector of the poor countries tends to be with capital-intensive, labor-saving technologies which accentuate unemployment problems and the maldistribution of income. The MNCs are dominant in the innovative sectors of durable consumer goods, machinery and equipment, electronics, computers, chemicals and drugs. A precondition for keeping the process of industrialization going, then, becomes dependent cooperation with their particular model of development.

A fourth element in the process of underdevelopment, mentioned by Cardozo and others, is the reinforcement of local domestic elites in the LDCs by international elites.[15] A class analysis shows that leadership in many LDCs—particularly those countries most integrated into the world market economy—is supported by the fabric of business, educational, social and political relationships built up over the years with leadership in developed countries. Thus it is understandable why many of the Third World elites view with displeasure a development process which would challenge these relationships.

The dependency-underdevelopment theories are not without their critics. Many development analysts believe that the case is overdrawn and the history sometimes distorted. But the fact remains that these theories enjoy considerable influence in developing countries today. Therefore the reason for sketching in some detail the elements of the theories is to provide a context for the evolving understandings of development which find expression in the call for a "New International Economic Order" (NIEO). More and more of the developing nations have urged that the problem of development is not to be defined merely in terms internal to their own situation but in terms of the environment within which they must function. There is a call for a new set of "rules of the game" regarding trade, aid, investment patterns, monetary relationships, decision-making, etc. Power to back this call is found in the formation of producer cartels (e.g., Organization of Petroleum Exporting Countries—OPEC; bauxite nations, etc.) and is manifested in demands for indexation of commodity prices to combat inflation of manufactured goods, in requests for increased representation in major international monetary and funding agencies such as the International Monetary Fund, and in increased aggressiveness regarding expropriation and nationalization of foreign investments.

In April, 1974, the Sixth Special Session of the General Assembly of the United Nations passed—over the reservations of the United States and other industrialized nations—a Declaration on the Establishment of a New International Economic Order.[16] Among other things, the NIEO document calls for respect for the sovereign equality of all nations, sovereign rights over natural resources, the regulation and supervision of MNCs, and preferential trade agreements. In December, 1974, the United Nations General Assembly passed the Charter of Economic Rights and Duties of Nations, repeating the thrust of a call for an NIEO. The UN Seventh

Special Session, September, 1975, began the hard bargaining necessary to implement the elements of the NIEO.

What is emphasized, therefore, in this third alternative to defining development is the problem of the international economic order, the structured relationships between rich and poor nations. "What is at stake," writes an African political scientist, "is indeed the belated but still sorely needed transition from an interdependence based on hierarchy and Western charity to an interdependence based on symmetry and mutual accountability."[17]

II
ALTERNATIVES: THE STRATEGIES FOLLOWED

As would be expected, definitions of problems tend themselves to offer at least initial directions toward solutions. And so it is in considering the alternative ways to define problems faced in development. For this reason, the strategies to be followed in development efforts will depend very much on what is considered to be the key issue. In presenting here a survey of alternative strategies, no effort is made to parallel precisely the definition of problems as outlined in the previous section, but certain patterns of relationships will be obvious.

A. Economic Growth

The most widely accepted strategy for development today continues to be one which "focuses upon the creation of conditions for self-sustained growth in per capita GNP and the requisite modernization of economic, social, and political structures implicit in the achievement of this goal."[18] This strategy rests upon a reading of the historical experience of Western Europe, North America, and the Soviet Union—a partial reading at that—and suggests that this experience should provide the model for LDCs today.

In its emphasis upon the engines of investment, production, and consumption, this strategy tends toward a dualistic development pattern. The industrial sector is given prime consideration in plans and programs. This is usually concentrated in cities and hence the nation experiences rapid urbanization. Factories are constructed for the production of domestic consumer goods and for the manufacture of export goods. An industrial infrastructure is built up which includes power plants, modern transportation systems and skilled technical training. Capital-intensive, labor-saving technology is emphasized as the most efficient approach to increasing production output.

While the industrial sector is thus being promoted, this strategy bypasses or ignores the more traditional sector (e.g., cottage industries) and subordinates the agricultural sector. Agriculture is seen principally in two ways: (1) a source for improvement of balance of trade through the sale of cash crops (cotton, sugar, cocoa, coffee, etc.) and (2) a support for the needs of urban dwellers engaged in the industrial sector. Full-scale in-corporation of the agricultural sector into development plans is frequently neglected in the strategies concentrating on economic growth.

In the strategy of promoting economic growth, the question of income distribution is postponed. Until sufficient economic growth has occurred, it is considered harmful to focus on distributive effects. Policies aimed directly at promoting more equitable income distribution are thought to hamper economic growth by (1) reducing entrepreneurial incentives through curtailing profits, (2) lowering the rate of savings of those most likely to invest, and (3) delimiting the choice of efficient technologies through favoring of labor-intensive production. It is expected that an ever-increasing output of goods and services will in fact mean a prosperity which through a "trickle-down" process will improve the lot of the masses.

B. Growth with Distribution

Despite the significant effects of concentrated efforts to increase GNP growth, there has been a growing dissatisfaction with a "grow first, distrib-ute later" strategy. This dissatisfaction has been heightened by the marked failure of such a strategy to achieve real human progress in terms of a decrease in poverty, increase in employment, and promotion of more equitable income distribution. Grant sums up the empirical evidence for this failure by citing the case of Mexico.

> The experience of most developing countries over the past decade indi-cates that a rising GNP growth rate alone is no guarantee against worsening poverty. Mexico, for example, has been very successful by traditional standards: its GNP has risen by 6 or 7 percent annually for the past 15 years. Yet, at the same time, unemployment in Mexico has been increasing, and the income disparity between the rich and the poor has clearly been widening. This is not only because of Mexico's very rapid population growth, which has been far greater than that experienced by any presently in-dustrialized country, including Japan. It is also because government policies have bypassed the small, labor-intensive producers throughout Mexico and encouraged production primarily through large farms and urban-based factories. Four-fifths of the increase in production has been coming from the less than 5 percent of farms employing only one-sixth of the farm labor force. Half of Mexico's industrial production has been located in its capital city. In addition, the jobs, housing, education, and health facilities provided by the government have generally favored higher income groups. In the early 1950's, the total income of the top fifth of the Mexican population was 10 times that of the lowest fifth; by 1969, it was 16 times as great.[19]

Similar cases have led to a challenge of the economic growth approach and prompted considerable "rethinking" of development strategies within recent years. One of the most public efforts at this "rethinking" can be found in recent addresses by World Bank President Robert McNamara. In 1971, McNamara spoke of the need to attend to agriculture and rural de-velopment and to promote jobs through labor-intensive industrialization which aims at production for foreign markets.[20] In his 1972 address to the Board of Governors of the World Bank Group, he told his audience:

If government policy were directed towards promoting a price structure which reflected the scarcity values of labor and capital more realistically, the technological choice would be different. The result would be greater employment, broader income distribution, and more competitive patterns of production of precisely those labor-intensive goods which labor-scarce affluent countries need, but cannot themselves produce inexpensively.[21]

As noted earlier in this paper, McNamara issued a strong and specific call in 1973 for the need to reorient development strategies in order to provide a more equitable distribution of the benefits of economic growth. He challenged the approach which would consider it to be "wiser to concentrate on the modern sector [rather than on increasing the productivity of small-scale subsistence agriculture] in the hope that its high rate of growth would filter down to the rural poor."[22] He admitted that the World Bank itself had paid very little attention to subsistence agriculture in its 25 years of operation, devoting to it less than $1 billion out of a total of $25 billion of lending.[23]

According to McNamara, the strategy for increasing the productivity of small-holder agriculture includes as essential elements: (1) an acceleration in the rate of land and tenancy reform—meaning, of course, shifts in power structures; (2) better access to credit, with significant restructuring of interest rates; (3) assured availability of water through irrigation projects which actually reach the small farmer; (4) expanded extension facilities backed up by intensified agricultural research which gives priority to low-risk, inexpensive technology that can be put to immediate use; (5) greater access to the public services of transportation, education, health care, electrification, etc.; and (6) "most critical of all: new forms of rural institutions and organizations that will give as much attention to promoting the inherent potential and productivity of the poor as is generally given to protecting the power of the privileged."[24]

In emphasizing the rural sector, this strategy does not neglect industrialization. But the criteria for evaluating the success of efforts to industrialize are not simply the rates of increase in GNP/capita. Rather the patterns of industrialization should attend especially to the creation of jobs, the use of intermediate technology, the production of basic necessities for the majority of the population rather than the provision of luxury items for the elite, decentralization of industrial sites away from urban concentrations, and the development of industry to service the agricultural sector. It seems clear, for example, that if the purchasing power of the poor, mainly rural majority is increased, greater mass markets will result for labor-intensive products such as hand tools, textiles, and shoes.

An analysis of development strategies which support the "growth with distribution" approach can be found in an influential study published in 1972, *Development Reconsidered.* Owens and Shaw distinguish between *dual* and *modernizing* societies:

> . . . The basic distinction lies in the way in which these societies view the relationship between government and people. This relationship in *dual* societies is an extension of the ruler-ruled relationship of traditional societies in which decisions are essentially made at the top and passed down to the people. In *modernizing* societies there are explicit efforts to involve the populace in planning their own futures.[25]

Dual society governments encourage economic growth but do not attempt to reach the mass of people. Both investments and profits are concentrated in the hands of a few that are considered to possess more of the necessary expertise and initiative. Modernizing governments, on the other hand, attempt to bridge the gap between traditional elites and the masses, particularly by establishing and strengthening local institutions and systems in which the people work out solutions to their own local problems. The strategy emphasized by Owens and Shaw aims to integrate the elements of local participation, national organization, increased employment, focus on small farmers, emphasis on non-formal education, and provision of public services.

This "growth with distribution" strategy has been utilized in several nations in the past decade, with some significant instances of success. One particular variant of the strategy stresses integration of the developing country's economy into the international market through export production. Five nations are repeatedly cited as examples of this approach: Israel, Japan, South Korea, Singapore, and Taiwan. Adelman has described three stages of a "dynamic sequence of strategies" which characterize this approach.

> Stage I: Radical asset redistribution, focusing primarily on land, but also imposing (at the very minimum) curbs upon the use and further accumulation of financial capital. This stage may involve negative growth rates, but is necessary to set the economic and political conditions to ensure that subsequent economic growth is not highly unequalizing.
>
> Stage II: Massive accumulation of human capital, far in excess of current demand for skills. In this stage ownership of human capital is redistributed, the human resource base is vastly enlarged, and both the economic opportunities and the political pressures for the next stage are generated. In all five countries, this stage was accompanied by relatively slow rates of economic growth and, at later times, by political instability, social tension, and unrest.
>
> Stage III: Rapid, human-resource-intensive growth. After the investment in human resources has been made, continuing depauperization requires that subsequent increases in growth rate be achieved through strategies that stress rapid labor-intensive growth. This implies that sufficient attention must be paid to the formulation of economic policy. In the smaller nations development will have to be oriented towards export markets. In large countries, on the other hand, industrialization can be oriented more towards satisfying domestic demand, particularly when a more equitable growth pattern generates a mass consumer market and when a more appropriate import-substitution technology is found.[26]

Adelman notes that the five nations taken as examples all have been aided by unusually large per capita infusions of foreign capital. For this reason, and because all are also small nations with nonrepresentative cultural traditions and attitudes, and have been subjected to exceptional challenges that legitimized their governments and made economic viability a major condition for national survival, some economists tend to dismiss these success stories as special cases. Whether or not their unique experience can be repeated elsewhere is questioned. "Special cases they may be," writes Adelman, "but five successful cases are certainly more encouraging than none, and the consistency of their experiences surely weakens the 'uniqueness' argument."[27]

C. Self-Reliant Development

A development strategy which is closely related to the "growth with distribution" strategy, but has notably different *organizational* and *motivational* patterns, is that followed by the Peoples' Republic of China. In some senses it can be said to be a variant of the strategy discussed above in that it emphasizes rural development, promotes labor-intensive technology, relies on decentralized patterns of local control, and takes seriously the input of ordinary citizens into decision-making processes.

But one significant organizational difference is immediately obvious in viewing China as compared with Taiwan, South Korea, or Singapore. Whereas these latter nations are integrated into the international economic order through strong reliance on export-oriented production, China has stressed self-reliance with little or no integration. What integration does occur takes place on that nation's own terms. Mass-produced consumer goods are oriented towards satisfying domestic demands.

Another aspect of China's self-reliance is its independence from the influence of foreign investment. Weisskopf notes that as a matter of policy the Chinese have deliberately pursued conservative international financial policies to avoid long-term indebtedness after the 1960s. They allocated more resources and efforts to the development of indigenous technological capacities rather than relying on imported technologies introduced by foreign private enterprise. The turning point in this strategy, of course, was "the termination of Soviet aid to China in the late 1950's and the lack of aid opportunities from other sources. . . ."[28]

Recent events on the international scene do raise questions about future developments in China's strategy of self-reliance. Since the visit of President Nixon to China in 1972, new linkages with the international economic order are probable—but, again, on China's terms. Lin observes:

> It remains to point out that Chinese self-reliance, while ruling out acceptance of conditional aid, does not preclude normal trade and international cooperation as accessory stimulants to development. As China rapidly expands her foreign trade, she is also ensuring that it reinforces rather than distorts her own pattern of development and that the basic domestic economy is insulated from any disruptive effects of linkage with the world market. My own conjecture is that China will move logically towards setting up a complete export economy (including production facilities) parallel to the domestic, targeted at not too high a ratio to total national income, which would be geared to the competitive international market. The domestic market would draw on the proceeds but would not be caught in the crippling trap of fluctuations in the world market.[29]

The motivational differences between China's development strategy and strategies followed by other nations should also be noted. That particular articulation of Marxist-Leninist thought found in the directives of Mao Tse-tung provides a set of motivations which deeply influence the patterns of "growth with distribution." This value-orientation will be explored in detail in the next section of this study. But one example can be pointed to here in noting that Maoist ideology discourages consumption and encourages saving and investment. It thereby promotes the growth of capital stock —a development factor which appears to belong to that core of development theory acceptable both to proponents of a free-market strategy and of a socialist strategy. The values espoused in China promote this by preventing the rise of a "middle class" which is marked by high consumption patterns, and by fostering the virtues of plain living and aiding others rather than promoting a privileged status based on accumulation.[30]

Another effort at self-reliant development is that being made by Tanzania. President Jules Nyerere has emphasized a pattern of growth which focuses on the village—the "Ujaama" program. And he has made a tremendous effort to maintain independence in relating to outside investments and trade. Terrible poverty conditions, heightened by drought and famine situations, have crippled this effort in many ways, however, and Tanzania must presently rely heavily on outside assistance. This assistance does not always come without conditions, many of which bring into question the future viability of this distinct African development strategy.

III
ALTERNATIVES: THE VALUES GUIDING

As should be clear from the analysis being offered in this paper, no development strategy is "value-free." Hence, a survey of development alternatives must make some effort to explicate the value presuppositions which guide particular approaches. For our purposes here, two sets of value-systems will be discussed, one clustering around the dominance of technology and the other relating to a coherent ideological position.

A. Technology

The role of technology in development strategies is critical. In almost all cases, modernization has meant a commitment to technology. This at least implies a systematic approach to control of production through labor-saving techniques and a sophistication of communication and transportation operations. Although technology is but one element in overall development strategies, its influence is massive. And it is not simply a neutral instrument. The choice to emphasize technology involves the acceptance of certain societal structures and orientations. As a result, the introduction of technology into a developing country brings with it certain values and endangers other values already present.

Goulet, who has done some of the most important research in the area of technology and values in a development context, suggests three values that are embedded in Western technology and are transmitted in a technological development process:[31]

1. A particular approach to rationality. The technological mind wants to treat any phenomenon as something to be broken down into component parts, put together again, and verified. There is consequently a tendency to change things, to extract more out of nature, to organize human efforts so as to get results. In the process, Western technology shows less appreciation of myth and symbol, of the power of the mysterious.

2. A cult of efficiency. Technology goes after efficiency and expresses its goal in industrial terms of productivity. The final output is all-important. A cost-benefit analysis is vigorously applied to determine what is esteemed and sought after in the development process.

3. A predilection for problem-solving. Technologists do not view nature so as to discover a harmony with it. Rather the effort is to manipulate and dominate nature. Problem-solving thus has a tendency to distort reality, because it reduces reality only to those dimensions which can be treated as mere difficulties to be solved.

When technology is transferred from a developed country to a developing country—most frequently through the operations of multinational corporations—certain tensions frequently arise. Goulet outlines five of these, in noting the value conflict areas.[32] First, there is a difference in how technology is viewed: as a marketable commodity (the consequence of proprietary knowledge) or as a free good, something to be as freely available as scientific information or public statistics. Second, does technology reinforce the consumption patterns of the upper classes or does it benefit the poor? In short, what is the relationship of technological processes to inequalities among social classes? Third, there is a tension between the repeated demand of developing countries for autonomy and independence and the prohibitive costs of importing technology. This cost, it is frequently argued, is the compelling reason why poor countries must rely on (depend on?) technological assistance from developed countries.

Fourth, more advanced ("high") technology has a tendency to standardize for the sake of efficiency, economies of scale, and avoidance of duplication costs in research and development. This standardizing emphasis conflicts with the values of cultural diversity and pluralistic social patterns of work. Fifth, tensions arise over the search for intermediate technology (which is inexpensive, labor-intensive, small-scale, and requires low skill levels and unsophisticated local materials) and the drive for the status of more expensive and wasteful "high" technology which appears more "modern" and "first rate."

These tensions, of course, are not completely inevitable when commitments are made to modernization. What needs to be emphasized here, however, is that the values of technology can be determinative of the values of development. They need to be made explicit, if choices are to be made on the basis of values desired and not simply of availability of technologies.

B. Ideology

An ideological position can also be a dominant force in guiding national development. Such a position is a complex of values—either explicit or implicit—and sets the goals to be pursued relating to the overall transformation of society. It touches the attitudes, motivations, and behavior patterns of all the people. The Peoples' Republic of China provides an important example of this guidance of development by ideology.

In analyzing the guiding values that energize China's transformation and development, Lin distinguishes between "development values" and "superordinate goals"—"the former representing the policy norms as well as values in themselves, and the latter representing the ultimate ends of development."[33] The former can be seen as instrumental values for the attainment of the latter. Three principal development values are suggested by Lin.

1. Power to the People, with Its Corollary, Reliance on the People. A people-oriented development strategy requires that political power be held in the hands of the producer classes (peasants and workers) by every institutional means, formal and informal. This has certain policy derivatives, including: the choice of leaders for their identity with the people and their adherence to strategies and policies reflecting the peoples' interest (hence, the great importance of the Cultural Revolution which helped both to re-educate leaders and re-assert the influence of the masses); mass activation, or reliance on the people to emancipate themselves, which emphasizes that even technical innovation (or "R and D" efforts) must utilize "three-in-one" (administrator-technician-worker) teams in order to tap the resources of full worker participation; and participatory management, with direct representation from the basic, working level and avoidance of bureaucratic hindrances in order to bring initiative from below into full play.

2. The Serve-the-People Ethic. This value aims at rooting-out the individualistic spirit and any self-serving policies. It becomes a premise in planning and developing both production and distribution, both industrialization and environmental protection. "To keep this value operational at all levels, Mao Tse-tung has laid special emphasis on the constant re-identification and re-merging of cadres with the masses."[34] Institutional means to promote this, for example, have been such efforts as the May 7th Cadre Schools and the mass movement of high school graduates to settle in the countryside to help build up the rural areas (where 80 percent of the people live and work).

3. Self-Reliance and Autonomy in Development. This value—already referred to in our earlier discussion of a self-reliant strategy—requires the optimal use of all available human, natural, and technological resources throughout the country. A balanced, congruent development is necessary especially in the relationships between industry and agriculture. (China's astounding ability to feed its people attests to at least some success in its endeavor to place priority emphasis—as a human value—on agriculture.) Also necessary is a dual approach of "walking on two legs"—i.e., utilizing "both indigenous and advanced technologies; both smaller, low-investment, quickly built plants and big industrial complexes; both mechanized and semi-mechanized technologies. . . ."[35] Serious attention is also paid to the avoidance of waste, to large-scale recycling efforts, and to patterns of austerity.

These three sets of development values provide the possibility, according to Lin, of achieving in China what he calls the "end" values (or "super-ordinate goals") of development. These "end" values can be grouped under four headings:

1. Social justice based on freedom from exploitation, with human relations of egalitarianism, cooperation, and respect for work.
2. Economic welfare for all in a society of abundance, with special attention to raising the level of life of marginalised groups (such as women and national minorities) and regions that have been resource-poor or historically oppressed.
3. Maximum cultural and aesthetic fulfilment. This includes full popular participation in the production of culture.
4. An aesthetically and ecologically sound environment. This value is not posed *against* growth, but as *part of* development, fulfiling the same purpose of service to the people as growth.[36]

In citing China as an example here, no more is intended than to illustrate the organizing and motivating power of a coherent ideology. What appears to an increasing number of outside observers as a truly remarkable instance of development success (not without shortcomings, of course) can at least partially be explained as the consequence of what Goulet refers to as the creation of a shared value system based on solidarity, revolutionary consciousness, and the primacy of moral over material incentives. "The Chinese lesson is that values commands politics (the primary value is to construct revolutionary consciousness); politics (which includes ethics) commands economics; and economics commands technique."[37]

NOTES

1. Benjamin Higgins, *Economic Development: Problems, Principles, and Policies* (revised edition; New York: W. W. Norton and Company, Inc., 1968), p. 189.
2. W. W. Rostow, *The Stages of Economic Growth: A Non-Communist Manifesto* (Cambridge: Cambridge University Press, 1960).
3. See the statistical data presented in James W. Howe, ed., *The U.S. and World Development: Agenda for Action, 1975* (New York: Praeger Publishers, 1975), p. 258.
4. Edgar Owens and Robert Shaw, *Development Reconsidered: Bridging the Gap Between Government and People* (Lexington, Massachusetts: Lexington Books, 1972), p. 1.
5. Dudley Seers, "The Meaning of Development," *International Development Review*, Vol XI, No. 4 (December 1969), p. 3.
6. Irma Adelman, "Development Economics: A Reassessment of Goals," *The American Economic Review*, LXV (May 1975), p. 302.
7. Robert S. McNamara, "Address to the Board of Governors," Nairobi, Kenya, September 24, 1973, World Bank reprint, pp. 10–11.
8. See Donald V. McGranahan, *Contents and Measurements of Socio-Economic Development* (New York: Praeger Publishers, 1972).
9. See, for example, " 'New Directions' in Development Assistance: Implementation in Four Latin American Countries," report to the Committee on International Relations, U.S. House of Representatives, August 31, 1975.
10. See Denis Goulet, " 'Development' . . . or Liberation?" in this anthology, pp. 379–386.
11. Paulo Freire, *Pedagogy of the Oppressed*, translated by Myra Bergman Ramos (New York: Herder and Herder, 1970).
12. Theotonio Dos Santos, "The Structure of Dependence," *American Economic Review*, Vol. LX, No. 2 (May 1970), pp. 231–236.

13. See Andre Gunder Frank, "The Development of Underdevelopment," in James D. Cockcroft *et al.*, eds., *Dependence and Underdevelopment: Latin America's Political Economy* (Garden City, N.Y.: Anchor Books, 1972), pp. 3–18. Also in this anthology, pp. 103–113.

14. Celso Furtado, "The Concept of External Dependence in the Study of Underdevelopment," paper presented to the Union for Racial Political Economics, Washington, D.C. November 10, 1972.

15. Fernando Henrique Cardosa and Enzo Faletto, *Dependencia y Desarrollo en América Latina* (Santiago: ILPES, 1967).

16. United Nations General Assembly, "Declaration on the Establishment of a New International Economic Order," May 1, 1974, CESI.E21.

17. Ali A. Mazrui, "The New Interdependence: From Hierarchy to Symmetry," in Howe, *op. cit.*, p. 134.

18. Adelman, *op. cit.*, p. 306.

19. James P. Grant, "Growth From Below: A People-Oriented Strategy," Development Paper 16, December 1973 (Washington, D.C.: Overseas Development Council), p. 7.

20. Robert S. McNamara, "Address to the Board of Governors," Washington, D.C., September 27, 1971, World Bank reprint.

21. Robert S. McNamara, "Address to the Board of Governors," Washington, D.C., September 25, 1972, World Bank reprint, p. 14.

22. Robert S. McNamara, "Address to the Board of Governors," Nairobi, Kenya, September 24, 1973, World Bank reprint, p. 13.

23. *Ibid.*, p. 14.

24. *Ibid.*, p. 17.

25. Owens and Shaw, *op. cit.*, p. 4.

26. Adelman, *op. cit.*, p. 308.

27. *Ibid.*, p. 309.

28. Thomas E. Weisskopf, "China and India: Contrasting Experiences in Economic Development," *The American Economic Review*, LXV (May 1975), p. 361.

29. Paul T. K. Lin, "Development Guided by Values: Comments on China's Road and Its Implications," in Saul H. Mendlovitz, ed., *On the Creation of a Just World Order: Preferred Worlds for the 1990's* (New York: The Free Press), p. 272.

30. John W. Gurley, "Maoist Economic Development: The New Man in the New China," in this anthology, pp. 334–346.

31. Denis Goulet, "On the Ethics of Development Planning," address at the University of California at Los Angeles, March 6, 1975 (mimeo), pp. 13–15.

32. Denis Goulet, "The Paradox of Technology Transfer," *The Bulletin of the Atomic Scientists*, XXXI (June 1975), 39–46.

33. Lin, *op. cit.*, p. 267.

34. *Ibid.*, p. 269.

35. *Ibid.*, p. 271.

36. *Ibid.*, p. 272.

37. Goulet, "On the Ethics of Development Planning," *op. cit.*, p. 23.

2

Underdevelopment in Theory

Keith Griffin

Most of the theorizing on economic development has been done by economists who live and were trained in the industrial West. Some economists, in
fact, have written about the underdeveloped countries before they have
seen them,[1] and others—although they may have visited an underdeveloped
country—write as if they have seen only the capital and perhaps a few of
the other major cities. Almost all of these economists, moreover, are
ignorant of much of the economic history of the countries about which
they are theorizing. Thus many writers on the poverty of nations have suffered from two serious handicaps: lack of knowledge about the broad
historical forces associated with underdevelopment and ignorance of the
institutions, behaviour responses and ways of life of the largest sector
within the underdeveloped countries, the rural areas. Research now available or in progress is gradually reducing our ignorance of the causes of
underdevelopment and the conditions under which most of mankind lives.
It is almost certain that once additional evidence is accumulated many of
the theories of development proposed in the last two decades will have to
be abandoned.

THEORIES OF DUALISM

Perhaps the most pervasive theory is that of the dual economy. There are
numerous models of economic dualism, but their common feature is the
division of the economy into two broad—largely independent—sectors.[2]
The names given to these two sectors vary. In some cases the division is
between a "capitalist" and a "non-capitalist" sector (Lewis); in other cases
it is a division between an "enclave" and the "hinterland," between a
"modern" and a "traditional" sector of society[3] or, more generally, between
"industry" and "agriculture" (Jorgenson).

The two sectors are separate and radically different. The "modern,"
"capitalist," "industrial" sector is receptive to change, is market oriented
and follows profit-maximizing behaviour. The "traditional," "feudal," "agricultural" sector is stagnant; production is for subsistence; little output

Reprinted from the author's *Underdevelopment in Spanish America* (London: George Allen & Unwin,
1969), pp. 19–31, by permission of the author and the publishers. U.S. edition published by the M.I.T.
Press, Cambridge, Massachusetts.

passes through a market; the leisure preferences of producers are high and they do not follow maximizing behaviour. Unemployment, although "disguised," is assumed to be widespread throughout the agricultural sector and, indeed, the marginal product of labour is zero if not negative.[4] Income is at a subsistence level, which is variously interpreted as either a physiological[5] or a culturally determined minimum.[6]

The methods of production are very different in the two sectors. "The output of the traditional sector is a function of land and labour alone; there is no accumulation of capital . . . ."[7] In the manufacturing sector "output is a function of capital and labour alone."[8] The only link between the two sectors is a flow of unemployed labour (of homogeneous quality) from agriculture to industry. No flows of capital or savings are permitted—since production in the agricultural sector is done without the use of capital, and entrepreneurs are not allowed to engage in activities in both sectors—since motivations and behaviour in the two sectors differ. The economy is essentially closed and growth occurs through a transfer of labour from agriculture to industry in response to demand generated by capitalist businessmen reinvesting their profits. This process continues until all the disguised unemployed are eliminated, labour becomes scarce and the traditional sector is forced to modernize.

Dualistic models of growth, sometimes explicitly but more often implicitly, have constituted the basis on which broad development strategies have been created. The general neglect of agriculture and the bias in favour of industry, which until recently have been such a notable feature of development policy, stem directly from these models. Moreover, within agriculture, the concentration on large commercial farmers (who may be considered to belong to the modern sector) reflects the opinion that small peasants will not respond to ordinary economic incentives. Similarly, within industry, the concentration on manufactured consumer goods which use imported inputs and the failure to take advantage of opportunities to process locally available raw materials reflect the belief that the "traditional" sector is incapable of supplying the "modern" sector with the inputs it requires.

The assumptions on which dualistic models are constructed are highly suspect. First, there is very little evidence of widespread unemployment throughout the year. There may indeed be pronounced seasonal unemployment in some countries,[9] although even this has been denied in at least one densely populated underdeveloped country.[10] The usual pattern, at least in countries where imports of cheap manufactured goods have not destroyed the handicraft industries, is for seasonally available rural manpower to be fully engaged in non-agricultural activities—leather work, food processing, textile spinning and weaving, etc.[11] There is little surplus labour. Secondly, the assumption that rural incomes or wages exceed the marginal product of labour (even if the latter is not zero) could be correct only if there are no commercial farming activities whatever (e.g. share cropping, fixed rental farming), no employment opportunities outside the (extended) family farm and if all farm labour is provided by members of the family.[12] Our knowledge of tenure conditions (e.g. the interdependence of latifundia and minifundia in Latin America), the role of migrant labour (e.g. in Africa) and the practice of small farmers of hiring labour during the peak of the harvest season (e.g. in Asia) contradicts the assumption of the dual economy model. In other words, there is no reason to suppose that rural labour receives more than its marginal product. If there is a discrepancy between opportunity costs and incomes this is more likely to be due to the presence of monopolistic market power than to non-maximizing behaviour or a work-and-income-sharing ethic.

The presumption that members of the "traditional" sector of a dual economy are not maximizers is used to explain the alleged fact that labour supply curves are backward sloping and that peasants will not increase output when profit opportunities arise. In other words, dualistic models tend to suppose that if wages or farm prices increase the response will be to reduce the supply of labour or agricultural output. This view is clearly presented by a Dutch economist, J. H. Boeke:

> When the price of coconut is high, the chances are that less of the commodities will be offered for sale; when wages are raised the manager of the estate risks that less work will be done; . . . when rubber prices fall the owner of a grove may decide to tap more intensively, whereas high prices may mean that he leaves a larger or smaller portion of his tappable trees untapped.[13]

The extraordinary thing is that there is absolutely no empirical evidence to support the view that labour will work less if paid more. Indeed there is much evidence to the contrary. It is probable that the backward bending supply curve is a myth left over from the colonial era when the colonized peoples frequently were forced to offer their services to Europeans in order to earn sufficient cash income to pay their taxes. Obviously, in such a situation, if wages are raised, taxes can be paid more easily and the volume of labour services offered to the colonialists will correspondingly decline. Thus this third assumption of dualistic models—the perverse response of workers to wage incentives—must be dismissed.

Fourth, a large number of detailed econometric studies have demonstrated beyond a doubt that the assumption that farmers in underdeveloped countries do not respond to price signals is untenable.[14] We now know that Punjabi peasants, whether Hindus in India or Muslims in Pakistan, respond actively to agricultural policies.[15] Thai farmers, under appropriate conditions, will introduce new crops and new technologies.[16] African farmers can be induced by pricing policies to improve the quality of the output of their tree crops.[17] If in many countries the rate of growth of agriculture is too low the explanation should be sought not in the motives, values and behaviour of the inhabitants of rural areas, but in land tenure conditions, in the distribution of economic power and in government policy.

Finally, the assumption that peasants cannot save because they are too poor must be questioned, even if sufficient information is not yet available to reject it completely. Nurkse presumes that savers are found "mostly among the urban commercial classes"[18] and that "peasants are not likely to save . . . voluntarily since they live so close to subsistence level."[19] Lewis argues that only capitalists save and the reason savings are low in the underdeveloped countries is because the capitalist sector (and hence the proportion of income received in the form of profits) is small.[20]

Unfortunately, data to test these hypotheses are very scarce. One study of rural and urban incomes and savings habits in East and West Pakistan is worth mentioning, however, despite the fact that the quality of the statistical information is rather poor.

The two wings of Pakistan are separated by a thousand miles of Indian territory. East Pakistan is the poorer of the two wings.

. . . Personal incomes in West Pakistan were about 28 per cent higher than in East Pakistan. What is noteworthy is that personal savings (expressed as a percentage of gross personal income before taxes) in the rural areas of Pakistan were higher than in the urban areas and that rural savings in East Pakistan were higher than in West Pakistan. When private corporate saving is added to personal saving, so as to obtain a measure of private saving, it turns out that urban areas save more than rural but that East Pakistan still saves more than West Pakistan. In general, "rural areas . . . appear to have contributed at least three-fourths of the total private savings in the country."[21]

. . .

Clearly one cannot reject the hypothesis that the "traditional" sector does not save on the basis of a single study of one country in one year, but enough information has been provided to create a certain amount of doubt as to the validity of theories which are dependent upon this assumption. Indeed it now seems most unlikely that the assumptions of the model of economic dualism—and particularly the assumptions about the extent of rural unemployment, the relationship of wages to the marginal product of labour, the willingness of peasants to save and the response of workers and farmers to economic incentives—can withstand empirical scrutiny.

One can always maintain that the assumptions of a theory are less important than its predictions and that it is more important to foresee the development path of an economy than to describe accurately its structure and behaviour patterns. Let us, therefore, briefly examine the trends and tendencies the dual economy models would lead one to expect.

The most obvious feature of these models is the tendency for real income in the agricultural sector to remain constant. It cannot rise because there is surplus labour and it cannot fall because incomes already are at a subsistence level. Given that the marginal product of labour is zero, it must follow that all available amounts of land are fully utilized, otherwise it is very difficult to understand why the surplus labour does not combine with uncultivated land. If labour is redundant and land is fully utilized any increase in population will lead to falling *per capita incomes*—unless the increase in population is exactly offset by technical progress. The technical progress may not be of the embodied type, however, because capital accumulation in the "traditional" sector is assumed not to occur; thus the increase in technical knowledge must be entirely disembodied, i.e. it must fall like manna from heaven at precisely the rate of population increase.

These, in fact, are the assumptions many development theorists make. Jorgenson, for example, assumes that his production function "will shift over time so that a given bundle of factors will generate a higher level of output at one date than at an earlier date."[22] He also assumes "that so long as there is disguised unemployment population expands at the same rate as the growth of agricultural output."[23] Thus *per capita* income in the agricultural sector cannot fall by assumption, and since the modern, industrial sector is assumed to be increasing its relative importance in the economy the *per capita* income of the nation as a whole must rise.

Dualistic theories thus make three specific predictions about the development path of an underdeveloped country: first, aggregate *per capita* income will rise; second, agricultural output will increase at the same rate as the population; and, third, *per capita* income in rural areas will remain constant. What evidence is there that these predictions are generally correct?

In the first place, there are several areas in which *per capita* income has declined. In Africa north of the Sahara, for example, gross domestic product *per capita* declined by 0.3 per cent a year between 1960 and 1967. Looking at individual countries over the period 1960–66, GNP *per capita* grew at an annual rate of −0.1 per cent in Ghana, −0.5 per cent in Morocco, −2.6 per cent in Rhodesia, −0.4 per cent in the Dominican Republic and −1.4 per cent in Uruguay.[24] Evidently, a few countries are engaged in a process of underdevelopment which dual economy models are incapable of explaining. It is quite likely, as we shall see below, that if the economic history of today's poverty-stricken nations were examined it would become apparent that many of them descended into underdevelopment from a level of material prosperity and social well-being that was once considerably greater than that observed at present.

Next, there is abundant evidence that in many countries agricultural output, and particularly production of food for domestic consumption, has failed to keep pace with the rate of population increase. Comparing 1966 with the average of the period 1957–59 it appears that *per capita* agricultural production had declined in the following countries: Algeria, Burundi, Congo (Kinshasa), Liberia, Malagasy Republic, Morocco, Rwanda, Tunisia, Uganda, Iran, Iraq, Egypt, India, Burma, Cambodia, Indonesia, South Vietnam, Argentina, Bolivia, Brazil, Chile, Colombia, Costa Rica, Dominican Republic, Ecuador, Haiti, Paraguay, Peru, Trinidad and Tobago.[25] Clearly the theories of dualism have failed this simple test on a massive scale.

Finally, there is the question of whether *per capita* incomes in rural areas have remained constant. There is some evidence that rural incomes have been falling in several Spanish American countries. It is possible, of course, that our data on Spanish America are wrong or that for some reason this area constitutes a special case. Hence it is worth considering briefly what is happening in another country in a rather different part of the world.

In 1965 it was suggested, on the basis of the then existing statistical information on the *per capita* availability of foodgrains and average rural incomes, that despite the rapid growth in GNP and *per capita* income that Pakistan has enjoyed, particularly during the Second Five Year Plan, "the vast majority of the Pakistani population probably have a lower standard of living today than when the country achieved its independence in 1947."[26] Two years later additional evidence became available which showed that *per capita* agricultural output in East Pakistan declined from Rs.197 in 1949–50, to Rs.184 in 1954–55, and finally to Rs.174 in 1959–60; it then increased to Rs.188 in 1964–65 but was still lower than the level achieved in the earliest recorded period. Exactly the same pattern was followed in West Pakistan except that by 1964–65 *per capita* agricultural output had fully regained the previous peak.[27] Clearly a strong presumption exists that the standard of living in rural areas, particularly in East Pakistan, has declined in the last two decades.

The author of a more recent study has investigated in great detail the trends in rural incomes in East Pakistan since 1949.[28] According to the evidence collected by Mr. Bose agricultural value added per head of rural population declined from Rs.200.5 in 1949/50–1950/51 to Rs.182 in 1962/63–1963/64; in the same period agricultural value added per head of agricultural population declined from Rs.229 to Rs.202.5 and *per capita* rural income declined from Rs.272.5 to Rs.268.5.[29] Because of increased population density in rural areas the number of landless male workers seeking wage employment rose from 14.1 per cent of the male agricultural labour force in 1954 to 19.4 per cent in 1961.[30] The real wages of these landless agricultural labourers declined from an index of 100 in 1949 to 82.3 in 1966.[31]

In view of this evidence it seems rather pointless to construct a model of an underdeveloped economy in which the central feature is the constancy of real incomes in the largest sector. Ironically, it was during the period of falling rural incomes in Pakistan that two visiting economists published the first version of their model of a dual economy based on the assumption of a fixed "institutional or subsistence level of real wages in the agricultural sector."[32] The Fei and Ranis model subsequently became famous, particularly in the United States,[33] but in its country of origin it remains pathetically irrelevant.

It is conceivable, however, that some theorists would claim that models of economic dualism are not really concerned with the agricultural sector but are concerned with describing the pattern of growth of the modern industrial sector. In other words, it might be claimed that the dual economy models put a spotlight on one—often very small[34]—sector and leave the rest of the economy in relative obscurity.[35] If this is the correct interpretation, the validity of the theory should be tested by comparing its predictions with the performance of the "modern" sector, and the "traditional" sector should be ignored.

A prominent characteristic of the dual economy cum surplus labour theory is the lack of employment opportunities in agriculture and the growth of employment opportunities in the "modern" sector. This is a fundamental asymmetry in the model, and it is this difference in the treatment of the growth and employment potential of the two sectors which determines the development path of the economy. Given the structure of the model it is obvious that development can occur only through a process of capital accumulation in the "modern" sector and the absorption of labour in industry. In other words, the proportion of the labour force occupied in industry should increase, and in the classical version of the model "the rate of growth of manufacturing employment is, of course, equal to the rate of growth of manufacturing output."[36]

These hypotheses are contradicted by a great deal of empirical evidence. Nowhere, I believe, has industrial output and employment increased at the same rate; there has always been some increase in the productivity of labour in industry. More important, there are many countries in which the proportion of the labour force employed in industry has increased much less than the theory would lead one to expect (e.g. Turkey and Malaysia), others in which the relative size of the industrial labour force has remained constant (e.g. Egypt), and still others in which the proportion has even declined (e.g. Cyprus). . . . In a few Spanish American nations there was a smaller proportion of the labour force employed in manufacturing in 1960 than in 1925.

. . .

In a few countries, especially in Africa, there has been a decline not only in the *proportion* of the work force employed in industry and the "modern" sector, but in the *absolute level* of employment in non-agricultural activities as well. Output of the "modern" sector has increased while employment has fallen. For instance, between 1955 and 1964 the trend rate of increase of non-agricultural employment was −1.0 in the Cameroons, −0.5 in Kenya, −0.7 in Malawi, −0.4 in Tanzania, −0.1 in Uganda and −0.9 in Zambia.[37] The dual economy model is incapable of explaining these trends.

The theories we are examining make predictions not only about the level of employment in industry, but also about the aggregate rate of savings and investment in the economy. Arthur Lewis asserts that an understanding of how the savings and investment ratios rise from 4–5 per cent to 12–15 per cent of national income is the "central problem in the theory of economic development."[38] His explanation of the rise is in terms of a redistribution of income from the "subsistence" to the "capitalist" sector. Similarly, Professor Jorgenson's model implies that "if the proportion of manufacturing output to agricultural output increases, the share of saving in total income also increases."[39]

Once again, there is statistical evidence that suggests that there is no simple association between a growing modern, capitalist, industrial sector and rising savings and investment. For instance, in Colombia between 1953 and 1965 industrial output rose from 15.5 per cent of GDP to 19.0 per cent, while the gross investment ratio *declined* from 16.5 to 16.0 per cent. Similarly, in Guatemala between 1950–51 and 1962–63 the share of industry in GDP rose from 12.0 to 14.0 per cent, while private savings as a per cent of net national product *declined* from 2.6 to 2.3. The same phenomenon has occurred in Brazil: during the period 1946–48 to 1958–60 industrial production increased from 21 to 34 per cent of GDP and the ratio of gross domestic savings to GNP declined from 16.4 to 16.0 per cent. Indeed it appears that the savings ratio in Brazil has remained roughly constant since at least the late 1930s.[40] The lack of a strong positive correlation between the degree of industrialisation and the domestic savings ratio is not, of course, peculiar to Latin America; a similar lack of association can be found elsewhere. For example, in Turkey between 1954 and 1965 industrial output rose from 13.0 to 15.0 per cent of GDP, while the gross investment ratio—despite the availability of considerable amounts of foreign aid—fell from 14.5 per cent to 13.0 per cent of GDP. Thus once more the predictions of the theory are refuted by the facts.

In summary, dualistic models of development make an unhelpful division of the economy into a "traditional" and a "modern" sector. The assumptions of the theory regarding the characteristics of the "traditional" agricultural sector are not credible and, indeed, can be shown to be erroneous by even the most casual empiricism. The predictions of the theory are likewise incorrect. It has been demonstrated that in not a few countries the growth of national income *per capita*, the level of rural wages, the expansion of agricultural output, the evolution of employment in industry and the behaviour of the aggregate savings and investment ratios have differed markedly from what the theory would lead one to expect. In almost every conceivable way the theory fails to conform to the reality of a great many underdeveloped countries.

In many respects this theory of growth and development is curiously static and a-historical. Models of the dual economy assume a given and constant subsistence wage rate, a given pool of disguised unemployment and unchanged, i.e. "traditional," agrarian institutions. The real problem arises, however, when population growth rates exceed the capacity of the economy to adjust its institutions (e.g. land tenure), attitudes (e.g. toward birth control) and composition of output (e.g. the degree of industrialisation) so that real wages *fall*, seasonal unemployment in agriculture *increases* and the proportion of the labour force employed in large-scale industry *declines* or at best remains roughly constant. One cannot even begin to analyse these problems if the conceptual framework being used is one of static, unchanged, constant "subsistence" incomes and "traditional" institutions, values and modes of behaviour.

.   .   .

CONCLUSIONS

Underdevelopment as it is encountered today in Spanish America and elsewhere is a product of history. It is not the primeval condition of man, nor is it merely a way of describing the economic status of a "traditional" society. Underdevelopment is part of a process; indeed, it is part of the same process which produced development. Thus an interpretation of underdevelopment must begin with a study of the past. It is only from an examination of the forces of history—i.e. of the historical uses of power, both political and economic—that one may obtain an insight into the origin of underdevelopment.

The study of the uses of power in the past must be complemented by an analysis of the distribution of power in the present. The opportunities for development are conditioned by the functioning of the world economy in which the underdeveloped countries find themselves. There are some international economic forces which obviously tend to stimulate development, but there are many other forces which perpetuate inequalities and tend to retard development. . . . The transfer of ideas, knowledge, factors of production and commodities may all increase rather than decrease the obstacles to development.

The internal barriers to development—e.g. inappropriate institutions, attitudes and values—are as important as the external obstacles. . . . The types of barriers one finds, and their strength, frequently are related to the way economic and political power are distributed within the country. The concentration of purchasing power and the instruments of legitimate political force in a few hands, and the use to which this force is put, inevitably affect the country's aggregate economic performance and the welfare of its inhabitants.

Broadly speaking, the object of development policy is to turn historical constants into variables. Occasionally this can be achieved merely by changing the pattern of expenditure and the composition of investment. For example, the government might spend more of its revenues on rural education and less on central administration; investment in military installations might be reduced and expenditures on directly productive activities increased. In many cases, however, policy is underdeveloped countries cannot be concerned exclusively with allocating resources in the usual sense; it must also be concerned with creating new institutions and reforming existing ones. The major purpose of development planning, in fact, is to undertake the required structural transformation of a country in a conscious, explicit, orderly and rational manner.

The essence of development is institutional reform.[41] This process of institutional reform can act as an independent variable stimulating growth, e.g. an educational reform can stimulate growth by increasing the supply of relevant skills and improving the quality of the labour force. Alternatively, institutional reforms may be a prerequisite to development, e.g. large-scale investment in some minifundia zones may be virtually impossible unless fragmented land holdings are consolidated. Most important, institutional reforms may be complementary to other development policies and increase their effectiveness, e.g. a reorganization of the government's administrative machinery may be essential if development policies are to be properly formulated and implemented.

The three reforms we have mentioned—of the educational system, land tenure and public administration—are just a few of the many that are required. Furthermore, most of these reforms are linked to others. For example, the government administration cannot be improved unless the educational system is altered; education reform is contingent upon increased tax revenues; tax reform is impossible unless the political power of the wealthy is reduced and this, in turn, requires a land reform. The outcome of such a series of reforms is little short of a revolution. This is what Paul Baran meant when he said that "economic development has historically always meant a far-reaching transformation of society's economic, social, and political structure."[42]

NOTES

1. The most candid confession is by C. P. Kindleberger: "The book is written by one who has not been there." (*Economic Development*, McGraw-Hill, 1958, 1st edition, p. ix.)

2. The most frequently cited authors in this literature are W. Arthur Lewis, "Economic Development with Unlimited Supplies of Labour," *Manchester School*, May 1954, and "Unlimited Labour: Further Notes," *Manchester School*, January 1958; J. C. H. Fei and G. Ranis, *Development of the Labour Surplus Economy: Theory and Policy*, Yale University, 1964; D. W. Jorgenson, "The Development of a Dual Economy," *Economic Journal*, June 1961, and "Surplus Agricultural Labour and the Development of a Dual Economy," *Oxford Economic Papers*, November 1967.

3. See W. W. Rostow, *The Stages of Economic Growth*, Cambridge University Press, 1960.

4. See R. Nurkse, *Problems of Capital Formation in Underdeveloped Countries*, Oxford University Press, 1957; P. N. Rosenstein-Rodan, "Problems of Industrialization of Eastern and South Eastern Europe," *Economic Journal*, 1943; K. Mandelbaum, *The Industrialization of Backward Areas*, Basil Blackwell, 1945.

5. Leibenstein defines the subsistence level as one where "equality between high fertility and high mortality rates exist. These are the maximum rates consistent with the survival of the population." (H. Leibenstein, *Economic Backwardness and Economic Growth*, John Wiley and Sons, 1960, p. 154.)

6. W. Arthur Lewis, *op. cit.*

7. D. W. Jorgenson, "Surplus Agricultural Labour and the Development of a Dual Economy," *loc. cit.*, p. 291.

8. *Ibid.*, p. 292.

9. See, for example, K. B. Griffin, "Algerian Agriculture in Transition," *Bulletin* of the Oxford University Institute of Economics and Statistics, 1965.

10. M. Paglin, "Surplus Agricultural Labour and Development," *American Economic Review*, September 1965. Paglin's study is of India.

11. See, for instance, M. Herskovits, *Economic Anthropology: A Study in Comparative Economics*, 2nd edition, Knopf, 1952; G. Dalton, ed., *Tribal and Peasant Economies: Readings in Economic Anthropology*, Natural History Press, 1967; J. Ingram, *Economic Change in Thailand Since 1850*, Stanford University Press, 1955.

12. A useful discussion of some of these issues is found in A. Berry and R. Soligo, "Rural-Urban Migration, Agricultural Output, and the Supply Price of Labour in a Labour-Surplus Economy," *Oxford Economic Papers*, July 1968.

13. J. H. Boeke, *Economics and Economic Policy of Dual Societies*, New York, 1953, p. 40. The backward bending supply curve of effort is also supported by B. Higgins, *Economic Development*, Constable, 1959, pp. 286–7, 504.

14. See, for example, W. P. Falcon, "Farmer Response to Price in a Subsistence Economy: The Case of West Pakistan," *American Economic Review*, May 1964; P. T. Bauer and B. S. Yamey, "A Case Study of Response to Price in an Underdeveloped Country," *Economic Journal*, December 1959; J. R. Behrman, *Supply Response in Underdeveloped Agriculture: A Case Study of Thailand, 1937–1963*; D. Narain, *The Impact of Price Movements on Areas Under Selected Crops in India, 1900–1939*; E. Dean, *The Supply Responses of African Farmers: Theory and Measurement in Malawi*, Amsterdam, 1966.

15. W. P. Falcon and C. H. Gotsch, "Two Approaches with the Same Results," *Asian Review*, July 1968.

16. J. R. Behrman, "The Adoption of New Products and of New Factors in Response to Market Incentives in Peasant Agriculture: An Econometric Investigation of Thai Corn and Kenaf Supply Responses in the Post-war Period," University of Pennsylvania, Department of Economics, Discussion Paper No. 45, mimeo, February 1967.

17. P. T. Bauer and B. S. Yamey, *op. cit.*

18. R. Nurkse, *op. cit.*, p 37.

19. *Ibid.*, p. 43.

20. "Economic Development with Unlimited Supplies of Labour," *loc. cit.* Jorgenson assumes that "saving is equal to total profits in the industrial sector" (*op. cit.*).

21. A. Bergan, "Personal Income Distribution and Personal Savings in Pakistan, 1963/64," *Pakistan Development Review*, Summer 1967, p. 186.

22. "Surplus Agricultural Labour and the Development of a Dual Economy," *loc. cit.*, p. 292.

23. *Ibid.*, p. 293.

24. AID, Statistics and Reports Division, *Economic Growth Trends: Latin-America, East Asia, Near East and South Asia, Africa*, 1967/1968.

25. *Ibid.* Also see FAO, *The State of Food and Agriculture*, 1967.

26. K. B. Griffin, "Financing Development Plans in Pakistan," *Pakistan Development Review*, Winter 1965, p. 606.

27. G. F. Papanek, *Pakistan's Development*, Harvard University Press, 1967, Appendix Table 5B, p. 318.

28. S. R. Bose, "Trend of Real Incomes of the Rural Poor in East Pakistan, 1949–66—An Indirect Estimate," Pakistan Institute of Development Economics, Research Report No. 68, July 1968.

29. *Ibid.*, Table 1. The data are expressed in constant prices of 1959/60.

30. *Ibid.*, Table 3.

31. *Ibid.*, Table 4.

32. J. C. H. Fei and G. Ranis, "Unlimited Supply of Labour and the Concept of Balanced Growth," *Pakistan Development Review*, Winter 1961, p. 32.

33. See G. Ranis and J. C. H. Fei, "A Theory of Economic Development," *American Economic Review*, September 1961; J. C. H. Fei and G. Ranis, *Development of the Labour Surplus Economy: Theory and Policy, loc. cit.*

34. In Chad the non-agricultural labour force is 8 per cent of the total, in Kenya 12 per cent, in Thailand 18 per cent, in Nepal 8 per cent, in Yemen 11 per cent and in Haiti 17 per cent.

35. This rationalization certainly does not apply to Fei and Ranis who criticize Lewis for treating the agricultural sector "more or less as an afterthought" while claiming that their model "gives a more explicit treatment to the agricultural sector." ("Unlimited Supply of Labour and the Concept of Balanced Growth," *loc. cit.*, p. 29.)

36. D. W. Jorgenson, "Surplus Agricultural Labour and the Development of a Dual Economy," *loc. cit.*, p. 297.

37. C. R. Frank, Jr., "Urban Unemployment and Economic Growth in Africa," *Oxford Economic Papers*, July 1968, Table II, p. 254.

38. "Economic Development with Unlimited Supplies of Labour," *loc. cit.*

39. "Surplus Agricultural Labour and the Development of a Dual Economy," *loc. cit.*, p. 310.

40. See N. H. Leff, "Marginal Savings Rates in the Development Process: The Brazilian Experience," *Economic Journal*, September 1968.

41. In most of the literature on growth and development institutional reforms are ignored; in other cases reforms are treated in a purely formal way. For example, Mrs. Adelman writes her production function in the form $Y = f\ (K_t, \ldots, U_t)$, where K_t is the stock of capital at time t and U_t is the "socio-cultural environment." By differencing the production function one can determine the effect of institutional reform,

$$\sum_{g=1}^{w} \frac{\Delta Y}{\Delta Uj} \cdot \frac{\Delta Uj}{\Delta t}$$

This last expression, however, increases our knowledge of the role of institutional reforms by precisely zero. It tells us that if reforms lead to increased output, they lead to increased output; and if they don't, they don't. A more trivial result is hard to imagine. (See I. Adelman, *Theories of Economic Growth and Development*, Stanford University Press, 1961, Ch. 2.)

42. P. Baran, *The Political Economy of Growth*, Monthly Review Press, 1957, p. 3.

3

Balanced Thought and Economic Growth

Warren Frederick Ilchman and Ravindra C. Bhargava

> In framing an ideal we may assume what we
> wish, but should avoid impossibilities.
> —Aristotle, *Politics*

In no field does orthodoxy seem to last less long than in development economics. Today's general strategy for economic growth becomes tomorrow's barrier. A factor considered crucial in one schema becomes a highly dependent variable in another. Often the whole strategy is premised on a tautology: to develop economically, a nation must develop economically. The attempts to discover basic psychological sources of the process, such as motivational patterns in a society, have pushed the answers back to deviant minority groups and the *leit-motif's* of children's fairy tales.[1] For the economic strategist in a low-income country, these latter studies, while important and interesting, are as useful in guiding his investment decisions as the studies by Max Weber.

But are the more exclusively economic strategies of greater value? It is the contention of this article that the major strategies so far advanced by economists are relevant operationally only in highly specific situations. These situations, furthermore, are not defined by economic factors alone. They are determined by crucial political, sociological, and administrative factors as well. A further contention of this article is that the only operational strategies for "development" are the products of a cross-disciplinary social science perspective with a strong contribution from political scientists.

To prove this contention, the authors have analyzed several major theorists concerned with three potentially operational strategies—"Big Push" balanced growth, unbalanced growth, and capital formation through unlimited supplies of labor.[2] These theories are not assessed in terms of their economic merits. Instead, they are analyzed in terms of the major social problems that might arise from undertaking them and the political regime and administrative systems they presuppose.[3] In other words, these strategies are analyzed in terms of what they assume about the rest of the social system. Among the questions asked are: What is the character and membership of the elite? What is the degree of organization of two of the affected sectors—the urban working force and the peasantry? How responsive is the political system to group demands? What is the expected role of government in the strategy? How many civil servants will be required, and to what extent and in what way must they be trained? How much and what

Reprinted from *Economic Development and Cultural Change*, Vol. XIV, No. 4 (July 1966), pp. 385–399, by permission of The University of Chicago Press and the authors. Copyright 1966 by The University of Chicago.

types of data are required? Detailed answers to these questions, of course, cannot be given in an article of this length. But, despite the necessary abstractions, a clear idea will be given of the "non-economic" criterion by which these strategies must be judged before they can be considered operational.

I

Balanced Growth

The "Big Push" balanced growth strategy for the development of underdeveloped countries may be attributed to Ragnar Nurkse and Paul Rosenstein-Rodan. In general, the strategy argues that the low per capita incomes which prevail in underdeveloped countries are a consequence of the low levels of productivity and that substantial increases in productivity require increased capital formation. However, another consequence of the low levels of income is that the demand for most manufactured goods is small, most of the income being utilized for subsistence. This limitation to the extent of the market implies that no entrepreneur can profitably, even with a monopoly, set up a modern factory, as the indivisibilities of capital result in the unit being of such a size that, at its low levels of operation, the costs of production are too high. Consequently, capital formation in manufacturing is not feasible, productivity does not increase, and poverty continues. To break this vicious circle, the balanced growth theorists suggest that in a country a whole set of complementary investments should be made, such that factories themselves, as well as the workers in them, can buy up all the produce either as intermediate goods or for final consumption. This will then render all the investments profitable. Thus, it is proposed to solve the demand problem by means of investment itself. In this way, capital formation will be made possible and vicious circles broken.

The most striking feature of the "Big Push" strategy is that, whereas investments in general are not profitable in the economy, there are combinations of investments,[4] which if implemented simultaneously, will prove profitable. To achieve these "right" bundles of investments, qualitatively and quantitatively, together with the time schedule for execution, is not easy. It involves planning substantial changes in production patterns with little assistance from the market mechanism and requires anticipating the market requirements once these changes have been made. In a scheme of balanced growth, every component must be at the right place at the right time in the right quantity. The entire effort is based on the capability of a country to organize its relevant sectors, enact the proper controls and incentives, and acquire and submit to the best technical judgments on the combinations of investments for balanced growth.

The capital required for the "Big Push" will come from two sources—domestic and foreign savings. For domestic savings, taxation, higher profits, and inflation will be the chief means. However, with the large requirements of the strategy, domestic savings, even under the best of circumstances, will not be adequate, and foreign capital inflows will have to be substantial. The inflow would be in the form of government grants and loans and direct private investment.

What are the so-called "non-economic factors" which might enable an underdeveloped country to adopt successfully this strategy? Above all, there must exist in the country some authority or institutional arrangement capable of planning and implementing the combination of investments. This presupposes a political ruling elite with considerable unanimity of purpose and agreement on measures that may be taken to achieve this goal, a political system supportive, in the short and at least medium run, of the resulting programs, and an administrative system capable of bearing the technical burden of preparing and implementing the strategy.

Two ruling elites are possible. They are distinguished by their membership, especially private sector representation, and the role they conceive for government to play. The first is a modernizing elite made up largely of intellectuals, the military, and civil servants. It would be, in varying degrees, distrustful of the private sector. For this elite, the government is the obvious agent for balanced growth. Any role for the private sector, if allowed at all, would have to be subject to extensive controls. Reliance on incentives and indirect controls to secure the massive complementarity of investment would contain too much uncertainty. Government ownership and operation would be preferable for this elite.[5]

The membership of a second possible ruling elite would be distinguished by heavy representation from the business sector. This elite would have to be particularly small and closely knit to achieve the cooperation necessary to plan and organize the establishment of a whole complex of industries in the balanced growth pattern. Active government help and encouragement to provide the necessary incentives and business conditions would also be required. Taxes on industries and the elite must be low (or subventions high); high profits and monopolies permitted; infrastructure investments and technical assistance provided; trade union activity controlled; and internal security maintained. Indeed, it is unnecessary to distinguish between government and the private sector; they are virtually the same.[6]

Both ruling elites will have to be narrow in membership. A broadly based nationalist elite, drawing from several social sectors, such as the urban working force, would be too susceptible to the demands of its members, and this would impede the success of the strategy. This narrow base presupposes either a quiescent population, no political opposition of a formal or informal sort, heavy expenditures on coercion, or all three.[7] This is, of course, another way to describe an authoritarian situation, for it must be apparent that the "Big Push" cannot be undertaken unless the ruling elite can effectively restrict access by the broad mass of the public to the substance of the strategy. Furthermore, ideally, the technical considerations in the "Big Push" even subordinate the elite's judgment to that of the engineers and the economists.

Therefore, for the length of time required to break the "vicious circle of poverty," the political system cannot be sensitive to group demands. But in the "Big Push," this is highly unlikely for several reasons. First, the strategy requires that within a short period of time a country will find itself with a large industrial sector superimposed on an economically primitive base. Industrialization, and attendant urbanization, means the influx of large numbers of people from the rural areas into an entirely different set of social conditions. These people would find their values and ways of life unsuited to the new environment and would need considerable readjustment to be absorbed into industry and to attain stability. Their problems would be aggravated by the fact that it would be unlikely that adequate arrangements for housing, sanitation, medical attention, recreation, etc., would exist, since the numbers involved would be so large and the capital available for these purposes inadequate. Because of the nature and objectives of either ruling elite, trade union activity would be restricted and any liberal labor legislation unimplemented. All claims for redistribution would be unacceptable. This would tend to produce a restless and dissatisfied mass of people, who will have little to say in the political system and will constitute a constant threat to the social system, necessitating an elaborate coercive apparatus. It is true that the problems of adjusting the rural population to the modern sector always create tensions and difficulties, but in the "Big Push" strategy, the magnitudes would be much larger. Industrialization would not be arriving gradually, but would be more in the nature of a "once-and-for-all" process.

Second, the problems of regional disparities would constantly press for redress. The "Big Push" strategy, however, permits this only insofar as the redress fulfills a role in the total combination of investments. Probably, the dictates of location economics, and the possible bias of the ruling elite, would lead to the concentration of economic activity in certain areas, to the neglect of other regions. The experience in several countries, Pakistan, India, and Nigeria among them, has shown how serious a situation may result from this.

Third, the financing of the strategy renders it vulnerable to group demands. On one hand, major reliance on foreign capital would be unacceptable to nations which have recently won, and intend to sustain, freedom from foreign controls. Any restriction on their use of foreign capital, whether borrowed or granted, is considered compromising to their independence. Prohibitions against foreign capital imports, restrictions on the use of foreign capital, the universal condemnation of "strings" on foreign aid, the demands for trade rather than aid, the popularity of nationalization through confiscation are common manifestations of this.[8] Under these conditions, the capital-exporting and aid-giving countries will hardly be encouraged to fill the capital needs. And to remove these impediments requires a regime unmenaced by an opposition able to exploit this sensitive issue. On the other hand, the burden of domestic saving from taxation and inflation would be borne by the non-profit-earning classes—the urban working force, the middle class, the service professions, and the rural sector. At the same time, particularly in a predominately private sector strategy, there will be increasing disparities of income. The public in all regimes tolerate the above condition to a certain degree. But if the destabilization produced by massive foreign capital is to be avoided, or if the required capital is not available, increased reliance will be placed on mobilizing domestic savings. For the authority of a regime (and consequently the strategy) to remain unaffected in this case presupposes the existence of a long-suffering and tranquil non-profit-earning class or the existence of a widely effective coercive apparatus, whose costs the "Big Push" strategist externalizes. In reality, the demands for redistribution would be great and fully exploitable by any opposition in low-income countries.

Thus, at a time when social harmony is an essential and assumed part of the strategy for economic development, it is that same strategy that is least likely to produce it.

Administratively, the "Big Push" necessitates, in the public and/or private sector, an extensive and highly skilled bureaucracy. This would have to be in addition to the existing civil service, for retraining a civil service for development objectives is a long-term process, and the needs of "law and order" would undoubtedly increase greatly under the pressure of the "Big Push." These personnel would be needed for both the formulation and execution of the strategy. New skills of many kinds and in great quantities would be called for—managerial and technical skills for operating the new enterprises, organizational and administrative skills for over-all coordination and the various forms of controls, including coercion. The experience with the execution of comparative modest development programs in several countries has revealed the shortcomings in these fields. Furthermore, formulating the strategy requires a large quantity of reliable data, not only of economic variables like elasticities of demand, income distribution, price changes, and technologies, but also of non-economic variables like changes in taste, motivations, and values. The data-gathering and processing machinery will, therefore, have to be widespread and able—far more than what exists at present in any underdeveloped country.[9]

Unbalanced Growth

Albert Hirschman developed his theory of unbalanced growth in response to the "Big Push" idea. The different kinds of resources required for the "Big Push," he contended, are ones which low-income countries have in short supply. Indeed, that is why they are underdeveloped. He also insists that development is a gradual process, and it is unrealistic to think in terms of superimposing a large modern sector on a traditional economy. But the greatest shortage, according to his analysis, is the ability to perceive and take investment decisions, even when opportunities exist. The strategy of unbalanced growth seeks to remedy this shortage by creating situations in which people are forced to take investment decisions. Such situations are achieved by deliberately "unbalancing" different sectors of the economy. If certain parts of the economy are made to grow, the shortages in the complementary parts will create pressures for their growth also, forcing investments to be made. The areas which lead the development should be so selected that investments in the complementary areas are really compulsive rather than permissive.

The most important field of application of this strategy is to governmental decisions regarding investments in economic and social overhead capital. The role of government is usually defined to include the function of providing this infrastructure, in order that entrepreneurs may make profitable investments of a directly productive nature. Hirschman, however, points out that investments in infrastructure are basically permissive of directly productive investments. They do not create any compelling situation for the latter to be made. Consequently, infrastructure investments are often uneconomic, insofar as they remain underutilized for long periods. A better sequence would be for the government to provide only the barest minimum of infrastructure and to encourage entrepreneurs through incentives, such as tariff protection and subsidies, to invest in directly productive activities. As more of these investments are made, the deficiencies of overhead facilities become marked and increase the cost of production. Entrepreneurs would then press for provision of these services. This pressure would be an indicator to government for the more rational allocation of infrastructure investments. Thus, by having infrastructure lag behind productive activities, development would be quicker, and better use would be made of the available resources.

Hirschman applies this technique to other matters, such as the choice of investments, selection of technology, and ensuring maintenance of capital. To ensure the continuance of productive investments being made, he suggests that the initial activity chosen should be one that maximizes the backward and forward linkages. Instead of starting industrial efforts by making finished goods, the investments should be made in activities which are near the middle of a triangularly arranged input-output matrix. In choosing the technology, an attempt should be made to adopt "machine-paced" operations that compel labor to work at a predetermined rate, despite such a technique being more capital-intensive. Hirschman recommends that underdeveloped countries should choose complicated techniques, where the consequence of a breakdown would be more serious and hence compel adequate maintenance.

Finally, Hirschman does not favor central planning, for it tends to internalize both the external economies and diseconomies.[10] He believes that the net effect would not necessarily be positive, and more rapid growth can be achieved by encouraging aggressive entrepreneurship in the 19th-century fashion. He would also favor a certain amount of inflation in the interest of forcing savings and making investments more profitable.

Although Professor Hirschman has insights into the problems facing at least some of the underdeveloped countries, his strategy ignores important political, social, and administrative factors. What sort of regime is necessary for adopting the strategy of unbalanced growth? Dominant power in the country, needless to say, would be exercised by one group—the business class. A regime totally sympathetic to private sector development and serving its interests would be required. There would be no governmental responsibility for comprehensive central planning and execution, and government would best fulfill its functions by providing the right social overheads at the right time and maintaining law and order. This latter task will be particularly difficult, as the urban working force and the middle class will be subject to inflation, low wages, and increasing disparities of income. At the same time, the government will be observed to tax the businessman inadequately and even to grant him subsidies to swell his profits.

To compound this problem, the urban working force will be subject to the destabilizing effects of inadequate social overhead investments—in housing, education, and welfare programs. In addition, the adoption of machine-paced and capital-intensive operations would increase, or at least fail to reduce, unemployment. This would come at a time when trade union activity would be discouraged or completely curtailed by the state. Furthermore, the regime cannot be disturbed by any political objections to foreign business activity in the country. Nor would the demands of regional balance be permitted to affect the "unbalancing" decisions. This, of course, presupposes a high degree of national unity.

What regimes are excluded from adopting the strategy of unbalanced growth? Socialist regimes are, of course. So are those in which businessmen are held in low repute, and only a few businessmen, if any, are part of the core elite guiding decisions. Regimes are excluded in which trade union activity is strong and the political mechanisms sensitive to claims for redistribution. Finally, a regime which invested in social overhead for any reason other than on demonstrated need by directly productive activities would be considered hopelessly inefficient.

Administratively, the demands of the strategy, though less than those of the "Big Push," will nevertheless be considerable. The skill for taking profitable investment decisions is not the same as skills required to organize and operate enterprise. Government must gather data for rationally deciding between alternative infrastructure investments. Also, it will have to select the sectors and areas where activity is to be promoted on the basis of comparative advantage and the likely trends in the demand function. Determination of a suitable system of subsidies and sources of revenue will be necessary. Decisions, it might be added, on purely economic grounds would be difficult, owing to the differing degrees of political power various business interests would possess. Lastly, the administrative requirements for coercion would be considerable.

Capital Formation with Unlimited Supplies of Labor

W. Arthur Lewis believes that in several underdeveloped countries there are virtually unlimited supplies of labor which can be used for capital formation. Disguised unemployment in the agricultural sector, large numbers in domestic service, population growth at a rate faster than the rate of growth of productive employment, and women who can work if opportunities arise —these are the main sources.

The development of the economy takes place by the increase of the sector using reproducible capital—the capitalist sector. This sector has a higher level of productivity than the remaining part of the economy, which is at subsistence level. As development takes place, the capitalist sector expands, while the subsistence sector grows smaller. Lewis also assumes that the capitalist class, which owns the reproducible capital, has a propensity to save and reinvest a large proportion of its profits. Hence, for the growth of the capitalist sector, it is necessary for profits to grow. It is immaterial to the argument whether the state itself is the capitalist.

The capitalist sector has to hire labor to work the capital it owns. As the sector expands, the requirements for labor keep increasing. Since the model assumes virtually unlimited supplies of labor, the process of growth cannot stop because of lack of workers, at least until all the surplus labor has been absorbed. Moreover, as capital accumulates, it causes labor productivity to rise, while technological innovations have the effect of increasing the productivity of both labor and capital. Consequently, the volume of profits, and possibly the profit rate also would keep rising, assuming other factors remain unchanged, and the process of growth would continue. However, growth can be slowed, or even stopped, if the wages increase at such a rate that, despite increases in productivity, the volume of profits falls. This will lead to a decrease in savings and investments. Thus, for the success of this model, keeping wages in check is essential.

The wages paid by the capitalist sector are determined by the wages and the average product of workers in the subsistence sector. To attract workers away from the farms and the villages, the capitalist has to offer an adequate incentive in the form of higher wages. As workers are drawn away from the subsistence sector in quantities large enough to decrease the absolute numbers, the average product rises, and hence the capitalist wages also have to rise in order to maintain the differential. An even more important cause for wages to rise in the capitalist sector would be the relative increase in the price of foodstuffs, as compared with the price of industrial products. The process of drawing workers into the capitalist sector would raise real incomes and increase the demand for food, necessitating larger supplies of food being brought to the market by the farmers. If this does not happen, owing to output being inelastic, food prices would rise, and hence the wages of the capitalist sector workers must rise correspondingly. Further, as the real wages in the subsistence sector would also be increasing, the maintenance of the differential would mean a rise in the capitalist wages. However, if food output does continue to increase, wages would still have to keep rising to keep pace with the average product of the subsistence sector. The solution is twofold: increasing the output of food and, by drawing away the surplus in the form of a land tax, preventing the farmer from taking advantage of this increase. If this can be successfully done, capital formation would continue until all the surplus labor was absorbed and the productivity of the two sectors raised to a high and almost equal level.

Nurkse has a somewhat similar model. He also proposes to utilize the disguised unemployed to form productive capital, i.e., roads, dams, irrigation canals. To minimize the cost of this operation, he intends that these workers be fed from the existing food production by keeping unchanged the consumption of those remaining on the farms. This will be accomplished by the imposition of a land tax or by compulsory requisitioning of food. Nurkse realizes that the workers transferred from the farms need to be given some small increase in consumption. He also recognizes the necessity of making all the surplus population work to avoid the "demonstration effect" inducing people to return to the villages.

As with other strategies of development, these models also appear to require a specific set of conditions. Lewis's model can work either with complete state ownership of the means of production, or with a government dominated by a business elite. In either case, the rural population and the industrial working force will not be in a position to influence the allocation of resources or the distribution of income and wealth. The government has to follow a policy of keeping the wages of the subsistence sector and the industrial workers at the minimum possible level. The tools for this will largely be heavy doses of land taxation, control of the activities of organized labor, non-implementation of any liberal labor legislation, and coercion. If the industries are being developed by private entrepreneurs, the economy will have to be geared to maximize their profits, to encourage investments. Accordingly, monopolies will presumably be allowed and taxes on business and high incomes kept at low levels. The state would provide the infrastructure investments, credit facilities, and other institutional arrangements to enable entrepreneurs to make investments. Consequently, the state will have few resources to invest in general welfare activities. In any case, income transfers to the working class would not be in accordance with the logic of the model.

The model assumes that the rural and urban working population will either be docile enough to accept this situation or the state able to coerce a condition of stability. But growing income disparities, regressive taxation, and suppression of the right of organization are policies which are difficult to adhere to for long. Nurkse's model has the added complication of labor conscription to make it operational. Finally, the social problems of adjustment, arising from industrialization and accentuated by the living conditions which the industrialists are likely to provide, would be as acute as in the balanced and unbalanced growth theories. Few underdeveloped countries today could undertake this strategy.

Administratively, the major task would be the maintenance of internal stability, coercion of the working class, and prevention of expressions of disaffection. An elaborate and reliable machinery for the collection of land tax would be required—a machinery not prone to leakages through corruption. In countries where land holdings are small, this problem would be even more difficult. Further, the success of the model demands rapid increase in food output. While imposing and collecting land taxes, the government would also have to embark upon an extensive program of agricultural extension. Experience in several countries has shown in recent years that this is not an easy matter and calls for high technical, administrative, and organizational skills. This has been true even where the farmers were generally cooperative, and the frictions of high taxes were not present.[11] Another task requiring substantial and advanced skills is the planning and implementing of a consistent program. If the state participated in the productive investments, the additional problem of making public enterprise efficient will have to be solved.

II

The three strategies analyzed claim that their implementation will probably lead to economic growth. No demands are made explicitly on the regime undertaking them, except, by implication, that the regime follow generally the prescribed program. From a social scientist's and a planner's point of view, however, certain questions need to be asked of these and other strategies.

1. What type of regime is required for undertaking the strategy? To what extent are a regime's values or the ruling elites' composition limitations? Must there be separate strategies for economic growth for "liberal" regimes, "radical" regimes, "tutelary democracies," pro-business regimes, anti-business regimes, regimes in which labor and/or small landholders are important components of the ruling elite, regimes in which taxes cannot be effectively collected, or where there is a low tolerance for bilateral foreign assistance or foreign private investment? Is a moratorium on politics necessary for the period during which the strategy is being implemented? Can there be permitted opposition parties which might try to exploit grievances against the regime and its new policies?

2. How does the strategy affect various social and economic sectors? Will substantial disorganization result for many existing economic and social institutions and functions? How long must this disorganization be endured before "growth" provides new institutions and articulates new functions? Is the strategy profligate of a society's integrative institutions, values, and beliefs? What have been or might be some of the unintended consequences of implementing the strategy? An increase in the number of landless laborers? Greater urban unemployment because of increasing capital intensiveness of investment and advancing requirements for skills?

3. What is implicit in the strategy for the distribution of wealth? Will this "formula" change? If so, how and when will it change? What new demands might be made on the political system as a consequence of implementing the strategy? Will there be greater demands for welfare expenditures and urban amenities? Does the strategy allow for them? Does the strategy "internalize" their costs?

4. To what degree is the strategy dependent on coercion? Persuasion? What, from the experience of other regimes, might be the short-term economic costs of coercion? Are they internalized in the strategy? What might be the long-term economic and social costs of a policy of coercion? Are social deviancy, anomie, and extremist movements likely "prices" to pay?

5. What does the strategy demand of the administrative system? Will more personnel and new skills be needed? Will the needs of the strategy for administrators in one sector starve the other sectors in their needs?[12] Will existing machinery for supervision and coordination be adequate? Are new data, and hence data-gathering machinery, required? Are these costs internalized in the strategy?

The authors of these strategies might insist that models are necessarily abstract and that implementation must be moderated to meet each country's particular situation. At this point, the relevant political, social, and administrative information is added. But this answer will not do. First, the authors of the strategies were inspired by the process of economic growth in specific countries. In each instance, this process took place in a sociopolitical context from which the process acquired effectiveness and without which it would be virtually meaningless. Professor Nurkse's balanced growth strategy found many precedents in the Soviet Union, Professor Hirschman's proposals in a composite of occurrences in Latin America, and the advocates of capital formation through unlimited supplies of labor in Japanese and, less enthusiastically, Soviet experience.[13] Answers to the questions posed previously are also part of the record. Advice, hence, could also be given on the political, social, and administrative prerequisites, requisites, and consequences. Important costs can be calculated. Whether or not the strategy is relevant, with the addition of the appropriate information, can be assessed. Only then, the strategy for economic growth really becomes a strategy for social, political, and administrative change as well. Second, the strategies are, in different ways, unsusceptible to moderation in economic terms. Balanced growth requires a massive complementarity of supply and demand. Anything short of a total package of investments would fail in the "Big Push." Although most countries have unbalanced growth all the time, a substantially moderated "unbalance" will probably fail to achieve Professor Hirschman's objectives. Also, most conscious efforts in this direction, despite moderated intensity, might still be destabilizing to civil authority. Any moderation in the capital formation through the use of unlimited supplies of labor strategy would be difficult, because of the small size of the profit-making sector and the declared rate of economic growth of most underdeveloped countries. For these countries, moderating any one of the three strategies really means abandoning it. Finally, the strategies might tend, if followed only "moderately," toward self-justification. For example, failure to achieve high rates of capital formation through the Lewis and Nurkse models would set up pressures to remove the political and social barriers to "efficiency." Judgment on the strategy's effectiveness would have to be postponed until a country's social and political system approximated the strategy's "hidden" requirements.

One major reason for the difficulties inherent in implementing the economic strategies is that they were constructed by tools developed for nations with different problems and needs. While this assertion is not novel, it has usually been argued within the terms of economic analysis. Part of the justification for the allegation here is an interpretation of the history of ideas. The key problems confronting underdeveloped countries are the survival of the centralized polity and the existing regime. Neither can claim the likelihood of permanence. The centralized polity, often the rather recent creation of a former colonial power, has institutions too new or too dubious to be accorded deference and legitimacy by various elites in the country. Even the nation's existence is menaced from many sources: threats of and attempts at secession; over-weening neighbors, allies, and would-be allies; and retreats into regional and village loyalties and consequent starving of resources and support for the central government's objectives.[14] The existing regime is always a changing coalition, resting in varying proportions on charisma, promises, and coercion. Each of these has built-in limitations—limitations insofar as many demands are exclusive of others in their fulfillment, limitations to the endurance of coercion and restraints by various groups, limitations in resources (which are much more than economic resources) to meet promises, limitations to the mystique of the nationalist movement, "the hero of Independence," the popular military figure. Much of modern economic analysis, however, was developed for an economic sub-system in a larger social system in which the political problems confronted by most underdeveloped countries had been largely solved or the pace of industrialization had not raised them as starkly. The centralized polity's existence could be assumed, and the ruling regime was expected primarily to help make the market mechanism more efficient and more authoritative.[15] This assumed virtual autonomy of the economic sphere was and is theoretically more acceptable for, say, Great Britain or the United States than it can be in the foreseeable future for underdeveloped countries. In the latter, the initial political prerequisites for a functioning national market are not yet met, and it is, furthermore, the intention of most of the regimes to rely (optimistically, of course) on the political marketplace in the first instance as the authoritative allocator of resources and power.

There are other reasons as well for the difficulty inherent in implementing these economic strategies. One is the extreme division of labor and consequent assumptions dominant in the social sciences.[16] Each discipline has staked out a process, defined perhaps too sharply the relevant variables, developed intrinsic indices, and tended to erect boundaries against trespassing from the other social sciences. When representatives of other social sciences have, nevertheless, successfully crossed the boundaries, the "host" social science incorporates a previously exogenous variable into its system. But there is seldom a cross-disciplinary attempt to penetrate the interrelationship of "each discipline's variables" in terms of the social system as a whole.[17] The three economic strategies analyzed in this article are premised on an essentially autonomous economic sphere in which government and/or private persons make decisions about directly productive activities and related social overhead. The strategies accept as evidence of success, among other economic indicators, an increase in gross national product or a decrease in the incremental capital/output ratio. But these decisions subsume other crucial decisions and judgments. The major judgment is simply that there *will be* a long run for which the short-term sacrifice in consumption is made. This judgment, which is more explicit in underdeveloped countries than can be imagined by analysts from politically well established nations, is the product of other judgments and decisions: a nation's laws will be honored; social conflict can be contained in the institutions of the state; the administrative apparatus is adequate and predictable enough to make just and rapid decisions; material productivity is a "good"; the present distribution of privilege, power, and resources is desirable and/or sufficiently supported, etc. As can easily be seen, the underlying judgments are narrowly social and political in character. The relevant data are not simply economic and cannot be viewed so restrictively.

Another reason stems from a misunderstanding of the mandate given by rulers of underdeveloped countries. The mandate is never a *carte blanche* for development in the most efficient way. In addition to the usual limitations on productive factors, economic development programs are limited by the character and intentions of the existing political regime and social system. The concept of "rising expectations" refers to different sectors (social and economic) and their differing demands, not a unanimous "general will" in this direction.[18] Phrases like "Arab Socialism," "communocracy," and "socialist pattern of society" may imply a "general will," but they must always be interpreted in terms of the elites endorsing these phrases. Furthermore, no nation has ever had or could have an exclusive, secular goal of economic development to which all others must be subordinated. The elites and mobilized publics of every nation, rich and poor, have many objectives for public policy: national survival, national grandeur, distributive-welfare goals, political stability, maximum public choice, maintaining a particular elite combination in power, and the "higher life" among them.[19] While it is true that economic development is necessary for some of these goals, it is also true that economic development is not sufficient. In other goals, it is dysfunctional.[20] In most cases, the other public goals and economic development are mutually necessary. Ignoring this, some economic strategists complain about "prestige" expenditures and concentration on "unproductive" activities. These complaints, heard often from professional economists in underdeveloped countries, place a great burden on the political system. Trained as they and their Western counterparts are in a discipline concerned with the most productive use of scarce resources, they are uncomfortable in the face of politics and the ambiguities of social structure and cultural values.[21] There is a growing feeling among these people that anything short of exclusive concentration on the goal of economic growth is treason by the politicians. A political system able to arbitrate many claims and move toward many common goals cannot long bear this alienation.

III

How would a more integrated social science be of greater relevance for the problems of underdeveloped countries? Basically, a new question must replace the "economic growth" question. Rather than "How should a nation allocate its scarce resources to achieve economic growth?" the question should be, "How should a government allocate its scarce resources to modernize?" This permits the social scientist and the policy-maker to look at a total social system and its institutions and puts economic growth where it belongs, as part of a broader process—the process of modernization. Modernization can be defined generally as a process of improving the capability of a nation's institutions and value system to meet increasing and different demands.[22] Theoretically, a modern nation is one in which the institutions and values are able to meet or adequately handle the increasing and different demands made on them. Political modernization, for example, involves improving the capability of the political system. The general modernization process is dependent on securing a centralized polity, its penetration into the various spheres of life, and obtaining for the polity free-floating resources, unattached to any ascriptive group, to pursue further modernizing goals. It is also dependent on changing certain values: acquiring a new time perspective, a different valuation of the objectives of the state, a changed allegiance from particularistic to broader, more functionally specific associations and institutions, and, finally, new assessments of human activity and achievement. Developing the capability to meet changing and increasing demands is by no means a settled achievement of the underdeveloped nations.[23]

How do "modernization" and "economic growth" differ? The latter becomes part of the former. As a process, modernization is social and political as well as economic. Indeed, to separate the activities is to suggest a divisible character of the phenomena which does not exist. Although economic growth is one way of increasing the stock of free-floating resources to meet demands, it is not exhaustive. The range of demands includes claims for prestige, status, and power; these demands may or may not require economic resources. But like economic growth, modernization must be planned and, above all, invested in as rationally as in the too narrowly conceived directly productive activities and social overhead capital.

Viewed from the perspective of modernization, the concept of social overhead becomes useful in formulating strategy. Social overhead or "infrastructure" permits thinking about essential conditions for building a modernized nation. In doing so, it makes more explicit the character of the social system and, particularly, the role of the state. Society must be seen in terms of developing within it new structures and sanctioning different values: institutions to integrate the members of society, who were forced to leave traditional institutions and values, into new, more materially productive relationships, values to justify modernization as a process. These, too, constitute infrastructure—social infrastructure. Likewise, a modernization strategy casts the state into a more realistic role. The state becomes more than a "fomentor" or the best instrument for capital formation, as it is for the economic development strategies; it becomes the authoritative allocator of society's scarce values and resources—even when the authoritative decision is in favor of the private sector. For the objectives of public policy, the state becomes the arbiter of claims—economic, social, ideological, and philosophical—made by the sectors of society. To fulfill these functions, particularly as they expand in later phases of modernization, a solid political infrastructure must be built: institutions to contain conflict; institutions to aggregate and simplify claims; value systems which accept the legitimacy of the state's authoritative allocations. Just such institutions and values preceded and became more implicit in the modernization of the West and were subsumed in the development of modern economic thought. Finally, an administrative infrastructure is needed. This is the economic development strategists also recognize. But the modernization perspective does not allow the glib suggestion that administration must switch from "law-and-order values" to development values! Modernization brings in its wake intensified social problems for which increased expenditures on law-and-order institutions and values are required. At the same time, the administrative infrastructure must be expanded in new directions, with emphasis on values of expedition in non-law-and-order fields; on skills—economic, sociological, and managerial—to comprehend the wider range of relevant phenomena and activity; and on institutions designed to cope with the needs for coordination. Infrastructure, hence, is too inadequately conceived by strategists for economic development. The viable modernized state which would have as a major activity economic development requires conscious and rational investments in social, political, and administrative infrastructure as well.

Perhaps the concept of modernized values needs further explanation. How does a state encourage in its citizens the longer time perspective, the revised valuation on the objectives of the state, the shifting allegiance from particularistic to more universalistic associations and the new assessments of human activity and achievements? The answer is: in terms of rational planned investments. One difference, however, is that the concept of resources for investment, as understood by economic development strategists, must be expanded. Resources, as used here, include coercion, threats of coercion, economic resources, power to command resources, prestige, and security. These "factors" are brought together in different proportions for the major investments to obtain the needed value changes.[24]

Three major types of investments can be thought of for modernization of the state: stability investments, legitimacy investments, and solidarity investments. The contents, proportions, and amount of resources for each differ. Stability investments are allocations aimed at reducing potential and probable opposition to civil authority. Opposition, in this case, might take the form of secessionist groups, radical trade unions, or an urban mob of unemployed. In content, the "investment" would mainly include coercion, threats of coercion, and economic resources. By proportion and amount, there would be a heavy emphasis on coercion and meeting demands with economic resources. Legitimacy investments are very similar to stability investments, but go farther. They are investments aimed at inculcating acceptance of civil authority as right and correct, as discouraging in the public any feeling that they have a right to make authoritative allocations except through civil authorities. These investments, made for instance in educational programs, are comprised of coercion, threats of coercion, power to command economic resources, and economic resources. But the proportion of resources and coercion decreases. The decrease in coercion is primarily due to the fact that the state can rely on the traditional acceptance of authority by most citizens, and the threat of coercion, usually handled in terms of consequences resulting from the deprivation of authority, is adequate. Legitimacy investments can also be made by sharing the power to command economic resources—hitherto reserved by the central government—with local governments. Panchayati Raj is conferring legitimacy on the Indian state and its authoritative acts by sharing power with local governments.

But this last example could easily be used to illustrate the third investment level—solidarity investments. These investments are aimed at securing emotional commitments to the state and a willingness to sacrifice personal resources and forego demands for it. Coercion and threats of coercion are absent in these investments, except insofar as they define people outside the state. Prestige, security, power to command economic resources—all are involved. Identifying a sector (such as private business) as patriotically useful, an important role at the United Nations, safeguarding the population against the "enemy," participation through representative bodies, and allocations of resources for "regional balance," stadia, national air lines—all conduce to integration into the structures and values of a modernized state. In all three types of investment, the size of each decreases over time, though reduced recurrent expenditures continue.

Free primary education might be useful in illustrating this concept. Some economic development strategists are increasingly finding free primary education a luxury consumption expenditure and argue for greater expenditures in higher and more technical education or more directly productive activities.[25] On the other hand, a modernization strategy might use free primary education in several ways. As a stability investment, it might be useful as a way of pacifying dissident groups, as part of a *quid pro quo* for civil obedience. Or, in the context of a rapidly modernizing society, the denial of free primary education might be destabilizing to large numbers of status-conscious parents. But free primary education is mostly relevant as an investment in legitimacy and solidarity. Not only does this means of human improvement (status and income) come from the state, but it provides an opportunity to teach "the rules of the game" to a modernizing nation's young citizens. As a solidarity investment, it provides a common experience for citizenship, avoids the extremes of education and the resulting social friction, provides an opportunity to stress the importance of the state, modernization, and all its other values. As an economic investment, the arguments for free primary education are obvious.

Most economic development strategists do not recognize these social and political investments. They make little room for them in their writings and calculations. When these investments are made, as they will be, the strategists label them "compromises," "politically motivated," "prestige items," and "unproductive." Yet, these investments provide the basis for subsequent investments in directly productive activities. Without these prior investments, "correct decisions" will not be made or maintained. These are investments in modernization values. And, if understood from a modernization perspective, they can be made with greater rationality and efficiency. Indeed, many of these investments would be acceptable as sound under the stricter criterion of economic development strategy.

If the appropriate question is "modernization" and not "economic growth," then social scientists must work on strategies jointly. For data, they have the tools and findings of survey research, the growing compilations of political and social quantitative indicators, and the record of modernizing activities of, among many others, Napoleon, Bismarck, the Bolsheviks, the Congress Party of India, Mexico's PRI, Nasser, and Mao Tse-Tung. Much needs to be known about the character of social change; greater precision must be achieved in defining problems and seeking relationships of variables within the wider social system. Indeed, it might be suggested that modernization first began in the social sciences.

NOTES

1. Everett E. Hagen, *On the Theory of Social Change* (Homewood, 1962); David C. McClelland, *The Achieving Society* (Princeton, 1961).
2. "Big Push" balance growth—P. N. Rosenstein-Rodan, "Problems of Industrialization

of Eastern and South-Eastern Europe," in A. N. Agarwala and S. P. Singh, *The Economics of Underdevelopment* (New York, 1963), pp. 145–55; Ragnar Nurkse, *Problems of Capital Formation in Underdeveloped Countries* (New York, 1960), Ch. 1; Unbalanced growth—Albert O. Hirschman, *The Strategy of Economic Development* (New Haven, 1958); Capital formation through unlimited supplies of labor—W. Arthur Lewis, "Economic Development with Unlimited Supplies of Labour," in Agarwala and Singh, *op. cit.*, pp. 400–49; Nurske, *op. cit.*, Ch. 2.

3. Certain assumptions are made in this article about the social system and its response to economic change. First, the population is increasingly "mobilized," i.e., a population shifting to wages and a more complex division of labor, exposed to mass media and increasing education, and more easily susceptible to new forms of organization. See Karl W. Deutsch, "Social Mobilization and Political Development," *American Political Science Review* (September 1961), 493–514. Second, extreme inequalities of income, inflation over a long period of time without redistribution, and accelerated urbanization without adequate social overhead expenditures and provision for the maintenance of primary group relationships or acceptable alternatives are destabilizing to a social system. See, for example, Bert F. Hoselitz, "Urbanization and Economic Growth in Asia," *Economic Development and Cultural Change* (October 1957), 42–54; Neil J. Smelser, "Mechanisms of Change and Adjustment to Change," in Bert F. Hoselitz and Wilbert E. Moore, eds., *Industrialization and Society* (UNESCO, The Hague, 1963), pp. 32–54; Philip M. Hauser, "The Social, Economic, and Technological Problems of Rapid Urbanization," in *ibid.*, pp. 199–217; Richard D. Robinson, "Turkey's Agrarian Revolution and the Problem of Urbanization," *Public Opinion Quarterly*, XXII (Fall 1958), 397–405; Joseph A. Kahl, "Some Social Concomitants of Industrialization and Urbanization," *Human Organization* (Summer 1959), 53–74 (especially bibliographical section). An act is destabilizing when it threatens the legitimacy of the institutions of civil authority and their means of handling conflict and distribution. See, for example, Seymour Martin Lipset, *Political Man, The Social Bases of Politics* (Garden City, New York, 1960), Ch. 3; Ronald C. Ricker, "Discontent and Economic Growth," *Economic Development and Cultural Change*, XI (October 1962), 1–15. For the authors' general approach to the social system and its sub-systems, see Marion J. Levy, Jr., *The Structure of Society* (Princeton, 1953); S. N. Eisenstadt, *Essays on the Sociological Aspects of Political and Economic Development* (The Hague, 1961); David E. Apter, "System, Process and the Politics of Economic Development," in Hoselitz and Moore, *op. cit.*, pp. 135–58.

4. The probability of formulating alternative combinations of investments in underdeveloped countries is small. Indeed, at present, it is rare even to find alternative projects to choose from. See, for example, Government of Pakistan, Planning Commission, *Final Report of the Committee on Review of On-going Schemes* (Karachi, 1961), pp. 3–16.

5. See Zbigniew Brzezinski, "The Politics of Underdevelopment," *World Politics*, IX (October 1956), 55–75; Alexander Eckstein, "Individualism and the Role of the State in Economic Growth," *Economic Development and Cultural Change*, VI (January 1958), 81–87.

6. The "Big Push" strategy can also be formulated by differing proportions of authoritarian and oligarchical rule, but authoritarian and/or oligarchical, nonetheless.

7. A fourth possibility is a population almost unanimous in its commitment to economic development. This is relevant, in the authors' view, to no country now in existence. Even when a large proportion of the "effective" population has economic development as *one* of its top priorities—even its top priority—the interpretations of what "development" means, who is to sacrifice, what is to be foregone, and who is to prosper are legion, and the view of the economic strategist, or the ruling elites, is never accepted as definitive.

8. See, for example, Donald Hindley, "Foreign Aid to Indonesia: Its Political Implications," *Pacific Affairs*, XXXVI (Summer 1963), 107–19; M. Bronfenbrenner, "The Appeal of Confiscation in Economic Development," *Economic Development and Cultural Change*, III (1954), 201–18.

9. See, for example, Albert Waterston, " 'Planning the Planning' Under the Alliance for Progress," in Irving Swerdlow, *Development Administration, Concepts and Problems* (Syracuse, 1963), pp. 141–62; "Progress in Planning in Latin America," *Economic Bulletin for Latin America*, VIII (October 1963), 129–46; John P. Lewis, *Quiet Crisis in India* (Garden City, New York, 1964), pp. 129–40.

10. Professor Hirschman has since modified his position. See Albert O. Hirschman, "Economics and Investment Planning: Reflections Based on Experience in Colombia,"

Investment Criteria and Economic Growth (Bombay, 1961), pp. 38–39. This modification, however, does not affect this article's analysis.

11. See, for example, Government of India, Planning Commission, *Reports of the Programme Evaluation Organization*, especially nos. 6 and 7; Kusum Nair, *Blossoms in the Dust* (London, 1961), *passim.*

12. See Joseph LaPalombara, "Bureaucracy and Political Development: Notes, Queries, and Dilemmas," in Joseph LaPalombara, ed., *Bureaucracy and Political Development* (Princeton, 1963), pp. 34–61.

13. Nurkse, *op. cit.*, pp. 15–16, 43, 76, 90–91, 143, 148–50; Hirschman, *op. cit.*, pp. 14, 112–13; see also Albert O. Hirschman, *Journeys Toward Progress* (New York, 1963), *passim.*; W. Arthur Lewis, *op. cit.*, pp. 422–23, 434. The experiences of other nations were also relevant, but this does not alter the argument.

14. See, for example, Reinhard Bendix, "Public Authority in a Developing Political Community: the Case of India, *Archives Europeennes de Sociologie*, IV (1963), 39–85; Selig S. Harrison, *India: the Most Dangerous Decades* (Princeton, 1960).

15. This point cannot be adequately developed in an article of this length. Indirectly, a similar argument can be inferred from: Joseph A. Schumpeter, *History of Economic Analysis* (New York, 1954), pp. 143–208; Bert F. Hoselitz, "The Scope and History of Theories of Economic Growth," *Revista de Economia Politica*, V (May 1953), 9–28; William Letwin, *The Origins of Scientific Economics* (London, 1963), *passim.*; Karl Polanyi, *The Great Transformation* (New York, 1944), Chs. 10 and 19.

16. See also Fred W. Riggs, *Administration in Developing Countries: The Theory of Prismatic Society* (Boston, 1964), pp. 19–31.

17. An obvious "heroic" exception is Talcott Parsons and Neil J. Smelser, *Economy and Society* (London, 1956).

18. An interesting study of a nation's sectors and their demands is Myron Weiner, *The Politics of Scarcity, Public Pressure and Political Response in India* (Bombay, 1963).

19. See, for example Rupert Emerson, "Nationalism and Political Development," *Journal of Politics*, XXII (February 1960), 3–28.

20. See, for example, Bert F. Hoselitz and Myron Weiner, "Economic Development and Political Stability in India," *Dissent*, VIII (Spring 1961), 172–84.

21. For an example of an economist handling the political preconditions of economic development in terms of an autonomous (i.e., less subject to the influence of the political sub-system) economic system and the consequent role for the state to play, see Joseph J. Spengler, "Economic Development: Political Preconditions and Political Consequences," *Journal of Politics*, XXII (August 1960), 387–416. Among other things, Professor Spengler argues, "Only a well-entrenched party, or a pair of parties strongly committed to economic development, is likely to be able to keep the ideology of development effectively alive, to impose the necessary costs of development on the population, and yet to remain in office long enough to get economic growth effectively underway. A dictatorship might find itself in a somewhat similar position, given that it sought to promote economic growth and had fairly widespread support. . . . a multi-party system is not compatible with economic growth; it is too likely to give in to ever-present demands for 'liberal' welfare-state provisions." In other words, a moratorium must be called on politics to achieve the optimum product of a nation's scarce resources.

22. See S. N. Eisenstadt, "Modernization: Growth and Diversity," *India Quarterly*, XX (January–March 1964), 17–42; S. N. Eisenstadt, *The Political Systems of Empires* (New York, 1963), pp. 3–32.

23. See the excellent study by Lucian W. Pye, *Politics, Personality and Nations Building: Burma's Search for Identity* (New Haven, 1962), pp. 3 ff. See also Herbert Feith, *Decline of Constitutional Democracy in Indonesia* (Ithaca, 1962).

24. An increasing example of how the economist is now widening his concept of investment is in the sphere of education. The usual practice, when projecting future demand and production patterns, by means of input-output models or linear programming models, has been to treat the labor inputs as given, along with the capital inputs. However, it is obvious that labor is no homogeneous input, which is given, like any natural resource. Investments have to be made to create the skills required for different productive activities. The amounts of such investments are dependent on the level and nature of these activities. Therefore, if in a linear programming model, an attempt is being made to obtain the optimal allocation of all available resources, the activity by which human skills are created should also be included along with the other activities, and not as a primary input. Only in this way can the

economically optimal allocation be approximated. If, however, the investments in creating skills are treated as exogenous, to be determined on the basis of the optimal investment pattern, it is unlikely to obtain the "optimal results." For if the costs of creating the skills were attributed to different activities, the model would in all likelihood give a different pattern. This is a fact which economists are only realizing now. This article's contention is that there are other activities in which resources have to be invested, even if the only goal is the maximization of output.

25. See, for example, Sixto K. Roxas, "Investment in Education: The Philippine Experience," *The Philippine Economy Bulletin*, II (September–October 1963), 32–38. The authors are not including in the above statement the excellent recent work of Professors Harbison and Myers, although their "human resource development orientation" is concerned essentially with skills, not values. See Frederick Harbison and Charles A. Myers, *Education, Manpower, and Economic Growth* (New York, 1964).

4

Population and Methodological Problems of Development Theory

Charles K. Wilber

The purpose of this paper is twofold. First, it is to describe more precisely the role that population has played in Western economic thought since Adam Smith. Of necessity this survey must be selective and schematic. Second, it is to formulate some hypotheses as to the reasons for this role of population.

THE HISTORY OF POPULATION IN ECONOMIC THOUGHT

The Classical School

Although there were writers on economic subjects in Ancient Greece, the Middle Ages, and particularly during the seventeenth and eighteenth centuries, modern economics is usually dated from the publication in 1776 of Adam Smith's, *The Wealth of Nations*. Economic writings from Adam Smith to John Stuart Mill in the mid-nineteenth century have become known as the classical school in the history of economic thought. The core of classical economic analysis is the model of competitive market capitalism. Since an uncoerced person can be depended upon to act rationally to maximize his or her individual self-interest, it was thought possible to set up an automatic, self-regulating mechanism to manage economic affairs. These free choices were expected to overcome scarcity and result in the common good through the automatic adjustments of free exchange in markets. The forces of competition ensured that the economy produced those goods that people desired and that there would be maximum output at minimum cost.

The fact that all economies were characterized by widespread poverty, unemployment, and low wages was explained in two ways. First, there were the countries that restricted the free operation of markets. If such restrictions were removed, much of the poverty, it was argued, would be eliminated by the resulting economic growth. Malthus made an exception for international trade and argued that tariffs on agricultural products were necessary to protect the landlords, who, in turn, played a vital role in the economy. Second, in those countries that had free market systems, continuing poverty was explained as the result of the "niggardliness" of physi-

Adapted from a paper prepared for Institute of Society, Ethics and the Life Sciences, May 1977.

cal nature and the improvidence of human nature in the form of population growth.

Adam Smith, Thomas Malthus, David Ricardo, and John Stuart Mill all explained poverty as the result of the interaction of physical scarcity and population growth. In each version of classical economic theory, economic growth ultimately culminates in a stationary state where net per capita investment is zero and wages have settled at the subsistence level. The tendency of the wage level to subsistence is brought about by the assumption of a perfectly elastic supply of labor in the long run: that is, a certain increase in wages brings forth a proportionate increase in population which drives wages back down. Increased wages leads to a decrease in mortality because families can afford better nutrition and health care.

The Neoclassical School

Neoclassical economics, beginning in the 1870s, turned away from the classical concern with economic growth and concentrated instead on the problem of efficient resource allocation. In this abstract model, input supplies, including labor, were taken as given and, thus, population receded into an *ad hoc* explanation that was trotted out whenever the free market was blamed for continuing poverty.

Modern Development Theory

As the colonized territories of Africa and Asia gained their independence after World War II, concern for the process of economic development was renewed among economists and politicians alike. The per capita GNP had increased enormously in Europe and the United States since the days of Smith, Malthus, and Mill. The Malthusian prediction that increases in production would elicit proportionate increases in population clearly proved false in the developed countries. The explanation given was that technological change had offset the tendency toward diminishing returns and the practice of birth control had broken the link between income and population.

The first post-war development theories focused on why the countries of Africa, Asia, and Latin America failed to experience a growth of per capita GNP similar to that of the developed countries. The answer suggested was insufficient capital investment, and thus stagnant technology, and excessive population growth. It was argued that excessive population growth left those countries so poor that the Smithian market system did not lead to self-sustaining economic growth.[1] There was little possibility of profitable investment because of low purchasing power.[2] Risk-taking entrepreneurs were led to invest in non-growth-producing sectors of the economy.[3] Since the impact of the population growth was assumed to be simple and easily understood, much of the economic work focused on why the market mechanism was not working to generate growth in *total* GNP. Most economists focused on obstacles to the workings of the free market: cultural dualism, technological dualism, and government restrictions on the free working of markets. Where there was significant growth in total GNP but little or no growth in per capita GNP, the cause was typically held to be the swamping effect of population growth. This theory of the "low-level equilibrium trap,"[4] created to explain the lack of growth of per capita GNP, became the standard approach to poverty in underdeveloped countries and still occupies a prominent place in some development textbooks.[5]

As the complexities of underdeveloped countries became better known to development economists, population growth decreased in importance as a primary factor in programmatic development models. Economists learned from demographers that economic development affected population growth as well as the other way around. Thus was born the "demographic transition" wherein population growth would decrease as development proceeded but only with a time lag. The crucial problem of development became one of controlling population growth until the "transition" was completed. Population control, therefore, was seen as the *sine qua non* for any successful development program.[6] Once it was agreed that population control was necessary, the attention of some economists shifted to more purely economic problems: investment criteria, import substitution, planning techniques, and so on. Other economists developed models of how overpopulated economies could develop using their agricultural labor surplus in industrial development.[7] By the 1970s population growth had become one obstacle among many for most development economists. Despite recognition of the inadequacy of the evidence supporting the importance of population growth as a deterrent to economic development, it still remained an obstacle: "little support is found for any strong positive or negative relationship between growth of population and that of real output, but it seems clear that at least among poor developing countries a slowing down of population growth must facilitate the growth of per capita output."[8]

Economists specializing in development have been and are arrayed across a spectrum of opinions on population issues. Most see population growth as one problem among many, a few actually see it as a potential stimulus to development,[9] and a significant minority place so much importance on population issues that it frequently appears that they consider population to be the only development problem.[10] They have had influence out of all proportion to their numbers in agencies such as United States Agency for International Development and the World Bank. They have been believed and backed by special interest groups, such as The Population Council, the UN Fund for Population Activities, The Pathfinder Fund, and the International Planned Parenthood Federation. There has been a passion to their work that "appears to reflect the existence of a powerful 'cult of population control.' The strength of that cult, its control over limited available research resources, the evangelical fervor with which its objectives are pursued, and the dispatch with which agnostic or heretical viewpoints are dismissed all militate against the appearance of agnosticism or heresy."[11] The influence of this "cult" is such that most Western development economists have not thoroughly investigated the evidence for themselves but have tended to join the consensus by at least accepting the *sine qua non* position mentioned above.

The consensus is based upon three "seemingly irrefutable" hypotheses.

The first hypothesis is that the relationship between changes in age structure and additional capital requirements means that the rate of population growth and the rate of growth in per capita GNP are inversely related. The second is that very large expenditures—on the order of $100 to $200—per prevented birth are economically justifiable. The third is that investments in birth control programs are substantially more productive than investments in directly productive activities.

These three hypotheses are based, in turn, upon three types of economic research. First is the use of simplified analytic models of economic growth that incorporate some effects of a population variable.[12] Second are complex numerical simulation models derived from the analytic models.[13] Third are individual partial studies of the impact of birth prevention on income.[14]

The influence of the population cult was such that dubious assumptions were not questioned, and contradictory evidence was explained away or ignored. The conflicting work of Colin Clark[15] was written off as that of a Catholic apologist, and the work of Paul Baran as that of a dogmatic Marxist.[16] Despite the fact that by the mid-1960s most development economists were aware of the severe limitations of the three hypotheses championed by some of their colleagues, the population consensus held sway in the aid agencies[17] and was important in the chapters on economic development in introductory textbooks[18] and dominated the public imagination.[19]

Over the last five years a substantial body of work has appeared that challenges the assumptions and empirical evidence of the population establishment; some of this work is within that establishment.[20] In addition, the revolt of the underdeveloped countries at the United Nations World Population Conference in Bucharest in August, 1974, has emboldened dissenters among Western economists and has shattered the Malthusian consensus of the population establishment.

Why have so many Western economists clung to these hypotheses as if they were self-evident truths and others acquiesced in the consensus by their silence?

REASONS FOR THE CENTRAL ROLE OF POPULATION IN ECONOMIC THOUGHT

Methodological Reasons

Western economics, particularly since World War II, has patterned itself after the physical sciences. The goal of economics as a science is to provide a system of generalizations (theories) that can be used to make predictions about the consequences of any change in circumstances. Economic science is carried forth by logically deducing an hypothesis from a theory or model. These hypotheses act as predictions of correlational relationships in the real world. That is, the economist tests the degree of correspondence between his or her predictions and the empirical evidence provided by the real world. A high degree of correspondence confirms or verifies the theory. A low level or lack of correspondence indicates a flaw in the theory. It is by testing that disputes are resolved, and testing leads to the accumulation of general laws that constitute theory. If the predictions derived from one model prove "better" than the corresponding predictions drawn from another model, the former model is tentatively selected as preferable. In any case, the theory preferred is the one that best explains the observable phenomena of the economic world. However, practice falls far short of the ideal.

Successful prediction is extremely difficult in economics. In the past several years experience with unemployment, inflation, the energy crisis, and so on, has highlighted this problem. However, economists have achieved a high degree of insulation from the failure of their predictions. This is due to the highly conditional nature of economic predictions, which are dependent upon the *ceteris paribus* (assuming other conditions unchanged) clauses holding and upon the data being representative of economic reality. These conditionals give the positivist an escape clause for rationalizing the failure of a prediction. When his model repeatedly fails to predict correctly, the physicist blames his model. The economist, on the other hand, is tempted to blame the *ceteris paribus* conditions, the data, or the specific testing procedure itself. Consequently, for the economist, hypotheses are seldom proved false and general theory rarely or never disproved. Economics thus becomes highly insulated from refutation.

Since economists use accuracy of predictions for verification of the validity of a theory, this insulation of predictions from refutation is worth exploring further. Why do positive economists resist disconfirmation of their hypotheses? At the heart of the issue is Thomas Kuhn's concept of a paradigm.[21] An economist normally has some general theory that guides his choice of problems, provides analytic tools, and supplies a general vision of how reality is structured. This general theory—whether it is neoclassical economics, Malthusianism, Marxism, or some other—is usually so much a part of his very thought processes that empirical disconfirmation of some particular hypothesis is almost automatically rejected. The three specific conditions that were briefly mentioned above make it easy for the economist to reject a disconfirmation as invalid and, thus, protect his basic theory or paradigm.

First is the *ceteris paribus* problem. Hypotheses in economics must always be stated in the form of "if . . . then" propositions. Since the "ifs" do change, an econometric test that disconfirms the theory can always be rejected as "misspecified."[22] In addition, since hypotheses are stated in probabilistic terms, a nonoccurrence of the predicted event cannot be used as a refutation of the general law from which the particular hypothesis was deduced.

Second is the difficulty of constructing a clear-cut test of an hypothesis in economics. Most of the traditional statistical tests, for example null hypotheses, are very weak, and a large number of different theories can pass them. The choice among alternative theories, therefore, cannot be settled on empirical grounds. Instead, the desirable qualities of a logical model—simplicity, generality, specificity, and aesthetic quality—are used, and the relative evaluation of these qualities is probably determined by one's own paradigm.[23]

Finally, both the methods of collection and construction of economic data are unreliable. Furthermore, the data that are statistically constructed frequently are not conceptually the same as the corresponding variables in the theory. Therefore, econometricians engage in data "massaging." If a test disconfirms an hypothesis, the investigator can always blame the data —they have been "massaged" either too much or not enough.

The structure of Malthusian population theory makes it particularly difficult to falsify any of its constituent propositions. Its survival and attractiveness derive from the theory's tendency to shift from interesting empirical, though false or misleading, propositions to true, though empty, tautologies. For example, from the *truism* that population growth is *limited* by food supply, Malthus deduced the *empirical proposition* that population growth is *regulated* by the food supply.[24] However, when confronted with evidence that the food supply was *actually* growing faster than population, he retreated to a comparison of *potential* differences: in the long run population has a tendency to grow faster than the means of subsistence. Thus an apparent empirical falsification can always be sidestepped by comparing a long run abstract potentiality (population growth) with concrete data (food supply, per capita GNP, etc.). Tautologies take such forms as the proposition that any nation will have higher per capita income with fewer people (assuming that output does not decline proportionately). This is merely a statement about the rules of arithmetic rather than a proposition about empirical reality. Whenever conflicting evidence is raised, population theory retreats to this type of true but empty tautology.[25] This ability to avoid falsification (empirical refutation) certainly accounts for some of the continued vitality of Malthusianism.[26]

Ideological Considerations

When a theory has achieved such a high level of insulation from falsification, it might best be termed an ideology or, less pejoratively, an ideal type. As an ideal type, the Malthusian theory of population that has been dominant in Western economic thought has had two essential and related effects. It has restricted the scope of economic inquiry and it has served as a policy stance for molding society in its image, while legitimating certain aspects of the status quo.

In terms of restricting or defining the scope of economic inquiry into the causes of poverty, the Malthusian theory of population focuses attention on natural scarcity and the improvidence of human nature. As such, universally applicable hypotheses are devised which ignore the environmental influence of institutional, systemic, and historical variations. The Malthusian population theory, coupled with competitive economic theory, focuses potential economic research upon and, in effect, constrains attention to, the behavior of individuals and households. Thus, people are poor because they have made the wrong decisions, for example about family size. This provides a universal explanation for poverty that exonerates particular economic institutions from blame.

Concentration on the actions of atomistic actors camouflages the existence and exercise of power in an economic system and the fact that poverty is perpetuated, if not created, by social institutions that benefit certain social classes at the expense of others. Ultimately, the theory of population becomes a conservative defense of the status quo. Thus, poverty is said to be caused by the weaknesses of human nature and can be overcome only by educating people to use available technology for birth reduction. Under those circumstances, changing economic systems would not make any difference except to the extent that existing social institutions misdirect the decisions of rational individuals.

As already mentioned, the Malthusian view of population has been challenged on analytical and empirical grounds. It has also been attacked for ideological reasons. Probably the most important ideological dissent comes from Marx and his followers.[27] Marx held that "every special historic mode of production has its own special laws of population, historically valid within its limits alone. An abstract law of population exists for plants and animals only, and only in so far as man has not interfered with them." However, Malthusianism plays an important role in bourgeois economics. It is "far more convenient and much more in conformity with the interests of the ruling classes . . . to explain this 'overpopulation' by the external laws of nature, rather than by the historical laws of capitalist production."[28] But such overpopulation as exists at any stage of historical development is overpopulation not in relation to natural resources but in relation to productive plant and equipment. In the words of Engels, "the pressure of population is not upon the means of subsistence but upon the means of *employment.*"[29] The supply of "means of employment" is not a natural datum but a social phenomenon that can be understood only in terms of its *systemic nature.*

Marxists argue that the so-called race between population growth and the food supply is misconceived. The race, if any, is between population growth and economic development. Only economic development can solve both aspects of the so-called overpopulation problem. It increases the supply of food and at the same time reduces the growth of population.[30] Thus, to the Marxists, population change is a function of changes in income and economic institutions, not the other way around.

The Marxist objection to the Malthusian population theory is that it postulates population growth as an independent variable; that is, it operates independently of socioeconomic institutions and thus exonerates those institutions from blame for the existence of poverty. Marxian theory can be criticized on the same grounds. Marxists insist that population growth is a dependent variable because they *believe* that the existing socioeconomic system is to blame for poverty. Therefore, they focus on changing the economic system and claim that population will take care of itself. However, once in power, Marxist regimes have all resorted to population control. The ideological factor is clearly a two-edged sword.

One final comment on the ideological issue is in order. For those of us in the developed world, Malthusianism is both frightening and comforting. It is frightening to contemplate "Asiatic hordes" overrunning the world and threatening our own means of existence. It is comforting because we cannot be held liable for the plight of the poor around the world. They have only themselves to blame. We can even convince ourselves that foreign aid is useless because it will be just swamped by population growth.[31]

Cultural Traditions

The individualist/rationalist tradition of the West, with its emphasis on achievement and attribution of responsibility to individuals, has lent credence to Malthusian views. Economics developed primarily in the individualist societies of England and the United States. Explaining poverty by an appeal to human nature fits very well with the values of an individualist, achievement-oriented culture. Hard work, thrift, and prudence always have been seen as the keys to success. Failure has been attributed to a lack of these values. Systemic causes of poverty have been ignored in favor of personal characteristics. For example, the main explanation for poverty in the United States is the "human capital" theory, which states that people are poor because they do not have enough skills to sell, thus totally ignoring the structural characteristics of labor markets.

A second aspect of the cultural tradition of the West, particularly of the United States, is a fascination with technique and technological solutions. In addition, as scientists, economists have been trained to believe that technological solutions are far easier than political ones. Thus, education, training programs, and birth control appear to be the obvious technological response to the problem of poverty.

Historical Conditions

Particular historical and contextual circumstances must be noted in explaining the importance of population theory in economics. During the last quarter of the eighteenth century population was growing rapidly in England but, more importantly, population was shifting from rural to urban areas under the impetus of technological change, the expansion of job opportunities in the cities, and the expanded enclosure movement in agriculture. Thus there was a serious relative overpopulation problem caused by a crowding of people into the cities with the consequent increase in visible unemployment, crime, and riots. Writers such as Malthus were influenced by these events.

In most Third World countries today a similar phenomenon has taken place. This relative overpopulation in the cities certainly must give impetus to the Malthusian position.

CONCLUSIONS

Mainstream economists since Adam Smith have looked to factors exogenous to the economic system for explanations of poverty. They have focused on the scarcity of natural resources and the improvidence of human nature. The creation of a viable market economy and the control of population became the twin foundations of the strategy to overcome poverty and underdevelopment. Proper economic policies, education, and family planning were the tactics necessary to implement the general strategy.

The newly emerging position of the Third World is much closer to the Marxist tradition than to the Malthusian. This new "developmentalist" view stresses that population growth *per se* is not an important variable in economic development. The emphasis of development policy should be on rapid economic change with change in socioeconomic institutions. These changes in socioeconomic institutions, in turn, will lead to a decrease in fertility. From this viewpoint, a direct attack upon population growth is seen as a diversion from the main problems. It is also thought that such attacks are generally unsuccessful. This does not imply that there is no need for family planning programs—clearly there is a need for such programs. This does imply that these programs must be supportive of general development strategies, not the main thrust of development policy itself. Perhaps the breakup of the population consensus at Bucharest will be the first step in a general reevaluation of development priorities and strategies.

NOTES

1. P. N. Rosenstein-Rodan, "Problems of Industrialization of Eastern and South-Eastern Europe," *Economic Journal* (June/September 1943).

2. Ragnar Nurkse, *Problems of Capital Formation in Underdeveloped Countries* (New York: Oxford University Press, 1953).

3. Albert O. Hirschman, *The Strategy of Economic Development* (New Haven: Yale University Press, 1958).

4. See H. Leibenstein, *A Theory of Economic-Demographic Development* (Princeton: Princeton University Press, 1954); and R. N. Nelson, "The Low-Level Equilibrium Population Trap," *American Economic Review* (December 1956).

5. See Charles Kindleberger, *Economic Development* (2nd ed., New York: McGraw-Hill, 1965); and Benjamin Higgins, *Economic Development* (3rd ed., New York: Norton, 1975).

6. See Hans W. Singer, *International Development: Growth and Change* (New York: McGraw-Hill, 1964); Kindleberger, *op. cit.* (1965); and Joseph A. Raffaele, *The Economic Development of Nations* (New York: Random House, 1971).

7. W. Arthur Lewis, "Economic Development with Unlimited Supplies of Labour," *The Manchester School of Economic and Social Studies* (May 1954); and John C. H. Fei and Gustav Ranis, *Development of the Labour Surplus Economy* (Homewood, Ill.: Richard D. Irwin, 1964).

8. Robert H. Cassen, "Population and Development: A Survey," *World Development*, Vol. 4, Nos. 10/11 (1976), p. 785. Also see Everett Hagen, *The Economics of Development* (rev. ed., Homewood, Ill.: Richard D. Irwin, 1975); Charles P. Kindleberger and Bruce Herrick, *Economic Development* (3rd ed., McGraw-Hill, 1977).

9. See Hirschman, *op. cit.*, as the best known example.

10. See A. J. Coale and E. M. Hoover, *Population Growth and Economic Development in Low Income Countries* (Princeton: Princeton University Press, 1958); Stephen Enke, *Economics for Development* (Englewood Cliffs, N.J.: Prentice-Hall, 1963); Joseph J. Spengler, "Demographic Patterns," in H. F. Williamson and J. A. Butrick, *Economic Development: Principles and Patterns* (Englewood Cliffs, N.J.: Prentice-Hall, 1954); and Kingsley Davis, "The Amazing Decline of Mortality in Underdeveloped Areas," *American Economic Review*, Vol. XLVI (May 1956).

11. Michael E. Conroy and Nancy R. Folbre, "Population Growth as a Deterrent to Economic Growth: A Reappraisal of the Evidence," Hastings-on-Hudson: Institute of Society, Ethics and the Life Sciences (February 1976), pp. 4–5. Most of what follows is based on this study. Also see H. A. Meilink, "The Population Factor in Economic Growth Theory," *Kroniek van Afrika* (1974/1), pp. 6–19. Cassen, *op. cit.*,

provides a critical but sympathetic review of the same material as Conroy and Meilink.

12. See Leibenstein, *op. cit.*; Nelson, *op. cit.*; and Jurg Niehaus, "Economic Growth with Two Endogenous Factors," *Quarterly Journal of Economics*, Vol. 77, No. 3 (August 1963), pp. 350–371.

13. See Coale and Hoover, *op. cit.*; Peter Newman and P. H. Allen, *Population Growth and Economic Development in Nicaragua*, prepared for the Government of Nicaragua and the U. S. Agency for International Development (Washington, D.C.: Robert R. Nathan Associates, 1967); Peter J. Lloyd, "A Growth Model with Population as an Endogenous Variable," *Population Studies*, Vol. 23, No. 3 (November 1969), pp. 463–478; and Richard Brown, *Survey of TEMPO Economic-Demographic Studies* (Washington, D.C.: G. E. TEMPO Center for Advanced Studies, 1974).

14. See Stephen Enke, "The Gains to India from Population Control: Some Money Measures and Incentive Schemes," *Review of Economics and Statistics* (1960), pp. 175–181; Stephen Enke, "The Economics of Government Payments to Limit Population," *Economic Development and Cultural Change*, Vol. 8 (July 1960), pp. 339–348; and Paul Demeny, "Demographic Aspects of Savings, Investment, Employment, and Productivity," Background Paper A 9/11/3/460 for the U. N. World Population Conference, Belgrade, Yugoslavia, 1965.

15. Colin Clark, "Population Growth and Living Standards," *International Labour Review* (August 1953). He has a number of other relevant works.

16. Paul A. Baran, *The Political Economy of Growth* (New York: Monthly Review Press, 1957), pp. 237–248.

17. See the relevant case studies in the *Occasional Population Papers* series of the Cultural Values and Population Policy Project, Institute of Society, Ethics and the Life Sciences.

18. See Robert L. Heilbroner and Lester C. Thurow, *The Economic Problem* (4th ed., Englewood Cliffs, N.J.: Prentice-Hall, 1975); Edwin Mansfield, *Economics* (2nd ed., New York: W. W. Norton, 1977); Richard G. Lipsey and Peter O. Steiner, *Economics* (4th ed., New York: Harper & Row, 1975); George L. Bach, *Economics* (9th ed., Englewood Cliffs, N.J.: Prentice-Hall, 1977). In every one of these books, rapid population growth is seen as a, if not *the*, main impediment to economic development.

19. See W. Paddock and P. Paddock, *Famine 1975* (Boston: Little, Brown, 1967); Paul Ehrlich, *The Population Bomb* (New York: Ballantine Books, 1968); Garret Hardin, "The Tragedy of the Commons," *Science*, Vol. 162 (1969). These are some of the more recent and better known popular treatises that sound the neo-Malthusian alarm.

20. See particularly Conroy, *op. cit.* Also see the work cited in Meilink, *op. cit.*; Mahmood Mamdani, *The Myth of Population Control* (New York: Monthly Review Press, 1973); Michael S. Teitelbaum, "Population and Development: Is a Consensus Possible?" *Foreign Affairs* (July 1974); Cassen, *op. cit.*; J. E. Kocher, *Rural Development, Income Distribution and Fertility Decline*, Occasional Paper (New York: Population Council, 1973); William Rich, *Smaller Families Through Social and Economic Progress* (Washington, D.C.: Overseas Development Council, 1973); and Julian Simon, "Population Growth May Be Good for LDC's in the Long Run: A Richer Simulation Model," *Economic Development and Cultural Change*, Vol. 24, No. 2 (January 1976), pp. 309–337.

21. T. S. Kuhn, *The Structure of Scientific Revolutions* (Chicago: University of Chicago Press, 1970).

22. See Fritz Machlup, "The Problem of Verification in Economics," *Southern Economic Journal*, Vol. 22 (July 1955), pp. 1–21.

23. See Jeffery B. Nugent, "Methodology in Economics: Some Implications of Pessimism and Some Suggested Alternatives," *American Economist*, Vol. 11 (Fall 1967), pp. 49–55; and Jack Melitz, "Friedman and Machlup on the Significance of Testing Economic Assumptions," *Journal of Political Economy*, Vol. 73 (February 1965), pp. 37–60.

24. See Thomas Sowell, *Classical Economics Reconsidered* (Princeton: Princeton University Press, 1974), pp. 89–95.

25. See Cassen, *op. cit.*, for an example of this tendency. After reporting all the contradictory evidence, he concludes, "but . . . a slowing down of population growth must facilitate the growth of *per capita* output," p. 785. This is a demonstration of the rules of arithmetic (*given* assumptions about savings rates, capital-labor ratios in production, etc.), not a falsifiable statement.

26. Malthusian population theory is not the only theory characterized by swings from short run empirical propositions to long run tautologies when confronted with contradictory evidence. The structure of both Marxism and Rostow's "stages-of-growth" theory lend themselves to this type of manipulation. See Paul Streeten, "Strength Through Tautology," *The New Republic* (September 4, 1971), pp. 27–29.

27. See Karl Marx, *Marx and Engels on Malthus*, ed. Ronald Meek (London: Lawrence & Wishart, 1953); Sydney Coontz, *Population Theories and the Economic Interpretation* (London: Routledge and Kegan Paul, 1961); and Baran, *op. cit.*, pp. 237–248.

28. Karl Marx, *Capital*, Vol. 1 (New York: Modern Library, 1906), pp. 580, 593.

29. Letter to F. A. Lange, March 29, 1865, in Marx and Engels, *Selected Correspondence* (New York: International Publishers, 1942), p. 198.

30. Baran, *op. cit.*, p. 243.

31. Signs of the times are the reclassification of poor countries into Third World and Fourth World, where there is much less hope for the Fourth World; and the theories of Triage and Life Boat ethics which, in effect, write off the poorest of the poor as hopeless.

part two

Economic Development and Underdevelopment in Historical Perspective

because the essence of economic development is rapid and discontinuous change in institutions and the value of economic parameters, it is impossible to construct a rigorous and determinate model of that process. An economist must be willing to settle for less. Elegance and rigor are important attributes of economic theory, but they take second place to relevance and applicability. The more rigorous the model, the higher its degree of technical success may be, but the greater its inability to explain economic development. Such a model necessarily omits too many of the most significant variables in economic development. An inquiry into the origin of economic development and underdevelopment ought not to commence with a highly generalized and abstract model. If a rigorous and determinate model cannot be utilized to study the process of economic development, a less rigorous but more richly textured model that accounts for the most important socioeconomic variables must be constructed. The use of economic history together with theoretical concepts, such as economic surplus, holds out the greatest prospect for success. Most of the readings in this section use the concept of the social surplus (outlined in the introduction to the first part) to organize and analyze the historical and empirical evidence of the process of development and underdevelopment.

Probably the greatest weakness of economic theorists is their lack of understanding of the process of development in the West between the seventeenth and twentieth centuries. The development of capitalism in the West was faced with the need for change in the social structure so that the progress-oriented middle class could become the leaders of society. This change often involved a violent struggle for supremacy between the old social order and the emerging new one. The English Revolution of 1640, ending with the Supremacy of Parliament in 1688, replaced the feudal lords with the landed gentry and urban middle class as the dominant classes in England, thus preparing the way for later economic progress. The French Revolution of 1789 replaced the old aristocracy with the new middle class. The lack of such social change was a major factor in the economic stagnation of Spain after the seventeenth century.

This change in social structure enabled the social surplus to be productively used. As Dudley Dillard points out in the first reading in this part: "Productive use of the 'social surplus' was the special virtue that enabled capitalism to outstrip all prior economic systems." Dillard's article outlines some of the crucial elements in the historical development of capitalism in the West.

Keith Griffin and Andre Gunder Frank emphasize the importance of seeing the history of the underdeveloped countries in the context of the worldwide development of capitalism; the underdevelopment of Africa, Asia, and Latin America was part of the same process that led to development in Europe and North America. Griffin emphasizes the actual historical events, while Frank attempts to formulate a series of hypotheses based upon historical experience.

Paul Baran argues that because of the unique historical experiences of the underdeveloped countries, their class structure evolved in a substantially different way than in the West. Capitalism entered most underdeveloped countries the "Prussian way"—not through the growth of small, competitive enterprise, but through the transfer from abroad of advanced, monopolistic business. Thus, capitalist development in these countries was not accompanied by the rise of a strong, property-owning middle class and by the overthrow of landlord domination of society. Instead, an accomodation was reached between the newly arrived monopolistic business and the socially and politically entrenched agrarian aristocracy.

Therefore, there was neither vigorous competition between enterprises striving for increased output, nor accumulation of the social surplus in the hands of entrepreneurs, who would be forced by the competitive system to reinvest in the expansion and modernization of their businesses. The result was that production was well below the potential level, with agriculture still being operated on a semifeudal basis and with waste and irrationality in industry protected by monopoly, high tariffs, and other devices.

For these and other reasons the actual social surplus was much lower than the potential social surplus. A large share of the potential social surplus was used by aristocratic landlords on excess consumption and the maintenance of unproductive laborers. In addition, a large share of the actual social surplus was taken by businessmen for commercial operations promising large and quick profits, or for the accumulation of investments or bank accounts abroad as a hedge against domestic social and political hazards. Furthermore, in order to obtain social status and the benefits and privileges necessary for the operation of a business, they emulated the dominant aristocracy in its mode of living. The actual social surplus was further reduced by the substantial quantity of resources used to maintain elaborate and inefficient bureaucratic and military establishments.

Although many factors brought about the inadequate amount and composition of investment, the waste of a large portion of the social surplus through the prevailing social structure was probably one of the major causes of economic stagnation. This process, described in the Griffin, Baran, and Frank readings, has been speeded up and changed somewhat since World War II.

The last article in this part focuses on the historical development of what Latin American economists call "dependency." It emphasizes the importance in underdeveloped countries of the upper income groups' adoption of the consumption patterns of their counterparts in the developed countries. It elaborates on the Furtado hypothesis that the concentration of the economic surplus in the hands of a few and its expenditure on luxury goods has shaped both the import and domestic manufacturing sectors of the underdeveloped countries. The demands for luxury goods by the upper-income group have been catered to instead of the subsistence needs of the vast majority. Because of the unequal income distribution, the small upper-income class is unable to support a full range of industrialization. The resultant dependency has gone through three historical stages. First, countries on the periphery were shaped by following a process of international comparative advantage. Second, in an attempt to overcome this dependency, such countries began a process of import substitution. However, this process merely strengthened the structure of dependency. Third, in the last two decades multinational corporations (MNCs) have played the leading role in furthering dependence on this particular pattern of consumption and on the type of technology necessary to produce those consumer goods.

5

Capitalism

Dudley Dillard

Capitalism [is] a term used to denote the economic system that has been dominant in the western world since the breakup of feudalism. Fundamental to any system called capitalist are the relations between private owners of nonpersonal means of production (land, mines, industrial plants, etc., collectively known as capital) and free but capital-less workers, who sell their labour services to employers. Under capitalism, decisions concerning production are made by private businessmen operating for private profit. Labourers are free in the sense that they cannot legally be compelled to work for the owners of the means of production. However, since labourers do not possess the means of production required for self-employment, they must, of economic necessity, offer their services on some terms to employers who do control the means of production. The resulting wage bargains determine the proportion in which the total product of society will be shared between the class of labourers and the class of capitalist entrepreneurs.

. . . . .

HISTORICAL DEVELOPMENT

1. Origins of Capitalism

Although the continuous development of capitalism as a system dates only from the 16th century, antecedents of capitalist institutions existed in the ancient world, and flourishing pockets of capitalism were present during the later middle ages. One strategic external force contributing to the breakup of medieval economic institutions was the growing volume of long-distance trade between capitalist centres, carried on with capitalist techniques in a capitalist spirit. Specialized industries grew up to serve long-distance trade, and the resulting commercial and industrial towns gradually exerted pressures which weakened the internal structure of agriculture based on serfdom, the hallmark of the feudal regime. Changes in trade, industry and agriculture were taking place simultaneously and interacting with one another in highly complex actual relations, but it was chiefly long-distance

Reprinted from *Encyclopaedia Britannica*, pp. 839–842, by permission of the publisher and the author. © *Encyclopaedia Britannica*, 1972.

trade which set in motion changes that spread throughout the medieval economy and finally transformed it into a new type of economic society.

Flanders in the 13th century and Florence in the 14th century were two capitalist pockets of special interest. Their histories shed light on the conditions that were essential to the development of capitalism in England. The great enterprise of late medieval and early modern Europe was the woolen industry, and most of the business arrangements that later characterized capitalism developed in connection with long-distance trade in wool and cloth.

In Flanders revolutionary conflict raged between plebeian craftsmen and patrician merchant-manufacturers. The workers succeeded in destroying the concentration of economic and political power in the hands of cloth magnates, only to be crushed in turn by a violent counterrevolution that destroyed the woolen industry and brought ruin to both groups. A similar performance was repeated in Florence, which became one of the great industrial cities of Europe during the 14th century. Restless, revolutionary urban workers overthrew the ruling hierarchy of merchants, manufacturers and bankers, and were in turn crushed in a bloody counterrevolution. Thus both Flanders and Florence failed to perpetuate their great industries because they failed to solve the social problem arising from conflicting claims of small numbers of rich capitalists and large numbers of poor workers.

2. Early Capitalism (1500–1750)

By the end of the middle ages the English cloth industry had become the greatest in Europe. Because of the domestic availability of raw wool and the innovation of simple mechanical fulling mills, the English cloth industry had established itself in certain rural areas where it avoided the violent social strife that had destroyed the urban industries of Flanders and Florence. Although it was subject to many problems and difficulties, the English rural cloth industry continued to grow at a rapid rate during the 16th, 17th and 18th centuries. Hence, it was the woolen industry that spearheaded capitalism as a social and economic system and rooted it for the first time in English soil.

Productive use of the "social surplus" was the special virtue that enabled capitalism to outstrip all prior economic systems. Instead of building pyramids and cathedrals, those in command of the social surplus chose to invest in ships, warehouses, raw materials, finished goods and other material forms of wealth. The social surplus was thus converted into enlarged productive capacity. Among the historical events and circumstances that significantly influenced capital formation in western Europe in the early stage of capitalist development, three merit special attention: (1) religious sanction for hard work and frugality; (2) the impact of precious metals from the new world on the relative shares of income going to wages, profits and rents; and (3) the role of national states in fostering and directly providing capital formation in the form of general-purpose capital goods.

Capitalist Spirit. The economic ethics taught by medieval Catholicism presented obstacles to capitalist ideology and development. Hostility to material wealth carried forward the teachings of the Christian fathers against mammonism. Saint Jerome said, "A rich man is either a thief or the son of a thief." Saint Augustine felt that trade was bad because it turned men away from the search for God. Down through the middle ages commerce and banking were viewed, at best, as necessary evils. Moneylending was for a time confined to non-Christians because it was considered unworthy of Christians. Interest on loans was unlawful under the anti-usury laws of both church and secular authorities. Speculation and profiteering violated the central medieval economic doctrine of just price.

Expansion of commerce in the later middle ages stirred controversies and led to attempts to reconcile theological doctrines with economic realities. In Venice, Florence, Augsburg and Antwerp—all Catholic cities—capitalists violated the spirit and circumvented the letter of the prohibitions against interest. On the eve of the Protestant Reformation capitalists, who still laboured under the shadow of the sin of avarice, had by their deeds become indispensable to lay rulers and to large numbers of people who were dependent upon them for employment.

The Protestant Reformation of the 16th and 17th centuries developed alongside economic changes which resulted in the spread of capitalism in northern Europe, especially in the Netherlands and England. This chronological and geographical correlation between the new religion and economic development has led to the suggestion that Protestantism had causal significance for the rise of modern capitalism. Without in any sense being the "cause" of capitalism, which already existed on a wide and expanding horizon, the Protestant ethic proved a bracing stimulant to the new economic order. Doctrinal revision or interpretation seemed not only to exonerate capitalists from the sin of avarice but even to give divine sanction to their way of life. In the ordinary conduct of life, a new type of worldly asceticism emerged, one that meant hard work, frugality, sobriety and efficiency in one's calling in the market place similar to that of the monastery. Applied in the environment of expanding trade and industry, the Protestant creed taught that accumulated wealth should be used to produce more wealth.

Acceptance of the Protestant ethic also eased the way to systematic organization of free labour. By definition, free labourers could not be compelled by force to work in the service of others. Moreover, the use of force would have violated the freedom of one's calling. Psychological compulsion arising from religious belief was the answer to the paradox. Every occupation was said to be noble in God's eyes. For those with limited talents, Christian conscience demanded unstinting labour even at low wages in the service of God—and, incidentally, of employers. It was an easy step to justify economic inequality because it would hasten the accumulation of wealth by placing it under the guardianship of the most virtuous (who were, incidentally, the wealthiest) and remove temptation from weaker persons who could not withstand the allurements associated with wealth. After all, it did not much matter who held legal title to wealth, for it was not for enjoyment. The rich like the poor were to live frugally all the days of their lives. Thus the capitalist system found a justification that was intended to make inequality tolerable to the working classes.

The Price Revolution. Meanwhile treasure from the new world had a profound impact on European capitalism, on economic classes and on the distribution of income in Europe. Gold and silver from the mines of Mexico, Peru and Bolivia increased Europe's supply of precious metals sevenfold and raised prices two- or threefold between 1540 and 1640. The significance of the increased supply of money lay not so much in the rise in prices as in its effect on the social and economic classes of Europe. Landlords, the older ruling class, suffered because money rents failed to rise as rapidly as the cost of living. The more aggressive landlords raised rents and introduced capitalistic practices into agriculture. In England the enclosure movement, which developed with ever increasing momentum and vigour during the 17th and 18th centuries, encouraged sheep raising to supply wool to the expanding woolen industry. Among labourers, money wages failed to keep pace with the cost of living, causing real wages to fall during the price revolution. The chief beneficiaries of this century-long inflation were capitalists, including merchants, manufacturers and other employers. High prices and low wages resulted in profit inflation, which in turn contributed to larger savings and capital accumulation. Profit inflation and wage deflation created a more unequal distribution of income. Wage earners got less and capitalists got more of the total product than they would have received in the absence of inflation. Had the new increments of wealth gone to wage earners instead of to capitalists, most of it would have been consumed rather than invested, and hence the working classes of the 16th century would have eaten better, but the future would have inherited less accumulated wealth.

Mercantilism. Early capitalism (1500–1750) also witnessed in western Europe the rise of strong national states pursuing mercantilist policies. Critics have tended to identify mercantilism with amassing silver and gold by having a so-called favourable balance of exports over imports in trading relations with other nations and communities, but the positive contribution and historic significance of mercantilism lay in the creation of conditions necessary for rapid and cumulative economic change in the countries of western Europe. At the end of the middle ages western Europe stood about where many underdeveloped countries stand in the 20th century. In underdeveloped economies the difficult task of statesmanship is to get under way a cumulative process of economic development, for once a certain momentum is attained, further advances appear to follow more or less automatically. Achieving such sustained growth requires virtually a social revolution.

Power must be transferred from reactionary to progressive classes; new energies must be released, often by uprooting the old order; the prevailing religious outlook may constitute a barrier to material advancement. A new social and political framework must be created within which cumulative economic change can take place.

Among the tasks which private capitalists were either unable or unwilling to perform were the creation of a domestic market free of tolls and other barriers to trade within the nation's borders; a uniform monetary system; a legal code appropriate to capitalistic progress; a skilled and disciplined labour force; safeguards against internal violence; national defense against attack; sufficient literacy and education among business classes to use credit instruments, contracts and other documents required of a commercial civilization; basic facilities for communication and transportation and harbour installations. A strong government and an adequate supply of economic resources were required to create most of these conditions, which constitute the "social overhead capital" needed in a productive economy. Because the returns from them, however great, cannot be narrowly channeled for private gain, such investments must normally be made by the government and must be paid for out of public revenues.

Preoccupation with productive use of the social surplus led mercantilist commentators to advocate low wages and long hours for labour. Consumption in excess of bare subsistence was viewed as a tax on progress and therefore contrary to the national interest. Mercantilist society was not a welfare state; it could not afford to be. Luxury consumption was condemned as a dissipation of the social surplus. Restrictions on imports were directed especially at luxury consumption.

Opportunities for profitable private investment multiplied rapidly as mercantilist policy succeeded in providing the basic social overhead capital. Rather paradoxically, it was because the state had made such an important contribution to economic development that the ideology of *laissez-faire* could later crystallise. When that occurred, dedication to capital accumulation remained a basic principle of capitalism, but the shift from public to private initiative marked the passage from the early state of capitalism and the beginning of the next stage, the classical period.

3. Classical Capitalism (1750–1914)

In England, beginning in the 18th century, the focus of capitalist development shifted from commerce to industry. The Industrial Revolution may be defined as the period of transition from a dominance of commercial over industrial capital to a dominance of industrial over commercial capital. Preparation for this shift began long before the invention of the flying shuttle, the water frame and the steam engine, but the technological changes of the 18th century made the transition dramatically evident.

The rural and household character of the English textile industry continued only as long as the amount of fixed capital required for efficient production remained relatively small. Changes in technology and organization shifted industry again to urban centres in the course of the Industrial Revolution, although not to the old commercial urban centres. Two or three centuries of steady capital accumulation began to pay off handsomely in the 18th century. Now it became feasible to make practical use of technical knowledge which had been accumulating over the centuries. Capitalism became a powerful promoter of technological change because the accumulation of capital made possible the use of inventions which poorer societies could not have afforded. Inventors and innovators like James Watt found business partners who were able to finance their inventions through lean years of experimentation and discouragement to ultimate commercial success. Aggressive entrepreneurs like Richard Arkwright found capital to finance the factory type of organization required for the utilization of new machines. Wealthy societies had existed before capitalism, but none had managed their wealth in a manner that enabled them to take advantage of the more efficient methods of production which an increasing mastery over nature made physically possible.

Adam Smith's great *Inquiry Into the Nature and Causes of the Wealth of Nations* (1776) expressed the ideology of classical capitalism. Smith recommended dismantling the state bureaucracy and leaving economic decisions to the free play of self-regulating market forces. While Smith recognized the faults of businessmen, he contended they could do little harm in a world of freely competitive enterprise. In Smith's opinion, private profit and public welfare would become reconciled through impersonal forces of market competition. After the French Revolution and the Napoleonic wars had swept the remnants of feudalism into oblivion and rapidly undermined mercantilist fetters, Smith's policies were put into practice. *Laissez-faire* policies of 19th-century political liberalism included free trade, sound money (the gold standard), balanced budgets, minimum poor relief—in brief, the principle of leaving individuals to themselves and of trusting that their unregulated interactions would produce socially desirable results. No new conceptions of society arose immediately to challenge seriously what had become, in fact, a capitalist civilization.

This system, though well-defined and logically coherent, must be understood as a system of tendencies only. The heritage of the past and other obstructions prevented any full realization of the principles except in a few cases of which the English free trade movement, crystallised by the repeal of the Corn Laws in 1846, is the most important. Such as they were, however, both tendencies and realizations bear the unmistakable stamp of the businessman's interests and still more the businessman's type of mind. Moreover, it was not only policy but the philosophy of national and individual life, the scheme of cultural values, that bore that stamp. Its materialistic utilitarianism, its naive confidence in progress of a certain type, its actual achievements in the field of pure and applied science, the temper of its artistic creations, may all be traced to the spirit of rationalism that emanates from the businessman's office. For much of the time and in many countries the businessman did not rule politically. But even noncapitalist rulers espoused his interests and adopted his views. They were what they had not been before, his agents.

More definitely than in any other historical epoch these developments can be explained by purely economic causes. It was the success of capitalist enterprise that raised the bourgeoisie to its position of temporary ascendancy. Economic success produced political power, which in turn produced policies congenial to the capitalist process. Thus the English industrialists obtained free trade, and free trade in turn was a major factor in a period of unprecedented economic expansion.

The partition of Africa and the carving out of spheres of influence in Asia by European powers in the decades preceding World War I led critics of capitalism to develop, on a Marxist basis, a theory of economic imperialism. According to this doctrine, competition among capitalist firms tends to eliminate all but a small number of giant concerns. Because of the inadequate purchasing power of the masses, these concerns find themselves unable to use the productive capacity they have built. They are, therefore, driven to invade foreign markets and to exclude foreign products from their own markets through protective tariffs. This situation produces aggressive colonial and foreign policies and "imperialist" wars, which the proletariat, if organized, turn into civil wars for socialist revolution. Like other doctrines of such sweeping character, this theory of imperialism is probably not capable of either exact proof or disproof. Three points, however, may be recorded in its favour; first, it does attempt what no other theory has attempted, namely, to subject the whole of the economic, political and cultural patterns of the epoch that began during the long depression (1873–96) to comprehensive analysis by means of a clear-cut plan; second, on the surface at least, it seems to be confirmed by some of the outstanding manifestations of this pattern and some of the greatest events of this epoch; third, whatever may be wrong with its interpretations, it certainly starts from a fact that is beyond challenge—the capitalist tendency toward industrial combination and the emergence of giant firms. Though cartels and trusts antedate the epoch, at least so far as the United States is concerned, the role of what is popularly called "big business" has increased so much as to constitute one of the outstanding characteristics of recent capitalism.

4. The Later Phase (Since 1914)

World War I marked a turning point in the development of capitalism in general and of European capitalism in particular. The period since 1914 has witnessed a reversal of the public attitude toward capitalism and of almost all the tendencies of the liberal epoch which preceded the war. In the prewar decades, European capitalism exercised vigorous leadership in the international economic community. World markets expanded, the gold standard became almost universal, Europe served as the world's banker, Africa became a European colony, Asia was divided into spheres of influence under the domination of European powers and Europe remained the centre of a growing volume of international trade.

After World War I, however, these trends were reversed. International markets shrank, the gold standard was abandoned in favour of managed national currencies, banking hegemony passed from Europe to the United States, African and Asian peoples began successful revolts against European colonialism and trade barriers multiplied. Western Europe as an entity declined, and in eastern Europe capitalism began to disintegrate. The Russian Revolution, a result of the war, uprooted over a vast area not only the basic capitalist institution of private property in the means of production, but the class structure, the traditional forms of government and the established religion. Moreover, the juggernaut unleashed by the Russian Revolution was destined to challenge the historic superiority of capitalist organization as a system of production within less than half a century.

Meanwhile, the inner structure of west European economies was tending away from the traditional forms of capitalism. Above all, *laissez-faire*, the accepted policy of the 19th century, was discredited by the war and postwar experience.

Statesmen and businessmen in capitalist nations were slow to appreciate the turn of events precipitated by World War I and consequently they misdirected their efforts during the 1920s by seeking a "return to prewar normalcy." Among major capitalist countries, the United Kingdom failed conspicuously to achieve prosperity at any time during the interwar period. Other capitalist nations enjoyed a brief prosperity in the 1920s only to be confronted in the 1930s with the great depression, which rocked the capitalist system to its foundations. *Laissez-faire* received a crushing blow from Pres. Franklin D. Roosevelt's New Deal in the United States. The gold standard collapsed completely. Free trade was abandoned in its classic home, Great Britain. Even the classical principle of sound finance, the annually balanced governmental budget, gave way in both practice and theory to planned deficits during periods of depressed economic activity. Retreat from the free market philosophy was nearly complete in Mussolini's Italy and Hitler's Germany. When World War II opened in 1939, the future of capitalism looked bleak indeed. This trend seemed confirmed at the end of the war when the British Labour party won a decisive victory at the polls and proceeded to nationalize basic industries, including coal, transportation, communication, public utilities and the Bank of England. Yet a judgment that capitalism had at last run its course would have been premature. Capitalist enterprise managed to survive in Great Britain, the United States, western Germany, Japan and other nations [with a] remarkable show of vitality in the postwar world.

.   .   .

6

Underdevelopment in History

Keith Griffin

STAGE THEORIES

Economic history, and theories firmly based upon historical knowledge, would appear to be essential in understanding the nature of underdevelopment. Unfortunately, however, most of the theories which claim to view development in historical perspective begin by assuming that the underdeveloped countries are in a "low-level equilibrium trap."[1] This presumption, of course, largely precludes endogenous change, since the very essence of an equilibrium position is absence of movement.

A common procedure is to assume that all nations, rich and poor, were once equal, i.e. suffered from an equivalent degree of poverty and state of underdevelopment. The implications of Kuznets' findings that "the present levels of *per capita* product in the underdeveloped countries are much lower than were those in the developed countries in their pre-industrialization phase"[2] have been totally ignored. Instead economists have argued from an assumption of equality when inequality obviously exists. Professor Leibenstein could not be more explicit. In defining "the abstract problem" he says, "We begin with a set of economies (or countries), each 'enjoying' an equally *low* standard of living at the outset. . . . Over a relatively long period of time (say, a century or two) some of these countries increase their output per head considerably whereas others do not."[3] This being so, the thing to do is determine how today's wealthy countries escaped the "low-level equilibrium trap," and then apply the lessons to the backward countries which were left behind.

The most self-conscious attempt to do this is found in Rostow's book, *The Stages of Economic Growth: A Non-Communist Manifesto*. The terminology and analytical categories employed in this book, although severely criticized,[4] have permeated Western thinking on development problems.[5] The reasons for this have more to do with sociology than economics.

Rostow believes that all countries pass through five stages. The initial stage is called "the traditional society" and its features are similar to those of the "non-capitalist" sector of dual economy models. Next comes a "pre-conditioning" stage, followed by the "take-off," the "drive to maturity" and, finally, an "age of high mass-consumption." How a nation gets from one

Reprinted from the author's *Underdevelopment in Spanish America* (London: George Allen & Unwin, 1969), pp. 31–48, by permission of the author and publishers. U.S. edition published by The M.I.T. Press, Cambridge, Massachusetts.

stage to another is unclear, since all Rostow presents, in effect, is a series of snapshots which freeze the development process in five different moments of time. What is clear, however, is that the present "traditional society" stage is the initial stage, and that development occurs essentially as a result of internal efforts which are largely unaffected by the workings of the wider international economy.

As Gunder Frank has stressed, Rostow's theory "attributes a history to the developed countries but denies all history to the underdeveloped ones."[6] Rostow neglects the past of the underdeveloped countries but confidently predicts a future for them similar to that of the wealthy nations. In this respect Rostow's views differ little from the Marxist doctrine that "the most industrially advanced country presents the less advanced country with the image of its future."

Marx and Rostow notwithstanding, it is exceedingly improbable that one can gain an adequate understanding of present obstacles and future potential for development without examining how the underdeveloped nations came to be as they are. To classify these countries as "traditional societies" begs the issue and implies either that the underdeveloped countries have no history or that it is unimportant.[7] No proof has yet been provided to substantiate either of these claims. Indeed it is clear that the underdeveloped countries do have a history and that it is important. Furthermore, evidence is gradually being accumulated that the expansion of Europe, commencing in the fifteenth century, had a profound impact on the societies and economies of the rest of the world. In other words, the history of the underdeveloped countries in the last five centuries is, in large part, the history of the consequences of European expansion. It is our tentative conclusion that the automatic functioning of the international economy which Europe dominated first created underdevelopment and then hindered efforts to escape from it. In summary, underdevelopment is a product of historical processes.

Historical research is gradually reconstructing the past of the underdeveloped countries for us. Enough is known to enable us to say with confidence that "by the end of the sixteenth century . . . the agricultural economies of the Spice Islands, the domestic industries of large parts of India, the Arab trading-economy of the Indian Ocean and of the western Pacific, the native societies of West Africa and the way of life in the Caribbean islands and in the vast areas of the two vice-royalties of Spanish America [were] all deeply affected by the impact of Europeans. . . . The results [of European expansion] on non-European societies were . . . sometimes immediate and overwhelming. . . ."[8]

The expansion of Europe throughout the world was an outcome of the competition among mercantilist-capitalist states for trading advantages. This competition was both peaceful and violent and its object was to obtain monopoly control of the most lucrative trading areas. In practice the quest for monopoly control led inevitably to the forceful acquisition of colonies, satellites, dependent territories and spheres of influence. But the initial impulse, from the time when the Portuguese first began to explore the Orient, was to dominate trade, not to gain territory; that came later. "The object of Portuguese colonization was not the possession of the Indies themselves, but of the trade of the Indies. Their approach was based on a concept of a *mare clausum*, secured to them under papal authority, which should save them from the inroads of other Christian states, and on a system of forts and garrisons which should save them from native opposition." The Portuguese had no wish to engage in production but "merely to divert to their own sea-routes a trade which was based on a competent native economy. Their purpose was to make the king of Portugal the only merchant trading between India and Portugal."[9]

Ironically, it was the combination of Europe's military superiority and her relative material poverty which shaped events in the early phase of European expansion. Western ascendancy was made possible by advanced military technology and it was made necessary by the inability of Europe to engage in trade on equal terms with the wealthy nations of the East. Asia had much that Europe wanted but Europe could offer almost nothing that was desired in Asia. As Professor Rich has said, "the spice trade was conditioned by the fact that the Spice Islands wanted very little of the produce of Europe save firearms."[10]

An historian of Indonesia notes that "when the first Dutch merchants and sailors had come to the island world of the Indies, they had been amazed by the variety of its nature and civilization, and the more observant among them had recognized that southern and eastern Asia were far ahead of western Europe in riches as well as in commercial ability and mercantile skill."[11] Similarly, an historian of the Middle East has written that "when Islam was still expanding and receptive, the Christian West had little or nothing to offer, but rather flattered Islamic pride with the spectacle of a culture that was visibly and palpably inferior."[12] Europe's subsequent ability to dominate the rest of the world depended not upon her cultural superiority or economic strength but upon two technological breakthroughs: the construction of large ocean-going sailing vessels and the development of gunpowder and naval cannons.[13] Indeed, Europe owed a great technological debt to the rest of the world, and particularly to China. Without Chinese science the industrial revolution would have been impossible.[14] It was European advances in specific military techniques rather than general progress in the peaceful arts of civilization which enabled her to establish hegemony in Latin America, Asia and Africa.

In the early period of expansion, in fact, a large volume of trade between Europe and the rest of the world would have been impossible because of the European tendency to run a substantial balance of payments deficit. If Europe was to obtain the products from the East which were desired she either had to force down the price of oriental products or increase the demand for goods which Europe could supply. In practice she did both. The Dutch, for instance, exacted an annual tribute in spices; for other crops they enforced compulsory deliveries at favourable prices. The English destroyed the Indian textile industry and then proceeded to supply India with cotton goods from Great Britain. How Britain was to finance the imports of tea from China presented great problems, for as the Chinese emperor said to George III, "our celestial empire possesses all things in prolific abundance" and, presumably, therefore, China had little need for English goods. This knotty problem was finally resolved by forcing opium on the

Chinese and encouraging addiction. This created a large demand for the drug which the East India Company was able to supply from Bengal. The Chinese made many vain attempts to restrict the trade. Finally, Britain forced China to permit the trade and fought the Opium War of 1839–42—"a war that was precipitated by the Chinese government's effort to suppress a pernicious contraband trade in opium, concluded by the superior firepower of British warships, and followed by humiliating treaties that gave Westerners special privileges in China."[15]

It is still a matter of debate whether domination of the rest of the world was the vital ingredient in Europe's recipe for rapid economic growth. There is little doubt, however, that resources were transferred to the West, and especially to Great Britain, on a massive scale. British India had a large trading surplus with China and the rest of Asia. These surpluses, in turn, were siphoned off to England "through the (politically established and maintained) Indian trading deficit with Britain, through the 'Home Charges'—i.e. India's payments for the privilege of being administered by Britain—and through the increasingly large interest-payments on the Indian Public Debt. Towards the end of the [nineteenth] century these items became increasingly important. Before the First World War 'the key to Britain's whole payments pattern lay in India, financing as she probably did more than two fifths of Britain's trade deficits'."[16]

Going back still further, the East India Company, according to Keynes, had its origin in privateering. "Indeed, the booty brought back by Drake in the *Golden Hind* may fairly be considered the fountain and origin of British Foreign Investment. Elizabeth paid off out of the proceeds the whole of her foreign debt and invested a part of the balance (about £42,000) in the Levant Company; largely out of the profits of the Levant Company there was formed the East India Company, the profits of which during the seventeenth and eighteenth centuries were the main foundation of England's foreign connections; and so on."[17]

. . .

[W]e are concerned not with whether European expansion enriched the West, but with whether it impoverished the rest of the world. It is conceivable that the benefits to Europe of its hegemony were slight and accrued in the form of temporarily increased consumption (rather than greater investment and growth), while the costs of her dominance were heavy and fell primarily upon the dependent countries. It is to this final question that we now turn.

FRAGMENTS OF HISTORY

The concept of "underdevelopment" as it is used [here] is all-inclusive. It refers to a society's political organization, economic characteristics and social institutions. Poverty is neither a synonym for underdevelopment nor a cause of underdevelopment; it is only symptomatic of a more general problem. Poverty, in other words, forms part of a culture. Oscar Lewis had the following to say about this culture: "The culture of poverty is both an adaptation and a reaction of the poor to their marginal position in a class-stratified, highly individuated, capitalistic society. It represents an effort to cope with feelings of hopelessness and despair. . . . Most frequently the culture of poverty develops when a stratified social and economic system is breaking down or is being replaced by another. . . . Often it results from imperial conquest in which the native social and economic structure is smashed and the natives are maintained in a servile colonial status, sometimes for many generations."[18]

As Lewis is the first to recognize, however, the culture of poverty is not identical in all settings; the slums of Puerto Rico produce a different culture from those of Mexico City;[19] the culture of poverty varies from place to place and from one era to another. The culture both shapes and is shaped by a people's history. It is for this reason that the differences between the developed and the underdeveloped countries cannot be explained exclusively in statistical terms; the two types of countries differ qualitatively as well as quantitatively. For similar reasons, it is almost certainly incorrect and misleading to assume that the circumstances of today's underdeveloped countries were always the same. Yet this is the view that at present prevails. Nurkse's notion of the "vicious circle of poverty"—the proposition that "a country is poor because it is poor," and presumably always has been—expresses the conventional doctrine perfectly.[20] As an alternative approach one might advance the hypothesis that the wellbeing of today's poor countries was not always so low and that their descent into underdevelopment did not occur independently of what was happening in the rest of the world.

It is our belief that underdeveloped countries as we observe them today are a product of historical forces, especially of those forces released by European expansion and world ascendancy. Thus they are a relatively recent phenomenon. Europe did not "discover" the underdeveloped countries; on the contrary, she created them. In many cases, in fact, the societies with which Europe came into contact were sophisticated, cultured and wealthy.

This is well illustrated by the case of Indonesia, an archipelago which today includes about half of the inhabitants of South-East Asia and the region which formerly acted as a magnet to Western traders and precipitated European expansion. At the beginning of the sixteenth century Indonesia was a prosperous region. "Local emporia were the equal of anything Europe had to offer: indeed Malacca was at that time regarded by Western visitors as the greatest port for international commerce in the world, clearing annually more shipping than any other."[21] The Dutch, operating through the Netherlands' United East India Company, aimed first to establish a monopoly of trade with the region. This aim was accomplished by 1641. They next established a monopsony over the purchases of the output of the islands. Finally, in the eighteenth century, the Dutch established a system of forced deliveries, forced cultivation and even the legal obligation to grow specific commercial crops on peasant holdings. Specialization was not dictated by the market but by the Company. As a consequence of this so-called Culture System "so little time was left to the Javanese for the cultivation of food crops that serious famines occurred in the eighteen-forties. The fertile island had been transformed into a vast Dutch plantation, or, from the point of view of the people, a forced labour camp."[22]

Agriculture was not the only sector that was adversely affected. The Dutch systematically discouraged and prevented local enterprise outside agriculture, and even brought in Chinese as ubiquitous middlemen. Java's indigenous commercial and industrial activities were utterly destroyed: ship building, iron-working, brass and copper founding all disappeared; weaving and peasant handicrafts declined; the merchant marine vanished and the merchants devoted themselves to piracy.

By the beginning of the present century the Indonesian economy was in a state of crisis and the Dutch government announced its intention in 1901 to "enquire into the diminishing welfare of the people of Java." Some indication of the extent to which the wellbeing of the people had declined is provided by Mr. Caldwell's figures:

Table 1   Average Annual Rice Consumption Per Head in Java and Madura

Period	Quantity (kilogrammes)
1856–70	114.0
1881–90	105.5
1891–1900	100.6
1936–40	89.0
1960	81.4

Source: M. Caldwell, *Indonesia*, Oxford University Press, 1968, p. 21.

Indonesia's experience was not unique. Indeed, President Roosevelt's comment to Lord Halifax in January 1944 that the French had possessed Indochina ". . . for nearly 100 years, and the people were worse off than they were at the beginning" is applicable to Asia as a whole. In some cases the destruction of the indigenous society was largely inadvertent. The decimation of the population of the South Pacific islands through the introduction of alien diseases is an example of this.[23] In other cases the destruction of the native economy and its institutions was deliberate. A second great example of this is India.

As late as the early seventeenth century India was more advanced economically than Europe. She had a fairly large manufacturing sector which produced mostly luxury goods—including gold and silver objects, plus glassware, paper, iron products and ships. Many of these items as well as cotton cloth, silk, indigo and saltpetre were exported to the West for payment in bullion.[24] The decline of India's industry was due to a combination of several factors: technical progress in Europe associated with the industrial revolution, domination of the East India Company and the imposition of the free trade doctrine under unequal conditions by the British. After 1833 the process of de-industrialization was accelerated and emphasis was placed on developing cash crop agriculture for export. Industrial decay was complete by the 1880s.

Parallel to the destruction of the manufacturing sector, agricultural institutions were profoundly altered and the economic wellbeing of rural inhabitants declined. Throughout the nineteenth century the proportion of the total population dependent upon agriculture increased, and the propor-

tion of the rural population composed of agricultural labourers also increased. Data from the Madras Presidency of South India indicate that
the real wages of agricultural labourers (measured in *seers* of common rice)
declined sharply even as late as the last quarter of the last century. In only
one of the seven districts for which data are available did real wages actually rise; in the others they declined from 13 to 48 per cent.

Table 2 Change in Real Wages of Agricultural Labour in Seven Districts
of South India, Average 1873–75 to Average 1898–1900

	per cent
Ganjam	−43
Vizagapatam	−48
Bellary	−20
Tanjore	+29
Tinnevelly	−40
Salem	−13
Coimbatore	−39

Source: Dharma Kumar, *Land and Caste in South India*, Cambridge University Press, 1965,
p. 164.

Conditions in the rest of India were roughly comparable. René Dumont
summarizes the experience of Bengal as follows: "On 22 March 1793 Lord
Cornwallis and the East India Company proclaimed that *zamindars* and
talukhars (the men who had been charged with the collection of tribute)
would henceforth be considered as permanent and irrevocable owners of
the lands on which they had gathered taxes. This proclamation had far-
reaching consequences. Of course, it is easy to see that the East India Company regarded it both as an improved way of obtaining a better return of
tributes, and also as an easy means of making firm allies. But they never
realized that, in depriving the peasant of his traditional and permanent
right to occupy the land, they were making him, throughout the greatest
part of India, a slave of new owners; and that exploitation of the peasant
now took the place of exploitation of resources. Rural societies were not
only compelled to pay taxes, but also rents which demographic development soon made outrageous; some peasants took to running away. A new
law gave the *zamindars* the right to catch them, and this completed the
dismemberment of traditional rural society. On the one hand great landowners; serfs on the other; the former with no incentive to improve the
land; the latter with no means to do so."[25]

The conversion of tax collectors into landlords, the emphasis on production of cash crops for export, and the population explosion which began at
the end of the nineteenth century were jointly responsible for the final
disaster. The mass of the people were reduced to a subsistence income
which hovered precariously above the famine level. Using 1900–01 as an
index base of 100, agricultural production *per capita* had declined to 72 a
half century later, while production of food *per capita* had plunged to the
miserably low figure of 58.[26]

None of the preceding discussion should be taken to imply that all of the underdeveloped countries were once wealthy societies and advanced civilizations. Some of the peoples with whom the Europeans came into contact were, of course, relatively primitive. But nearly all of the people encountered in today's underdeveloped areas were members of viable societies which could satisfy the economic needs of the community. Yet these societies were shattered when they came into contact with an expanding Europe. The manner in which the indigenous societies were destroyed varied from one region to another and depended upon the precise form taken by European penetration and the wealth, structure and resilience of the native civilization. Although the method of destruction varied, the outcome was always the same: a decline in the welfare of the subjugated people. Writing about Africa, Professor Frankel notes that attempts at modernization under colonialism are "in greater or lesser degree accompanied by increasingly rapid disintegration of the indigenous economic and social structure. However primitive those indigenous institutions may now appear in Western eyes, they did in fact provide the individuals composing the indigenous society with that sense of psychological and economic security without which life loses its meaning."[27]

Although our knowledge of African history is rudimentary, it is perhaps correct to say that no continent has felt the impact of European expansion more thoroughly than Africa. The introduction, especially by the Portuguese, of large-scale trading in slaves during the sixteenth century completely disrupted West Africa from Guinea to Angola.[28] Slavery created chaos in vast areas of the continent. The population declined; wars among formerly peaceful tribes were incited; the native economy fell into decay; and the social organization of the community and the authority of the chief frequently were corrupted. The entire way of life in Africa was altered. "The increased demand for slaves arising from the plantation owners of North and South America in the seventeenth and eighteenth centuries was responsible for depopulating large parts of Africa, and for degrading what had once been settled agricultural peoples back to long-fallow agriculture or nomadism."[29]

The slaughter of the indigenous people and the depopulation of the land did not cease with the end of slavery, however. In 1919 the Belgian Commission for the Protection of the Native estimated that the number of inhabitants of the Congo had declined by as much as 50 per cent since the beginning of occupation forty years earlier. In South-West Africa during the German-Herero War of 1904 General von Trotha, after the campaign was over, issued his notorious Extermination Order which required every Herero man, woman and child to be killed.[30] As a result of this the tribe was reduced from 80,000 to 15,000, and today it has regained only half of its former strength.

As pervasive as slavery and indiscriminate slaughter may have been, they can hardly be considered the typical pattern of European penetration in Africa. One must also consider the more "normal" economic activities of colonization and mineral extraction. One cannot, of course, accurately describe in a few paragraphs all the forms which colonialism adopted in North, East and Southern Africa, but it is possible to reconstruct a simplified scheme of the effects of European activity upon the indigenous society.

The process began with the acquisition of all the good land, mineral deposits and water resources by the colonialists. Excluding West Africa, this was nearly a universal phenomenon, and was not confined to the acknowledged cases of white settlers in Kenya, Algeria and the Republic of South Africa, but was also prevalent in less prominent places. For instance, the Bechuana tribes of Botswana were continually forced to give up their most productive lands in the south and northwest in order to avoid becoming a colony and to maintain their status as the Bechuanaland Protectorate.[31] In Liberia the descendants of freed slaves (Americo-Liberians) have installed themselves as aristocratic absentee landlords of rubber farms, have required the indigenous people to supply one fourth of the labour supply gratis, and pay the remainder four cents an hour or less.[32] The mandate territory of South-West Africa is a classical example of Europeans monopolizing the land. "Whites, though only one in seven of the total population, enjoy the exclusive use of two-thirds of the land."[33]

Having lost the best lands, the indigenous population was then confined to the less desirable and more remote areas—the "bush," Reserves, the veld or Bantustans. The high population densities led inevitably to increased erosion, declining yields of food crops in native areas and falling consumption levels. Colonialism in Africa—like that in Latin America, as we shall soon see—led to underemployment both of land (in the European areas)

Table 3 Per Capita Output of Indigenous Agriculture in Algeria

	Cereals (kilos)	Cattle (head)	Sheep (head)
1863	1000	n.a.	4.5
1911	377	0.2	1.5
1938	231	0.1	0.8
1954	202	0.1	0.7

Source: R. Murray and T. Wengraf, "The Algerian Revolution," *New Left Review*, No. 22, p. 32, who cite A. Gorz, *"Gaullisme et neo-colonialisme,"* Temps Modernes, March 1961.

and labour (in the African areas). *Per capita* food consumption, at least in some cases, has fallen over a considerable period of time. For example, food consumption in Algeria was perhaps between five and six times higher in 1863 than it was in 1954.

It was not sufficient, however, simply to dispossess the natives of their land and confine them to Reserves. The colonial economy—particularly the mines—also required cheap manpower; the Africans had to be compelled to emigrate and work for the Europeans. In some cases, e.g. in the Belgian and Portuguese colonies, the authorities relied to a great extent on forced labour. In most of the other colonies, however, a more subtle device was used—fiscal policy. A high tax, payable in money, was imposed on the natives. This forced them to enter a monopsonistic labour market and work for the white men at extremely low wages in order (i) to pay their taxes and (ii) to supplement the declining income obtainable from indigenous agriculture. Positive inducements in the form of incentive goods also were occasionally provided. Often this was unnecessary, however. A common technique, as in Basutoland, was to assign the responsibility for collecting taxes to the chief and allow him to take a rake-off. In this way the authority of the chief was used to favour the ambitions of the colonialists rather than the interests of his own people. The system of colonialism and indirect rule was designed to generate abundant supplies of cheap unskilled labour for Europeans who monopolized all other resources. The material wellbeing of the African was systematically lowered and his institutions were intentionally destroyed. It was this process of impoverishment and growing degradation which contributed to the urgent demands for independence in the late 1940s. By this time Africa and the other underdeveloped countries had gone through a lengthy period of growing misery which culminated in the collapse of primary commodity prices in the 1920s, the world depression of the 1930s, and the Second World War of the first half of the 1940s. The crisis of colonialism was not exclusively or even primarily a political crisis; its roots lay in the inability of the colonial system to generate economic progress and distribute it equitably.[34]

Even this rather superficial discussion of conditions in Africa and Asia should give us a broader perspective from which to consider the historical origins of underdevelopment in Latin America.

. . .

In general, colonialism in Latin America, as in the rest of the world, was a catastrophe for the indigenous people. In the areas of more primitive civilization the population virtually disappeared within less than thirty years. In the areas of advanced civilization the people were completely subjugated.

Spanish penetration of Latin America began in the Caribbean area. There they encountered Arawak, Carib and Cueva tribes with large populations tilling the soil in permanent clearings and on *conucos*. The native culture in the West Indies and on the Isthmus was not as advanced as some other civilizations, but the tribal societies were well organized and the economy was perhaps as productive as that of Indonesia. Yet within a generation the indigenous society and economy had been ruined and the native population had virtually disappeared.[35]

The Spaniards gained control over the natives by breaking their political structure. The chiefs were liquidated and the rest of the community were allocated to individual claimants. These allocations were originally called *repartimientos* and subsequently formed the basis of the *encomienda* system. These colonial institutions, in turn, were the origin of the latifundia system, under which individual rights to labour services were transformed to include the land as well. One of the features of the *repartimientos* was that the number of natives allocated to a Spaniard depended upon how much work he could extract from them, i.e. originally, how much gold for export he could get them to produce. In this way strong incentives to exploit labour were created.

The combination of brutality, slaughter, high tribute, slavery, forced labour for gold mining, destruction of the social framework, malnutrition,[36] disease and suicide led to the extinction of the indigenous population. "It has been reckoned that at the approach of the Spaniards, in 1492, total Carib population in Hispaniola was about 300,000. By 1508 it was reduced to about

60,000. A great decline had brought it to about 14,000 by 1514, as serious
settlement began; and by 1548 it had reached a figure which indicated virtual extermination, about 500."[37] The population of the other islands declined even more rapidly. The Bahamas lost their population first. Puerto
Rico was decimated in little more than a decade, and Cuba followed soon
after. By 1519 Jamaica was almost uninhabited. Those who survived were a
pitiable lot. "A well-structured and adjusted native society had become a
formless proletariat in alien servitude. . . ."[38]

As the population declined the *conucos* on the islands were abandoned
and the terrain became rangeland for cattle and pigs; in Central America
the continuous savanna reverted to a tropical rain forest. The Spaniards
responded to the labour shortage by introducing extensive grazing on their
estates. The few natives who managed to escape fled to the jungle and
adopted the slash-and-burn shifting agriculture that can still be observed
today.

A similar story may someday be told, perhaps, of the sparsely settled
regions of the Amazon basin. It is usually assumed that this region was
inhabited by extremely primitive people: this assumption, however, may
well turn out to be incorrect. The inhabitants of this area may once have
had a more advanced civilization and a higher standard of living than is
currently believed. A noted anthropologist who has had considerable research experience in Brazil, Claude Lévi-Strauss, is too cautious to advance
a positive hypothesis, but the question he poses is worth pondering. "Is it
not also possible to see them [the tribes in Brazil] as a regressive people,
that is, one that descended from a higher level of material life and social
organization and retained one trait or another as a vestige of former conditions?"[39]

We do not know what the answer to his question is as regards Brazil,
but in the two cases of Mexico and the Inca Empire the answer is clearly
"yes." Space does not permit us to recount the downfall of the Aztecs. Let
us only note that the native population of Mexico was decimated. From
about 13 million at the time of the Spanish Conquest, the population had
declined to about 2 million by the end of the sixteenth century.

In the Inca Empire, which covered a very large portion of western
South America, the impact of the Spanish was not quite so fatal, yet it is
still true that one of the greatest tragedies in Latin America was the destruction of this civilization. The Spanish Conquest of Peru was accompanied by profound social, institutional and demographic changes. The wars,
the epidemics and the fierce exploitation of the Indians reduced the indigenous population by one-half to two-thirds.[40] It was only towards the end
of the nineteenth century that the Indian population began to increase
again, and it is now estimated that this population only slightly exceeds the
number of inhabitants of the Inca Empire. The catastrophic decline in
population was accompanied by the utter ruination of the Andean civilization. Cities vanished; the communal customs of the Inca became an historical curiosity; terraced hillsides were abandoned; agricultural productivity
declined. The survivors of the conquest became a miserable, starving,
diseased and disorganized mass of humanity. In short, they became an
underdeveloped people.[41]

The new civilization constructed from the debris of the earlier indigenous society was markedly different. The colonizing Spaniards and their descendants enslaved what remained of the indigenous population. Indians were sent to the mines by the thousands to extract the mineral wealth of the continent. Following the precedent established in the Caribbean, the best lands were appropriated and huge estates were distributed to the favoured few. The great mass of the underprivileged, on the other hand, were pushed on to the mountain slopes where they attempted to eke out a living on small plots. In this way the distinctive economic system of Spanish America—the latifundia-minifundia complex—was created.

The essential feature of the new economic system was the monopolization of land. This by itself was sufficiently important to shape the social and political relationships of the colonial civilization, since in a predominantly agricultural economy one's livelihood depends almost entirely upon access to land. Exploitation did not stop here, however. Water rights were tightly controlled by the large landowners; the majority of the population had very little access to credit; rural education was practically non-existent. Thus the latifundium acquired a monopoly of the major factors of production—land, capital, water and technology, and its position as virtually the only large employer gave it a strong monopsonistic position in the labour market as well. The economic power of the minifundium was nil; its role in the system was to provide an abundant supply of cheap, unskilled labour.

Low productivity and an unequal distribution of income were inevitable characteristics of the new social and economic system. The universal syndrome of the latifundia-minifundia complex was the continuous pressure upon the Indians to move to poorer lands, the consequent accelerated erosion of the mountain slopes, falling yields of food crops on the subsistence plots, and a decline in consumption standards of the mass of the population. In contrast to the intensive agriculture of the minifundium and its declining productivity, the latifundium adopted highly labour extensive techniques of production and the large landowners were able to prosper at the expense of the rest of the community. Thus it was the social and political systems imposed by the colonists, in combination with the demographic changes which followed the Conquest, which were responsible for creating underdevelopment in Spanish America. One cannot explain the poverty of the region today without referring to the region's history.

NOTES

1. The phrase is taken from R. R. Nelson, "A Theory of the Low-Level Equilibrium Trap in Underdeveloped Economies," *American Economic Review*, December 1956. Also see by the same author, "Growth Models and the Escape from the Low-Level Equilibrium Trap: The Case of Japan," *Economic Development and Cultural Change*, July 1960.

2. S. Kuznets, *Economic Growth and Structure*, London, 1966, p. 177.

3. H. Leibenstein, *Economic Backwardness and Economic Growth*, John Wiley and Sons, 1960, p. 4. Italics in the original.

4. See, for example, P. A. Baran and E. J. Hobsbawm, "The Stages of Economic Growth," *Kyklos*, 1961; S. Kuznets, "Notes on the Take-Off," in W. W. Rostow, ed., *The Economics of Take-Off into Sustained Growth*, Macmillan, 1964.

5. For instance, in presenting their dualistic model Ranis and Fei claim that Rostow's "well-known intuitive notion has been chosen as our point of departure." ("A Theory of Economic Development," *American Economic Review*, Sept. 1961, p. 533.)

6. A. G. Frank, "Sociology of Development and Under-Development of Sociology," *Catalyst*, Summer 1967, p. 37.

7. A typical view is exemplified by Trevor-Roper's arrogant assertion that "the history of the world, for the last five centuries, in so far as it has significance, has been European history." (*The Rise of Christian Europe*, 1965, p. 11.)

8. E. E. Rich, "Preface," in E. E. Rich and C. H. Wilson, eds, *The Cambridge Economic History of Europe*, Vol. IV, *The Economy of Expanding Europe in the Sixteenth and Seventeenth Centuries*, Cambridge University Press, 1967, p. xiii. The contributions of Professor Rich to this volume, and especially the "Preface," are brilliant.

9. E. E. Rich, "Colonial Settlement and its Labour Problems," *ibid.*, p. 304.

10. *Ibid.*, p. 368.

11. B. H. M. Vlekke, *The Story of the Dutch East Indies*, Harvard University Press, 1946, p. 178.

12. B. Lewis, *The Emergence of Modern Turkey*, Oxford University Press, 1961, p. 40.

13. See C. M. Cipolla, *Guns and Sails in the Early Phase of European Expansion, 1400–1700*, Collins, 1965.

14. See J. Needham and W. Ling, *Science and Civilization in China*, Vol. IV, Part II, Cambridge University Press.

15. J. K. Fairbank, E. O. Reischauer and A. M. Craig, *East Asia: The Modern Transformation*, George Allen and Unwin, 1965, p. 136.

16. E. J. Hobsbawm, *Industry and Empire*, Weidenfeld and Nicolson, 1968, p. 123, citing S. B. Saul, *Studies in British Overseas Trade 1870–1914*.

17. J. M. Keynes, *A Treatise on Money*, Vol. II, *The Applied Theory of Money*, Macmillan, 1930, p. 156.

18. Oscar Lewis, *La Vida*, Secker and Warburg, London, 1967, p. xli.

19. See Oscar Lewis, *The Children of Sanchez*, Secker and Warburg, 1961.

20. R. Nurkse, *Problems of Capital Formation in Underdeveloped Countries*, Oxford University Press, p. 4.

21. M. Caldwell, *Indonesia*, Oxford University Press, 1968, p. 39.

22. *Ibid.*, p. 47.

23. See A. Moorehead, *The Fatal Impact*, Hamish Hamilton, 1966, Part I.

24. S. C. Kuchhal, *The Industrial Economy of India*, Chaitanya Publishing House, 1965, p. 64.

25. R. Dumont, *Lands Alive*, Merlin Press, 1965, p. 139.

26. See K. Mukerji, *Levels of Economic Activity and Public Expenditure in India*, Asia Publishing House, 1965.

27. S. H. Frankel, *The Economic Impact on Underdeveloped Societies*, Basil Blackwell, 1953, p. 134.

28. See J. Duffy, *Portuguese Africa*, Harvard University Press, 1959, especially Ch. VI. See also the well-known study by E. Williams, *Capitalism and Slavery*, University of North Carolina Press, 1944. J. Pope-Hennessy, *Sins of the Fathers: A Study of the Atlantic Slave Trade, 1441–1807*, 1967, is a lively popular account.
    Slave raiding in Eastern and Central Africa had been introduced earlier by Arab traders operating out of Zanzibar and Khartoum. This naturally disturbed the native economy and society, but the effects were insignificant in comparison with the devastation created by European and American slaving expeditions.

29. Colin Clark, *Population Growth and Land Use*, Macmillan, 1967, p. 136.

30. See R. First, *South-West Africa*, Penguin, 1963, pp. 69–83.

31. E. S. Munger, *Bechuanaland*, Oxford University Press, 1965, Ch. II.

32. G. Dalton, "History, Politics, and Economic Development in Liberia," *Journal of Economic History*, December 1965.

33. R. First, *op. cit.*, p. 142.

34. See B. Davidson, *Which Way Africa?*, Penguin, 1964, Ch. 6.

35. See C. O. Sauer, *The Early Spanish Main*, University of California Press, 1966, especially chapters III and VII.

36. There was never a deficiency of cassava bread and sweet potatoes on the islands.

Malnutrition occurred after the Spaniards suppressed native fishing and hunting and the supply of protein and fat declined.

37. E. E. Rich, "Colonial Settlement and its Labour Problems," *loc. cit.*, p. 319. The author adds that "European diseases had played their parts in this decimation of the Carib population, but the main cause was without doubt a passive revulsion from the changes which white occupation brought."

38. C. O. Sauer, *op. cit.*, p. 204.

39. Claude Lévi-Strauss, *Structural Anthropology*, Anchor Books, 1967, p. 101. Also see by the same author, *Tristes Tropiques*, 1958.

40. In Latin America as a whole Colin Clark estimates that the population declined from 40 million in 1500 to 12 million in 1650. (*Population Growth and Land Use*, p. 64.)

In North America the indigenous population was not very large, but the Indian was destroyed nevertheless. A former U.S. Commissioner of Indian Affairs has described in detail how "a policy at first implicit and sporadic, then explicit, elaborately rationalized and complexly implemented, of the extermination of Indian societies and of every Indian trait, of the eventual liquidation of Indians, became the formalized policy, law and practice," (John Collier, *Indians of the Americas*, Mentor, 1948, p. 103.)

41. The classic study of this process is W. H. Prescott, *The Conquest of Peru*.

7

On the Political Economy of Backwardness

Paul A. Baran

I

The capitalist mode of production and the social and political order concomitant with it provided, during the latter part of the eighteenth century,
and still more during the entire nineteenth century, a framework for a
continuous and, in spite of cyclical disturbances and setbacks, momentous
expansion of productivity and material welfare. The relevant facts are well
known and call for no elaboration. Yet this material (and cultural) progress
was not only spotty in time but most unevenly distributed in space. It was
confined to the Western world; and did not affect even all of this terri-
torially and demographically relatively small sector of the inhabited globe.

. . .

Tardy and skimpy as the benefits of capitalism may have been with
respect to the lower classes even in most of the leading industrial countries, they were all but negligible in the less privileged parts of the world.
There productivity remained low, and rapid increases in population pushed
living standards from bad to worse. The dreams of the prophets of capitalist
harmony remained on paper. Capital either did not move from countries
where its marginal productivity was low to countries where it could be
expected to be high, or if it did, it moved there mainly in order to extract
profits from backward countries that frequently accounted for a lion's share
of the increments in total output caused by the original investments. Where
an increase in the aggregate national product of an underdeveloped country
took place, the existing distribution of income prevented this increment
from raising the living standards of the broad masses of the population.
Like all general statements, this one is obviously open to criticism based on
particular cases. There were, no doubt, colonies and dependencies where
the populations profited from inflow of foreign capital. These benefits, however, were few and far between, while exploitation and stagnation were the
prevailing rule.

But if Western capitalism failed to improve materially the lot of the
peoples inhabiting most backward areas, it accomplished something that
profoundly affected the social and political conditions in underdeveloped
countries. It introduced there, with amazing rapidity, all the economic and
social tensions inherent in the capitalist order. It effectively disrupted whatever was left of the "feudal" coherence of the backward societies. It
substituted market contracts for such paternalistic relationships as still

Reprinted from *The Manchester School* (January 1952), pp. 66–84, by permission of the publisher.

survived from century to century. It reoriented the partly or wholly self-sufficient economies of agricultural countries toward the production of marketable commodities. It linked their economic fate with the vagaries of the world market and connected it with the fever curve of international price movements.

A *complete* substitution of capitalist market rationality for the rigidities of feudal or semi-feudal servitude would have represented, in spite of all the pains of transition, an important step in the direction of progress. Yet all that happened was that the age-old exploitation of the population of underdeveloped countries by their domestic overlords, was freed of the mitigating constraints inherited from the feudal transition. This superimposition of business *mores* over ancient oppression by landed gentries resulted in compounded exploitation, more outrageous corruption, and more glaring injustice.

Nor is this by any means the end of the story. Such export of capital and capitalism as has taken place had not only far-reaching implications of a social nature. It was accompanied by important physical and technical processes. Modern machines and products of advanced industries reached the poverty stricken backyards of the world. To be sure most, if not all, of these machines worked for their foreign owners—or at least were believed by the population to be working for no one else—and the new refined appurtenances of the good life belonged to foreign businessmen and their domestic counterparts. The bonanza that was capitalism, the fullness of things that was modern industrial civilization, were crowding the display windows—they were protected by barbed wire from the anxious grip of the starving and desperate man in the street.

But they have drastically changed his outlook. Broadening and deepening his economic horizon, they aroused aspirations, envies, and hopes. Young intellectuals filled with zeal and patriotic devotion travelled from the underdeveloped lands to Berlin and London, to Paris and New York, and returned home with the "message of the possible."

Fascinated by the advances and accomplishments observed in the centers of modern industry, they developed and propagandized the image of what could be attained in their home countries under a more rational economic and social order. The dissatisfaction with the stagnation (or at best, barely perceptible growth) that ripened gradually under the still-calm political and social surface was given an articulate expression. This dissatisfaction was not nurtured by a comparison of reality with a vision of a socialist society. It found sufficient fuel in the confrontation of what was actually happening with what could be accomplished under capitalist institutions of the Western type.

II

The establishment of such institutions was, however, beyond the reach of the tiny middle-classes of most backward areas. The inherited backwardness and poverty of their countries never gave them an opportunity to gather the economic strength, the insight, and the self-confidence needed for the assumption of a leading role in society. For centuries under feudal rule they themselves assimilated the political, moral, and cultural values of the dominating class.

While in advanced countries, such as France or Great Britain, the economically ascending middle-classes developed at an early stage a new rational world outlook, which they proudly opposed to the medieval ob-scurantism of the feudal age, the poor, fledgling bourgeoisie of the under-developed countries sought nothing but accommodation to the prevailing order. Living in societies based on privilege, they strove for a share in the existing sinecures. They made political and economic deals with their domestic feudal overlords or with powerful foreign investors, and what industry and commerce developed in backward areas in the course of the last hundred years was rapidly moulded in the straitjacket of monopoly—the plutocratic partner of the aristocratic rulers. What resulted was an economic and political amalgam combining the worst features of both worlds—feudalism and capitalism—and blocking effectively all possibilities of economic growth.

It is quite conceivable that a "conservative" exit from this impasse might have been found in the course of time. A younger generation of enterprising and enlightened businessmen and intellectuals allied with moderate leaders of workers and peasants—a "Young Turk" movement of some sort—might have succeeded in breaking the deadlock, in loosening the hide-bound social and political structure of their countries and in cre-ating the institutional arrangements indispensable for a measure of social and economic progress.

Yet in our rapid age history accorded no time for such a gradual transi-tion. Popular pressures for an amelioration of economic and social condi-tions, or at least for some perceptible movement in that direction, steadily gained in intensity. To be sure, the growing restiveness of the under-privileged was not directed against the ephemeral principles of a hardly yet existing capitalist order. Its objects were parasitic feudal overlords appropriating large slices of the national product and wasting them on extravagant living; a government machinery protecting and abetting the dominant interests; wealthy businessmen reaping immense profits and not utilizing them for productive purposes; last but not least, foreign colonizers extracting or believed to be extracting vast gains from their "develop-mental" operations.

This popular movement had thus essentially bourgeois, democratic, anti-feudal, anti-imperialist tenets. It found outlets in agrarian egalitarian-ism; it incorporated "muckraker" elements denouncing monopoly; it strove for national independence and freedom from foreign exploitation.

For the native capitalist middle-classes to assume the leadership of these popular forces and to direct them into the channels of bourgeois democracy—as has happened in Western Europe—they had to identify them-selves with the common man. They had to break away from the political, economic, and ideological leadership of the feudal crust and the monopolists allied with it; and they had to demonstrate to the nation as a whole that they had the knowledge, the courage, and the determination to undertake and to carry to victorious conclusion the struggle for economic and social improvement.

In hardly any underdeveloped country were the middle-classes capable of living up to this historical challenge. Some of the reasons for this portentous failure, reasons connected with the internal make-up of the business class itself, were briefly mentioned above. Of equal importance was, however, an "outside" factor. It was the spectacular growth of the international labor movement in Europe that offered the popular forces in backward areas ideological and political leadership that was denied to them by the native bourgeoisie. It pushed the goals and targets of the popular movements far beyond their original limited objectives.

This liaison of labor radicalism and populist revolt painted on the wall the imminent danger of a social revolution. Whether this danger was real or imaginary matters very little. What was essential is that the awareness of this threat effectively determined political and social action. It destroyed whatever chances there were of the capitalist classes joining and leading the popular anti-feudal, anti-monopolist movement. By instilling a mortal fear of expropriation and extinction in the minds of *all* property-owning groups the rise of socialist radicalism, and in particular the Bolshevik Revolution in Russia, tended to drive all more or less privileged, more or less well-to-do elements in the society into one "counterrevolutionary" coalition. Whatever differences and antagonisms existed between large and small landowners, between monopolistic and competitive business, between liberal bourgeois and reactionary feudal overlords, between domestic and foreign interests, were largely submerged on all important occasions by the over-riding *common* interest in staving off socialism.

The possibility of solving the economic and political deadlock prevailing in the underdeveloped countries on lines of a progressive capitalism all but disappeared. Entering the alliance with all other segments of the ruling class, the capitalist middle-classes yielded one strategic position after another. Afraid that a quarrel with the landed gentry might be exploited by the radical populist movement, the middle-classes abandoned all progressive attitudes in agrarian matters. Afraid that a conflict with the church and the military might weaken the political authority of the government, the middle-classes moved away from all liberal and pacifist currents. Afraid that hostility toward foreign interests might deprive them of foreign support in a case of a revolutionary emergency, the native capitalists deserted their previous anti-imperialist, nationalist platforms.

The peculiar mechanisms of political interaction characteristic of all underdeveloped (and perhaps not only underdeveloped) countries thus operated at full speed. The aboriginal failure of the middle-classes to provide inspiration and leadership to the popular masses pushed those masses into the camp of socialist radicalism. The growth of radicalism pushed the middle-classes into an alliance with the aristocratic and monopolistic reaction. This alliance, cemented by common interest and common fear, pushed the populist forces still further along the road of radicalism and revolt. The outcome was a polarization of society with very little left between the poles. By permitting this polarization to develop, by abandoning the common man and resigning the task of reorganizing society on new, progressive lines, the capitalist middle-classes threw away their historical chance of assuming effective control over the destinies of their nations, and of directing the gathering popular storm against the fortresses of feudalism and reaction. Its blazing fire turned thus against the entirety of existing economic and social institutions.

III

The economic and political order maintained by the ruling coalition of owning classes finds itself invariably at odds with all the urgent needs of the underdeveloped countries. Neither the social fabric that it embodies nor the institutions that rest upon it are conducive to progressive economic development. The only way to provide for economic growth and to prevent a continuous deterioration of living standards (apart from mass emigration unacceptable to other countries) is to assure a steady increase of total output—at least large enough to offset the rapid growth of population.

An obvious source of such an increase is the utilization of available unutilized or underutilized resources. A large part of this reservoir of dormant productive potentialities is the vast multitude of entirely unemployed or ineffectively employed manpower. There is no way of employing it usefully in agriculture, where the marginal productivity of labor tends to zero. They could be provided with opportunities for productive work only by transfer to industrial pursuits. For this to be feasible large investments in industrial plant and facilities have to be undertaken. Under prevailing conditions such investments are not forthcoming for a number of important and interrelated reasons.

With a very uneven distribution of a very small aggregate income (and wealth), large individual incomes exceeding what could be regarded as "reasonable" requirements for current consumption accrue as a rule to a relatively small group of high-income receivers. Many of them are large landowners maintaining a feudal style of life with large outlays on housing, servants, travel, and other luxuries. Their "requirements for consumption" are so high that there is only little room for savings. Only relatively insignificant amounts are left to be spent on improvements of agricultural estates.

Other members of the "upper crust" receiving incomes markedly surpassing "reasonable" levels of consumption are wealthy businessmen. For social reasons briefly mentioned above, their consumption too is very much larger than it would have been were they brought up in the puritan tradition of a bourgeois civilization. Their drive to accumulate and to expand their enterprises is continuously counteracted by the urgent desire to imitate in their living habits the socially dominant "old families," to prove by their conspicuous outlays on the amenities of rich life that they are socially (and therefore also politically) not inferior to their aristocratic partners in the ruling coalition.

But if this tendency curtails the volume of savings that could have been amassed by the urban high-income receivers, their will to re-invest their funds in productive enterprises is effectively curbed by a strong reluctance to damage their carefully erected monopolistic market positions through creation of additional productive capacity, and by absence of suitable investment opportunities—paradoxical as this may sound with reference to underdeveloped countries.

The deficiency of investment opportunities stems to a large extent from the structure and the limitations of the existing effective demand. With very low living standards the bulk of the aggregate money income of the population is spent on food and relatively primitive items of clothing and household necessities. These are available at low prices, and investment of large funds in plant and facilities that could produce this type of commodities more cheaply rarely promises attractive returns. Nor does it appear profitable to develop major enterprises the output of which would cater to the requirements of the rich. Large as their individual purchases of various luxuries may be, their aggregate spending on each of them is not sufficient to support the development of an elaborate luxury industry—in particular since the "snob" character of prevailing tastes renders only imported luxury articles true marks of social distinction.

Finally, the limited demand for investment goods precludes the building up of a machinery or equipment industry. Such mass consumption goods as are lacking, and such quantities of luxury goods as are purchased by the well-to-do, as well as the comparatively small quantities of investment goods needed by industry, are thus imported from abroad in exchange for domestic agricultural products and raw materials.

This leaves the expansion of exportable raw materials output as a major outlet for investment activities. There the possibilities are greatly influenced, however, by the technology of the production of most raw materials as well as by the nature of the markets to be served. Many raw materials, in particular oil, metals, certain industrial crops, have to be produced on a large scale if costs are to be kept low and satisfactory returns assured. Large-scale production, however, calls for large investments, so large indeed as to exceed the potentialities of the native capitalists in backward countries. Production of raw materials for a distant market entails, moreover, much larger risks than those encountered in domestic business. The difficulty of foreseeing accurately such things as receptiveness of the world markets, prices obtainable in competition with other countries, volume of output in other parts of the world, etc., sharply reduces the interest of native capitalists in these lines of business. They become to a predominant extent the domain of foreigners who, financially stronger, have at the same time much closer contacts with foreign outlets of their products.

The shortage of investible funds and the lack of investment opportunities represent two aspects of the same problem. A great number of investment projects, unprofitable under prevailing conditions, could be most promising in a general environment of economic expansion.

In backward areas a new industrial venture must frequently, if not always, break virgin ground. It has no functioning economic system to draw upon. It has to organize with its own efforts not only the productive process *within* its own confines, it must provide in addition for all the necessary *outside* arrangements essential to its operations. It does not enjoy the benefits of "external economies."

There can be no doubt that the absence of external economies, the inadequacy of the economic milieu in underdeveloped countries, constituted everywhere an important deterrent to investment in industrial projects. There is no way of rapidly bridging the gap. Large-scale investment is predicated upon large-scale investment. Roads, electric power stations, railroads, and houses have to be built *before* businessmen find it profitable to erect factories, to invest their funds in new industrial enterprises.

Yet investing in road building, financing construction of canals and power stations, organizing large housing projects, etc., transcend by far the financial and mental horizon of capitalists in underdeveloped countries. Not only are their financial resources too small for such ambitious projects, but their background and habits militate against entering commitments of this type. Brought up in the tradition of merchandizing and manufacturing consumers' goods—as is characteristic of an early phase of capitalist development—businessmen in underdeveloped countries are accustomed to rapid turnover, large but short-term risks, and correspondingly high rates of profit. Sinking funds in enterprises where profitability could manifest itself only in the course of many years is a largely unknown and unattractive departure. The difference between social and private rationality that exists in any market and profit-determined economy is thus particularly striking in underdeveloped countries.

. . .

But could not the required increase in total output be attained by better utilization of land—another unutilized or inadequately utilized productive factor?

There is usually no land that is both fit for agricultural purposes and at the same time readily accessible. Such terrain as could be cultivated but is actually not being tilled would usually require considerable investment before becoming suitable for settlement. In underdeveloped countries such outlays for agricultural purposes are just as unattractive to private interests as they are for industrial purposes.

On the other hand, more adequate employment of land that is already used in agriculture runs into considerable difficulties. Very few improvements that would be necessary in order to increase productivity can be carried out within the narrow confines of small-peasant holdings. Not only are the peasants in underdeveloped countries utterly unable to pay for such innovations, but the size of their lots offers no justification for their introduction.

Owners of large estates are in a sense in no better position. With limited savings at their disposal they do not have the funds to finance expensive improvements in their enterprises, nor do such projects appear profitable in view of the high prices of imported equipment in relation to prices of agricultural produce and wages of agricultural labor.

Approached thus *via* agriculture, an expansion of total output would also seem to be attainable only through the development of industry. Only through increase of industrial productivity could agricultural machinery, fertilizers, electric power, etc., be brought within the reach of the agricultural producer. Only through an increased demand for labor could agricultural wages be raised and a stimulus provided for a modernization of the agricultural economy. Only through the growth of industrial production could agricultural labor displaced by the machine be absorbed in productive employment.

Monopolistic market structures, shortage of savings, lack of external economies, the divergence of social and private rationalities do not exhaust, however, the list of obstacles blocking the way of privately organized industrial expansion in underdeveloped countries. Those obstacles have to be considered against the background of the general feeling of uncertainty prevailing in all backward areas. The coalition of the owning classes formed under pressure of fear, and held together by the real or imagined danger of social upheavals, provokes continuously more or less threatening rumblings under the outwardly calm political surface. The social and political tensions to which that coalition is a political response are not liquidated by the prevailing system; they are only repressed. Normal and quiet as the daily routine frequently appears, the more enlightened and understanding members of the ruling groups in underdeveloped countries sense the inherent instability of the political and social order. Occasional outbursts of popular dissatisfaction assuming the form of peasant uprisings, violent strikes or local guerrilla warfare, serve from time to time as grim reminders of the latent crisis.

In such a climate there is no will to invest on the part of monied people; in such a climate there is no enthusiasm for long-term projects; in such a climate the motto of all participants in the privileges offered by society is *carpe diem*.

IV

Could not, however, an appropriate policy on the part of the governments involved change the political climate and facilitate economic growth? In our time, when faith in the manipulative omnipotence of the State has all but displaced analysis of its social structure and understanding of its political and economic functions, the tendency is obviously to answer these questions in the affirmative.

Looking at the matter purely mechanically, it would appear indeed that much could be done by a well-advised regime in an underdeveloped country to provide for a relatively rapid increase of total output, accompanied by an improvement of the living standards of the population. There are a number of measures that the government could take in an effort to overcome backwardness. A fiscal policy could be adopted that by means of capital levies and a highly progressive tax system would syphon off all surplus purchasing power, and in this way eliminate non-essential consumption. The savings thus enforced could be channelled by the government into productive investment. Power stations, railroads, highways, irrigation systems, and soil improvements could be organized by the State with a view to creating an economic environment conducive to the growth of productivity. Technical schools on various levels could be set up by the public authority to furnish industrial training to young people as well as to adult workers and the unemployed. A system of scholarships could be introduced rendering acquisition of skills accessible to low-income strata.

Wherever private capital refrains from undertaking certain industrial projects, or wherever monopolistic controls block the necessary expansion of plant and facilities in particular industries, the government could step in and make the requisite investments. Where developmental possibilities that are rewarding in the long-run appear unprofitable during the initial period of gestation and learning, and are therefore beyond the horizon of private businessmen, the government could undertake to shoulder the short-run losses.

In addition an entire arsenal of "preventive" devices is at the disposal of the authorities. Inflationary pressures resulting from developmental activities (private and public) could be reduced or even eliminated, if outlays on investment projects could be offset by a corresponding and simultaneous contraction of spending elsewhere in the economic system. What this would call for is a taxation policy that would effectively remove from the income stream amounts sufficient to neutralize the investment-caused expansion of aggregate money income.

In the interim, and as a supplement, speculation in scarce goods and excessive profiteering in essential commodities could be suppressed by rigorous price controls. An equitable distribution of mass consumption goods in short supply could be assured by rationing. Diversion of resources in high demand to luxury purposes could be prevented by allocation and priority schemes. Strict supervision of transactions involving foreign exchanges could render capital flight, expenditure of limited foreign funds on luxury imports, pleasure trips abroad, and the like, impossible.

What the combination of these measures would accomplish is a radical change in the structure of effective demand in the underdeveloped country, and a reallocation of productive resources to satisfy society's need for economic development. By curtailing consumption of the higher-income groups, the amounts of savings available for investment purposes could be markedly increased. The squandering of limited supplies of foreign exchange on capital flight, or on importation of redundant foreign goods and services, could be prevented, and the foreign funds thus saved could be used for the acquisition of foreign-made machinery needed for economic development. The reluctance of private interests to engage in enterprises that are socially necessary, but may not promise rich returns in the short-run, would be prevented from determining the economic life of the backward country.

The mere listing of the steps that would have to be undertaken, in order to assure an expansion of output and income in an underdeveloped country, reveals the utter implausibility of the view that they could be carried out by the governments existing in most underdeveloped countries. The reason for this inability is only to a negligible extent the nonexistence of the competent and honest civil service needed for the administration of the program. A symptom itself of the political and social marasmus prevailing in underdeveloped countries, this lack cannot be remedied without attacking the underlying causes. Nor does it touch anything near the roots of the matter to lament the lack of satisfactory tax policies in backward countries, or to deplore the absence of tax "morale" and "discipline" among the civic virtues of their populations.

The crucial fact rendering the realization of a developmental program illusory is the political and social structure of the governments in power. The alliance of property-owning classes controlling the destinies of most underdeveloped countries cannot be expected to design and to execute a set of measures running counter to each and all of their immediate vested interests. If to appease the restive public, blueprints of progressive measures such as agrarian reform, equitable tax legislation, etc., are officially announced, their enforcement is wilfully sabotaged. The government, representing a political compromise between landed and business interests, cannot suppress the wasteful management of landed estates and the conspicuous consumption on the part of the aristocracy; cannot suppress monopolistic abuses, profiteering, capital flights, and extravagant living on the part of businessmen. It cannot curtail or abandon its lavish appropriations for a military and police establishment, providing attractive careers to the scions of wealthy families and a profitable outlet for armaments produced by their parents—quite apart from the fact that this establishment serves as the main protection against possible popular revolt. Set up to guard and to abet the existing property rights and privileges, it cannot become the architect of a policy calculated to destroy the privileges standing in the way of economic progress and to place the property and the incomes derived from it at the service of society as a whole.

Nor is there much to be said for the "intermediate" position which, granting the essential incompatibility of a well-conceived and vigorously executed developmental program with the political and social institutions prevailing in most underdeveloped countries, insists that at least *some* of the requisite measures could be carried out by the existing political authorities. This school of thought overlooks entirely the weakness, if not the complete absence, of social and political forces that could induce the necessary concessions on the part of the ruling coalition. By background and political upbringing, too myopic and self-interested to permit the slightest encroachments upon their inherited positions and cherished privileges, the upper-classes in underdeveloped countries resist doggedly all pressures in that direction. Every time such pressures grow in strength they succeed in cementing anew the alliance of all conservative elements, by decrying all attempts at reform as assaults on the very foundations of society.

Even if measures like progressive taxation, capital levies, and foreign exchange controls could be enforced by the corrupt officials operating in the demoralized business communities of underdeveloped countries, such enforcement would to a large extent defeat its original purpose. Where businessmen do not invest, unless in expectation of lavish profits, a taxation system succeeding in confiscating large parts of these profits is bound to kill private investment. Where doing business or operating landed estates is attractive mainly because it permits luxurious living, foreign exchange controls preventing the importation of luxury goods are bound to blight enterprise. Where the only stimulus to hard work on the part of intellectuals, technicians, and civil servants is the chance of partaking in the privileges of the ruling class, a policy aiming at the reduction of inequality of social status and income is bound to smother effort.

The injection of planning into a society living in the twilight between feudalism and capitalism cannot but result in additional corruption, larger and more artful evasions of the law, and more brazen abuses of authority.

V

There would seem to be no exit from the impasse. The ruling coalition of interests does not abdicate of its own volition, nor does it change its character in response to incantation. Although its individual members occasionally leave the sinking ship physically or financially (or in both ways), the property-owning classes as a whole are as a rule grimly determined to hold fast to their political and economic entrenchments.

If the threat of social upheaval assumes dangerous proportions, they tighten their grip on political life and move rapidly in the direction of unbridled reaction and military dictatorship. Making use of favourable international opportunities and of ideological and social affinities to ruling groups in other countries, they solicit foreign economic and sometimes military aid in their efforts to stave off the impending disaster.

Such aid is likely to be given to them by foreign governments regarding them as an evil less to be feared than the social revolution that would sweep them out of power. This attitude of their friends and protectors abroad is no less short-sighted than their own.

The adjustment of the social and political conditions in underdeveloped countries to the urgent needs of economic development can be postponed; it cannot be indefinitely avoided. In the past, it could have been delayed by decades or even centuries. In our age it is a matter of years. Bolstering the political system of power existing in backward countries by providing it with military support may temporarily block the eruption of the volcano; it cannot stop the subterranean gathering of explosive forces.

Economic help in the form of loans and grants given to the governments of backward countries, to enable them to promote a measure of economic progress, is no substitute for the domestic changes that are mandatory if economic development is to be attained.

Such help, in fact, may actually do more harm than good. Possibly permitting the importation of some foreign-made machinery and equipment for government or business sponsored investment projects, but not accompanied by any of the steps that are needed to assure healthy economic growth, foreign assistance thus supplied may set off an inflationary spiral increasing and aggravating the existing social and economic tensions in underdeveloped countries.

If, as is frequently the case, these loans or grants from abroad are tied to the fulfillment of certain conditions on the part of the receiving country regarding their use, the resulting investment may be directed in such channels as to conform more to the interests of the lending than to those of the borrowing country. Where economic advice as a form of "technical assistance" is supplied to the underdeveloped country, and its acceptance is made a prerequisite to eligibility for financial aid, this advice often pushes the governments of underdeveloped countries toward policies, ideologically or otherwise attractive to the foreign experts dispensing economic counsel, but not necessarily conducive to economic development of the "benefitted" countries. Nationalism and xenophobia are thus strengthened in backward areas—additional fuel for political restiveness.

For backward countries to enter the road of economic growth and social progress, the political framework of their existence has to be drastically revamped. The alliance between feudal landlords, industrial royalists, and the capitalist middle-classes has to be broken. The keepers of the past cannot be the builders of the future. Such progressive and enterprising elements as exist in backward societies have to obtain the possibility of leading their countries in the direction of economic and social growth.

What France, Britain, and America have accomplished through their own revolutions has to be attained in backward countries by a combined effort of popular forces, enlightened government, and unselfish foreign help. This combined effort must sweep away the holdover institutions of a defunct age, must change the political and social climate in the underdeveloped countries, and must imbue their nations with a new spirit of enterprise and freedom.

Should it prove too late in the historical process for the bourgeoisie to rise to its responsibilities in backward areas, should the long experience of servitude and accommodation to the feudal past have reduced the forces of progressive capitalism to impotence, the backward countries of the world will inevitably turn to economic planning and social collectivism. If the capitalist world outlook of economic and social progress, propelled by enlightened self-interest, should prove unable to triumph over the conservatism of inherited positions and traditional privileges, if the capitalist promise of advance and reward to the efficient, the industrious, the able, should not displace the feudal assurance of security and power to the well-bred, the well-connected and the conformist—a new social ethos will become the spirit and guide of a new age. It will be the ethos of the collective effort, the creed of the predominance of the interests of society over the interests of selected few.

The transition may be abrupt and painful. The land not given to the peasants legally may be taken by them forcibly. High incomes not confiscated through taxation may be eliminated by outright expropriation. Corrupt officials not retired in orderly fashion may be removed by violent action.

Which way the historical wheel will turn and in which way the crisis in the backward countries will find its final solution will depend in the main on whether the capitalist middle-classes in the backward areas, and the rulers of the advanced industrial nations of the world, overcome their fear and myopia. Or are they too spell-bound by their narrowly conceived selfish interests, too blinded by their hatred of progress, grown so senile in these latter days of the capitalist age, as to commit suicide out of fear of death?

8

The Development of Underdevelopment

Andre Gunder Frank

We cannot hope to formulate adequate development theory and policy for the majority of the world's population who suffer from underdevelopment without first learning how their past economic and social history gave rise to their present underdevelopment. Yet most historians study only the developed metropolitan countries and pay scant attention to the colonial and underdeveloped lands. For this reason most of our theoretical categories and guides to development policy have been distilled exclusively from the historical experience of the European and North American advanced capitalist nations.

Since the historical experience of the colonial and underdeveloped countries has demonstrably been quite different, available theory therefore fails to reflect the past of the underdeveloped part of the world entirely, and reflects the past of the world as a whole only in part. More important, our ignorance of the underdeveloped countries' history leads us to assume that their past and indeed their present resembles earlier stages of the history of the now developed countries. This ignorance and this assumption lead us into serious misconceptions about contemporary underdevelopment and development. Further, most studies of development and underdevelopment fail to take account of the economic and other relations between the metropolis and its economic colonies throughout the history of the world-wide expansion and development of the mercantilist and capitalist system. Consequently, most of our theory fails to explain the structure and development of the capitalist system as a whole and to account for its simultaneous generation of underdevelopment in some of its parts and of economic development in others.

It is generally held that economic development occurs in a succession of capitalist stages and that today's underdeveloped countries are still in a stage, sometimes depicted as an original stage of history, through which the now developed countries passed long ago. Yet even a modest acquaintance with history shows that underdevelopment is not original or traditional and that neither the past nor the present of the underdeveloped

Reprinted from *Monthly Review*, Vol. 18, No. 4 (September 1966), pp. 17–31, by permission of Monthly Review Press. Copyright © 1969 by Andre Gunder Frank. All Rights Reserved.

countries resembles in any important respect the past of the now developed countries. The now developed countries were never *under*developed, though they may have been *un*developed. It is also widely believed that the contemporary underdevelopment of a country can be understood as the product or reflection solely of its own economic, political, social, and cultural characteristics or structure. Yet historical research demonstrates that contemporary underdevelopment is in large part the historical product of past and continuing economic and other relations between the satellite underdeveloped and the now developed metropolitan countries. Furthermore, these relations are an essential part of the structure and development of the capitalist system on a world scale as a whole. A related and also largely erroneous view is that the development of these underdeveloped countries and, within them of their most underdeveloped domestic areas, must and will be generated or stimulated by diffusing capital, institutions, values, etc., to them from the international and national capitalist metropoles. Historical perspective based on the underdeveloped countries' past experience suggests that on the contrary in the underdeveloped countries economic development can now occur only independently of most of these relations of diffusion.

Evident inequalities of income and differences in culture have led many observers to see "dual" societies and economies in the underdeveloped countries. Each of the two parts is supposed to have a history of its own, a structure, and a contemporary dynamic largely independent of the other. Supposedly, only one part of the economy and society has been importantly affected by intimate economic relations with the "outside" capitalist world; and that part, it is held, became modern, capitalist, and relatively developed precisely because of this contact. The other part is widely regarded as variously isolated, subsistence-based, feudal, or precapitalist, and therefore more underdeveloped.

I believe on the contrary that the entire "dual society" thesis is false and that the policy recommendations to which it leads will, if acted upon, serve only to intensify and perpetuate the very conditions of underdevelopment they are supposedly designed to remedy.

A mounting body of evidence suggests, and I am confident that future historical research will confirm, that the expansion of the capitalist system over the past centuries effectively and entirely penetrated even the apparently most isolated sectors of the underdeveloped world. Therefore, the economic, political, social, and cultural institutions and relations we now observe there are the products of the historical development of the capitalist system no less than are the seemingly more modern or capitalist features of the national metropoles of these underdeveloped countries. Analogously to the relations between development and underdevelopment on the international level, the contemporary underdeveloped institutions of the so-called backward or feudal domestic areas of an underdeveloped country are no less the product of the single historical process of capitalist development than are the so-called capitalist institutions of the supposedly more progressive areas. In this paper I should like to sketch the kinds of evidence which support this thesis and at the same time indicate lines along which further study and research could fruitfully proceed.

II

The Secretary General of the Latin American Center for Research in the Social Sciences writes in that Center's journal: "The privileged position of the city has its origin in the colonial period. It was founded by the Conqueror to serve the same ends that it still serves today; to incorporate the indigenous population into the economy brought and developed by that Conqueror and his descendants. The regional city was an instrument of conquest and is still today an instrument of domination."[1] The Instituto Nacional Indigenista (National Indian Institute) of Mexico confirms this observation when it notes that "the mestizo population, in fact, always lives in a city, a center of an intercultural region, which acts as the metropolis of a zone of indigenous population and which maintains with the underdeveloped communities an intimate relation which links the center with the satellite communities."[2] The Institute goes on to point out that "between the mestizos who live in the nuclear city of the region and the Indians who live in the peasant hinterland there is in reality a closer economic and social interdependence than might at first glance appear" and that the provincial metropoles "by being centers of intercourse are also centers of exploitation."[3]

Thus these metropolis-satellite relations are not limited to the imperial or international level but penetrate and structure the very economic, political, and social life of the Latin American colonies and countries. Just as the colonial and national capital and its export sector become the satellite of the Iberian (and later of other) metropoles of the world economic system, this satellite immediately becomes a colonial and then a national metropolis with respect to the productive sectors and population of the interior. Furthermore, the provincial capitals, which thus are themselves satellites of the national metropolis—and through the latter of the world metropolis—are in turn provincial centers around which their own local satellites orbit. Thus, a whole chain of constellations of metropoles and satellites relates all parts of the whole system from its metropolitan center in Europe or the United States to the farthest outpost in the Latin American countryside.

When we examine this metropolis-satellite structure, we find that each of the satellites, including now-underdeveloped Spain and Portugal, serves as an instrument to suck capital or economic surplus out of its own satellites and to channel part of this surplus to the world metropolis of which all are satellites. Moreover, each national and local metropolis serves to impose and maintain the monopolistic structure and exploitative relationship of this system (as the Instituto Nacional Indigenista of Mexico calls it) as long as it serves the interests of the metropoles which take advantage of this global, national, and local structure to promote their own development and the enrichment of their ruling classes.

These are the principal and still surviving structural characteristics which were implanted in Latin America by the Conquest. Beyond examining the establishment of this colonial structure in its historical context, the proposed approach calls for study of the development—and underdevelopment—of these metropoles and satellites of Latin America throughout the following and still continuing historical process. In this way we can understand why there were and still are tendencies in the Latin American and world capitalist structure which seem to lead to the development of the metropolis and the underdevelopment of the satellite and why, particularly, the satellized national, regional, and local metropoles in Latin America find that their economic development is at best a limited or underdeveloped development.

III

That present underdevelopment of Latin America is the result of its centuries-long participation in the process of world capitalist development, I believe I have shown in my case studies of the economic and social histories of Chile and Brazil.[4] My study of Chilean history suggests that the Conquest not only incorporated this country fully into the expansion and development of the world mercantile and later industrial capitalist system but that it also introduced the monopolistic metropolis-satellite structure and development of capitalism into the Chilean domestic economy and society itself. This structure then penetrated and permeated all of Chile very quickly. Since that time and in the course of world and Chilean history during the epochs of colonialism, free trade, imperialism, and the present, Chile has become increasingly marked by the economic, social, and political structure of satellite underdevelopment. This development of underdevelopment continues today, both in Chile's still increasing satellization by the world metropolis and through the ever more acute polarization of Chile's domestic economy.

The history of Brazil is perhaps the clearest case of both national and regional development of underdevelopment. The expansion of the world economy since the beginning of the sixteenth century successively converted the Northeast, the Minas Gerais interior, the North, and the Center-South (Rio de Janeiro, São Paulo, and Paraná) into export economies and incorporated them into the structure and development of the world capitalist system. Each of these regions experienced what may have appeared as economic development during the period of its respective golden age. But it was a satellite development which was neither self-generating nor self-perpetuating. As the market or the productivity of the first three regions declined, foreign and domestic economic interest in them waned; and they were left to develop the underdevelopment they live today. In the fourth region, the coffee economy experienced a similar though not yet quite as serious fate (though the development of a synthetic coffee substitute promises to deal it a mortal blow in the not too distant future). All of this historical evidence contradicts the generally accepted theses that Latin America suffers from a dual society or from the survival of feudal institutions and that these are important obstacles to its economic development.

IV

During the First World War, however, and even more during the Great Depression and the Second World War, São Paulo began to build up an industrial establishment which is the largest in Latin America today. The question arises whether this industrial development did or can break Brazil out of the cycle of satellite development and underdevelopment which has characterized its other regions and national history within the capitalist system so far. I believe that the answer is no. Domestically the evidence so far is fairly clear. The development of industry in São Paulo has not brought greater riches to the other regions of Brazil. Instead, it converted them into internal colonial satellites, de-capitalized them further, and consolidated or even deepened their underdevelopment. There is little evidence to suggest that this process is likely to be reversed in the foreseeable future except insofar as the provincial poor migrate and become the poor of the metropolitan cities. Externally, the evidence is that although the initial development of São Paulo's industry was relatively autonomous it is being increasingly satellized by the world capitalist metropolis and its future development possibilities are increasingly restricted.[5] This development, my studies lead me to believe, also appears destined to limited or underdeveloped development as long as it takes place in the present economic, political, and social framework.

We must conclude, in short, that underdevelopment is not due to the survival of archaic institutions and the existence of capital shortage in regions that have remained isolated from the stream of world history. On the contrary, underdevelopment was and still is generated by the very same historical process which also generated economic development: the development of capitalism itself. This view, I am glad to say, is gaining adherents among students of Latin America and is proving its worth in shedding new light on the problems of the area and in affording a better perspective for the formulation of theory and policy.[6]

V

The same historical and structural approach can also lead to better development theory and policy by generating a series of hypotheses about development and underdevelopment such as those I am testing in my current research. The hypotheses are derived from the empirical observation and theoretical assumption that within this world-embracing metropolis-satellite structure the metropoles tend to develop and the satellites to underdevelop. The first hypothesis has already been mentioned above: that in contrast to the development of the world metropolis which is no one's satellite, the development of the national and other subordinate metropoles is limited by their satellite status. It is perhaps more difficult to test this hypothesis than the following ones because part of its confirmation depends on the test of the other hypotheses. Nonetheless, this hypothesis appears to be generally confirmed by the non-autonomous and unsatisfactory economic and especially industrial development of Latin America's national metropoles, as documented in the studies already cited. The most important and at the same time most confirmatory examples are the metropolitan regions of Buenos Aires and São Paulo whose growth only began in the nineteenth century, was therefore largely untrammelled by any colonial heritage, but was and remains a satellite development largely dependent on the outside metropolis, first of Britain and then of the United States.

A second hypothesis is that the satellites experience their greatest economic development and especially their most classically capitalist industrial development if and when their ties to their metropolis are weakest. This hypothesis is almost diametrically opposed to the generally accepted thesis that development in the underdeveloped countries follows from the greatest degree of contact with and diffusion from the metropolitan developed countries. This hypothesis seems to be confirmed by two kinds of relative isolation that Latin America has experienced in the course of its history. One is the temporary isolation caused by the crises of war or depression in the world metropolis. Apart from minor ones, five periods of such major crises stand out and seem to confirm the hypothesis. These are: the European (and especially Spanish) Depression of the seventeenth century, the Napoleonic Wars, the First World War, the Depression of the 1930's, and the Second World War. It is clearly established and generally recognized that the most important recent industrial development—especially of Argentina, Brazil, and Mexico, but also of other countries such as Chile—has taken place precisely during the periods of the two World Wars and the intervening Depression. Thanks to the consequent loosening of trade and investment ties during these periods, the satellites initiated marked autonomous industrialization and growth. Historical research demonstrates that the same thing happened in Latin America during Europe's seventeenth-century depression. Manufacturing grew in the Latin American countries, and several of them such as Chile became exporters of manufactured goods. The Napoleonic Wars gave rise to independence movements in Latin America, and these should perhaps also be interpreted as confirming the development hypothesis in part.

The other kind of isolation which tends to confirm the second hypothesis is the geographic and economic isolation of regions which at one time were relatively weakly tied to and poorly integrated into the mercantilist and capitalist system. My preliminary research suggests that in Latin America it was these regions which initiated and experienced the most promising self-generating economic development of the classical industrial capitalist type. The most important regional cases probably are Tucumán and Asunción, as well as other cities such as Mendoza and Rosario, in the interior of Argentina and Paraguay during the end of the eighteenth and the beginning of the nineteenth centuries. Seventeenth- and eighteenth-century São Paulo, long before coffee was grown there, is another example. Perhaps Antioquia in Colombia and Puebla and Querétaro in Mexico are other examples. In its own way, Chile was also an example since, before the sea route around the Horn was opened, this country was relatively isolated at the end of the long voyage from Europe via Panama. All of these regions became manufacturing centers and even exporters, usually of textiles, during the periods preceding their effective incorporation as satellites into the colonial, national, and world capitalist system.

Internationally, of course, the classic case of industrialization through non-participation as a satellite in the capitalist world system is obviously that of Japan after the Meiji Restoration. Why, one may ask, was resource-poor but unsatellized Japan able to industrialize so quickly at the end of the century while resource-rich Latin American countries and Russia were not able to do so and the latter was easily beaten by Japan in the War of 1904 after the same forty years of development efforts? The second hypothesis suggests that the fundamental reason is that Japan was not satellized either during the Tokugawa or Meiji period and therefore did not have its development structurally limited as did the countries which were so satellized.

VI

A corollary of the second hypothesis is that when the metropolis recovers from its crisis and re-establishes the trade and investment ties which fully re-incorporate the satellites into the system, or when the metropolis expands to incorporate previously isolated regions into the world-wide system, the previous development and industrialization of these regions is choked off or channelled into directions which are not self-perpetuating and promising. This happened after each of the five crises cited above. The renewed expansion of trade and the spread of economic liberalism in the eighteenth and nineteenth centuries choked off and reversed the manufacturing development which Latin America had experienced during the seventeenth century, and in some places at the beginning of the nineteenth. After the First World War, the new national industry of Brazil suffered serious consequences from American economic invasion. The increase in the growth rate of Gross National Product and particularly of industrialization throughout Latin America was again reversed and industry became increasingly satellized after the Second World War and especially after the post-Korean War recovery and expansion of the metropolis. Far from having become more developed since then, industrial sectors of Brazil and most conspicuously of Argentina have become structurally more and more underdeveloped and less and less able to generate continued industrialization and/or sustain development of the economy. This process, from which India also suffers, is reflected in a whole gamut of balance-of-payments, inflationary, and other economic and political difficulties, and promises to yield to no solution short of far-reaching structural change.

Our hypothesis suggests that fundamentally the same process occurred even more dramatically with the incorporation into the system of previously unsatellized regions. The expansion of Buenos Aires as a satellite of Great Britain and the introduction of free trade in the interest of the ruling groups of both metropoles destroyed the manufacturing and much of the remainder of the economic base of the previously relatively prosperous interior almost entirely. Manufacturing was destroyed by foreign competition, lands were taken and concentrated into latifundia by the rapaciously growing export economy, intraregional distribution of income became much more unequal, and the previously developing regions became simple satellites of Buenos Aires and through it of London. The provincial centers did not yield to satellization without a struggle. This metropolis-satellite conflict was much of the cause of the long political and armed struggle between the Unitarists in Buenos Aires and the Federalists in the provinces, and it may be said to have been the sole important cause of the War of the Triple Alliance in which Buenos Aires, Montevideo, and Rio de Janeiro, encouraged and helped by London, destroyed not only the autonomously developing economy of Paraguay but killed off nearly all of its population which was unwilling to give in. Though this is no doubt the most spectacular example which tends to confirm the hypothesis, I believe that historical research on the satellization of previously relatively independent yeoman-farming and incipient manufacturing regions such as the Caribbean islands will confirm it further.[7] These regions did not have a chance against the forces of expanding and developing capitalism, and their own development had to be sacrificed to that of others. The economy and industry of Argentina, Brazil, and other countries which have experienced the effects of metropolitan recovery since the Second World War are today suffering much the same fate, if fortunately still in lesser degree.

VII

A third major hypothesis derived from the metropolis-satellite structure is that the regions which are the most underdeveloped and feudal-seeming today are the ones which had the closest ties to the metropolis in the past. They are the regions which were the greatest exporters of primary products to and the biggest sources of capital for the world metropolis and which were abandoned by the metropolis when for one reason or another business fell off. This hypothesis also contradicts the generally held thesis that the source of a region's underdevelopment is its isolation and its precapitalist institutions.

This hypothesis seems to be amply confirmed by the former super-satellite development and present ultra-underdevelopment of the once sugar-exporting West Indies, Northeastern Brazil, the ex-mining districts of Minas Gerais in Brazil, highland Peru, and Bolivia, and the central Mexican states of Guanajuato, Zacatecas, and others whose names were made world famous centuries ago by their silver. There surely are no major regions in Latin America which are today more cursed by under-development and poverty; yet all of these regions, like Bengal in India, once provided the life blood of mercantile and industrial capitalist development —in the metropolis. These regions' participation in the development of the world capitalist system gave them, already in their golden age, the typical structure of underdevelopment of a capitalist export economy. When the market for their sugar or the wealth of their mines disappeared and the metropolis abandoned them to their own devices, the already existing economic, political, and social structure of these regions prohibited autonomous generation of economic development and left them no alternative but to turn in upon themselves and to degenerate into the ultra-underdevelopment we find there today.

VIII

These considerations suggest two further and related hypotheses. One is that the latifundium, irrespective of whether it appears as a plantation or a hacienda today, was typically born as a commercial enterprise which created for itself the institutions which permitted it to respond to increased demand in the world or national market by expanding the amount of its land, capital, and labor and to increase the supply of its products. The fifth hypothesis is that the latifundia which appear isolated, subsistence-based, and semi-feudal today saw the demand for their products or their productive capacity decline and that they are to be found principally in the above-named former agricultural and mining export regions whose economic activity declined in general. These two hypotheses run counter to the notions of most people, and even to the opinions of some historians and other students of the subject, according to whom the historical roots and socio-economic causes of Latin American latifundia and agrarian institutions are to be found in the transfer of feudal institutions from Europe and/or in economic depression.

The evidence to test these hypotheses is not open to easy general inspection and requires detailed analyses of many cases. Nonetheless, some important confirmatory evidence is available. The growth of the latifundium in nineteenth-century Argentina and Cuba is a clear case in support of the fourth hypothesis and can in no way be attributed to the transfer of feudal institutions during colonial times. The same is evidently the case of the postrevolutionary and contemporary resurgence of latifundia particularly in the North of Mexico, which produce for the American market, and of similar ones on the coast of Peru and the new coffee regions of Brazil. The conversion of previously yeoman-farming Caribbean islands, such as Barbados, into sugar-exporting economies at various times between the seventeenth and twentieth centuries and the resulting rise of the latifundia in these islands would seem to confirm the fourth hypothesis as well. In Chile, the rise of the latifundium and the creation of the institutions of servitude which later came to be called feudal occurred in the eighteenth century and have been conclusively shown to be the result of and response to the opening of a market for Chilean wheat in Lima.[8] Even the growth and consolidation of the latifundium in seventeenth-century Mexico—which most expert students have attributed to a depression of the economy caused by the decline of mining and a shortage of Indian labor and to a consequent turning in upon itself and ruralization of the economy —occurred at a time when urban population and demand were growing, food shortages became acute, food prices skyrocketed, and the profitability of other economic activities such as mining and foreign trade declined.[9]

All of these and other factors rendered hacienda agriculture more profitable. Thus, even this case would seem to confirm the hypothesis that the growth of the latifundium and its feudal-seeming conditions of servitude in Latin America has always been and still is the commercial response to increased demand and that it does not represent the transfer or survival of alien institutions that have remained beyond the reach of capitalist development. The emergence of latifundia, which today really are more or less (though not entirely) isolated, might then be attributed to the causes advanced in the fifth hypothesis—i.e., the decline of previously profitable agricultural enterprises whose capital was, and whose currently produced economic surplus still is, transferred elsewhere by owners and merchants who frequently are the same persons or families. Testing this hypothesis requires still more detailed analysis, some of which I have undertaken in a study on Brazilian agriculture.[10]

IX

All of these hypotheses and studies suggest that the global extension and unity of the capitalist system, its monopoly structure and uneven development throughout its history, and the resulting persistence of commercial rather than industrial capitalism in the underdeveloped world (including its most industrially advanced countries) deserve much more attention in the study of economic development and cultural change than they have hitherto received. Though science and truth know no national boundaries, it is probably new generations of scientists from the underdeveloped countries themselves who most need to, and best can, devote the necessary attention to these problems and clarify the process of underdevelopment and development. It is their people who in the last analysis face the task of changing this no longer acceptable process and eliminating this miserable reality.

They will not be able to accomplish these goals by importing sterile stereotypes from the metropolis which do not correspond to their satellite economic reality and do not respond to their liberating political needs. To change their reality they must understand it. For this reason, I hope that better confirmation of these hypotheses and further pursuit of the proposed historical, holistic, and structural approach may help the peoples of the underdeveloped countries to understand the causes and eliminate the reality of their development of underdevelopment and their underdevelopment of development.

NOTES

1. *América Latina*, Año 6, No. 4, October–December 1963, p. 8.
2. Instituto Nacional Indigenista, *Los centros coordinadores indigenistas*, Mexico, 1962, p. 34.
3. *Ibid.*, pp. 33–34, 88.

4. "Capitalist Development and Underdevelopment in Chile" and "Capitalist Development and Underdevelopment in Brazil" in *Capitalism and Underdevelopment in Latin America*, New York, Monthly Review Press, 1967.

5. Also see, "The Growth and Decline of Import Substitution," *Economic Bulletin for Latin America*, New York, IX, No. 1, March 1964; and Celso Furtado, *Dialectica do Desenvolvimiento*, Rio de Janeiro, Fundo de Cultura, 1964.

6. Others who use a similar approach, though their ideologies do not permit them to derive the logically following conclusions, are Aníbal Pinto S.C., *Chile: Un caso de desarrollo frustrado*, Santiago, Editorial Universitaria, 1957; Celso Furtado, *A formaçao económica do Brasil*, Rio de Janeiro, Fundo de Cultura, 1959 (recently translated into English and published under the title *The Economic Growth of Brazil* by the University of California Press); and Caio Prado Junior, *Historia Económica do Brasil*, São Paulo, Editora Brasiliense, 7th ed., 1962.

7. See for instance Ramón Guerra y Sánchez, *Azúcar y Población en las Antillas*, Havana, 1942, 2nd ed., also published as *Sugar and Society in the Caribbean*, New Haven, Yale University Press, 1964.

8. Mario Góngora, *Origen de los "inquilinos" de Chile central*, Santiago Editorial Universitaria, 1960; Jean Borde and Mario Góngora, *Evolución de la propiedad rural en el Valle del Puango*, Santiago, Instituto de Sociología de la Universidad de Chile; Sergio Sepúlveda, *El trigo chileno en el mercado mundial*, Santiago Editorial Universitaria, 1959.

9. Woodrow Borah makes depression the centerpiece of his explanation in "New Spain's Century of Depression," *Ibero-Americana*, Berkeley, No. 35, 1951. François Chevalier speaks of turning in upon itself in the most authoritative study of the subject, "La formación de los grandes latifundios en México," Mexico, *Problemas Agrícolas e Industriales de México*, VIII, No. 1, 1956 (translated from the French and recently published by the University of California Press). The data which provide the basis for my contrary interpretation are supplied by these authors themselves. This problem is discussed in my "Con qué modo de producción convierte la gallina maíz en huevos de oro?" *El Gallo Ilustrado*, Suplemento de *El Día*, Mexico, Nos. 175 and 179, October 31 and November 28, 1965; and it is further analyzed in a study of Mexican agriculture under preparation by the author.

10. "Capitalism and the Myth of Feudalism in Brazilian Agriculture," in *Capitalism and Underdevelopment in Latin America*, cited in note 4 above.

9

Patterns of Dependency: Income Distribution and the History of Underdevelopment

Charles K. Wilber and James H. Weaver

I

Development has been seen traditionally as the attainment of a "high mass consumption" society, to use Rostow's term. It is, therefore, understandable that economists have traditionally measured the level of economic development by the level of per capita income or product. It is a simple, logical extension of this approach to focus on growing per capita income as the *deus ex machina* that will solve all development problems.

However, in the past few years serious doubt has been cast upon this approach. Several countries—Brazil, Pakistan, even Mexico—have had rapid growth rates of per capita income while unemployment, inequality, and the level of poverty of the mass of the population have remained unchanged or even increased. A thin upper layer has prospered while the vast majority of the population remains entrapped in the backwaters of underdevelopment.

II

One result of this typical process of development has been substantial increases in the GNP of many underdeveloped countries. During the period from 1960 to 1971 per capita GNP grew at an average annual rate of 3.3 percent in Jamaica, 3.5 percent in Mexico, 2.7 percent in Brazil, 6.5 percent in Iran, 7.1 percent in Taiwan, 3.1 percent in Malaysia, 3.7 percent in Turkey, 4.6 percent in Ivory Coast, 7.4 percent in Korea, 4.8 percent in Thailand, 3.5 percent in Kenya, and 3.7 percent in Pakistan.[1]

In addition to the growth in GNP, however, there was growing income inequality. Irma Adelman and Cynthia Morris have recently completed a massive cross-sectional study of income distribution in 44 noncommunist, underdeveloped countries during the post-World War II period.[2] Their results strongly suggest that as economic growth begins in very poor countries, the share of income going to the richest 5 percent of the population shows a "striking" increase, while the income going to the bottom 60 per-

Paper delivered at The Conference on Third World Development Strategies, University of Notre Dame, April 1975. An earlier version was published in *Economic Analysis and Workers' Management*, Vol. IX, Nos. 3–4, pp. 202–221.

cent of the population falls relatively (which was already known) and, in certain cases, *absolutely*, as well. That is, the bottom 60 percent of the population have less to live on after growth begins than they had before. As the growth process widens and spreads throughout the economy, Adelman and Morris found that while the top 5 percent continues to gain, the income of the bottom 40 percent of the population continues to fall both relatively and absolutely. This increase in income inequality and mass poverty continues until countries reach an annual income level of roughly $400–$500 per capita.

A recent World Bank study of 66 countries at various income levels has presented confirming data on the distribution of income.[3] The study found that the bottom 40 percent of the people get less than 10 percent of the national income in 15 countries, including Kenya, Iraq, Ecuador, Turkey, Colombia, Peru, Jamaica, Brazil, Panama, and Venezuela. This same study found that the top 20 percent receive more than 60 percent of the national income in 15 countries, including Kenya, Ecuador, Iraq, Turkey, Brazil, Peru, Jamaica, Mexico, and Venezuela. In Senegal, the bottom 40 percent of the population gets 10 percent of the income, and the top 20 percent of the population gets 64 percent of the income. In South Africa, the figures are 6.2 percent and 58.0 percent; Tanzania, 13 percent and 61 percent; Brazil, 10.0 percent and 61.5 percent; and Peru, 6.5 percent and 60.0 percent.

The World Bank study also confirms the impression formed by Adelman and Morris—that the situation worsened during the 1960s. Cross-section data for many countries are substituted for unavailable time-series data for a single country. This is the best we can do to measure changes in income distribution over time. In Table 1 countries have been grouped accord-

Table 1 Per Capita GNP and Income Distribution

Per Capita GNP	% of GNP Received Top 20%	Bottom 40%
$100 or less	46.1	16.4
$101 – $200	57.9	13.4
201 – 300	67.9	11.1
301 – 500	57.6	11.6
501 – 1,000	54.0	13.5
Above $1,000	46.6	16.1

Source: Data compiled from Chenery, et al., *Redistribution with Growth* (London: Oxford University Press, 1974).

ing to level of per capita GNP and the income distribution for each grouping has been computed. Inequality increases until an annual per capita GNP level of $501–$1,000 is reached, and the equality of the lowest GNP group isn't regained until the level increases above $1,000. As will be argued later in the paper, the "natural" operations of the capitalist development process generate this inequality. It is only when a relatively high level of per capita GNP is reached that the state intervenes to counter this "natural" outcome. A disturbing implication of all this is that if the underdeveloped countries of the world duplicate the historic long-run rate of growth (2 percent) of per capita GNP achieved by the now-developed countries, it will take more than 150 years to move from a $75 per capita GNP to a $1,000 per capita GNP.

Evidence from some Latin American countries support this picture of a growing inequality of income distribution. In Mexico, the ratio of per capita income of the richest 20 percent of the population to the poorest 20 percent increased from 10 to 1 in 1950 to 16 to 1 by 1969.[4] In Brazil, between 1960 and 1970, the top 1 percent of the income-earning population increased its share from 11.7 percent to 17.8 percent; the next 4 percent of the population increased its share from 15.6 percent to 18.5 percent; the next 15 percent of the population held steady with a change from 27.2 percent to 26.9 percent; the next 30 percent of the population decreased its share from 27.8 percent to 23.1 percent; and the bottom 50 percent of the population decreased its share from 17.7 percent to 13.7 percent.[5]

The same type of information from other countries adds further evidence of growing poverty and income inequality. In India, the bottom 45 percent of the population is now living below the poverty line where malnutrition begins ($50 per year income), and more importantly, the per capita income of this group has declined over the past 20 years while the per capita income of the country has increased.[6] In Pakistan during the period of rapid economic growth in the 1960s, real wages in the industrial sector declined by one-third.[7] In his fine study of development in Senegal (1958–1974), Professor Sheldon Gellar concludes, "In terms of income distribution . . . the gap between rural and urban incomes has increased and . . . most of the gains in the urban areas have been made by the educated inheritance elite. . . ."[8]

Another consequence of most growth-oriented development programs has been increasing unemployment (or at least no decrease). In Trinidad, from 1953 through 1968, per capita income increased more than 5 percent per year while unemployment increased each year as well.[9] An OECD study estimated urban unemployment at 15 percent in Ceylon, 14 percent in Colombia, 12 percent in the Philippines, and 21 percent in Guyana.[10] Pakistan's experience of rapid growth also shows unemployment increasing each year.[11] Hans Singer has recently estimated that unemployment in underdeveloped countries (not counting disguised unemployment) amounts to at least 25 percent of the labor force.[12] Turner, in a study of 14 underdeveloped countries, found unemployment growing at a rate of 8.5 percent per year.[13] The Prebisch Report concluded that for Latin America, GNP would have to grow at a rate of 6 percent per year between 1970 and 1980 just to maintain the unemployment levels of 1960.[14]

III

During the past 20 years increasing GNP has been accompanied by increasing income inequality, increasing unemployment, and little, if any, decrease in the level of poverty for the majority of the population. Reliance on capitalist development methods, combined with highly unequal income distribution, is the main cause of this trend.

The continuation of highly unequal income distribution patterns in underdeveloped countries means that development programs *must* be based on the consumption demands of the rich minority. This necessity leads to the perpetuation of underdevelopment—of mass poverty, unemployment, and inequality. To illustrate this point, a simplified model of the impact of income distribution on economic development that stresses the relationship between income distribution and the economic structure that emerges will be presented.

The structure of final demand for consumer goods is determined by consumer preferences and the distribution of personal income. The composition of the output of consumer goods is determined, in turn, by the structure of final demand in conjunction with relative costs of production. In an economy with very unequal income distribution, the demand for most commodities (beyond the basic necessities of life) is primarily determined by the distribution of income. Income distribution is more important than the position that commodities occupy in an absolute scale of preferences of consumers. For example, in a poor country, a highly unequal income distribution means that clinics for organ transplants will be built in the capital city instead of water purification systems in the villages, automobiles will be manufactured instead of buses, country clubs will be constructed instead of schools, Coca Cola plants will be built instead of dairies, and so on. Both types of output cannot be produced simultaneously in a country having a low level of national income.

In the context of economic development, a highly unequal income distribution means that the growth process in the private sector proceeds primarily by providing new, modern, consumer goods for upper-income people. Often, the demand for these new consumer goods can be met only by imports. In other cases domestic production of these goods can take place only by using capital-intensive techniques that are not able to achieve economies of scale because of the small size of the market.[15] In either case, the impact on employment and, therefore, on income distribution and the level of poverty may very well be negative.[16]

In addition, emphasis on individual, rather than collective, consumption means that many more durable consumer goods will be produced than is necessary. Individually owned washing machines, television sets, and lawn mowers that sit idle most of the time use resources that could have been used to supply those same consumer durables to all of the people on a collective basis (for example, laundromats and community centers).

A time-honored theory of economic development is that inequality of income is necessary to provide incentives for investment. If self-interested, maximizing individuals are allowed to seek differential rewards for their efforts and risk taking, then income will be maximized. Then, according to a conservative analysis, the benefits will eventually "trickle down" to the less successful portion of the population in the form of higher wages; or, according to a liberal analysis, the state could redistribute the benefits when society is rich enough so that incentives will not be drastically impaired. Unfortunately, as we have seen, the results of these two strategies in underdeveloped countries are not very encouraging. Sixty percent of the people in these countries live and die all too early in the meantime.

An unequal income distribution means that the bulk of the economic surplus is controlled by the upper-income classes. The surplus is then used to purchase consumer goods of a type that does little to reduce poverty—television sets, expensive clothes, and so on. The portion of the surplus that is saved is invested in those same industries. Other portions of the surplus may be sent abroad as a hedge against domestic inflation, for safety in case of a revolutionary overturn, or simply for better and safer investments in the developed countries.

IV

The importance of income distribution to the process of economic development and underdevelopment can be elaborated by tracing that process over the past three centuries in the underdeveloped world, particularly in Latin America.[17]

If there is lack of understanding of the history of development in the West, there is almost total ignorance about the history of underdeveloped countries. The typical level of understanding is illustrated by Rostow's stages of growth model.[18] The use of the stages of growth (or most other development models) as a framework for analysis of the process of development assumes that present-day underdeveloped countries correspond to the "Traditional Society" stage or, at best, the "Preconditions" stage in the Western developed countries. That is, the present-day developed countries were once underdeveloped, and that all countries move through all these stages. This theory obscures, more than it illuminates, historical reality. It denies that underdeveloped countries have had any history.

· · ·

For example, India is today radically different than it was 300 years ago. The stage approach totally ignores that 300-year history, including British colonial control, except to praise colonialism as the "intrusion" that broke through the crust of traditionalism and triggered the stage of "Preconditions."

It would be more illuminating to have two alternative stages—one, Rostow's "Preconditions" stage, which is a transition from "Traditional Society" to the "Take-off"; and two, the "Underdevelopment" stage, which follows the breakup of traditionalism wherein the economy becomes distorted and frozen, developing the characteristics that identify underdeveloped countries.[19] India and Japan were both traditional societies 300 years ago—neither was underdeveloped. Today Japan is developed and India is underdeveloped. Why did Japan pass from "Traditional Society" through the "Preconditions" to "Take-Off," and why did India get sidetracked into underdevelopment?

The answer to this question requires study of the history of the developed countries, the history of the underdeveloped countries, and the history of their interrelations. Questions must be asked about the role of imperialism and dependency (and most particularly the resulting income distribution) in *creating* underdevelopment. An examination must be made of the relation between the *process of development* in Europe and America and the *process of underdevelopment* in Africa, Asia, and Latin America. The now-developed countries were never *under*developed in the sense previously defined. They were *un*developed at one time, just as the now-underdeveloped countries were once *un*developed. Underdevelopment and development are both results of a historical process.

Although the economic histories of low-income countries show great diversity, there is a striking common pattern that captures the essential causes of underdevelopment. It is recognized that this model does not fit every country, but it is useful in understanding the nature of many underdeveloped countries. The description of the typical pattern of underdevelopment that follows should be read with this limitation in mind.

Because of the particular historical experience of contemporary underdeveloped countries, the class structure typically evolved in a substantially different way than in the West. Capitalism entered most underdeveloped countries through what the late Paul Baran called the "Prussian Way"—not through the growth of small, competitive enterprise, but rather through the transfer from abroad of advanced monopolistic business.[20] Thus, capitalist development in these countries was not accompanied by the rise of a strong property-owning middle class, the overthrow of landlord domination of society, and the redistribution of the economic surplus to that middle class. Rather, an accommodation was reached between the newly arrived monopolistic business and the socially entrenched agrarian aristocracy. Therefore, there was little competition between enterprises striving for increased output and rationalized production. Nor was there accumulation of economic surplus in the hands of entrepreneurs. The resulting social structure yielded an extremely unequal distribution of income. The typical result was production well below the potential level. Agriculture continued to be operated on a semifeudal basis. Waste and irrationality in industry were protected by monopoly, high tariffs, and other devices.

For these and other reasons the actual economic surplus was much lower than the potential surplus. Typically, a large share of the potential economic surplus was used by the tiny upper-income group on luxuries and maintenance of unproductive laborers (servants, soldiers, and bureaucrats, for example). In addition, a large share of the actual economic surplus was taken by businessmen for commercial operations promising large and quick profits or for the accumulation of investments or bank accounts abroad as a hedge against domestic social and political hazards. Because of unequal income distribution, a small group controlled the society's economic surplus and disposed of it in ways that furthered rapid growth of a narrow, elite-controlled industrial sector and economic stagnation for the country as a whole.

Starting with the historical studies of underdevelopment pioneered by Celso Furtado, Andre Gunder Frank, Keith Griffin, Osvaldo Sunkel, and others, an entirely new approach to this characteristic process of development and underdevelopment has been in the making, particularly in regard to Latin America. This "structural" approach builds on the historical perspective presented above. The development of capitalism and the world market is seen as a two-fold process. A highly dualistic *process of underdevelopment* of Africa, Asia, and Latin America is the consequence of the *process of development* of Europe and North America. This two-fold process has created a situation of dependence in which the underdeveloped countries have become appendages of the developed countries.

The structural approach tries to get behind statistical indicators, such as the value of exports or imports, and attempts to identify the social forces that are responsible for generating those indicators. This new approach emphasizes the role of dependence in shaping the internal economic, social, and political structures (and thus the income distribution) and in shaping the external relations of underdeveloped countries. The structural approach leads to an examination of the multifaceted links between developed and underdeveloped countries that impede genuine development of the Third World.

As a result of the highly unequal income distribution, a condition created by narrowly based growth stimulated by foreign business, the upper-income groups adopted the consumption patterns of their counterparts in the developed countries. Thus, the economic surplus was not reinvested, but rather dissipated on imports of luxury consumer goods. This shaped both the import and domestic manufacturing sectors of the underdeveloped countries. The luxury demands of this group were catered to instead of the subsistence needs of the vast majority. But the small upper-income class was unable to provide a market for full industrialization.[21]

This process of underdevelopment has usually gone through three historical stages.[22] Each of these stages was characterized by the creation or aggravation of income inequalities that produced a structure of consumption and investment strikingly unfavorable to economy-wide economic growth. The first stage was characterized by domestic and international investment on the basis of the static comparative advantage of most poor countries in producing primary products. In the second stage, the emphasis shifted to investment for import substitution. The third phase is typically characterized by the domination of the multinational corporation in domestic manufacturing.

Comparative Advantage. When the now-developed countries were developing, they moved into contact with what are now the underdeveloped countries. This contact took many forms. However, all were characterized by the subordination of the now-underdeveloped countries (of Africa, Asia, and Latin America) to the technological superiority of the then-developing countries (of Europe and North America).

During the first stage the countries of the West undertook certain kinds of investments in their colonies and semicolonies. These investments were essentially of two types. One type of investment was the expansion of tropical agriculture through the creation of large plantations. There was a comparative advantage in geography or climate in growing certain crops on these plantations. Thus, sugar, coffee, cocoa, banana, coconut, pineapple, tea, and rubber plantations were established throughout Africa, Asia, and Latin America. These plantations used essentially the same type of capital for production as had been used before the Europeans or Americans arrived. They did achieve substantial economies of scale through reorganization; they shifted land from subsistence to market crops; and they introduced modern methods of transporting the crops to the coast and from there to Europe and North America. These investments brought about a large increase in output. However, this increase in productivity was the result primarily of a reallocation of resources that captured the gains from static comparative advantage through international trade. There was little in the way of technological change and thus almost no transformation in the structure of the society toward self-sustaining growth. No industrial transformation took place because of this expansion of agricultural output as was taking place in the European countries.

The second type of investment made by European and North American countries was in extractive industries. Minerals of all kinds were found in Africa, Asia, and Latin America. The copper mines of Chile and Katanga, the tin mines of Bolivia, the bauxite mines of Jamaica, and the oil fields of Venezuela, the Middle East, and North Africa were the sources of an enormous inflow of minerals to the industrializing economies of the West. Again, the effect of these investments on the economies of countries on the "periphery" of what was fast becoming a capitalist world system was of little consequence. There was no industrial transformation. There were no major technological changes in production that affected anything but the particular extractive industry itself. Some transportation networks were established to move the minerals to the ports so they could be transported to the "center" countries of the developing capitalist world system—Europe and North America. The majority of people living in the periphery countries experienced few, if any, changes in their lives as the result of these investments. The extractive type of investments typically resulted in an even greater income inequality than did plantation agriculture because the linkages with other parts of the economy were fewer. This type of investment may also have left fewer of the benefits in the underdeveloped country than did plantations.

Thus neither type of investment—plantation agriculture nor mineral extraction—had a transforming effect on the economies of the periphery countries. If these foreign investments had "spread" their effects throughout the economies of the underdeveloped countries, there would have been a technological transformation. But, as Hans Singer and Gunnar Myrdal have argued, this has not happened, and instead, "backwash" effects have predominated.[23] These export-oriented industries have never become a part of the internal economic structure except in the purely geographical and physical sense. Economically speaking, they have really been an extension of the economies of the more-developed countries. The major secondary multiplier effects have taken place not in the underdeveloped country where the investment is physically located but in the developed country from which the investment has come. For example, because extractive industries often have a high capital/labor ratio, there has been little impact on local factor markets, particularly the labor market.

Thus, the countries of Africa, Asia, and Latin America were now well along to becoming underdeveloped. Their market economies were becoming appendages of and dependent on the center countries of Europe and North America. As plantation agriculture and mineral extraction grew (financed by the center countries), the economies of the periphery became more and more dependent on the needs and demands of the center countries and on the vicissitudes of the world market. For example, as plantation agriculture was introduced into the periphery countries, workers were needed on the plantations. How were they recruited? The practices differed from one country to another, but gradually, in the typical case, a class of property-less workers was created, often from previously self-sufficient farmers. The land they had formerly farmed for themselves or as customary tenants was taken over for plantations to produce cash crops for export.[24] As a re-sult, formerly self-sufficient farmers became subject to the vagaries of world demand (primarily from the center countries) for the crops grown by the plantations. Seasonal unemployment of landless day laborers became the most visible sign of their dependency on what was happening far away in the center countries.

There were large and obvious gains from the vast increase in productiv-ity that came about as specialization took place more or less along lines of static comparative advantage. Many of the gains went to the investors and traders of the center countries. Others who gained from the increased productivity were Europeans and Americans who settled in the periphery countries and served as managers and overseers in the mines and planta-tions and local residents who became foremen and supervisors over the indigenous work force or who were involved in the limited commercial expansion associated with the foreign investment.

What did these expatriate and local elites do with their gains? The answer is so obvious that it is often overlooked and so important to an understanding of the process of underdevelopment that it must be placed squarely in the center of an analysis of development and underdevelopment. They imported those goods from Europe and North America that would make it possible for them to live in much the same way as their European and North American counterparts. The elites imported bottled water from Vichy, wine from Bordeaux, suits from Saville Row, automobiles from Detroit, and so on. This standard of living was imported from Europe and North America for the benefit of that tiny minority of the people who were beneficiaries of the gains from participation in the international divi-sion of labor based on static comparative advantage.

The consumer preferences of this tiny minority were critically de-termined by American and European movies, television programs, and magazines. They lived in Accra or Santiago, but their minds were, to an important extent, formed in Paris and New York. To maintain this level of consumption they had to receive very high incomes, as high as their com-patriots in Europe and North America. And this was indeed the case. A pattern of consumption was introduced into the poor countries that was the result of enormous inequalities of income and that led to a structure of production that further aggravated these inequalities. These inequalities deepened underdevelopment and frustrated attempts to carry out a success-ful development program.

Import Substitution. Typically, the process of underdevelopment began with the creation of a primary commodity exporting economy. The gains from trade were realized by the center countries together with their agents and an associated indigenous elite in the periphery countries. The resulting concentration of income created a pattern of consumption among the well-to-do minority that was based to a large extent on imports from the center countries.

The second stage of underdevelopment began with the shift to a policy of import substitution. This shift was precipitated by many factors. One factor was the balance of payments crisis in the underdeveloped countries triggered by the Great Depression in the center countries. This crisis was dramatic evidence of just how dependent poor countries had become during the first phase of underdevelopment. A further push toward a policy of import substitution occurred in the 1950s. Restrictive trade policies in the center countries made it difficult for poor countries to earn enough foreign exchange to pay for their imports.

Usually this policy of import substitution took the form of local manufacture of the products that were previously imported for consumption of the well-to-do minority.[25] Because of the great inequalities in income distribution, the primary source of market demand for products other than necessities was limited to the rich minority. Therefore profit-seeking firms found it most lucrative to produce for that minority market.

The economic structure that resulted from import substitution in the periphery country exhibited a number of striking characteristics. The market for manufactured goods became bifurcated. One segment provided consumer goods for the bulk of the population with very low incomes. The other segment catered to the demands of the rich minority.

The basket of consumer goods produced for the poor majority contained little diversity, was dominated by traditional necessities, and tended to remain unchanged because the real per capita income of this group remained more or less constant or even declined. The two major industries producing for the poor, food and textiles, had weak linkages (in an input-output sense) because they drew their input directly from primary production and sell their output directly to the final consumer. They were subject to few economies of scale or external economies.

The basket of consumer goods produced domestically for the rich minority, on the other hand, was characterized by the diversity of the products it contained. This wide range of modern and constantly changing products required a complex array of industries, both domestic and foreign, for their production. Because the proportion of income going to the rich minority expanded while the proportion of income going to the poor majority was stagnant or falling, economic growth in the typical underdeveloped country was based on the expanding consumer demand of that minority. The essence of economic growth in the context of underdevelopment, dependence, and unequal income distribution was the introduction of a wide range of new luxury consumer goods. The developed center countries were the source of this never-ending stream of new consumer goods.

One result of this pattern of consumption and production was to place a heavy drain on foreign exchange earnings.[26] Many items had to be imported to produce the import substitutes. The factories, spare parts, intermediate inputs, sometimes even the raw materials had to be imported to produce modern consumer goods for the rich minority. The foreign exchange necessary to produce these goods was clearly higher than would have been necessary if economic growth had consisted of increased production of food, basic clothing, and housing for the poor majority.[27] These industries would have used primarily domestic, not imported, materials and equipment.

A second and more important aspect of this characteristic pattern of production was that the capital requirements in the industries geared to production of consumer goods for the rich minority were generally much higher than they were in industries producing for the poor majority.[28] Thus, the industries established during the import substitution phase were relatively capital intensive. Generally, the industries producing for the rich minority used more relatively scarce resources (capital, skilled labor, and foreign exchange) than the industries producing for the poor majority. This meant a further concentration of income in the hands of the small, if somewhat expanded, minority of property owners, managers, technicians, professionals, and skilled workers. This continued concentration of income was necessary to generate the demand profile appropriate to the structure of output. That is, inequality of income had to be maintained if the new consumer goods that were being produced were to be sold.

There was some "trickling down" of benefits to the poor. There were increased employment opportunities in the new factories. However, since employment per unit of investment was much lower in the industries producing the new consumer goods, less employment was created than there would have been if the investment had been in production of traditional consumer goods. The social overhead capital (roads, schools, hospitals) that was created for the benefit of the new industries certainly also benefitted some of the poor. Again, however, these developments were not as beneficial as alternative public investments (rural water purification systems instead of urban hospitals, basic literacy programs rather than universities for the elite) that would have been possible with a more equal distribution of income. Infant mortality rates fell as the result of modern medical practices. Some of the poor who moved to urban areas had electricity and running water available in their favelas, something they probably didn't have in the rural villages they left.

Our point should be clear. The import substitution phase typically brought no transformation of the economies of the periphery.[29] No technological breakthrough took place in the way most work was done. In most such countries the lives of most people were not much improved, if at all, as the result of the import substitution phase of development.

Multinational Corporations. The third and current phase in the structural process of underdevelopment is characterized by the movement of multinational corporations (MNCs) into the manufacturing sector of periphery countries.[30] Once a fair-sized domestic market had been established during the import substitution phase, the MNCs realized that it would be profitable to set up production facilities within the underdeveloped countries for production for the local market.

In the developed countries, competition between large corporations has long taken the form of product innovation instead of price reductions. Thus, growth in the developed countries has more and more relied on the introduction of new consumer goods. As the MNCs moved into the underdeveloped countries they brought this philosophy with them. In addition, they found that this philosophy fit into the prevailing structure of income distribution and the consequent structure of "tastes" for goods. Thus, the MNCs concentrated on producing new consumer goods for the rich minority.

When the MNCs built factories in the underdeveloped countries, they almost invariably introduced the same technology they were using in the developed countries. This technology was readily available—the technology was already embodied in physical capital (including used machinery and equipment whose commercial life could be extended by transferring it to underdeveloped countries)—and the companies knew how to manage factories using this technology. To have designed new technologies that would better fit the factor endowments of the underdeveloped countries might have required a vast expenditure on research and development. By lowering profits, this would have made the investments less attractive to the individual MNCs.

Since the technologies used by the MNCs tend to be labor saving, the impact on income distribution must be to increase inequality if there are no government transfer programs. There is a lesser increase in employment with capital-intensive technologies. The extent of the labor-saving nature of this technology is revealed by a recent study of 257 manufacturing firms throughout Latin America, which found that compared with local firms, MNCs use only about one-half the number of employees per $10,000 of sales. The study also found that, although MNCs use fewer employees than do local firms, there seems to be no appreciable capital saving.[31]

A good example of the effect of capital-intensive technology in an economy of unequal ownership of productive property and of highly unequal income distribution is the impact of the "Green Revolution" on the poor in Mexico. In 1960 more than half the total agricultural output of the country was produced on just 3 percent of the farms. The same farms accounted for 80 percent of the increase in agricultural production between 1950 and 1960. "Owners of the large-scale, capital-intensive, irrigated farms were by far the largest beneficiaries of the [Green Revolution] . . . In a ten-year period, the number of landless laborers increased 43 percent, while the average of days worked each year dropped from 194 to 100."[32] Also, Martin Fransman, in analyzing South African development, says, "the increasing capital-intensity led to the expulsion of labour from the industries where these changes were taking place as the production process became more mechanised following the local production and import of labour-saving technology."[33] A United Nations report concludes that for underdeveloped countries generally, "the problem of urban unemployment and underemployment is . . . more than anything else one of rapid population growth and inappropriate technologies."[34] They specifically argue that capital-intensive technologies are creating unemployment. This, of course, further concentrates income in the hands of those at the top.

Recent research indicates that private businesses and government agencies in underdeveloped countries tend to use modern, capital-intensive technologies even when labor-using, capital-saving alternatives are available.[35] Modern technologies are better known to many involved in the process of choosing technologies; they give more prestige to those involved; and control from the top is easier. This reinforces the propensity of MNCs to utilize capital-intensive technologies.

A typical structure is emerging in this third phase of underdevelopment. This emerging structure is characterized by the development of three separate sectors in the economy.

One sector is dominated by the MNCs. In this sector, because product innovation is so rapid, control of technical progress is the most important source of market power. Products such as durable consumer goods, machinery and equipment, electronics, computers, chemicals, and drugs fall into this category.

The second sector is more and more coming under the control of the governments of the underdeveloped countries (at least of the most active ones). In this sector production consists of standardized, intermediate products, such as steel and petroleum, in which innovation of productive techniques is more important than product innovation. Since products are more standardized and the turnover of fixed capital is slow, the rate of innovation tends to be slower and thus less crucial as a source of market power. A second part of this sector is the growing physical infrastructure of roads, docks, electric power facilities, and so on.

The third sector has been left to local capitalists. This sector consists of the industries that produce nondurable, traditional consumer goods for the mass of the population, such as food and textiles. Since these industries in underdeveloped countries are characterized neither by product innovation nor by innovation of productive techniques, control of technical progress is not of major importance as a source of market power. Also, firms in these industries have lower effective rates of return. For these reasons, MNCs, to date, have not moved into these industries except in certain speciality lines, such as luxury foods, where product innovation once again becomes of major importance.

A good illustration of this emerging structure is Brazil. The Brazilian "miracle" is largely the creation of the state and MNCs. Of the 50 largest Brazilian companies, 31 are state-owned, 14 are owned by MNCs, and only five are owned by Brazilians.[36]

In addition to increased income inequality and unemployment, capitalist development methods have brought something of even greater import to the underdeveloped countries—the ideology of individual consumption-oriented development. If the priority of development policy is to attack the three main problems of mass poverty, unemployment, and inequality, then the transfer of this ideology to the rich and poor alike in the underdeveloped countries has had negative effects. Along with their investments, multinational corporations have brought the awesome power of modern advertising into the underdeveloped world. The existing rich minority, of course, were more than willing to buy the message that the good life comes from increases in consumption of individually marketable goods and services. But there is more to it than this. When the rich minority believes that they *must* have individual washers and dryers instead of laundromats, private automobiles instead of public transportation, and when they control the economic surplus because of the inequality of income distribution, more and more of the surplus flows into the purchase of the new products introduced and promoted by the multinationals. This leaves relatively less and less available for development, whether directly through investment or indirectly through taxation. As the rich minority becomes more and more accustomed to these consumption levels, the less they will accept development programs that restrict those privileges.

This consumption ideology has even "trickled down" to the poor majority in the underdeveloped countries. The poor, believing they will never change their basic lot in life except by luck (such as winning the local lottery), find they can at least share vicariously in the "good life" through television and even participate on the fringes by drinking Coca Cola, wearing the latest lipstick, and eating white bread. Many would ask, what is wrong with consumption? Is not the alternative to consumer democracy totalitarian control? Some people even argue that the psychological benefits to the poor from spending their money on transistor radios may outweigh the physical benefits of spending that money on basic subsistence goods. This argument is somewhat ingenuous when one considers the poor in underdeveloped countries such as Peru, where a significant number of babies suffer irreparable brain damage due to malnutrition. Creating and satisfying wants for lipstick, Coca Cola, white bread, and transistor radios while the basic necessities remain unfulfilled help maintain the mass poverty characteristic of underdevelopment. Multinational and local corporations determine, through their promotion and advertising campaigns, which products give psychological satisfaction. To speak of consumer democracy, when the producer has such power to manipulate consumers' tastes and where income is so unequally distributed, is to obfuscate the real issues.

The fact that underdeveloped countries do not have unlimited resources means that if they are to escape underdevelopment, they must find an entirely different type of development strategy than that based on the consumption pattern of the rich minority. The reliance on growth rates of GNP to eliminate poverty must be rejected. Instead, a direct attack upon the worst forms of mass poverty, inequality, and unemployment must be mounted. The elemental health, food, housing, and clothing needs of all the people must be met before luxury consumption goods are introduced.

The key question is whether such a strategy of development can be conceived and implemented given the constraints of the present political and economic structures in the underdeveloped countries and in the world. The economy that prevails in most underdeveloped countries combines the worst features of capitalism and state or centrally planned socialism—the inequalities of capitalism without its incentives and the bureaucracy of state socialism without its equality and welfare. Obviously sweeping political and economic changes are needed. Whether the underdeveloped countries can manage such a change, or will be allowed to change by the developed countries, without violent revolutions is possibly the critical question of our time.

NOTES

1. IBRD, *World Bank Atlas: Population, Per Capita Product and Growth Rates* (1973).
2. Irma Adelman and Cynthia Taft Morris, *Economic Growth and Social Equity* (Stanford: Stanford University Press, 1973).
3. H. B. Chenery, M. Ahluwalia, C. L. G. Bell, J. Duloy, and R. Jolly (eds.), *Redistribution with Growth* (London: Oxford University Press, 1974).
4. William Rich, *Population Explosion: The Role of Development* (Communique, Overseas Development Council, Washington, D.C., April 13, 1972).
5. Phillip Berryman, "The 'Miracle' and 'Distensão'," *America*, Vol. 132, No. 20 (May 24, 1975), p. 398.
6. Chenery, et al., *op. cit.*
7. Mahbub ul Haq, "Employment in the 1970's: A New Perspective," *International Development Review*, Vol. 13, No. 4 (December 1971), pp. 9–13.
8. Sheldon Gellar, "The Inheritance Situation and Post-Colonial Development Strategies: The Senegal Case" (Paper prepared for the Conference on Third World Development Strategies, University of Notre Dame, April 1975).
9. Dudley Seers, "The Meaning of Development," *International Development Review*, Vol. 11, No. 4 (December 1969).
10. David Turnham and Ingeles Jaeger, "The Employment Problem in Less Developed Countries," *OECD* (December 1970).
11. Ul Haq, *op. cit.*
12. Hans Singer, "Dualism Revisited," *Journal of Development Studies* (1971).
13. *Ibid.*
14. Raul Prebisch, *Change and Development: Latin America's Great Task* (Report submitted to the Inter-American Development Bank, Washington, D.C., 1970).
15. There are exceptions where domestic demand plus export demand is sufficient to avoid excess capacity.
16. James W. Land and Ronald Soligo, "Income Distribution and Employment in Labor Redundant Economies," Paper No. 9 (1971), Program of Development Studies, Rice University.
17. We are aware of places such as Taiwan, South Korea, Singapore, and Hong Kong that do not fit the model. They would all seem to be somewhat special cases, where, for whatever reasons, there have been progressive changes in income distribution and significant reductions in unemployment.
18. Even Marx did not escape this ethnocentrism: "The country that is more developed industrially only shows, to the less developed, the image of its own future." Karl Marx, *Capital*, Vol. I (New York: Modern Library, 1906), Author's Preface to the first German edition, p. 13.
19. The simplest way to understand the meaning of underdevelopment is to see it as a process whereby an undeveloped country, characterized by subsistence agriculture and domestic production, progressively becomes integrated as a dependency into the world market through trade or investment. Its production becomes geared to the demands of the world market and particularly of the developed countries; there is a consequent lack of integration between the parts of the domestic economy. The key, however, is asymmetrical interdependence, i.e., dependency.
20. Paul Baran, "On the Political Economy of Backwardness," in this anthology, pp. 91–102.
21. It is difficult to be quantitatively precise about the size of the market necessary for full industrialization. Generally, however, the smaller the country's population, the more equal the income distribution must be. Even in large countries (Brazil, India, Nigeria), the distribution of income must be equal enough to incorporate 40–60 percent of the population into the modernizing sectors.
22. Celso Furtado, "The Concept of External Dependence in the Study of Underdevelopment," in Wilber, *The Political Economy of Development and Underdevelopment.*
23. H. W. Singer, "The Distribution of Gains Between Investing and Borrowing Countries," *American Economic Review*, Vol. XL, No. 2 (May 1950), pp. 473–485; and Gunnar Myrdal, *Economic Theory and Underdeveloped Regions* (London: Gerald Duckworth & Co., 1957).

24. This is truer in Latin America than in Africa where communal self-sufficient agriculture persisted for years alongside plantation agriculture.

25. African countries, however, are barely into this stage.

26. The ensuing balance of payments disequilibria helped generate runaway inflation in certain Latin American countries, which further reduced the consumption levels of the poor.

27. International Labour Organization, *Towards Full Employment: A Programme for Colombia* (Geneva: ILO, 1970).

28. Ronald Soligo has summarized the findings of several attempts to measure the factor intensities of the goods consumed by the rich and the poor. All the studies have found that the goods consumed by the rich and by the poor are markedly different. In addition, the capital intensity of the goods consumed by the rich is higher and the labor intensity lower than of the goods consumed by the poor. Ronald Soligo, "Consumption Patterns, Factor Usage, and the Distribution of Income: A Review of Some Findings," Rice University, 1974 (mimeo).

29. There are obvious exceptions, e.g., Korea, Taiwan, Japan.

30. This phase is much more typical of Latin America than of sub-Saharan Africa. But see Gellar's paper on Senegal.

31. Ronald Müller, "The Multinational Corporation and the Underdevelopment of the Third World," in this anthology, pp. 151–178.

32. Rich, *op. cit.*

33. Martin Fransman, "The Political Economy of Southern Africa." Also David Chaplin points to the importance of capital-intensive technology for unemployment. See Chaplin, "Corporatism and Development in Peru" (papers prepared for the Conference on Third World Development Strategies, University of Notre Dame, April 1975).

34. United Nations, World Population Conference, *Population Change and Economic and Social Development*, Report of the Secretary General. E/CONF. 60/4, 1974, p. 52.

35. See Louis T. Wells, "Economic Man and Engineering Man: Choice of Technology in a Low Wage Country," *Economic Development Report*, No. 226, Center for International Affairs, Harvard University, November 1972; and John W. Thomas, "The Choice of Technology in Developing Countries," Agency for International Development, 1973 (mimeo).

36. Berryman, *op. cit.*

part three

Economic Development in a Revolutionary World: Trade and Dependency

the historical studies of underdevelopment pioneered by Celso Furtado and Andre Gunder Frank[1] stimulated a new approach to the study of the process of development and underdevelopment in Latin America. This approach is based on the historical perspective presented in the previous section and emphasizes the interdependence between the developed and underdeveloped countries. It is this interdependence that shapes the internal economic, social, and political structures and external relations of underdeveloped countries that impede any real development.

In the first article in this part Thomas Weisskopf places the concept of dependency within a broad Marxian analysis of capitalist imperialism. He focuses on recent trends in the relationship between the capitalist center and periphery to determine the extent to which the character of imperialism has changed. The article concludes with an examination of certain contradictions that seem likely to arise from contemporary imperialism; one such contradiction is the *dependent* nature of capitalist growth in the periphery.

In the second reading in this part, Ronald Müller analyses the specific ways in which multinational corporations (MNCs) contribute to the development (or underdevelopment) of underdeveloped countries. *Dependentistas* refer to the post-World War II period as "the new dependence." This new type of dependence is based on MNCs, which began to invest in industries geared to the internal market of the underdeveloped countries. This form of dependence is considered as basically technological-industrial in form. Utilizing the results of recent research, Müller analyses the contribution of MNCs to technological, financial, and balance-of-payments requirements. His conclusions are that MNCs have had a negative impact in these three areas and that the main result has been an increased dependence of the underdeveloped countries on the MNCs.

In the final article in this part, Mahbub ul Haq examines the impact of the international economic system upon the development prospects of the Third World countries. He argues that the central issue is whether the present world order systematically discriminates against the interests of the Third World or is the demand by Third World countries for a New International Order mere empty rhetoric against imagined grievances.

Ul Haq argues that the present world market system is systematically biased toward the needs and interests of the developed nations. In the face of a highly skewed world distribution of income, wealth, and power, the market mechanism has failed to deliver the promised fruits for the struggling "bottom forty percent."

It is ul Haq's contention that although poor countries have made modest absolute income gains in past years, the distribution of relative income and wealth has largely stagnated. This stagnation is precipitated by the prevailing institutional structures of the world economic order.

Ul Haq contends that the causes of the inequities in these international structures lie in the history of underdevelopment (i.e., colonial rule, a legacy of dependence). He concludes that the only long-term solution for development is a fundamental revamping of world institutional structures that places an upper boundary on the opportunity for balanced and continuing economic growth.

The call for a New International Order, detailed in the Dag Hammerskjöld Report (included in the last part of this book), is the Third World's suggested revamping of world institutional structures.

1. See CELSO FURTADO, *The Economic Growth of Brazil* (Berkeley: University of California Press, 1957); Andre Gunder Frank, *Capitalism and Underdevelopment in Latin America* (New York: Monthly Review Press, 1967).

10

Imperialism and the Economic Development of the Third World

Thomas E. Weisskopf

I. INTRODUCTION

Since the early days of capitalism, the imperialist relationship between the center and the periphery has had an inherently dual, and consequently ambivalent, character. On the one hand, the center is in a position to dominate the periphery by virtue of its superior power. The result can be that the center exploits the resources of the periphery to the advantage of the former and to the disadvantage of the latter. On the other hand, the center, in the process of penetrating the periphery, can break down its traditional modes of production and promote the growth of a modern capitalist social and economic order. This result may be progressive in the sense that pre-capitalist barriers to development are destroyed and the basis for participation in world capitalist development is established. Which of these dual aspects of imperialism is predominant depends on the particular historical context and the geographical area under analysis.

In most parts of the third world,[1] at least until the middle of the twentieth century, the regressive aspect of the imperialist relationship dominated the progressive aspect. Economic relations with the major capitalist powers, and the gradual extension of the capitalist mode of production, did little to stimulate sustained economic growth in the countries and territories of Asia, Africa, and Latin America. The huge differences in current levels of per capita product shown in Table 1 attest to the highly unequal participation of the center and the periphery in capitalist economic growth over the past few centuries.

In the last few decades, however, there is evidence that a significant number of third-world countries have begun to experience more rapid rates of growth than in the past.[2] Moreover, they have done so without breaking out of the world capitalist economic system. Indeed, many of them have intensified their economic relations with the major capitalist powers. This suggests that we may now be entering a new stage of imperialism in which the economically progressive aspect of the relationship may be dominating the regressive aspect in at least some parts of the third world.

In this essay I will examine recent trends in the relationship between

Thomas E. Weisskopf, "Imperialism and the Economic Development of the Third World" in *The Capitalist System,* Revised Edition, © 1978, Prentice-Hall, Inc., pp. 500–514. Reprinted by permission of Prentice-Hall, Inc., Englewood Cliffs, New Jersey.

Table 1 Per Capita Output by Country Groups: 1971

Area	Per Capita Output[1] (U.S. $)	Population (millions)	Total Output[1] (billion U.S. $)
North America	5,064	228	1,155
Australia, New Zealand	2,797	16	45
Western Europe	2,296	375	861
Japan, Israel, South Africa	1,890	132	249
U.S.S.R., Eastern Europe	1,358	371	504
Latin America	591	288	170
Middle East[2]	376	69	26
Africa[3]	170	343	58
Asia[4]	144	1,853	267
WORLD	907	3,675	3,335

[1] Output measured by gross national product at market prices, converted to U.S. $ at official exchange rates.
[2] Excluding Israel.
[3] Excluding South Africa.
[4] Excluding Japan and the Middle East.
Source: *World Bank Atlas* (Washington, D.C.: World Bank, 1973).

the capitalist center and periphery in order to determine the extent to which the character of imperialism has changed. I will begin in section II by reviewing the nature of imperialism before World War II, and the reasons why it generally retarded the economic development of the periphery. In section III I will discuss certain changes in the world capitalist system which have significantly affected economic relations between the metropolis and the periphery in the postwar period. In section IV I will describe the character of the economic development which has been taking place in the third world since 1950. Finally, in section V I will examine certain contradictions which seem likely to arise from contemporary imperialism.

II. SOURCES OF UNDERDEVELOPMENT IN THE PERIPHERY

The capitalist mode of production unquestionably generated a momentous long-run expansion of productivity and economic output in the nations of the present-day center. Why did capitalism not bring to the periphery the same growth stimulus that it brought to the center? The primary reason is that the shaping of the periphery to the requirements of the center resulted in a very different development of *class relations* in the two areas.[3]

In the center countries, capitalism was introduced and spearheaded by a dynamic indigenous bourgeois class that had to struggle persistently against the old feudal order in order to gain control of the state apparatus and win a dominant position within the society. It was very much in the class interest of the bourgeoisie to destroy the social and economic institutions of the feudal era and thereby to eradicate pre-capitalist fetters on the expansion of capitalist production. Bourgeois revolutions in England (the

Civil War of the seventeenth century), France (the Revolution of 1789), and Japan (the Meiji Restoration of 1868) were part of this process; in North America, Australia, and New Zealand, no such revolutions were needed because white settlers from already bourgeois-dominated countries destroyed most of the precapitalist inhabitants and their institutions.[4] Either way, the stage was set for rapid and unrestrained capitalist growth.

In the periphery, however, nothing equivalent to a bourgeois revolution occurred because of the impact of Western colonization and economic domination by the capitalist center. Western colonialists and capitalists introduced certain features of capitalism—growing commercialization of the economy, increased domestic and foreign trade, new investments in raw material extraction and transportation—but they did not stimulate the development of an indigenous bourgeoisie or a free wage-labor force. On the contrary, colonial administrators reinforced the power of certain traditionally powerful classes—e.g., the landed aristocracy—in order to facilitate their rule. And foreign capitalists, benefiting from friendly governments and/or their greater wealth and experience, inhibited the emergence of local competitors. Consequently, to the extent that an indigenous bourgeoisie did arise in the peripheral areas, it was small, weak, highly dependent on foreign capital and/or the local state, and quite unable to provide the dynamic leadership necessary for a thorough-going transformation of traditional society into an expanding capitalist economy.

As Paul Baran described it:

> While in advanced countries, such as France or Great Britain, the economically ascending middle-classes developed at an early stage a new rational world outlook, which they proudly opposed to the medieval obscurantism of the feudal age, the poor, fledgling bourgeoisie of the underdeveloped countries sought nothing but accommodation to the prevailing order. Living in societies based on privilege, they strove for a share of the existing sinecures. They made political and economic deals with their domestic feudal overlords or with powerful foreign investors, and what industry and commerce developed in backward areas in the course of the last hundred years was rapidly moulded in the straitjacket of monopoly—the plutocratic partner of the aristocratic rulers. What resulted was an economic and political amalgam combining the worst features of both worlds—feudalism and capitalism—and blocking effectively all possibilities of economic growth.[5]

Granted that there was no indigenous bourgeoisie capable of promoting economic growth in the periphery, why could not foreign capitalists play a progressive role in the development of the peripheral economy? In general, foreign capital could not promote long-run growth in the periphery because it was concentrated primarily in export-oriented extractive activities (e.g., mines, and plantations), with little positive impact on most of the peripheral economy. In effect, foreign investment typically created small enclaves geographically located in the periphery but economically representing simply extensions of the domestic economies of the center. Capital and technology were brought from the center to extract food products and raw materials from the periphery and ship them back home; very few of the material inputs were purchased from the domestic economy; very little of the output was sold there; virtually none of the profits remained there. Thus, the domestic society received little or nothing in exchange for the depletion of its natural resources.

Whether or not a colonial administration was formally in power, foreign investors sought to ally themselves with and strengthen reactionary domestic elites in order to preserve political stability and their own freedom to continue their extractive activities. Thus, parasitic landed and trading classes would be favored over potentially dynamic and productive entrepreneurs. Foreign capitalists and their indigenous allies did not promote the development of capitalist social relations of production in the periphery. Instead, they generally preferred to incorporate pre-capitalist relations into a system of international exchange dominated by foreign capital. Thus capitalism made use of—and in many cases helped to establish—pre-capitalist labor systems based on slavery, debt-serfdom, contract labor, and various other forms of unfree labor. These practices served to keep down labor costs in the production of agricultural and mineral commodities for export to the center, while they inhibited capitalist development in the periphery.

Thus the periphery remained primarily a supplier of cheap primary products to the center and a purchaser of manufactured products therefrom. Instead of fostering capitalist development, imperialism led to a form of underdevelopment in the periphery in which economic growth was limited and industrialization was blocked. In those few regions of the third world where rapid economic growth did occur, the growth was almost always linked to a boom in the export of primary products. Often the boom would eventually peter out, leaving the exporting region little better off than before. Even where the market for the exported products remained strong (e.g., in the case of oil), the economic growth was rarely accompanied by any significant degree of structural change that could lay the basis for a sustained and diversified pattern of economic growth long into the future.[6]

This overall analysis of imperialism and underdevelopment is applicable to most of the periphery up to the time when the Great Depression and World War II disrupted the world capitalist economy and brought the second stage of imperialism to an end.

III. RECENT CHANGES IN RELATIONS BETWEEN THE CENTER AND THE PERIPHERY

The period following World War II ushered in several changes in the world capitalist system with potentially great significance for the periphery.[7] The most obvious change was the dissolution of the bulk of the European colonial empires in Asia, Africa, and the Caribbean. As a result, formally independent national governments assumed power throughout most of the third world. This development also had the effect of changing the character of rivalries among the major capitalist powers. Where in the nineteenth century each power maintained a degree of economic monopoly over its own colonies and/or spheres of influence, in the modern postwar period there is much greater scope for economic competition in the periphery among the capitalist powers. This reality was only latent in the early postwar period when the United States dominated the international capitalist order, but it has become increasingly evident with the revival of the European and Japanese economies and the consequent intensification of "inter-imperialist" rivalries. Finally, a third important difference between the postwar period and earlier historical eras is that there now exists a substantial group of state socialist nations competing with the capitalist powers for influence in the third world. The international capitalist system no longer dominates the entire world but faces significant economic, military, and ideological rivalry from these socialist nations.

Such changes in the international setting have had several consequences for relations between the capitalist center and periphery. Governments of third-world countries have found themselves under mounting popular pressure to promote economic growth and industrialization as well as to reduce their dependence on the major capitalist powers. Political independence has meant that these governments have somewhat greater control over their domestic economies, and rivalries between capitalist powers and between capitalist and socialist states have improved their bargaining position vis-à-vis foreign states and corporations. Moreover, farsighted capitalists in the center now tend to see economic growth in the periphery as a possible antidote to socialist revolution. The significance of such changes has, of course, varied greatly from one country to another. For example, governments in small countries like Honduras or Malawi will necessarily remain in a much weaker position than in large countries like India or Brazil. But the direction of change is applicable to most of the third world.

These changing circumstances are reflected in corresponding changes in economic relations between the capitalist center and periphery. In the first place, the increased bargaining power of third-world governments has helped to bring about a substantial flow of financial aid from the rich to the poor countries.[8] To be sure, the aid is given not for altruistic reasons but to serve the foreign policy interests of the donors; much of the aid has been directed to support friendly governments and allied military establishments in the third world; and the real economic value of aid to the recipient countries is generally overstated by its nominal value. Nonetheless, the flow of aid from rich to poor capitalist countries does make available resources to third-world governments on an unprecedented scale; during the colonial era the flow of official capital was generally in the other direction, as colonial territories paid heavily to be administered by their rulers in the center.

A second significant development in the postwar period has been a change in the character of private foreign investment in the periphery. The traditional type of investment in primary product extraction—especially petroleum—has continued to grow. However, its developmental impact is no longer so limited as it used to be because host governments have been able to capture, in the form of taxes, an increasing share of the huge monopoly profits generated by the petroleum and mineral companies.[9] The most dramatic change in the character of investment in the periphery has resulted from a rapid growth of foreign investment in the manufacturing sector. Policies adopted by host country governments to promote indus-trialization—e.g., tariff protection for local industries—have induced multi-national corporations to set up local subsidiaries to produce commodities within the countries whose markets are to be served. This has been espe-cially true of those third-world countries with large internal markets—e.g., Brazil, Mexico, India—but it has occurred on a smaller scale in other countries as well. More recently there has been significant growth in a different kind of foreign investment in the manufacturing sector, known as "offshore sourcing." This involves the establishment by multinational cor-porations of enterprises in the periphery designed to produce certain inter-mediate products for re-export back to the center either for further processing or for sale on the domestic market. The point is to take ad-vantage of cheap and disciplined labor in certain third-world countries to perform relatively labor-intensive activities, such as electronic component assembly, at a much lower cost than would be possible in the center. Countries such as Taiwan, South Korea, Singapore, and Mexico (especially near the U.S. border) have been among the major recipients of this kind of investment.

All of the above developments have greatly increased the extent of economic linkage between foreign capital and the domestic economies of the periphery. No longer does foreign investment simply create an export enclave that is but an extension of the home economy. Rather, foreign capital is now penetrating into the peripheral economies and inducing changes on a much greater scale. By the same token, the governments and capitalists of the center nations no longer necessarily support the tradi-tional pre-capitalist elites of the periphery, nor the pre-capitalist relations of production with which they are associated. They now have more of an interest in collaborating with those classes in the periphery who will pro-mote the growth of capitalism—its markets, its infrastructure, its labor force—so long as foreign capital retains access to the local economy.[10]

IV. CONTEMPORARY CAPITALIST DEVELOPMENT IN THE PERIPHERY

As a consequence of the changes described above, one would expect the impact of imperialism on the periphery to have become somewhat more favorable to economic growth and industrialization than in the past. In fact, the available data do tend to confirm the view that conditions within the world capitalist system are developing in such a way as to favor growth in the periphery.

Table 2 presents some statistical evidence on rates of growth of ag-gregate output and manufacturing output in the capitalist center and periphery from 1950 to 1973.[11] According to the data in the table, aggregate output in the periphery as a whole grew at an annual rate of roughly 5 per-cent from 1950 to 1973; per capita aggregate output increased by roughly 2.5 percent per year, and manufacturing output by more than 7 percent per year. Although comparable figures are not available for earlier periods, there can be no doubt that these growth rates are much higher than ever

Table 2   Economic Growth in the Center and the Periphery: 1950–1973

Area	Total Output[1]	Per Capita Output[1]	Manufacturing Output
	(Average annual % rate of growth, 1950–1973)		
Capitalist world[2]	4.7	2.6	5.5
Center	4.5	3.4	5.4
Periphery	5.1	2.6	7.2
Latin America	5.4	2.6	7.0
Middle East[3]	7.8*	4.8*	10.5*
Africa[4]	4.9*	2.3*	7.0*
Asia[5]	4.4	2.0	7.1

* Figures apply to the period 1960–1973 only.
[1] Output measured by gross domestic product.
[2] Defined here to exclude the U.S.S.R., Eastern Europe, China, Mongolia, North Korea, and North Vietnam.
[3] Excluding Israel.
[4] Excluding South Africa.
[5] Excluding Japan and the Middle East.
Source: Growth rates calculated from index numbers published in the United Nations, *Statistical Yearbook, 1968* and *1974* (New York: United Nations, 1969 and 1975), Table 4.

before. Moreover, they compare very favorably with the performance of the center in the postwar period. Aggregate output and manufacturing output actually grew more rapidly in the periphery than in the center.

Rapid as the growth of output has been in the periphery as a whole, it has not been rapid enough to prevent a widening of the gap between average levels of living in the center and the periphery. The best single quantitative measure of the average level of living in a country is its per capita income, equivalent to its per capita output.[12] To reduce the enormous differentials shown in Table 1, it would be necessary for per capita output to grow more rapidly in the periphery than in the center. But as Table 2 shows, the growth of *per capita* output in the periphery has been somewhat lower than in the center, even though the growth of *total* output has been higher. And it is in the poorest areas of the periphery (Africa, and South and East Asia) that per capita output is growing the most slowly.

The above figures on aggregate economic growth suggest that imperialism has begun to have a more progressive impact on the periphery than in the past. It does appear that capitalism is now generating forces that are conducive to some degree of economic growth and industrialization in the third world. Any effort to analyze this phenomenon, however, must go beyond aggregate growth rates to study in more detail the *nature* of capitalist growth in the periphery. As we will see below, this growth—like all capitalist development—has been highly uneven and exploitative in character.

Before examining evidence on the character of capitalist development in the periphery, it will be useful to review the context of class relations in which this development is occurring. Although nationalist movements have taken over power from earlier colonial rulers in almost every part of the periphery, there has been in most cases no revolutionary redistribution of power among the indigenous classes. Workers and peasants, and the lower- and middle-income classes in general, have very little political influence. Power tends to be concentrated among various elite classes—landlords, indigenous businesspeople, highly placed bureaucrats, and foreign capitalists—in combinations that vary from one country to another. But, as writers like Baran have stressed, the indigenous bourgeoisie tends to be weak or virtually nonexistent, and it therefore cannot play the role of a dominant elite as it did in the capitalist center.

Yet since World War II, unlike in earlier times, economic growth and industrialization have not been stunted by the absence of a strong and independent indigenous bourgeoisie. It appears now that capitalist growth can be promoted in the periphery if foreign capitalists can be induced by the peripheral state to play the economically progressive role classically performed by an indigenous bourgeoisie. In fact, capitalist growth in the periphery has been largely dependent on foreign initiative, foreign technology, and—often—foreign capital. While some of the countries of the present-day capitalist center drew on foreign resources at various stages of their economic development, the growth process as a whole was led by an indigenous bourgeoisie with varying degrees of support from the state. In the present-day periphery the indigenous bourgeoisie has always been and remains relatively weak and ineffectual vis-à-vis the bourgeoisie from the capitalist center. The stimulus for growth and industrialization in the periphery has typically come from the state, which has had to turn to foreign enterprise for many of the key resources required for economic advancement. The multiplying rates of foreign investment attest to the prominent role played by foreign *capital* in the growth of the periphery. These figures do not account for the ever-increasing dependence of peripheral economies on foreign *technology*, which can remain in effect even where local firms or the local state have financial control over productive enterprises.

It is precisely the need for an alliance between the peripheral state and capitalists from the center (with the peripheral bourgeoisie as a junior partner at best) that imparts to capitalist growth in the periphery a particularly uneven and repressive character. The class relations characteristic of the periphery no longer necessarily inhibit economic growth *per se*, but they serve to aggravate some of the negative qualities that have always characterized the capitalist growth process.

In the first place, economic growth in the periphery has been very unevenly distributed among the peripheral nations. Table 3 lists the twenty third-world nations (among those with populations exceeding one million) whose output has grown most rapidly since 1950. These are the "success stories" of the capitalist periphery, where the average rate of economic growth has exceeded 6 percent per year and per capita output has risen by roughly 3 percent or more per year. The remaining sixty-five peripheral nations and territories (with populations exceeding one million) have had at best very mixed success, with per capita output rising slowly or—in some cases—not at all. It is worth noting that among the twenty "success stories" are five major oil-producing nations (Libya, Saudi Arabia, Iran, Iraq, and Venezuela), two commercial city-states (Hong Kong and

Table 3 Economic Growth in Selected Peripheral Countries: 1950–1973

Rank	Country	Total Output	Per Capita Output
		(Average annual % rate of growth, 1950–1973)	
1	Libya	12.7	8.7
2	Israel	9.9	5.5
3	Saudi Arabia	9.8	7.8
4	Taiwan	9.3	6.0
5	Hong Kong	9.1	5.4
6	Iran	8.1	4.9
7	Singapore	8.0	4.6
8	Iraq	7.8	4.5
9	South Korea	7.6	5.0
10	Greece	7.0	6.3
11	Puerto Rico	6.9	5.7
12	Spain	6.7	5.7
13	Brazil	6.7	3.7
14	Thailand	6.7	3.5
15	Jamaica	6.6	5.1
16	Dominican Republic	6.5	3.2
17	Panama	6.4	3.4
18	Venezuela	6.4	2.7
19	Jordan	6.4	3.3
20	Mexico	6.3	2.9

Source: Growth rates for the full period 1950–1973 calculated from growth rates for various subperiods presented in the World Bank *World Tables* (Washington, D.C.: World Bank, 1971 and 1976).

Singapore), five of the major per capita beneficiaries of U.S. foreign aid (Israel, Taiwan, Greece, Jordan, South Korea) and a U.S. territory (Puerto Rico). Needless to say, conditions for economic growth in these countries have been unusually favorable and atypical of the third world as a whole.

The uneven incidence of economic growth in different parts of the periphery can be explained largely in terms of the degree of interest shown by foreign capital in different third-world countries. For the investor from the center the most attractive countries are those with one or more of the following attributes: (1) large deposits of key industrial raw materials; (2) large internal markets for manufactured goods; and (3) a disciplined low-wage labor force.[13] Thus, major oil producers (e.g., Iran, Saudi Arabia, Venezuela) and aluminum producers (e.g., Jamaica), countries with relatively high levels of per capita income and population (e.g., Brazil, Mexico, Spain) and countries with reliable cheap labor (e.g., Taiwan, South Korea, Hong Kong) can expect to attract foreign capital on a considerable scale. Such countries then have at least the *potential* for generating economic growth and industrialization with the help of foreign capital, provided their respective governments can form a workable alliance—neither scaring away foreign capital nor becoming totally subservient to it. Countries that for political/strategic reasons received substantial amounts of foreign aid from the center (e.g., Israel, Jordan, Greece) clearly also have their growth potential raised. In countries with little appeal to foreign investors or governments, the prospects for economic growth would depend on the ability of the state itself to play the role of a dynamic bourgeoisie. This is a remote possibility as long as the dominant elites are still very much identified with past privilege and the old order.

Just as economic growth has been very unevenly distributed *among* peripheral nations, economic gains have been very unevenly distributed *within* these nations. In most areas of the third world both inequality and unemployment appear to be worsening. The available data show that income distribution is even more unequal in the capitalist periphery than in the center.[14] Data on the time trend of income distribution within countries is as yet rather unreliable, but what evidence there is suggests to most observers that there has been an increase in inequality in the great majority of the countries of the third world. Moreover, urban/rural disparities seem to be widening, as much of the economic expansion is concentrated in industries located in or near large cities. As a high official of the World Bank wrote, in introducing a volume on economic growth and income distribution:

> It is now clear that more than a decade of rapid growth in under-developed countries has been of little or no benefit to perhaps a third of their population. Although the average per capita income of the Third World has increased by 50 percent since 1960, this growth has been very unequally distributed among countries, regions within countries, and socio-economic groups.[15]

Evidence on trends in unemployment is similarly hard to come by, but again there seems to be little doubt among observers that the problem is becoming increasingly acute.[16] One fact is quite clear: the rate of growth of industrial employment in the periphery has been much slower than the rate of growth of industrial output, so that the ability of even a rapidly growing industrial sector to provide employment opportunities has been rather limited. Moreover, the population in urban areas has been increasing much more rapidly than the availability of jobs in the modern sector of the economy, with the result that increasing numbers of urban dwellers have joined the ranks of the marginalized "lumpenproletariat." In general, the beneficiaries of capitalist economic growth in the third world appear to have been confined largely to the well-to-do classes, and particularly those living in major urban centers with close links to the capitalist center.

The persistence and exacerbation of inequalities among regions and socioeconomic classes within third-world countries is a natural consequence of the nature of capitalist growth and the class relations that underlie it. The very logic of capitalist expansion is "to build on the best"—i.e., to invest in those areas and favor those people that are already the most economically advanced, because it is more profitable to do this than to try to develop backward areas or provide opportunities for the poorer classes. Inequality is inherent in the operation of capitalist institutions,[17] and it is often indispensable for capitalist accumulation because it concentrates income in the hands of those with the highest propensity to save and invest—the capitalist class. Similarly, unemployment plays a functional role in any capitalist society by holding down wages and maintaining labor discipline,[18] thereby stimulating capitalist profits and accumulation.

There are several aspects of the situation in contemporary third-world countries which tend to aggravate the forces that generate inequality and unemployment in any capitalist economy. The fact that economic growth and industrialization is propelled largely by foreign rather than indigenous capital and technology means that types of products and techniques of production based on conditions in the center are likely to play an undue role in the periphery. In particular, relatively capital-intensive products and technology tend to be transferred to the periphery, where they generate large economic gains for a small and privileged group of people while displacing many local small businesspeople and workers and failing to provide alternative employment opportunities for them. At the same time, the domination of power by privileged classes limits the political effectiveness of demands for redistributive measures, employment-creating projects, and more equitable growth in general.

Finally, successful capitalist growth in the periphery has generally been associated with highly authoritarian political rule.[19] Many of the more rapidly growing nations in the capitalist periphery (listed in Table 3) are characterized by unusually repressive regimes—most notable are the examples of Taiwan, South Korea, Spain, and Brazil. Most of the remaining countries in the table have been subject to authoritarian and/or colonial rule for much of the postwar period. Only Israel stands out as a nation in which a wide range of bourgeois democratic rights have been maintained continuously since 1950 (and only for the majority Jewish population). Greece, Mexico, Jamaica, and Venezuela have at times had democratic institutions functioning with a moderate degree of effectiveness. But—with the exception of the special case of Israel—the most democratic political systems in the third world over the past twenty-five years are to be found in countries that are *not* among the capitalist success stories—e.g., in Ceylon, Chile (until recently), Costa Rica, India, Lebanon (until recently), and Uruguay (until recently).

The particularly authoritarian political context of capitalist growth in most third-world countries may be attributed in part to the absence of a revolutionary bourgeois triumph over the old order in those countries. Instead of being led by an indigenous bourgeoisie rebelling under a democratic banner against pre-capitalist bastions of privilege, capitalist growth in the periphery has been fostered by an alliance of elites—both traditional and modern—operating through a relatively powerful state. Even in some of the "late developers" among the nations of the center—notably Germany and Japan—the relative weakness of the indigenous bourgeoisie, its inclination to ally with rather than struggle against feudal elites, and the emergence of the state as a major force promoting capitalist growth had markedly authoritarian implications.[20]

In the third-world countries that are presently experiencing some economic growth, these same sociopolitical circumstances are modified primarily by the addition of foreign capitalists to the alliance of dominant classes. This modification serves only to reinforce authoritarian tendencies, for foreign capitalists and foreign governments have much to fear from the nationalist and populist forces that are likely to gain strength with the inclusion of middle and lower classes into the political process. It is no accident that so many of the authoritarian regimes of the contemporary third world—in Brazil, Chile, Indonesia, etc.—have come to power with the active assistance of the United States government and its Central Intelligence Agency.[21]

Both foreign and domestic capitalists tend to see in strong, authoritarian regimes the best hope for political and economic stability in the periphery today. In a context of growing worker militance, increasing public demands for a wider distribution of economic benefits, and nascent as well as active revolutionary movements in many parts of the third world, political repression often seems to be the surest way to insure a docile labor force willing to work at wage levels that ensure a high rate of profit on invested capital. In the capitalist center, bourgeois democracy serves an important legitimizing function without seriously threatening capitalist economic interests.[22] In the capitalist periphery, however, democracy usually serves to inhibit the process of capital accumulation.

It is important to recognize that the inequality, the unemployment, the dependence, and the authoritarianism that have characterized capitalist development in the periphery are not inevitable requisites of economic growth. One need only study the example of the People's Republic of China to learn that it is possible for a poor third-world country to achieve rapid economic growth and industrialization while promoting a high degree of equity and self-reliance as well as full employment.[23] While China's political system remains authoritarian in important respects, there is also evidence of a substantial degree of popular participation in decision-making at the "micro" level of the neighborhood and the enterprise (farm, factory, or office). There is therefore good reason to believe that there are viable alternatives to the pattern of development that has occurred in the capitalist periphery; and the existence and awareness of such alternatives heightens the contradictions that are developing there.

In conclusion, it appears that the contemporary stage of imperialism has proven somewhat more progressive in its overall impact on the third world than earlier stages. To a greater extent than in the past, capitalism has begun to play in the periphery as well as in the center the historical role Marx foresaw for it in advancing the forces of production. Yet this does not imply that the unequal international relations of the world capitalist system will come to an end, nor that the periphery will come to resemble the center.

In the first place, capitalist growth is taking place only in certain favored regions of the periphery; the prospects for capitalist growth in many other regions remain highly uncertain. Secondly, even where it is taking place, capitalist growth in the periphery remains in many important ways dependent on the center and its capitalists. Thus the underlying hierarchy that characterizes imperialism remains a reality, although it is taking a new form. Especially because of continuing technological dependence, the capitalist success stories of the periphery will find it very difficult to join the center. Most of them can expect to become, at best, junior partners intermediate between the center and the periphery.

V. CONTRADICTIONS OF IMPERIALISM IN THE PERIPHERY

Even where imperialism is successful in advancing the forces of production in the periphery, it generates certain contradictions which threaten the stability of the process and offer opportunities for revolutionary change. These contradictions are more intense than those that arose out of early capitalist growth in the center because of the different setting in which growth now takes place in the periphery.

First, the unequal character of capitalist growth in the periphery is likely to give rise to serious tensions. When some classes in a society are quite obviously benefiting from economic growth while the masses of people see little improvement in their standard of living, discontent is bound to grow. The perception of inequality is heightened by continual improvements in transportation and communications media. The poor in the periphery are becoming more and more aware of the affluent standards of living enjoyed by some of their compatriots and by most foreigners resident in the periphery or at home in the center; as a consequence, their economic aspirations are raised. This so-called "demonstration effect" operates much more powerfully in the modern era than it did in the early stages of growth in the capitalist center.

Rising aspirations conflict with a largely unchanging reality for the masses of people who benefit little from economic growth. Thus demands for more widespread participation in economic progress begin to mount. In response, the dominant classes can either turn toward tighter repression or begin to share the benefits of growth. The first course will sooner or later lead to intensified conflict and possibly a revolutionary movement; the second course may threaten the foundations of capitalist growth by reducing the surplus available for accumulation and lowering the private profitability of investment. Only in countries where unusually favorable circumstances create the potential for very rapid economic growth can capitalist accumulation proceed while at the same time the standard of living of the masses rises appreciably. For most of the third world, the contradiction of unequal capitalist growth cannot long be circumvented.

A second contradictory aspect of capitalist growth in the periphery arises from its effect on the traditional socioeconomic structure. The increasing penetration of capitalist social relations serves to undermine the paternalistic and/or communal sources of security in traditional precapitalist societies. Peasants, serfs, and artisans are separated from their means of production and their niche in rural society and thrown into the impersonal free market for labor, seeking employment on large capitalist farms or in industrializing urban areas. The brutal proletarianization of the labor force is part of the history of capitalist development in every part of the world. But again it is particularly acute in the contemporary periphery because employment opportunities are now much scarcer than before. As I have argued earlier, new products and improved techniques of production, developed primarily in the rich countries, usually involve a capital-intensive bias appropriate to conditions in the center. Whether introduced by foreign capitalists or by local capitalists borrowing from abroad, these new products and techniques tend to have a limited potential for absorbing labor. Thus, capitalism in the periphery erodes traditional bases of stability without providing an adequate substitute in the form of wage employment. The ranks of the "reserve army" of unemployed or marginalized workers are growing, and they are exacerbating the conflict between capital and all but the (usually small) minority of workers who manage to get the limited number of secure jobs available.

A third contradiction arising out of capitalist growth in the periphery results from its politically authoritarian character. Repression can promote stability—but not forever. In the long run the most stable kind of capitalist society is one in which bourgeois democratic freedoms can thrive sufficiently so as to legitimize the *status quo* by obscuring the fundamentally authoritarian nature of the economic order. With few exceptions, the governments in third-world countries experiencing capitalist growth derive no legitimacy from popular involvement in the political process. What legitimacy they can claim is based upon their ability to deliver economic improvement, and even this source of legitimacy is compromised by the uneven distribution of the gains. Continued authoritarian rule with limited popular legitimacy is at best an uncertain and unstable proposition. It is likely to breed either popular revolt on the part of the repressed masses or military coups carried out in the name of the people or with the intent of "restoring stability." The recent history of third-world countries is replete with popular uprisings and sudden changes of government. While they do not always necessarily inhibit the process of capitalist economic growth, they can lead to serious economic reverses and the possibility of revolutionary upheavals.

To be sure, some of the negative aspects of capitalist economic growth that I have described as potentially contradictory in the periphery have also characterized capitalist growth in the center. Capitalism has always generated resistance from the many people who suffer from its expansion: those whose traditional kinship systems, communities, and occupations are destroyed; those who are excluded from the growing wealth of the economy; those who are thrown into the reserve army of the unemployed; those who experience directly the repressive arm of the state; and so on. Yet so far, at least, capitalism has proven durable in the center. For all of its potential contradictions, it has rarely been seriously vulnerable to a revolutionary challenge. Why should we expect capitalism to be any less viable in the contemporary periphery, as long as it does succeed in generating economic growth?

Part of the answer is that the potentially contradictory aspects of capitalist growth are stronger in the periphery today than they were in the center in the past. For reasons discussed earlier, inequality, unemployment, and authoritarianism are likely to be particularly acute in the circumstances under which capitalist growth can take place in the contemporary third world. Even more important, however, is the fact that there now exist concrete examples of an alternative to capitalism in the form of the state socialist nations of the world. These nations have not avoided all the shortcomings of capitalist economic growth. But their experience serves to heighten the contradictory elements of capitalist growth in the periphery and strengthen revolutionary anticapitalist movements in several ways.

First, the very existence of the state socialist nations is important in exploding the conservative myth that there simply is no alternative route to economic improvement than a capitalist one. Second, the model projected (if not always realized) by the state socialist nations provides a forward-looking inspiration for anti-capitalist movements. In the past history of the capitalist nations of the center, opposition to the growth of capitalist hegemony was usually doomed from the beginning because it was predominately backward-looking. It encouraged the smashing of machines and extolled the virtues of traditional ways of life; but it offered no vision of the future and could develop no positive program capable of resisting the increasing power that capitalism derived from its harnessing of technological progress. The socialist model, however, provides a socially, economically, and technologically progressive focus for anti-capitalist resistance in contemporary third-world countries. At the same time, some of the state socialist nations are in a position to provide direct material assistance—as well as political and ideological support—to revolutionary movements struggling against capitalist domination in the periphery.

One final important new element in the contemporary situation is the *dependent* character of capitalist growth in the periphery. Because the indigenous elites and their state become dependent on foreign capital for much of the impetus to economic growth, they find it difficult to harness the forces of nationalism to their own advantage. The very presence of foreign capitalists and their growing role in the economy serve to inflame nationalist feelings on the part of the indigenous population. The elites must respond to growing nationalist pressures by at least an escalation of nationalistic rhetoric and a show of tougher bargaining with foreign capitalists and governments. Up to a point they may be able to improve the terms of their alliance with foreign capital, but they cannot afford to push too far. In the last analysis they are inextricably tied to an internationalist outlook and cannot maintain ideological hegemony over popular nationalist forces. Thus, their participation in the capitalist economic growth process makes them increasingly vulnerable to oppositional movements which can raise more effectively the banner of nationalism.

It is precisely the opportunity of anti-capitalist opposition movements to link their struggles with nationalism that gives them a potentially powerful basis for carrying out a successful revolution. Within the center—both in the past and at present—socialist movements have had to struggle primarily against an indigenous capitalist class, and nationalism could not play much of a role. But in the periphery anti-capitalist movements can be simultaneously anti-imperialist, and thereby draw upon a broader base of opposition to the *status quo*. It remains quite possible that indigenous national capitalists will attempt to use anti-imperialist struggles to serve their own ends and to co-opt potentially revolutionary socialist movements. But the logic of capitalist development in the periphery ultimately leads in an internationalist direction. In the long run, it is socialist movements that are likely to reflect most effectively the nationalist aspirations of third-world peoples.

In the foregoing discussion I have stressed the contradictions that arise even when imperialism is successful in stimulating capitalist economic growth in the periphery. In those parts of the third world where

imperialism has yet to show much of its progressive side, significant contradictions are also likely to develop. In the first place, a lack of economic
growth is likely to be a source of instability in itself, given increasingly widespread demands for economic improvement. Moreover, the slower the rate
of economic growth, the less tolerance there will be for existing inequalities,
the less successful the economy will be in providing employment opportunities, and the weaker will be the classes supportive of foreign capital.
Where imperialism fails to build a local base of support by promoting some
degree of capitalist economic growth in alliance with indigenous elites, it
renders itself all the more vulnerable to nationalist opposition. Whether
under these circumstances the anti-imperialist forces become anti-capitalist
as well depends largely on the effectiveness of revolutionary socialist organization. And the success of any revolutionary socialist movement in the
third world ultimately depends both on its own strength and on the ability
and desire of the imperialist powers to defend their empire with military
might.

NOTES

1. I will use the term "third world" synonymously with the "periphery"—i.e., all
those nations and territories which do not belong to the capitalist center (the advanced capitalist nations) and which have not become state socialist nations.

2. See Tables 13-G and 13-H, p. 506 and p. 507 of Richard C. Edwards, Michael Reich,
and Thomas E. Weisskopf (eds.), *The Capitalist System*, Revised Edition (Englewood Cliffs, N.J.: Prentice-Hall, 1978).

3. The analysis of underdevelopment outlined here is based on the work of neo-
Marxist authors such as Paul Baran and Andre Gunder Frank.

4. The "American Revolution" involved much less an anti-feudal than an anti-colonial
struggle, in which the nascent national bourgeoisie and its allies threw off the
fetters of British Imperial rule. For more details, see the introduction to Chapter
6, p. 217 of Edwards et al., *op. cit.*

5. Paul Baran, "On the Political Economy of Backwardness," in this anthology, pp.
91–102.

6. Andre Gunder Frank, in his essay "The Development of Underdevelopment," in this
anthology, pp. 103–113, points out that the limited amount of industrialization that
did occur in the third world before the second half of the twentieth century almost
always happened when and where there were relatively *weak* links between the
metropolis and the periphery. For example, spurts of industrial growth took place
in Argentina, Brazil, and Mexico precisely when trade and investment relations with
the metropolis were sharply reduced by the Great Depression and World War II.
This negative correlation between the strength of imperialism and industrialization
supports the argument that the economically regressive aspect of imperialism was
dominant up to the postwar period.

7. These changes, and their implications for the neo-Marxist analysis of imperialism and
underdevelopment, have been forcefully spelled out by Bill Warren in his essay,
"Imperialism and Capitalist Industrialization," *New Left Review*, No. 81 (September
10, 1973). Unfortunately, Warren's analysis tends to overstate the case; for a useful
antidote, see Philip McMichael, James Petras, and Robert Rhodes, "Imperialism
and the Contradictions of Development," *New Left Review*, No. 85 (May/June 1974).

8. Since the early 1960s the annual flow of official development assistance funds from
the capitalist metropolis to the periphery has ranged from roughly $5 billion to $10
billion; see Everett Hagen, *The Economics of Development* (Homewood, Ill.: Irwin,
1975), Table 17.4, for data from 1962 to 1972. For reasons discussed in detail by
Gunnar Myrdal, *Challenge of World Poverty* (New York: Pantheon, 1970), Chap. 11,
such figures overstate the actual value of the aid to the recipient countries.

9. For example, Raymond Vernon, *Sovereignty at Bay* (New York: Basic Books, 1971),
p. 54, reports that the host country share of pretax profits of foreign investors in

oil and copper rose from roughly 10–15 percent in the 1920s to 65–70 percent in the 1960s; the percentage has no doubt increased further in the 1970s with the increasing power and collaboration of governments from the oil- and mineral-exporting nations.

10. This is not to suggest that foreign capital always supports pro-capitalist forces in the periphery. Under certain circumstances pre-capitalist institutions can enhance the profitability of foreign investment—for example, by maintaining a semi-prole-tarianized labor force whose cost of reproduction is lower than that of a fully developed proletariat.

11. The United Nations data from which these growth rates have been calculated are not perfectly reliable; for reasons suggested by Simon Kuznets, "Problems in Comparing Recent Growth Rates for Developed and Less Developed Countries," *Economic Development and Cultural Change*, 20, No. 2 (January 1972), the rates of growth in the periphery are probably overstated. Nonetheless, the broad conclusions that I draw from the data are adequately supported.

12. Many elements of economic welfare are not captured by per capita income figures —e.g., the distribution of income, nonmonetized sources of welfare, etc. Moreover, international comparisons of income levels are fraught with both theoretical and empirical problems. Still, the comparative figures in Table 13-F, p. 501, Edwards et al., *op. cit.*, do provide a rough indication of the vast differences in average standards of living prevailing in different parts of the world.

13. Note that these attributes correspond to the three types of foreign investment discussed earlier: investment in primary product extraction, investment in manufacturing for the local market, and investment in offshore sourcing.

14. See Felix Paukert, "Income Distribution at Different Levels of Development: A Survey of the Evidence," *International Labor Review*, 108 (July–December 1973).

15. Hollis Chenery, introduction to Chenery et al., *Redistribution with Growth* (London: Oxford University Press, 1974), p. xiii.

16. For a detailed review of the evidence, see David Turnham and Ingeles Jaeger, *The Employment Problem in Less Developed Countries: A Review of the Evidence* (Paris: Organization for Economic Cooperation and Development, 1971).

17. See the introduction to Chapter 8, p. 293, in Edwards et al., *op. cit.*, for an analysis of the relationship between capitalism and inequality.

18. *Ibid.* See Weisskopf, Section 12.2, p. 441, and Crotty and Rapping, Section 12.4, p. 461, on the role of the "reserve army of the unemployed" in maintaining profitability in advanced capitalist economies.

19. Every capitalist society is authoritarian in the sense that the most important decisions reflect disproportionately the interests of the dominant capitalist class. But there are nonetheless real and significant differences in the degree of responsiveness of different kinds of political institutions to the will of the people. For all its short-comings, a bourgeois democracy often permits sections of the working class to obtain certain concessions that could not be wrung from a fascist police state. For a detailed discussion and documentation of the degree of democracy and authoritarianism in different countries throughout the world, see the annual *Comparative Survey of Freedom* published by Freedom House (New York).

20. See Barrington Moore, Jr., *Social Origins of Dictatorship and Democracy* (Boston: Beacon Press, 1967), for a comparative historical analysis illustrating—among many other things—the importance of a bourgeois revolution for nonauthoritarian capitalist development.

21. The experience of Chile provides a perfect illustration of this point. Chile's unusually democratic political framework resulted in a trend toward increasing nationalism and populism in public officials, culminating in the electoral victory of socialist Salvador Allende in 1970. Allende proved to be more than ITT or Henry Kissinger could stand, so three years later the U.S. government (via the CIA) helped to overthrow Allende and install one of the most brutal and repressive military governments in the third world.

22. See Edwards and Reich, Section 6.5, p. 252, on the role of democracy in the United States.

23. There is a rapidly growing literature on the development achievements of the People's Republic of China. For a brief survey of the Chinese experience, see John W. Gurley, "Maoist Economic Development: The New Man in the New China," in this anthology, pp. 334–346.

11

The Multinational Corporation and the Underdevelopment of the Third World

Ronald Müller

INTRODUCTION

In the two decades since World War II, there has been an increasing awareness that two revolutionary phenomena have occurred in the less developed countries of the Third World. The first phenomenon is reflected in the most recent recognitions of the plight of less developed countries (LDCs) after some twenty years of so-called development attempts. This phenomenon, revolutionary in terms of its impact on the lives of roughly two-thirds of the world's people which it affects, is the maintenance of underdevelopment. It is a phenomenon which is unique to the Third World and which is mirrored in the statistical findings on increasing unemployment, the growing inequality in income distribution, and the fact that anywhere from 40 percent to 60 percent of the populations of most LDCs have suffered not only relative but also absolute declines in consumption compared to ten, fifteen, twenty years ago.[1]

A second revolutionary phenomenon, which has occurred in the past twenty years but which is not unique to the Third World, is the occurrence of a new institution in the political economy of nations, the multinational corporation (MNC). Although it had its historical antecedents in the late nineteenth and early twentieth centuries, the multinational corporation in its modern form has been the subject of concern in a recent deluge of books, Ph.D. dissertations, and articles in newspapers, magazines, and scientific journals. Part of this deluge has focused on definitions (is an MNC a company which makes a certain percentage of its sales overseas or should the criterion be a certain percentage of its profits) while at the same time debating terminology (some choose to call the MNC a transnational corporation while others prefer the terminology of a global corporation).

Whatever we choose to call it, a multinational corporation is a company with its parent headquarters located in one country and subsidiary operations in a number of other countries. The central characteristic of a multinational corporation is that it seeks to maximize the profits not of its individual subsidiaries, but rather of the center parent company. This, as we shall see, may even mean operating certain of its subsidiaries at an "official" loss. The best way to define an MNC is to name a few, for they are

This article was written expressly for this book of readings. © 1973 by Ronald Müller.

familiar to us whether we reside in a more developed or a less developed part of the world. They are companies such as Du Pont, Ford Motor, National Biscuit, ITT, Bayer, Unilever, Procter & Gamble, Dow Chemical, Volkswagen, Squibb, etc.

The objective of this present work is to explore whether these two phenomena, the maintenance of underdevelopment, a human condition, and the rise of a new worldwide institution, the modern multinational corporation, are related to each other. Specifically our exploration of this question will focus on three main aspects: (a) the empirical reality of the role played by MNCs in the economies of the Third World, with a specific focus on Latin America as an illustrative case; (b) the methods and practices utilized by MNCs in their Third World operations; and (c) the results of these operations and their impacts on the development potential of LDCs.

Since many readers may not be intimately familiar with the operations of MNCs and/or the political economy of Third World nations, we have chosen a particular breakdown for the remainder of our discussion that should be sufficiently intelligible to both the expert and non-expert alike. The discussion will be broken down into the most-often-cited contributions of multinational corporations to the economic development of LDCs. For example, it is often said that the multinational corporation makes a fundamentally important *technological contribution* to the development of Third World countries. In what follows, this and other contributions will be individually examined to see whether or not they represent myth or reality.

Before proceeding, however, it is critical to an understanding of the impact of MNCs in LDCs to have a certain degree of familiarity with the institutional conditions and economic structure of these economies. This familiarity coupled with the use of some simple tools of economic analysis can aid us in analyzing the contributions of MNCs. In addition, a familiarity with the politico-economic circumstances of LDCs will shed further light on why it cannot be assumed that the contributions of, for example, a United States corporation's subsidiary in West Germany to that economy are the same as the contributions of that corporation's subsidiary in Peru to the Peruvian economy.

MNCs AND THE MEANING OF UNDERDEVELOPMENT

Underdevelopment: The Institutional Setting

In turning to the economic environment of Third World nations, let us first review the reasons why these countries are called "less developed." First, there is a lack of adequately trained civil servants to examine and investigate whether or not commercial and business laws are being complied with by MNCs or locally owned companies. Secondly, the implications of this lack of expertise indicate that the very laws themselves are usually quite old, designed for times past, when the holding of a patent, the legal institution which sets the limits on the market power of technology, had far different implications than it does today. The laws, as well as taxation practices and other governmental functions, have remained unrevised too long to take cognizance of the major changes in the origins of economic power. And lastly, whereas we normally think of the institutions of organized labor in advanced countries as a countervailing force or check upon the power of the corporation, this is not the case in most LDCs where organized labor is either weak or absent.

Thus, a basic part of the meaning of underdevelopment is a set of institutions which are either lacking or malfunctioning relative to similar institutions in industrialized societies. For those of us accustomed to life in the advanced nations, a fundamental understanding of this basic aspect of underdevelopment is essential when analyzing the impacts of MNCs on Third World economies. Whether we look at legal institutions or those of organized labor or those of financing, we shall find that the "bargaining power" of the MNC to maximize profits is far greater in the Third World than in rich countries because of the absence or weakness of institutional mechanisms to control the behavior of subsidiaries. Stated in Galbraithian terms, Third World countries are characterized by an absence of the "countervailing" power of government and organized labor for setting limits on the power of the modern corporation.

The institutional conditions characterizing underdevelopment are one aspect explaining the power of the multinational corporation in LDCs, but there is another aspect of underdevelopment which further intensifies this power, and that is the economic structure of societies in underdevelopment. In assessing the power of MNCs, there are two key characteristics of this economic structure which are important to grasp: first, the need for and the sources of *technology;* and second, the need for and the sources of investment *financing.*

Underdevelopment: The Structure of Technology

Fortunately or unfortunately, most Third World countries have already set in motion a process of industrialization highly similar to that found in the advanced capitalist nations of the West. This industrialization is not only similar in terms of the output of industry (capital goods and private consumption goods), but also in terms of the mechanical technology and human technical skills needed for its implementation. In other words, the voluntary or involuntary institutionalization of Western consumption values as the goal of economic growth has, in turn, brought about the need for a technology which can satisfy this pattern of consumption. Given this need, what are the sources of this technology? Tables 1 and 2 provide the answer.

The meaning of these statistics is clear. LDCs are virtually entirely dependent upon foreign sources, specifically the advanced nations of North America, Western Europe, and Japan, for their technology. Not even these figures reflect the absolute dependency involved, however, for if we look at the ownership of patents actually utilized for producing goods versus patents granted but not utilized in production we find that:

. . . if the number of patents is weighted by their economic or technological worth (i.e. volume of sales or value added) most developing countries
are likely to find that the so weighted patents belonging to their own na-
tionals amount to a fraction of 1 percent of the total patents granted by
such countries.[2]

Table 1   Patents Granted to Foreigners as a Percentage of Total Patents Granted
Between 1957 and 1961 Inclusive

"Large" Industrial Countries		"Smaller" Industrial Countries		Developing Countries	
U.S.A.	15.72	Italy	62.85	India	89.38
Japan	34.02	Switzerland	64.08	Turkey	91.73
West Germany	37.14	Sweden	69.30	United Arab	
United Kingdom	47.00	Netherlands	69.83	Republic	93.01
France	59.36	Luxemburg	80.48	Trinidad and	
		Belgium	85.55	Tobago	94.18
				Pakistan	95.75
				Ireland	96.51

Source: Statistical information appearing in United Nations, "The Role of Patents in the
Transfer of Technology to Developing Countries," New York, 1964, pp. 94–95, as cited in
Constantine Vaitsos, "Patents Revisited: Their Function in Developing Countries," *The Jour-
nal of Development Studies* (1973), p. 6.

Table 2   Percentages of Patents Registered in Chile

Year	Owned by Nationals	Owned by Foreigners
1937	34.5	65.5
1947	20.0	80.0
1958	11.0	89.0
1967	5.5	94.5

Sources: Corporacion de Fomento de la Produccion (CORFO), "La Propiedad Industrial en
Chile y su Impacto en el Desarrollo Industrial," preliminary unpublished document, Santiago
(September 1970), p. 15; also in Vaitsos, "Patents Revisited . . . ," *op. cit.*, p. 8.

Also, the foreign versus local control of technology does not indicate
the actual concentration of control in the hands of a very small number of
foreign corporations. In the United States, for example, of the five hundred
largest industrial corporations, the top thirty own 40.7 percent of the
patents in their respective industries.[3] The mirror image of this concentration of technology control in the advanced nations is found to an even
greater extent in the underdeveloped areas. In Colombia, for instance, in
the pharmaceutical, synthetic fiber, and chemical industries 10 percent of
all patent-holders own 60 percent of all patents, and these 10 percent are
all foreign MNCs.[4]

Concentrated control of technology is one of the most effective means
to establish oligopoly power over the market place, restricting the development of local competition and permitting, as we shall see, an astounding
rate of profits, the greater majority of which leave the country. Once such

a process is under way, it becomes cumulative and self-perpetuating (see Table 2). The initial institutional purpose of patent rights, i.e., to stimulate *domestic* inventiveness, is self-defeating, since the wherewithal to pursue research and development (R&D) goes increasingly to foreign firms. Over time local business enterprises lose access not only to mechanical technology to compete, but perhaps more importantly to the human technical skills which can be accumulated only through experience in order to allow further development. In the end domestic firms are either absorbed by the MNCs or must resort to the "licensing" of their technology, as is the actual case today in Latin America. With such licensing comes a number of restrictions, enumerated below, on the ability of these enterprises and their nations to develop in the future.

Underdevelopment: The Structure of Finance

Such are the vicious circles which emerge in the interplay between the economic structure of underdevelopment in the LDCs and the technological power of the MNCs. A similar set of vicious circles is also at play in the financial patterns of these countries. Of first importance in assessing the investment financing aspects of the particular industrialization process described above is the expensiveness of the technology being used. It is also well-known that in almost all LDCs there is a scarcity of local savings available to be channeled into financial capital for productive investments. This scarcity of savings is due not only to the LDCs' low level of income, but also to the fact that a certain portion of savings leaves the country. That is, foreign firms repatriate a significant part of their profits, and indigenous wealth-holders also channel a part of their savings out to MNCs (the so-called phenomenon of "capital-flight"). Adding to the outflow of savings through repatriated profits and capital-flight is the increasing debt-repayments to bilateral (e.g., AID) and multilateral (e.g., World Bank) aid agencies on loans granted in the 1960s. Taken together, the magnitude of these outflows has led a number of writers to comment that in aggregate terms the poor countries of the world are now ironically helping to finance the rich countries, that is, the financial outflows from LDCs far exceed the inflows.[5]

There is thus a twofold dilemma in the financial structure of LDCs. On the one hand, there is a growing gap between the supply of *available* local savings and the demand for investment funds to alleviate the growing poverty *and* the growing awareness of it by the people of these countries, via increased literacy, improved communications, and the ensuing demonstration effects. On the other hand, the particular technology which the industrialization process necessitates not only is expensive, but must be paid for in foreign, not local, exchange. The relative reduction in LDCs' exports[6] which has reduced their ability to generate foreign exchange,[6] plus the relative increase in foreign exchange outflows versus inflows, has brought about the well-known problem of the "foreign exchange bottle-neck." Even when there are sufficient savings to finance needed investment projects, the investment may not take place because savings in local currency cannot be translated into foreign exchange for the purchase of the imported technology required by the project.

The upshot of this twofold dilemma (inadequate amounts of local savings and foreign exchange), from the viewpoint of domestic enterprises, is a rather perverse form of non-competitive financing patterns in most LDCs. Contrary to accepted notions about multinational companies in poor countries, these firms do not bring their own finance capital from abroad, but rather the overwhelming majority of their financing is derived from local (host country) sources. This fact will be given statistical clarity below, but what is important for the present discussion is the impact on domestic enterprises. Namely, the subsidiaries of MNCs in LDCs borrow from local financial institutions with the credit rating and financial resources backup of the entire global network of the parent MNC of which they are a part. This is in contrast to the credit rating and financial resources backup of the infinitely smaller, typical local business enterprise when it attempts to obtain finance capital. The vicious circle begins to close. The local financial institution, faced with limited loan capital relative to its demand and, like any other business, interested in risk-minimization and profit-maximization, will inevitably show a lending pattern biased toward the subsidiaries of MNCs.

This conclusion is even more obvious when the local financial institution is, in fact, a branch or subsidiary of a so-called private multinational bank, such as Bank of America, First National City Bank of New York, etc. These banks are playing a powerful role in the financial structures of the Third World where in many instances they control close to 50 percent of the private deposits of a country.[7] The LDC operation of a multinational bank will prefer lending to the subsidiaries of MNCs for the same reasons that locally controlled financial institutions do. In addition, in such a lending operation there is more at stake than just the particular profitability of one or a series of loans in a single country.

It is a well-established fact that the worldwide parent networks of banks and corporations are not two distinct entities, separated "at arm's length" by a competitive market in which one is a seller and the other a buyer. Instead there are interlocking interests of common ownership, management, and technical personnel in the groups that control banks and corporations.[8] Furthermore, whatever the consequences of these interlocking interests may be, there is a second well-established fact of a near perfect correlation between the worldwide expansion of MNCs and the commensurate expansion by multinational banks.[9] Whether the banks or the corporations led in this expansion is not of key importance; rather, what is important is that a mutual process of interdependent expansion characterized by common familiarity, experience, and objectives has developed. The commonalities lock together in a theme of expansion, where the expansion is based on the facilitation of an industrialization model most particularly suited to the competitive advantages of the MNC and, therefore, to the multinational banks. Thus, even if domestic businesses in LDCs could offer the branch offices of multinational banks better borrowing terms than MNCs, it is highly unlikely that these banks would forego their long-range global interests for the short-range local interests of a branch office.

The vicious circles emanating from the financial structures of under-development are now closed. The results for the development of national enterprises are similar to those in the case of our analysis of the technology structures: the bargaining power of MNCs to obtain finance capital is far greater than for local competitors, the degree of this financial bargaining power being greater the more dynamic a particular industry is.[10] This relatively greater bargaining power in finance has, over time, the same consequences as it does in technology. It becomes the equivalent, as noted above, of what the economist calls oligopoly power, meaning the power to erect "barriers to entry" against potential new competition or, on the other side of the same coin, the power to eliminate existing competition usually through the absorption of or buying into local firms.

Structural Impact of MNCs: Concentration and Power

Our analysis of the economic structure of LDCs, with reference to technology and finance, has shown why MNCs have a relatively high and ever-growing degree of oligopoly power in contrast to national firms in LDCs. Just how great this power is can be determined from the empirical reality of societies in underdevelopment. A focus on pre-1970 Chile will reflect this reality for almost all LDCs in which MNCs operate. In the industrial sector between 1967 and 1969, foreign participation (in terms of assets owned) increased from 16.6 to 20.3 percent, while domestic participation diminished from 76.1 to 63.0 percent, the difference between the two being made up of state owned firms. Of the 100 largest industrial firms (on the basis of asset size) in the country, 49 were effectively controlled by MNCs; when the sample was expanded to the largest 160 firms, over 51 percent were under the control of MNCs. Even these figures do not accurately convey the degree of concentration involved. When we look at control by industry, we see that in 7 of the more important industries of Chile, 1 to 3 foreign firms controlled not less than 51 percent of production in each industry. In a behavioral analysis of 22 of the largest MNC operations in the country, 5 of the MNC subsidiaries were monopolists in their respective industrial markets, 6 were duopolists, and 8 were oligopolists with each of these 8 being the largest supplier in its market. For 18 of these subsidiaries for which rate of growth in sales data were available, 16 showed a growth rate much higher than the average for the industrial sector as a whole. These figures reflect not only the reality of Chile prior to 1970, but are representative of most LDCs where MNCs are currently operating. Taken together, these concentration indicators demonstrate the degree of oligopoly power of MNCs in the Third World as well as their ability to increase that power over time.[11]

Thus far this work has attempted to convey to the reader a basic understanding of the meaning of underdevelopment as it relates to the power of MNCs. This understanding of the economic environment of Third World countries should facilitate the analysis of the impacts of MNCs on these nations, which follows in the next section. We have shown that the bargaining power, or its equivalent, the oligopoly power of the multinational corporations, is a function of the institutional conditions and the economic structure of LDCs. As the term underdevelopment implies, the institutions of poor countries are either weak and outdated or largely non-existent. Thus, compared to the more developed countries, there is little countervailing power or "checks and balances" via government and organized labor to set limits on the power of the modern international corporation. The institutional conditions described refer basically to non-business institutions which, because of their malfunctioning and/or absence, make the MNC in a Third World country a different institutional force than need necessarily be the case when it operates in an advanced industrial society.

If the non-business institutions of government and organized labor cannot act as a sufficient check on the power of the MNC in a Third World country, there still remains the check of other business institutions, namely, domestic competition. But the nature of the economic structure of underdevelopment, exemplified in the technological and financial spheres, makes it highly unlikely that domestic business institutions will be able to perform this function, because most LDCs have embarked upon an industrialization process, highly similar to those of advanced industrialized nations, as the chief means of bringing about economic growth. Given this industrialization process and the nature of the technological and financial needs to implement it, the result is a diminution in the power of domestic enterprises to compete and a further augmentation in the oligopoly power of MNCs. Having presented the rationale and evidence for the manner in which MNCs achieve their relatively powerful positions in the economies of LDCs, we turn now to an analysis of how that power reflects itself in their day-to-day operations and of the resulting impact upon the people of these countries.

MYTH OR REALITY:
THE CONTRIBUTIONS OF MULTINATIONAL CORPORATIONS

The description and evaluation of the behavior of MNCs in the Third World will be divided into three specific sections. The choice of this breakdown for our analysis is based on what many believe to be the three most potentially important areas in which MNCs can contribute to the development of LDCs: in technology, in financial inflows, and in the alleviation of balance of payments problems. Within each of these sections, we shall proceed from a description of operational behavior to an evaluation of its impact. It is important here to mention briefly the overall criterion which serves as the basis of our evaluation.

The criterion is a simple one, although one which until recently has been relatively ignored by students of development, particularly by economists who have been trained in the orthodoxy of neo-classical analysis. We shall employ the analytical tools of the latter, but our definition of development, i.e., our evaluation criterion, shall be different than that most frequently used. It will not be assumed that an increase in average per capita income constitutes "development." Instead, a MNC activity and its impact will be judged a contribution to development only if it results in an increase in the consumption potential of the poorest 60 percent of a LDC's population. For we believe that unless economic growth brings some alleviation to those suffering most, such growth is a contribution not to development but rather to the continued underdevelopment of Third World nations.

The Technology Contribution: Employment, Income Distribution, Costs

The United Nations estimated that in 1960 approximately 27 percent of the population of Third World countries were unemployed. By 1970, the estimate of the percentage of the active population unemployed had gone beyond 30 percent.[12] Even these global macro figures for LDCs as a whole, however, underestimate the dramatic dimension of the unemployment problems in Latin America, ironically called the "more developed" region of the Third World relative to Asia and Africa. A 1968 study estimated that by 1971, 36 percent of Colombia's labor force would be unemployed, and later studies from Colombia have confirmed that the estimate is more than being fulfilled.[13] A 1965 analysis of manpower in Peru showed that of the available Peruvian labor force, "43 percent are not needed in the production of that nation's national product."[14] In 1960 (the last year for which comparative country estimates are available), the unemployment equivalent ranged from 22 percent in Argentina, Brazil, and Mexico to 42 percent in the poorer countries of Central America and the Caribbean, and as noted, unemployment has been progressively increasing since then.[15]

Employment: Causes and Impact. Is there any hope for at least a partial diminution of the problem in the near future? If the past is any indication, the answer is no. All projections indicate that the problem will worsen, not diminish. The Prebisch report concluded that with population growing at approximately 3 percent in many countries of the region, total output would have to grow by 8 percent per annum between 1970 and 1980 in order to absorb current unemployment as well as the new additions to the labor force. To maintain the 1960 unemployment levels, total output would have to grow at a yearly rate of 6 percent for 1970 to 1980, a rate never before achieved in the region.[16]

An underlying cause of the unemployment crisis rests in the particular industrialization process being utilized to bring about economic growth. One important impact of this process was emphasized earlier, namely, that almost all of the technology in LDCs comes from, and is controlled by, foreign sources, that is, the MNCs. There is yet another and equally important impact of this industrialization process and the technology it necessitates; the technology transferred to the Third World by the MNCs has been designed for the resource conditions of the advanced industrialized nations where there is a relative abundance of capital and a relative scarcity of labor. In other words, this technology is incapable of absorbing labor because it has been designed to do just the opposite, i.e., to be "labor saving and capital using." Thus the MNC drug companies use a technology in which only 3.4 percent of total costs are due to labor.[17] There is, of course, an obvious contradiction to have such technology entrenched in the industrialization processes of Third World countries where the resource conditions are an abundance of labor and an acute scarcity of capital. An example of the change in the employment capacity of the industries where MNCs have their most intensive expansion will show the dimensions of the contradiction in which the MNCs are pivotally involved.

A recent study in Colombia has derived an estimated index of the capital to labor requirements for the five modern manufacturing industries in which MNCs have concentrated most of their investments between 1960 and 1967.[18] In all five industries similar results were found. In the chemical products industry in 1960, it took 1.63 units of capital investment to employ 1 unit of labor; by 1967 it took 4.45 units of capital for 1 unit of labor employment. Thus, within the eight-year period, the investment requirements to employ a unit of labor almost tripled. This study also revealed that the increase in fixed investment to employ a unit of labor was smaller for the industrial manufacturing sector as a whole compared to the five specific industries where MNCs were concentrating their new investments. The International Labor Organization, in its independent analysis of Colombian unemployment, came to almost identical conclusions. It found that in the period 1957–1961 it took an average fixed investment of 45,000 pesos to employ one person in a modern manufacturing industry in which MNC technology was most used; in contrast, during the 1962–1966 period the figure had risen to 100,000 pesos (the figures are in constant 1958 pesos, corrected for inflation).[19] Finally, in a still more recent study of 257 manufacturing firms throughout Latin America, it was found that MNCs use almost one-half the number of employees per $10,000 of sales as do local firms.[20]

It is this process of ever more intensive substitution of capital for labor in the technology transferred by the MNCs which is one of the prime causes of the startling degree of unemployment in the Third World, a situation which Africa and Asia only recently have begun to face but which has been gnawing at Latin America since the 1920s. Between 1925 and 1960 the manufacturing sector was able to absorb only 5 million of the 23 million people who migrated into urban centers from the countryside,[21] and while the total output of modern manufacturing industries expanded relative to other activities so that it increased its share of national product from 11 percent in 1925 to 25 percent in 1970, the percent of the Latin American work force which it employed actually decreased from 14.4 to 13.8 over the same time period.[22] This, then, is the employment contribution of the technology of the multinational corporation to Third World countries: MNCs are eliminating many more jobs than they are creating.

Unemployment is only one dimension of poverty; the other is income distribution. It is clear that when a person becomes unemployed, without the assistance of social security and/or unemployment insurance, which is the case in LDCs, he will become economically impoverished. What many, particularly those unfamiliar with economics or LDCs, forget, however, is that poverty can also be the reflection of a highly unequal distribution of a country's income. Technology is a key variable in explaining unequal income distribution in countries undergoing increasing industrialization based to a large degree on private ownership of the required technology and in which there are no governmental programs for redistribution, again the case in LDCs.[23]

Income Distribution: Causes and Impact. In focusing on the relationship between MNCs' technology and income distribution in LDCs, we find that capital is replacing labor at a growing rate. Who receives the income generated by capital resources? Most LDC economies are based on the legal institutions of capitalism, meaning that the owners of capital resources receive the income generated by those resources. Where there are only a very small number of owners (and thus a very large number of non-owners) of capital, and where the technology used generates a larger proportion of income from capital than labor resources, then, by definition, income distribution will be highly unequal. In addition, where there is a relatively rapid change in technology biased toward labor saving techniques, and where capitalist legal institutions are not modified via, for example, more progressive tax rates to keep pace with this change, then, again by definition, income distribution will become even more unequal over time. This then is the second dimension of the growing poverty in LDCs, namely, the impact of the modern technology of the MNCs on the income distribution of these nations. Just how unequal is the distribution of national income in LDCs and how has it changed over time?

Irma Adelman and Cynthia Taft Morris, in a worldwide study of income distribution, noted a profound change in income distribution from a subsistence level to an average per capita income level of $800 during the industrialization period in Third World countries undergoing the type of industrialization described above. During this "take-off," the richest 5 percent of LDC populations experienced a "striking" increase in incomes both relatively and absolutely compared to the poorest 40 percent of the population.[24] Latin American countries in the midst of this industrialization provide a dramatic verification of this finding. In the 1960s, for example, Chile's average per capita income was approximately $600, but the richest 10 percent were receiving 40 percent of the national income or an actual per capita income of some $2,400, giving a family income higher than the majority of families in Western Europe.[25] In Mexico and Brazil, the situation is worse, and it is notable that these two countries have been by far the most favored investment targets of the MNCs in Latin America.

In Mexico in the early 1950s the ratio of individual income of the richest 20 percent to individual income of the poorest 20 percent was 10 to 1. By the middle 1960s, the ratio had increased to 17 to 1.[26] Yet even these aggregate figures becloud the actuality of what is taking place in the urban industrial zones where MNC investment is concentrated. For example, in the Mexico City area, the richest 20 percent received 62.5 percent of the area's income, while the poorest 20 percent attempted survival on 1.3 percent of the income.[27] In Brazil, where unprecedented increases in industrial output are being achieved, almost all of the benefits of that increase are going to the richest 5 percent. In the short span of ten years, their share of national income went from 27.8 percent (a U.S. Government estimate) or, depending on the source, 44 percent (a U.N. estimate) to a 1970 figure of 36.8 percent (U.S.) or 50 percent (U.N.).[28] And the income share of the poorest 40 percent, some 40 million of the Brazilian people, using the U.S.

Government figures as the conservative estimate, dropped from 10.6 to 8.1 percent during the ten years between 1960 and 1970.

This then is the second aspect of the contribution of the modern technology being transferred to the Third World by the MNCs. It is a contribution to the richest 5, 10, or 20 percent of these populations, but an absolute disservice to the human condition of the greater majority of the populations of LDCs.

The Dollar Cost of MNC Technology. We have one final note on the technology contribution, and this refers to the dollar value that MNCs place on their technology when it is transferred as part of their overall investment in their subsidiaries in LDCs. The sum of the investment value in establishing a subsidiary operation of an MNC is made up largely of the costs of plant and equipment. Of this sum, anywhere from 50 to 65 percent represents the cost of the subsidiary's technology, as valued by and received from the parent MNC. The dollar value placed on this technology is crucial to the overall investment figure claimed to have been made by the MNC and is important for both economic and political reasons. In many LDCs, for example, the tax rate on profits and/or excess profits is based on the dollar sum of profits calculated as a percentage of the value of fixed investment. This is the "rate of return"; it will be lower, and so too will be the tax liability of the subsidiary, the higher the value of fixed investment claimed. In addition, many LDCs place limitations on the amount of profits that can be repatriated by an MNC subsidiary in any given period, based on the value of the fixed investment; thus, the higher the fixed investment, the greater will be the dollar amount of profits that can be transferred out of the LDC.[29]

The declared fixed investment via the declared rate of return also has political significance to the managers of the MNCs. To maintain political stability in hospitable host countries is always a sensible business objective of MNC management. A key operational criterion then is to avoid charges of "exploitation" or, in the parlance of Western economists, charges of "excess profits." Since the empirical basis of such charges relies on the rate of return in the first instance, it is wise to keep that rate as "normal" as possible. MNCs thus wish to keep their declared values of transferred technology, and therefore fixed investment, as high as possible.

We can now look at some of the findings on the actual values of MNCs' transferred technology. From Mexico there have been numerous reported cases of secondhand technology being transferred to subsidiaries declared as either new equipment or valuated at prices much higher than could have been obtained on independent markets.[30] In Colombia, where detailed investigations have been undertaken, excessive overvaluation of the technology was found in *all* cases. For example, a parent MNC was selling machinery to its own subsidiary at prices 30 percent higher than those it was charging an independent Colombian firm for the identical items.[31] In another case, investigation revealed that the valuation of machinery declared at $1.8 million was in fact overstated by 50 percent, the true figure being $1.2 million. In the paper industry, an MNC subsidiary applied for an import permit for *used* machinery which it claimed had a value in excess of $1 million. The government agency then asked for competitive bids internationally on *new* models of the same machinery. The MNC's declared value for the used machinery was found to be 50 percent higher than bids received on the new machinery. Finally, in research conducted by the author, interviews were held with managers of subsidiaries in LDCs. In a number of cases, after a lengthy discussion of the impact of their operations on the host countries, these managers admitted that overvaluing their technology was a common practice.[32]

It is not difficult to understand how MNCs are able to commit these practices when we recall the introductory remarks on the meaning of underdevelopment in the sense of inadequate alternative sources of technology intensified by relative ignorance of international markets on the part of LDC buyers relative to their contemporaries in advanced industrialized nations.

The Financial Contribution and Absorption of Domestic Firms

A traditional argument in favor of MNC expansion in the Third World has been that they bring much needed finance capital. This argument holds that LDCs cannot generate sufficient savings in the form of foreign exchange holdings to purchase the foreign technology needed to implement investment projects. Another variant of this argument contends that even in the cases where there is no foreign exchange shortage, there is still a general shortage of domestic savings relative to the investment needs of these countries. Thus, the MNC is envisaged as contributing foreign savings, i.e., finance capital, to alleviate the general dearth of domestic savings and/or foreign exchange. The key assumption here is, of course, that the MNCs in fact do utilize foreign savings to finance their LDC operations. This assumption, incidentally, is also made by Marxist scholars who have held that MNCs expand from their capitalist home countries because of an excess of surplus finance capital relative to inadequate domestic investment opportunities.

The Origins of MNCs' Finance Capital. Upon investigation of the empirical facts, however, the assumption proves to be incorrect. Table 3 shows the argument to be more myth than reality.

Only 17 percent of the total finance capital used by MNCs in their gross investments came from non-local savings. It should be noted that in the last three years of the overall 1957–1965 period the figure dropped to 9 percent. Of more importance is the use of local savings in manufacturing, the most rapidly expanding of the three sectors. Here the figure of 78 percent of total local financing has been constant since 1960. Individual country studies covering 1965–1970 have also shown no change in this constancy.[33]

Of the finance capital being used by MNC subsidiaries in manufacturing, 38 percent comes from local "internal" sources, largely reinvested earnings, and 40 percent from local capital markets. While in an official accounting sense reinvested earnings are classified as funds from the home country, such a classification misses the real economic meaning of these reinvested earnings. That is, they were generated by the use of largely local resources to start with, both local financial and other resources. These reinvested

Table 3   Percentage of U.S. MNC Gross Investments in Latin America
Financed from Local versus Foreign Savings

		Origin of Finance Capital 1957–1965		
	(A)	(B) Reinvested Earnings and	(C) Local, Host	(D) Total Local
Area and Sector	USA	Depreciation	Country*	(B + C)
Latin America, total	17	59	24	83
Mining and Smelting	8	78	14	92
Petroleum	13	79	8	87
Manufacturing	22	38	40	78

* The original source labels "Local, Host Country" as "Local and Third Countries." Since the participation of third countries is such a small part, we have omitted the designation to avoid misleading labels.

Source: Fernando Fajnzylber, *Estrategia Industrial y Empresas Internacionales: Posicion Relativa de America y Brasil* (Rio de Janeiro: Naciones Unidas, CEPAL, November 1971).

earnings are local savings in the same sense that they are for a 100 percent domestically owned and controlled corporation, with one big exception. Whereas the future net profits (after taxes) from earnings reinvested today constitute, in the case of local firms, a net gain to the income of the LDC that most likely will stay *internalized* to the country, this is not the case for an MNC subsidiary. For the MNC's profit, although it represents a net gain in income for itself, will be largely *externalized* from the LDC and, therefore, will not be for the consumption or investment benefit of the local citizenry. This is borne out by the fact that over the period 1960–1968 MNCs repatriated on the average some 79 percent of their net profits, not to mention the additional remissions of royalties, interest, and other fees.[34] In manufacturing, repatriated profits were somewhat lower but increasing, going from 42 percent of net profits in 1960–1964 to 52 percent in 1965–1968.[35] For each dollar of net profit earned by an MNC subsidiary, 52 cents will leave the country *even though* 78 percent of the investment funds used to generate that dollar of profit came from local sources. If we look at all sectors in which MNCs operate in Latin America, the inflow-outflow accounting gets even worse. Each dollar of net profit is based on an investment that was 83 percent financed from local savings; yet only 21 percent of the profit remains in the local economy.[36]

MNCs not only use local savings to finance their equity investments, but also draw more heavily than domestic firms on local credit markets for short-term working capital loans. In fact, studies show that the MNCs operate on roughly one and one-half to two and one-half times the level of indebtedness of their domestic competition for any given level of total assets.[37] Again the use of largely local savings, in this case working capital, makes possible a productive activity, the profits of which largely benefit recipients external to the local economy.

Do the MNCs make a financial contribution to LDCs, that is, do they make a net addition to the supply of available local savings over time? The answer is no. Although we cannot make an exact quantitative estimate of this loss, from the magnitudes of the above indicators it is clear that there is a net decrease in the amount of local savings that are being utilized for the benefit of either indigent consumers or investors in the local economies of LDCs.

The Buying Out of Domestic Firms. The preceding paragraphs have attempted to correct the first of the two most prevalent misconceived notions about the financial contributions of MNCs to the economies of Third World nations. We turn now to the second of these two notions, namely, the specific use to which MNCs put their finance capital. It is commonly held that when a MNC invests in a LDC, even if it uses largely local savings, it at least channels that investment into the creation of *new* production facilities, facilities which otherwise would have been absent from the local economy. In turn, it is concluded that these new facilities represent a net addition to the productive assets of the LDC.

Again reference to the facts shows this notion to be more myth than reality and its implications therefore largely erroneous. The error can be seen when we refer to the information available on the "method of entry" by the MNCs into LDC economies. By method of entry is meant the use of the MNCs' investment capital, i.e., creation of a new production facility, expansion of a branch office into a subsidiary operation, or the buying out of a local, domestically controlled business. We have argued earlier that the vicious circles of the technology and financial structures of LDCs generate a process whereby the multinational corporations slowly and then increasingly absorb local business enterprises. This, in fact, is actually happening in Latin America.

Data now available on the 187 largest United States MNCs, which account for some 70 percent of all United States foreign investment in the region,[38] show that between 1958 and 1967 these firms established 1,309 subsidiaries. Of the 1,136 subsidiaries for which information on method of entry was available, the breakdown is as follows: 477 or more than 36 percent of these subsidiaries were formed by buying out local enterprises; of the 642 new subsidiaries, 503 or 45 percent of the total 1,309 actually were for new production, with the other 139 established as sales subsidiaries only; the remaining 17 of the total represented the expansion of branch into subsidiary operations. The figures become even more convincing when we examine the method of entry of new subsidiaries in the manufacturing sector in which the majority of the total were established and in which the MNCs are expanding fastest. For the 717 known new manufacturing subsidiaries, 331 or 46 percent did not establish new production but rather purchased existing domestic firms. Compared to the percentage of finance capital devoted to such acquisitions since 1929, the rate of increase is notable throughout. In addition, it was observed that in industries where the percentage of foreign investment going to acquisitions had decreased, the decline was "probably attributable in part to the scarcity of local firms (remaining) in these industries."[39]

The implications of this analysis for the Third World are clear in regard to the so-called financial contributions of MNCs. In the manufacturing sector, currently the most important to the future of development of Latin America, 78 percent of MNCs' foreign investments are financed from local savings. Of this finance capital, 46 percent is used to buy out existing locally controlled firms, whose profits would otherwise be retained domestically and thus contribute to local consumption and/or savings. But from the date of the acquisition and henceforth, some 52 percent of those profits leave the country, resulting in a net decrease in the LDCs' savings which would have been available *and* a net increase in their already acute shortage of foreign exchange. Given these results, it is impossible to see how the MNCs' financial impact on Third World countries could possibly assist in the alleviation of their underdevelopment.

Balance of Payment Contributions: Restrictions, Pricing, Actual Profits

We have already alluded to the acute foreign exchange shortages, termed "the balance of payments problem," which most Third World countries experience. It is well known that Latin America is experiencing the severest of difficulties in maintaining its ability to pay off foreign debts. There is an increasing negative gap between exports and imports, and the region's foreign debts are growing at a rapid rate in terms of repayments of past public and private loans. Concomitantly, outflows continue to mount on payments of profits, royalties, and interests for past MNC direct investment. While in the period 1951–1955 these latter items accounted for some 13 percent of the annual export earnings of the Latin American countries, by the 1966–1969 time period, they took 21 percent of those earnings.[40]

Thus it is not surprising that experts in both the offices of Wall Street and the government buildings of the Third World are taking an intense interest in the balance of payments impacts of the multinational corporations. And it is perhaps also not surprising that experts come to different conclusions on the matter.[41]

Our prior discussion of the sources and uses of MNCs' financial capital indicated that the impact on foreign exchange is largely negative. In this section, we shall go beyond an analysis of the sources and uses of finance capital to explore a second dimension of the balance of payments impacts of MNCs, the export and import behavior of these global corporations and their remittances of royalties and service fees. The latter item is the so-called managerial fee paid to the parent MNC for technical assistance rendered to its own subsidiaries and joint ventures, as well as to licensees of technology. These royalty and fee payments have reached significant proportions, accounting for some 25 percent of the total returns from all United States MNCs' foreign investments in 1970.[42] As for the significance of MNCs' export and import operations, in 1968 United States MNCs were responsible for 40 percent of Latin America's manufactured exports and in 1966, some 33 percent of its total exports, while accounting for more than a third of the region's imports from the United States in 1964.[43] It should be emphasized here that these percentages refer only to so-called *intracompany transactions*, exports and imports between subsidiaries of the same parent network. From the United States side, these intra-company transactions were very important, reflected by the fact that United States MNCs shipped some 33 percent of *total* United States exports directly to their subsidiaries overseas.[44] Thus the internal, intra-company transactions of exports and imports and the payments of royalties and fees between subsidiaries of the same parent are both a significant part of the MNCs' total revenues and an important component of the foreign exchange outflows and inflows of the countries in which they are located.

It has been claimed that the MNCs can make a significant contribution to raising the foreign exchange earnings of Third World countries through their ability to export, particularly manufactured goods. On the surface this argument would appear correct, given the competitive advantages of the technology and worldwide marketing systems of the MNCs compared to local firms. There are a number of considerations, however, which this argument overlooks. First, if MNCs have subsidiaries manufacturing similar products in many countries, which most of them do, would the subsidiaries of the same parent want to compete with each other through exports? Second, even where the parents have complementary production between subsidiaries so that intersubsidiary exports and imports are desirable, what are the prices on such exports and imports since they are internal transactions and not subject to the competitive pressures of the open market? Third, what are the tax and other financial criteria at work which would make these prices different from those received or paid by local firms dealing with independent buyers and sellers on the international market? Fourth, what does the available empirical evidence tell us concerning the initial argument and the considerations we have introduced? Finally, besides the exporting by MNC subsidiaries, what impact does the licensing of their technology to local firms have on the latter's ability to export?

The MNCs and Exports: Restrictions. We shall start with the last question first. One study, investigating the licensing agreements between local firms in LDCs and the MNCs, has shown that in most cases there are total prohibitions on using this technology in the production of exports. The study was based on 409 "transfer of technology" contracts in the five countries of the Andean Group, i.e., Bolivia, Colombia, Chile, Ecuador, and Peru. The results showed that 92 percent of the nationally owned firms and 79 percent of the wholly owned MNC subsidiaries were totally prohibited from exporting by the MNC parent from whom they had licensed their technology.[45]

As telling as these figures are, they are, nevertheless, biased downward. In many of the contracts which permitted some exporting, the effect was really total prohibition, since either they limited the firms to a small neighboring market in which the MNCs had no interest or they limited exports to distant countries which local firms could not hope to penetrate. And these practices are not unique to the Andean countries. Similar results have been revealed by government and U.N. studies in India, Pakistan, the Philippines, Mexico, Iran, etc.[46] There is a profound impact of these "restrictive business practices," to use the formal language of the U.N., on the export capacity of domestic firms and their LDC economies. At a time when the political leaders[47] of the more developed countries are encouraging Third World countries to export more, their own MNCs are making it virtually impossible for them to enter the one export market which in the long run is viable, namely, manufactured exports.

We turn now to the question of the export performance of the MNC subsidiaries themselves. As the above study illustrates, it does not necessarily follow that the MNCs will export from LDC locations even though they may have the technological and marketing prerequisites. For in the Andean Group 79 percent of the MNC subsidiaries were prohibited by their parents from engaging in exporting, and these findings are again not unique to these countries. In fact, studies have found that in Latin America, manufacturing MNCs on the average export less than 10 percent of their total sales; while in Europe, United States firms average about 25 percent.[48] There are exceptions, however. Some MNC subsidiaries do export significant *volumes*, depending on the country and industry in which they are located.

MNCs and Exports: Performance and Pricing. American MNCs account for some 40 percent of Latin America's manufactured exports, and they have achieved this level of export participation within the span of the past twenty years. Yet the figure is a deceptive one if it is intended to imply that MNCs are therefore making a significant positive impact on the balance of payments of Third World countries in general. Manufactured exports constitute only 16.6 percent of the region's total exports, and well over half of these exports are from only three of the twenty-one countries, Argentina, Brazil, and Mexico.[49] Further, a detailed econometric analysis has determined that, relative to local firms, MNC subsidiaries performed significantly better only in these three countries and only in terms of export sales to other Latin American countries.[50] In contrast, for exports to the rest of the world, where one would expect the technological and marketing superiority of the MNCs to be most crucial, their export performance was not significantly different from domestic enterprises. For the remaining countries of the region, the MNCs were outperformed on exports to the rest of the world by firms which had substantial domestic participation, while on exports to other Latin American countries the MNCs performed no differently than their domestic counterparts.[51]

Finally, in terms of the potential export contribution of MNCs, we turn to the question of the prices they received for exports relative to domestic companies trading with independent buyers. Let us first note, however, some of the reasons why the export price received by an MNC subsidiary will be different from the international market price received by a local firm exporting a similar item.

The price put on an export or import between MNC subsidiaries of the same parent is termed in the business literature an intra-company transfer price, or "transfer price." The business literature is also replete with reasons and documentation on why and how transfer prices frequently deviate sharply from the market price of these goods.[52] For example, if a subsidiary exporting in country X is faced with higher corporate tax rates than the importing subsidiary of the same parent in country M, then the parent will pay less *total* taxes for both subsidiaries and earn more *total* net profits by directing the exporting subsidiary to undervalue its exports. Another and even more profitable variant of this pricing technique is to direct the underpriced exports first to a tax-free port (so-called tax-havens) and then re-export the goods at their normal market value (or perhaps now overvalued) to the subsidiary of final destination. Either way total profits are higher than they would be had the MNC followed the "spirit of the law." Of more importance here, however, is the obvious impact on the local economy of the LDC in which such exports originate. LDC governments severely short of needed tax revenues to service the masses of illiterate, undernourished, and unemployed people in their countries are now deprived of that much more tax revenue so that a MNC can "maximize," as economists are prone to say, their global profits. All this through a simple but modern accounting technique called transfer pricing.

But we are getting ahead of our facts at this point. Let us first look at the information on export pricing and then import pricing by MNCs in Latin America. A look at the export pricing of a large number of MNCs in manufacturing industries in Mexico, Brazil, Argentina, and Venezuela shows that 75 percent of these firms sold exports only to other subsidiaries of the same parents. In turn, these 75 percent on the average *underpriced their exports by some 40 percent* relative to the prices being received by local firms.[53] The bulk of the exports of these countries and these MNCs were going to Latin American destinations, and it was for these destinations that the underpricing took place. Moreover *an average level of underpricing of 50 percent* was found in six other Latin American countries where MNCs were engaged in exporting to subsidiaries in rest of the world destinations.[54]
MNCs and Imports: Tie-in Clauses. The transfer price placed on the imports of an MNC subsidiary will be *higher* than the normal market price in the event that the parent desires to transfer funds extra-legally from that subsidiary to some other part of its network. In other words, the overpricing of imports accomplishes the same objectives and is done for similar reasons as the underpricing of exports. As a professor of business administration has recently observed:

> . . . there is the problem of transfer pricing: in a cluster of corporations (subsidiaries) controlled by the same top management, earnings may be changed at will by changing the charges for goods and services within the cluster. Presumably, rational management will use the mechanism of transfer prices in a way that will minimize the total tax burden on the (parent) company, showing higher earnings in countries where the rate of taxation is lowest.[55]

Before examining the empirical facts of overpricing of imports, we should first mention an additional "restrictive clause" in the transfer of technology contracts negotiated between MNC parents and their subsidiaries and licensees. This is the so-called "tie-in clause" which requires the subsidiary or the licensee (depending on who is acquiring the technology) to purchase intermediate parts and capital goods from the same parent MNC which supplies the basic technology. This practice is quite common and part of the day-to-day operational behavior of MNCs in the Third World. For example, in the Andean Group study, 67 percent of the investigated contracts had tie-in clauses.[56] The results were no different in other countries like India, Pakistan, etc.[57]

It is ironical that although this type of clause is in basic violation of the antitrust laws of the MNC's home countries, it continues to be put into practice in LDCs.[58] The fact that the legal institutions of LDCs cannot yet cope with these problems strongly underlines the differences in the oligopoly power of MNCs in advanced industrialized versus Third World countries.

MNCs and Imports: Pricing. Having noted this oligopoly power of the parent MNCs with reference to the imports of both subsidiaries and domestic companies, we can now examine the empirical evidence on import overpricing. Since the information is relatively unknown to economists and non-economists alike, particularly outside of Latin America, we shall devote some detail to it in Table 4.

The Colombian data on overpricing are not unique to that country. Similar results have been discovered in other parts of Latin America and in other regions, such as the Philippines and Pakistan. In Chile, overpricing ranges from 30 to more than 700 percent, in Peru from 50 to 300 percent, and in Ecuador from 75 to 200 percent. Apparently the techniques for extra-legally transferring funds out of LDCs does not stop short of overpricing actual imports. During a two-day interview with the head of a European MNC subsidiary in a South American country, the author was shown shipping crates which had just cleared local customs. In this isolated case, the shipping crates contained less than 30 percent of their declared contents although the payment to an offshore subsidiary of the parent was for 100 percent of the declared contents at an overpricing of 2500 percent.[59] One can only speculate as to what extent this case represents the day-to-day behavior of MNCs in the Third World.

But even these *average* figures on overpricing, as high as they are, do not portray the actuality of what was happening in the case of specific products. Thus, tetracycline, a modern antibiotic increasingly replacing penicillin, was overpriced by 948 to 987 percent. And in the case of librium and valium, drugs used in the treatment of mental illness, the overpricing reached figures of 6500 and 8200 percent, respectively; while in electronics transistors were overvalued by 1100 percent and electric motors by 404 percent.[60] Who paid for the overpricing of such items as tetracycline? The Colombian consumer paid, in a country where the average per capita income is around $300. The total value of the overpricing for the *actually sampled* items in the four industries was more than $4 million. If the average overpricing is extended and assumed to hold for the rest of the products and MNCs in the drug industry, and there is no reason to assume otherwise, then the total loss to the 1968 Colombian balance of payments was on the order of $20 million with a loss in governmental tax revenues of some $10 million, and this from one industry alone![61]

The Triangular Trade: Pricing and Royalties. In the Colombian investigation, it was found that a large proportion of the overpriced imports involved a "triangular trade." That is, they were shipped from a United States or European based parent or subsidiary of the parent to a holding company in Panama. In Panama, a tax-haven, the prices of these articles were raised to their stated overpriced levels and then re-exported to Colombia.[62] Thus, the MNCs involved avoided tax payments on their true profits *both* in the country of export origin and in Colombia.

Panama also serves another function. The holding companies of many United States and European MNCs in Panama are the companies for which

Table 4 Overpricing of Imported Intermediate Parts by Foreign Ownership Structure: Colombia 1968

Ownership Structure	Pharmaceutical Industry			Rubber Industry			Chemical Industry			Electronics Industry		
	a	b	c*	a	b	c	a	b	c	a	b	c
Foreign Owned	50%	25%	155%	33%	60%	40%	30%	12%	25.5%	40%	90%	16%–60%
Joint Ventures	n.a.	n.a.	n.a.	n.a.	n.a.	n.a.	45%	37%	20.2%	50%	90%	6%–50%

Code: a: approximate percentage of sales of sample firms relative to total sales of firms with a similar ownership structure
b: total volume of imports sampled and evaluated as a percentage of the firm's total imports
c: weighted average of overpricing of evaluated imports
n.a.: not available

* Individual firm data are as follows (in percent): #1: 253.6; #2: 133.7; #3: 132.8; #4: 306.2; #5: 483; #6: 39.5; #7: 179.4; #8: 79.1; #9: 58.3; #10: 73.8; #11: 475.4; #12: 374.7; #13: 177.5; #14: 164.8; #15: 60.4; #16: 476.9; #17: 34.4.

Source: Constantine Vaitsos, "Interaffiliate Charges by Transnational Corporations and Intercountry Income Distribution," submitted in partial fulfillment of the requirements for the degree of Doctor of Philosophy at Harvard University, June 1972, p. 48.

many of their foreign investments in Latin America are registered. In Peru, for instance, Panama is the second largest foreign country in which foreign investments are registered.[63] This procedure permits the channeling of royalty and fee payments to Panama, thereby giving the MNCs a substantial flexibility as to where they ultimately report their income. The income generated from royalties and fees alone is large and, in fact, most often considerably greater than reported profits received from subsidiaries. In the Andean Group, for MNC subsidiaries, royalties paid to the parent are fixed at anywhere from 10 to 15 percent of gross or net sales, depending on the particular company.[64] Since a considerable part of the final sale price is based on imported parts which are overvalued, the MNCs multiply their unearned profits, first via the import overpricing and second through that component of royalties derived from an inflated sales price due to the overpricing. The earnings thus generated are impressive relative both to the MNCs' reported profits and to the foreign exchange shortages of these countries. Thus in Chile the outflow of royalties is three times greater than profit remittances, and in Colombia the payments for royalties alone use up approximately 10 percent of non-coffee export earnings.[65]

Reported vs. Actual Rates of Return. The above figures speak well enough for themselves. We can now add these figures to the "reported profits" and the payments of royalties and fees from MNC subsidiaries. Taken together, overpricing of imports plus reported profits, royalties, and fees give the total dollar value of profits generated by a subsidiary in a given year. This total dollar value of "effective profits" can then be divided into the subsidiary's declared net worth of its investment (including reinvested earnings). The resulting answer is called the "annual rate of return on investment." Vaitsos and his group have performed this exercise for 100 percent parent owned MNC drug subsidiaries in Colombia. The results are shown in Table 5.

Table 5   On Investment: Annual Rate of Return:
Wholly Owned MNC Drug Subsidiaries: Colombia, 1968

MNC Subsidiary	Rate of Return	MNC Subsidiary	Rate of Return	MNC Subsidiary	Rate of Return
#1	197.3%	#6	38.1%	#11	88.8%
#2	94.4%	#7	402.3%	#12	256.8%
#3	247.0%	#8	126.1%	#13	56.5%
#4	708.3%	#9	44.2%	#14	378.9%
#5	962.1%	#10	138.0%	#15	352.8%

Average of Declared Returns to Colombian Tax Authorities   6.7%
Average of Effective Returns   136.3%

Source: Vaitsos, "Interaffiliate Charges . . . ," *op. cit.*, pp. 69–73.

As astoundingly high as these rates of return are, they undoubtedly *understate* the actual sums earned by these MNCs. First, the above calculations do not include the probability of export underpricing, which as previously shown is quite high. Second, these returns are based on the net worth of investment as declared by the subsidiaries. As pointed out earlier, all evidence to date indicates there is substantial overvaluation of declared investment of approximately 30 to 50 percent. Thus, the correction for this overvaluation would significantly raise the above figures. One Colombian economist has commented on the fact that between 1960 and 1968 the average *reported* rate of return for MNCs in all manufacturing sectors of the country was 6.4 percent. He found it "difficult to accept" that these MNCs would continue to enter Colombia at this rate of reported profitability while national firms were showing higher returns and the interest rate in financial markets was running between 16 and 20 percent.[66] Hopefully, the foregoing analysis helps to explain why the MNCs continue to expand in Third World countries like Colombia.

SUMMARY AND CONCLUSIONS

There can be little doubt as to our overall conclusions concerning the impact of MNCs on Third World nations. We have found more myth than reality in the claims made about the three most important contributions of MNCs. Our analysis of the contribution in technology revealed a basic cause of further unemployment and a further concentration of already extremely unequal income distribution, while noting the excessive prices being charged by the MNCs in transferring this technology. Upon examination, the financial contribution turns out to be a financial drain, decreasing both current consumption and available local savings and, thus, future consumption for the vast majority of LDC inhabitants. The third area of analysis, the balance of payments contribution, led to similar conclusions. In contrast to a contribution, the empirical information showed no superior export performance by MNCs relative to local firms unless it was accompanied by export underpricing. Concomitantly, exports were further limited via restrictions placed on their technology by the MNCs. While potential inflows were minimized, the balance of payments outflows were accentuated through import overpricing and inflated royalty payments.

There can be little doubt that such an impact can only contribute to the further inpoverishment of the poorest 60 to 80 percent of Third World populations. Summing up the specific consequences discussed in this paper, however, leads to an overall consequence which should be briefly mentioned. In the Third World, the MNCs are involved in a structural process which cannot be ignored. We have already referred to the fact that this process permits an ever greater control over the technology and finances of the majority of LDCs, resulting in what Celso Furtado, among others, has shown to be an ever-growing external dependency of the poor nations on the few rich nations of the world. Besides the transfer-in of inappropriate technology and the transfer-out of financial resources, this process includes one further destabilizing force, the transfer, via advertising and mass-media programming, of a consumption ideology, the goals of which only 30 percent at best and, more realistically, 20 percent of LDC populations can hope to achieve in the foreseeable future. These consumption goals do not go unheeded by the greater majority of these countries; rather, they are observed, absorbed, and become part of the poor, the not-so-poor, and the rich. Thus, just as the MNCs are involved in the restructuring of the production sector, so too are they a major force in restructuring the consumption "sector." Yet there is a rather blatant contradiction at work here, for the new structure of consumption is in serious imbalance with the inadequate consumption capacity generated by the very production structure which the MNCs have so pivotally helped to create; and, therefore, the MNCs themselves have negated any possibility for attaining the new consumption goals by all except a small minority. It is perhaps here that we can discover a major cause for the profound and growing frustration that is often found in underdeveloped countries. When many share the same basic and intense frustration, the problem goes beyond the realm of economics and becomes truly a social and political one.

Latin America, the region which has nurtured this frustration relatively longer than any other Third World area, has already witnessed three patterns of political response to this problem. The political decision of Brazil and Mexico has been to continue the present reliance on the MNCs via the expedient of growing political oppression. Cuba and Chile are attempting to detach themselves from industrialization via the MNCs by establishing socialist institutions. And the Peruvian military appears to be in the midst of deciding to what extent it desires, let alone is able, to minimize and/or modify the role of MNCs in order to pursue a new form of national development. What the long-run viability of any of these three responses will be cannot be dealt with here. There is, however, a clear message. The continued and unaltered expansion of the MNCs into the Third World will increase the instability of these societies and bring about significant political change.

To the extent that such political change will reduce the bargaining power of the MNCs in these countries and thereby diminish the transfer of income to MDCs, the result will be a negative impact in the general level of affluence in advanced nations. Such an interpretation could, in fact, be given to the creation of the Organization of Petroleum Exporting Countries (OPEC) and the growing "Energy Crisis" being faced in the United States and other MDCs. OPEC has succeeded in significantly reducing the flow of income from poor to rich nations. This means that by the late 1970s the rising price of energy, the backbone of modern industrial society, will have negatively affected the consumption levels of the greater majority of people residing in MDCs. If new mechanisms for increasing Third World bargaining power over MNCs in the manufacturing sector are found, then there will be even more profound implications for maintaining present consumption styles in the rich nations. Whether or not the United States, Japan, and Western Europe will permit such mechanisms to become reality can only be speculated upon and such speculation lies within the domain not of economics but of an analysis of power and the use of power by the major actors in the world political economy.[67]

NOTES

1. On unemployment, see Dudley Seers, "Poverty in the Third World," lecture for The American University's Social Science Seminar, Washington, D.C., December 16, 1972; also International Labor Organization (ILO), *Hacia el Pleno Empleo*, Un Programa para Colombia, Preparado por una Mision Internacional Organizada por la Oficina Internacional del Trabajo, Ginebra 1970. On income distribution, see Cynthia Taft Morris and Irma Adelman, "An Anatomy of Income Distribution Patterns in Developing Nations: A Summary of Findings," Economic Staff Paper No. 116, IBRD (September 1971). On income distribution in Brazil, see H. P. Miller, unpublished study (Washington, D.C.: U.S. Bureau of the Census, 1971). On income distribution in Latin America, see United Nations Economic Commission for Latin America (ECLA), *The Distribution of Income in Latin America* (E/CN-12/868) (New York: UN, 1970); UN-ECLA, *Economic Survey for Latin America, 1971* (E/EN-12/935) (New York: UN, June 1972); UN-ECLA, *Economic Survey for Latin America* (New York: UN, 1969); UN-ECLA, *The Process of Industrial Development in Latin America* (New York: UN, 1966).

2. Constantine Vaitsos, "Patents Revisited: Their Function in Developing Countries," *The Journal of Development Studies* (1973).

3. John M. Blair, *Economic Concentration: Structure, Behavior and Public Policy* (New York: Harcourt Brace Jovanovich, Inc., 1972), p. 205.

4. Vaitsos, "Patents . . . ," *op. cit.*, p. 12.

5. See R. Prebisch, *Change and Development: Latin America's Great Task*, report submitted to the Inter-American Development Bank, Washington, D.C., July 1970; UN-ECLA, *Economic Survey for Latin America, 1971, op. cit.*

6. From 1950 to 1970 LDCs' exports decreased from 33 percent of world exports to 19 percent. Peter Peterson, Presidential Task Force on International Development, *U.S. Foreign Assistance in the 1970's: A New Approach* (Washington, D.C.: Government Printing Office, 1970), p. 8.

7. Miguel Wionczek, "La Banca Extranjera en America Latina," report prepared for Novena Reunion de Technicos de los Bancos Centrales del Continente Americano, Lima, 17–22 de Noviembre, 1969; Aldo Ferrer, "El Capital Extranjero en la Economia Argentina," *Trimestre Economico*, No. 150 (Abril–Junio, 1971); Aldo Ferrer, "Empresa Extranjera: Observaciones sobre la Experiencia Argentina," seminar on *Politica de Inversiones Extranjeras y Transferencia de Technologia en America Latina*, organized by ILDIS/Flasco, Santiago, 1971.

8. See John M. Blair, *op. cit.*, pp. 75 ff.

9. Miguel Wionczek, *op. cit.*

10. Celso Furtado, "The Concept of External Dependence in the Study of Underdevelopment," paper presented to the Union for Racial Political Economies, Washington, D.C., November 10, 1972.

11. The figures for Chile are taken from Luis Pacheco, "La Inversion Extranjera y las Corporaciones Internacionales en el Desarrollo Industrial Chileno," in *Proceso a la Industrializacion Chilena* (Santiago: Ediciones Nueva Universidad, Universidad Catolica de Chile, 1972); Corporacion de Fomento de la Produccion (CORFO), *Las Inversiones Extranjeras en la Industria Chilena Periodo 1960–1969*, Publicacion No. 57-A/71 (Febrero 1971). For an analysis of Mexico, see Ricardo Cinta, "Burguesia Nacional y Desarrollo," in *El Perfil de Mexico en 1980*, III (1972), pp. 165–209. Mexico: Siglo Veintiuno. For an analysis of Argentina, see Aldo Ferrer, "El Capital Extranjero . . . ," *op. cit.*

12. The estimate of the "equivalent of the population" is based on the percentage of unemployment plus the percentage (weighted) of underemployment (i.e., less than substantial full employment throughout one work year) of the labor force. United Nations Economic and Social Council, *Development Digest*, No. 4 (1969).

13. *Survey of the Alliance for Progress, Colombia—A Case History of U.S. AID*, a study prepared at the request of the Subcommittee on American Republic Affairs by the staff of the Committee on Foreign Relations, U.S. Senate, together with a report of the Comptroller General, February 1, 1969 (Washington, D.C.: Government Printing Office, 1969). For more recent works, see William C. Thiesenhusen, "Latin America's Employment Problem," *Science*, CLXXI (March 5, 1971), pp. 868–874; ILO, *op. cit.*; Erik Thorbecke, "Desempleo y Subempleo en la America Latina," IBD/UN Seminar on Marginality in Latin America, Santiago, November 23–27, 1970.

14. Erik Thorbecke, *Employment and Output: A Methodology Applied to Peru and Guatemala* (Paris: Development Center, OECD, 1970), p. 4.

15. *Ibid.*

16. Prebisch, *op. cit.*

17. Pedroleon Diaz, *Analisis Comparativo de los Contratos de Licencia en el Grupo Andino* (Lima: Andean Group Document, Octubre 1971).

18. Dario Abad, "Las inversiones extranjeras—divergencia de interesse y posibilidades de una reconciliacion de intereses," in Albrecht von Gleich (ed.), *Las inversiones extranjeras privadas en Latin America* (Hamburg: Instituto de estudios Iberoamericanos, 1971).

19. ILO, *op. cit.*, p. 121.

20. Ronald Müller and Richard Morgenstern, "The Impact of Multinational Corporations on the Balance of Payments of LDCs: An Econometric Analysis of Pricing in Export Sales," paper presented to the Econometrics Society Program of the American Economics Association Annual Meetings, Toronto, December 28, 1972.

21. UN-ECLA, *The Process of Industrial Development, op. cit.*

22. Inter-American Development Bank (IDB), *Socio Economic Progress in Latin America* (Washington, D.C., 1971); Thorbecke, *Employment and Output, op. cit.*, p. 10.

23. As an aside, let us briefly mention another institutional aspect of the term underdevelopment, i.e., the inability of LDC governments to enforce redistribution institutions such as social security, medical and educational assistance, progressive income taxation, etc.

24. Morris and Adelman, *op. cit.*

25. Osvaldo Sunkel, "Subdesarrollo, Dependencia y Marginacion: Proposiciones para un Enfoque Integrador," IDB/UN Seminar on Marginality in Latin America, Santiago, November 23–27, 1970.

26. James P. Grant, "Multinational Corporations and the Developing Countries: The Emerging Job Crisis and its Implications" (Washington, D.C.: Overseas Development Council, January 1972).

27. UN-ECLA, *Economic Survey for Latin America, op. cit.*

28. The United States estimate is from Miller, *op. cit.* The Latin American UN estimate is from UN-ECLA, *The Distribution of Income, op. cit.*

29. For further elaboration of these reasons, see James A. Shulman, "Transfer Pricing in Multinational Business," unpublished Ph.D. dissertation, Harvard Graduate School of Business Administration, 1966; also Michael Z. Brooke and H. Lee Remmers, *The Strategy of Multinational Enterprise: Organization and Finance* (New York: American Elsevier Publishing Company, Inc., 1970).

30. See citations in Leopoldo Solis, "Mexican Economic Policy in the Post-War Period: The Views of Mexican Economists," *American Economic Review*, XVI, No. 3, Part 2, Supplement (June 1971); also Miguel Wionczek, "Nacionalismo Mexicano e Inversion Extranjera," *Comercio Exterior* (December 7, 1967), pp. 980–985.

31. This and the other cases in Colombia are presented in Constantine Vaitsos, "Interaffiliate Charges by Transnational Corporations and Intercountry Income Distribution," submitted in partial fulfillment of the requirements for the degree of Doctor of Philosophy at Harvard University, June 1972, pp. 55–56.

32. Richard Barnet and Ronald Müller, *Global Reach: The Power of Multinational Corporations* (New York: Simon and Schuster, 1974).

33. Abad, *op. cit.*; Ferrer, "El Capital Extranjero . . . ," *op. cit.*; Ferrer, "Empresa Extranjera . . . ," *op. cit.*; Corporacion de Fomento de la Produccion (CORFO), *Analisis de la Inversiones Extranjeras en Chile . . . Periodo 1954–1970*, No. 20 (Enero 1972); CORFO, *Comportamiento de las Principales Empresas Industriales Extranjeras Acegidas AL D. F. L. 258*, Publicacion No. 9-A/70 (Santiago: Division de Planeficacion Industrial, Departmento de Diagnostico y Politica, 1970); CORFO, *Las Inversiones Extranjeras, op. cit.*; CORFO, *La Propiedad Industrial en Chile y Su Impacto en el Desarrollo Industrial*, Santiago (Septiembre de 1970) (documento preliminar); ODELPLAN, *El Capital Privado Extranjero en Chile en el Perido 1964–1968 a Nivel Global y Sectorial*, #R/PL/70–007, Santiago (Agosto de 1970).

34. Fernando Fajnzylber, *Estrategia Industrial y Empresas Internacionales: Posicion Relativa de America y Brasil* (Rio de Janeiro: Naciones Unidas, CEPAL, November 1970), p. 59. On royalties and fees, see pp. 143–145 in this article.

35. Fajnzylber, *loc. cit.*

36. Tax revenues, which for LDCs constitute internalized local savings from MNCs, are so low that they do not change the basic conclusion of this paragraph. In addition, to be shown later, the amount of tax revenue lost due to unreported and extra-

legally repatriated profits more than compensates for the omission of collected tax revenues in the present argument.

37. See sources in note 33 above, particularly Dario Abad.

38. The data and its breakdown are from J. W. Vaupel and J. P. Curhan, *The Making of Multinational Enterprise* (Boston: Harvard Business School, 1969), pp. 254–265.

39. *Business Latin America* (January 15, 1970). Parentheses are mine.

40. Felipe Pazos, "El Financiamiento Externo de la America Latina: Aumento Progresivo o Disminucion Gradual?" *Trimestre Economico*, No. 150 (Abril–Junio 1971).

41. For a pro-MNC analysis of impacts, see: Herbert K. May, *The Effects of United States and Other Foreign Investment in Latin America* (Council for Latin America, January 1970); also Herbert K. May and J. A. Fernandez, *Impact of Foreign Investment in Mexico* (Washington, D.C.: National Chamber Foundation, undated, ca. 1971).

42. Susan B. Foster, "Impact of Direct Investment Abroad by United States Multinational Companies on the Balance of Payments," *Monthly Review of the Federal Reserve Bank of New York* (July 1972), p. 172.

43. United Nations Conference on Trade and Development (UNCTAD), *Restrictive Business Practices*, TD/122/Supp. 1, Santiago de Chile, January 7, 1972, p. 32; May, *op. cit.*, 1970; Samuel Pizer and Frederik Cutler, "U.S. Exports to Foreign Affiliates of U.S. Firms," *Survey of Current Business*, XLV, No. 12 (Washington, D.C.: U.S. Department of Commerce, 1965).

44. Foster, *op. cit.*, p. 174.

45. Constantine Vaitsos, "The Process of Commercialization of Technology in the Andean Pact: A Synthesis," Andean Group Document, Lima, October 1971, pp. 20–26; Diaz, *op. cit.*, pp. 10–14.

46. UNCTAD, *Restrictive Business Practices, op. cit.*, pp. 9–11.

47. See Peterson, *op. cit.*

48. Andean group statistics are from Vaitsos, "The Process of Commercialization . . . ," *op. cit.* For micro-derived Latin American figures, see Müller and Morgenstern, *op. cit.* For aggregates in Latin America and Europe, see David R. Belli, "Sales of Foreign Affiliates of U.S. Firms," *Survey of Current Business*, L, No. 10 (Washington, D.C.: U.S. Department of Commerce, October 1970), p. 20.

49. IDB, *op. cit.*; UN-ECLA, *Economic Survey for Latin America, 1971, op. cit.*

50. Müller and Morgenstern, *op. cit.*

51. *Ibid.*

52. See Shulman, *op. cit.*; Brooke and Remmers, *op. cit.*, Part II; Charles Levinson, *Capital, Inflation, and the Multinationals* (London: George Allen and Unwin Ltd., 1971), pp. 99 ff.

53. Müller and Morgenstern, *op. cit.*

54. *Ibid.*

55. Yair Aharoni, "On the Definition of a Multinational Corporation," in A. Kapoor and P. D. Grubs (eds.), *The Multinational Enterprise in Transition* (Princeton: Darwin Press, 1972), p. 11. Parentheses are mine, added for explanation.

56. United Nations Conference on Trade and Development (UNCTAD), *Transfer of Technology Policies Relating to Technology of the Countries of the Andean Pact: Their Foundations; A Study by the Junta del Acuerdo de Cartagena*. TD/107, December 29, 1971, pp. 14–15.

57. UNCTAD, *Restrictive Business Practices, op. cit.*, pp. 44–45. These technology contracts also include many other restrictions, e.g., the MNC can determine final selling prices and volume, select key personnel in the licensee's business, etc.

58. Diaz, *op. cit.*, pp. 19–23; Vaitsos, "Interaffiliate Charges . . . ," *op. cit.*, p. 52.

59. Further details on this and other interviews are given in Barnet and Müller, *op. cit.*

60. *El Espectador* (daily newspaper) citing the official Colombian Court transcripts, "Overpricing by Foreign Drug Companies," Bogota, Colombia, February 6, 1970, pp. 1A, ff; Vaitsos, "Interaffiliate Charges . . . ," *op. cit.*, Appendix 3.

61. *Ibid.*, pp. 49–50.

62. *Ibid.*, p. 49.

63. Diaz, *op. cit.*, pp. 24–25.

64. *Ibid.*

65. CORFO, *La Propiedad Industrial en Chile, op. cit.*, pp. 26–27. Diaz, *op. cit.*, pp. 18–19; UN-ECLA, *Economic Survey for Latin America, 1971, op. cit.*

66. Abad, *op. cit.*, p. 43.

67. A detailed analysis of the changing nature of bargaining power between MNCs and LDCs and its implications for advanced nations can be found in Barnet and Müller, *op. cit.* For an analysis of the variables affecting bargaining power and policy tools for increasing bargaining power over MNCs by LDC governments, see Ronald Müller, "The Political Economy of Direct Foreign Investment: An Appraisal for Latin American Policy Making," prepared Summer 1969 for the Prebisch Group (Washington, D.C.: Inter-American Development Bank, Special Studies Division, 1970), Chapters 1–3 and Appendix 1.

12

The Inequities of the Old Economic Order

Mahbub ul Haq

The Third World is not merely a catchword today. It is just becoming a political and economic force. A new trade union of the poor nations is emerging. It is united by its poverty—and by its heritage of common suffering. In fact, a "poverty curtain" has descended right across the face of our world, dividing it materially and philosophically into two different worlds, two separate planets, two unequal humanities—one embarrassingly rich and the other desperately poor. The struggle to lift this curtain of poverty and unequal relationships is certainly the most formidable challenge of our time. And it is likely to cover many decades and consume many generations.

Most of the required changes lie right within the control of the Third World—whether in the restructuring of domestic political power, or in the fashioning of new development styles and strategies, or in the search for new areas of collective self-reliance. But a part of this struggle is at the international level—the need to change the past patterns of hopeless dependency to new concepts of equality, partnership, and interdependence. These pages are addressed to this struggle at the international level, though I must make quite clear my own conviction that fundamental reforms in the international order will be meaningless, and almost impossible to achieve, without corresponding reforms in the national orders.

In the pages on the international economic order that follow, I intend to review the workings of the existing world economic order and analyze the concrete basis of the accusation by the poor nations that the present international institutions systematically discriminate against their interests.

· · ·

Let me also make clear that I am speaking not as an official of the World Bank or as a Pakistani or as an individual. I venture to speak as a citizen from the Third World, in utter frankness and candor, sharing the aspirations and the belief in the common cause that unite all of us in the Third World. Let me turn now to an analysis of the prevailing world economic order from the vantage point of the Third World.

The vastly unequal relationship between the rich and the poor nations is fast becoming the central issue of our time. The poor nations are beginning to question the basic premises of an international order that leads to ever widening disparities between the rich and poor countries and to a

Reprinted with permission from *The Third World and the International Economic Order* by Mahbub ul Haq, Development Paper No. 22 (Washington, D.C.: Overseas Development Council, 1976), pp. 1–11.

persistent denial of equality of opportunity to many poor nations. They are, in fact, arguing that in the international order—just as much as within national orders—all distribution of benefits, credit, services, and decision making gets warped in favor of a priviliged minority and that this situation cannot be changed except through fundamental institutional reforms.

When this is pointed out to the rich nations, they dismiss it casually as empty rhetoric of the poor nations. Their standard answer is that the international market mechanism works, even though not too perfectly, and that the poor nations are always out to wring concessions from the rich nations in the name of past exploitation. They believe that the poor nations are demanding a massive redistribution of income and wealth which is simply not in the cards. Their general attitude seems to be that the poor nations must earn their economic development, much the same way as the rich nations had to over the last two centuries, through patient hard work and gradual capital formation, and that there are no shortcuts to this process and no rhetorical substitutes. The rich, however, are "generous" enough to offer some help to the poor nations to accelerate their economic development if the poor are only willing to behave themselves.

In reviewing this controversy, we must face up to the blunt question: Does the present world order systematically discriminate against the interest of the Third World, as the poor nations contend? Or is the demand for a new order mere empty rhetoric against imagined grievances, as the rich nations allege?

There is sufficient concrete evidence to show that the poor nations cannot get an equitable deal from the present international economic structures—much the same way as the poorest sections of the society within a country and for much the same reasons. Once there are major disparities in income distribution within a country, the market mechanism ceases to function either efficiently or equitably, since it is weighted heavily in favor of the purchasing power in the hands of the rich. Those who have the money can make the market bend to their own will. When we start from a position of gross inequalities, the so-called market mechanism mocks poverty, or simply ignores it, since the poor hardly have any purchasing power to influence market decisions. This is even more true at the international level, since there is no world government and none of the usual mechanisms existing within countries that create pressures for redistribution of income and wealth.

But this is not a time to make a general case all over again. The Third World has done it many times over. Rather, it is time for our universities and our research institutions to do some serious work in documenting specific instances of inequities in the world order. In undertaking such a serious analysis, I believe that two "staple diets" we have used so often in the past should be played down. First, we cannot keep the rich nations feeling either guilty or uncomfortable by simply pointing out that three quarters of the world income, investment, and services are in the hands of one quarter of its population. The rich nations are increasingly turning around and saying: "So what? We worked for it and so should you." World income disparities, per se, are not an issue. We also must demonstrate that the prevailing disparities are creating major hurdles for the poor nations to execute their own development and are denying them equality of opportunity. Second, the Third World has often used the argument of instability of commodity prices and worsening terms of trade. This has been overdone and is probably not the heart of the problem. If low earnings are stabilized, they still remain low. It may give our policymakers a little peace of mind but it does not solve anything fundamental. Surely the argument must be that international structures deny us a fair price.

KINDS OF INEQUALITY

Ultimately, the reasons for unequal relationships must be sought in international structures and mechanisms which put the Third World at a considerable disadvantage and which cry out for thorough-going institutional reforms. Let me explore some of these areas.

There is a tremendous *imbalance* today *in the distribution of international reserves.* The poor nations, with 70 per cent of the world population, received less than 4 per cent of the international reserves of $131 billion during 1970–1974, simply because the rich nations controlled the creation and distribution of international reserves through the expansion of their own national reserve currencies (mainly dollars and sterling) and through their decisive control over the International Monetary Fund (IMF). For all practical purposes, the United States has been the central banker of the world in the post-Second World War period, and it could easily finance its balance-of-payments deficits by the simple device of expanding its own currency. In other words, the richest nation in the world has had an unlimited access to international credit facilities, since it could create such credit through its own decisions. This has been less true of other developed countries, though Britain and Germany have enjoyed some of this privilege at various times. This certainly has not been true of the developing countries, which could neither create international credit through their own deficit-financing operations nor obtain an easy access to this credit because of the absence of any genuine international currency and because of their limited quotas in the International Monetary Fund. The heart of any economic system is its credit structure. This is controlled entirely by the rich nations at the international level. The poor nations merely stand at the periphery of monetary decisions. This is nothing unusual. As in any normal national banking system, the poor get very little credit unless a concerned government chooses to intervene on their behalf.

The distribution of value added to the products traded between the developing and the developed countries is heavily weighted in favor of the latter. The developing countries, unlike the developed, receive only a small fraction of the final price that the consumers in the international market are paying for their produce, simply because many of them are too poor or too weak to exercise any meaningful control over the processing, shipping, and marketing of their primary exports. A rough estimate indicates that final consumers pay over $200 billion (excluding taxes) for the major primary exports (excluding oil) of the developing countries (in a more processed, packaged, and advertised form), but these countries receive only $30 billion, with the middle men and the international service sector—mostly in the hands of the rich nations—enjoying the difference. On the other hand, the rich nations have the resources and the necessary bargaining power to control the various phases of their production, export, and distribution—often including their own subsidiaries to handle even internal distribution within importing countries. In fact, if the poor nations were able to exercise the same degree of control over the processing and distribution of their exports as the rich nations presently do and if they were to get back a similar proportion of the final consumer price, their export earnings from their primary commodities would be closer to $150 billion. Again, there is a parallel here between national and international orders: within national orders as well, the poor receive only a fraction of the rewards for their labor and lose out to the organized, entrenched middle men unless the national governments intervene.

The protective wall erected by the developed countries prevents the developing world from receiving its due share of the global wealth. The rich nations are making it increasingly impossible for the "free" international market mechanism to work. In the classical framework of Adam Smith, the cornerstone of the free market mechanism is the free movement of labor and capital as well as of goods and services so that rewards to factors of production are equalized all over the world. Yet immigration laws in almost all rich nations make any large-scale movement of unskilled labor in a worldwide search for economic opportunities impossible (except for a limited "brain drain" of skilled labor). Not much capital has crossed international boundaries, both because of poor nations' sensitivities and because of the rich nations' own needs. And additional barriers have gone up against the free movement of goods and services—e.g., over $20 billion in farm subsidies alone in the rich nations to protect their agriculture and progressively higher tariffs and quotas against the simple consumer-goods exports of the developing countries, such as textiles and leather goods. The rich, in other words, are drawing a protective wall around their lifestyles, telling the poor nations that they can compete neither with their labor nor with their goods but paying handsome tributes at the same time to the "free" workings of the international market mechanism. Unfortunately, while the rich can show such discrimination, the poor cannot—by the very fact of their poverty. They need their current foreign exchange earnings desperately, just in order to survive and to carry on a minimum development effort, and they can hardly afford to put up discriminatory restrictions against the capital-goods imports and technology of the Western world. There is again a parallel here between national and international orders. Within national orders as well, the poor generally have very little choice but to sell their services to the rich at considerable disadvantage just in order to earn the means of their survival.

Another area in which the unequal bargaining power of the poor and the rich nations shows up quite dramatically is the *relationship between multinational corporations and the developing countries.* Most of the contracts, leases, and concessions that the multinational corporations have negotiated in the past with the developing countries reflect a fairly in-equitable sharing of benefits. In many cases, the host government is getting only a fraction of the benefits from the exploitation of its own natural resources by the multinational corporations. For instance, Mauritania gets about 15 per cent of the profits that the multinational corporations make from extracting and exporting the iron ore deposits in the country. Simi-larly, in Liberia, the foreign investors export an amount equivalent to nearly one fourth of the total GNP of the country in profit remittances. Such examples are numerous. In fact, it would be useful to tabulate all the concessions, contracts, and leases which have been negotiated between the multinational corporations and the developing countries and to present to the world an idea of what is the present sharing of benefits between host governments and multinational corporations in case after case. Such a factual background not only would illustrate the concrete and specific fashion in which the poor nations get discriminated against in the present world order but also could be a very useful prelude to the necessary re-forms.

The poor nations have only a *pro forma participation in the economic decision making of the world.* Their advice is hardly solicited when the big ten industrialized nations get together to take key decisions on the world's economic future; their voting strength in the Bretton Woods institutions (the World Bank and International Monetary Fund) is less than one third of the total; and their numerical majority in the U.N. General Assembly has provided no real influence so far on international economic decisions. In fact, it may well be an indicator of the sense of accommodation that the rich nations are willing to show that they have started protesting against the "tyranny of the majority" at a time when the majority resolutions of the poor nations carry no effective force and when the Third World coun-tries are not even being allowed to sit as equals around the bargaining tables of the world.

To take an example from the world of ideas, these *unequal relationships pervade the intellectual world and the mass media as well.* The developing countries have often been subjected to concepts of development and value systems that were largely fashioned abroad. While economic development is the primary concern of the developing countries, so far it has been written about and discussed largely by outsiders. The mass media, which greatly shape world opinion, are primarily under the control of the rich nations. The Nobel Prize, which is presumably given for excellence of thought, is given to very few in the Third World, even in non-technical fields such as literature. Is it because our societies are not only poor in income but also poor in thought? Or is it because our thought is being judged by standards totally alien to our spirit and we have no organized forums for either the projection or the dissemination of our thinking? The answer is quite obvious. There is no international structure, including intellectual endeavor, which is not influenced by the inequality between rich and poor nations.

There is much other evidence of instances in which unequal economic relationships have led to a denial of economic opportunities to the poorer nations, but the basic point already has been made: in the international order, just as much as within national orders, initial poverty itself becomes the most formidable handicap in the way of redressal of such poverty unless there is a fundamental change in the existing power structures.

In this context, a net bilateral transfer of about $8 billion of official development assistance to the poor nations every year is neither adequate nor to the point: the quantitative "loss" implicit in the just-quoted examples of maldistribution of international credit, inadequate sharing of benefits from the export of their natural resources, and artificial restrictions on the movement of their goods and services (not to speak of labor) would easily amount to $50–$100 billion a year. More pertinent, the poor nations are seeking greater equality of opportunity, not charity from the uncertain generosity of the rich.

EQUALITY OF OPPORTUNITY

The demand for a new international economic order must be seen in its proper historical perspective. On one level of reasoning, it is a natural evolution of the philosophy already accepted at the national level: governments must actively intervene on behalf of the poorest segments of their populations ("the bottom 40 per cent"), which will otherwise be bypassed by economic development. In a fast-shrinking planet, it was inevitable that this "new" philosophy would not stop at national borders; and, since there is no world government, the poor nations are bringing this concern to its closest substitute, the United Nations.

On yet another level, the search for a new economic order is a natural second stage in the liberation of the developing countries. The first stage was marked by movements of political liberation from the 1940s to the 1960s; the second stage constitutes a struggle for not only political but also economic equality, since the former is unattainable and meaningless without the latter. The demand for a new international economic order must be seen, therefore, as part of an historical process, which neither can be achieved by the poor nations in one single negotiation nor will go away quietly by the simple indifference of the rich nations (or by their misinterpreting it as the faint rumblings of "British socialism," as Mr. Moynihan, former U.S. Ambassador to the United Nations, has argued). In fact, the movement for greater equality of economic opportunity is likely to dominate the next few decades—as much within nations as among them.

At the same time, the developing countries must recognize the intimate link between the reform of the national and international orders. If national economic orders in the poor nations remain unresponsive to the needs of their own poor and if their development strategies continue to benefit only a privileged few, much of the argument for a fundamental reform in the international order will disappear because any benefits flowing from such a reform would go only to a privileged minority in these countries. Moreover, when the international and national orders are dominated by privileged minorities, the possibilities of a tacit collusion between their natural interests are quite unlimited. The developing countries have to learn, therefore, that reforms in their own national orders are often the critical bargaining chip they need in pressing for similar reforms at the international level.

The reforms in the national orders of the poor nations, however, are not in themselves a sufficient condition for a major improvement in the economic condition of their masses. According to a recent World Bank study, if present national and international policies continue unchanged, the poorest developing countries (those with per capita incomes below $200) face the prospect of virtually no increase in their low levels of income between 1975–1980. The increase for other developing countries also will be fairly small. A major change will be required in their internal policies (in saving and investment policies and in the distribution of rewards of economic growth) if such a grim prospect is to be averted. But a good part of this effort will be frustrated if these countries cannot import the needed machinery and technology and if critical foreign exchange shortages persist because of their limited access to the international market either through trade or through international resource transfers. The solution for this is not piecemeal international reforms—via selective trade "concessions" or somewhat larger foreign assistance—since these achieve exactly the same purpose and provide as temporary a relief as limited social security payments to the poor within a national system. The long-term solution is to change the institutional system in such a way as to improve the access of the poor to economic opportunities and to increase their long-term productivity, not their temporary income.

The basic principles for such a change can be easily established and follow logically from the above analysis of institutional imbalances. For instance, any long-term negotiating package should make provision for:

(a) Revamping of the present international credit system by phasing out national reserve currencies and replacing them with an international currency;

(b) Gradual dismantling of restrictions in the rich nations on the movement of goods and services as well as labor from the poor nations;

(c) Enabling the developing countries to obtain more benefit from the exploitation of their own natural resources through greater control over various stages of primary production, processing, and distribution of their commodities;

(d) Introduction of an element of automaticity in international resource transfers by linking them to some form of international taxation or royalties or reserve creation;

(e) Negotiation of agreed principles between the principal creditors and debtors for an orderly settlement of past external debts;

(f) Renegotiation of all past leases and contracts given by the developing countries to the multinational corporations under a new code of ethics to be established and enforced within the United Nations framework; and

(g) Restructuring of the United Nations to give it greater operational powers for economic decisions and a significant increase in the voting strength of the poor nations within the World Bank and the International Monetary Fund.

These ideas will be further developed in my specific proposals for the establishment of a new international economic order.

A NEW WORLD ORDER?

The debate on the establishment of a new international economic order has only recently begun. The battle lines are still being drawn; the battle plans of the rich and the poor nations are hardly clear at present. Our world may well be poised uneasily between a grand new global partnership or a disorderly confrontation. Unfortunately, there are very few examples in history of the rich surrendering their power willingly or peacefully. Whenever and wherever the rich have made any accommodation, they have done so because it had become inevitable, since the poor had gotten organized and would have taken away power in any case. The basic question today, therefore, is not whether the poor nations are in a grossly unfavorable position in the present world order. They are, and they will continue to be, unless they can negotiate a new world order. The basic question really is whether they have the necessary bargaining power to arrange any fundamental changes in the present political, economic, and social balance of power in the world.

Let me conclude with three main observations.

1. Tremendous responsibility rests on our universities, our research institutions, our intellectual forums in the Third World. It is for them to work out carefully concrete instances of systematic discrimination built into the existing economic order—whether the inadequate return from raw material exports, or inequitable sharing of gains from multinationals, or unequal distribution of world liquidity. This should be done in a spirit of serious, objective analysis so that there is concrete documentation available to our negotiators to press this point in international forums. There is no excuse for our not producing sufficient studies on this subject. If we do not attempt these exercises, the rich nations have no built-in incentive to carry them out. And, in the last analysis, facts are far more powerful ammunition than words can ever be.

2. We must keep stressing, as often as we can, that the basic struggle is for equality of opportunity, not equality of income. We are not chasing the income levels of the rich nations. We do not wish to imitate their lifestyles. We are only suggesting that our societies must have a decent chance to develop, on an equal basis, without systematic discrimination against us, according to our own value systems, and in line with our own cultural traditions. We are not asking for a few more crumbs from the table of the rich. We are asking for a fair chance to make it on our own.

3. Let us make quite clear in our future negotiations that what is at stake here is not a few marginal adjustments in the international system: it is its complete overhaul. We are not foolish enough to think that this can

happen overnight. We are willing to wait. And we are willing to proceed step by step. But we are not willing to settle for some inadequate, piecemeal concessions in the name of a step-by-step approach. The advice of Prime Minister Burnham of Guyana at the time of the Commonwealth Heads of Government meeting in May 1975 is pertinent:

> There is another danger that needs to be guarded against if we are all serious in our commitment to programmes of positive action which will give life to a new international economic order. It is the danger of deceiving ourselves that we can somehow achieve fundamental change by marginal adjustments and devices of a piecemeal and reformist nature. This is not to say that there is no value in particular approaches. It is to emphasize that we will not make real progress unless we evolve an integrated programme designed to fulfill not merely the aspirations of the developing world but the necessities for survival of the global community.

part four

Agricultural Institutions and Strategy

according to Johnston and Mellor, there are five important ways in which agriculture contributes to economic development. First, economic development expands the demand for food, which, if unfulfilled, impedes further development. Second, exports of agricultural products increase badly needed foreign exchange earnings. Third, the agricultural sector must supply a significant part of the expanding labor needs of the industrial sector. Fourth, as the dominant sector in a peasant economy, agriculture must provide capital for industry and social overhead investment. Fifth, rising cash incomes in agriculture can be an important source of demand.[1] In addition, if we abandon the economic growth meaning of development, increases in the income of the poorer rural classes *is development* by definition since poverty is being reduced.

There is little disagreement that in the long run the agrarian structure in most underdeveloped countries must be radically transformed if agriculture is going to make its contributions and development is not going to be seriously impeded. But this transformation is not easy to carry out, for as George Beckford points out in the first reading, it involves fundamental social and economic change.

Beckford develops a typology of major rural socioeconomic systems based on (1) the relations of production and (2) the nature of exchange. The systems include subsistence-peasant, feudal, "special case" (commercial farm-firm in capitalist economies), plantation, bureaucratic socialism, and people's communalism. Beckford explains the persistence of underdevelopment by demonstrating that different systems of agricultural (rural) organization possess different inherent potentials for development.

Beckford's model of underdevelopment is "institution centered." His holistic analysis incorporates both economic variables (for example, productivity, technical change, and market structures) and social and political factors (for example, the power of elites and the correlation between race and class). Examining the persistence of underdevelopment in each of his systems, Beckford lists a number of weaknesses (or inherent biases) in the social framework of economic relations. Based on this analysis, the author is able to suggest a ranking of rural systems according to the sum total of underdevelopment biases: socialist-people's communal, "special case," socialist-bureaucratic, subsistence-peasant, feudal, and plantation in descending order of development potential.

To achieve either a capitalist farm-firm or a productive subsistence-peasant type of agrarian structure would require substantial land reform. In the second article, Peter Dorner and Don Kanel analyze the impact of land reform (essentially, a choice between farm enlargement and farm subdivision) on employment, income distribution, and productivity. After surveying a variety of land-tenure systems—European, American, Soviet, Latin American—they found that the efficacy of a particular system depends mainly upon institutional and technical conditions, the "stage" of development, and development goals and priorities. A choice between farm enlargement and subdivision depends mainly on existing factor proportions and relative real factor costs. This article focuses on the economic variables of land reform. However, the social and political issues may be of even greater importance.

Most land reform involving subdivision (that is, the creation of small peasant holdings) has been of such limited scope and of such recent date that no valid generalizations about its efficacy can be made. Mexico has the longest standing land reform of this type. While Mexican agricultural production has increased greatly since 1940, small-scale peasant farming has not been responsible for this increase. The private sector produces the vast bulk of the agricultural output, and within the private sector it is the holdings over 100 hectares that account for the bulk of the output.

Corn, the most important subsistence crop, occupies nearly one-half the total harvested area and makes up the vast bulk of the produce of all small holdings. Most of the corn is grown by traditional methods, and it yields less per acre in Mexico than anywhere else in Latin America, a region of low corn yields compared with the rest of the world. Professor Rene Dumont says in his study of the Mexican agrarian reform that:

> Mexican agriculture doubled its production between 1945 and 1955, and is progressing very much faster than that of any other Latin American country: so the agrarian reform after all can be called progress. But, instead of being due to the peasants who have "inherited," the success comes from the irrigation works and from the efforts of the so-called "victims" of the reform; the agents of success are the dynamic expropriated haciéndéros cultivating smaller estates, and doing their best to recoup by higher yields what they have lost in extensive area.[2]

He goes on to say, however, that without the agrarian reform and the revolution of 1910–1921, agriculture might have remained stagnant. The revolution and reform acted as catalysts in transforming the basis of Mexican agriculture from a semifeudal one to a modern capitalist one.

The foregoing is not an attempt to demonstrate that subdivision cannot provide the basis for development, only that in Mexico it is the large capitalist farm that has done so. If anything, the small holding has been a drag on Mexican economic development. It is true, however, that subdivision may lead to the growth of large-scale capitalist farming through the more successful buying out the less successful.

A second type of agrarian structure is large-scale capitalist "family" farms. There is no question that capitalist farming in the West has been the most efficient and productive agricultural system ever known. This is particularly true in the United States. The major problem is how to establish and nurture this type of agricultural structure in a present-day underdeveloped country. There seem to be four basic ways of doing so. The first, applicable in countries where the bulk of land is held in landed estates, would be the creation of incentives to turn feudal landlords into capitalist farmers. To some degree this is what occurred in German agriculture in the nineteenth century. The major problem is that this would involve radical revision of the existing tenure system, since the majority of these large estates are actually cultivated in small plots by tenant farmers.

The second approach would involve the settlement of relatively virgin land where ownership rights have not already been established, such as occurred in the United States, Canada, Australia, and New Zealand (the ownership rights and tenure system of the local inhabitants in each case were easily eradicated). A number of underdeveloped countries are presently attempting to utilize this approach. Its virtue, of course, is that it does not infringe upon existing property rights. The major drawback is that there is not enough virgin land available in most countries for this approach to be of much importance.

A third way would be to follow the example of England and Germany and inaugurate an enclosure movement to remove the peasants from the land and consolidate the holdings into capitalist farms. However, this process takes time and a docile peasant class (or the power to suppress peasant discontent). It appears unlikely that social and political conditions in most underdeveloped countries today make this approach feasible. Of course some "enclosure" will occur simply by the "pull" exerted by an industrializing urban center.

The final approach to establishing a capitalist agricultural structure appears to be the most feasible and likely. This approach would involve an agrarian reform that gave free title to the land to individual peasants. Then, with free sale, the more successful would buy out the less successful. Many peasants would be "pushed" or "pulled" to the industrializing urban areas (presuming they exist), and eventually a capitalist agricultural structure would emerge. This process seems to be happening in Mexico on the privately held lands. Aside from the question of political feasibility, there is the problem of how long it will take to carry out this transformation.

Since effective land reform does involve a radical transformation, capitalist governments have turned to a technological solution for the agricultural problem. That technological solution is the "Green Revolution." In the third reading, Harry Cleaver evaluates this "revolution" and argues that the results so far have been to increase inequities among regions and classes, to increase MNC control of the agricultural sector through control of the new input, and to threaten massive ecological damage.

Since neither economic growth strategies nor the Green Revolution have increased the economic welfare of the rural population, and piecemeal land reform has been less than effective, many have turned to what Albert Waterston calls "integrated rural development." Waterston argues that rural development requires a self-supporting agriculture that benefits a substantial number of poor farmers in rural communities. He further argues that the elements of such a development model can be gleaned from the experience of the People's Republic of China, Taiwan, Tanzania, and Israel.

The final article in this part is primarily a case study of the development experience of the People's Republic of China, although the author is, in part, concerned with the usefulness of the Chinese experience as a replicable "model of development." The Chinese experience corresponds to Beckford's model of people's communalism.

Wong concentrates on three broad "successful aspects" of the Chinese agricultural development program. These include: (1) institutional preconditions for agricultural transformation, (2) balanced development strategies for agriculture, and (3) integration of production with overall rural development. With respect to institutional preconditions, the appropriate institutional framework (cadres) enabled the Chinese to deal more effectively with social tension arising out of technological change. The Chinese arrived at a balanced development strategy by experimentation. Integration of production with rural development was accomplished by a policy of rural diversification (public works and cottage industry) to utilize off-season surplus labor and to accelerate the diffusion of technical progress to agriculture.

In concluding, Wong says that it is not appropriate to speak of a Chinese model as such but rather of the Chinese *experience* as a process of experimentation and the trying of alternative strategies until the optimum plan emerges.

1. BRUCE F. JOHNSTON and JOHN W. MELLOR, "The Role of Agriculture in Economic Development," *American Economic Review*, Vol. LI, No. 4 (September 1961), pp. 571–572.
2. RENE DUMONT, *Lands Alive* (London: The Merlin Press, 1965), p. 93.

13

Comparative Rural Systems, Development and Underdevelopment

George L. Beckford

INTRODUCTION

A vast literature exists on the subject of "underdeveloped" agriculture, but very few of the writings tell us *why underdeveloped agriculture remains underdeveloped*. Unless we know the answer to that question, there is very little chance of stimulating development—either by evolutionary policy measures or by revolutionary social change. The present paper is offered to professional colleagues as a small attempt to find the answers to the questions raised. (I deliberately say "answers" because I am convinced that there is no single answer; and, therefore, no single solution to the problem.)

This prologue outlines the general conceptual framework of the exercise; and it locates my approach to the question within the context of other contributions to date.

The main thesis of the paper is that different systems of agricultural (and rural) organization possess different inherent *endogenous* potentials for development.[1] That is to say, within each system of rural social organization, there are certain inherent factors which stimulate or retard development. Furthermore, there are different *exogenous* influences which affect different underdeveloped countries—depending on what international system a particular economy is locked into. In the modern world, no economy is an island unto itself. And the international capitalist and socialist systems generate somewhat different exogenous influences on underdeveloped countries.

Following from this general thesis, we need to develop a typology of agricultural (rural) systems to facilitate the analysis. This is done in the first section of the paper. In the second section, I examine the economics of resource allocation and use, by type of system. This is important, because if we do not understand how resources are allocated and used, we cannot understand the phenomena of development and underdevelopment.[2]

The groundwork should, by then, be well established for a consideration of the political economy of underdevelopment in Section III. And, again, the analysis is by type of system. The "plantation case" and the "special case" provide the backdrop for that analysis. It is simply assumed that readers are familiar with the backdrop. The brevity of exposition may,

Reprinted with permission from *World Development*, Vol. 2, No. 6, George L. Beckford, Comparative Rural Systems, Development and Underdevelopment," 1974, Pergamon Press, Ltd.

therefore, fail to persuade those who are unfamiliar with the literature on those two cases.

The final section of the paper is a brief comment on certain issues relating to employment, unemployment, and technology.[3]

The immediate conceptual concern of the paper is with "economic development"—that is, how a people utilize their resources to advance their material welfare. Some rural peoples have achieved this; others have not. And so we must explain why this is so.

In my opinion, conventional "models" of agricultural development do not explain enough. Ruttan and Hayami are the authors of the most recent of these models—the induced development model.[4] By regarding technical changes as endogenous, they have improved on the earlier "high pay-off input model" of T. W. Schultz. That model itself was an advance on the earlier "diffusion model." Each of those models treats technology as the central factor in rural change. They are, therefore, productivity-centred. The "conservation model" of the early classical English and German writers is resource-centred. And the "urban-industrial impact model" originally developed by von Thunen and extended by T. W. Schultz is market-centred. That model is concerned with explaining how imperfections in both product and factor markets create regional disparities within industrial nations.

In that general tradition, the approach which I take in the present exercise can be said to be "institution-centred." My concern is to explain global poverty in different rural situations.[5] In other words, why are rural people in, say, Jamaica generally poorer in material terms than those in, say, the US Mid-West, or those in New Zealand, or in Cuba!

To explain such situations, we need a holistic analysis that integrates productivity, technical change, market structures, and other economic phenomena with social and political factors. That is a tall order to accomplish in a short paper. Therefore, one must expect to find many deficiencies in the exposition that follows.

ECONOMIC THEORY AND RURAL REALITY:
A VIEW OF WORLD AGRICULTURE

Different writers have developed typologies of world agriculture for different purposes. There are geographers (like Wagner) using typologies based on differences in exchange patterns (i.e., market relations). There are farm management approaches (such as that by Phillips Foster) which emphasize differences among decision makers and between types of land tenure arrangements. That approach is also useful but too disaggregated for present purposes. It is production-relations oriented.[6]

Then among the formal general economists and political economists, we have on the one hand the "pure" Marxist approach based on the social relations of production. And on the other hand we have the pure so-called "mainstream" economists who view economics narrowly and who treat development and underdevelopment in terms of the "modernity" and "backwardness" of observed techniques of production.

Finally we have a group of eclectic social philosophers, like Weber and Polanyi. They emphasize the importance of value systems or preference hierarchies of different peoples in different places and times.

Of the different approaches mentioned above, the least useful is that taken by "mainstream" economists. Yet the largest number of scholars are to be found in that stream. That school is really caught in the trap of the "special case" which, in the agricultural development context, is the US Mid-West rural situation. (We return to this point, later in this section, after presenting our working typology.)

The most useful approaches are those of the eclectic philosophers and the Marxists scholars; while elements drawn from the geography and farm management streams can be used to improve the typology we choose. The easiest way to combine all these approaches is to look for "historically-determined" types of rural social systems which we all understand to a certain degree. But before that, a little bit on each of the more important contributions just mentioned above.

Exchange relations are important in the Wagner sense. But since Polanyi and others deal with that we can, to some extent, ignore Wagner. Land tenure arrangements and decision-making as emphasized by Foster are crucial. So we keep those in mind.

Now the Marxist school is somewhat confused. The approach of the school is what I call "macrosocioeconomic," and their analysis is based on real historical experiences emanating from two distinct real world cases:

(a) The European sequential change of feudal–capitalist–socialist ("communist"?); and

(b) The Non-European sequential change of precapitalist–capitalist–socialist (?)–("communist").

Among the school, problems and inconsistencies arise in two directions. First, we get the exchange-centred point of view of Sweezy and Gunder Frank *vis-à-vis* the production-relations centred view of Dobb and Laclau (i.e., social organization of production). Secondly, we get some differences between the Sweezy analysis that is based on empirical validation using Europe back to the Middle Ages and the Gunder Frank analysis using Latin America only back to the sixteenth century. The Marxist school will need to sort out these differences in due course, to the benefit of all social scientists.

The eclectic philosophers[7] have a smaller following; but there is greater consistency within the school. The leaders of the school have made the important distinction between "formal" and "substantive" economics and rationality—a distinction which clearly exposes the sterility of the mainstream school. Weber and Polanyi make the distinction between formal rationality and substantive rationality. And we have Polayni and others exploring exchange relations in depth.

"Substantive" rationality is said to be equivalent to the implementation of given values. That is to say, given the limits of knowledge and information, a people will seek to get the most value from their resources, *depending on their particular value system or preference hierarchy.*

"Formal" rationality is said to be equivalent to the matching of means and ends, *for a given abstract end.* As such, this kind of behaviour tran-

Chart 1 A view of world agricultural and rural systems

Subsistence	Capitalist (ca. 2/3 World rural population)		Corporate capitalism	Socialist (ca. 1/3 World rural population)	
	Subs.[1]	*"Special case"* Commercial farm-firm in capitalist economies (e.g., US. Mid-West.)			
	Peasant[2] (a) Individual (e.g., W.I.) (b) Tribal or communal (e.g., W.Africa) (c) Peasant within wider regressive social frame-work		*Plantation*[4] (diff. types up to MNC)	*Bureaucratic socialism* (e.g., USSR.)	*People's communalism* (e.g., China)
	Feudal[3] (e.g., Latin America & Asia)		*Integrated*[5] *corporate capitalism* (internal) (e.g., Del Monte & Heinz farms in USA.)		

1. So-called "primitive" isolated communities (e.g., Amerindian "reservations," etc.).
2. Pure and adulterated. (For the adulterated, see (c) where peasant society is subordinate to a different and more powerful social framework.) The categories above in the chart are not mutually exclusive.
3. Pure and semi-feudalism exist in *parts* of Latin America and *parts* of Asia.
4. See *Persistent Poverty* for elaboration on the different types of plantation organization.
5. A minor type up until now (ca. mid-20th century).

197

scends institutional constraints to define a course of action which leads to a *defined* "optimum."

Thus we always find a bias in formal (mainstream) economics—value biases towards abstractions like "efficiency," "productivity," etc., as end goals—whereas what we really need are considerations of efficiency and productivity *as means to improving the welfare of people*.[8]

If we are to follow this general and most useful approach, thereby, to develop substantive economics for explaining rural development and underdevelopment, we need a typology of rural economy which incorporates the ideas that appear useful and enlightening. Accordingly, Chart 1 emerges as our analytical view of the world situation.

The typology seems rather old. But it is based on a combination of factors governing (i) the relations of production, and (ii) the nature of exchange. We are essentially concerned with decision making, tenure relationships, and exchange arrangements. In short, with both the modes of production and of exchange. Within that general conceptual mould we wish to explain differences in patterns of resource allocation and of development and underdevelopment, in the present exercise.

Before that, a few words on Chart 1. This paper will analyse neither the "special case" nor the socialist patterns of organization: and for two different reasons. The special case dominates economic theorizing about agricultural and rural development, and I am not yet sufficiently familiar with the socialist patterns.

As is suggested schematically, the bulk of the world's rural population falls under the capitalist systems designated in the chart. A few paragraphs, then, on the reality of these cases.

Global subsistence *production* is not common in the world; though global subsistence consumption exists among many rural people. The pure subsistence case will therefore be treated rather briefly.

Peasants, on the other hand, dominate the world, in terms of numbers and of different social situations. Everywhere, the peasantry is interlocked in some larger social framework—state capitalism in the Soviet Union; tribal systems in West Africa; plantation systems in the West Indies; and semi-feudal arrangements in Latin America and Asia. It is the larger social framework that determines the rate of advance of the peasantry in each case.

What do we mean by the term "peasant" in this classification? The simple answer is: whenever the decision maker utilizes his own labour and that of his family to transform resources into output; and when he *consciously* plans production with an eye on the market. He may or may not utilize hired labour at certain times. Thus we have different classes of peasants—big, middle and small—categories that relate to the nature of the labour régime but not necessarily to size of farm.[9]

In the analysis to follow in the next two sections, the special case is used as a background for analysing resource allocation and use. While the plantation case will provide general background for analysing development and underdevelopment.

THE ECONOMICS OF RESOURCE ALLOCATION AND USE

The "special case" allocation problem is familiar. The decision maker in agriculture sets out *consciously* to maximize profit and to minimize risk. Risk is critical in all agricultural situations. Accordingly, choice criteria are relative output prices and relative input prices. Where perfect (or near-perfect) market conditions exist, economic efficiency is achieved in the circumstances.

So long as producers have sufficient resources at their command, they will achieve reasonable and decent levels of living even though other groups of people in the same economy may surpass their consumption achievements. If resource distribution is relatively even, the rural society does not exhibit major disparities in income distribution. And local government will allocate resources to agricultural research and extension of a kind that ultimately serves further to improve the material welfare of the rural people.[10] So much for the special case, for now.

The pure *subsistence producer* need not detain us very long either. Such a producer sets out *consciously* to maximize consumer satisfaction (i.e., of himself and family) from the set of resources at his command. Meat or vegetables, or any combination of these which they happen to enjoy. There is no exchange; therefore, no relative prices to guide choice. Choice is determined by the consumer indifference surface and the production possibilities from owned (or controlled) resources and from the pool of technical knowledge. This point is elaborated in Part A of Chart 2. The solution to the allocation problem is a tangency one which equates the marginal rate of substitution on the consumption side with marginal rate of technical substitution in production.

What needs further discussion in the pure subsistence case is attitudes to risk, and hence to innovation and change. In this connection, I find the analysis developed by Miracle to be quite useful.[11] Part B of Chart 2 reproduces the Miracle analysis. That author uses two basic concepts in his analysis—the minimum physiologic level of consumption living (the *MPL*, which is fixed by nature); and the minimum desirable level of consumption (the *MDL*, which is culturally determined). The producer's attitude to risk is conditioned by his output performance relative to these two levels.

According to Miracle, in a situation such as Case (1), producer *A* has a greater incentive to minimize risk than does producer *B*, because *A* cannot take the chance of falling below the *MPL*. However in Case (2), producer *A* will take bigger risks relative to producer *B*, because he is close to his *MDL* and far enough above the *MPL*; while producer *B*, having achieved his *MDL*, has no great incentive for increasing output.

Since the peasant case is perhaps the most confusing, we will leave that for the last and treat, briefly, the plantation and feudal cases. I have dealt with the *plantation* case at length elsewhere.[12] Different types of plantations face different situations. . . . the family plantation may set out consciously to maximize the social welfare of the owner; while the corporate MNC subsidiary may maximize production, as part of an over-all corporate strategy to maximize profits for the international complex.

Chart 2   The subsistence allocation problem

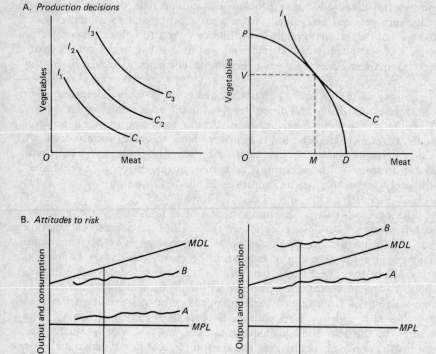

A. *Production decisions*

B. *Attitudes to risk*

Case (1)   Case (2)

Accordingly, different production decisions lead to different patterns of resource allocation and use. For example, whereas the corporation plantation is likely to substitute capital for labour, the family-owned plantation is less likely to do so. Generally speaking, we should expect to find greater changes in both "mechanical" (labour-saving) and "biological and chemical" (land-saving) technology in the corporate case, as compared with the family case.[13]

Now the *feudal* case is a kind of hybrid between the family plantation and the pure peasantry. The peons provide labour for the manorial lord (*haciendado*) part of the time; and they produce for their own subsistence (and surplus) the rest of the time. Accordingly we have a backward system of resource allocation and exploitation, in which technical change is slow and output is both limited and unequally distributed among the population, as in the general plantation case.

The *peasant* case is extremely interesting analytically. Production decisions are made within a complex matrix of social and economic variables. "A peasant economy is one which links purchaser and producer, resource allocation, and product allocation in a network of ties which are *personal*." Personal relationships affect:

(i) rights to the use of land,
(ii) the mobilization of labour,
(iii) the objectives of the decision maker,
(iv) the accumulation of capital, and
(v) the choice of technology.

There are two sets of such "personal" relationships: household influences, and community influences. In addition, there is the "super" power of the state which imposes taxes and/or rent.

Household influences affect present and future consumption,[14] labour inputs, land inputs, and capital inputs. Community influences affect inputs too, in addition to defining the social imperatives to which the peasant must accommodate in making decisions. Furthermore, the community affects the structure of markets and of exchange relationships.

Generally speaking, we would expect to find that the individual decision-maker in peasant economy sets out *consciously to maximize family welfare* —a rather vague objective which includes a mixture of profit maximization constrained by generally acceptable standards of peasant society. In such situations, "the rewards for economic effort may lie to a greater degree in the fulfilment of social obligations and social roles; and patterns of decision making are regulated accordingly."[15]

Chart 3 presents a summary position on the nature of decision making in the peasant case. Part A of the chart assumes a coincidence of market and household solutions; the price line is tangential to the production possibilities curve at the same output mix as determined by the household preference in terms of consumption. This is a unique and unstable solution. A more realistic choice situation is depicted in Part B of the chart. The peasant producer participates in market production by choice; and the choice is determined by prevailing market prices in conjunction with his own household preferences relevant to both farm and non-farm goods and services. Thus this producer converts resources into output both for sale in the market *and* for his own consumption.

In the peasant case, although the price line comes into the picture the household preference map is still relevant as a source of risk minimization; whether or not all output is actually marketed. In Chart 3 B, we get three different solutions which result from given market prices and a particular household preference. If the effective price line is P_bL_b, the particular output mix will be V_b of vegetables and M_b of meat. If the price line is P_aL_a, the output mix will be V_a of vegetables and M_a of meat. Now if the market price is not right, the producer will choose a $C_v + C_m$ combination for his own consumption. This is the case where market conditions generate a *forced* subsistence solution on the peasant farmer.

In peasant economy, the production possibilities frontier tends to re-

Chart 3 The peasant case.

A. *The Simple Case*

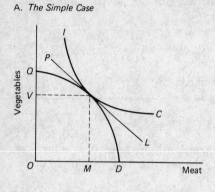

B. *The More Complex Case*

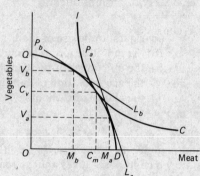

Note: $C_v + C_m$ if market situation is not "right"
(i.e., *forced* subsistence solution)

main relatively static over time as tradition tends to dominate economic and social life. Nevertheless, the society has a relatively even pattern of income distribution and full employment, albeit at generally low levels of income. Accordingly, the market for non-farm output remains small; and expansion comes mainly from exogenous shocks which either raise desirable levels of consumption, or shift the production frontier to the right, or a combination of both.[16]

DEVELOPMENT AND UNDERDEVELOPMENT

Agriculture contributes to general economic growth in the following directions: (i) providing output of food and raw materials for the whole population; (ii) providing factor supplies (especially labour and capital) to the non-agricultural sectors; (iii) providing linkages with other sectors of the economy—both at the final demand level and at the level of intermediate supplies (forward and backward linkages).

In these contexts agriculture's contribution is greatest where food output is geared heavily in initial stages, to satisfying internal demand (and where export is a surplus); where incomes are evenly distributed and output is rising; and where there are no great disparities in social relationships between groups that make up the society.

Agriculture is also an important earner of foreign exchange in many countries. However, the secular contribution of agriculture in this connection depends on terms of trade adjustments over time. For most underdeveloped countries these adjustments have been unfavourable in the past.[17] Consequently, we find that the export performance of underdeveloped countries has not had as dramatic an effect on their development as we would expect.

Agricultural Development[18]

The interaction of agriculture with other sectors during the process of economic development is important. But, in the present exercise, we are more concerned with the process of agricultural development. That is to say, the major concern is to examine what factors promote or retard sustained improvements in the material welfare of rural peoples.

If we assume that labour is already fully employed, then it is clear that the development process requires an expansion of agricultural output at the same time that labour must be transferred from agriculture to facilitate the expansion of other sectors. This means that the productivity of the labour force remaining in agriculture must increase substantially. Technological change is crucial in this regard. For this, research plays an important role since it serves to increase knowledge of new inputs and of possibilities for raising the productivity of old inputs. Capital accumulation is also essential to the process as the increased competition for labour resulting from the growth of other sectors increases the need for more capital-intensive techniques of production in agriculture.

The dynamic effects of technological change and capital accumulation can only come into play if certain preconditions for agricultural development exist. Among these are a highly motivated population to provide the basic human resources (managerial and technical skills, and adaptable labour power), adequate supplies of complementary resources—land and capital, and appropriate institutional arrangements for uniting all the available resources in the productive effort.

Economists have frequently noted these general preconditions; but of the three listed above, least consideration has been given to the need for appropriate institutional arrangements. Next to the need for a highly motivated population, we consider this neglected area to be of greatest importance. Shortage of land and capital is generally of much lesser significance. This ordering is based on our view of the development experience and performance in the underdeveloped world as a whole. The primary importance we attach to a highly motivated population—the human element —is based largely on the achievements of Israel where in spite of severe natural limitations in regard to land a viable agriculture has emerged. As concerns the importance we attach to institutional arrangements, it is to be noted that in spite of abundant supplies of land and capital throughout Latin America agricultural development in those countries has been extremely slow, mainly because structural factors have inhibited the unity of available resources.

Both the human element and the institutional arrangements in any situation are largely influenced by the pattern of social organization. It is the social environment that determines whether the population of a country is highly motivated in the service of the development effort or not. This motivation is intensified in societies where there is normative consensus with social and cultural homogeneity; but it becomes severely retarded in societies where dissensus prevails along with social and cultural plurality. The institutional arrangements determine whether or not large-scale units of collective action can be organized; and, as Brewster has emphasized, this largely determines whether the opportunities for agricultural development can be seized.[19]

The particular institutional arrangements that exist in any situation are determined by social structure and organization, tradition, values, beliefs and attitudes—all of which derive their flavour from the particular dominant rural institution existing in a country. Thus we should expect to find differences between agricultural systems, such as plantation, peasant, feudal, or state-controlled. It is the particular system which determines the nature of the social institutions, and, therefore, the kind of institutional arrangements that exist for uniting resources in the productive effort and for promoting agricultural development.

For agricultural development to proceed at a satisfactory rate it is necessary for available resources continuously to be made available to those people in the society best able to transform resource services into products for consumption. And it is clear that there is need for flexibility in resource use in order to bring about output adjustments necessitated by changing income opportunities. To achieve these, the required social institutions must be such as to facilitate the greatest possible degree of resource mobility— particularly in respect of access to land and capital by the more capable farmers, and the flexibility that exists for adjustments in patterns of land use over time. In addition, the social and economic institutions must be capable of ensuring a continuous extension of technical knowledge relating to agricultural production, adequate means of supplying farmers with new inputs and providing marketing and credit services, incentive for effort, progress-oriented values, and good government. Obviously different social systems have different inherent capacities for providing all these prerequisites for agricultural development.

Of all the capitalist systems identified in Chart 1, the "special case" appears, prima facie, to be best endowed with the prerequisites for development. In other cases, we will need to examine the persistence of underdevelopment by exposing weaknesses in the social framework of economic relations. But before proceeding to that we pause, briefly, to consider the question of the transition from *pure* subsistence to commercial agriculture.

The Transition from Subsistence

The transition from subsistence production occurs as a result of one of two processes: endogenous transition and/or exogenous change.

The endogenous sequence is the one outlined by Boserup.[20] The dynamic is population growth which places increasing pressure on natural resources; resulting in technical change, both in methods of husbandry and in techniques of production. This model seems adequately to describe the historical experience of Western Europe.

The exogenous sequence seems more applicable to contemporary underdeveloped countries. We can identify three possibilities in this connection. First, forced contact with the rest of the world, as when the Europeans invaded New World Indian society. Second, export cash crop incorporation into a food economy, as in the West African cocoa case. And, thirdly, fortuitous non-agricultural developments, like the discovery of minerals, tourism, etc., which create markets for foodstuffs, where none existed before.

In each of these cases, it is unlikely that subsistence production could survive for long. Patterns of exploitation would either exterminate the subsistence producers (the New World Indian case) or incorporate them in some way into the larger economic system (West Africa, the West Indies and Asia are three different patterns of such incorporation).

The final result of the exogenous sequence under capitalism is persistent impoverishment of the former subsistence producers by small minorities of ruling *élite* groups, nationally and internationally. These *élite* groups expropriate the bulk of the surplus for their own advancement. This is the foundation on which contemporary monopoly capitalism has been built. The final result remains entrenched as capital accumulation and technical change proceed to widen disparities internationally and within national communities.

Underdevelopment—Patterns and Results

Whereas, the "special case" generates even development and increasing rural welfare, the other cases within the capitalist international give evidence of uneven development and gross disparities in welfare among rural people. This unevenness and the corresponding disparities are found in varying degrees, as we move from one system to another along the continuum of types within the capitalist world.

In what follows, we use the plantation system as our main point of reference in analysing the underdevelopment biases of the different types of agriculture identified earlier. Chart 4 provides a summary picture. In an earlier analysis of the plantation system the 19 factors identified in Chart 4 were positively associated with the persistence of underdevelopment.[21] Development will proceed in the "normal" way in situations where these factors are *not* present in the social framework. In the chart "Yes" indicates the presence of the particular underdevelopment bias identified; and "No" indicates its absence. A "No (Yes)" or "Yes (No)" entry indicates an uncertainty; while "No-Yes" entries mean that the factor is present in some real-world cases and absent in others.

Now an examination of Chart 4 reveals that whereas underdevelopment is endemic to the plantation system, development is highly attainable in the capitalist "special case" and with the socialist peoples communalism. The feudal system has more underdevelopment biases similar to the plantation than has the peasant system. Bureaucratic socialism has several limitations for rural development. These derive principally from the centralization of power (B5 + B6) and from the presence of an authoritarian tradition (B9).

As in our earlier analysis of resource allocation and use, the peasant case is perhaps the least clear-cut regarding its development potential. This results from the fact that there are different peasant categories in different parts of the Third World. And these real world situations reflect

Chart 4 Underdevelopment biases in types of world agriculture

	Capitalist			Feudal	Socialist	
	"Special case"	Plantation	Peasant		(USSR) Bur. socialist	(China) Peoples
A. Economic factors						
1. Fracture of resource supply and demand	No	Yes	No	Yes	No	No
2. Unequal distribution of wealth and income	No	Yes	No	Yes	No	No
3. Foreign ownership of production	No	Yes	No	No (Yes)	No	No
4. Export orientation	No (Yes)	Yes	No (Yes)	No (Yes)	No	No
5. Low skill content of labour	No	Yes	No	Yes	No (Yes)	No
6. Resource use distortions	No (Yes)	Yes	No	Yes	No (Yes)	No
7. Metropolitan enterprise linkages	No	Yes	Yes	Yes	No	No
8. MNC resource allocation	No	Yes	Yes	Yes	No	No
9. Limited technical knowledge	No	Yes	Yes	Yes	No	No
B. Non-economic factors						
1. Weak community and loose family organization	No	Yes	No	No	No	No
2. Rigid social structure	No	Yes	No	Yes	No (Yes)	No
3. Correlation between race & class	Yes	Yes	No Yes	Yes	No	No
4. Absence of social responsibility	No	Yes	No	Yes	No	No
5. Strong central govt. administration	No	Yes	No	Yes	Yes	No
6. Excessive power of elites	No	Yes	No Yes	Yes	Yes	No
7. Low incidence of progress-oriented values	No	Yes	No Yes	No Yes	No	No
8. Strong individualism	No	Yes	No	No Yes	No	No
9. Authoritarian tradition	No	Yes	No	Yes	Yes	?
10. "Great House" value aspirations	No	Yes	No Yes	No (Yes)	Yes	?

somewhat different modes of over-all social organization. For example, land may be communally owned in certain tribal situations; but it may be individually owned elsewhere.

What Chart 4 really suggests is a *ranking* of systems according to the sum total of underdevelopment biases as follows:

1. Socialist—Peoples communal
2. "Special Case"
3. Socialist—Bureaucratic
4. "Pure" Peasant
5. Feudal
6. Plantation

The plantation comes last because it is the most dehumanizing of the systems considered here. The "feudal" system is almost as bad but because, in most instances, relations are more personal it is somewhat less dehumanizing.

All systems within the capitalist international, except the "special case," suffer from capitalist exploitation, as *economic* factors A7–9 indicate. As well they are subject to terms of trade backwash, resulting from A4. Consequently, countries in these categories have a common bond; that is, they have to break with the international capitalist system in order to secure economic advancement.

However, they will need to go beyond this to correct internal imbalances that inhere in each system. And that calls for political action to redress economic and social inequalities. How to achieve that is beyond the scope of the present exercise.

A COMMENT ON EMPLOYMENT AND TECHNOLOGY

Employment and unemployment are critical factors when we are considering the welfare of people. In most underdeveloped situations in the Third World today, unemployment and underemployment are significant and appear to be on the increase. The reasons for this derive *partly* from the international transfer of technology in two main directions.

The first dimension was the transfer of medical technology which brought down death rates, leaving birth rates unaltered. High rates of population growth resulted in a veritable explosion in Latin America, the Caribbean and parts of Asia. Resource pressure became great as more output was demanded, during the same period when monopoly capital was extending its control over more and more Third World resources. Considerable underemployment was the stark result of this process of change.

The second dimension is the more contemporary transfers of mechanical (labour-saving) technology and of biological and chemical technology (land-saving—the so-called "Green Revolution").

Mechanical technology directly displaces labour and creates unemployment. Biological and chemical technology has a less direct impact on employment. But that transfer favours the better-off farmers in underdeveloped countries and, thereby, aggravates inequalities in the distribution of wealth and income. Underemployment and unemployment are the chief results of this latter transfer.

Technology is not neutral. It comes with the biases of the countries exporting it; and it affects everything, including education, people's values, and the pattern of consumption mix that people aspire to achieve. Thus technological transfer locks the colonial economy tighter into the international capitalist system, and it makes a break with that system more difficult to achieve.[22]

Ultimately, however, Third World nations will have to develop indigenous technology to suit their particular resource endowments and the value aspirations of their peoples. That is the only path that will generate full employment and high levels of material welfare for the rural people and for non-rural people as well.

NOTES

1. I made an attempt to demonstrate this for the "plantation" case in *Persistent Poverty* (New York: Oxford University Press, 1972). It is no accident that I started my analysis with that case. It is the same reason why North American economists start with what I describe below as the "special case." We all start with what is most familiar (i.e., the system into which we have been socialized). The term "special case" is borrowed from Dudley Seers, writing in a somewhat different context: see "The limitations of the special case," *Oxford Economic Papers* (February 1959).

2. From a pedagogic point of view, the conventional distinction between "micro" and "macro" economics does not enlighten students of the discipline. *The particular micro makes the relevant macro.* Otherwise macro has no meaning at all!

3. These are among some of the central issues which cause economists most concern in dealing with agricultural development.

4. See V. Ruttan and Y. Hayami, "Strategies for agricultural development," *FRI Studies*, Vol. XI, No. 2 (1972); my comment in the same journal; and Hayami and Ruttan, *Agricultural Development An International Perspective* (Baltimore, Md., 1971) pp. 1–63.

5. I am not here concerned with pockets (or lacunae) of poverty in rich countries and of prosperity in poor countries. Those phenomena do exist but to understand them requires a level of analysis which is different from that used in the present exercise.

6. The references for these generally unfamiliar names are, Philip L. Wagner, "On classifying economies," in Norton Ginsburg (ed.), *Essays on Geography and Economic Development* (Chicago, 1960); Woytinsky and Woytinsky, *World Population and Production* (New York, 1953) Ch. 13; and Phillips Foster, "Systems of agricultural organization," *Journal of Farm Economics* (May 1966).

7. We should really add Joseph A. Schumpeter to the list of eclectic philosophers mentioned earlier.

8. The fact is that *all* societies exhibit substantive rationality by definition; only some societies have the techniques, the value system and institutional arrangements to achieve formal rationality.

9. The literature on the peasantry and on subsistence agriculture is really quite confusing. But I hope that our working definition here is clear enough.

10. Cf. the "land-grant" colleges and universities in the US Mid-West as examples of that kind of social capital input.

11. See Marvin P. Miracle, " 'Subsistence agriculture': analytical problems and alternative concepts," *American Journal of Agricultural Economics* (May 1968) pp. 292–310.

12. See my "The economics of agricultural resource use and development in plantation economies," *Social and Economic Studies* (December 1969); and *Persistent Poverty, op. cit.*, Ch. 6.

13. I have borrowed the terminological classifications here from Hayami and Ruttan, *op. cit.*

14. Consumption of both farm and non-farm goods and services. Present consumption has a high premium at low levels of income. Future consumption (investment) assumes greater significance as levels of income rise.

15. As an example, the "ceremonial fund" (for baptisms, weddings, funerals, etc.) is of direct relevance in this connection.

16. West African peasant-based export cocoa production is a good example of such a combination.

17. For further discussion on this point, see W. A. Lewis, *Aspects of Tropical Trade 1883–1965*, Wicksell Lectures (Stockholm, 1969).

18. The discussion below is drawn from my *Persistent Poverty, op. cit.*, pp. 193–6.

19. John M. Brewster, "Traditional social structures as barriers to change," in H. M. Southworth and B. F. Johnston (eds.), *Agricultural Development and Economic Growth* (Ithaca, NY, 1967) pp. 66–98.

20. See Ester Boserup, *The Conditions of Agricultural Growth* (London, 1965).

21. See my *Persistent Poverty*, Ch. 7 and pp. 216–17. The way in which each of these factors contributes to underdevelopment is analysed in the book.

22. The situation is aggravated by the association of technology transfer with increased foreign investment by metropolitan capitalist economy in the Third World.

14

The Economic Case for Land Reform: Employment, Income Distribution, and Productivity

Peter Dorner and Don Kanel

Though ideological arguments on the best ways of organizing agriculture continue, no land tenure system can be adjudged best in the abstract. Any judgements concerning a particular system must take note of the institutional and technological conditions in the society and the stage at which that society lies in the transformation from an agrarian to an industrial economy. Judgements must also consider what specific groups and individuals in that society are attempting to accomplish.

Several kinds of transitions from agrarian economies to industrial economies have occurred. The consequent reorganization of the agricultural sector in each of the following examples took place within a particular set of social and economic circumstances.

The system of European feudalism of several centuries ago is today, by most any standard, an anachronism. Although comprising a total system of political, social, and economic institutions, it was at base an agrarian system built around the control of land. Eventually that system conflicted with the evolving goals of creating strong nation states; proved ill-equipped to respond to the requirements of expanding markets and too inflexible to accommodate the increased use of capital; and failed to meet the needs of man's evolving conception of himself.

Yet despite its inadequacies, its injustices, and its rigidities by present standards, the feudal system was an adaptation to the times. Growing out of a crumbling and disintegrating world empire, it organized people according to strict and rigid class structures with mutual obligations between classes, thereby assuring some degree of internal harmony and a measure of security from potential enemies external to the feudal manor.

But these feudal structures were inconsistent with the requirements of changing from an agrarian system to an industrial society. The various attempts at reforming these agrarian systems, and their eventual transformation, define major landmarks in the economic history of the European states.

Russian collectivization may not have provided the individual incentives or the decision making freedom that family farms did; however, the Russian planners' major concern was rapid industrialization. Russian agriculture was producing a substantial export surplus at the time collectivization policy was implemented, and a key need was to free labour

Reprinted from *Land Reform, Land Settlement and Cooperatives*, No. 1, 1971, by permission of Food and Agriculture Organization of the United Nations.

from work in agriculture to provide manpower for the new factories. In addition, the state had to "squeeze" some of the surplus production from the agricultural sector in order to provide relatively cheap food for the growing population in the industrial sector. And of course collectivization of agriculture was perhaps necessary to assure party control over the economic system and to prevent decentralized political developments. The collective system functioned to achieve these ends (24, 25, 26). In recent years modifications have been introduced, presumably because the system was not achieving present objectives and goals.

When the Soviet system was instituted more than forty years ago, the country had a relatively slow population growth and a low man-land ratio —a sharp contrast with the current situations in South and Southeast Asia, most of Latin America, and much of Africa. In the latter areas, the rapid population growth of recent decades (and capital intensive, low labour-absorptive industrialization) makes it imperative that the agricultural sector hold people rather than being forced to release them.

Throughout the nineteenth century the United States was also charac-terized by a low man-land ratio; despite massive immigration, population growth was low relative to that in many of today's less developed countries. Furthermore, industrialization in the nineteenth century was generally more labour absorptive than it is today. United States development, like Russian development, required production of an agricultural surplus and the release of labour from agriculture to meet the demands of the growing industrial sector, but the means employed in achieving these ends were wholly different from those used by the Soviet Union a century later. United States policy placed primary emphasis on new technology to in-crease the productivity of land and especially the productivity of labour, and relied on competition among small producers for allocation of produc-tion factors among alternative uses (26).

In the past three decades U.S. agriculture has been substantially re-organized. The number of farms is now less than half what it was thirty years ago. Farms have been combined and their average size continues to grow. The 80 acre or even the 160 acre farm is an inefficient unit for most types of farming in the U.S. today. Present technology and factor costs and availabilities make them inefficient in terms of labour productivity and since labour is relatively scarce compared with land and capital, labour productiv-ity is a reasonably good measure for judging efficiency under U.S. con-ditions.[1]

When the design of a U.S. system of land tenure and economic organiza-tion of agriculture was being debated, the major alternative to family farms appeared to be a system of large estates and plantations with some features of European feudalism. The latter had been challenged on both political and economic grounds and was in various stages of disintegration. Further-more, the large land mass to the West had to be secured from threats by other nations. The family farm system was perhaps the only reasonable way in which a relatively weak government, lacking major communication and transportation networks, could assure that this large land mass would be rapidly settled and incorporated into the nation.

There are very few places in the world today where such circumstances exist. For the most part, the problems then faced by the U.S. are not now central issues in agricultural development in most of the less developed countries. For both the Soviet Union and the United States, then, the land tenure systems reflect specific historical, geographic, and political conditions; both systems continue to be modified as development occurs.

In most of Latin America, the land tenure system is dominated by the large estate or *hacienda*. There are of course some family farms, communal holdings, plantations, and large numbers of very small holdings—*minifundios*—in most countries, but the prevalent form of land tenure, in terms of the area of land controlled, is the large estate.

The tenure system resulting from Spanish conquest reflected the purposes of the *conquistadores* and the Spanish Crown: to gain control over, and to settle this part of the new world, much of which had a larger indigenous population than then existed in North America.

However useful this land tenure system originally was for the Spanish colonizers, or is for national elites that now hold power, it has become obsolete and stands in direct conflict with the achievement of development goals. It needs to be changed to meet changing conditions, just as the land tenure systems of the industrialized nations have been modified and reformed in the process of development. Specifically, the basic land tenure institutions in Latin America must be reformed in order to create more employment, to achieve a more equal distribution of income, and to provide necessary increases in productivity.

The above sketches are not intended to imply a neat, logical relationship between tenure systems and concurrent social problems and policy needs. Tenure systems emerge from conflict and debate among contending groups —witness the Soviet debate on the rapidity and method of industrialization and the many U.S. experiments with land settlement policies in the nineteenth century. Tenure systems, as hammered out by experience and conflict, are nevertheless adaptations to prevailing circumstances. They cannot be easily transplanted into an entirely different set of conditions.

Even in the industrialized countries, agriculture still makes substantial contributions to overall economic development. However, its contribution to the supply of non-agricultural manpower, to capital formation, and to demand generation for industrial goods certainly becomes less critical in a highly industrialized country where the labour force in agriculture may be less than 10 percent of the total. In the developing countries, by contrast, especially in countries with 50 percent or more of their labour force engaged in farming, agriculture's contribution is critical in all these areas (19). Although labour must move from agriculture to industry in the process of development, the problem under conditions of rapid population growth is not how to release labourers, but how to keep from releasing too many too quickly (32). Under present circumstances rapid population growth seems to accompany and even to precede development rather than to follow the nineteenth century pattern where population growth seemed a response to development.

The less developed countries need a labour-intensive, capital-saving approach with heavy reliance on yield-increasing technical innovations in earlier phases of agricultural development, followed by a capital-intensive, labour-saving approach only in the later phases. These phases are determined by changing conditions in the areas of (a) demand for food and (b) employment opportunities.

Changes in the demand for food are determined largely by population growth and by the income elasticity of demand for food (which declines as average incomes rise). These changes are readily seen in the following formulation: $D = p + \eta g$, where D, p and g are annual rates of growth of demand for food, population, and per capita income, and η is income elasticity of demand for food. As an illustration, assume that in a less developed country $p = 2$ and $\eta = .8$, while in an industrialized country $p = 1$ and $\eta = .2$, and that $g = 2$ in both cases. Then the demand for food will grow at a rate of 3.6 percent in the less developed country and at 1.4 percent in the industrialized country. The difference would be even wider if the population growth rate in the less developed country was more than 2 percent, while a higher growth rate of income in the industrialized country would make little difference because of the low income elasticity. Thus the less developed countries need considerably larger increases in food output than more developed countries do.[2] The need to earn foreign exchange increases even more the importance of increasing agricultural production.

On the employment side the crucial considerations are high rates of population growth and the difficulty of absorbing a large share of this growth in the small urban sector. Even with large rural to urban migration, rural population typically continues to grow, though at a slower rate than total population. Urban population grows rapidly, and much of it is absorbed in precarious, low productivity urban jobs. Absolute numbers of rural people decline only in later stages of development, and only then is it necessary to reorganize agricultural production in a way that would decrease labour requirements (12).

The combination of the above two sets of circumstances yields the Johnston and Mellor policy prescription: a labour-intensive approach with reliance on yield-increasing technical innovations in the earlier phases of agricultural development (19). This policy approach both produces the required increases in agricultural production and avoids displacing labour prematurely from agriculture. It is a prescription for agricultural research, for large increases in the use of yield-increasing inputs such as fertilizer, improved seeds, insecticides and pesticides, for increases in irrigation facilities and for building of service institutions in extension, marketing, and credit. It is also a prescription to minimize mechanization, especially when it serves to displace labour.

Under the large farm system in Latin America, however, it has been difficult to gain acceptance of such policies. Labour-saving machine technology is available from the industrialized countries. So long as investment decisions are made on the basis of private profit, large farm entrepreneurs may find it in their best economic interest to import labour-saving machinery. In fact it may be easier to transplant this type of technology than the biological type, which often requires additional research before it can be adapted to the specific conditions in new areas. The wide range of available production techniques now affecting employment contrasts with the more restricted options open to agricultural entrepreneurs in the nineteenth century. In this earlier period, labour-saving technology was largely a response to labour supply conditions, and the major innovations emerged from within the industrializing countries of the time—especially the United States and Western Europe.

The employment problem is worsened by the capital intensive-labour extensive patterns of development in manufacturing industries. In Latin America, manufacturing output is estimated to have increased by 140 percent from 1950 to 1965. During this same period, manufacturing employment grew by only 45 percent (1).

Widespread population growth rates of 3 percent and higher are a relatively recent phenomenon, but the relatively low capacity of the manufacturing sector to absorb labour in early phases of economic development has been a feature of development in earlier times. Though manufacturing has become increasingly capital intensive over the past century, the early phases in the development of manufacturing have always had both a positive and a negative effect on employment. The shift from handicraft and cottage type industries to assembly-line manufacturing has resulted in less employment for a given amount of output (23).

If agriculture were strictly comparable to industry, this employment dilemma would seem all but insoluble. In certain industries at least, capital intensive developments are frequently inevitable because the pattern of machine technology is set by that used in and available from industrialized countries. This technology may place limits on the substitution of factors (e.g., labour for capital) in production processes. If agricultural production were similarly restricted, there would be few alternatives to capital intensive developments in this sector since agriculture in developed countries is also capital intensive. But agriculture is different. There are alternative means of economic organization in agriculture which permit greater flexibility in production processes. Factor proportions (land, labour, and capital) can more nearly be utilized in a manner consistent with their relative cost and availability. Market imperfections continue to obstruct more rational use of factors, but it is precisely at these imperfections (in land, labour and capital markets) that land reform is directed.

An important element in this argument concerns the factor proportions to be used in agricultural production. As one writer says, ". . . the assumption of only a few alternative processes and a quite limited range for substitution of factors does not seem to fit well technological characteristics of a number of important industries, as for example, agriculture" (13). If factor substitution is possible over a fairly wide range, as here hypothesized, then the problem of major misallocations of resources is likely to be found in various market imperfections. The large, often redundant agricultural labour force in most Latin American countries lacks the economic and political power to gain control (either ownership or rental) over sufficient land and capital resources to increase its productivity. Nevertheless, present distribution patterns show a gross misallocation in terms of resource availabilities—too much land and capital and too little labour on the large farms, and too little land and capital and too much labour on the small farms. In Latin America, 30–40 percent of the active agricultural population typically lives on and works less than 10 percent of the land (12).

Why don't farmers with large extensions of land employ more labour? There are many possible reasons. Farm owners may have outside interests that hold greater economic importance for them than farming. Abundant labour is not always cheap labour; minimum wages and a variety of social welfare laws may make the price of labour higher than it would be in their absence. A large unskilled hired labour force becomes difficult to manage on labour intensive enterprises. It also increases the risk in dealing with expensive machinery, improved livestock, and modern production practices which require constant use of judgement on the part of labourers. Given these circumstances, owners of large farms will frequently reduce their labour force and move in the direction of capital intensive, mechanized operations with a relatively small force of skilled workers (supplemented when needed by seasonal labour) (31). On the apparent assumption that a developed agriculture must have the factor proportions now existing in the agriculture of the developed countries, government policy often encourages importation of farm machinery through favourable foreign exchange rates. Furthermore, most of the credit goes to the large farms sector (more credit-worthy by bankers' standards), with inflation often making effective interest rates minimal or even negative. Resource misallocations and poor performance are not surprising given the underlying assumptions and the monopolized control over land and capital, but the profitable course for the individual entrepreneur results in costs to society which cannot forever be postponed.

Reasoning from analogy, U.S. and European experience with farm enlargement and mechanization provides support for this type of development, but only if one ignores the widely differing situation with respect to factor proportions and real factor costs (in contrast to existing factor prices which are often controlled and distorted by some of the above policies). Given the rapid population growth (and the inevitable continuing absolute increase in farm populations in most of the developing countries) and the inadequate labour-absorptive capacity of industry, agriculture must be organized to provide much more productive employment than it does at present (33).

The size of farm operating units is a basic determinant in the development of a labour intensive agriculture. Data from India, the U.S. (Illinois), and Chile show the following relationships: the smallest farm group has 1.6, 74, and 1.1 acres while the largest farm group has 15.6, 219, and 16.6 acres per worker, for the three countries respectively (20). These data certainly indicate some adaptation to the factor proportions existing in each country. They also, however, illustrate the greater employment capacity of small farm units, even though output per man may be (and usually is) lower on the small units. These figures also suggest the wider range of production techniques: for example, the ratio of acres per man on large over small farms is about 3 in the United States but ranges from 10 to 15 in the cases of India and Chile.

A study of the Chateaulin area of Brittany reports the following results: "When one moved from holdings of less than 5 hectares to those of more than 25, the number of workers per 100 hectares fell from 105 to 18.7, the number of per-annum working hours per hectare from 1,500 to 480. Working capital also fell, but less markedly, from 210,000 to 119,000 francs, and gross yield from Index 163 to 88 (average for the area: 100)" (5).

Commenting on Mexico, Dovring notes that small-scale, labour intensive production is less costly than large-scale production in terms of the goods that are scarce in the Mexican economy. The large private farms are using more of the hardware that might otherwise have been invested toward even more rapid industrialization of the country. "There is no doubt," concludes Dovring, "that the owners or holders of large private farms make a good income by using more machines and somewhat less labour, but they render a less useful service to the struggling and developing economy of a low-income, capital-scarce country" (11).

In the case of West Pakistan, Johnston and Cownie make a strong case for employment of more labour rather than more tractors in agriculture. They argue that "the existence of yield-increasing innovations which are neutral to scale and consistent with the existing systems of small scale agriculture increases the advantages of the labour-intensive, capital-saving alternative" (18).

Additional cases could be cited, but the evidence is quite clear that a small farm agriculture can absorb more labour than a large farm agriculture. Some have cautioned that a small farm agriculture of peasant proprietors may lead to an excess of capital equipment on small holdings (i.e., much duplication and under-utilization of buildings and equipment) (14). However, the Japanese case shows clearly that technology can be adapted to fit small farms if research is specifically directed to achieve these results (10). Or, on the other hand, a reorganization of a large farm system on cooperative or communitarian principles can be designed to assure both labour absorption and efficiency in the use of capital.

Agricultural production processes, as mentioned, have characteristics which make many comparisons with developments in industry invalid. The superiority of a large farm system, argued on the basis of economies of scale, is an old idea. Marshall and Mill expressed serious doubts about its validity, but as Owen has pointed out, "It is probably fair to say that most economists have since attempted to resolve his (Marshall's) dilemma by avoiding it" (26).[3]

Moreover, Raup (27) comments that the investment processes in agriculture and industry differ:

> The process of economic growth in agriculture follows a distinct pattern. In its early stages, slow gains in capital stocks predominate. Investment decisions are typically made in small segments, spread over many seasons or gestation periods. Impressive amounts of capital are formed, but by many small, plodding steps. This is quite different from the large-scale, dramatic investment programmes emphasized in much current economic development planning. The image of development conveyed by a hydroelectric dam or by a steel mill is misleading if applied to agriculture. Capital formation in farming is rarely concentrated either in space or time. It accumulates by an incremental process that is best described as accretionary.

The development of a nation's livestock herds is a good example. But likewise is the use of available labour (due to the sequential nature of operations noted above in which slack periods inevitably occur) to construct buildings, drainage ditches, fences, maintenance of irrigation systems, etc. Raup concludes:

> Wherever there is surplus agricultural labour and shortage of working capital the task of the land tenure system is to put people to work. This is when proposals for land distribution are most strongly compelling.
>
> The prospect that subsequent economic development may create non-farm employment opportunities has led many economists to condemn land distribution programmes because of the "uneconomic" size of farm units that may result. In the long run this argument may have validity. In the shorter run, the waste of capital-forming potential represented by underutilized labour is the more serious concern. In this sense, the political pressures leading to drastic land distribution programmes may also be good economics.

It is very difficult to make a case for large-scale, labour extensive units in farming at early stages of economic development, especially in countries with a high man-land ratio. "Under a labour technology, costs cannot be cut by increasing the size of farm. Most of the cost economies from using modest capital items are largely exhausted as soon as the bullock team, horse or camel which provides the power are fully employed" (16).

The above argument presents the rationale for recommending farm enlargement under one set of circumstances (e.g., in the U.S.) and farm subdivision with smaller units (or in any event a more labour intensive agriculture) under another set of circumstances (e.g., in Latin America). The choice depends largely on the existing factor proportions and their relative real cost to society. What is good (i.e., profitable) for the individual entrepreneur may entail disastrous social costs.

The small farm cannot divert the cost of unemployed (or underemployed) labour onto society as can the large farm or industry working primarily with hired labour. It thus becomes a better vehicle for what Owen has referred to as farm financed social welfare (26). A small farm agriculture (or one organized in such a way as to provide a greater correspondence between private and public costs and benefits) also has advantages in providing a more equal distribution of income and thereby an enlarged demand for the growing industrial sector.

It may be conceded that a small farm or reformed agricultural system has the above noted advantages—more employment, more equitable distribution of income, a wider and more relevant demand structure for the growing manufacturing sector, a better base for farm-financed social welfare, and more rational (in terms of existing factor availabilities) investment policies in both the agricultural and non-agricultural sectors of the economy. Yet all these advantages may seem less significant if increasing agricultural production, both for export and for feeding rapidly growing populations, is viewed as the main issue, and if the problems of unemployment and redistribution are thought to be resolved indirectly (rather than through policies directed specifically at their resolution) in the course of increasing agricultural output. None can deny the great importance of increased agricultural production, for which Ruttan (28) has provided this rationale:

> Demographic and economic forces are resulting in annual increases in the demand for agricultural output of 3–5 percent. Sustained rates of growth in the domestic demand or in the supply of farm products in this range are completely outside the experience of presently developed countries. The annual rate of growth of agricultural output in the United States has not exceeded 3 percent for a sustained period since 1860.

But given the experience with agricultural modernization in Latin America, it is probably not feasible to institute a continuous process of development without specific attention to the growing problems of unemployment and redistribution.

Why should many agricultural production technicians (and some economists too) fail to give adequate recognition to the problems of unemployment and redistribution and concentrate instead on the more technical aspects of increasing production? (This is particularly true of U.S. technicians.) There is a general assumption that the large farm is more efficient. Under this assumption, it is natural to concentrate on ways and means of increasing the productivity of the larger farms through more favourable (incentive) cost/price ratios, improved practices, better markets, more credit, etc. Speaking of U.S. research, Ruttan points out that "Research has been primarily oriented to providing information relevant to private rather than public decision-making. The same orientation is characteristic of American farm management and production economics specialists and U.S. trained farm management and production economics specialists working in less developed countries" (28).

This erroneous assumption has arisen because of the particular measure of productivity of efficiency employed. It is true that labour productivity is consistently higher on larger farms, but this is hardly a measure relevant to policy in a labour surplus economy. Higher labour productivity on large farms is primarily related to mechanization and labour-saving techniques. Land-saving technologies such as improved seed varieties, fertilizers, insecticides, and improved weeding can usually be applied equally well and efficiently on small farms. Under conditions of abundant rural labour and continuous rapid population growth, productivity per unit of land is the most relevant measure for policy purposes for the next several decades. Obviously it is the purpose of economic development to raise labour's productivity—but not only for the few. And in order to raise labour productivity broadly for all those now in farming and those yet to be absorbed by the agricultural sector, land and capital must be redistributed—land reform must be implemented. Long (21) has stated the case well when, writing on Indian agriculture, he notes:

> Literally hundreds of American studies have confirmed that larger farms normally have correspondingly higher operator incomes, i.e., higher returns to the managerial and labour contributions of the farm operator and his family. In common usage this has erroneously been too often taken to be synonymous with greater "efficiency," leading to the conclusion that large farms are more "efficient" than small farms. They are! But only with reference to management and labour, i.e., with reference to returns to the human agent. They are not necessarily the most "efficient" in the use of other (non-human) resources. In the United States and similarly developed countries, this error creates little difficulty because the human agent is from

a social viewpoint the most scarce factor of production. Much more importantly, in the United States maximum returns to the human agent in agriculture, which is obviously the economic goal of the individual farmers, is also roughly congruent with the broad objectives of public agricultural policy. And since management and labour are usually supplied by the same social unit, the individual farm family operator's net income is the most relevant measure of the relative efficiency of farms of different sizes. Maximum operator's income serves as an adequate criterion of both private and public policy action. The situation in India and similar countries is very different.

[T]he results from a number of recent studies on the relationship between farm size and output per unit of land (30) . . . [are] generally consistent with the hypothesis that output per unit of land is inversely related to farm size. Some may say that this does not *prove* an inverse relationship between farm size and productivity per unit of land. However, the data do show that the general presumption of a highly positive relationship—which underlies most arguments against land reform—is highly suspect.

In a Chilean study Morales analysed output per hectare for farm size groups ranging from 10 to 500 hectares of irrigated land. In this study, soil quality, distance to market, and even type of farming were held constant. Even under these rigidly controlled circumstances there were no statistically significant differences in output per hectare for farms in the various size groups despite the small farms' greater difficulties in obtaining credit and water for irrigation (22).

. . . In his analysis of India, Long has suggested that similar analysis from societies whose agriculture has had more dynamics might be more relevant. The data from Mexico, Taiwan and Japan are especially revealing in this regard. As Long points out, "if data for such countries (as Japan) reveal a negative relationship between size-of-farm and gross value productivity per acre above variable capital costs as the end result of a highly dynamic agricultural development process, then indeed the pre-suppositions of most land reform discussions—and also of much technical assistance work—need intense re-examination" (21).

The data for Japan certainly are not inconsistent with this view. In fact the multiple cropping ratio is consistently smaller as farm size increases. For the case of Taiwan, [there is] a very consistent inverse relation between farm size and net farm income per unit of land. From 1940 to 1965, cultivated land per farm was reduced by almost one half while output per hectare *more than* doubled (6, p. 41). The Mexican data also support this view. The ejido sector in 1960 had only one fourth of the land but accounted for over one third of all marketed farm produce. In terms of sales as a percent of total output, the ejido sector sold practically the same proportion (65.2) as did the large farm sector (67.7) (11).

It might be argued that the higher productivity per unit of land on existing small farms is no real evidence that new units to be created by splitting up large farms would achieve increased productivity. But the evidence available on post-reform experiences in Mexico, Bolivia, Chile, Japan, Taiwan, and Egypt shows that although in some cases there was an initial drop, average productivity per unit of land increased rather substantially after these reforms. All cases involved a reduction in the average size of farm (30).

There has been much discussion of the drop in agricultural output following the Bolivian revolution and reform, yet this decline was not so much in output as in the amount marketed (7). In fact, even the amount marketed was not reduced by as much as official statistics indicate because marketing channels were altered. Some of the produce marketed through the new channels did not get counted since market reports were obtained only at the traditional outlets.

These points are *not* presented to argue for small holdings per se or necessarily for a family farm system. Certainly the man-land ratio in Latin America, for instance, is immensely more favourable than in Japan or Taiwan, and presenting information on these countries is in no way meant to suggest such small farm systems for Latin America. The figures are meant to show that even in a system of extremely small holdings, the inverse relationship between farm size and output per unit of land exists.

Differences exist between today's less developed nations and those parts of Europe, the United States, and Canada where the family farm system was established some time ago. What is required for development is an agriculture organized in such a way as to (a) provide incentives for productive work and investment, and (b) use a combination of production factors consistent with the cost and availability of these factors at a given time.

In the United States, land tenure research has concentrated largely on improving leasing arrangements and on "modifications designed to help the tenant become an owner operator" (28). This research emphasis is also fitting for many of the landlord-tenant small farm systems in Asia (where land reform is a simpler process than in Latin America since such systems are already characterized by small operating units and the key to reform is to sever the landlords' control over the tenants). But such a research emphasis does not get at the issues in the Latin American situation. There, if the agricultural sector is to contribute to overall development, basic reorganization and redistribution of land and capital is required in order to: productively employ more people in agriculture, contribute more to capital formation in both the agricultural and the industrial sectors, and provide the income distribution necessary for broadening the market for locally manufactured goods as well as for the increased production from agriculture.

NOTES

1. Labour productivity as a measure of efficiency in the agricultural sector ignores the social costs of people becoming stranded in rural communities and of large numbers of unskilled workers migrating to cities but failing to find employment within an occupational structure largely determined by the technological developments in industry. These are serious problems in the United States, and they are likely to become all but insoluble in the less developed countries if means cannot be found to hold more people in agricultural employment (32; 9).

2. This discussion also assumes that the rate of growth in per capita income is widely shared. If increases in incomes are highly skewed in their distribution, the full im-

pact of the income elasticity of demand for food would not be realized. For similar reasons, there may not be a one-to-one relationship in population growth and increased demand for food.

3. With regard to the nature of employment in agriculture, Owen quotes John Stuart Mill: "Agriculture . . . is not susceptible of so great a division of occupations as many branches of manufactures, because its different operations cannot possibly be simultaneous. One man cannot be always ploughing, another sowing, and another reaping. A workman who only practiced one agricultural operation would be idle eleven months of the year. The same person may perform them all in succession, and have, in most climates, a considerable amount of unoccupied time." Mill's insight has been elaborated by Brewster (3).

REFERENCES

1. BARRACLOUGH, S., "Employment problems affecting Latin American agricultural development," *FAO Monthly Bulletin of Agricultural Economics and Statistics* 18 (7–8): 1–9.
2. BARRACLOUGH, S., & DOMIKE, A. L., "Agrarian structure in seven Latin American countries." *Land Economics* 42(1966): 391–424.
3. BREWSTER, J. M., "The machine process in agriculture and industry," *Journal of Farm Economics* 32(1950): 69–81.
4. "Changes in Agriculture in 26 Developing Nations," *ERS Foreign Agricultural Report No. 27*, Department of Agriculture, Washington D.C. (1965).
5. CHOMBART DE LAUWE, J. B., & MORVAN, F., "Les possibilités de la petite entreprise dans l'agriculture française," Paris (1954). Cited by M. Cepede in *Rural Development Reader*, R. Weitz (ed.).
6. CHRISTENSEN, R., "Taiwan's agricultural development: its relevance for developing countries today," *ERS Foreign Agricultural Economic Report No. 39*, Department of Agriculture, Washington D.C. (1968).
7. CLARK, R., "Land reform and peasant market participation on the Northern Highlands of Bolivia," *Land Economics* 45(1968): 153–172.
8. COMITE INTERAMERICANO DE DESARROLLO AGRÍCOLA, "Tenencia de la tierra y desarrollo socioeconómico del sector agrícola: Guatemala," Pan American Union, Washington D.C. (1965).
9. DORNER, P., "Fourteen million rural poor," book review of "The People Left Behind," Report of the President's Advisory Commission on Rural Poverty, 1967. *The Yale Review* 58(1969): 282–292.
10. DORNER, P., & FELSTEHAUSEN, H., "Agrarian reform and employment: the Colombian case," *International Labour Review 102* (September 1970): 221–240.
11. DOVRING, F., "Land Reform and Productivity: The Mexican Case, Analysis of Census Data," *Land Tenure Center Paper No. 63*, University of Wisconsin, Madison, Wis. (1969).
12. DOVRING, F., "The share of agriculture in a growing population," *Monthly Bulletin of Agricultural Economics and Statistics* 8(1959): 1–11.
13. ECKAUS, R. S., "The factor proportions problem in underdeveloped areas," *American Economic Review* 5(1965): 539–565.
14. GEORGESCU-ROEGEN, N., "Economic theory and agrarian economics," *Oxford Economic Papers* 12(1960):1–40.
15. HANEY, E., "The economic reorganization of minifundia in a Highland Community of Colombia," Ph.D. dissertation, University of Wisconsin (1969).
16. HEADY, E. O., "A recipe for meeting the world food crisis," *CAED Report No. 28*, Iowa State University, Ames, Iowa (1966).
17. JOHNSON, R. G., & BUSE, R. C., "A study of farm size and economic performance in Old Santa Rosa, Rio Grande do Sul," *Land Tenure Center Research Paper No. 27*, University of Wisconsin, Madison, Wis. (1967).
18. JOHNSTON, B. F., & COWNIE, J., "The seed-fertilizer revolution and labour force absorption," *American Economic Review* 59(1969): 569–582.
19. JOHNSTON, B. F., & MELLOR, J. W., "The role of agriculture in economic development," *American Economic Review* 51(1961): 566–593.
20. KANEL, D., "Size of farm and economic development," *Indian Journal of Agricultural Economics* 22(1967): 26–44.
21. LONG, E. J., "The economic basis of land reform in underdeveloped economies," *Land Economics* 37(1961): 113–123.
22. MORALES, J. H., "Productividad presente y potencial en 96 predios de la Provincia

de O'Higgins y su relación con el tamaño de las propiedades," Memoria (1964), Universidad de Chile.

23. MYRDAL, G., "The United Nations, agriculture and the world economic revolution," *Journal of Farm Economics 47:* 889–899.

24. NICHOLS, W. H., "The place of agriculture in economic development," in C. Eicher and L. Witt (eds.), *Agriculture in Economic Development* (New York: McGraw-Hill: 1964).

25. NOVE, A., "The decision to collectivize." Paper presented at the Conference on the Agrarian Question in Light of Communist and Non-Communist Experience, 23–26 August, 1967, University of Washington.

26. OWEN, W. F., "The double developmental squeeze on agriculture," *American Economic Review 56*(1966): 43–70.

27. RAUP, P. M., "Land reform and agricultural development," in H. M. Southworth and B. F. Johnston (eds.), *Agricultural Development and Economic Growth* (Ithaca, Cornell University Press: 1967).

28. RUTTAN, V. W., "Production economics for agricultural development," *Indian Journal of Agricultural Economics 23*(1968): 1–14.

29. RUTTAN, V. W., "Tenure and productivity of Philippine rice producing farms," *The Philippine Economic Journal 5*(1966): 42–63.

30. SCHMID, L., "Relation of size of farm to productivity," *Land Tenure Center Annual Report 1968* (Madison, Wis., University of Wisconsin: 1969).

31. SCHMID, L., "The role of migratory labour in the economic development of Guatemala," Ph.D. dissertation, University of Wisconsin (1967).

32. THIESENHUSEN, W. C., "Population growth and agricultural employment in Latin America with some U.S. comparisons," *American Journal of Agricultural Economics 51*(1969): 735–752.

33. TODARO, M. P., "A model of labour migration and urban employment in less developed countries," *American Economic Review 59:* 138–148.

15

The Contradictions of the Green Revolution

Harry M. Cleaver, Jr.

Radical intellectuals have been noticeably absent from recent discussion of the Green Revolution. This neglect is surprising given the importance being openly attached to this new agricultural strategy by the same foreign policy institutions which are often targets of radical research. The Ford and Rockefeller Foundations, the Development Advisory Service, the World Bank, and USAID have all provided either financing or managers for the Green Revolution. The neglect is also strange in a generation of radical economists who have been more impressed by the peasant revolutions of China and Vietnam than by Marx's vision of revolution by an industrial proletariat. Even a cursory review of the easily available literature shows an omnipresent fear on the part of capitalist policy makers that in parts of Asia the Green Revolution may have a sizable negative impact on social stability and increase the possibility of peasant insurgency. This paper attempts to bring the Green Revolution to the attention of radical economists and to open a discussion about the importance of the phenomena to U.S. imperialism and revolutionary strategy at home and abroad.

I. THE GREEN REVOLUTION AND IMPERIALISM

Narrowly defined, the Green Revolution is the rapid growth in Third World grain output associated with the introduction of a new package of tropical agricultural inputs. The package consists essentially of a combination of improved grain varieties, mainly rice and wheat, heavy fertilizer usage and carefully controlled irrigation. Without fertilizer or without controlled irrigation the new varieties usually yield no more and sometimes less than traditional strains. With them they give substantially higher yields per acre.

The development of this new technology is very much a part of the efforts of the American elite to direct the course of social and economic development in the Third World. With a foreign policy devoted to facilitating the expansion of U.S. multinational business, the elite is always concerned with creating new investment and sales markets. But it also tries to plan for the longer-run problem of economic or political upheaval which might upset the stability of those markets. Although overt military

Reprinted from *American Economic Review*, Vol. LXII, No. 2 (May 1972), pp. 177–186, by permission of the American Economic Association and the author.

and covert CIA type intervention is used whenever necessary to put down threats, the more lucid members of the elite have tried to develop ways of warding off instability before it irrupts.

The Growth of a Strategy

The Rockefellers sent plant pathologist J. George Harrar to Mexico in 1943 to develop an agricultural research program. The resulting research effort can be seen as a friendly gesture to soften rising nationalism and to hang on to wartime friends, but the Green Revolution it produced has clearly developed into one aspect of a Third World strategy to open profitable new markets and to avoid both rural and urban turmoil caused by growing hunger and poverty. The focus on agriculture is designed to increase the availability of basic foodstuffs in potentially unstable areas and to create outlets for agribusiness products. Population control is another part of the strategy and is aimed at slowing the growth of an unemployable, unproductive labor force. Publicly the diagnosis of Third World nationalism and revolts against U.S. imperialism has been population versus food supplies.

By 1963 the Mexican research project had grown from a small team to a large organization: the International Center for the Improvement of Corn and Wheat (CIMMYT). CIMMYT became the nucleus for research and the training of native technicians. The Foundations and AID have also carried on this work. But technicians are not enough to manage an empire and a new organization. The Agricultural Development Council (ADC) was set up to provide a special focus and analysis capability for the training of a higher level elite. The goal was the formation of agricultural economists and managers who could take over agricultural policy formulation in their home countries and, with help from their teachers, mold it into forms compatible with stability and profit.

The ADC was founded by J. D. Rockefeller III in 1953. At that time the capitalist world, still reeling from the loss of China, was fighting in Korea; and much of Asia was wracked by rural guerrilla war. That same year Rockefeller made a survey trip to the Far East. Soon after, ADC advisors were dispatched to Asia to set up new programs in the universities and to ferret out promising young students for stateside training. While small in terms of the number of personnel and students it supports, the ADC, together with the U.S. universities, has helped coordinate much of the research and thinking on agricultural development policy and foreign student training.

As this new effort was getting underway to save Southeast Asia, the earlier Mexican research was beginning to pay off. Rust resistant wheat strains had been widely distributed by 1951 and a new wheat package was developed that gave high yields in the newly opened irrigation lands of Mexico's northwestern deserts. A rapid increase in yields coupled with expansion of acreage caused dramatic increases in total wheat production throughout the 1960's. Mexico, which had been a sizable net importer of wheat at the time of the Rockefeller team's arrival, was able to achieve "self-sufficiency" by the early 1960's and is today exporting a portion of her crop.

Encouraged by these successful results the Rockefeller Foundation joined with the Ford Foundation to expand research operations into Asia. In 1962 they founded the International Rice Research Institute (IRRI) in the Philippines to develop new rice varieties comparable to the Mexican wheats. The Philippine project gave results even quicker than the effort in Mexico. Within barely four years "miracle" rices were boosting yields in the Philippines. Like the Mexican wheats the new rice varieties were dwarfs and their similar requirements for a lot of inputs seemed to open new vistas for agribusiness salesmen.

The new Institute began to train agricultural technicians for Asia to complement the economists and managers being trained under Foundation, AID, and ADC auspices. These trainees and their mentors came to form an international team of agricultural experts ready and willing to spread the seeds of the Green Revolution. Their big push began in 1965, the same year as the beginning of a major turnaround in U.S. aid policy toward the capitalist Third World.

That turnaround was of great importance in opening the way for the Green Revolution and the expansion of rural markets. Since the war the U.S. government had been stopgapping socially disruptive food shortages in the Third World by the provision of grain supplies from U.S. surpluses, first on an *ad hoc* basis and then from 1954 on under P.L. 480. This program, which began as a subsidy to U.S. agribusiness, bought time for the new agricultural strategy to be put together. But in 1965 Johnson announced the reversal of this policy. No longer would U.S. surpluses be handed out freely. Future deliveries were made dependent on the satisfaction of a number of conditions by the receiving countries—primarily a shift of emphasis from industrialization to agricultural development, expansion of population control, and an open door to U.S. investors.

The crunch came with the application of this "short-tether" policy to India during the 1965–66 famine. Successive droughts had brought about major food shortages and U.S. capital was knocking at the door with plans for new fertilizer plants and demands for control over prices and distribution. Faced with upheaval at home and Johnson's intransigence, the Indian government opened her doors to some U.S. capital and most of the Green Revolution.

Since 1965 the international team handling the spread of the new technology has had mixed success. In the capitalist Third World only about 17 percent of its wheat acreage and 8 percent of its rice acreage have been planted with the new seeds. In some particular countries on the other hand, the new varieties have been diffused with considerable success. There can be little question that a Green Revolution has come to India, West Pakistan, and the Philippines. In India and Pakistan the growth rates of wheat production have increased dramatically while in the Philippines the growth rate of rice production has risen moderately.

Spreading Capitalism

The integration of the agricultural sector into the capitalist market is achieved through the adoption of the new technological package which itself makes the peasant producer more dependent on the market. He must now buy the manufactured inputs and sell part of his crop for cash in order to be able to buy next year's inputs. The international team has also been making an effort to teach personal gain and consumerism where it feels peasants lack sufficient motivation. In his handbook, ADC president Arthur T. Mosher harps repeatedly on the theme of teaching peasants to want more for themselves, to abandon collective habits, and to get on with the "business" of farming. Mosher goes so far as to advocate extension educational programs for women and youth clubs to create more demand for store-bought goods. The "affection of husbands and fathers for their families" will make them responsive to these desires and drive them to work harder. These tactics of the ADC are more than efforts to bring development to rural areas. They are attempts to spread capitalism with all its business-based social relations and the markets such relations support.

Profits from Progress?

Many Green Revolutionists have had an eye to international corporate profits all along. Lester Brown has hailed the multinational corporation as "an amazingly efficient way of institutionalizing the transfer of technical knowledge in agriculture." He sees international agribusiness as a major source of new investment in both inputs and international marketing.

In Jalisco, Mexico, an experiment financed by AID is underway to involve foreign private capital investment in a new kind of corporation which would provide inputs to "independent" peasants and then market their combined output (in this case corn). Such a corporation is designed to earn an annual income of 50 percent on equity after the third year. Its involvement in "fighting hunger" is expected to provide a good public relations cover to the foreign capital involved.

But for all the best laid plans of apologetic economists and corporate planners, exploitation is not always an easy business and market creation can be costly. Bilateral and multilateral financing for complementary irrigation systems, fertilizer and tractor imports, and joint production ventures have provided large profits to international agribusiness. Local government grain support prices, overvalued currencies, and special tariff structures have cheapened the costs of importing inputs and have helped increase sales. But ESSO recently sold its oft cited fertilizer distribution network in the Philippines because of low profits. And after all the arm twisting in India the actual amount of foreign investment in fertilizer was limited. The increase in input sales to countries adopting the new technology seems to be far less than expected and the marketing of food-grain output almost nil. It seems unlikely for now that international agribusiness will be able to move into Third World grain marketing in a big way. If projects like that at Jalisco work out, they may eventually make headway, but such a development is not around the corner.

The most profitable international investments in agriculture are outside the area of food grains and in traditional export crops like meat, oil palm, fruit, and vegetables. If the aid lobby succeeds in increasing economic aid appropriations for agricultural development, input sales and profits will probably increase, though it is likely that they will continue to be financed more through foreign aid than through direct commercial contracts. This will add to the growing debt burden of aid recipients and bring them even more closely under imperial control.

In sum, the new agricultural strategy is giving mixed results in terms of its planners' aims. Corporate investment and profit opportunities have not been as great as hoped. On the other hand, there have been sizable increases in food output in some of the biggest and most important Third World countries. How much this increased output will insure stability in those countries remains in doubt. In the process of trying to resolve one contradiction of neocolonialism—that between a rapidly growing, poverty stricken population and the inability of satellite capitalism to provide food —the Green Revolutionists appear to be creating or accentuating a whole series of other contradictions which not only threaten national social stability but the ecological balance of wide areas.

II. THE EFFECTS OF THE GREEN REVOLUTION ON THE CONTRADICTIONS OF CAPITALIST DEVELOPMENT

The simultaneous existence of poverty and wealth is a fundamental characteristic of capitalism. That unevenness, which results from investing where the private rate of return is greatest, is what John Gurley has called "building on the best." The Green Revolution is now intensifying this pattern in the Third World.

Contradictions between Regions

By breeding new grain varieties that give maximum results only on carefully irrigated land, the Rockefeller scientists insured that only limited areas of Third World agriculture would benefit. This was partly due to their concentrating on the best potential lands. It was also because within capitalist systems there is little hope of reversing the dictates of "efficiency" by transferring wealth from rich regions to poor ones. Irrigated land represents only a small proportion of the total cultivated land in most countries and well-controlled irrigation is even rarer. The resulting regional bias of the new technology has been obvious from the beginning. In Mexico the new wheats were planted overwhelmingly in the new, irrigated districts of the Northwest, and it has been this area alone which is responsible for the rapid growth in wheat output. The rest of the country, where most of the people live, has remained virtually untouched by the new varieties. India has only some 20 percent of her cultivated land under irrigation and only about half of that has assured water supplies. The adoption has thus been primarily in the north and northwestern states like the Punjab where irrigation facilities are concentrated. In Turkey wheat adoption has been limited to the coastal lowlands. In Thailand, their new rice varieties have been confined largely to the Central Lowlands.

The most striking case of uneven regional development being exacerbated by the Green Revolution is that of Pakistan. In West Pakistan, where nearly all the cropland is under controlled irrigation, the spread of the new wheats was very successful. There has been hardly any success in flood-irrigated Eastern Pakistan. The result has been to transform the West into a food surplus area while leaving the East heavily dependent on food imports and its people in greater relative poverty than before.

In all of these countries the Green Revolution is benefiting those regions which are already the most developed and neglecting the poorest and least developed areas. Moreover, the prospects for future extension into these latter areas are not very promising. There has been some work but very little success with the development of new varieties adaptable to dry or flood areas. It is also unlikely that the bulk of current drylands and flooded areas will be able to develop adequate irrigation facilities.

Contradictions between Classes

Just as the Green Revolution appears to be accentuating regional contradictions in capitalist development, there is also evidence that it is intensifying inequalities within the regions it has affected directly. Foundation and government officials often turned first to established, commercial farmers for initial field trials. The results of numerous studies on both rice and wheat have been far from unanimous, but if there is a trend it is that "them what has gets." This usually has meant larger, commercial farmers but it also has meant small peasants close to extension and market centers, and sometimes tenants where landowners supplied financing. At least two of the studies show that in some areas where the initial adoption rate was higher for larger farmers, there was a rapid catching up by others. The problem with most of these studies is that they concentrate on the diffusion of the new seeds alone, whereas the real question is that of the package. There is some indication that while more wealthy farmers may not use a higher percentage of seeds they do use more of the complementary inputs.

How representative these studies are is hard to judge, but they do indicate that, while the new combination of inputs is largely neutral with respect to technical economies of scale, there are other costs like financing and education which are not.

For those wealthier farmers who can adopt the new grains and afford all the complementary inputs, the change can be a very profitable one. A study by AID shows impressive differentials in average cash profits between traditional and new methods. Viewed together with the higher adoption rate for the entire package by large farmers, the implied greater profit differential suggests that the Green Revolution is resulting in a serious increase in income inequality between different classes of farmers in those areas where it is being adopted.

Wolf Ladejinsky claims that in the Indian Punjab such high profits have resulted in an increased demand for land which has driven its price up as much as 500 percent. He says there is a growing effort by landlords to acquire more land and to convert their tenants into hired laborers in order to reduce their costs. Under some situations this does seem to be an optimal strategy for a landlord trying to optimize his own profits. Such a change could have significant implications for the class structure of the countryside. A shift from a quasi-feudal structure of tenancy and share-cropping to a concentration of land in large operational units dependent on wage labor suggests a trend toward some variation of the classical capitalist two-class dichotomy.

With the growth of a rural proletariat, already sizable in India, is also coming the "reserve army" of the unemployed. Encouraged by increasing profits and new land acquisitions, capitalist farmers are accumulating more and more of their capital in the form of mechanical equipment. Investment in such capital is also being encouraged by the structure of input prices. Overvalued currencies and government subsidies have sharply reduced the relative cost of equipment to farmers. "Labor shortages" in some Green Revolution areas are also accentuating this trend by raising cash wage rates. Mechanical pumps, tractors, threshers, reapers, and combines all contribute to raising yields and output. There is considerable evidence that their net effect is to be labor displacing. These labor-displacing effects are tending to offset the much heralded positive impact on labor utilization caused by the new seed-fertilizer package. In the absence of mechanical equipment the new technology not only requires more labor for planting and cultivation but also, by increasing output and, in some cases, permitting double cropping, there is a considerable increase in harvest labor require-ments. The impact of reapers, threshers, and combines during harvest periods will be dramatic because the absolute number of men displaced will be higher during harvest, the one period of relatively sure employment for the seasonally unemployed rural laborers.

The overall outlook indicated by the various available studies points in the direction of considerable increase in rural unemployment in those areas where mechanization proceeds rapidly. This effect, especially if combined with the eviction of an appreciable number of tenants, will generate a growth in both size and insecurity of the rural landless labor force.

Growing numbers of the unemployed undoubtedly will leave the coun-tryside and join the migration to the cities—swelling the urban slums. This movement, coupled with the inability of neocolonial capitalism to create urban jobs through industrial growth, is affecting the class structure of the cities. The rising tide of urban unemployment threatens to transform an already large urban "reserve army" into a vast and permanently unemploy-able lumpen proletariat which will swamp even the new rush by multi-national corporations to capitalize on cheap foreign labor.

To date there has been little government action either to increase capital costs or to bring about land reform. Pakistan recently abandoned its 50 percent subsidy of fertilizer—a non-labor-displacing input. Another land reform law, which appears no more effective than those which came before it, has been passed by the Philippines. The United States and the puppet regime in Saigon have introduced land reform as part of their war effort. There has been no substantial recent land reform at all in the other major countries affected by the Green Revolution. Indeed, in some countries the discussion of land reform without action may have hastened the process of tenant eviction.

Contradictions in Price and Trade Relations

The Green Revolution countries are now experiencing one of the fundamental contradictions of capitalist agriculture: to achieve higher output of rice and wheat, their prices must be raised to make the necessary investment profitable to farmers. This has and is being done. But maintaining high support prices keeps consumer prices up and encourages surplus accumulation. High consumer prices are a cost of living increase that hits all who must buy food for cash. It does not hit all classes equally. In India, for example, lower income groups often pay more than the rich for the cereal foods that make up so much of their diet.

Any fall in support prices will result in decreased incentives to capitalist producers and perhaps a reduced output. Such a fall will hit the poorer peasants with narrower profit margins more than the big commercial adopters of the whole new package. A sufficient decline might push many of these small producers back into subsistence or off the land. Rising production must be either sold domestically or exported to avoid downward pressure on prices and surpluses. The chances of substantially raising the incomes of the millions of rural and urban poor through employment or welfare programs in order to increase domestic demand sufficiently to absorb the rising production is out of the question. Unemployment is getting worse, not better, and the size of the welfare program needed would bankrupt the United States, not to mention the countries of the Third World.

It is increasingly being said that continued success of the new agricultural strategy will depend on the readiness of the developed countries to import the increased grain production of the Third World. As Third World imports are being replaced with surpluses only the rich countries appear to have the potential effective demand to absorb the excess. There is little reason to believe that these countries are about to open their doors to food grains from others when they themselves are major exporters. It is the entry of Japan's highly subsidized rice exports and substantial increases in U.S. subsidized rice exports which are major factors in the growing glut of the international rice market. "Rice prices have declined to the lowest levels of the past decade and a half and export earnings from rice of the developing countries have been drastically reduced." The share of the underdeveloped countries in world rice exports has dropped from 66 percent in 1959–63 to only 45 percent in 1969, while that of the imperialist countries has risen from 19 percent to 40 percent in the same period. The current glut on the world wheat market is due to an unnoticed "Green Revolution" which has been taking place in the imperialist countries. Yields have been rising for both traditional importers and traditional exporters.

England has drastically reduced her imports. Production has been rising

University of Minnesota
Morris

April 1, 1993

To: All UMM Faculty Members

From: CAC Films Committee
         Tami Hanson and Joy Flugge, Co-Chairs

Subject: 1993 Fall Quarter Film Schedule

The CAC Films Committe is starting to select movies for Fall Quarter 1993. If you have any films that you would like to suggest as a class supplement, or that you would like to see on campus for Fall Quarter please submit them along with your name to CAC films Committe in care of Student Activities by April 12. The committee will consider all ideas when selecting the films. We appreciate your input. Thank you!

in Canada, the United States, and Australia, all traditional exporters. Rather than the Third World countries turning to the developed world for markets the opposite is taking place.

If the Third World governments are forced to strangle the Green Revolution by lowering prices radically to avoid surpluses and budget deficits, we have an idea of what could happen—marginal producers for the market may be pushed back into subsistence and further spread of the new technology would be limited. The widespread hopes stimulated by the new programs would be demolished either slowly or all at once.

Ecological Contradictions

The most difficult to foresee but the most potentially devastating of all the contradictions of the Green Revolution are those involving the ecosystem. The extension of capitalist agriculture to the tropics brings with it all of the serious ecological contradictions that we have been discovering in the United States. These contradictions are more than just technical problems because the technology itself is a product of the capitalist economic system. Pesticides, which are widely required in heavy doses for the new varieties, are primarily developed in the laboratories of private business. Their efforts to minimize research costs and to reach as wide a market as possible are dictated by capitalist competition. The resultant products are both undertested and designed to kill a broad spectrum of pests. The lack of kill specificity is bad enough in the United States. When transferred to the much more complex tropics, the results can be catastrophic. It is one thing to kill a few bald eagles. It is quite another to poison fish ponds and their protein supply while spraying rice fields. The runoffs from the heavy inorganic fertilizer applications called for by the new technology will also add to the process of protein destruction as it results in massive eutrophication of lakes, streams, and rivers.

The rapid distribution of a few plant varieties has created the danger of oversimplified ecosystems. The recent southern corn leaf blight in the United States is an example of what may be in store for Green Revolution areas. There were over 50 percent losses in many areas of the Gulf states and a one billion dollar loss to the country as a whole. The vulnerability of the crop was apparently due to the efforts of commercial hybrid breeders to reduce labor costs involved in detasseling corn plants. They used a particular kind of sterility gene which eliminated detasseling, but also conferred susceptibility to the leaf blight. Serious problems of this kind have already impeded wheat production in Turkey in 1968 and 1969. The Philippine rice boom was set so far back in 1971 by a virus disease that rice will have to be imported. The United States can afford a limited number of such "mistakes"; the Third World cannot. When such crises arise a team of breeders may patch things up. But patchwork won't solve the basic problem of having food production tied to a profit-maximizing system where the input manufacturers profit but don't have to bear the cost of error.

If the Third World is to avoid widespread ecological crises, then it must be freed from a system that insists on selling them its most deadly technology. Whether the Third World accomplishes this before the ecological contradictions of the Green Revolution negate all of its successes remains to be seen.

III. THE IMPACT OF THE NEW STRATEGY ON REVOLUTION

The most important effects of the Green Revolution on political tensions might be grouped into four categories: intensified regional conflict, changes in the form of rural class struggle, the growth of an urban lumpen, and the speedup of change.

There can be little doubt that while the Green Revolution didn't cause the victory of the Awami League in East Pakistan it certainly added to the regional bitterness which did. The differential regional success of the new technology came on top of a history of exploitation of the East by the West. This exploitation has been accomplished through capitalist institutions in a kind of internal imperialism.

How important is the factor of regional exploitation and neglect for revolution? Eric Wolf has commented on the important rule of "frontier areas" in his studies of revolution in Mexico, Vietnam, Algeria, and Cuba. Today we can see this tendency to revolt by neglected or exploited regions within many of the Green Revolution countries: Bangladesh in Pakistan, Assam and West Bengal in India, the North and Northeast in Thailand, the North in Malaya, West Irian in Indonesia, Guerrero in Mexico, as well as in countries untouched by the Green Revolution, such as Eritrea in Ethiopia, the South in the Sudan, and the North in Chad.

The impact of the Green Revolution on class structure will also have an influence on the form of revolutionary activity. A major restructuring of rural society would destroy the stability of both quasi-feudal and village relationships and lay a broader basis for a struggle for land and higher wages. The example most often cited was a clash between organizing laborers and scabs which occurred in the Green Revolution area of Tanjore, India, in 1968. Forty-three peasants were burned to death in a fight over wages. India has also seen the rise of the Naxalites, a coalition of Maoist intellectuals and landless peasants. This guerrilla group has carried on an increasing campaign of assassination and land seizure. In some areas the Naxalites developed before the new technology was introduced. How much and what kind of influence it is having on their activities, support, and tactics I don't know.

In the Philippines a guerrilla force is reported to be growing both in the Green Revolution areas of the Central Luzon rice bowl and in the outer islands. Most of its recent activities have been centered on struggle against landlords and in defense of small farmers.

Perhaps the most important effect of the Green Revolution is on the rate of urbanization. Shifts in rural class structure call for a rethinking of optimal strategy in the countryside but do not call into question the basic Maoist or Cuban "models" of revolution based on peasant support.

An increased rate of urbanization, caused by unemployment and impoverished peasants pouring into the cities, however, raises serious questions about the continued applicability of these models in some countries. In the Third World the rate of change in the distribution of the population between countryside and city has been great. This has led some revolutionary groups to abandon the rural areas and to try and develop new forms of urban guerrilla war such as the Tupamaros in Uruguay.

A final and very important question raised by the Green Revolution is one of time. How fast are these effects taking place in relation to the development of revolutionary groups capable of leading revolt toward socialist goals? In Pakistan the independence of Bangladesh has come before such a political group, based on popular support, could develop. Finally, lurking ominously behind the social turmoil is the ultimate question: can capitalism be replaced in these countries before its profit-born technology destroys all hope for survival by poisoning the environment?

For radicals in the developed countries there is at least one lesson. The Green Revolution provides a striking illustration of how imperialist intervention, no matter how well-intentioned, can have far-reaching negative effects on the Third World. The problem of hunger in the capitalist world has rarely been one of absolute food deficits, particularly when the productive capacity of the developed countries is taken into account. It is one of uneven distribution caused by a system that feeds those with money and, unless forced to do otherwise, lets the rest fend for themselves

16

A Viable Model for Rural Development

Albert Waterston

Regional and subregional planning may be comprehensive, in the sense that it covers all functional sectors, or it may be partial when it covers only a few or even one. It may concentrate on rural or urban areas and, within rural areas, on agricultural as opposed to rural development. Agricultural development is an essentially sectoral activity, one which is concerned with occurrences within the agricultural sector, as usually defined. In contrast, rural development is generally conceived of as a multisectoral activity which includes, besides agricultural development and rural industry, the establishment or improvement of social overhead facilities or infrastructure (schools, clinics, roads, communications, and water supply), and welfare services or programs, which could be for disease control, improved nutrition, widening adult literacy, or family planning.

Some rural development projects or programs are "selective" rather than "integrated" in the sense that they cover a particular nonagricultural activity like health, education, or family planning. However, as generally employed, and as employed here, rural development is an integrated multisectoral activity which includes the development of agriculture and social overhead facilities.

While the primary objective of agricultural development is usually increased growth of agricultural output, the primary objective of rural development is the enrichment of the material and social welfare of the rural population, always including poor farmers, and sometimes, landless farm workers and others in rural areas.

AGRICULTURE: AN ESSENTIAL PART OF RURAL DEVELOPMENT

Although it may not have been intended specifically, agricultural development has frequently benefited the rich rather than the poor farmers in developing countries, because the rich have, and the poor often lack, the education, credit, and other attributes required to respond adequately to new opportunities. Studies of the green revolution, for example, suggest that programs which concentrate on the adoption of improved techniques for the use of new seeds and fertilizers have tended to benefit the middle income and rich farmers rather than the poor. In fact, productivity in-

Reprinted from *Finance and Development* (December 1974), pp. 22–25, by permission of the publisher.

creases concentrated on larger farms can undermine the position of small farmers by reducing agricultural product prices, putting pressure on tenancy, and restricting the access of small farmers to credit and other resources. This has increasingly led the World Bank and other donor agencies and countries to concentrate on promoting development that provides poor farmers in developing countries with the infrastructure and services required to enlarge their share of increases in agricultural output and incomes. However, prodigious difficulties stand in the way of mounting rural development programs which will provide a sustained increase in the welfare level of a significant proportion of poor farmers in an underdeveloped country. While governments in these countries may provide social overhead facilities and services to the rural poor, it is difficult to make these facilities and services self-sustaining, since they contribute only marginally to economic development.

For rural development to be self-sustaining, it is essential that it include a self-supporting agriculture which can consistently provide surpluses for financing social overhead facilities and services. This is not only because people's expectations of what can be supported become excessively inflated when central governments provide rural areas with water supply, drainage, roads, buildings, and other facilities at little or no cost, but also because most developing countries do not have the resources to finance the establishment, operation, and maintenance of rural infrastructure and services indefinitely. While it is true that agricultural development, by itself, often ends up by benefiting rich farmers more than poor ones, it is also true that if agricultural development does not have a high priority in a rural development program, rural communities are unlikely to be able to accumulate funds from current income to establish, maintain, and operate clinics, schools, access roads, and other infrastructure and services. When communities look to governments for continued support, rural development programs become little more than welfare. Even Tanzania has run into this problem.

Governments in many countries have devoted considerable sums to social overhead facilities in rural areas, at the expense of allocations to improve agricultural production, and have been left with schools without teachers, clinics without doctors, and chronic unemployment on their hands. In contrast, countries which have given priority to production have been able to generate the resources required to finance social overhead facilities. Communes in the People's Republic of China, for instance, have expanded health and education facilities from their own savings, which is the only way they are permitted to do this.

THE MODEL

Since self-supporting agriculture is the key to self-sustaining rural development, a rural development model is needed which, unlike the usual one for agricultural development, benefits a substantial number of poor farmers in rural communities. The elements of such a model are suggested by the experience in the People's Republic of China, the Republic of China, Tanzania, and Israel.

First, since surplus agricultural labor is a problem in most developing countries, low cost labor-using, rather than capital-using, techniques must be employed to the greatest extent possible in agriculture.

Although the ultimate solution to rural underemployment in many countries probably lies in the permanent migration out of agriculture of labor not required for farm production, a viable program of rural development can provide preparatory training for rural workers who eventually migrate to urban centers and spread the migration over time. Low-cost labor-intensive techniques imply that the capital (including working-capital) cost per unit of labor, as well as capital output ratios, should be kept as low as possible.

Second, since even labor-intensive agriculture is unlikely to provide year-round full employment in rural areas with surplus labor, "employment generating" minor development works with high labor content—the construction of feeder roads, irrigation, and other waterworks—as well as social overhead facilities, such as schoolhouses, or clinical buildings, should be carried out with underemployed and seasonally unemployed rural labor. To minimize housing and transport costs, productive activities should be concentrated as much as possible in areas with the greatest excess labor. Local materials should be used wherever possible, to provide employment and reduce transport costs. By using local labor to create some of the infrastructure needed in rural communities, the handicap of underemployment of the labor force can be converted into an advantage. In the People's Republic of China, peasants have constructed irrigation, flood control, terracing, and other works and have reforested local areas. Rural populations in Pakistan at the *thana* (or *tehsil*) and union levels were used in the Rural Public Works' Program to construct roads, bridges, embankments, and other works. In India, small capital formation projects have provided work and supplemental incomes to small cultivators and landless agricultural workers.

Third, small-scale, labor-using, light industries with low capital requirements should be established in rural areas to supplement employment opportunities in agriculture. However, certain light industries are better than others. For best results, as experience in the People's Republic of China and Israel has shown, light industry should concentrate mainly on two kinds: (a) the processing of agricultural commodities produced in the area concerned, which might include fruit and vegetable canneries, flour and rice mills, woodworking factories, slaughterhouses, creameries and milk powder plants, sugar refineries, paper mills, and processing units for cotton ginning and edible oils; and (b) the fabrication of inputs for agriculture such as cattle, pig, and poultry feed mills, fertilizer mixing plants, small toolmaking shops, and clay, brick, and tile works. However, wherever it was "economically feasible," rural industry could also produce consumer goods and building materials for capital construction and infrastructure projects.

To be "economically feasible" requires that considerations of efficiency not be abandoned to solve the unemployment problem. In this connection,

India's experience in attempting to foster rural industry during the period of the First Five-Year Plan is instructive. The rural industrialization program emphasized consumer goods, particularly textiles, produced with traditional labor-using village technology. Efforts to revive traditional industry failed for several reasons. There, although the traditional textile industry was labor intensive, it sometimes used as much capital per unit of labor as was used in India's modern textile plants. Traditional industry also required large quantities of working capital for the procurement of raw materials and distribution of output. Because traditional industry was highly dispersed, it also raised management and coordination problems which were beyond the capacity of the managers. Moreover, demand for the textiles produced by rural industry was not high enough to attract investment, and capital could not easily be obtained for rural industry. In contrast, the greater demand for textiles produced in the modern sector permitted economies of scale which made it possible to sell textiles produced in this sector at much lower prices than those produced in the traditional sector. Although the public sector eventually provided financing for the program, it had to be abandoned as a failure.

The agro-industries of the type using agricultural inputs all involve weight or bulk losing processes, and therefore have locational advantages if established near their sources of raw materials. Some of the second type of agro-industries (those producing products intended primarily for the use of farmers in an area) have transport advantages when located near their markets. This is especially true if their products are heavy (such as brick, tile, and concrete blocks) or bulk gaining (harrows, chicken brooders, and seed drills), or if their major inputs can be purchased in large quantities (fertilizer for mixing or steel and wrought iron for toolmaking). Many kinds of agro-industries are therefore well-suited to small- or medium-scale production in rural areas.

SELF-HELP AN ESSENTIAL FOUNDATION

Fourth, to be self-sustaining, the model must rest on a foundation of local self-reliance or self-help. Simply stated, this means that those communities which benefit from rural development must assume responsibility for raising a reasonable proportion of the resources. What constitutes a reasonable proportion depends on the circumstances, but in each situation criteria for judging the success of any rural development program would include a measure of the extent to which local or regional jurisdictions contribute to the support of rural social services. A second criterion would measure how quickly, as well as how far, local or regional jurisdictions take over the support of rural facilities initially financed by the central government or other outsiders.

Where regional, subregional, or local areas are completely dependent on grants and loans from above, rural development planning becomes a matter of drawing up shopping lists for outside funding, without making the hard allocative choices which realistic planning requires. If the lower jurisdictions are to participate in the planning process, as good planning demands, it is likely that the quality and reliability of rural investment choices, as well as their management, will be improved if they have to raise and risk significant quantities of their own resources. Moreover, the total quantity of resources raised for rural development in most poor countries is likely to fall short of what is needed unless a portion of the funds come from the countryside itself. The best way of raising this is to challenge local authorities and institutions to provide parts of the funding, through taxation or otherwise, with government producing matching grants or using other appropriately devised incentives to reward results.

Self-reliance is becoming increasingly important as the basis for rural development. Kenya, Tanzania, and other countries have emphasized "self-help" as integral parts of their rural development programs. As already indicated, in the People's Republic of China, communes can expand health and educational facilities only from their own savings. However, the county government provides teachers and doctors once a commune has built the basic facilities. The People's Republic of China has probably gone further than any other poor country in this respect. For example, when major campaigns were launched to control the five major parasitic diseases—malaria, filariasis, hookworm, kala azar, and schistosomiasis—great emphasis was placed on having the "masses" take specific action whenever possible, rather than have everything done for them by outside "experts."

SUCCESS RESTS ON A PRECISE COMBINATION OF ALL FACTORS

Experience indicates that this combination—labor-intensive agriculture; labor-using, minor development works; agriculturally oriented, small-scale, light industry, using labor-intensive techniques with low capital requirements; and an atmosphere of self-reliance—offers the best prospect for developing a self-supporting agriculture which can, in turn, provide the increased incomes and savings for the social overhead facilities and services required for self-sustaining rural development. Since self-supporting agriculture is the backbone of self-sustaining rural development, it should have the highest priority of all the elements in the model; and since it is difficult to organize effective agricultural development based on labor-using techniques, time should be allowed to make it viable. The precise combination of agriculture and industry, as well as the timing for introducing industry, will depend on the circumstances in each country. In Pakistan's Punjab, for instance, farmer demand led to the establishment of more than 100 small factories employing a total of over 1,000 workers to produce diesel engines, principally from local materials, for tube wells and grain mills. In the Punjab of India, which has a dynamic agricultural sector with a broad-based distribution of income, there was a significant increase in the effective demand for consumer goods and services. Some of these, like milk and milk products, were old items of consumption, while others, like bicycles and sewing machines, shoes and soap, were new consumption items. Increased demand and the consequent increase in the profitability of investment often brought about a significant mobilization of rural savings for the provision of goods and services. While government may find it expedient to make available some social overhead facilities and services, these should be correlated with the development of the agricultural component over time to insure that earnings from local agricultural output will ultimately be sufficient to take over support of these facilities. The provision of social services in rural areas of Africa has been found to be effective in sustaining people's interest in development projects and in mobilizing self-help efforts in rural areas, particularly for capital works projects. On the other hand, experience in Africa also leads to the conclusion that unless the rural community accepts the principles of self-help and self-financing, social services are unlikely to be viable.

The preparation and implementation of a program of self-sustaining rural development is necessarily a long-term task which requires much planning and farmers' support. This means, therefore, that it must be a product evolved by the country concerned, as well as its farmers; and by the same token that it cannot be the product of short-term missions of international or national lending agencies. These agencies can do much to support rural development by financing components of rural development programs, but it would be unreasonable to expect them to provide the continuing, long-term effort which viability requires. Only the country concerned can do that.

ORGANIZATION FOR RURAL DEVELOPMENT

The preparation and implementation of a self-sustaining rural development program also requires major changes in government organization. This is so because each ministry, department, or agency tends to concern itself only with its own functional sector or subsector. However, a rural development program requires coordinated action among ministries, departments, and agencies which cuts horizontally across the vertical organization typical of most governments.

Experience in countries such as the People's Republic of China, the Republic of China, and Israel make it clear that where rural development has been adopted as a national policy, it is normal for government structures and procedures to be adjusted accordingly. Each ministry establishes appropriate groups and administrative procedures to facilitate the coordination of its own activities with those of others on a continuing basis. Moreover, at national and regional levels, interministerial or other bodies, under the chairmanship of the minister of agriculture or another suitable person, are established to synchronize the related activities of the different ministries, departments, and agencies. Thus, what are exceptional activities for ministries when individual rural development projects or programs are involved become normal routine when rural development is national policy.

In the absence of a national policy for country-wide rural development, it is unlikely that conventional ministries, departments, and agencies will be able to deviate from their normal structures and procedures to deal effectively with the requirements of a rural development program in one or a few regions of a country. This is also true of crop programs, e.g., for high-yielding varieties of rice or wheat, which may be concentrated in a few regions of a country. In these cases, experience shows that it is best to establish a special agency to deal with the program or regions concerned.

ADDENDUM

In the article, "A Viable Model for Rural Development," which appeared in the December 1974 issue of **Finance & Development,** I wrote that experience had indicated that the combination of four elements—labor-intensive agriculture; labor-using minor development works; agriculturally oriented, small-scale light industry; and self-reliance constituted the elements of a model which offered the best prospect for rural development in poor countries. The article also stated that a serious rural development effort usually required major organizational and institutional adjustments.

Research carried out since publication of the article indicates that for the model to be self-sustaining, institutional and organizational arrangements *must* be made which will permit the activities covered by the first four elements of the model to proceed on a continuing basis. These arrangements should include farmers' organizations as well as government and (where pertinent) private agencies and institutions. Too often failure to establish institutional and organizational structures which allow rural development to become self-sustaining accounts for the failure of otherwise worthy rural development programs. Because of this, I believe that establishment of the appropriate institutional and organizational arrangements should be included as a fifth element of the rural development model I espoused in the original article.

Moreover, experience reveals that viable rural development also required a hierarchy of development centers to bridge the wide gap between rural villages and the metropolis, which is characteristic of less developed countries. The typical development hierarchy is composed of three levels: small basic marketing and servicing centers for rural villages at the lowest level, with small and large towns at the two higher levels where more advanced marketing and other services are provided to rural people. The establishment of an appropriate hierarchy of development centers therefore constitutes the sixth and final element of a viable rural development model.

17

Some Aspects of China's Agricultural Development Experience: Implications for Developing Countries in Asia

John Wong

INTRODUCTION

In recent years agriculture in many Third World countries seems to have been in disarray and poor performance has prompted many of these countries to actively re-assess their existing development policies and to search in earnest for more effective alternative strategies. On the other hand, the thawing of the Cold War and the opening up of China to the world have led to a "rediscovery" of China. In the process, a growing interest has been focused on China's rural development, bringing to the fore the issue of whether the Chinese experience is relevant to the needs of the Third World.

The appeal of the Chinese "model" seems to rest more on the observation that Chinese development in the past had followed some "unorthodox" paths and the structure of her development programmes had, if judged against the mainstream approach, embodied many "unconventional" elements. It is thus seen that Chinese innovations in rural development, though many are still experimental in nature, could inspire other developing countries to consider new alternatives to their established patterns, even though it might not be possible to extrapolate directly from the Chinese experience to their own situations.

In essence, China's agricultural development since the Communist revolution has been a process of the economy responding to three conditioning factors. The first is the ideological prescription of development. Chinese agriculture had to develop within the socialist framework based on collective production and egalitarian distribution, although the extent of ideological commitment at times tended to fluctuate in inverse proportion to the degree of pragmatism displayed by the Chinese leadership. The second is the continuing influence of traditional elements. Farming in China has always been and still is very much a way of life bearing the hallmarks of China's history, society, culture as well as the ecosystem—although this is decreasingly so, owing to rapid structural transformation in the recent years. The third is related to the developmental requirements. From the outset, China shared with other developing countries the universal attributes of an underdeveloped agriculture with low productivity and

Reprinted with permission from *World Development*, Vol. 4, No. 6, John Wong, "Some Aspects of China's Agricultural Development Experience: Implications for Developing Countries in Asia," 1976, Pergamon Press, Ltd.

extensive rural underemployment. Much of the Third World's rising interest in China is actually geared to the developmental implications of the Chinese experience. The fact that China started off with many similar conditions of underdevelopment but has now apparently come to grips with her immense problem of rural poverty more effectively than many other developing countries, has naturally stirred the imagination in the Third World over the usefulness and relevance of the Chinese "model."

Whether or not a nation should and can emulate another has long been highly controversial. According to one school, every "success story" is a special case by itself, being a product of its entire historical circumstances. The question will become more debatable if it is posed rather precisely: can Third World countries really imitate the Chinese development patterns under different ideological assumptions, or adapt them to different political and social contexts? Such an issue is immensely complicated in nature. As a limited exercise, this paper addresses itself to the question of the usefulness of the Chinese experience by distilling the relatively *successful* aspects of the Chinese innovations and then considering their "export" potential from the standpoint of the Southeast Asian countries in general.

We will concentrate on the macroeconomic implications of the Chinese development experience in three broad areas: (1) institutional precondition for agricultural transformation, (2) balanced development strategies for agriculture, (3) integration of production with overall rural development.

1. Institutional Precondition for Agricultural Transformation

It is not unusual for developing countries on the threshold of launching their agricultural development programmes to engage their scholars or experts in a sort of "development debate" focusing mainly on two basic issues. First, they would raise the question of whether the agricultural underdevelopment in their country had been an expression of such unfavourable physical factors as a high man-land ratio and technological stagnation in production, or had been caused by the backward socio-economic (institutional) framework. Second, even allowing that backwardness had been caused by the combination of both sets of forces, they would still have to agree on where the central focus of their development strategy should be: an emphasis on institutional reform or a straight commitment to technological transformation?

One can trace such a "debate" in China before the War. Amidst such growing agrarian abuses as landlordism and the increasing trend towards rapid pauperization of the peasants, many Chinese rural reformers had passionately advocated radical social reforms both as a remedy and as a prelude to any form of agricultural development.[1] On the other hand, there was a "technical school" which gave little consideration to the socio-economic obstacles in agricultural development. Prominent among the latter proponents was the eminent American agricultural economist, J. L. Buck, who saw the Chinese agrarian problem mainly in terms of lack of capital, shortage of institutional credit and insufficient support from modern extension services. Hence the growth of production was seen as an increasing function of technical progress and the consolidation of fragmented uneconomic holdings.[2] Essentially, the implications of the "technical arguments" were much akin to the view held today by the "Chicago School," which hypothesizes that peasant agriculture by itself is already efficient with its resources having been intensively utilized so that any reallocation of resources along the same traditional production patterns would not significantly enhance productivity.[3] From a narrow angle such a purely technical argument might well be true. But the problem of Chinese agriculture then, as in some Third World countries today, amidst growing rural unrest, had clearly got beyond the realm of a simplistic technico-economic argument. While Chiang Kai-shek let his experts debate on land reform in Nanking, the Communists were already carrying it out in the villages. The outcome was pretty clear, as events have shown.

No such "debate" was entertained after the Chinese Communists came into power, who chose to approach the long-term strategy of agricultural development on the basis of their own ideological disposition. From the outset, they held that Chinese agriculture was underdeveloped because its institutional set-up was "feudalistic" which, to put it in Marxian terms, means that "production relations" were impeding the development of "production forces." Such a basic contradiction had to be resolved before any development could proceed, thus requiring the substitution of new production relations based on socialistic organization. In other words, the institutional transformation of traditional agriculture was to take precedence over any form of developmental changes including the technological transformation.

Hence the ideological rhetoric for China's rigorous institutional revolutions, starting with the land reform and culminating in the formation of the People's Communes. A stereotyped misconception has been formed that the institutional revolutions in China had been too radical, socially and economically too disruptive, resulting in high political costs that only a totalitarian government would be willing to pay. Excesses reported in the early stages appeared to be quite inevitable in so far as the Chinese Government relied on mass mobilization techniques to carry out institutional reforms. However, the extremist nature of the various reforms had been over-exaggerated for a time outside China. Take, for instance, the Chinese land reform, once viewed as a very radical movement because of its early association with the revolutionary violence before the Communists came to power, but actually conducted with considerable moderation and restraint. In terms of economic revolution, it was only a limited exercise: it sought to expropriate the landlords *as a class* while at the same time instituting measures to protect the rich peasants (as opposed to the outright liquidation of the Kulaks in the Soviet land reform). Furthermore, less than 50% of the total land, and considerably lower proportions of other means of production such as draught animals and farm implements, had actually been expropriated for redistribution. The distribution ratio was no higher than that found in most of the conventional types of distributionist land reform in other developing countries.[4]

The Chinese land reform did not stabilize the small-peasant agriculture but actually led to conditions of instability, which called for continued institutional adjustments culminating first in the collectivization and then in the communization. Socialization of agriculture, which met with so much disruption and difficulty in the Soviet Union under Stalin, was achieved in China only four years after the completion of the land reform. A number of factors have been advanced by scholars to explain the relatively smooth and, considering the scale of operations involved, almost painless institutional reorganization: (1) The Chinese implemented the programmes by stages, starting with the MATs and moving on to higher forms, thus overcoming the initial frictions. (2) One can trace some strong historical connection to rural collectivism in China.[5] (3) Above all, China had a successful land reform, which enabled the Government to establish a high degree of control in the rural areas and brought a drastic redistribution of political and social power in the villages, thus removing the conservative rural elements who might have opposed such an institutional shake-up.

What then has contributed to the success of the Chinese land reform? To a large extent, the Chinese style of land reform could only be implemented effectively by a revolutionary government, which would not be opposed to, but actually stand to gain from, a reshuffle in the rural power relationships. Needless to say, such a government must not be dominated by the traditional rural élite. Chiang Kai-shek's regime had never got beyond the stage of talking, writing about and even legislating land reform in the capital city, simply because the leadership could not shake off its connection with the rural landed interests.[6] After having been driven by the Communists to exile in Taiwan, Chiang's government, which had little connection with the local landed interests in Taiwan, rigorously pushed ahead with the land reform programme to success! For institutional land reforms, no amount of legislation can substitute for the political will to implement.

The land reform expert, Folke Dovring, recently complained that the recognition of institutional reform as an important variable for economic development had been slow in coming.[7] In the past most discussions of land reform were focused on its political aspects, which were unduly permeated with emotive judgements.[8] The recent thawing of the Cold War not only defused much of the former ideological rhetoric surrounding the subject but also removed the unwarranted fear of the potential of land reform in radicalizing the peasantry.[9] The major "pure" economic argument for land reform today is centred on the appropriate factor proportions in capital-scarce small agriculture. By bringing about more secure tenure conditions, land reform is conducive to the land-intensive type of development. With economists increasingly concerned with the problem of rural employment generation, land reform has thus come back into the limelight of the mainstream economics.

A dispassionate advocate of land reform today is therefore not so likely to run the risk of being labelled as "reform-mongering," for even the "position of the World Bank in regard to land reform has changed over the decade, reflecting a reconsideration of the objectives of development and the most appropriate strategies for attaining those objectives."[10] Admittedly, it would be exceedingly difficult for a government in a developing country under normal conditions to consider launching a revolutionary land reform of the Chinese variant without fear of subsequent uncontrollable confrontation. On the other hand, there is a strong probability that the *threat* of a revolution as a result of mounting social and political pressure might be sufficient to force some governments to undertake more drastic reform measures. The recent reintroduction of land reform in the Philippines under martial law and the revival of land reform interest in Thailand following the change of political situation in Indochina are cases in point. Albert Hirschman has long argued that just as the difficulty of "non-antagonistic" reforms (e.g., a public health programme) had in the past been underestimated, there had been a tendency to overestimate the obstacles of "antagonistic" changes (e.g., a confiscatory land reform).[11] Given a sufficiently strong reformist will, even well-entrenched barriers to reform could be successfully outflanked or neutralized without resort to actual revolutionary cataclysm.

In the post-Vietnam Asia, it is not over-optimistic to say that there is a much better chance today for some countries to arrive at a durable coalition of interests which would see that the best way of maintaining the status quo is to carry out reforms in a gradual manner.[12] Some members of the rural élite may agree to an orderly land reform either out of enlightened self-interest or out of fear, having fully appreciated the maxim that it is better to give up something in order not to lose all in a total revolution. Others, thanks to industrialization in these countries, have built up a sizable stake of economic interests in the urban centres so that they are more in a position to give up some amount of their declining rural interests for the sake of overall stability. In some countries the various power groups might well be closely linked to one another through various social ties, as reported in one UN study.[13] Nonetheless there is a strong likelihood that the rising industrial bourgeoisie will clash with the conservative rural elements over institutional reforms on grounds of conflicting economic interests, e.g. the urban groups have an interest in obtaining cheap food and in preventing the peasants from being over-exploited by the landlords.[14] In short, the preconditions for genuine reforms today might be less remote than has ever been commonly realized.

The other equally remarkable feature about the Chinese experience in institutional transformation is that it is not an end in itself, but is a means to lead the technological transformation in agriculture. Throughout the 1950s, the Chinese Government relied on the institutional reorganization to increase production—"developing production forces through changes in production relations." After institutional reorganization had exhausted its potential for increasing production following the formation of the communes, the basic development strategy shifted to technological progress, which thus gave birth to the Chinese equivalent of the "Green Revolution."[15] The mainspring of China's agricultural growth today does not lie in social organization but in technological change.

Many Asian countries, in their pursuit of the pure "technocratic style" of rural development, have hastily plunged into the "Green Revolution" with a weak institutional framework, unsupported by an "organizational

revolution." The shortcomings of the Green Revolution, especially its unfavourable welfare aspects, are all too familiar.[16] Suffice it to stress that a
successful technological transformation means more than just a "seed-
fertilizer" revolution; it needs to be buttressed by proper institutional
changes. From the very start, the Chinese had not fallen into what Myrdal
called "technological euphoria."[17] Further, the "Green Revolution" was never
allowed to steer out of its proper institutional context. Consequently, China
has been more effective in coping with social tension arising from technological change.

In short, the Chinese experience serves to highlight that institutional
changes of an egalitarian nature are not incompatible with technological
progress. If anything, the institutional revolution has only facilitated the
diffusion of the benefits of the technological revolution to all the peasants.

2. Balanced Development Strategies for Agriculture

As a legacy of equating economic development with "Industrial Revolution"
in the context of the Western experience, most developing countries have
followed development strategies which consistently assign low priorities to
agricultural development. Hence the prevalance of urban-biased development patterns in the Third World. Such a bias is fully reflected in the
economic literature dealing with growth and development. Many macroeconomic growth models do not even treat agricultural growth as an
important endogenous variable! In the dualistic development theories of the
Lewis-Ranis-Fei variant which are primarily designed to explain growth in a
developing economy, the industrial sector is regarded as the dynamic-
growth sector and development is treated as a process of transferring surplus resources from agriculture to the urban centres.

The Marxists, with their traditional obsession with the efficiency of
large-scale production and scorn for small peasantry, have equally been
responsible for inspiring many less developed countries to follow a wrong
development path.[18] In fact, China had gone through the experience of
such a bias when she took on the so-called Stalinist model of development
for her First Five-Year Plan. In essence, the Plan relegated agriculture to
the role of subserving industrial growth by contributing the maximum
surplus, which was to be generated with as little resource feedback as
possible.[19] Consequently, the agricultural sector was virtually starved of
development funds as is evident in the official investment allocation plan,
which earmarked only 9.9% of state funds to agriculture as opposed to
64.5% to industry. Towards the end of the First Five-Year Plan, the
Chinese leaders began to be increasingly concerned over the applicability of
the Soviet strategy to the Chinese economy with markedly different structural characteristics, demographic patterns and degree of underdevelopment. As a reaction against the lopsided development programme, the
Chinese Government launched the Great Leap Forward Movement, 1958–
60, which emphasized the simultaneous development of both the modern
and the traditional sectors ("walking on two legs"). Apart from some ro-
mantic idea about the way human resources could be mobilized to increase

economic progress, Mao Tse-tung did perceive in the Great Leap Forward campaign certain functions which were realistic for the Chinese economic conditions, e.g. the appropriate utilization of China's vast underemployed rural manpower, the greater role played by small industries in the rural areas, and the proper choice of techniques of production, particularly the labour-using and capital-saving type. However, the Great Leap Forward was miscarried on account of a combination of factors, including bad weather, the sudden Soviet withdrawal of aid, and the mismanagement of the newly-formed communes. During the retreat from the Great Leap Forward, the Chinese did not revert to the Soviet style of planned development based on industrial priority with a bias towards capital-intensive projects. Instead, the Chinese moved on to consolidate what is now called the "Maoist model" of economic development, which is essentially based on a distinctly pro-agriculture policy and the policy of self-reliance.[20]

Most development planners recognize that the proper strategy for promoting overall economic growth and agricultural transformation is to exploit the "positive interrelations between agricultural and other economic sectors."[21] In practice, however, country after country has tended to follow policies which are inherently biased against the peasants, whether it is import-substitution industrialization or subsidizing rice consumption in the urban centres.

In the process of modern economic growth, there arise conditions and trends which seem to consistently work against the agricultural sector. What makes China succeed where many others have failed in upholding an unbiased development strategy is that the Chinese have developed and implemented a package of concrete measures calculated to counteract those unfavourable forces working against agriculture.

To begin with, the Chinese leadership, comprised mainly of members of rural origin, has a greater understanding of the peasants and their problems than most administrations in other Asian countries. Such a close affiliation of the high-level leaders with the peasants has prevented the usually articulate urban interest groups from unduly influencing the government's overall economic policy. On the contrary, the urban bureaucrats in China are deliberately "rusticated" through being sent down to the countryside from time to time to work with the peasants and "learn from the rural masses."

Regardless of the economic system, agriculture has to generate a surplus over and above what is needed for rural subsistence consumption in the process of development. However, there is considerable variation in the ways and means as well as in the degree of "extracting" such surplus. The test of whether the extraction has been too severe can be seen in (a) whether the peasants have unduly suffered from such an acquisition and (b) whether the transferred surplus has been productively utilized in other economic sectors. Thus the traditional Soviet agricultural policy under Stalin had been too harsh, because it had led to "over-squeezing" the Russian peasants to the extent of producing disincentive effects. Under the regressive Meiji land tax system, the Japanese peasants in the late 19th century also suffered, but not unbearably, especially since the burden they carried was eventually paid off as the economy had soon achieved take-off.

Many developing countries today have carried economic policies biased against the rural sector because they tend to make the peasants suffer *unnecessarily,* and worse still, there seems to be no signs that the hardship of the peasants will pay off in the foreseeable future as the resources channelled out of the agricultural sector have not been properly and productively utilized—hence a case of misallocation of resources. By contrast, the Chinese economic policy has been distinctly more favourable to agriculture than was the case with traditional Soviet policy. Agriculture was not tightly squeezed even during the industrialization drive of the 1950s.[22]

In China, the mechanism by which agricultural surplus is transferred to other sectors operated through the agricultural tax in kind, together with both compulsory and voluntary after-quota sales by the production units at fixed official prices. In the early 1950s, the rate of agricultural tax amounted to 13% on the average of the total agricultural output, which declined to about 10% in the late 1950s. Currently, agricultural taxation is known to take from 5–6% of the gross agricultural output in the communes. Any government acquisition of grain either through compulsory or voluntary sales by the production units no doubt contains elements of "squeezing the peasants." The exact extent of such a "squeeze" in China is not known on account of the limited role price is allowed to play in the market. In the early 1960s, it was reported that the government delivery prices were 25–50% lower than the free market prices based on supply and demand. Such differentials are clearly not confiscatory, especially compared with the Russian equivalent of over 200%.[23]

The agricultural surplus can also be skimmed off by turning the terms of trade against agricultural products. In China, the opposite is known to have happened. The Chinese government has consistently lowered the prices of modern agricultural inputs of industrial origin close to their costs of production. In fact, the prices for rice and wheat paid by the state to the farms are higher than the retail prices for these products charged to consumers in government stores. The difference thus represents an agricultural subsidy.[24]

In most developing countries the issue of channelling off what is considered to be the appropriate portion of the investible surplus from the agricultural sector is admittedly a delicate one. Agricultural products must be priced in such a way as to generate some capital for industrial development. On the other hand, the agricultural sector should not be overtaxed before it has achieved sustained growth; and in no circumstances should such policy be ruthlessly pursued as to overstep the limit of what is politically and socially acceptable to the peasants. In China, two built-in measures have effectively worked against over-exploitation of the peasants. First, the Chinese Government has rejected both the socialistic Stalinist model and the capitalistic Ranis-Fei type of development, since both embody the narrow concept that only industry forms a dynamic sector capable of leading the development of the economy. The Chinese believe that agricultural surplus must not be totally drained off for a "big push" development centering on the industrial-urban sector, and that some amount of agricultural savings must be left for adequate reinvestment within the agricultural sector. Second, the Chinese Government is constantly aware of the crucial role played specifically by the peasant incentive in the collectivized system of farming.[25] They know only too well the counter-productive outcome of the Soviet over-exploitation of the *Kolkhoz* in the 1930s. As a matter of fact, it is in this policy of not over-squeezing the peasants that the main explanation lies as to why China, having declared self-sufficiency in food production, has continued to purchase wheat from advanced countries of the West at great cost to her foreign exchange reserve. In 1973, for instance, China spent US$840 million to import wheat for consumption in her big urban centres. Given a government less inclined to support agriculture, such an amount of import, totalling 7 million tons or half a kilogram per person per month, could have been easily scraped out from the peasant consumption.[26]

Another significant pillar for sustaining the pro-agriculture policy in China has been the successful regulation of rural–urban migration. Historically speaking, internal rural–urban migration has brought about intersectoral labour reallocation which contributed significantly to the economic development of the West and led to the coupling of urbanization with overall economic development.[27] In the developing countries, however, rural–urban migration in recent decades has caused the problem of over-urbanization, resulting in open urban unemployment and the growth of urban plight. Worse still, the outflow of people from the villages has not significantly relieved rural overpopulation but has, for some countries at least, created instead the problem of labour shortage in the rural areas during the peak farming seasons.

The Chinese approach to the issue of rural–urban migration carries a distinctly Maoist brand. As noted earlier, the Chinese leaders are much at home with "agrarian socialism." Ideologically Mao has long believed that the urban élite can have a great deal to learn from the peasants through actually working in the fields, and that it is necessary to break down the barriers between the urban and rural society. Thus the Chinese Government not only sought to restrict population movements from the countryside to the cities but also actually operated a reverse system of decentralizing the existing urban centres.

In restraining the outflow of rural labour to the urban areas, the Chinese authorities have resorted to a system of control comprising: (1) population registration regulations, which require formal approval for legitimate movement; (2) regulations governing changes in employment, e.g. enterprises must apply to a municipal employment bureau to hire additional labour, thus ensuring that the potential labour supply from the existing urban population would be fully utilized before rural labour could be brought over; and (3) regulations governing housing allocation and the control of primary foodstuffs in the urban areas.[28] No amount of control, however stringent, could be completely effective in stemming urban in-migration unless the rural sector has also worked out its own strategies to provide employment for the surplus rural labour. This topic will be discussed in detail in the next section. Suffice it to say that extension of rural industrial activities has been one of the effective measures in retaining the rural labour. "Instead of letting the peasants drift into urban industry, industry is brought to the peasants."[29]

The Chinese innovation in the area of rural–urban migration does not lie in the various control measures as outlined above, but in the policy of reversing the flow of labour in the other direction. Such is the celebrated *hsia fang* ("sending down to the countryside") movement, first started in 1955 and now institutionalized. Apart from its ideological underpinning of bridging the gap between the urban élite and the rural masses, the *hsia fang* represented a conscious effort to support the state's employment strategies for the urban areas. First, it was one of the long series of campaigns to return short-term migrant peasants and those who had been attracted to the cities in search of material glamour to the countryside to join agriculture production. Second, it was related to the nation-wide drive to eliminate bureaucracy and reduce overstaffing in various city organizations. Third, it was designed to solve the student unemployment problem. Since 1968, more than 10 million high school leavers in the cities have been sent down to work in the countryside. Admittedly, it has not been an easy task to move urban graduates, who often shirk manual labour, into the rural areas. The Government has expressly ruled out any coercive approach as such a method is self-defeating in the end. Instead, the *hsia fang* movement depends on mass persuasion, which in China inevitably involves some amount of involuntary "ideological mobilization."[30]

By itself the *hsia fang* is not sufficient to de-concentrate the urban centres. Thus it is also supported by regional development planning which includes industrial relocation and decentralization. As a result, for the two decades between 1953 and 1973, the ratio of urban to total population in China increased from 13% to only 16%, a remarkably low ratio for a rapidly industrializing country. Apart from stabilizing urban population growth and solving the problem of the unemployable urban intellectuals, the *hsia fang* has indeed produced in the long run a profound economic and social impact on rural development, which can be summarized by the observation of a China expert:[31]

> Moreover, the transfer of large numbers of trained, educated, and skilled personnel from urban to rural areas has strengthened the regime's capacity to innovate in the countryside. The knowledge and skills of those "transferred downward" (or *hsia fang*) have been regarded as important assets for improving Commune management, developing local industries, expanding rural education and health services, and generally promoting modernization in the countryside.

3. Integration of Production with Overall Rural Development

Agricultural production in China today is not an isolated activity but one that is closely linked to distribution, rural capital formation, rural industrialization, and a range of other broad-based non-farm economic operations. In short, production is part of the overall integrated rural development programme organized by the communes.

The Chinese approach to organizing agricultural production has undergone several changes until it has reached what may be called the "optimum" form. To begin with, the Government recognized that land reform has therefore immediately taken to organize the small peasants into Mutual created numerous economically unviable small owners, and steps were

Aid Teams (MATs). The teams were soon merged to form cooperatives, which evidently came close to being the optimal unit of organizing production in the context of China because they had eliminated the structural shortcomings inherent in small peasant farming while at the same time avoiding the diseconomies of mismanagement due to over-size. The subsequent measures to convert the cooperatives into the still larger collectives and then communes were primarily motivated by the ideological obsession with large-scale farming on the part of some high-ranking Chinese leaders, and also by the consideration of maximizing non-farm employment. The setback during the Great Leap Forward had brought home the lesson to the Chinese leadership that there is a scale limit to mobilizing peasants for farm production, as opposed to non-farm activities, such as building a dam. In the ensuing decentralization of the commune organization, the teams and brigades were thus brought back as the basic units for organizing production and carrying out planning.

The present communes have remarkable scale flexibility in managing farm production. Since the size of a commune is not predetermined, the size of the production brigades and production teams can vary according to specific economic requirements and local conditions.[32] This virtually implies that the commune has a wide range of production functions, with the input proportions being capable of adjusting upward and downward to suit a specific task.

In China, agricultural production is not an independent activity on the part of the operators but is highly coordinated with other economic programmes in the commune. Two significant developments come out of such an integrated approach. First, it leads to specialization in economic functions. Not all the teams have to engage in paddy production and some may well take up commercial crops or indeed a whole range of side-line activities from forestry, fisheries and animal husbandry to small-scale industrial production. Such a degree of diversification of activities is clearly not possible under the system of individual farming with numerous small subsistence peasants carrying out uncoordinated activities. In the labour-surplus areas, the advantage of the commune will bear out even more distinctly. Here we actually find the Ranis-Fei type of theory more operational in the commune context if we visualize the commune as a small labour-surplus economy and development as a process of transferring the surplus from the food-producing to the non-food-producing teams! As diversification opens up opportunities in other areas, the production teams need not be over-burdened with redundant labour.

Second, production planning facilitates rural capital formation through utilizing either excess labour or seasonally under-employed labour for labour-intensive development projects—("turning labour into capital"). In fact, the early commune movement in China was a history of mobilizing rural labour for large-scale public works. For the period 1949–60, a total of 70 billion cubic meters of earthworks and masonry were completed, predominantly by labour-intensive methods, which were equivalent to 960 Suez Canals.[33] Many observers have been ready to point out that not all of the conservancy works, erected in haste during the Great Leap Forward period have proved effective in times of great calamities. Subsequently, the

Chinese Government had enforced a tighter control over the design and execution of the public works projects and prohibited the communes from undertaking unplanned mobilization of labour at the expense of agricultural production. There can be no doubt that over the long run such labour-intensive works of the communes as land improvements, flood control and water management, have borne fruit as reflected in the extension of the irrigated areas from 20% to 78% between 1952–71 and the increase in the multiple crop index from 130 to 185 for the same period. That Chinese agriculture today is much less vulnerable to weather is not the result of the massive investment from the Central Government in large-scale water conservancy works, but the cumulative effect of the numerous small improvements undertaken by the communes through mobilizing their excess labour during the slack seasons.

Much of the current setback of the "Green Revolution" in many developing countries in Asia can be traced to the failure in water control and irrigation improvement. The governments in these countries cannot mount extensive rural public works programmes because of financial constraints. For lack of wage goods, the only alternative to bring about such vital infra-structural development in the rural areas seems to lie in organizing the peasants to undertake labour-intensive public works on a cooperative basis during their off-peak seasons.

The rural diversification programme in China cannot be divorced from the small rural industries. One of the major motivations behind the Great Leap Forward Movement was to up-grade and develop the small-scale rural industries by integrating them into the commune system. Today, tens of thousands of small- and medium-sized workshops and factories have been set up by the communes with local resources—local capital, raw materials, and labour. Broadly, three kinds of rural industries can be distinguished in China. (1) The first refers to the process industries (officially called "five small industries") producing iron and steel, cement, chemical fertilizer, energy (coal and electricity) and machinery, which had been established by 1971 in over half of China's counties as part of the effort to increase local self-reliance and responsibility. (2) The second refers to the repair and manufacture of agricultural machinery and tools (officially called "the three-level agricultural machinery repair and manufacturing network") in the rural areas. By 1971, over 90% of the counties had achieved this. (3) The third category of local industry is made up of plants processing agricultural and side-line products.[34]

The importance of the rural industrial sector in China can be gauged by the fact that in 1973, 63% of her total chemical fertilizer output, and 50% of cement output came from small industries scattered in the communes. Apart from the output effect, the great merit of the small industries in China "lies not in the superiority of their capital/labour or capital/output ratios but in the overall savings in resources they make possible."[35] Further, it is also part of the programme for bringing about a gradual mechanization of agricultural production. Beyond such economic rationale lie even greater social considerations associated with the rise of industrialism in the rural areas. "Rural industrialization also makes it possible for many people to participate in making decisions which have great consequences for their children and themselves."[36]

Until recently the importance of small-scale industries has not been properly recognized. In so many developing countries one finds that existing government regulations tend to hinder the development of small-scale industry while substantial subsidies and concessions are given generously to inefficient large firms. In others, policy planners have wrongly treated small industries as an "urban phenomenon" and confined their promotion to only urban centres. The Chinese experience should serve to show that small rural industries can generate far-reaching economic and social consequences in the rural areas, from accelerating technological progress (usually the "disembodied" type) in agriculture to serving as the carrier of overall rural modernization.

Last but not least, the integrated approach based on the communes aims at increasing not only total output but also employment. China has claimed that the rural unemployment problem has been successfully solved. Both employment generation and employment absorption certainly depend on the successful operation of a unified rural development programme. The rural economy of traditional China was characterized by a low degree of labour utilization—the average peasants in the 1930s in northern China worked only 100–120 days a year, and 80–100 days in southern China. The creation of the communes has made it possible to increase the labour intensity in agricultural activities, resulting in the average increase of three to four times the labour inputs in agriculture as compared to the pre-war level.[37] Furthermore, the widely diversified side-line activities and numerous infrastructural development programmes have certainly absorbed a large proportion of labour not directly required for crop production. While the rural industrial employment is not yet growing fast enough—only about 5% of the rural work force is estimated to be regularly employed in various small rural industries run by the communes—the recent expansion of education, health and other public services in the communes has opened up employment opportunities and has increasingly absorbed a substantial amount of labour.[38] Hence an American economist has aptly summarized:[39]

> All in all, it appears that the claims of full employment in the rural sector are valid. Some of this employment, to be sure, has a low marginal yield per man-hour; for example, creating new land with great effort by carrying baskets of earth from some other area. The available labour time is apparently regarded as a fixed factor, and any small addition it can make to output is considered worthwhile. China is thus still a "labour surplus economy" in the sense that there are many rural workers whose marginal product is below their consumption. But until there is a demand for these workers in urban industries, their use in low-productivity rural activities is sound social policy.

A CHINESE MODEL?

The Chinese might have devised many innovative solutions to the myriads of problems that they faced. However, the summation of those solutions do not necessarily form a "model." Many China experts would be quick to point out that China had not worked out any *consistent* measures for the purpose of solving her problems and that at various times in the past quarter-century, China had actually experimented with different opposing strategies. It is therefore more valid to speak of the "Chinese experience" emerging from their shifting strategies of development than to speak of a "Chinese model."

Even the talk of "Chinese experience" can run up against objections from certain quarters, in so far as the phrase implies that China has something to teach other countries. First, even at the peak of the Cold War when China was often accused of exporting her revolution to the Third World, she never failed to belabour the point that any revolution or any programme of change, to succeed, must grow out of that particular society's traditions through the genuine support of the masses, rather than have it imported ready-made. Turning to the "economic revolution," the Chinese were even more emphatic about the *sui generis* nature of their development effort, particularly with respect to such innovative institutions as the communes. Second, modern Chinese studies, which have been supported predominantly by American resources, have until recently been much affected by what many young American scholars called the "Cold War scholarship," partly due to the legacy of McCarthyism and partly due to the influence of some leading emigré Chinese-American scholars still holding allegiance to Taiwan. The Chinese agricultural system was often analyzed in terms of the paradigm of "command farming" derived from Sovietology and unbalanced conclusions were drawn based on selected downward-biased statistical estimates.[40] Thus the noted Cornell economist, Professor Liu Ta-chung in his testimony to the United States Congress in April 1967, remarked:[41]

> The economic performance of the Communist regime during 1952–65 as a whole is unimpressive, significantly poorer than that of most other underdeveloped countries. What is often not realized by the people in this country is that per capita consumption on the mainland in the best year of the regime (1957) was still significantly below that in 1933 when China suffered Japanese occupation of Manchuria and the Chinese economy was under constant threat of Japanese intrusion into north and central China . . . The Chinese people suffered unprecedented misery and deprivation on massive scales at least twice since 1949, and the group hit hardest was the peasants.

If the Chinese economy was found to be not even holding its own ground, what has it got to show to other countries?

With the détente, discussion of Chinese economic development has become less susceptible to unwarranted political value judgements. With many economists becoming increasingly disenchanted with some aspects of neo-classical economics, particularly its relevance to underdeveloped economies, the economic profession as a whole has thus become more open-minded and receptive to unorthodox experiments such as those going on in China.

However, the removal of barriers to relatively free and impartial analysis and interpretation of China's economic development should not blind us to the fact that the unique factors in the structure of the Chinese development experience would present great obstacles to its transferability elsewhere. In refraining from publicizing its success as a model to other countries, perhaps the Chinese Government knew only too well that its agricultural development strategies had evolved through long periods of experience and practice based on China's specific agronomical environment and socio-economic structure. Ironically, the type of agriculture which bears the greatest structural similarities to Chinese agriculture is to be found in Korea, Taiwan or Japan, all belonging to the Sinic-cultured East Asia; but these are precisely the same countries which have also undertaken successful agricultural development under a different system. To the extent that the majority of the innovative features in Chinese agricultural development are associated with the organizational strategy centred on the communes, can the Chinese-style commune organizations be actually transplanted onto a different social and ideological setting? The question amounts to whether the existing non-socialist Asian countries can actually emulate the Chinese strategy of development without having undergone a thorough political and social revolution beforehand. Further pursuit along this line would lead to the inevitable *cul-de-sac* that Maoist economics cannot operate in the land without Mao.

Nevertheless, it would be a mistake to dismiss the whole Chinese experience of agricultural development as totally irrelevant to other developing countries in Asia. The Chinese development performance has been the result of, among other things, what Professor Barry Richman termed "the willingness and ability of people to work relatively hard and effectively on a national scale for goals that inspire them."[42] These and other similar factors of a pragmatic nature, which clearly transcend the ideological boundary, have made the Chinese "model" work for China, just as they have made for Japan and other success stories. Many of these factors, as have been demonstrated in this paper, should be very instructive to other Third World countries, at least in highlighting the problematic areas in their existing agricultural development policies.[43]

NOTES

1. See, e.g. *Agrarian China: Selected Materials from Chinese Authors* (London: 1939).

2. J. L. Buck, *Land Utilization in China* (Nanking: 1937).

3. See T. W. Schultz, *Transforming Traditional Agriculture* (New Haven: Yale University Press, 1964). For the criticism, see Michael Lipton, "The theory of optimizing peasant," *Journal of Development Studies* (April 1968), pp. 527–531.

4. See John Wong, *Land Reform in the People's Republic of China: Institutional Transformation in Agriculture* (New York: Praeger, 1973).

5. See John Wong, "Peasant economic behaviour: the case of traditional agricultural co-operation in China," *Developing Economies*, Vol. IX, No. 3 (September 1971).

6. See Ping-ti Ho, *Studies on the Population of China, 1368–1953* (Harvard University Press, 1959), Chapter IX.

7. "Land reform: a key to change in agriculture," in Nurul Islam, ed., *Agricultural Policy in Developing Countries*, Proceedings of a Conference held by the International Economic Association at Bad Godesberg, West Germany (London: Macmillan, 1974).

8. As Doreen Warriner puts it, "Some people think that the object of land reform should be to defeat communism, and that this object should override all other considerations. Others will assert that land reform is communism," in "Land reform and economic development," in C. Eicher and L. Witt, eds., *Agriculture in Economic Development* (New York: McGraw-Hill, 1964), p. 274.

    Recent studies have shown how the possibility of the Communists making use of the peasant movement for revolution in some Asian countries had in the past been exaggerated. See John Wilson Lewis, ed., *Peasant Rebellion and Communist*

Revolution in Asia (Stanford University Press, 1974). (Donald Zagoria stated that land reform does not radicalize the peasantry and that "the forces upholding the status quo played an important role in determining how the peasantry acts," p. 58.)

9. The shift of opinion regarding land reform in the American development "establishment" is fully reflected in the "self-confession" of the US AID, which frankly stated in its 1970 *Spring Review:* "In the past the United States has been notably reluctant to become involved in any aspect of land reform and its attitude has sometimes actually prevented progress."

10. The World Bank, *The Assault on World Poverty: Problems of Rural Development, Education and Health* (Baltimore: John Hopkins University Press, 1975), p. 226.

11. Albert O. Hirschman, *Journeys Toward Progress: Studies of Economic Policy-Making in Latin America* (New York: The Twentieth Century Fund, 1963).

12. For a lucid discussion of the reformist pre-condition, see C. L. Bell and John H. Duloy, "Rural target groups," in Hollis Chenery, et al., eds., *Redistribution with Growth* (London: Oxford University Press, 1974), also Chapter III.

13. United Nations, Department of Economic and Social Affairs, *1970 Report on the World Social Situations* (1971), p. 11.

14. See A. D. Lehmann, ed., *Agrarian Reform and Agrarian Reformism* (London: Faber, 1974). Also Keith Griffin, "Policy options for rural development," *Oxford Bulletin of Economics and Statistics*, Vol. 35, No. 4 (November 1973).

15. See Benedict Stavis, *Making Green Revolution: The Politics of Agricultural Development in China*, Cornell University Rural Development Committee Monograph Series No. 1 (1974).

16. See, e.g. Keith Griffin, "Policy options for rural development," *Oxford Bulletin of Economics and Statistics*, Vol. 35, No. 4 (November 1973); and Kazuo Saito, "On the Green Revolution," *The Developing Economies*, LX, No. 1 (March 1971).

17. Gunnar Myrdal, *The Challenge of World Poverty* (New York: Pantheon Book, 1970).

18. See Alexander Erlich, "Stalin's views on Soviet economic development," in E. J. Simmons, ed., *Continuity and Change in Russian and Soviet Thought* (Harvard University Press, 1955); and Michael Kaser, "The Soviet ideology of industrialization," *Journal of Development Studies* (October 1967).

19. Anthony M. Tang, "Agriculture in the industrialization of Communist China and the Soviet Union," *Journal of Farm Economics*, Vol. 49, No. 5 (December 1967).

20. For further discussion of Maoist economic development strategies, see E. L. Wheelwright and Bruce McFarlane, *The Chinese Road to Socialism: Economics of the Cultural Revolution* (New York: Monthly Review Press, 1970).

21. Bruce F. Johnston and Peter Kilby, "Interrelations between agricultural and industrial growth," in Nurul Islam, ed., *Agricultural Policy in Developing Countries*, *op. cit.*, p. 51.

22. L. G. Reynolds, "China as a less developed economy," *The American Economic Review* (June 1975), p. 421.

23. See H. V. Henle, *Report on China's Agriculture* (Rome: FAO, 1974), p. 37.

24. Some quantitative data may be useful to substantiate the arguments in this paragraph. For the commodity price index, with 1950 as the base year, the change for 1971 is as follows: for wholesale, 93.0; retail, 96.0; agricultural acquisition, 166.0; and retail prices of industrial input to agricultural products, 88.0. *Ibid.*, p. 38.

25. For discussion of the peasant incentive problem in China, see John Wong, "Socialization of agriculture and peasant response to economic incentives in China," *Review of Southeast Asian Studies*, Vol. II. Nos. 1–4 (December 1972), pp. 14–26.

26. Of course, there is also some amount of economic considerations behind the Chinese wheat import. China also exports rice every year (in 1974 alone, her rice exports amounted to almost 2 million tons), and for each ton of rice she sold abroad she could buy 2 tons of wheat, at the current world prices.

27. Some recent studies point out that the Western models of modernization and economic growth in which urbanization plays a crucial role, show a distinct middle class bias, with the cities giving rise to conditions which primarily satisfy the middle class style of life. Hence there is a need for a new conceptualization of the development process in the developing countries. In fact, careful analysis of South Asian cities has called into question whether urbanization is really an instrument of modernization in the Western sense, for cities there still contain much that is similar to rural areas. See M. A. Qadeer, "Do cities 'modernize' the developing countries? An examination of the South Asian experience," *Comparative Studies in Society and History*, Vol. 16, No. 3 (June 1974), pp. 256–283.

28. See Christopher Howe, *Employment and Economic Growth in Urban China, 1949–1957* (Cambridge University Press, 1971).

29. Jan. S. Prybyla, "The Chinese economic model," *Current History* (September 1975), p. 82.

30. After the Cultural Revolution, many Red Guards and young radicals in Shanghai, who had formed the backbone of the Cultural Revolution, were dispatched in the *hsia fang* movement to the remote regions of Northwest China. This can be interpreted, depending on one's ideological persuasion, as a punitive action against the Red Guards for their former disruptive deeds, as a political move for clearing the cities of young radicals to avoid unnecessary agitation, or as a progressive move for letting the young revolutionaries reform the relatively conservative rural areas.

    For a detailed discussion on this subject, see Jan. S. Prybyla, "Hsia Fang: the economics and politics of rustication in Communist China," *Pacific Affairs* (Summer 1975).

31. A. Doak Barnett, *Uncertain Passage, China's Transition Post-Mao Era* (Washington, D.C.: The Brookings Institution, 1974), p. 150.

    Cf. the Indian case, Michael Lipton has analyzed how various forces and policies have worked to drain away the factors in support of population—skills, private savings and forced savings, producing adverse effects on the economy. Even the taxation of agriculture has exceeded the "fair" amount. "Transfer of resources from agriculture to non-agricultural activities: the case of India" (Brighton: University of Sussex, Institute of Development Studies, 1972).

32. For a detailed analysis of the commune organization, see Frederick W. Crook, "The commune system in the People's Republic of China, 1963–74," in Joint Economic Committee of the United States Congress, *China: A Reassessment of the Economy* (Washington, D.C.: US Government Printing Office, June 1975).

33. State Statistical Bureau, *Ten Great Years* (Peking: Foreign Languages Press, 1960).

34. For a detailed discussion of this topic, see Jon Sigurdson's "Rural industrialization in China," in the Joint Economic Committee of the United States Congress, *China: A Reassessment of the Economy, op. cit.*

35. *Ibid.*, p. 413.

36. John Sigurdson, "Rural industry—a traveller's view," *China Quarterly*, No. 50 (April/June 1972), p. 332.

37. H. V. Henle, *op. cit.*, p. 158.

38. See Martin Karcher, "Unemployment and underemployment in the People's Republic of China," mimeo (Harvard University Center for International Affairs, 1973).

39. Lloyd G. Reynolds, "China as a less developed economy," *American Economic Review*, Vol. 65, No. 3 (June 1975), p. 425.

40. The typical case in point was the insistence by some US Department of State officials to use the low estimate of China's grain output which implied that for a decade since 1957, China had made no progress in grain production while population continued to grow! As late as 1970, Werner Klatt, former advisor to the British Foreign Office, gave the figure of China's grain output as 200 million tons, which would imply an increase of only 30% since 1952 or less than 1.4% annually—a rate which is intolerably below the population growth. See John Wong, "Grain output in China: some statistical implications," *Current Scene* (US Information Agency, Hong Kong), Vol. XI, No. 2 (February 1973).

41. *Mainland China in the World Economy:* Hearings before the Joint Economic Committee, Congress of the United States, April, 1967 (Washington, D.C.: US Government Printing Office, 1967), pp. 39–40.

42. Barry Richman, "Chinese and Indian development: an interdisciplinary environmental analysis," *American Economic Review* (May 1975), p. 345.

43. Similar reaction has been recently voiced by development specialists from the Third World; e.g. Sartaj Azis (formerly of the FAO, the Pakistan Planning Commission and the World Bank) remarked: "What can these countries learn from China? . . . These questions are not easy to answer, but one has only to study Israel's Kibbutz and Tanzania's *Ujamaa* to discover the scope that exists for adapting to local conditions at least some of the basic principles revealed by the Chinese approach towards rural development." ("The Chinese approach to rural development," *International Development Review*, Vol. XV, No. 4 (1973), p. 7.) For similar view, see also, Mahbub ul Haq, "Employment in the 1970s: A new perspective," *International Development Review*, Vol. 13, No. 4 (1971).

part five

Industrial Institutions and Strategy

Industrialization has always been considered to be the basis of economic development. And rapid growth has been seen as the means to industrialization. In the first reading in this part, Charles Wilber uses the historical experience of rapid growth in the Soviet Union as a basis for analyzing questions of industrial development strategy. The article is both a critique of development *theory* and of development *practice.* The article analyzes the policy issues of the role of central planning, the choice of investment rate, balanced vs. unbalanced allocation of investment, and choice of production techniques. The reader might consider the employment effects of a dual technology (that is, combining labor-intensive techniques with modern processes of production). It is not clear that the pursuit of a high growth rate and the use of advanced technology are incompatible with a policy of maximizing employment. In the Soviet Union, for example, the policy of a dual technology was combined with on-the-job training and overstaffing (compared with Western standards) that substantially reduced unemployment.[1] These policies would be difficult to transfer to an underdeveloped country with a capitalist economy because they would be considered inefficient by the business community (but it would not be inefficient for the economy as a whole) and therefore, unprofitable. However, a subsidy system could encourage firms to do so.

Paul Streeten, in the second reading, demonstrates that the strategy of industrialization in developing economies is inseparable from a unified, self-reliant development program. Insofar as development involves both identifying and satisfying real human needs, industrialization must provide a form of economic growth that will meet the needs of the country's mass of poor people. Certain development objectives, such as efficient growth, reduced inequality, diversification, and integration, are discussed with respect to a variety of constraints, including environmental damage, scarce factor endowments, and the institutional structure of the present world economic order.

Streeten discusses the relationship between collective self-reliance and international trade, the role of MNCs as instruments for achieving certain social (as well as economic) objectives, and the relationship between interventionist strategies and efficiency, in the context of well-defined developmental objectives. Throughout the article, Streeten argues that once clear development objectives are identified, solutions to seemingly unrelated problems tend to emerge. This comprehensive approach avoids myopic strategies, uneven and unequal development, and insures consistency and coherence in a country's development package.

In the third article, Frances Stewart criticizes the methodology of social cost-benefit analysis (SCB) as a means of assessing alternative projects in underdeveloped countries. She argues that any ranking of "socially desirable" projects depends on the values of the analyst. When specifying the practical definitions of "social" welfare, "social" objectives, and "social" costs, Stewart shows that a weighting system for values necessarily underlies any SCB. To illuminate the role of conflicting values in project selection Stewart suggests the use of class analysis.

For Stewart a class is an interest group with common values. In terms of SCB, for each alternative set of values (or for each class) there is a corresponding different set of "shadow prices" and therefore a different rank-order of projects. Consequently, the choice between projects will ultimately depend on whose values the policy maker is taking. Use of government values as a proxy for social values, as widely advocated in the current literature, is found unacceptable since governments typically represent certain class interests. Thus, Stewart concludes, SCB is primarily an instrument of class struggle rather than a practical tool for achieving a social welfare optimum.

---

1. CHARLES K. WILBER, *The Soviet Model and Underdeveloped Countries* (Chapel Hill: University of North Carolina Press, 1969), pp. 101–103.

18

Economic Development, Central Planning and Allocative Efficiency

Charles K. Wilber

INTRODUCTION

This paper is concerned with the question of central planning and allocative efficiency in the context of a backward economy trying to achieve the one overriding goal of economic development. No pretense is made of constructing a complete theory of a centrally planned economy. Rather, the aim is much more limited. This study is concerned only with the development process and within this process only with the problem of resource allocation.

This paper will first present a critique of the usefulness of static equilibrium analysis in evaluating allocative efficiency under conditions of rapid economic development. Second, the paper will construct a model of dynamic allocative efficiency derived mainly from the historical development experience of the Soviet Union, modified where appropriate by the later experience of the other Socialist countries.

CRITIQUE OF STATIC EQUILIBRIUM ANALYSIS

A persistent criticism levied against Soviet-type central planning by Western economists is that it leads to a misallocation of resources. It is argued that since there is no market for intermediate goods, no interest charge on capital, and subsidies and taxes are used to arrive at final prices, prices do not reflect relative scarcities and thus distort resource allocation.

It is true that there are many examples of miscalculation and misallocation in centrally planned economies. However, similar examples of misallocation can be found in every economy including market economies. No economy does a perfect job of allocating resources. Rather, the important question is, in what type of economy do the fewest misallocations occur. While this writer feels an advanced market economy (not, however, an underdeveloped one) probably allocates resources better than a centrally planned economy, there is insufficient empirical evidence to give a conclusive answer.

Reprinted from *Jahrbuch der Wirtschaft Osteuropas*, Band 2, 1970, pp. 221–243, by permission of Günter Olzog Verlag.

Since empirical proof is not available, Western economists have turned to static equilibrium analysis to prove the inefficiency of Soviet-type central planning. With the recent advances in linear programming, input-output-analysis, and similar mathematical tools, equilibrium analysis has become an invaluable method for solving the problem of constrained maximization of an objective function for sub-units within an economy. Despite the problem of quantifying costs and benefits, General Motors and the U.S. Defense Department can use equilibrium analysis to increase the efficiency of resource allocation within their respective units.

However, recent advances in welfare economics, and particularly the theory of second best, show that static equilibrium analysis breaks down when it comes to evaluating the efficiency of resource allocation for an economy as a whole and particularly for an economy in the process of rapid economic development. Static equilibrium analysis indicates that maximum efficiency is attained when available resources are allocated in such a way as to maximize the particular output mix determined by consumers' preferences (in a market economy) or planners' preferences (in a centrally planned economy). To achieve this allocation the first-order welfare conditions, which for simplicity can be summarized as price equals marginal costs, must be fulfilled in all markets. These first-order or marginal conditions are derived from the rules of the calculus regarding maximization of functions. They constitute a set of necessary conditions for the attainment of maximum efficiency, but are not sufficient conditions. They do not guarantee that it is maximum efficiency being attained; it might be minimum efficiency.

In addition, it is necessary to have second-order, convexity conditions of all cost and utility functions. Even with this, however, one cannot be sure a *maximum maximorum* has been reached. There is nothing in the first-order and second-order conditions to differentiate the top of a molehill from that of a mountain.

For efficiency to be at a maximum, the "total conditions," as J. R. Hicks calls them, must also be satisfied. They state that if efficiency is to be maximized, it must also be impossible to increase efficiency by introducing a new product or by withdrawing an old product.

If the marginal, second-order, and total conditions are all satisfied, static efficiency will be a maximum. However, it is not a unique maximum; it is merely one of an infinite number of Pareto optima because it presupposes a given distribution of income that is not itself determined by the conditions of maximum efficiency. Changes in the distribution of income will cause variations in the most efficient outputs of the various products and allocations of the various inputs.

A Pareto optimum as a position of maximum efficiency loses its validity when external effects (i.e., external economies and diseconomies, interdependence of preference functions) in consumption and production and public goods are taken into account.

Since there are institutional or technical obstacles that preclude the satisfaction of at least some of the conditions of maximum efficiency in all economies, static equilibrium analysis breaks down as an evaluative tool. There is no logical way of determining whether an economy with only one sector failing to attain the price-equals-marginal-cost condition is more efficient in resource allocation than an economy with no sector fulfilling the first-order conditions. That is, if any one price does not reflect relative scarcities (i.e., price equals marginal cost) there is no way of theoretically saying that one set of prices is more rational than another. The conclusion from this is that probably ". . . it is impossible to demonstrate the irrationality—or rationality—of centrally planned economies on the basis of standard welfare economies."[1]

CENTRAL PLANNING AND DYNAMIC EFFICIENCY

All of the above is concerned with a static welfare analysis of resource allocation. If the problem of resource allocation is placed in the context of economic development, then an entirely different approach to evaluation is required. In a developmental setting, the questions of external economies and changing resource scarcities become of prime importance.

The Soviet Union's approach to the specific resource allocation problems of investment rate (choice between present and future), investment allocation and choice of production techniques (including factor proportions) will be analyzed in the next section. For now it is enough to say that their approach centered on the capture of external economies and economizing the obviously scarce factors—capital and skilled labor.

In addition, recognition of constantly changing resource scarcities led to the use of a pricing system that deviated markedly from current resource scarcities. It is worthwhile to analyze the Soviet price system in some detail at this time.

The Pricing System

To repeat, almost every Western specialist on centrally planned economies has argued that the Soviet pricing system is irrational, that is, it does not reflect the relative scarcities of resources derived from the structure of planners' preferences. Two important points are made. First, it is argued that Soviet prices do not include an interest rate on capital. While an appropriate interest rate is theoretically determinable, practically it is very difficult. The Soviet use of the "coefficient of relative effectiveness" has been a rough, if inadequate, substitute.[2] Second, it is argued that Soviet subsidization of some capital goods and taxation of consumer goods distorts present relative scarcities, and, more importantly, the low price of capital relative to the price of labor does so also. However, as seen above, these arguments cannot be logically derived from static equilibrium theory. Furthermore, in the context of economic development this pricing system might even be rational.

A centrally planned economy attempts to secure a coordinated set of investment decisions *ex ante*, that is, in advance of any commitment of resources. In a market economy the allocation of investment is the result of the estimates and expectations of independent entrepreneurs, revised in the long-run by *ex post* movements of market prices. The differences between the planned and market approach are important. Current investment changes both productive capacity and employment and thus exercises an important influence upon market prices by changing relative scarcities. Accordingly, the present structure of market prices cannot be used as a sure measure of the future structure of prices, or, therefore, of what will be the return on any particular investment project. Professor Kenneth Boulding argues that "there is not the slightest reason . . . to suppose that the equilibrium price set, in the sense of classical or neoclassical equilibrium theory, is the price set which will go with the maximum rate of economic development."[3]

The appropriate price structure will depend on a number of considerations. Where there is a divergence between the private and social returns on investment in a particular area due to external economies:

> . . . there is a strong argument for distorting the price structure away from what would be a market equilibrium by deliberately lowering the relative prices and hence discouraging investment in those industries where the external economies or the nonfinancial returns are small, and raising prices and encouraging investment in those industries where the external economies or the nonfinancial returns are large.
> . . . (or) the general principle of the taxation of vice and the subsidization of virtue can be extended to include the taxation of those commodities the production of which we wish to discourage from the point of view of economic development and the subsidization of those the production of which we wish to encourage.[4]

The Soviets accomplished this end by subsidizing strategic material and industries such as steel, engineering, chemicals, and electrical equipment; and taxing low priority products such as textiles and most consumer goods.[5]

In the context of economic development, "personal consumption should have a low claim on resources, and the static welfare criterion of equating price to marginal cost must recede in the background."[6] This the Soviets have done by imposing high turnover taxes on most consumer goods. Some consumer goods which have significance for development, such as paper which plays an important role in the spread of literacy, are favored. Soviet pricing policies, thus, have a rationale in a development context.

Central Planning

The process of industrialization and economic development was facilitated in the Soviet Union by the centralized disposal of economic resources. All of the country's resources were concentrated on certain objectives and their dissipation on other objectives which were not conducive to rapid industrialization was avoided. The lack and weakness of industrial cadres made it desirable to concentrate the available talent on high priority objectives. Thus in the Soviet Union planning in the early stages of development was characterized by administrative management and administrative allocation of resources on the basis of priorities centrally established. The Soviet model in the early stages of the development process can be best described as a *"sui generis* war economy."[7]

A major advantage of public ownership and central planning is its ability to overcome Nurkse's famous "vicious circle of poverty."

> On the supply side, there is the small capacity to save, resulting from the low level of real income. The low level of real income is a reflection of low productivity, which in its turn is due largely to the lack of capital. The lack of capital is a result of the small capacity to save, and so the circle is complete.
>
> On the demand side, the inducement to invest may be low because of the small buying power of the people, which is due to their small real income, which again is due to low productivity. The low level of productivity, however, is a result of the small amount of capital used in production, which in its turn may be caused, at least partly, by the small inducement to invest.[8]

The Soviet Union was able to break the circle on the supply side (i.e., raise the savings rate) because of its ability to collect the economic surplus from the agricultural sector and its control over the division between consumption and investment in the industrial sector.[9] Public ownership allowed the former luxury consumption from property income to be converted into savings for investment purposes. The ability of central planning to concentrate on the one goal of development permitted the Soviet Union to channel savings and thus resources into the most productive purposes and to reduce the proportion of savings going into (from the point of view of rapid growth) unproductive investment.

The demand side of the problem did not exist in the Soviet Union. Long-range development, not short-run profits, was the goal. The problem of finding buyers for what was produced did not exist. The state, through central planning, created the necessary demand by its decision to produce.[10] In making decisions about the allocation of resources between the production of capital goods and consumer goods, the state made *ipso facto* a savings decision. In real terms both investment and savings must refer to the difference between total production and consumer goods production. Thus, there is an identity of savings decisions and investment decisions.[11]

A closely related problem is that of external economies.[12] If an economy is far from equilibrium, current market prices and profit maximization are poor signals for investment decisions. In neo-classical terms, equilibrium occurs when firms (and the industry) are at the bottom of their long-run cost curves, that is, where there are constant or decreasing returns to scale. In addition, *ex ante* coordination of investment decisions is excluded. However, in underdeveloped countries such as the Soviet Union in the 1930's firms (and industries) are likely to be on an increasing return section of the cost curve. And since they are far from the technological frontier, the cost curves will shift downward over time. The presence of potential external economies makes pre-planned coordination among development projects highly desirable. Moreover, in many development schemes there exists a high degree of physical interdependence among different projects such that the productivity of anyone cannot be maximized in isolation. Multipurpose river basin planning, hydroelectricity generation, organization of an iron and steel industry, and the development of chemicals are examples of this nature. The individual project within such a scheme can seldom be examined by itself and in estimating its operational efficiency it has to be jointly considered with its related units.

In underdeveloped countries, private marginal productivity of capital frequently falls short of its social marginal productivity. In developed economies, external economies of various industries support each other and thus help to bridge the gap between private and social productivity. However, lack of basic industrial structures and of social overhead capital does not permit the capture of potential external economies and complementarities in underdeveloped countries. The net productivity of capital, therefore, does not attain a sufficiently high level to stimulate productive private investment. Thus, since a modern industrial structure is highly interdependent, any particular investment project, by itself, frequently appears uneconomic, unless viewed in the perspective of interrelated growth of other firms and industries. Since "the lifetime of equipment is long . . . the investor's foresight is likely to be more imperfect than that of the buyer and seller or of the producer. The individual investor's risk may be higher than that confronting an overall investment program."[13] The volume and cost of production have to be computed on the basis of the anticipated future, and since each project has to be so viewed, the plans for any one project cannot be finished until the plans for all the others are known. The price system fails in these computations because the external economies of individual projects get interrelated and the supply prices depend upon the levels of outputs, which in turn are related to the overall input requirements of the entire development scheme. It is important to remember that when the economy is far from equilibrium, present prices are poor indicators of future prices, and there is no guarantee that the *sequence* of investment dictated by the market will maximize the rate of growth toward equilibrium. To promote coordinated industrial expansion, therefore, the perspective of growth must be known well in advance. This is what the state, through central planning, provided in the Soviet Union.

The most important question is where are most of the external economies and complementarities to be found. In the present context, they can be classified into two types—horizontal external economies and complementarities of demand and vertical externalities and complementarities of forward and backward linkage. These two types lie at the heart of both the debate over balanced growth versus unbalanced growth and the question of investment criteria. As such they will be considered in detail in the next section of this paper when the strategy of resource allocation in the Soviet Union is discussed. For now it is enough to say that because of interdependence of demand and of industries, a system of central planning more easily maximizes the potential external economies.[14] Individual investors will be less motivated to do so because the benefits of external economies accrue to society as a whole, or at least to some members of it, without bringing a direct return to the investor that can be anticipated by using profit maximization and current prices as criteria.

DEVELOPMENT STRATEGY AND RESOURCE ALLOCATION

In discussing resource allocation within the context of economic development, three major problems arise. First is the problem of allocation between the present and future, that is, the choice of an optimum rate of investment. Second is the allocation of investment among sectors and projects. The third problem is the choice of production technique.

The Rate of Investment

What is the optimum rate of investment for a poor country beginning a development program? There is no uniquely determinate economic solution to this question. Increasing the rate of investment today means lowering the share of consumption in gross national product (though not necessarily the absolute amount) in the present in exchange for a larger income and consumption in the future. A lower rate of investment will yield greater consumption in the present, but lower amounts in the future, than would higher rates of investment. The key to the solution, therefore, is the trade-off between present and future consumption.

In an ideal market economy individuals' time preferences would determine the relative values of present and future consumption. A market rate of interest or discount of future income streams would emerge from the particular configuration of time preferences. The market determined rate of investment would be the rate at which the marginal productivity of investment equals the market rate of discount that emerges from the interplay of unilateral decisions of savers and investors. Economists are fairly well agreed that this market determined rate is not necessarily an optimum rate from either a welfare or a growth viewpoint.

> . . . we reject the twin notions (1) that the rate of interest determined in an atomistic competitive market need have any normative significance in the planning of collective investment, and (2) that the market-determined rate of investment, and hence the market-determined rate of economic growth, need be optimal in any welfare sense.[15]

The market rate of interest as a device for discounting the worth of future income streams, however it may be justified for an individual, is inappropriate for the community as a whole, at least within the context of economic development. By determining the rate of saving and investment, time preferences of individuals would decide not only their own future income and consumption but that of future generations as well. There seems to be an inevitable short-sightedness in the individual's choice, owing to the limited perspective in time from which the individual, *qua* isolated individual, necessarily views the range of available alternatives. This limitation in regard to time has often been referred to as the deficiency of the "telescopic faculty" of the individual with regard to the future, and the fact that it gives rise to a "psychological discount" of his future income does not appear to be relevant to planning economic development.[16] In fact, even ". . . the accuracy of its basic assumption that an anticipated satisfaction is always less attractive the more distant the future date to which the actual satisfaction is assigned appears to be questionable, as anticipation can also be enjoyable."[17] This last point is valid both for an individual at different points during his lifetime and even, beyond his lifetime, in the case where satisfaction is received from passing on wealth to heirs.

Professor Holzman points out several other problems[18] of time preference. The present evaluation of the present versus the future will differ from the future evaluation of the present versus the future. The hindsight of the future will overcome the "weakness of imagination" and "defective telescopic faculty" of the present. Thus, he argues, the rate of investment undertaken in the present would be higher if it could be chosen by the population from the vantage point of the future instead of the present. In addition there is a particular time preference configuration for every possible income distribution. If the income distribution changes between the present and the future, then *ceteris paribus*, the investment rate will also change. He argues that the optimum rate is indeterminate between a lower limit set by the present evaluation and an upper limit set by the future evaluation.

Professor Sen introduces the concept of the "isolation paradox"[19] in arguing the limitations of time preference in choosing an investment rate. An individual may be unwilling to give up one unit of consumption today so that a future generation's consumption can be increased by three units. However, if someone else agrees to give up one unit of consumption now if he does likewise then he might very well change his decision. To the first individual, the loss of one unit today will be compensated by a gain of six units for the future. Therefore, while he is not prepared to make the sacrifice alone, he is ready to do so if others join in.

A central planning board cannot simply imitate the rate of investment that would emerge from individual time preferences. The social perspective of the future and the time horizon of a community differ significantly from those of an individual. The community cannot and does not discount its future in the same manner and at the same rate as an individual.[20] What rate of investment does the planning board choose? As noted above, Professor Holzman says it is indeterminate between the lower limit set by the present evaluation of the future and the upper limit set by the future evaluation of the future. Professor Sen argues that the rate is indeterminate between a lower limit set by the rate necessary to utilize existing productive capacity and to maintain a constant consumption level for a growing population and an upper limit set by the rate of investment which maintains the present level of consumption and does not yield negative marginal returns.[21] The indeterminancy in practice is not so great as these limits might imply. The rate of investment is not determined in isolation. The past allocation between consumption and investment production will physically limit the present alternatives. The rate of investment chosen in the present will, in turn, limit the alternatives in the future.[22] More importantly, the choice of investment rate cannot be determined independently of the choice of investment projects and technique.

> Once the specificity of productive capacity is recognized to have an important bearing on the question, the problem of the allocation of investment between different sectors becomes the present-day equivalent of

choosing future rates of saving. If, for example, we assume that investment goods are of two types, viz., those that make consumer goods and those that produce investment goods, the present-day allocation of productive *capital* between these two sectors comes to very much the same thing as the determination of the future division of national output between consumption and investment. The allocation of *investment* between the two becomes the means of influencing the rates of investment in the future.

If one assumes further specificity, so that investment goods to make investment goods to make consumer goods are different from investment goods to make investment goods to make investment goods, the decision has to be taken one further step backwards, and so on.[23]

Thus, the decision on investment rate is dependent on the *allocation* of investment and vice-versa. In a centrally planned economy particularly, the decision on allocation greatly affects the final determination of the rate of savings and investment. This problem of allocation between sectors and projects is the next aspect of resource allocation to be considered.

The Allocation of Investment

Exponents of "imbalanced growth," such as Hirschman, have stressed that if a country decides to industrialize, the correct development strategy is not to seek an optimal allocation of resources at any given time nor to dissipate scarce resources by attempting to advance on all fronts simultaneously, but rather to concentrate on a few major objectives most conducive to transforming the economy to a higher stage. Efficiency is attained in the dynamic sense of finding the most effective sequences for converting a stagnant, backward economy into one which is dynamic and modern. In other words, to be breathlessly climbing a peak in a mountain range is considered more important than standing poised on the crest of a ridge in the foothills.

There is not an infinite number of alternative investment allocation patterns. Because of complementaries and indivisibilities each individual investment project cannot be evaluated in isolation. The construction of a steel industry requires increased coal mining and investment in steel-using industries. The capture of external economies requires that the entire range of investment projects be evaluated as a whole.

> . . . problems of economic planning seem to acquire a resemblance to the problems of military strategy, where in practice the choice lies between a relatively small number of plans, which have in the main to be treated and chosen between as organic wholes, and which for a variety of reasons do not easily permit of intermediate combinations. The situation will demand a concentration of forces round a few main objectives, and not a dispersion of resources over a very wide range.[24]

Investment allocation in the Soviet Union gives us an historical example of this strategy. They pursued a "shock" strategy of bottlenecks successively created and resolved. Thus, Soviet planning concentrated on certain key branches in each plan to overcome particular bottlenecks. Scarce capital and managerial talent were then concentrated on these key targets. This gave Soviet planning its peculiar nature of planning by "campaigning." During the first Five Year Plan the main target was heavy industry with particular emphasis on machine building. During the second and third Five Year Plans the target was again heavy industry with metallurgy, machine building, fuel, energetics, and chemicals singled out for emphasis. This emphasis on key branches yielded high growth rates. The average annual rates of growth in Soviet heavy industry between 1928/29 and 1937 were 18.9 percent for machinery, 18.5 percent for iron and steel, 14.6 percent for coal, 11.7 percent for petroleum products, 22.8 percent for electric power, and 17.8 percent for all heavy industry.[25] Sectors which did not contribute directly to further growth (consumption) were neglected while sectors which enhanced growth (capital goods) were emphasized. Growth tempos such as these caused acute shortages and strains. The bottlenecks which appeared then became the new targets.

Much of the balanced growth versus imbalanced growth debate boils down to the question of where external economies are the greatest. One of the key questions in choosing investment criteria, in turn, hinges on how best to take advantage of external economies and avoid external diseconomies. Economic theorists usually argue that investment should be allocated in such a way that its social marginal product (SMP) is equal in all uses. While this is true as a formal statement it has little meaning unless the "empty box" entitled SMP can be filled with some content. To date no one has done so. One advantage of the imbalanced growth strategy is that it provides a practical signal for reallocating investment. When bottlenecks appear the planner can be sure that the SMP of investment is not equal in all uses. The industries that are the bottlenecks will have a high SMP and thus should receive large investment allocations in the next period. In this sense the SMP will be equated in all uses through time, that is, in a dynamic sense. Thus the campaign method of imbalanced growth, though crude, does have a logic. It also, of course, entails a large risk of waste. If the bottlenecks are not quickly opened they can seriously retard economic growth.

The logic of the campaign method does not ensure that any particular campaign is the right one. The search is for industries which are particularly potent in starting a chain reaction through the capture of external economies. An indication of which industries these are may be found, according to Hirschman, by calculating the backward and forward linkage effects of the industry.[26] Backward linkage represents the degree of input requirements or derived demand which every nonprimary economic activity generates. Forward linkage represents the degree to which output is utilized as an input for activities other than final demand. Thus, the establishment of a new industry with a high backward linkage will provide a new and expanding market for its inputs whether supplied domestically or from abroad. Similarly, the domestic production of a product will tend to stimulate the development of industries using this product. Of course, the domestic availability of a product will not "compel" the construction of industries using the product, but it will create conditions favorable to their development. Hirschman admits that backward linkages are much more clear cut in their stimulating effects than forward linkages. While backward linkage creates demand, forward linkage is dependent upon the existence or antici-pation of demand. Therefore, forward linkage cannot be regarded as an independent inducement mechanism. It acts, however, according to Hirsch-man, as an important and powerful reinforcement to backward linkage. Industries with a high combined backward and forward linkage should, therefore, play a powerful role in inducing industrial development through "creating the demand" or "paving the way" for other supplier or user industries. Indeed, examination of the process of development of a number of mature economies such as Great Britain, Germany, and the United States reveals the crucial role in development played by leading sectors with high-linkage effects.

The identification of high-linkage industries should enable us to put our finger on the crucial sectors or sub-sectors whose growth has maximum impact on an economy's development. Data prepared by Professors Chenery and Watanabe based on input-output tables for the United States, Italy, and Japan indicate that industries with the highest combined linkage effect include (in order of rank) iron and steel (144 of a possible combined 200); nonferrous metals (142); paper and paper products (135); petroleum prod-ucts (135); grain mill products (134); coal products (130); chemicals (129); textiles (124); metal mining (114); petroleum and natural gas (112); and coal mining (110). Two other industries, transportation equipment (80) and machinery (79), would certainly have scored substantially higher and been among the above group of industries had the sales of these industries not been construed in input-output tables as final demand under capital formation.[27]

The list of industries, derived without reference to Soviet experience, is very similar to a list of the "leading sectors" given priority in Soviet development. The Soviet Union did not give high priority to paper and paper products, and textiles. In the case of grain mill products the high linkage effect, in this case largely backward, is explained by the industry being a satellite of agriculture. It is an outgrowth rather than a cause of agricultural development and for this reason could properly be excluded from the original list. Of the industries given high priority by the Soviet Union only electric power production is omitted from the list. The relatively low combined linkage effect (86) would not apply in the Soviet Union, however, where a much smaller share of electric power output is used by households or for municipal lighting.[28] When these qualifications are taken into account, the lists very nearly overlap and the similarity of the two lists is surely not coincidental.

While linkage is not the same thing as external economies, it is probably a good indicator of where they lie. Hirschman, however, stresses the incentive effect of linkage. The creation of bottlenecks forces entrepreneurs to invest in the bottleneck industries. Presumably an overall plan would account for linkage effects and thus the incentives of linkage would be minimized. However, economic planning of the type used by the Soviet Union during the industrialization period and by extension in less developed countries today, is a relatively crude affair. "Campaigns," with their ensuing bottlenecks, substitute for the profit motive in keeping the planning bureauc-racy on its toes.

> . . . the entire *rationale* of the Soviet "campaign" approach to economic
> planning rests upon . . . the need to stimulate not only the executants but
> also the controllers. . . . Campaigns are, among other things, a means of
> goading the goaders, of mobilizing the controllers, of providing success in-
> dicators for officials at all levels. . . .
> . . . Hence the vital role of campaigns as controller mobilizers. Hence
> the value of bottlenecks as stimulators to effort.[29]

The Soviet campaign method of planning thus has logic when viewed
in the light of Hirschman's imbalanced growth theory and concept of
linkage. When the SMP of investment is viewed as containing the return
on external economies, allocation of investment to bottleneck industries
through time appears to be not only good practice but good theory as
well. This does not imply, of course, that the Soviets deliberately created
bottlenecks or that they understood the meaning of imbalanced growth.
Rather, the bottlenecks and imbalanced growth were necessary by-products
of the high growth tempos that the planners adopted. It is also true that
the Soviets have pushed imbalanced growth so far at times that waste
occurred with a consequent reduction in the potential growth rate. However, during periods of rapid growth and structural change misallocation
errors are of relatively minor importance.

> . . . Soviet development technique is more effective: choose a few "lead-
> ing branches" and concentrate on them. The details and the secondary in-
> dustries can catch up later. The fact that such a programme is unbalanced
> and violates "scarcity" rules matters less than its superior speed. . . . A
> certain increase in growth is worth any amount of minor allocation errors.
> . . . There are two main reasons for this. . . . The mere fact of growth
> floats off even a *permanent* misallocation of resources. . . . Secondly, the
> misallocation need not be permanent. . . . Scarcity need not be violated
> always in the same direction. . . . We have here again the dichotomy: good
> resource allocation versus rapid growth.[30]

Professor Wiles is referring, of course, to static resource allocation.
Because of external economies, imbalanced growth can lead to a proper
resource allocation through time, that is, in a dynamic sense. But even
when imbalanced growth is pushed too far the resulting allocation errors
may be a small price to pay, if concentration on leading sectors yields
a faster tempo of growth.

As an economy becomes more sophisticated, "campaign" planning
becomes less appropriate. The number of products multiply and "balance"
becomes more important. Since there is little structural change, and firms
and industries are operating closer to equilibrium, marginal calculations
become more feasible. This seems to be the present situation of the
economy of the Soviet Union. Failure to pull up lagging sectors, particularly
agriculture, and to develop more sophisticated planning methods is causing
the Soviets many problems and slowing their growth tempo.

Finally, it must be remembered that investment allocation is not independent of the investment rate and the investment rate is not independent
of the growth rate of national income. The decision on the pace of economic
growth determines both the share of national income that is to be devoted
to investment and also the physical nature of the required investment. To

attain a certain growth rate a certain investment rate must be maintained. To maintain this investment rate over time the physical output of the growing capital goods industries must match this rate. Thus, a high growth rate means a high investment rate, which in turn means a large allocation of investment to capital goods industries. Therefore, given the indivisibilities and complementarities of production, the range of choice in allocating investment becomes small. This makes the rather crude Soviet strategy of investment allocation more feasible.

The Choice of Production Technique

The final question which arises in regard to resource allocation in the context of centrally planned economic development is the choice of technique in production.

This problem usually resolves into a question of whether capital should be devoted to large-scale units using advanced and expensive technology or to smaller-scale enterprises using simple tools and employing relatively more workers. It is often argued that since, practically by definition, there is a shortage of capital and a surplus of labor in underdeveloped countries, labor-intensive techniques should be used wherever possible so as to conserve on capital and provide as much employment as possible.[31] But, to a large degree, this is a false issue. The decision on the type of technology to use cannot be divorced from the decision regarding the allocation of investment. Once the allocation of investment to sectors and industries has been decided, the choice of technologies is severely limited. The range of processes available for the production of steel, electric power, tractors, and machine tools is not a continuous function where capital and labor are substitutable at the margin in infinitesimal increments. More realistically, the production function in these key industries is sharply discontinuous with probably only two or three alternative processes which make any sense from the purely engineering point of view. Further, many of the most modern technologies tend to be both labor *and capital* saving, as witnessed by the declining capital/output ratios of the advanced countries during their industrialization.[32]

Since Great Britain each succeeding country to industrialize has capitalized on its ability to borrow the most advanced technology from the more developed countries. Professor Gerschenkron points out that "borrowed technology . . . was one of the primary factors assuring a high speed of development in a backward country entering the stage of development."[33] Professor Patel also argues that the explanation "of the progressively higher rates of growth of industrial output for each new entrant to the process of industrialization lies in the opportunity of benefiting from accumulated technological advance."[34] Since many of these modern technologies are both labor- *and capital*-saving the choice can be made on purely engineering grounds rather than economic.

Wholesale borrowing of the most advanced technologies that are labor-saving *but not capital-saving* would be desirable, however, only if the factor proportions in the underdeveloped country were somewhere near those in the developed country. This is seldom the case. Where it is not, redesigning and adapting the most advanced technology to its own factor proportions will yield a larger output.[35]

Soviet development policy has been aware of this conflict between requirements of progress and factor endowment and has dealt with it by adopting the strategy of a "dual technology." On the one hand, in the key industries, they utilized to the maximum the advantage of borrowing the most advanced technologies developed in economies with very different factor endowments. On the other hand, they allowed for these differences by utilizing manual labor in auxiliary operations and by aiming at high performance rates per unit of capital instead of per man.[36]

In many Soviet plants it is common to find the most advanced capital equipment in the basic processes and, at the same time, the most primitive labor intensive methods in maintenance, intra-plant transport, and materials handling. In such enterprises as the Gorky Automotive Plant, which was a direct copy of the Ford River-Rouge plant, they allowed for their lower level of skills by redesigning job descriptions so that each worker performed fewer and simpler tasks.[37] Thus, the Soviets obtained the advantages of advanced technology, conserved scarce capital in auxiliary operations that did not affect output, and utilized their relatively abundant labor.

In addition, the Soviets aimed at high performance rates per unit of capital instead of per man in further adapting advanced technology to their factor endowments. Typical are their records in output of pig-iron per cubic meter of blast furnace. In 1958 they obtained 1.25 tons of pig-iron per cubic meter of blast furnace capacity per day compared with about 0.92 tons per cubic meter in the United States. Without this utilization differential they would have needed an additional 39 blast furnaces to produce the same output.[38] Thus, again, they economized on the scarce factor.

Both use of labor-intensive techniques in auxiliary operations and the intensive utilization of capital tend to lower the capital/output ratio or at least keep it from rising. Thus, the benefits of modern technology are reaped while at the same time minimizing the demand for capital, which is the scarce factor. Undoubtedly the Soviets did not perfectly accommodate modern technology. There are many examples where they did not adapt borrowed technology but instead imitated it exactly.[39]

As indicated above, the key to adoption of this dualistic technology was the desire of Soviet planners to conserve scarce capital. In certain cases, such as the choice between hydroelectric and steam-generated electric power, a means for more accurately measuring the relative scarcity of capital is crucial. The Soviets have used the crude "period of recoupment," or its inverse, the "coefficient of relative effectiveness" as a substitute for an interest rate. While this leaves much to be desired it must be remembered, as was pointed out above, that no one has yet been able to measure the SMP of capital when it is being allocated through time. The capture of external economies and changes in relative scarcities make use of the interest rate derived from static equilibrium analysis inappropriate.

A final factor in the choice of technique, and another reason the determination of an appropriate interest rate is so difficult, is the external economies created by the stimulus of advanced technology to the creation of a disciplined industrial work force.

New technologies do much to educate industrial labour to become a reliable and disciplined social stratum, psychologically adjusted to the requirements of the modern factory. In order to operate with modern machinery some attitude of responsibility and some habits of punctuality are necessary. The education of such a stratum is a protracted process and involves no less difficulties than the creation of the necessary savings.[40]

CONCLUSION

As already seen above, static equilibrium theory has little to say about the efficiency of resource allocation where marginal-cost-equals-price conditions do not prevail in all markets. One of the major weaknesses of equilibrium analysis is the assumption of resource mobility. In reality, mobility of resources, at least in the short run, is not from one sector of employment to another, but, rather, from a state of unemployment or underemployment to a sector of employment. Further, it may be that the major cause of resource immobility in an economy and, therefore, of inefficient allocation is the full-employment of resources. As an economy approaches full-employment, the pool of skilled labor, for instance, dries up and all kinds of shortages and bottlenecks begin to appear.

The fact that centrally planned economies have typically aimed at full employment of capital and skilled labor may explain what seems to be their poor record of resource allocation. Constantly operating at full employment has left little slack to cover the inevitable shortages and rigidities. They have reduced the consequences of this tautness by diverting resources from low priority sectors (primarily the consumer goods sector) to cover the shortages in high priority sectors.

In market economies the normal slack in the use of capital goods' capacity and employment has provided greater flexibility. The normal pool of unemployed resources has been used to cover allocation errors. Whenever a market economy approaches sustained full employment, rigidities and shortages similar to those in centrally planned economies begin to appear.

Unemployed resources can be likened to an Army commander's troop reserves that are used to plug a gap that develops in the battle line. The conclusion seems to be that increased inefficiency in resource allocation may be an unavoidable concomitant of full employment. This makes centrally planned economies' efforts at reform more difficult. The system of central planning and resource allocation derived from Soviet experience was developed for use in a backward economy trying to achieve the one overriding goal of economic development. The methods are basically those of a war economy. As such, when the economy has reached some level of sophistication, the required economic strategy then changes from one of maximum concentration of available resources on a few main goals towards successively greater dispersion. Since a number of the centrally planned economies seem to have reached this stage, either the planning system will have to become much more effective or pools of unemployed resources will have to be allowed to develop since low priority sectors, particularly consumer goods, can no longer be drawn on to provide the necessary flexibility to cover allocation errors.

SUMMARY

This paper analyzes the question of allocative efficiency within the context of a backward economy using a system of central planning to achieve rapid economic development. The paper first critiques static equilibrium analysis and finds that its usefulness is limited in a developmental context. Second, the paper constructs a model of dynamic allocative efficiency derived mainly from the historical development experience of the Soviet Union, modified where appropriate by the later experience of the other socialist countries.

When the problem of resource allocation is placed in the dynamic context of economic development, the questions of external economies, complementarities, and *changing* resource scarcities become of prime importance. The resource allocation problems of investment rate (choice between present and future), investment allocation among sectors and projects, and choice of production techniques (including factor proportions) are analyzed in the light of the above questions. Central planning is analyzed in terms of its role in solving these resource allocation problems.

The model of central planning and resource allocation set forth in this paper is based on a backward economy trying to achieve the one overriding goal of economic development. The strategy is basically that of a war economy. As such, when the economy has reached some level of sophistication, the required economic strategy then changes from one of maximum concentration of available resources on a few main goals toward successively greater dispersion.

NOTES

1. Alastair N. D. McAuley, "Rationality and Central Planning," *Soviet Studies*, Vol. 18, No. 3 (January 1967), p. 353. There may not be a satisfactory second-best solution at all or a third-best, fourth-best, or nth-best, and if there is, the rules for achieving it may be almost impossible to implement. For a thorough treatment of resource allocation see E. J. Mishan's, "A Survey of Welfare Economics, 1939–1959," and "A Reappraisal of the Principles of Resource Allocation," both in E. J. Mishan, *Welfare Economics* (New York: Random House, 1964), pp. 3–97, 155–183.

2. The "coefficient of relative effectiveness" (CRE) is given by the formula $e = \dfrac{V^1 - V^2}{K^2 - K^1}$

where V^1 and V^2 represent the annual operating costs (including depreciation) of two alternative projects producing the same output, and K^1 and K^2 represent the corresponding capital outlays. Since capital outlays usually vary inversely with operating expenses, e represents the savings in operating expense realized per ruble of additional capital outlay. The choice between two projects depends on whether $e \gtrless E$, where E is some CRE taken as a standard. Thus K^1V^1 is chosen if $e < E$; K^2V^2 if $e > E$: and the two projects are equally desirable if $e = E$.

3. Kenneth E. Boulding and Pritam Singh, "The Role of the Price Structure in Economic Development," *American Economic Review*, Vol. LII, No. 2 (May 1962), pp. 29, 30.

4. *Ibid.*, pp. 29, 33.

5. Subsidizing an industry has the same effect as increasing the price of its output, and, conversely, taxation has the same effect as decreasing price. Also, the effect of subsidization can be achieved by simply taxing some goods less than others. The effect is that some goods are priced below and others above what their relative equilibrium prices would be in a free market.

6. Boulding and Singh, *op. cit.*, p. 35.

7. Oskar Lange, "Role of Planning in Socialist Economy," *Problems of Political Economy of Socialism*, ed. Oskar Lange (New Delhi: Peoples Publishing House, 1962), p. 18. During the First World War and even more so the Second World War, capitalist countries used war economy methods. Resources were concentrated towards the one basic objective of producing war materials. Resources were centrally allocated to prevent leakages to production not connected with the prosecution of the war. Essential consumer goods were rationed. The production of consumer durables such as automobiles and refrigerators was prohibited. The average work week was lengthened. Patriotic appeals were used to maintain labor productivity and discipline. The share of consumption in gross national product in the United States declined from 75.4 percent in 1940 to 53.9 percent in 1944. These same features characterized the Soviet economy during its war on economic underdevelopment. It is somewhat strange that Western economists who applauded war economy methods in the Second World War do not understand their analogous use in the Soviet Union's industrialization and by extension in underdeveloped countries today.

8. Ragnar Nurkse, *Problems of Capital Formation in Underdeveloped Countries* (Oxford: Basil Blackwell, 1958), pp. 4–5.

9. A planned economy is, of course, still limited in raising the savings rate by the minimum standard of living necessary to maintain the efficiency and morale of the agricultural and industrial work force, and, more importantly, by the absorptive capacity of the economy.

10. It is in a planned economy that Say's Law can be said to hold (at least for capital goods). Supply does create its own demand, or rather, more correctly, demand creates its own supply (within the limits of available resources, of course).

11. There are certain problems with the mechanism necessary to ensure this result. The amount of real investment is susceptible to market influence if enterprise managers have discretion as to the size of inventories they hold, and even under the most centralized planning they are bound to have considerable *de facto* discretion. See Maurice Dobb, *Soviet Economic Development Since 1917* (London: Routledge & Kegan Paul Ltd., 1960), pp. 356, 382. R. W. Davies, *The Development of the Soviet Budgetary System* (Cambridge: Cambridge University Press, 1958), pp. 158, 231.

12. At this point, external economies can be considered the divergence between private profit and public benefit. See Tibor Scitovsky, "Two Concepts of External Economies," *The Economics of Underdevelopment*, ed. A. N. Agarwala and S. P. Singh (Oxford: Oxford University Press, 1958), pp. 295–308. P. N. Rosenstein-Rodan, "Problems of Industrialization of Eastern and South-Eastern Europe," *The Economics of Underdevelopment*, pp. 245–256. Maurice Dobb, *An Essay on Economic Growth and Planning* (London: Routledge & Kegan Paul Ltd., 1960), pp. 5–13. Hla Myint, *The Economics of the Developing Countries* (New York: Frederick A. Praeger, Publishers, 1964), pp. 118–125.

13. P. N. Rosenstein-Rodan, "The Flaw in the Mechanism of Market Forces," *Leading Issues in Development Economics*, ed. Gerald M. Meier (New York: Oxford University Press, 1964), p. 417.

14. ". . . complete integration of all industries would be necessary to eliminate all divergence between private profit and public benefit." Scitovsky, *op. cit.*, p. 305. And, it is necessary that the ". . . whole of the industry to be created is to be treated and planned like one huge firm or trust." Rosenstein-Rodan, "Problems of Industrialization of Eastern and South-Eastern Europe," p. 248.

15. Stephen A. Marglin, "The Social Rate of Discount and the Optimal Rate of Investment," *Quarterly Journal of Economics*, Vol. LXXVII, No. 1 (February 1963), p. 111. Also see Franklyn D. Holzman, "Consumer Sovereignty and the Rate of Economic Development," *Economia Internazionale*, Vol. IX, No. 2 (1958), pp. 3–17. Maurice Dobb, *An Essay on Economic Growth and Planning*, pp. 15–28. A. K. Sen, "On Optimising the Rate of Saving," *The Economic Journal*, Vol. LXXI, No. 283 (September 1961), pp. 479–496.

16. Roy Harrod refers to pure time preference as ". . . a polite expression for rapacity and the conquest of reason by passion." Roy Harrod, *Towards a Dynamic Economics*

(London: Macmillan & Co., Ltd., 1948), p. 40. Also see S. S. Wagle, *Technique of Planning* (Bombay: Vora & Co., 1961), pp. 165–169.

17. G. L. S. Shackel, *Time in Economics* (Amsterdam: North-Holland Publishing Co., 1958), p. 37.

18. Holzman, *op. cit.*, pp. 8–10.

19. Sen, *op. cit.*, pp. 487–489.

20. "It should be noted that the problem of inadequate foresight on the part of individuals, where collective needs are under consideration, is not restricted to the rate of economic development undertaken by the state. A similar situation exists in the cases of both trade unions and large corporations. Union leaders may call a strike which they know will reduce the total income of their members over the subsequent five-year period but which, in their opinion, will strengthen the position of the union (and the labor movement) and the earnings of its members over the longer-run period. The conflict between rank and file stockholders and management of large corporations on dividend and reinvestment policy is too well-known to need repeating." Holzman, *op. cit.*, p. 11.

21. Professor Horvat argues that this upper limit is the optimum rate of saving and investment. His argument, in effect, ignores completely *any* discount of the future. See Branko Horvat, "The Optimum Rate of Investment," *The Economic Journal*, Vol. LXVIII, No. 272 (December 1958), pp. 747–767.

22. If the allocation between consumption and investment is changed too abruptly, excess capacity will appear in the sector receiving the reduced allocation.

23. Sen, *op. cit.*, pp. 493–494. Also see H. B. Chenery, "Comparative Advantage and Development Policy," *American Economic Review*, Vol. LI, No. 1 (March 1961), p. 41. Maurice Dobb, *Some Aspects of Economic Development* (Occasional Paper No. 3; Delhi: Delhi School of Economics, 1951), pp. 52–53.

24. Dobb, *Soviet Economic Development Since 1917*, p. 6.

25. Alexander Gerschenkron, "Soviet Heavy Industry: A Dollar Index of Output, 1927–1937," *Economic Backwardness in Historical Perspective* (New York: Frederick A. Praeger, Publishers, 1962), p. 247.

26. This approach is feasible only for a country with population and resources capable of maintaining a full industrial structure. Those too small to do so must modify the strategy by a much greater reliance on international trade.

27. Hollis B. Chenery and Tseunehiko Watanabe, "International Comparisons of the Structure of Production," *Econometrica*, October, 1958, p. 493, quoted in Albert O. Hirschman, *The Strategy of Economic Development* (New Haven: Yale University Press, 1958), pp. 106–107.

28. The United States uses about half its electric power for industrial purposes while the Soviet Union uses perhaps 80 percent, W. W. Rostow, "Summary and Policy Implications," *Comparisons of the United States and Soviet Economies*, Part III (Washington: Joint Economic Committee, GPO, 1959), p. 291.

29. Alec Nove, *The Soviet Economy* (New York: Frederick A. Praeger, Publishers, 1969), p. 292. Also see Gregory Grossman, "Soviet Growth: Routine, Inertia and Pressure," *American Economic Review*, Vol. L, No. 2 (May 1960), pp. 62–72.

30. P. J. D. Wiles, "Growth vs. Choice," *The Economic Journal*, Vol. LXVI (June 1956), pp. 244–255. Reprinted in *Capitalism, Market Socialism, and Central Planning*, ed. Jesse W. Markham (New York: Houghton Mifflin Co., 1963), pp. 296–297, 299. Also see Tibor Scitovsky, *Welfare and Competition* (Homewood: Richard Irwin, Inc., 1951), pp. 8–11.

31. See Nurkse, *Problems of Capital Formation in Underdeveloped Countries*, p. 45.

32. In the United States the capital/output ratio first rose, then fell. This was in part technological and in part reflected an initial buildup of capital ahead of demand; e.g. the railroads. See Simon Kuznets, "A Comparative Analysis," *Economic Trends in the Soviet Union*, ed. Abram Bergson and Simon Kuznets (Cambridge, Mass.: Harvard University Press, 1963), pp. 353–358.

33. Gerschenkron, *Economic Backwardness in Historical Perspective*, p. 8.

34. Surendra J. Patel, "Rates of Industrial Growth in the Last Century, 1860–1958," *The Experience of Economic Growth*, ed. Barry E. Supple (New York: Random House, 1963), p. 69.

35. For fuller theoretical treatments of this, see Joseph Berliner, "The Economics of Overtaking and Surpassing," *Industrialization in Two Systems*, ed. Henry Rosovsky (New York: John Wiley & Sons, 1966), pp. 170–174. R. S. Eckhaus, "Factor

Proportions in Underdeveloped Areas," *American Economic Review*, Vol. XLV, No. 4 (September 1955), pp. 539–565. Hirschman, *op. cit.*, pp. 150–152.

36. See Alfred Zauberman, "Soviet and Chinese Strategy for Economic Growth," *International Affairs*, Vol. XXXVIII, No. 3 (July 1962), pp. 347–349. Berliner, *op. cit.*, pp. 172–174. Gregory Grossman, "Scarce Capital and Soviet Doctrine," *Quarterly Journal of Economics*, Vol. LXVII (August 1953), pp. 311–343. Professor Granick's studies cite evidence for these Soviet policies but his evaluation is much more negative. See David Granick, *Soviet Metal-Fabricating and Economic Development* (Madison: The University of Wisconsin Press, 1967).

37. Berliner, *op. cit.*, p. 172.

38. Robert W. Campbell, *Soviet Economic Power* (Boston: Houghton Mifflin Co., 1960), p. 61.

39. See Berliner, *op. cit.*, p. 173. M. Gardner Clark, *The Economics of Soviet Steel* (Cambridge, Mass.: Harvard University Press, 1956), pp. 65–66, 84.

40. S. Swianiewicz, *Forced Labour and Economic Development: An Inquiry into the Experience of Soviet Industrialization* (London: Oxford University Press, 1965), p. 263.

19

Self-Reliant Industrialization

Paul Streeten

SUMMARY

This paper surveys the role of industrialization in developing countries in the light of certain objectives (efficient growth, reduced inequality, diversified jobs, integrated development) and certain constraints (environmental damage, scarcity of resources, protectionist policies by industrialized countries). It is argued that the basic objective of development provides a key to the solution of a number of problems that appear to be separate but on inspection are related: urbanization, protection of the environment, equality, a better international division of labor. This approach throws a new light on the demand for sources of energy and for sophisticated products, the transfer of inappropriate technologies, the role of the transnational enterprise, the relation between rural development and industrialization and the relation of domination and dependence.

Self-reliant development is a complex process in which many variables act upon one another and in which policies must act upon several objectives either simultaneously or in an appropriate sequence. Industrialization is clearly only a part of a unified, self-reliant development strategy. A unified, self-reliant strategy provides an opportunity to overcome the fragmentation that some critics have discerned in national policy-making and also in the organization of the United Nations specialized agencies. It is a challenge to organize and integrate all development efforts aimed at improving the lot of the poor people of the world.

In a concerted and unified strategy, industrialization has a special role to play. The poorer the country, the larger the proportion of the population that is engaged in producing food. To rise above poverty, industrialization is necessary, for industrialization means the application of power to production and transport. Output and consumption per head can rise toward desired levels only with the help of mechanical aids. In this sense, development, including rural development, is industrialization.

In addition, manufacturing industry is subject to increasing returns,

This article was written expressly for this book of readings. It draws on Paul Streeten's contribution to *Employment, Income Distribution and Development Strategy: Problems of the Developing Countries —Essays in Honour of H. W. Singer*, edited by Alec Cairncross and Mohinder Puri (Macmillan, 1976). © Paul Streeten.

to learning effects, and to cumulative processes. The exceptionally high growth potential of manufacturing industry (reflected in the annual average growth target of manufacturing output of 8 percent) has been demonstrated in several countries in recent years.

Rapid economic growth, and especially industrial growth, has come under attack from several directions. It has been argued that social objectives, such as income distribution and jobs, are more important than the rise in some abstract index number to which industrial growth contributes substantially. It has been said that the drive for industrial growth has destroyed the environment and has rapaciously used up exhaustible natural resources, particularly, sources of energy. It has been claimed that rapid growth, spurred by industry, increases inequalities and proceeds without regard to the damage inflicted upon its victims. Perhaps most convincingly, it has been argued that in countries where cultivable land and capital are scarce and where the labour force grows rapidly and mass emigration is ruled out, development must aim at raising the yield of the land; that food output can grow only if markets exist in which the food can be sold; and that, exports apart, these markets must be found in the countryside, amongst the mass of the rural population. Rural development, the argument goes, combined with income redistribution, is a necessary condition of economic growth.

In the face of all these charges against and criticisms of industrialization, it must be emphasized that to achieve the social objectives rightly advocated and to fight the evils of pollution, premature exhaustion of raw materials, unemployment, inequality, and market limitations, industrial growth is an absolutely essential condition. It must, of course, be growth that benefits the right groups. It must be correctly composed and measured so that social costs are fully accounted for and proper relative weights are given to different components, to the working conditions and to the human relations in which production is carried out.

Statistically there is no evidence of an inevitable conflict between high rates of industrial growth and the achievement of other development objectives; if anything, there is evidence to the contrary. In many, though not in all, cases, the achievement of social objectives has been consistent with high rates of industrial growth and, indeed, has depended on them. The causal links between these variables are complex, controversial, and still partly unknown, but the promotion of industrial growth is one of the strategic variables in the complex set of related national and international development policies.

The current combination of a worldwide energy crisis and worldwide cost-inflation has called into question the whole inherited framework of economic analysis and policy. If it needed underlining, the crisis has certainly underlined the fact that economic and political forces cannot be treated separately and in isolation, for the demands of the trade unions and the demands of the oil producers (and possibly of other producers of scarce raw materials and food) are economic exercises in political power. The role of industrialization in this new framework of thought and action also requires a thorough reappraisal.

INDUSTRIALIZATION FOR WHAT?

Many confusing and complex issues become clearer and simpler if we remind ourselves of the purpose of development and the place of industrialization in a development strategy. In particular, questions about energy, the environment, pollution, appropriate technology, appropriate products and consumption patterns, markets, international trade and integration, and the transnational corporation can be answered more easily if we know where we want to go. Many apparently technical and separate problems are seen to be connected and become amenable to a solution if we bear the basic objective in mind.

Development is not about index numbers of national income, it is not about savings ratios and capital coefficients: it is about and for people. Development must therefore begin by identifying human needs. The objective of development is to raise the level of living of the masses of the people and to provide all human beings with the opportunity to develop their potential. This objective implies meeting such needs as adequate nutrition and safe water, continuing employment, secure and adequate livelihoods, more and better schooling, better medical services, shelter, cheap transport, and a higher and increasing level of measured income. It also includes meeting nonmaterial needs, such as the desire for self-determination, self-reliance, political freedom and security, participation in making the decisions that affect workers and citizens, access to power, national and cultural identity, and a sense of purpose in life and work. Much of this can be achieved in ways that do not increase the measured output of commodities, while a high and growing index for national income growth can leave these basic needs unsatisfied.

If we approach development in these terms, the place of the private motor car, of heavy demand on sources of energy, of highly sophisticated luxury goods, of the transfer of inappropriate products and technologies, of the role of the transnational enterprise, of urbanization, of the relation between industrial and agricultural policies, and of domination and dependency, all appear in a different light.

The disenchantment with industrialization in recent writings and speeches has been based on confusion; it is a disenchantment with the form that economic growth has taken in some developing countries and with the distribution of its benefits. Certain types of modern products and modern technology have reinforced an income distribution and a style of development that is out of tune with the basic goals sketched out above. After a reorientation of goals, industrialization as the servant of development regains its proper place in the strategy. Industry should produce the simple goods required by the people, the majority of whom live in the countryside—hoes, simple power tillers, and bicycles, not air conditioners, expensive cars, and equipment for luxury flats.

An industrialization strategy guided by the goal of meeting the needs of the poor not only leads to a different composition of products and of techniques but also reduces the demand that rapid urbanization makes on scarce capital, scarce skills, and scarce natural resources. By raising the level of living of the poor people in the countryside, it may reduce the pressure to leave the farms and to expand expensive urban services.[1]

In subsequent sections, I shall survey several problem areas and reexamine the appropriate policy in the light of the basic objective. The conclusions depend upon countries opting for a style of development that gives priority to satisfying the simple, basic needs of the large number of poor people. Industries producing clothing, food, furniture, simple household goods, electronics, buses, and electric fans would thrive without the need for heavy protection in a society that had adopted this style of industrialization and development. Much of the recent criticism of inefficient, high-cost industrialization behind high walls of protection and quantitative restrictions should be directed at the types of product and of technique that cater to highly unequal income distribution and reflect entrenched vested interests. It is in no way a criticism of industrialization for the needs of the people.

This does not mean that opting for such a style is an easy matter. Among the enormously difficult tasks are the required changes in the thrust of research and development expenditure and of science policy; the attack on the living standards and power of those profiting from the present pattern of trade, technology, and products; the more complex system of decentralized administration of rural development; and the required coordination and changes in trade and investment policy. The point, however, is that no solution is possible unless the fundamental objective is borne in mind.

INDUSTRY AND AGRICULTURE

The dispute about whether to give priority to industry or agriculture is a sham dispute. The answer is not either/or, but both/and. Industry needs agriculture and agriculture needs industry, and for some purposes the very division into the two categories is wrong. Thus, when we are concerned with evaluating an agroindustrial project, the relevant project appraisal criteria cut across the demarcation line between industry and agriculture.

Still, some people might object by saying that the speed of progress of an economy in which the scope for substitution between sectors is limited is controlled by the speed of its slowest moving sector. For this reason in the last 15 years attention has been focused on agriculture. Although it is true that agriculture is the slowest moving sector, how do we identify it as such in the first instance? How do we unmask it as the laggard, so that we can bring pressure to bear upon it to improve its performance? It has been a platitude for many years now to say that nonexport agriculture, especially in dry zones, has been the lagging sector in many developing countries. But today's platitudes are yesterday's startling discoveries. In the 1930s, when all the talk was of agriculture surpluses, nobody would have believed what we find so obvious today. It is the very success of rapidly moving, dynamic industry combined with high growth rates of agricultural productivity in the advanced countries, and especially in the United States, that has shown up agriculture in the developing countries as the slow coach: an instance of the uses of unbalanced growth.

In spite of the Green Revolution and substantial, though patchy, progress in agriculture, we have not yet turned industry into the lagging sector. We need continuing advances in industry to provide agriculture with the input and with the markets; we need progress in agriculture to provide industry with food, raw materials and, again, markets (and in some cases, exports). If several things done together are essential for success, it does not make sense to ask which should have priority. There is less scope for substitution, even at the margin, than is sometimes thought.

Even at the margin, the choice is not between industry and argriculture. The choice is between projects and complexes of projects, many of which, like processing local raw materials (see below, p. 287), cut across the line between industry and agriculture. Priority must be given to a form of industrialization consistent with a strategy of rural transformation. Some plead for a type of agriculture that supports urban industrialization; others for industrialization that serves agriculture. The argument here is that mutual support and consistency are required.

URBAN AND RURAL LOCATION OF INDUSTRY

The concern with growing inequality has a regional dimension. There are both economies and diseconomies in the rapidly growing cities of the developing world. Urban centers offer businesses advantages of location; economies of scale; low costs of information; availability of suitable labor force; access to administrators, policy makers, and sources of learning; and opportunities to exchange information and coordinate actions. On the other hand, the inability of the rural sector to hold the growing working population has led to migration to the towns with the resulting shanty towns and slums and the growing burden of constructing urban public services for the rapidly expanding number of town dwellers. The more that is done to meet the needs of the urban immigrants through creation of jobs, clearance of slums, building of houses, and provision of public services, the more people flood in from the countryside. The social costs of urban industrialization diverge from its private costs. Even with the best policies, urban industry is incapable of providing anything like an adequate number of jobs or a satisfactory level of living for all those wishing to leave the country for the promises of the city.

This proposition is sometimes criticized by those who say migration to the towns is an improvement for the migrants and that economic progress consists in reducing the number of those in agriculture. But this view neglects the fact that the absolute number of people in agriculture and industry depends not only upon the rate of growth of the labor force and the rate of growth of employment opportunities in industry but also on the initial, relative size of the industrial sector. For the same growth rates in the labor force and in employment opportunities, the existence of an initially relatively small industrial sector implies that the absolute number (though not the proportion) of people in agriculture (or at any rate, in the rural sector and in the urban "informal sector") must increase. The belief that the absolute number of people in the rural work force and the "informal sector" can decline in the early stages of industrialization is false.

The creation of rural industries and rural public works could contribute to the absorption of some of the large and rapidly growing underutilized labor force. The purpose of these industries would be to use agricultural labor when it can be spared from seasonal peak demands, to use local materials, and to mobilize the underemployed labor force for the construction of rural public works, such as feeder roads, houses, and schools, which would support rural industries.

. . .

EXPORTS OF MANUFACTURED PRODUCTS: PROSPECTS OF GROWTH AND THE INTERNATIONAL DISTRIBUTION OF GAINS

The spectacular export performances of a few, but growing number of, countries (and by no means only those with high GNP growth records) have shown that breakthroughs into the markets of developed countries are possible in spite of existing tariff and nontariff barriers. However, there is evidence of growing restrictions against these exports whenever they begin to be seriously felt by the protected and local industry of an importing country. Annual growth rates in the 1960s of 10 to 15 percent of exports of manufactured products from the developing countries are liable to run into obstacles put up by importing countries. These would become more serious if the lesson were to be generalized and more developing countries were to engage in massive export drives, particularly if these exports were concentrated on a few "sensitive" products.

Policy restrictions are liable to be supported by a form of "adjustment assistance" that directs research and development and compensation expenditure at defensive investment to reequip the industry hit by the low-cost imports or simply to subsidize it to remain competitive.

Apart from restrictions by importing countries, there are also institutional limitations to increasing exports, limitations that cannot easily be classified under "supply and demand." Such limitations include absence of export credits, absence of marketing and sales organization, and lack of knowledge of required designs. Calling in a transnational corporation to overcome these obstacles may solve some of the problems while raising others (see below, pp. 291–294).

There are also supply limitations. These may lie in the lack of entrepreneurial ability to spot the type of products for which world demand is expanding and which can be produced at low costs; in weak organizational and administrative ability (in both the private and public sectors); in the inability of the economy to supply enough food for the workers engaged in manufacturing to keep industrial wages low and prices competitive; and in the inability to resist the power of the urban trade unions to extract ever higher money wages.

While organizational and other supply obstacles clearly account for part of the export failure of some countries, this failure contributed to the success of the successful exporters. If all developing countries had adopted the strategy of Taiwan and Korea, their exports and the exports of some other countries would have fared less well in the 1960s than they did.

There is also the question of the distribution of the gains from the rising volume and value of manufactured exports. When transnational corporations are engaged in producing and selling exports, part of the gain accrues to countries other than the exporting country. In conditions of oligopoly, low costs are not automatically passed on either to buyers, in the form of lower prices, or to workers, in the form of higher wages, but may only swell profits.

What is often considered to be the peculiar virtue of private foreign enterprise, viz., that it brings a "package" of capital, enterprise, management, and know-how, is also its peculiar defect: it means that monopoly rents and profits accruing to these factors go abroad and that only the reward for unskilled or semiskilled labor, in highly elastic supply and with little bargaining power, goes to the host country. If, on top of this, the country gives tax concessions to the foreign firm and subsidizes it through trading estates or import privileges, the division of the gains is very uneven, and export figures give a misleading picture of the host country's gain.[2] Alternatives might be subcontracting, the encouragement of indigenous firms with management contracts, national export sales corporations, or various forms of joint venture.

If we are interested in the limits to the growth of exports of manufactured products and the likely international and internal distribution of gains, a typology by product will be useful. We may then distinguish between the following products.

1. *Processed local primary products.* These include products such as vegetable oils, foodstuffs, plywood and veneer, pulp and paper products, and fabricated metal. The processing may be into semiprocessed, refined, or completely manufactured products. When these products are less expensive to transport in a processed form rather than in a raw state, countries processing them enjoy an advantage over the countries in which they are sold. Cascading tariffs (rising with the stage of processing) in developed countries discriminate against this type of export. Yet, processing is clearly not appropriate in all cases where a developing country has the raw material. But where appropriate, countries with highly sought after raw materials can insist that the materials be processed locally. This is another instance of a strategy directed at exploiting the scarcities of raw materials and food in combination with industrialization.

2. *Traditional labor-intensive goods.* These include garments, textiles, footwear, and simple engineering goods. While low labor costs make the exports of developing countries competitive in these products, they face particular obstacles in importing countries where the competing industries are often concentrated and politically well organized. Successful exporting may have to be combined with the mobilization of interests in importing countries. Independent retail chains, mail-order firms, trading houses, or consumers' associations are useful allies in organizing pressures against

the producers' organizations and their lobbies. A better system of international monetary adjustments would also give wider scope to increased
exports of these products.

3. *Newer labor-intensive goods.* Goods such as plastic and wooden
items, rattan furniture, glassware, pottery, and wigs have appeared in
recent years. The fact that their impact on importing countries is more
dispersed and less noticeable makes them better export prospects as
long as not too many countries compete in selling them.

4. *Processes, components, and assembly in a vertically integrated international firm.* A comparatively recent phenomenon is the location of a
wide range of activities in a vertically integrated transnational corporation
in developing countries. Semiconductors, tubes, and other electronic components are assembled in developing countries for the parent firm in
developed countries. Garments, gloves, leather luggage, and baseballs are
sewn together in Taiwan, South Korea, Thailand, and India; automobile
parts, such as radio antennas, piston rings, cylinder linings, headlights,
brakes, batteries, and springs are made in many countries. Data are flown
to Southeast Asia and the West Indies for punching on tape by low-wage
key punch operators; watchmakers fly jewels to Mauritius for precision
drilling. These industries are footloose, attracted by low wages, tax concessions, docile trade unions, relative absence of corruption, and political
stability. They also represent an organized interest in the importing country
opposing import-competing interests and sometimes enjoy tariff advantages.

5. *Import substitutes or local products turned exports.* These products,
often goods such as automobiles (Brazilian Volkswagen is an outstanding
example), car parts, steel pipes and tubes, electric wires and cables,
bicycles, electric motors, and diesel engines, were set up initially to replace
imports; having become established, they have entered the export market.
They represent the last stage in the product cycle. Marginal-cost pricing
for exports is common (i.e., export prices are lower than domestic prices),
and exports may be subject to antidumping measures.

This classification is useful for identifying problems of adjustment and
pressure groups in the importing countries, and hence for identifying the
possible limits to growth in the exporting country and the division of gains
between different factors of production and different countries. The classification also indicates that it would be rash to conclude that promotion of
exports of manufactured goods through price incentives is necessarily the
best strategy for all developing countries. A good deal has recently been
written about negative value added in import-substituting manufacturing
as a result of excessive protection. We should not forget that negative
value added can also occur in exports and that a recipe of universal export
promotion, extrapolated from the experience of the 1960s, supported by
transnational enterprises with concessions, privileges, and incentives, can
be as detrimental to the developing host country as high-cost import
substitution.

The next ten years will be a more difficult period, especially as more
and more countries adopt export-promoting strategies. Overexpansion may
turn the income terms of trade against the exporting countries (though
this would improve the terms of trade of developing primary producers);

import capacity and import willingness are not likely to keep in step with accelerated export expansion; and even when exports are successful, the gains to the developing countries may be small or, in extreme cases, negative. This does not mean that developing countries should not devote considerable efforts to promoting exports, or that export-oriented strategies do not have advantages over import-substituting ones. It does mean that institutional, political, and technological constraints will have to be investigated and overcome and that some coordination and cooperation between developing countries is essential if they are not to erode the benefits through excessive competition.

COLLECTIVE SELF-RELIANCE AND INTERNATIONAL TRADE

An industrialization strategy guided by the goal of meeting the needs of the poor also introduces different incentives and opportunities into international and intraregional trade: it implies a reorientation toward more trade between developing countries. Starting with similar factor supplies and similar levels of demand, developing countries can more appropriately produce for one another what they consume and consume what they produce.[3] This can be the basis of mutually beneficial trade. In simple goods for mass consumption, often produced in a labor-intensive, capital-saving way, the developing countries have a comparative advantage and could expand trade among themselves.

I have argued that even if the developed countries were to resume high rates of economic growth, their ability and willingness to absorb large increases of manufactured products from developing countries is limited. There are good arguments on grounds of comparative advantage for increasing trade among developing countries. Some developing countries, such as Brazil and Mexico, have been registering high rates of growth, and it might well be in the high-growth countries of the Third World, rather than in the OECD countries, that the future of the international division of labor lies. To interpret "collective self-reliance" in this sense is entirely compatible with the most conventional economic doctrine. Sir Arthur Lewis drew a historical parallel.

> Besides competing in the O.E.C.D. markets, the tropics can also compete in their own markets. In 1965 they imported manufactures, excluding metals, valued at $14.1 billion; to wit $2.3 billion of chemicals, $4.7 billion of light manufactures and $7.2 billion of machinery and transport equipment. At least $12.5 billion of this came from outside the region. It follows that the tropics do not have to depend on competing with O.E.C.D. countries in O.E.C.D. markets. They can just as well compete with O.E.C.D. in their own tropical markets.
>
> This point sometimes comes as a surprise to policy-makers in the tropics. We have got so accustomed to the idea that the tropics trades with the temperate world that we tend to assume that the chief way to expand tropical trade is to sell more to the temperate countries. Actually, as Germany industrialized in the second half of the nineteenth century, she did not concentrate primarily on breaking into the British and French markets, though she did this too. She looked rather to the countries around

her in Eastern and Central Europe, who were even more impoverished than she, and made big gains there. Similarly Japan's trade drive in the 1930's was directed not at the industrial nations but at Asia and Africa and Latin America. This is where the rising new exporters should surely be looking, rather than to European and North American markets, since it is surely easier to beat your competitors in third markets than it is to beat them at home, once you have established the machinery for making customer contacts.

The continuous discussion of the possibility of creating new customs unions or common markets in Africa and Asia and Latin America indicates that many people have seen the light, though the paucity of actual results also indicates how difficult the problem is. The basic difficulty centers in the fact that only a handful of tropical countries are currently in a position to benefit from expanded opportunities for exporting manufactures. Twelve of these accounted for 85 per cent of the trade.[4] The problem stands out clearly if one asks the following question: Since among themselves the tropical countries now import over $14 billion of manufactures, why do they have to wait for preferences for their exports in O.E.C.D. markets? Why do they not just accord preferences to each other in their own markets, in line with the already agreed principle that discrimination against developed countries is acceptable? The answer is because this would benefit the leading twelve at the expense of the remaining seventy, who might now have to pay higher prices to these twelve than they would have had to pay to O.E.C.D. countries. The problem differs only in scale when one shifts from global tropical preferences to more limited regional preferences, customs unions or free trade areas. In each region one or two countries stand out as the ones most likely to benefit at the expense of their regional partners, who are therefore not anxious to rush in without some clearer indication of what the balance sheet of profits and losses is likely to be.[5]

But there is another type of argument for increased trade between developing countries that does not rest on comparative advantage and a combination of protection in advanced countries and demand expansion in developing countries. It embraces variables not normally included in a narrowly economic analysis.

Orthodox arguments for protection are based on the principle that to protect one industry one has to *pull* resources *into* this type of activity. If there is full employment, so that no spare resources are available for this absorption, this implies that resources must be *pulled out of* some other type of activity. It would be nonsense to wish to protect *all* industries. Protection, according to this argument, always favors one type of production at the expense of some other type. Conventional arguments for protection based on increasing returns or external economies imply pulling resources out of agriculture or services into manufacturing industry.

The new argument that we are now considering requires some protection (though not autarky), at least in principle, for nearly *all* activities. By opening up a society indiscriminately and too widely, incentives and opportunities for the development of indigenous processes and products, appropriate for the low-income groups in developing countries, are reduced. The educational, psychological, and institutional arguments against a move toward world free trade, for capital flows and general openness, point to the need to protect *all* activities from the eroding influences of the advanced world economy. More important, they point to the need for constructive, indigenous efforts, which may be hampered by an *excessively* outward-looking strategy and by emulation of the style of the rich.

Something like this also underlies the distinction between self-reliance and dependence, between autonomy and domination. Countries and groups of countries that generate their own technological capability and their own social institutions and organizations (not only in technology and industry but also in land tenure and rural institutions) will be able to mobilize their efforts more effectively than those that look at how these things are ordered in the metropolis.

There are alternative styles of development, and one type of society may prefer to develop by adapting technologies and products from abroad, while another will find its identity by raising a curtain around its frontiers or around the frontiers of a group of like-minded countries with similar factor availabilities and similar income levels. A judicious selection of features of an outward- and inward-looking strategy is likely to give the best results (drawing on foreign research and developing indigenous research or drawing on and adapting foreign technology and products, for example). The lessons of industrializing Germany, France, Japan, and Soviet Russia, which used and adapted the foreign ways of blending new institutions with old traditions, are not directly applicable because international income gaps were narrower then and the dimensions of the demographic problem, which determine the scale of the need for jobs, were quite different. Yet, as the Lewis quotation shows, even these countries did not look at the established markets of England but at new opportunities and the growing markets of the future. The main point is that there may be a choice of styles of development that can be understood only if institutional and educational variables are included in the model and if a narrowly defined static economic model is transcended.

Some authors prefer to put the contrast more starkly and simply in terms of planning versus laissez-faire. According to them, it is the need for stronger, more effective, centralized planning according to social priorities and the search for independence from the vagaries of the world market that distinguishes the advocates of different trade policies.[6] Others, while in sympathy with the planning approach, see the differences in the areas of learning, education, and institutions. A third group sees them in the political power structure. Planning and controls in an inegalitarian society reinforce inequalities and encourage corruption; the use of prices in an egalitarian society will contribute to the eradication of poverty and increasing equality.

THE TRANSNATIONAL CORPORATION: ITS POTENTIAL ROLE IN INDUSTRIALIZATION

The role of the transnational corporation in industrialization is of growing importance. Policies must be evolved that enable governments, willing to admit the corporation, to harness its potential for the benefit of the development effort. It has been argued above that the basic objective of development (that is, meeting the needs of the hundreds of millions of poor) provides one rallying point around which many development issues can be grouped. The transnational corporation is not a goal but an instrument of achieving certain goals. It, too, provides a focus for a number of different issues.

1. *Regional integration.* Two distinct sets of problems arise here. One is an anxiety shared by many countries. When several developing countries form a customs union, a free trade area, or a closer region of cooperation, new profit opportunities arise for the already-operating and newly entering foreign companies. Policies have to be devised to ensure a fair sharing of these profits between the union and the foreign companies.

A second set of problems concerns the sharing of the gains from integration between different members of the union. The creation of a new form of international company, the shares of which are held by the member countries of the union, might be one way of solving this problem, though so far it has not been successful. The proposal would be for the company to combine low-cost and efficient location and operation with sharing of the gains between member countries.

Alternatively, there can be agreement on other forms of compensation, such as agreeing to pay higher prices for the exports of the less industrialized member countries, or to permit their citizens to migrate within the region or to locate universities and research institutes in the less developed partner countries.

2. *Environment.* In the new international division of labor that would be guided by differential pollution costs in different countries, the location of certain "dirty" processes in developing countries could be one of the functions of the transnational corporation. This function could be carried out either by locating "dirty" processes within the firm's vertically integrated system of operations in a developing country, where the social costs of pollution would be lower and the benefits from industrialization higher, or by transferring the whole operation to such a country. The argument would be analogous to that of locating unskilled- or semi-skilled-labor-intensive processes using unskilled and semiskilled workers in developing countries. The comparative advantage consists in one case in an unpolluted environment, in the other in inexpensive labor. One important point to be investigated here is whether the transnational corporation could be used as a pressure group to ensure access for the products to the markets of the developed countries.

3. *Technology.* In terms of technology, the objective would be to devote more research and development expenditure to the invention and dissemination of appropriate technologies and products either in the developed or in the developing countries. The potential, but as yet unrealized, contribution of the transnational corporation to transferring and adapting existing technology and to inventing new and appropriate technology may be substantial. It would raise the problem of the ability of the developing countries to absorb existing or new technologies and of the contribution that the transnational corporation could make, preferably through joint ventures, to training people, encouraging research, and fostering attitudes favorable to such absorption.

4. *Bargaining.* Since the transnational corporation has become one of the main vehicles for transferring technology from developed to developing countries, an important aspect of policy is the terms on which the technology is transferred. In settling the bargain and in drawing up the contract, a large number of items may be up for negotiation. Some may involve incentives, such as protecting the market for the product or improving the quality of input (public utilities, a disciplined labor force); others may lay down conditions for sharing the benefits with the host country, such as tax provisions, use of local materials, local participation in management, training workers, creating jobs, raising exports, and so on; others will relate to such policies as conditions for repatriation of capital and profits, raising local capital, and so forth.

Hitherto, multilateral technical assistance in negotiations of this type and in training negotiators has been given on a very small scale. International organizations could render vital technical assistance in strengthening the bargaining power of LDCs in negotiating such contracts and could contribute to an informed dialogue between managers of companies and public officials through training courses, in an area at present obscured by emotional and ideological fumes. What is needed is both direct technical assistance in drawing up contracts, possibly with the aid of model contracts, and indirect aid through training and the provision of information.

5. *Institutions.* Another important area of policy is the imaginative exploration of new legal and business institutions that combine the considerable merits of the transnational corporation with the maximum beneficial impact on development. This area comprises joint ventures— that is, joint both between private and public capital and between domestic and foreign capital. Such ventures would give developing countries access to information and a role in decision making; they would also include provisions for divestment and gradual transfer of ownership and management from foreigners to the host country. Thus, countries wishing to curb the power of large groups in their manufacturing sector might find investment reduced. This might make it advisable to institute a "joint sector" in which public capital is combined with private national management with or without an equity stake, or in which public capital is combined with private international capital. Another possibility would be a management contract with a national or international investor.

Thought and action in this area have suffered from poverty of the institutional imagination, which has lagged behind the scientific and technological imagination. Discussions have turned partly on the ideological dispute between private and public enterprise. Yet, the real issues have little to do with this type of ideology. Mixed companies can be devised that simultaneously harness private energy and initiative, yet are accountable to the public and carry out a social mandate. Equally arid has been the dispute over the virtues and vices of private foreign investment. Here again, the task should be to identify the positive contributions of foreign firms and the social costs, to see how the former can be maximized or the latter minimized, and to provide for gradual, agreed transfer to national or regional ownership and management. There is a need for a legal and institutional framework in which the social objectives that are not part of the firm's objectives can be achieved, while giving the firm an opportunity to contribute efficient management and technology.

COSTS AND BENEFITS OF ALTERNATIVE POLICIES OF INDUSTRIALIZATION

Since the last World War, many developing countries have attempted to promote their manufactures by a large number of direct interventions, such as physical controls, licenses, and so on. These were accompanied by a host of other incentives and deterrents, such as multiple exchange rates, import entitlements, export bonus vouchers, and subsidies. In some cases, there have been periodic reversions to more simplified and uniform policies, often under pressure from the World Bank and the International Monetary Fund, and the government of the United States. The theoretical pros and cons of both approaches are by now well known. At the same time, quantitative estimates of their practical significance are scarce, unsystematic, and usually out of date.

It would be useful to compare high levels of intervention and the incidence of decline in efficiency, not only in a narrowly allocative sense, but also through blunting of incentives and divergence between social and private productivity; between the pursuit of static comparative advantage and the mobilization and generation of new resources; between the costs of and returns to a sizeable bureaucratic control of industry; and between unified and multiple exchange rates. Such comparisons might be made in the light of certain social and economic objectives over time.

The debate is sometimes confused by an identification of the interventionist approach with protectionism and of the "market" approach with free trade. These distinctions, in turn, are occasionally confused with that between "inward-looking" and "outward-looking" policies. The issue here is *not* the well-rehearsed dispute between protectionists and free traders, nor the less understood dispute between those who advocate looking inward and those who advocate looking outward. The issue is *instruments*, and comparing the effects of a battery of direct controls and intervention with operation through prices and the market. Export-orientation and looking outward have been and can be pursued through intervention and directives, just as import substitution and looking inward have been pursued. An objective, quantitative appraisal would contribute to taking some of the ideological wind out of the sails of the better-known disputes between "freedom and planning" and similar choices presented to developing countries.

TECHNOLOGY AND ENTREPRENEURSHIP

Technologies both determine and are determined by the objectives of development strategy: growth, distribution, savings, employment. Capital-intensive, labor-saving methods will generate large profits and high salaries for a small labor aristocracy. Unless ownership of capital assets is widely shared or is public, these incomes will accrue to a small group of owners of physical assets and people with the required skills and access to education. Their consumption—often influenced by advertising, open communications, and foreign imitation—will reinforce the demand for capital-intensive, foreign-exchange-using luxury goods, the production of which will reinforce unequal distribution of income. It is often maintained, though not enough hard evidence has been produced as yet, that a more equal income distribution would give rise to a consumption pattern that is more capital-saving and labor-using. More capital-saving, labor-intensive techniques may distribute a larger *share* of income to the unskilled and semi-skilled and are likely to lead to a different consumption pattern. But the causal nexus in either direction is not yet established with any certainty.

These connections between choice of industrial technology, both in core processes and in ancillary activities, choice of industrial products, income distribution, wealth distribution, access to education and training, and consumption patterns are vital for policy decisions.

Inward-looking policies of import substitution have been blamed for distorting the price and incentive system; these distortions have been said to cause growing inequalities. At the same time, it has been argued that reliance on the price mechanism and outward-looking, freer trade policies also increase inequalities, though these have a different cause and take on a different form. Is it true that both inward-looking and outward-looking industrialization and trade policies increase inequalities? Are there forces inherent in rapid industrial growth that make for greater inequality? If so, institutional, structural, and technological changes are required to distribute the fruits of growth more evenly.

It is in the nature of modern technology that it reduces the scarcity value and hence the rewards of unskilled labor and traditional know-how, while modern medical science, by reducing mortality rates, increases the supply of unskilled labor. An important question arises here about strategies that proceed on "both legs" by simultaneously promoting the modern, capital-intensive, high-technology sector, and the nonorganized, self-employed, "informal" labor-intensive sector. Can rapid, modern industrialization proceed in a manner that will not destroy, but encourage, the nonorganized, low-income, low-productivity sector? Can the surplus from modern industry be used to create jobs, to raise productivity, and to generate incomes in that part of the economy that has not yet been absorbed in it?

Income distribution and employment are only two aspects of an entire cluster of social objectives. Different forms of industrial organization are accompanied by different degrees of workers' participation and different power structures.

The test of a successful self-reliant strategy of industrialization is the extent to which it reduces the gap between the high incomes in the high-productivity, high-technology sector and the low incomes in the low-productivity, low-technology sector, by raising the performance of the latter, without impeding progress in the former.

NOTES

1. On the other hand, the turmoil and disruption caused by rural modernization, with better roads, easier transport, better primary schools, the introduction of radios, cinemas, and other media of communication bring about more migration to the cities than if the villages had continued in their traditional ways. Nevertheless, sufficiently attractive rural opportunities, combined with limited opportunities in the towns, is bound to reduce the flow of migrants.

2. Paul Streeten, "Policies Towards Multinationals," *World Development*, Vol. 3, No. 6, June 1975.

3. It might be thought that having similar factor supplies and demand patterns there would be less scope for trade. Even without calling on Stefan Burenstam Linder's trade theory, according to which most trade takes place between countries with similar income levels, conventional trade theory would lead us to expect scope for trade where countries start off, under protection, with similar production and demand patterns but, as trade is opened, become complementary. Trade within the European Economic Community has confirmed that unions between similar but potentially complementary patterns are most promising.

4. The leading exporters of manufactures in 1965 were as follows: India, 799; Singapore, 295; Pakistan, 190; Mexico, 170; Brazil, 124; U.A.R., 123; Rhodesia, 116; Philippines, 66; Malaya, 64; Colombia, 34; El Salvador, 32; Trinidad, 28. Kenya is also a substantial exporter if her trade with Uganda and Tanzania is counted as foreign trade.

5. W. Arthur Lewis, *Aspects of Tropical Trade*, Wicksell Lectures, Stockholm, 1969, pp. 42–43.

6. Ignacy Sachs, *Trade Strategies for Development*, ed. Paul Streeten (Macmillan, 1973), Ch. 3.

20

A Note on Social Cost-Benefit Analysis and Class Conflict in LDCs

Frances Stewart

Social cost-benefit analysis is a technique of project evaluation designed to ensure that projects are selected in accordance with their *social* or *national* profitability. The two terms appear to be used interchangeably by most analysts. As UNIDO [21] puts it, "the object of social choice is to maximize social gains" (p. 27), and this will be achieved by selecting projects according to their *national economic profitability*. The UNIDO Guidelines are intended to describe the rules one has to apply to arrive at national economic profitability. Similarly, the Little–Mirrlees Manual [12] is concerned to "produce a practical method of analysis which could be systematically applied and which would, we believe, measure social benefit better than a profitability analysis" (p. 37).

In developed countries techniques of social cost-benefit analysis (SCB) were originally introduced, and have since been mainly used, for evaluation of projects in the public sector, in which the output is largely unmarketed, and for which therefore some method of choice, other than the market, is essential. In contrast, the techniques as developed for LDCs[1] are mainly concerned with *marketed* inputs and outputs.[2] Here the techniques are not primarily concerned to measure the normally unmeasured (though some attempt is also made to allow for various externalities), but to correct the measures provided by the market so that they coincide with social and not simply private valuation. Shadow prices[3] are to be used, which measure the social costs and benefits associated with different projects, and then social welfare may be maximized by maximizing the net present value of the stream of benefits, net of costs.

Although it is possible—as shown by the vast amount of literature on these questions—to disagree about the precise methodology of SCB (for example whether it is better to use world prices and a shadow wage rate or domestic prices and a shadow exchange rate; how one should take externalities or risk into account), it might seem difficult to object to the *intention* of SCB and, taken *very* broadly, its methodology. As Layard [8] puts it:

> The basic notion is very simple. If we have to decide whether to do A or not, the rule is: Do A if the benefits exceed those of the next best alternative course of action, and not otherwise. If we apply this rule to all possible

Reprinted with permission from *World Development*, Vol. 3, No. 1, Francis Stewart, "A Note on Social Cost-Benefit Analysis and Class Conflict in LDCs," 1975, Pergamon Press, Ltd.

choices we shall generate *the largest possible benefits*, given the constraints within which we live. *And no-one could complain at that.*[4]

It would seem *logically* perverse to object to maximization of benefits, or maximization of social welfare, as the aim of social choice. It also appears obvious that, in many developing countries, market prices do not correctly represent social evaluation of the resources used. For example, wages in the modern sector often exceed the opportunity cost of labour. Heavy and uneven protection means that domestic prices overstate the foreign exchange costs of resources used. Unsatisfactory income distribution makes market demand a poor guide to social gains. One could go on. The simple point, which is the basis of the need for SCB, is that it is difficult to claim that market prices produce the correct results.

All this seems unexceptionable: as Layard says, "no-one could complain at that." But the argument has skated over a major problem and raised a central puzzle. The puzzle is why, for marketed inputs and output, market prices, if incorrect, should not be altered, rather than using incorrect prices and relying on SCB to bring about the correct results. After all, a change in market prices affects all projects; SCB normally only affects a minority of cases. The problem arises in the definition and derivation of *social* welfare, *social* objectives, and *social* costs (all concepts which are logically related). Or, put in Layard's terms, what do we mean by "the largest possible benefits"? Light is shed on the puzzle from further analysis of the problem: we shall therefore discuss this first and return to the puzzle at the end.

The benefits of a project, that is its contribution to social welfare, can only be assessed once one knows what social objectives are and what weight is to be attributed to them. Suppose one is comparing two projects, both of which involve spending the same amount of foreign exchange, and which

Table 1

Consequences	Project A	Project B
Output	+10,000 shoes p.a.	+100,000 bushels of wheat p.a.
Employment:		
urban	+100	—
rural	—	No additional employees. Extra utilization of employed and self-employed
Incomes:		
urban middle class	+500 Rs	+50 Rs
urban working class	+1,000 Rs	—
rural landlords	—	+1,000 Rs
rural peasants	—	+500 Rs
Savings:		
urban	+100 Rs	—
rural	—	+500 Rs

Note. Figures are (obviously) fictional.

have the following consequences (as illustrated in Table 1). It is at once clear that the figures, as they stand, comparing the projects are incommensurable. Market prices would give one set of values and one solution. SCB experts might argue that this should be rejected as giving insufficient weight to, e.g., urban employment, or savings. SCB analysis would therefore give its own weighting, as shown in shadow prices. These prices are in part derived from (relatively) value-free facts. But most of the shadow prices of SCB depend on values as well as facts. Thus it may be a known fact that employment of an additional urban worker will, indirectly, reduce agricultural output by a known (in physical quantities) amount, but valuation of these physical quantities, in terms commensurable with other items in the calculation, or of the effects on consumption and savings of an extra urban employee, all depend on values as well as facts.

It is here that the key question arises. In any society there are individuals, groups and classes with different interests, and objectives.

Differences in objectives and their weighting, here described as values, arise from differences in tastes, and differences in interests. Differences in tastes (which form the basis of much of the analysis of individual and social preference in welfare economics) suggest an individualistic analysis, in which each individual is regarded as having a set of preferences, and the task of the social welfare function is to produce a set of orderings consistent with the individual orderings.[5] In contrast, differences in interests suggest a class analysis; individuals' differing interests arise in large part from their membership of a class—i.e., from their relationship to the modes of production, because, e.g., they are peasants, or because they are industrial workers—not because of their unique characteristics as individuals. Not all relevant classifications are strictly economic. For example, generations may, for some purposes, form a common interest group, so may bachelors, or large families. A class, or interest group, may be defined as having common values. The preference ordering of any individual is then an amalgam of his individual tastes and his preferences as determined by his interests, i.e., as deriving from membership of one or more interest groups. Since individual tastes are themselves largely determined by environment, and indeed by the class to which individuals belong, the distinction between tastes (individually determined) and interests (class determined) can be overemphasized.

To each set of values, there corresponds a set of shadow prices—i.e., those prices which would contribute most to the objectives. If used for project evaluation, a different set of projects would be chosen according to whose values, and hence which shadow prices, were being used. The choice between projects A and B below illustrates the point. The weighting given to the different consequences of two projects, and consequently which project gives maximum benefits, depends on whose values one is taking, as illustrated in Table 2.

The absolute value of the figures in the table is arbitrary and unimportant. But the sharp difference in ordering is not. It shows that to select projects in such a way that net benefits are maximized is meaningless as a criterion of selection, until one has defined whose benefits one is talking about. Conflicts which arise depend on the extent to which different

Table 2

Weighting given: by to	Urban			Rural	
	Middle class	Working class employed	Working class unemployed	Landlord	Peasants
Employment:					
urban	10	10	70	—	10
rural	—	5	5	—	10
Incomes:					
urban middle class	65	—	—	—	—
urban working class	5	85	20	—	10
rural landlord	—	—	—	70	—
rural peasants	—	—	5	—	60
Savings:					
urban	20	—	—	—	—
rural	—	—	—	30	10

Weighting chosen to add up to 100.

Value of project according to:	A	B
Urban middle class	40,500	3,250
Urban working class:		
employed	86,000	Zero
unemployed	27,000	2,500
Rural landlords	Zero	85,000
Rural peasants	11,000	35,000

* Assuming weighting is calculated so that weights may be applied by straight multiplication of values given in Table 1.

interests are differently affected by the projects being compared, and the extent to which the weighting of different classes does in fact differ. In the above example, though the figures differ, the ordering of all the urban classes is the same, and so is that of the rural classes. But it would be easy to devise examples in which the ordering of, e.g., the employed urban and the unemployed urban differed. Some overlap of interests has been allowed for in attributing the weights. For example, it is assumed that the urban middle classes have some interest in maintaining urban employment and working class incomes (so as to reduce threats of various kinds from the unemployed upon their security and conscience), and that the urban unemployed have some interest in maintaining rural (peasant) incomes and employment, because this represents an alternative opportunity for them, and because they have family interests in the rural areas. Obviously, the weighting differs from society to society and depends on the links between different parts of the productive structure, which is a product of the history of the political economy.

The table has chosen one class structure to illustrate potential conflicts. Other class structures are possible. So are other dimensions of conflict. For example, different generations (both among those alive, and also among those not yet born) have different interests and objectives. Race, religion, tribe and caste provide other possible sources of conflict. Whatever dimension is chosen it is clear that weighting attributed to different objectives depends on the characteristics of those making the valuation. There is no objective function or social welfare function independent of a *prior* weighting decision: this prior decision, which since it is prior cannot emerge from the social welfare function itself, is that of how to weight the weightings among conflicting classes, groups or individuals in society.

Methods of SCB do, of course, recognize the need to elucidate social values. The UNIDO Guidelines spend some time in describing the equiwelfare curves that enable one to arrive at the (socially) correct weighting of different objectives.[6] But this attempt misses the point since there is no single set of curves, but a number of sets according to whose valuation is being used, as illustrated in the diagram below. The problem is really not one of information at all, though lack of information may misleadingly make it appear so.

Suppose *PP* is the production possibility curve. For the urban population the best position would be U: for the rural population it is R. How can we say that either position maximizes *social* welfare, or even that some intermediate position maximizes social welfare, since which intermediate position one chooses depends on how one weights the objectives of the rural as against the urban sector; and such weighting is a question of values.

There is a connection between this problem and the debate, starting with the Kaldor-Hicks criterion [7, 6], as to what constitutes an increase in economic welfare: if one could unambiguously define an increase in economic welfare, this definition would provide a basis for SCB. Indeed the Kaldor-Hicks criterion provides the explicit basis for exercises in SCB

Diagram 1

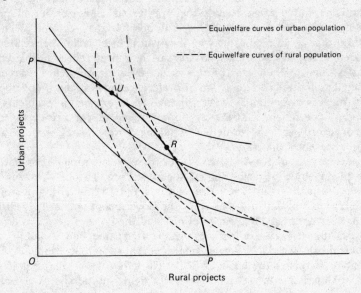

Equiwelfare curves of urban population

———— Equiwelfare curves of rural population

which do not use distributional weights—see Harberger [4]. However, none of those contributing to the debate succeeded in this since the criteria depend on the assumption that the question of distribution of costs and benefits has been dealt with satisfactorily, *independently* of the criteria,[7] and it is precisely this question of distribution that lies at the heart of the problem of definition of social welfare.

Subsequent attempts to replace the rather crude (and sometimes inconsistent[8]) bribery/compensation criteria with a social welfare function,[9] that in theory ordered all social states (like the UNIDO equiwelfare curves) failed to provide a solution to the question. They failed in two respects: first, purely logically Arrow showed that it was impossible, on quite unrestrictive assumptions, always to produce a *consistent* ordering. Moreover, and of greater relevance for our purpose, advocates of social welfare functions never clarified the key question with which we are concerned, namely, *who* should determine society's preferences, which as we have seen is crucial to the outcome.

However SCB is only meaningful if social values are established. Hence despite the manifold and well-established difficulties, advocates of SCB require a method of establishing values. Both LM and UNIDO solve the problem by looking to the Government to establish the values. They do so in two ways: by asking them directly, and by performing a sort of revealed preference exercise on the Government's choices, deducing the values it places on different objectives by its decisions on projects differently affecting the different objectives.[10]

There is an information problem about ascertaining the Government's values, especially since Governments are not monolithic, not consistent, and circumstances change. The revealed preference approach poses particular problems because behaviour alone does not reveal the assumptions about constraints, and the actions of others, that were being made, when the observed decisions were made.[11] For example, Governments may act in one particular way, not because that is their preferred course of action, considering their own action in isolation, but because they assume (rightly or wrongly) that by acting in this way they will induce certain behaviour in others. Hence, their action does not reveal their preferences as between possibilities open to them, as the theory of revealed preference assumes, but rather it constitutes an amalgam of preferences and assumptions about the consequences of action. However, though these are major problems in ascertaining Government values, they are not of central concern here. Here we are concerned with the principle of taking Government decisions and values to represent social values.

We have argued above that there is no correct weighting of conflicting values, and no objective definition of social welfare. To use Government values may be justified in two ways: one is simply by definition, defining social welfare and social values as what the Government wants. This either means that Governments, like Kings of old, and the Pope of new, can do no wrong, or that social welfare loses its prescriptive value. Few would accept that Governments can do no wrong (more, perhaps, that Governments can do no right): if this is the basis of SCB then it is a weak one. But if we accept that Governments are not necessarily right, and persist in claiming that social welfare is by definition that which Governments want to maximize, it is perfectly possible to question social welfare maximization as an aim. To return to Layard's quotation: if maximization of benefits means maximization of benefits as defined with reference to Government objectives, then we may certainly complain at that.

Much of the above may be agreed on. But it may be argued that decisions have to be made: while it is true that it is impossible to draw up a "correct" social welfare function, Governments represent the whole community and are in the best position to fulfil an impossible task—to draw up or elucidate a sort of general will, from the mass of conflicting interests. This is the second type of justification for using Government values, and depends on a theory of Governments as being above the fray, impartial, if sometimes misguided, brokers between the different interests in society. Governments are assumed to resemble Plato's Guardians (the UNIDO Guidelines actually refer to them as "guardians of public policy"), whose only concern is the good of all.[12] Here the earlier distinction between differences in values arising from differences in tastes, and differences arising from differences in interests becomes important. While it may be reasonable to expect Governments to decide how differences in tastes, based on individual differences, may best be resolved, it is not reasonable when it comes to conflicts in interests. Suppose, for example, some people would like their policemen to be dressed in blue, others in red, and yet others black, and all agree that a *single* colour is to be preferred. Choice of colour, it might be argued, can be left to the Government, since a decision must be made. But when we come to differences in interests this is not so, because the Government itself is part of the class and interest struggle. Representing a single interest (or an alliance of interests), their weighting of social objectives does not represent some sort of attempt at synthesis of the national interest, but rather primarily the interests on which they depend for their power.[13]

There are two distinct, but related questions; both need different treatment in conflict or class societies, and in no-conflict homogeneous societies. The first question is the conceptual one: that measurement of benefits (or social welfare) generated by a project cannot be separated from the distributional consequences, and that there is no single correct measure; the measure depends on the point of view adopted. The second question is pragmatic: accepting that we cannot establish a uniquely correct "social" view, should we turn to the Government, as *deus ex machina*, to do the impossible and provide one? While this would be a reasonable line to take if Governments were disinterested arbiters, in a class and conflict society, where Governments are part of the system, taking Government values to represent "social" values means taking the views of the particular class constellation represented by the Government. In homogeneous societies both problems tend to disappear: the conceptual question, which essentially arises out of the problem of how to weight the interests and views of different parts of society, disappears where there is no conflict. The general will can then be identified as the will of all. Similarly in such societies, Governments can be argued to be the best interpreters of social values. This is to say no more than that it is easy to identify what to do in homogeneous societies. But in conflict societies, the problem becomes acute: conflicts mean that there is a problem in identifying social values, while in such societies Governments generally are actively engaged in the conflict. Social cost-benefit analysis, in so far as it implies that social welfare maximization or national welfare maximization is meaningful (and also possible) in conflict societies, is highly misleading, and sometimes dangerously so, since it dresses up one set of activities—those of taking the objectives of one section of society, normally those represented by the Government, and showing how they may be more efficiently fulfilled—as another, that of maximizing the benefits to society. The former being a meaningful (and possible), but for many an undesirable, objective: the latter being meaningless and therefore impossible, though desirable.[14]

One way of defending SCB from these charges is to argue that SCB merely provides the technology or methodology of rational decision making. There is no need to take Government values. One can, if one likes, take any values one likes—one's own, those of the political opposition, etc. SCB does not claim to provide a unique or objective assessment of the net benefits of projects, but simply a method of assessment which will give different results according to the assessor. While this is, in one sense true, it is a specious argument for three reasons. In the first place, the manuals are explicitly addressed to Governments: "The Government requires a methodology for comparing and evaluating alternative projects . . . This volume is concerned with the formulation of such a methodology."[15] Secondly, the language adopted suggests, if it does not imply, the objectivity of the analysis, as if there were a well-defined social welfare function, which correctly represented *the* interests of the society. Thus the Guidelines argue[16] that "Projects should therefore be formulated and evaluated in such a way as to single out for implementation those that contribute most to *the ultimate objectives of the country*." (My emphasis.) The Guidelines show how to arrive at "the optimal welfare point" (p. 124). In the third place, the way in which a set of values is translated into shadow prices depends on the power of the decision maker.[17] If the volumes were really intended to provide a general decision-making framework for any individual or class, then this area would require serious attention. In fact, it is ignored, and the only power limitations discussed are those of the Government.

Regarding SCB as a method of translating Government objectives into reality brings us back to the puzzle mentioned earlier: if that is the correct view of SCB, why does the Government not use more direct means, particularly the price and tax system, to achieve its objectives. One reason why SCB is used is that for some things it is a more efficient instrument than other possibilities. The price and tax system may not be able to discriminate as finely (in time or by commodity) as project selection. For externalities, the price system tends to be a clumsy instrument, which is why SCB was initially devised in developed countries to deal with those cases where prices do not operate at all, or efficiently. But SCB for developing countries is intended to deal with marketed outputs, where, often, the price system does present an efficient alternative: indeed since it is likely that SCB will only deal with a minority of projects, the price system, which extends to all projects, would seem to be a more efficient instrument. The SCB analysts are aware of this puzzle and pose and answer it in the following terms:

> One could, of course, retort by asking why if the guardians of public policy do not like the income distribution (e.g., if they disapprove of the existing inequality), they do not reform it directly. Once the distribution is reformed, the project evaluator can simply treat the money prices offered as guides to welfare without worrying about income distribution. This retort, while not uncommon, is somewhat hollow, since there are constraints—political, economic and social—that prevent such reforms of income distribution, and given these limitations the exercise of project evaluation cannot be based on the notion that all appropriate income redistributions have already been carried out. (UNIDO, *Guidelines*, pp. 22–23.)

Little–Mirrlees pose, and answer, a similar question in similar vein:

> In the previous Chapter we raised the question whether a Government seriously wants to raise the rate of investment at the expense of current consumption, if it does not raise taxation when it can, and if it does not take other steps to see that public savings, including those of public enterprises are as high as reasonably possible. Of course governments want to stay in power. There is a limit to the extent to which they will try to squeeze more savings from the public even if it is believed on ethical grounds that a greater provision should be made for investment and growth, and thus for consumption in the future. This raises a very important point. The most important and normal way for a government to hold consumption in check and so increase savings is taxation; and taxation is notoriously unpopular. ([12], p. 42.)

Both answer the question in terms of *constraints* on Government action which prevent it going as far as it would like by the use of normal instruments. But why, then, should these constraints be removed by the introduction of SCB? If a Government's political supporters prevent it from raising taxation as much as it might like, this is surely because those who pay the taxes dislike, and are strong enough to resist, the cut in real income implied, not because they have taken a particular dislike to the form (taxation) which the cut takes. In the first instance, ignorance may prevent any public outcry against the use of SCB to achieve objectives which have been successfully thwarted as far as other instruments are concerned. But if the use of SCB is equally effective in achieving the objective, then it is likely to be subject to the same constraints as other instruments. Why should the *instrument* used influence the possibilities?

If the net effects are identical it seems unlikely, in the long run when the veil of ignorance has been eliminated, that constraints will be removed simply by the introduction of new tools. The unpopularity of taxation is not irrational but a consequence of its effects and will be shared by any other instrument, including SCB, which has the same effects. The possibilities of using SCB to achieve objectives such as income redistribution, where other tools are ruled out because they are unpopular, thus must rest on some peculiarities of SCB, as compared with other tools.

First, SCB has, to date, applied, and is likely to apply, to only a small minority of cases. Hence the over-all effect on interests is likely to be marginal as compared with more direct methods. Its use depends on its marginality, or ineffectiveness. As soon as it becomes more than a marginal instrument, it will be subject to the same constraints as other instruments.

Secondly, SCB is optional and not mandatory. With most systems of taxation, once a system (and rates) have been established, its enforcement is subject to the country's legal system. There has never been the same sort of legal enforcement of SCB. Governments may go against the recommendations of SCB with legal impunity. This means that it is easier to establish it as a system, than to change the tax system, because it is always possible, when the time comes, to ignore the recommendations. The third London Airport provides an example.

Thirdly, SCB, as an instrument, does not always have identical effects with the alternative instruments. Partly, this is because it only applies to a small number of cases, so the impact is much smaller—i.e., the same point as that above. For example, it may be politically attractive to put a high weight on redistribution of income in SCB, thus getting credit for pursuing the objective, while not actually meeting any costs to speak of, because of the small number of cases. But there are also cases where SCB involves a *different* distribution of costs and benefits from the alternative instruments. The premium put on savings is a good example. Raising savings by extra taxation involves placing the burden of reduced current consumption on current taxpayers, generally the employed and the richer members of society. Using SCB to achieve extra savings means that those whose consumption is cut are those who would be employed if no premium were put on savings, but are not if a premium is placed on savings and capital-intensive projects therefore selected. The burden is thus borne by the unemployed. The different class burden explains why a Government may be subject to constraints in the use of one instrument—taxation—but not another—SCB.

SCB is thus used as an instrument, rather than other instruments, because Governments do not represent the "social" interest, but their own class interests, and yet wish to appear to represent the "wider" social interests. SCB is used either because Governments do not wish the impact to be effective (reasons one and two above), or because they want a different class distribution of the costs and benefits than would be achieved by the use of more direct instruments (reason three). The answer to the puzzle thus supports the general analysis of this paper. SCB does not show Governments stepping outside their normal activities to represent the interests of all; rather, it is another instrument in the class struggle.

NOTES

1. In UNIDO[21] and Little and Mirrlees.[12]
2. Little–Mirrlees, p. 31.
3. Sometimes described (e.g., by Little–Mirrlees) as social accounting prices.
4. Layard,[8] p. 9. My emphasis.

5. See Arrow[1] and Sen.[17]
6. Though this does seem a somewhat clumsy device, since once one had enough knowledge about social objectives to draw up the curves one would not need the curves to tell one what to do.
7. Little's[11] criteria recognize the central importance of distribution by combining the Scitovsky criteria with the additional requirement that the distributional implications must be acceptable. But again this leaves completely unanswered our central question: who is to determine what is acceptable?
8. See Scitovsky[16] and Samuelson.[15]
9. See Bergson.[3]
10. A revealed preference exercise on other non-SCB decisions has also been suggested,[22] though this is a bit odd if it is assumed that SCB allows the Government to attain objectives, which it cannot obtain in its absence. Seton[20] uses this method to establish the weights the Government gives to income distributional objectives.
11. See Sen.[18]
12. Plato spends considerable time delineating the very stringent conditions in which the Guardians must be chosen, educated and live if they are to represent the general interest, and not sectional interests: so that "the whole State will grow up in noble order and the several classes will receive the proportion of happiness which nature assigns to them." (Book IV, p. 420.) They "may not touch or handle silver or gold." They should have no property beyond what is absolutely necessary. Even laughter was to be banned.
13. Some recent analyses show how interests dominate Government in a number of developing countries. Beckford[2] shows how the interests of the plantation companies are pursued in plantation economies by apparently "independent" Governments. Leys[9,10] (for Kenya) and Harris[5] (for India) analyze and explain Government action in terms of the interests they represent. For developed countries see Milliband.[13]
14. This does raise the interesting question of whether one can desire something which is meaningless.
15. Introduction to the Guidelines, UNIDO, p. 1.
16. Again in the Introduction.
17. This point is explored in Sen.[18]

REFERENCES

1. ARROW, K. J. (1951) *Social Choice and Individual Values*, Wiley.
2. BECKFORD, G. L. (1972) *Persistent Poverty, Underdevelopment in Plantation Economies of the Third World*, Oxford University Press.
3. BERGSON, A. (1938) "A Reformulation of Certain Aspects of Welfare Economics," *Quarterly Journal of Economics*.
4. HARBERGER, A. C. (1971) "Three Basic Postulates for Applied Economics: An Interpretative Essay," *Journal of Economic Literature*.
5. HARRIS, N. (1974) *India-China-Underdevelopment and Revolution*, Delhi.
6. HICKS, J. R. (1940) "The Valuation of Social Income," *Economica*.
7. KALDOR, N. (1938) "Welfare Propositions of Economics and Interpersonal Comparisons of Utility," *Economic Journal*.
8. LAYARD, R. G. (ed.) (1972) *Cost Benefit Analysis*, Penguin.
9. LEYS, C. (1971) "Politics in Kenya: The Development of Peasant Society," *British Journal of Political Science*.
10. LEYS, C. (1974) *Underdevelopment in Africa*, Heinemann.
11. LITTLE, I. M. D. (1957) 2nd ed. *A Critique of Welfare Economics*, O.U.P.
12. LITTLE, I. M. D., AND MIRRLEES, J. A. (1969) *Manual of Industrial Project Analysis in Developing Countries, Vol. II. Social Cost Benefit Analysis*, O.E.C.D.
13. MILLIBAND, R. (1969) *The State in a Capitalist Society*, Weidenfeld and Nicolson.
14. PLATO, *The Republic* (translation B. Jowett, 1908).
15. SAMUELSON, P. A. (1950) "Evaluation of Real National Income," *Oxford Economic Papers*.
16. SCITOVSKY, T. (1941) "A Note on Welfare Propositions in Economics," *Review of Economic Studies*.
17. SEN, A. K. (1970) *Collective Choice and Social Welfare*, Oliver & Boyd.

18. SEN, A. K. (1972) "Control Areas and Accounting Prices: An Approach to Economic Evaluation," *Economic Journal*.
19. SEN, A. K. (1973) *Behaviour and the Concept of Preference*, London School of Economics and Political Science.
20. SETON, F. (1972) *Shadow Wages in the Chilean Economy*, O.E.C.D.
21. UNIDO (1972) *Guidelines for Project Evaluation*, United Nations (by P. Dasgupta, S. A. Marglin and S. K. Sen).
22. WEISBROD, B. A. (1968) "Deriving an Implicit Set of Governmental Weights for Income Classes," Reading no. 16, in R. G. Layard (ed.) *Cost Benefit Analysis*, Penguin, 1972.

part six

Comparative Models of Development

In this part of the book, the readings present models of development
based on the historical experiences of particular countries. The term "model"
does not mean a detailing of every strategy, correct and incorrect, used by the
particular country. Rather, it is an abstraction of the most relevant patterns
from the historical experience of development in that country. Despite the
variation of development methods and strategies within and among countries,
it is possible, and indeed necessary, to abstract from the secondary attributes
of the individual cases and to concentrate on their essential common
characteristics. That the resulting "model" does not take into account every
peculiarity of the given case does not invalidate its usefulness. Its value lies in
the establishment of a framework that gives meaning to the facts and descriptions
assembled by quantitative research.

In the first two readings Irma Adelman looks at Israel, Japan, South Korea,
Singapore, and Taiwan and Celso Furtado looks at Brazil as contemporary
models of capitalist development. Adelman argues that the five countries she
studied have successfully combined accelerated economic growth with
improvements in the share of income accruing to the poor. They have done so
by stressing export-oriented growth "based on labor-and-skill-intensive exports.
That is, they have all adopted human-capital-intensive development strategies."
Vast disparities in wealth and further access to wealth have been redistributed
and broad-based, massive investment in education has been phased into the
subsequent creation of productive employment opportunities. She calls this the
"redistribute and educate now, grow later" strategy of development compared
with Brazil's strategy of "grow now, redistribute and educate later."

In his paper on the "Brazilian Model" Celso Furtado uses dependency as the
theoretical framework to analyze and evaluate the Brazilian experience. The main
feature of this experience is large-scale industrialization based on the demands
of a small minority of the population who possess an extraordinarily large
percentage of the national income. A corollary of this feature is a tendency to
exclude the mass of the population from the benefits of capital accumulation
and technical progress. Furtado argues that the structure of dependency created
by the capitalist world market is a major factor working against the success of
this contemporary model of capitalist development. In effect, Furtado argues
that the "grow-now redistribute and educate later" is not working to create an
equitable development.

It is only in the last twenty-five years that economic development has captured the attention of economists and statesmen alike. There are several reasons for this recent emphasis. First is the realization that international division of labor has not brought the benefits expected by nineteenth century economic theory. Second, the pressure for economic development exerted by the newly independent countries suggests that lack of freedom from want in underdeveloped countries may well mean lack of freedom from fear in developed countries. The third, and probably most important reason, is the emergence of socialism in the USSR and China as alternative models of development to capitalism.

In the final article, John Gurley presents an analysis of the Chinese model of development. He has two main points. First, even in conventional terms of GNP growth rate, Chinese development has been impressive. Second, and more important, the Chinese leadership is primarily concerned with creating a "new socialist man." When these two goals conflict, the first must give way. Gurley spells out in this context the meanings of such concepts as "walking on two legs" and "building on the worst." The reader should compare this Chinese version of socialist development with the general thrust of Albert Waterston's article in Part Four and Paul Streeten's article in Part Five. Gurley's discussion of the Chinese emphasis upon creating a "new socialist man" should also be reread after reading Paulo Freire's article on the "pedagogy of the oppressed" in Part Eight.

21

Growth, Income Distribution and Equity-oriented Development Strategies

Irma Adelman

I. INTRODUCTION

The paper begins with a summary of the findings in Adelman and Morris.[1] I shall then draw on these findings and on the recent historical experience of several developing countries to address the lessons, as I see them, that one might learn from the experience of those countries that have successfully combined economic growth with increases in the relative incomes of the poor. I shall next discuss both the politics and the economics of equitable growth, with emphasis on equity-oriented growth strategies and the relationship between growth and income distribution. Finally, I will give our conclusions with regard both to policies that may work and those that do not.

II. REVIEW OF ADELMAN–MORRIS FINDINGS

In an extension of the methodology of our previous work,[2] our study of growth and equity relates interactions among changes in economic and social structure to two dimensions of social equity, namely political participation and income distribution. The analysis relates to the period 1957–68 for 43 underdeveloped countries.

With respect to the distribution of income, the statistical technique is based on an analysis of variance which seeks to "explain" variations in the dependent variable. In fact, three dependent variables for the 43 countries are constructed from the basic income distribution data shown in Table 1. They are:

  (a) The income share of the lowest 60 per cent of the population;
  (b) The income share of the middle quintile of the population;
  (c) The income share of the wealthiest 5 per cent of the population.

The statistical analysis attempts to assess the relative importance of 35 independent variables in explaining inter-country differences in patterns of income distribution. The six most important variables are found to be: the rate of improvement in human resources; direct government economic

Reprinted with permission from *World Development*, Vol. 3, Nos. 2/3, Irma Adelman, "Growth, Income Distribution and Equity-oriented Development Strategies," 1975, Pergamon Press, Ltd.

Table 1 *Income Distribution Estimates* (Percentage shares by population groups)

	Country	0–40	40–60	0–60	60–80	80–100	95–100
1.	Argentina	17.30%	13.10%	30.40%	17.60%	52.00%	29.40%
2.	Bolivia	12.90	13.70	26.60	14.30	59.10	35.70
3.	Brazil	12.50	10.20	22.70	15.80	61.50	38.40
4.	Burma	23.00	13.00	36.00	15.50	48.50	28.21
5.	Ceylon	13.66	13.81	27.47	20.22	52.31	18.38
6.	Chad	23.00	12.00	35.00	22.00	43.00	23.00
7.	Chile	15.00	12.00	27.00	20.70	52.30	22.60
8.	Colombia	7.30	9.70	17.00	16.06	68.06	40.36
9.	Costa Rica	13.30	12.10	25.40	14.60	60.00	35.00
10.	Dahomey	18.00	12.00	30.00	20.00	50.00	32.00
11.	Ecuador	16.90	13.50	30.40	15.60	54.00	33.70
12.	El Salvador	12.30	11.30	23.60	15.00	61.40	33.00
13.	Gabon	8.00	7.00	15.00	14.00	71.00	47.00
14.	Greece	21.30	12.30	34.10	16.40	49.50	23.00
15.	India	20.00	16.00	36.00	22.00	42.00	20.00
16.	Iraq	8.00	8.00	16.00	16.00	68.00	34.00
17.	Israel	16.00	17.00	33.00	23.90	43.10	16.80
18.	Ivory Coast	18.00	12.00	30.00	15.00	55.00	29.00
19.	Jamaica	8.20	10.80	19.00	19.50	61.50	31.20
20.	Japan	15.30	15.80	31.10	22.90	46.00	14.80
21.	Lebanon	7.20	15.80	23.00	16.00	61.00	34.00
22.	Libya	.50	1.28	1.78	8.72	89.50	46.20
23.	Malagasy	14.00	9.00	23.00	18.00	59.00	37.00
24.	Mexico	10.50	11.25	21.75	20.21	58.04	28.52
25.	Morocco	14.50	7.70	22.20	12.40	65.40	20.60
26.	Niger	23.00	12.00	35.00	23.00	42.00	23.00
27.	Nigeria	14.00	9.00	23.00	16.10	60.90	38.38
28.	Pakistan	17.50	15.50	33.00	22.00	45.00	20.00
29.	Panama	14.30	13.80	28.10	15.20	56.70	34.50
30.	Peru	8.80	8.30	17.10	15.30	67.60	48.30
31.	Philippines	12.70	12.00	24.70	19.50	55.80	27.50
32.	Rhodesia	12.00	8.00	20.00	15.00	65.00	40.00
33.	Senegal	10.00	10.00	20.00	16.00	64.00	36.00
34.	Sierra Leone	10.10	9.10	19.20	16.70	64.10	33.80
35.	South Africa	6.11	10.16	16.27	26.37	57.36	39.38
36.	Sudan	15.00	14.30	29.30	22.60	48.10	17.10
37.	Surinam	22.26	14.74	37.00	20.60	42.40	15.10
38.	Taiwan	14.20	14.80	29.00	19.00	52.00	24.10
39.	Tanzania	19.50	9.75	29.25	9.75	61.00	42.90
40.	Trinidad & Tobago	9.42	9.10	18.52	24.48	57.00	26.60
41.	Tunisia	10.62	9.95	20.57	14.43	65.00	22.44
42.	Venezuela	13.40	16.60	30.00	22.90	47.10	23.20
43.	Zambia	15.85	11.10	26.95	15.95	57.10	37.50

Source: I. Adelman and C. Taft Morris, *Economic Growth and Social Equity in Developing Countries* (Stanford Press, 1973), p. 152.

activity; socio-economic dualism; the potential for economic development; *per capita* GNP; and the strength of the labour movement.[3]

It must be stressed that the generalizations that follow, in this section and elsewhere, depend crucially on a dynamic interpretation of the cross-section results. This assumes that in its growth path a typical under-developed country will embody the average characteristics of the group of countries which are associated with successive levels of development. These generalizations, though stated as fact, should thus properly be regarded as suggestive hypotheses, worthy of consideration by policy-makers and still in need of further study.[4]

The relationship between levels of economic development and the equity of income distribution is shown to be asymmetrically U-shaped, with more egalitarian income distributions being characteristic of both extreme economic underdevelopment and high levels of economic development. Between these extremes, however, the relationship is, for the most part, inverse: up to a point, higher rates of industrialization, faster increases in agricultural productivity, and higher rates of growth all tend to shift the income distribution in favour of the higher-income groups and against the low-income groups.

The beneficiaries of economic development as well as the processes by which the poor are penalized by economic development, vary with the level of development of the country. At the lowest level of development, as economic growth begins in a subsistence agrarian economy through the expansion of a narrow modern sector, inequality in the distribution of income typically increases greatly, the income share of the poorest 60 per cent declines significantly, as does that of the middle 20 per cent, and the income share of the top 5 per cent increases strikingly. In these countries the path toward sustained economic growth is eventually blocked unless either the country is sufficiently large or redistributive policies are sufficiently important to generate an internal market for growth.

Once countries move successfully beyond the stage of sharply dualistic growth, the middle-income receivers are the primary beneficiaries of the widening of the base for that economic growth which follows. The position of the poorest 40 per cent typically worsens both relatively and absolutely, even where a transition from sharply dualistic growth to more broadly based economic growth is accomplished. Even when relatively high levels of development have been attained and the capacity for more broadly based economic growth has been established, the poorest segments of the population typically benefit from economic growth only where widespread efforts are made to improve the human resource base.

Finally, it should be noted that, in order to reach the relatively small positively correlated portion of the equity-level-of-economic-development curve, a country must be among the upper half of those underdeveloped countries at the highest level of development. Indeed, in the absence of domestic policy action aimed specifically at redirecting the benefits of growth, a nation must attain a level of development corresponding to that which exists among the socio-economically most developed of the underdeveloped countries (Argentina, Chile, Taiwan, Israel) before the income distribution tends to become as even as it is in countries that have undergone virtually no economic development (e.g., Dahomey, Chad, Niger).

With regard to political participation, perhaps the principal lesson suggested by our results is that increases in political participation are by no means automatic consequences of socio-economic development in underdeveloped countries.[5] The early stages of social mobilization and economic modernization generate pressures for political and administrative reform and a general transformation of the political élite. For these pressures to lead to viable forms of political participation requires both the institutionalization of socio-economic interest groups and the evolution of mechanisms for sharing political and economic power among them which are sufficiently equitable to be generally accepted. Success in accommodating these demands on the political system tends to reduce social tensions, but the process of inducing the necessary political changes is fraught with social conflict and often accompanied with violence. If the resultant instability exceeds the capacity of the system to integrate conflicting claims peacefully, authoritarianism and the suppression of incipient participant institutions may postpone indefinitely the development of modern forms of participation.

III. THE POLITICS OF EQUITABLE GROWTH

The major unresolved question posed by equity-oriented development economics is: "Is equitable growth possible within existing sociopolitical structures?" A subsidiary question is: "If not, what socio-political structures are most conducive to equitable economic growth?"

Neither question can be answered unequivocally at this time, and I shall not theorize on the answers. Instead I shall limit myself to a few remarks based on empirical evidence that may be suggestive in developing answers to these questions.

1. Greater political participation, that favourite remedy of Western democracy for making equitable economic growth politically possible, does not appear to redistribute income to the poor. To the extent that it is effective at all, it tends to redistribute income from the upper- towards the middle-income groups.[6]

2. Greater government ownership of productive enterprise, that favourite remedy of the socialist world for making equitable economic growth politically possible, also does not appear to redistribute income to the poor. It reduces the income share of the upper 5 per cent dramatically, but the benefit of the redistribution redounds to the next quintile in the income scale.[7] It also tends to reduce the growth rate relative to the free enterprise growth rate, thus providing less to redistribute.

3. There appears to be an uncomfortable trade-off between freedom of action in the economic arena and the equity of the distribution of income. Such a conflict is evident in Yugoslavia, for example, where, after the adoption of a more liberal and decentralized economic policy, inequalities in the distribution of income have started reasserting themselves disconcertingly quickly. Theorizing for a moment, I would guess that this conflict is deeply rooted in human nature.

IV. THE ECONOMICS OF EQUITABLE GROWTH

A different view of human nature is held by most radical social scientists today. Economists and non-economists alike, radicals believe that the conflict between equity and growth is rooted not in human nature, but rather in the system. Observing the pervasive socio-political biases against equitable growth within and between nations, they conclude that radical political change is necessary before equitable growth can be attempted. This conclusion leads them to infer further that the economics of equitable growth is irrelevant and that it is only the politics of redistribution which matters.

Personally, I am convinced that, whatever the definition of radical political change may be and whatever the merits of the first part of the radical argument, that last inference does not follow. After all, most socialist countries, whose avowed purpose is growth with equity, disagree with the radicals on this point, in that they are clearly quite serious about economic policy for equitable growth. And it may be significant that much of the failure of Allende to combine democratic growth with massive redistribution is attributable to plain economic mismanagement, in the wake of major redistributive efforts.

The existence of a handful of successful equitable-growth countries with market economies (Israel, Japan, South Korea, Singapore, Taiwan) suggests that the first part of the radical argument is also not universally applicable. Clearly, in many developing countries the political power of conservative forces (such as traditional élites, expatriates, and international corporations) must be significantly weakened before growth with social justice can become a national goal. In others, it is just barely possible that the political and intellectual leaderships may be made to have a change in heart, once they realize that the trickle-down theory of economic development does not work effectively to improve the welfare of the poor.

The reason why the political climate is so important is that asset redistribution and the redistribution of opportunities for access to asset accumulation are a necessary first step for the initiation of equitable growth. (The latter has been an actual precondition in all successful equitable growth countries to date.) But in all successful countries that redistribution has been followed by a host of primarily growthmanship-oriented policies to maintain the value of the redistributed assets. Poor economic management or excessively slow growth rates have invariably negated the intent of redistributive efforts both by producing a drastic fall in the value of the redistributed assets (witness the host of abortive land reforms and enterprise nationalizations) and by providing unforeseen and undesirable windfall profits for the upper 20 per cent of the population.

V. EQUITY-ORIENTED DEVELOPMENT STRATEGIES

The results of the statistical analyses performed by Morris and myself suggest that equitable growth requires a major reorientation of development strategies. The most hopeful redirection to emerge from this work is towards human-resource-intensive development patterns.[8] It is significant that all five Western countries which have successfully combined accelerated growth with improvements in the share of income accruing to the poor have followed a strategy consistent with this result, in that each has stressed export-oriented growth based on labour-and-skill-intensive exports. That is, they have all adopted human-capital-intensive development strategies, in which broad-based massive investment in the improvement of the educational level of the population was phased into the subsequent creation of productive employment opportunities.

In Korea, for example, in 1964, the educational level of the population was approximately three times that of an average country at its level of *per capita* GNP;[9] at the same time, high school graduates were competing for jobs as municipal street sweepers, and the Minister of Education was fired for allowing too large an enrolment in universities to take place! Despite the disaffection and political unrest implied by the preceding facts, six years of very rapid human-resource-intensive growth (at an average rate of 10 per cent in real GNP, with a marginal capital-output ratio of 2.2 and a non-agricultural marginal labour-output ratio of 0.55) led, by 1970, to a situation in which unemployment had fallen from 7.7 per cent to 4.5 per cent,[10] real wage rates in manufacturing of unskilled and skilled labour were rising at an average annual rate of 20 per cent, and the wages of agricultural workers were rising at a rate of 12 per cent. These spectacular results were achieved only after the human resource development had taken place, and were accomplished by an economic development programme which involved two major elements: (a) the reorientation of development strategy from import-substitution-led industrialization to export-oriented development, and (b) the rationalization of the price system. The latter entailed a dramatic increase in the real cost of capital, a significant currency devaluation, and a substantial dismantling of the quantitative restrictions on trade.

In assessing the success of the Korean experience, it must be emphasized that the improvement in education preceding the growth phase of the Korean economy involved the achievement of universal primary education, as well as improvements in secondary schools and higher levels of education. In addition (and it is hard to know to what extent this may be relevant), the educational curricula were reoriented from the provision of an essentially classical education to an American-type educational system. In this process the educational pyramid was broadened substantially, while its content became more oriented towards the acquisition of basic skills.

This educational reorientation and broadening occurred also in Japan and, to a lesser extent, in Taiwan; a similar education policy typified Jewish Palestine (and hence Israel) from the beginning. Singapore, as well as Israel and Taiwan, built up much of their human capital resources through the immigration of skilled and semi-skilled labour. Given the immigration, all three nations proceeded to maintain and improve this resource, which permitted subsequent equity-oriented growth. This educational policy stands in sharp contrast to that of India, where the educational pyramid is quite narrow and the content remains largely classical.

All countries whose development process has successfully combined equity with growth have thus followed a similar dynamic sequence: a redistribution of assets (primarily but not exclusively land), followed by a massive buildup (or acquisition) of human capital, followed by an accelerated human-resource-intensive industrialization and growth strategy.

VI. GROWTH AND INCOME DISTRIBUTION

Before discussing policy implications, it may be worth-while to examine the relationship between growth and income distribution. Both cross-sectional and time series evidence suggest the following rather complicated relationship between the rate of economic growth and the change in the share of income accruing to the poorest 40 per cent of the population: [11]

1. Real rates of *per capita* economic growth below 3.5 per cent tend to be associated with declines in the share of income of the poor. At current rates of population growth, this puts the minimum required growth rate of real GNP around 5.5 per cent.

2. Higher rates of growth are a necessary *but not a sufficient* condition for substantial improvements in the share of income of the poor.

3. High growth rates tend to lead to improvements in the income of the poorest 40 per cent of the population only if accompanied by a human-resource-intensive development strategy pursued within a not sharply dualistic growth pattern. [12]

The economic responses underlying these observations (admittedly somewhat oversimplified) are:

1. Where growth is slow, the adverse equity effects of development are due primarily to deterioration of the position of the small farms in the agricultural sector and to the population impact of modern health measures on low-income families. Capital-intensive industrialization does not tend to generate sufficient employment to absorb the labour force released by higher agricultural productivity. Subsistence farmers, tenants, and other small farms cannot take full advantage of modern methods, and cannot compete with plantations or large mechanized farms. The resultant fall in real income (due both to lower product prices and higher money costs) is especially hard on the subsistence and tenant groups. In the industrial sector, modern industry tends to displace cottage and handicraft workers, while the wage gains of the employed are largely eroded by the inflationary impact of tariff-supported import-substitution industrialization.

2. Under moderately rapid capital-intensive growth, dualistic or otherwise, changes in product mix and technology within both agricultural and non-agricultural sectors, rapid expansion of the urban industrial sector, continued rapid population increases, migration to the cities, lack of social mobility, and inflation all operate to the detriment of the urban and rural poor.

As economic growth spreads, regional income inequality increases as the concentration of rapidly growing, technologically advanced enterprises in cities widens the gap between rural and urban *per capita* income. Within the urban sector, the spread of capital-intensive methods, which results from the ease with which owners of modern large-scale enterprises can obtain capital abroad, and from the preferences of entrepreneurs for advanced technologies, intensifies the accumulation of assets into the hands of a relatively small number of owners of modern enterprises. This labour-saving bias of technological advance, the rapidity of urban population growth, the migration to the cities of unemployed rural workers, and the lack of social mobility all tend to swell the numbers of the urban impoverished and decrease the income share of the poorest segments of the urban population.

In the rural sector, meanwhile, agricultural output expands, and the inelasticity of international and domestic demand for many agricultural products tends to reduce the real income of agricultural producers. Import substitution policies, which raise domestic consumers' goods prices above international levels, contribute further to decreasing real income among the poorest groups. Simultaneously, mechanization in industry continues to reduce greatly the earnings of large numbers of artisans and cottage workers; where cheap manufactures are permitted to flood domestic markets, the destruction of handicraft industries contributes further to reducing incomes and increasing unemployment among both the rural and urban poor. Finally, inflation depresses the real income of large groups of low-income workers.

An analogous process takes place at high rates of growth whenever the pattern is highly capital-intensive (and therefore dualistic).

3. When the rate of labour absorption in high productivity employment can exceed the rate of growth of the urban proletariat, wage rates and employment for both unskilled and semi-skilled workers will tend to rise faster than GNP. Wage differentials in industry will tend to narrow, as skilled and white-collar wage rates will not rise as fast. The consequent shift of the distribution of money income towards the lower 40 per cent will then tend to raise the demand for the outputs of agriculture. If, in addition, the industrialization process is export-oriented, domestic prices for light consumer goods need not rise above international prices and gains in money income need not be as thoroughly eroded. The differential between rural and urban incomes then narrows, both because of the continuing outward migration from agriculture and because the income elasticity of demand for agricultural products starts raising agricultural incomes more than price inelasticity will decrease them. In short, once the rates of increase of productive wage employment exceed additions to the labour force, the spread effects of growth can start outweighing its backwash effects and the benefits of growth can start percolating downwards.

As indicated earlier, the minimum rate of growth at which this scenario can take place is estimated empirically at 5.5 per cent. An independent semi-empirical approach leads to a similar figure. Thus, at current average labour-output ratios, labour absorption in industry proceeds at about half the rate at which industrial output rises. Since, for an average developing country, the current rate of urban population growth (natural increase plus immigration) is about 4 per cent per year, an annual rate of growth of industrial output of at least 8 per cent is required merely to absorb new increments. A growth elasticity for industrial output with respect to GNP of approximately 1.3 per cent leads to a figure of about 5 per cent as the minimum turnaround rate of GNP growth. If the process of industrialization is more labour-intensive, or if the elasticity of industrial growth with respect to output is higher, or the rate of population growth lower, the turnaround will occur at lower GNP growth rates; if the rate of growth of GNP is more rapid, the turnaround will occur sooner.

VII. INEFFECTIVE POLICY INSTRUMENTS

With this background in mind, we can now turn to a discussion of potential instruments of policy. A number of policy instruments have been shown in our analyses to be relatively unimportant for improving income distribution, and I shall discuss these first.[13] It should be noted that our studies indicate only that the unimportant instruments are unimportant if applied in isolation, i.e., under *ceteris paribus* conditions. As part of a policy package, which is part and parcel of a properly phased equity-oriented development strategy (see the next section), the instruments might not be ineffective.

Improvements in tax systems that include increases in the importance of direct taxes produced insignificant results. As confirmation, recent studies of Latin America show that neither tax structures nor government expenditure patterns typically favour a larger share for the poorest groups in the population. The reasons are complex, but they probably include the fact that the structure of political power typically stands in the way of effective progressivity. Also tax agencies are poorly developed and are administered unevenly.

Financial institutions are also less important mechanisms for favourable redistribution than one might expect. Their unimportance is consistent with John Gurley's hypothesis that the functioning of financial systems reflects closely the power structure of an underdeveloped country. In the absence of changes in the power structure, financial institutions operate unevenly.

The relative unimportance of agricultural structure and technology *by themselves* in our results is rather striking. With respect to land reform the reason is probably that redistribution of land favours higher incomes for the agricultural poor only when supported by measures to maintain the productivity of the redistributed assets. These supportive measures are often not carried out. The relationship expected *a priori*, therefore, is simply not observable.

Improvements in agricultural productivity also do not appear as significant as expected, in our analyses, a result which is consistent in the micro studies of the Green Revolution. This suggests that the primary beneficiaries of the adoption of improved techniques, and of the spread of new seeds and fertilizers, tend to be the middle-income and rich farmers, rather than the poor. Not only do the agricultural poor often not benefit from productivity increases that are concentrated on the larger farms, but (as indicated earlier) backwash effects from these improvements can undermine the position of small farmers by reducing agricultural product prices, putting pressure on tenancy, and restricting access to credit and other resources. These unfavourable consequences of agricultural modernization suggest rather strongly that agricultural policies that stress both rural development and technology rather than technological innovation alone are most desirable.

Industrialization, too, is less important in our results than one might expect. Short-term rates of change in the degree of industrialization are not significantly associated with the characteristics of the income distribution.

But when the means of groups of countries having successively higher scores on level of industrial technology are plotted against scores on the income share of the poorest 60 per cent, the resulting relationship is almost perfectly U-shaped. This finding is consistent with Kuznets's hypothesis and with our discussion above regarding the distributional impact of the early stages of industrialization in currently advanced nations. It suggests further that current policies to promote industrialization are likely to worsen income distribution until quite a high level of development is reached.

VIII. STRATEGIES CONDUCIVE TO EQUITABLE GROWTH

For countries at the lowest level of development, the policy implications of our results are rather depressing. No policy instrument emerges as systematically improving the position of the poor. The usual alternative to extreme inequality associated with expatriate domination of the socio-economic structure appears to be economic stagnation. Neither the expulsion of expatriates nor indigenous revolution appears likely to lead to economic growth, probably because of the very limited institutional and administrative capabilities found in countries at this level.

For countries at intermediate and higher levels of development, the prognosis is more hopeful. Our results suggest that improvements in human resources, more direct government control of enterprise and economic programmes, and increased stress on diversified manufacturing exports all have promise as strategies for improving income distribution. Even for these countries, however, the effective-policy instruments appear more likely, in the absence of direct governmental actions to the contrary, to increase the benefits accruing to the middle-income groups than to raise the level of living of the poorest two quintiles of the population.

If we recall the empirical observation that high rates of economic growth are necessary before growth can be equitable, we will recognize that effective measures for rapid improvement of the absolute welfare of the poor must vary significantly among country types, even at the intermediate and higher levels of development. In particular, a policy-maker interested in equitable growth must decide whether his country has an inherent potential for rapid growth (above the 5.5 per cent minimum) in the foreseeable future. If it does, he should first attempt to create the appropriate preconditions for equitable growth. The only proven way to accomplish this is by following the example of the five successful countries:

1. Reduce the vast disparities in wealth (particularly in land ownership), and
2. Redistribute access to further wealth by imposing controls on the use of capital and by engaging in a massive broad-based educational investment effort. This approach will generally lead to a decade or so of relatively slow growth of GNP, and will be accompanied by a substantial degree of political instability, social tension and unrest.

Once human resources have been upgraded, the subsequent acceleration of growth, if based on a human-resource-intensive industrialization strategy, can lead to growth with equity. However, it can do so only if proper attention is paid to economic policy. In small countries, the human-resource-intensive industrialization effort will have to be export oriented; in large countries, it can be aimed at satisfying the demands of the local market, particularly with a more equitable growth pattern which can provide the basis for a mass market domestically.

If the policy-maker does not believe that his country can meet the 5.5 per cent growth rate criterion within a reasonable time (and, realistically speaking, there are a significant number of LDCs for which this will be objectively the case), then he must make an explicit choice between deteriorating equity and continuing growth. The only policy I can see that works in the direction of improving equity under these conditions is through direct poverty-oriented transfer programmes. This will also reduce the already slow growth rate, a process that will contribute further to equity improvement, or at least reduce the rate of equity deterioration.

In deciding whether rapid growth potential exists, past economic performance may not be a reliable guide. During the 1950s, for example, South Korea was generally known in international circles as "the hell-hole of foreign assistance," and, even in the early 1960s, there was nothing in the performance of the economy to suggest that spectacular growth was just around the corner.

IX. CONCLUSION

To achieve equitable growth, two extreme strategies are in principle possible: (1) grow now, redistribute and educate later; (2) redistribute and educate now, grow later. The former strategy is the one that was followed typically by the currently-developed non-communist economies except for the United States and, according to its leaders, by Brazil currently; the latter strategy has been followed by those LDCs which have, within the past two decades, successfully achieved an equitable growth process.

I am convinced that, for equitable growth to become prevalent, there must be a deliberate application of the second strategy on a wide scale. My argument is one of efficiency; there is selective but consistent evidence that such a strategy can work, and significant evidence that the opposite strategy does not work in modern LDCs on an acceptable time scale. Once the difficult and politically dangerous massive-human-capital-accumulation, slower-growth phase is passed, the basis for a growth process which raises the welfare of the vast majority of the population is established, and the transition to a relatively highly developed stage can be accomplished in short order. In the five countries considered, the first phase lasted about a decade. After that, once economic incentives were rationalized to permit human-resource-intensive export-oriented industrialization, rapid economic growth led all of them into a phase of almost self-sustaining growth within a matter of another decade and a half.

The past, of course, is not necessarily a reliable guide to the future. Thus, one may object that the generally discouraging relationship of equity to growth may be merely the result of generally poor but readily rectified packages of economic policies. More appropriate relative prices, use of improved technologies, and a better balance between inward-oriented and export-oriented development strategies, it is often argued, will suffice to permit future growth to take place equitably. Unfortunately, however, the experience of the real world to date offers no evidence for equitable growth taking place without the preconditions described in this article.

By the same token, the success stories may be dismissed as special cases: small, with nonrepresentative cultural traditions and attitudes, subjected to exceptional challenges that legitimized the governments and made economic viability a major condition for national survival, benefited by unusually large *per capita* infusions of foreign aid. Special cases they are, but five successes are certainly more encouraging than none, and the consistency of their experiences surely weakens the "uniqueness" argument.

There is also evidence that the entire package—resource redistribution, massive education, and human-resource-oriented growth policies—must be adopted in that sequence in order to achieve rapid success. Incomplete versions of this programme—land reform alone, education without labour-intensive growth, etc.—just have not worked. And the different ordering of the package that was followed by most currently developed nations appears to have taken very much longer to achieve equitable growth than the specific ordering that was followed by our five successes.

In conclusion, I believe that our analyses, in combination with other empirical evidence, lead inescapably to the position that a major reorientation of development strategies is required to achieve equity-oriented growth. Marginal adjustments to current strategies simply will not work.

NOTES

1. I. Adelman and C. Taft Morris, *Economic Growth and Social Equity in Developing Countries* (Stanford Press, 1973).

2. I. Adelman and C. Taft Morris, *Society, Politics and Economic Development: A Quantitative Approach* (Johns Hopkins Press, 1967).

3. For a discussion of the statistical technique and its results, see Adelman and Morris, *Economic Growth and Social Equity, op. cit.*, Chapter 4. The indicators for the independent variables are defined in Chapters 1 and 2.

4. Apart from this methodological issue, on the validity of the data, *ibid.*, pp. 155–8.

5. *Ibid.*, Chapter 3.

6. *Ibid.*, p. 179.

7. *Ibid.*, p. 179.

8. It will be recalled that the rate of improvement in human resources is shown to be of great significance in the statistical analysis of variations in the dependent variables.

9. D. C. Cole and P. N. Lyman, *Korean Development* (Cambridge, Mass.: Harvard University Press, 1971), p. 130.

10. Between 1963 and 1968 employment increased from 92 to 95 per cent (*ibid.*, p. 138).

11. These relationships are supported by a cross-section regression analysis in Adelman and Morris, *Economic Growth and Social Equity, op. cit.*, Appendix C.

12. Panama, Mexico, and the Middle Eastern oil economies fail to meet either of these requirements.

13. See Adelman and Morris, *Economic Growth and Social Equity, op. cit.*, pp. 195–6.

22

The Brazilian "Model" of Development

Celso Furtado

The Brazilian economy constitutes a very interesting example of how far a country can go in the process of industrialization without abandoning its main features of underdevelopment: great disparity in productivity between urban and rural areas, a large majority of the population living at a physiological subsistence level, increasing masses of underemployed people in the urban zones, etc. The idea, implicit in the growth models of the genus started by Lewis, that steering the surplus of an underdeveloped economy toward the industrial sector (the activities absorbing technical progress) would ultimately create an economic system of increasing homogeneity (where the wage rate tends to increase in all economic activities *pari passu* with the average productivity of the system), has been thoroughly disproved.

The objectives of this paper are (a) to investigate why the worldwide diffusion of technical progress and the resulting increases in productivity have not tended to liquidate underdevelopment; and (b) to demonstrate that a policy of "development," geared to satisfy the high levels of consumption of a small minority of the population, such as that carried out in Brazil, tends to aggravate social inequalities and to increase the social cost of an economic system.

A significant element in our model is the hypothesis that underdevelopment is an aspect of the way industrial capitalism has been growing and spreading from the beginning. It is important to keep in mind that the industrial revolution took place inside an expanding commercial economy, in which foreign trade certainly was the most profitable activity; furthermore, the industrial revolution in turn spurred this trade. In the particular and fundamental case of Great Britain, the share of foreign trade in the economy increased enormously, giving rise to a complex system of international division of labor. The study of underdevelopment must start with the identification of the particular types of structures created in the periphery of the capitalist economy by this system of international division of labor. Therefore, to build a model of an underdeveloped economy as a closed system is totally misleading. To isolate an underdeveloped economy from the general context of the expanding capitalist system is to dismiss from the beginning the fundamental problem of the nature of the external

This paper originated in a talk given to the author's Seminar in Economic Development at the American University, Fall 1972. It was put into written form expressly for this book of readings. © Celso Furtado.

relationships of such an economy, namely, the fact of its global dependence. The first part of this paper will deal with this general problem, presented here in a rather schematic way. Most of the assumptions require additional empirical work to be adequately established. However, if the framework presented here helps in understanding better the different types of under-development, it will also be useful in providing more relevant interpretations of the vast empirical work currently being done on the so-called developing countries.

DEVELOPMENT AND MODERNIZATION

Let us define technical progress as the introduction of new productive processes capable of increasing efficiency in the utilization of scarce resources and/or the introduction of new products capable of being added to the basket of consumers' goods and services. And let us assume that economic development implies diffusion in the use of products already known and/or the insertion of new products into the basket of consumers' goods.

Because access to new products is with rare exceptions restricted, at least during a first phase, to a minority formed by high income people, development based mainly on the introduction of new products corresponds to a process of income concentration. And because diffusion means access of more people to the use of known products, development based mainly on diffusion corresponds to a process of greater equality in the distribution of income. Furthermore, a necessary condition in any process of economic development is accumulation of capital, as important for the diffusion of known products as for the introduction of new ones. But there are reasons to believe that the insertion of new products into the basket of consumers' goods requires relatively more capital accumulation than the diffusion of known products. For example: the introduction of a new model of auto-mobile of a certain class requires more investment (including research and development) per unit than the increase in the production of the corresponding model already being produced. A different way of focusing on this problem is as follows: the more diversified a basket of consumers' goods, the higher has to be the income of the person consuming these goods, and the larger the amount of capital required to satisfy the needs of that person. The average American citizen receives an annual income of approximately $4,000, and a certain basket of consumers' goods corresponds to that level of income. This basket of goods has been made possible by a process of capital accumulation that now adds up to something like $12,000 per person living in the country. The average Brazilian receives an annual income of something like $400 and the capital accumulated in Brazil adds up to something around $1,000. Thus, the basket of consumers' goods to which the average Brazilian has access has to be much less diversified than that available in the United States.

Increases in the income of a community may result from at least three different processes: (a) economic development, that is, accumulation of

capital and adoption of more effective productive processes; (b) the depletion of non-renewable natural resources; and (c) reallocation of resources
aiming at geographic specialization, through the pursuit of comparative
advantages in a system of international division of labor. Increases in
income entail diversification of consumption, adoption of new products,
etc. These increases, therefore, can be present in a community without
economic development, that is, without capital accumulation and introduction of more efficient productive processes. They may merely be the
result of an increase in income due to (b) and/or (c) above. Let us call
modernization this process of adoption of new patterns of consumption
corresponding to higher levels of income in the absence of economic
development.

The countries now known as underdeveloped are those where there
occurred a process of modernization: new patterns of consumption (introduction of new products) were adopted as a result of an increase in
income generated by the type of changes referred to in (b) and (c) above.
Brazil is a country where increases in income (economic productivity)
were, during a long period, basically the result of a simple reallocation of
resources aiming at maximization of static comparative advantages in
foreign trade. The shift from subsistence agriculture into commercial agriculture does not necessarily presuppose a shift from traditional into modern
agriculture. But, when generated by foreign trade, such a shift entails a
significant rise in economic productivity, and may initiate a process of
modernization. How important such a process will be depends on the institutional matrix at the time of its inception. In Brazil, because of the concentration of property in land and the abundance of labor in subsistence
agriculture, the increases in productivity benefited mainly a small minority.
However, because of the large population, the modernized minority was
sizable enough to allow a full urban development and a beginning of
industrialization.

In those countries where modernization occurred without economic
development, the process of industrialization presents very particular features. Thus, the market for manufactured products is formed by two completely different groups of people: the first, consumers of very low income
(the bulk of the population) and the second, a rich minority. The basket of
consumers' goods corresponding to the first group is only slightly diversified
and tends to remain without modifications because the real wage rate is
rather stable. Industries producing this basket of goods have weak linkages:
they use raw materials from agriculture (food and textile industries) and
produce directly for the final consumer. Furthermore, such industries
benefit little from economies of scale and externalities. The basket of consumers' goods corresponding to the second group, being fully diversified,
requires a complex process of industrialization to be domestically produced.
The main obstacle here stems from the dimension of the local market. This
is the sector of the market that is really expanding, however, and full
industrialization will only be possible if geared to it. Given the different
behavior of the two baskets of consumers' goods—one expanding slowly
and without introduction of new goods, and the other growing quickly,
mainly through the inclusion of new products—the two industrial sectors

compete only to a small degree for the same markets and may keep different standards of organization and marketing. But, once the sector catering to the rich minority comes to the fore, requirements in capital and modern technology tend to increase rapidly. Consequently, creation of new jobs per unit of investment declines and the need to keep up with the flow of new products increases. Furthermore, as a spin-off of the process of full industrialization, based on the second basket of consumers' goods, the industries catering to the mass of the population are bound to pass through important transformations. Economies of scale and externalities may also benefit the mass of the population, and products such as plastics and synthetic fibers be added to the popular basket of goods. As a consequence of the progressive integration of the industrial apparatus, more capital intensive processes tend to be adopted in the industries that first developed in competition with local handicraft activities. Technical progress is no longer a matter of buying a certain type of equipment, but a question of having access to the innovations pouring into the rich countries. In this phase, the branches of the multinational corporations (MNCs) will easily supersede the local firms, particularly in the industries geared to the diversified basket. More precisely, such a diversified basket of consumers' goods would never be locally produced if the flow of technical innovations had to be paid at market prices. In spite of the fact that for an MNC operating in an underdeveloped country the opportunity cost of such a flow of innovations is practically zero, the corporation would never make it available to independent local firms except for a very high price.

The industrialization of the economies that start with the process of modernization is bound to face a double difficulty: if the local industries remain producing for the first basket (industries with weak linkage) and the second basket has to be imported, the country will never reach the point required to form an industrial system; and if the local industries get into the production of the second basket, decreasing returns may show up because of the smallness of the local market. A few countries of large demographic dimensions and with a highly productive exporting sector have succeeded in overcoming these obstacles. Such has been the case with Brazil. This does not mean that industrial capitalism can operate in Brazil following the rules that prevail in a developed economy. In the latter case, expansion of production signifies parallel expansion in the cost of labor, that is, in the value added by labor during the production process. And because demand is mainly generated by payments to labor, expansion of demand is bound to follow the increase in production. In the underdeveloped economy, value added by labor is bound to decline in relative terms during the phases of expansion. Increases in productivity created by internal economies or externalities tend to benefit the owners of capital exclusively, and, given the structure of markets, nothing will press them to transfer the fruits of increased productivity to the consumers, the modernized minority. On the other hand, raising the wage rate would increase costs without enlarging the market, because the workers are linked to a different basket of goods. The fact is that the system operates spontaneously, benefiting too small a minority, the owners of capital. How should the process of income concentration, inherent to the system, be steered in order to create a link between the increase in productivity in the industries producing the second basket and the consumers who have access to that basket? In the third part of this paper we will examine the particular type of solution used in Brazil.

THE PERFORMANCE OF THE BRAZILIAN ECONOMY

In the last twenty-five years the Brazilian economy has been growing at a relatively high rate. Given "normal" levels of agricultural production, in terms of trade and public expenditures, a growth rate of about 6 percent a year could be expected. The very rich natural resources, the size of the population, and the average level of income attained in the past through maximization of static comparative advantages in foreign trade converge to produce this growth potential. Furthermore, fluctuations in the rate of growth of the gross domestic product (GDP) had little effect on the process of capital formation. The rates of saving and investment have been rather stable. Changes in the rate of growth of the GDP basically reflect modifications in the degree of utilization of the productive capacity already installed. In the elementary language of growth models, we would say that changes in the rate of growth are mainly caused by modifications in the parameter that represents the relationship between output and the stock of reproducible capital, and that the other parameter, representing the relationship between investment and income, tends to be stable.

In fact, the first parameter (output-capital ratio) doubled between 1964–67 and 1968–69, whereas the second (rate of investment) increased only slightly. No doubt, the process of accumulation has been much steadier than the performance of the economy in general. When performance is poor, the margin of unused productive capacity is increased, but in spite of that, the global capacity of production will grow as usual. We may infer from this that the rate of profit might be rather high even when the economy underutilizes its productive capacity; on the other hand, there is reason to believe that the economy has been unable to generate the kind of demand required to obtain adequate utilization of the productive capacity.

I have not referred to the level of demand but to the *kind of demand*. As a matter of fact, we are very far from the Keynesian hypothesis of insufficiency of effective demand. During the period considered, the Brazilian economy has been operating under strong pressure from excess money demand, with a high rate of inflation in the periods of rapid growth and relative stagnation as well.

My basic hypothesis is that the system has not been capable of spontaneously producing the demand profile that would assure a steady rate of growth, and that growth in the long run depends on the exogenous actions of the government. Account must also be taken of the fact that during the period being discussed, the industries catering to the modernized minority came to be increasingly controlled by multinational corporations, along the lines of the general process of expansion of capitalism referred to above.

Rapid industrial growth, in the particular conditions now prevailing in Brazil, implies an intense absorption of technical progress in the form of new products and the new processes required to produce them. For the MNCs the opportunity costs of such technical progress are at a minimum when they can reproduce what they create and amortize in the countries responsible for the financing of research and development, and are at a maximum when they have to introduce new R & D. Consequently, industrial expansion goes on through an interlocking of local industries with the dominant industrial systems from which the flow of new technology springs. On the one hand, the MNCs stick to their blueprints as the best way of maximizing growth and profits; on the other, the modernized minorities seek to keep up with *le dernier cri* in the metropolis. But, although the two social forces have convergent interests, these interests do not suffice to make the system generate the kind of demand required to assure growth.

The successive waves of industrial expansion in Brazil during the postwar period cannot be explained without taking into account the autonomous role of the government in either subsidizing investment or enlarging demand. The general framework was the process of import substitution, catering to the market formed during the period of expansion of the exports of raw materials. Creating new jobs, this process enlarged the market for wage goods, but given the small size of the market for durable consumers' goods, local production of such goods tended to increase their relative prices, causing a decline in demand. Such a negative effect was checked up to the middle of the fifties by actions of the government to reduce prices of imported equipment by means of differential exchange rates, and also to subsidize industrial investments (particularly in industries that produced import substitutes) largely through loans with negative rates of interest. Part of the resources used to implement such a policy came from an improvement in the terms-of-trade which took place during this period. Cutting the real cost of the fixed capital by half helped the industries producing durable consumers' goods to realize profits, even if they had to operate with a large margin of unused capacity. In the second half of the fifties, when the terms-of-trade had deteriorated, the government embarked on a policy of external indebtedness that allowed it to proceed with the subsidies. At the same time, the government engaged in a policy of huge public works: the building of Brasilia and the construction of a national network of roads, including pioneering roads like the Belem-Brasilia. More recently, as we will see, action has been taken directly in the area of income distribution in order to produce the quality of demand that better fits the plans of expansion of the MNCs and the expectations of the modernized minority.

THE NEW STRATEGY

Brazil's high rate of growth in industrial production, attained in the last five years (1968–72) after a period of seven years of relative stagnation (1961–67), has been obtained through a very successful governmental policy which aims at attracting the MNC and fostering the expansion of the branches of such corporations already installed in the country. By various means the government has been guiding the process of income distribution in order to produce the demand profile most attractive to the MNCs. Consequently, the basket of consumers' goods which attempts to reproduce the patterns of consumption of the rich countries has expanded rapidly in both absolute and relative terms.

The State also has been playing important complementary roles by investing in physical infrastructure, in human capital (in an attempt to enlarge the supply of professional cadres and personnel), and in those industries with a low capital turnover. Industries producing homogeneous products such as steel, non-ferrous metals, and other standard inputs of the industrial system do not rely on innovation of products to compete or generate market power. They rely on innovation of productive processes and, because the turnover of fixed capital is low, the flow of innovation tends to be much slower. Furthermore, a policy of low prices, followed by such industries through concealed subsidies, may be defended as essential to foster the process of industrialization. Thus, keeping this block of industries in the hands of the State, totally or partially, may be the best way for MNCs to obtain a rapid payoff, and may maximize profits and expansion.

The firms controlled by local capitalists also have a role in this system. Industries producing for the mass of the population face a sluggish demand because the real wage rate of the unskilled worker is declining or stagnating. The markets for such industries expand horizontally, however, because of the increase in population and the transfer of people from subsistence activities into the sector paying the basic wage rate guaranteed by social legislation. Because this basket of consumers' goods does not include the introduction of new products, control of technical progress is not so important as a source of market power. Consequently, the MNCs in this sector do not have the same advantages in competing with local capitalists.

Considering the industrial system as a whole, we perceive that MNCs control the activities which rely mainly on technical progress (the activities where the flow of new products is more intense), namely, production of durable consumers' goods and equipment in general. The State has an important share in industries producing intermediate products, and local capitalists are very strong in industries producing non-durable consumers' goods. Furthermore, local firms operate under contracts as an auxiliary line of production for MNCs and for the enterprises of the State, adding flexibility to the system. No doubt, MNCs are passing through a process of vertical integration in certain sectors, absorbing local firms, and are also expanding in important sectors of non-durable consumers' goods. The food industry, under the control of MNCs, is catering to the upper income groups, introducing a myriad of products that fill the supermarkets of the rich countries. Nevertheless, the basic lines of the system are those presented above, and we may say that the three sub-sectors pursue different roles and, up to a point, are complementary. It is important to stress, however, that the dynamism of the system rests upon the intensity of transmission of technical progress as visualized by MNCs. In other words, when the opportunity costs of technical progress are practically zero for the branches of multinational corporations, the rate of growth of the industrial system tends to be maximized.

Given the characteristics of the Brazilian economy, formed by a rather small highly diversified market and another relatively large market of low diversification, durable consumers' goods industries benefit much more from economies of scale than existing consumers' goods industries. Consequently, the more concentrated is the distribution of income, the greater is the positive effect on the rate of growth of GDP. Thus, the same amount of money when consumed by rich people causes a faster rate of growth of GDP than when consumed by poor people. Let us suppose that the consumers' goods whose demand is in rapid expansion are automobiles; most probably, the building of the infrastructure will not keep pace with the increase in the stock of automobiles, and efficiency in the use of the vehicles is bound to decline. This means more consumption of fuel and more repairs per mile as a consequence of traffic jams, etc. All this will also contribute to an increase in the rate of expansion of the GDP. We can push this further. Concentration of income creates the possibility of price discrimination. In fact, some touches added to certain cars (new models) allow overpricing to occur, and the producer's rent thus created will also add to the increment of the GDP. In short, squandering resources for the superfluous consumption of a rich minority contributes to the inflation of the growth rate of GDP, and may also inflate the prestige of people in government.

Another factor to be taken into account is the rate of inflow of foreign capital. If the demand profile fits with the requirements of MNCs, the possibilities of mobilizing financial resources abroad will obviously be greater. As a matter of fact, things are not so simple, because prospects for the balance of payments depend on other factors linked to the anticipated capacity to export. Other things being equal, however, if the anticipated rate of profit of MNCs is higher, then the inflow of foreign capital will be greater, adding to local savings and giving flexibility to the economy, at least in the short run.

To sum up: a certain profile of demand, corresponding to an increasing concentration in the distribution of income and to an increasing gap between the level of consumption of the rich minority and that of the mass of the population, entails a composition of investments that tends to maximize the transfer of technical progress through MNCs, and to increase the inflow of foreign resources. Thus, the policy aiming at producing that demand profile will also tend to maximize the expansion of the GDP.

Within this general framework, the Brazilian government has been pursuing four basic objectives:

1. fostering and steering the process of income concentration (a process inherent to the underdeveloped capitalist economies in general) to benefit the consumers of durable goods, that is, the minority of the population, with patterns of consumption similar to those of the rich countries;

2. assuming that the transfer of people from the subsistence sector into the sectors benefiting from the minimum guaranteed wage rate attains a minimum critical level;

3. controlling the differential between the minimum guaranteed wage rate and the level of real income in the subsistence sector. In six years the

government reduced the guaranteed wage rate and succeeded in reconciling the transfer of some people from the subsistence sectors with an intense process of income concentration; and

4. subsidizing the export of manufactured goods in order to reduce the pressure on those sectors producing non-durable consumers' goods with a sluggish demand due to income concentration, and also to improve the balance of payments.

The objectives referred to under (2) and (3) are instrumental social variables required to tackle the social tensions stemming from the process of income concentration, particularly when the real wage rate is declining. Creation of new jobs is a way of reducing the burden on people already working; since the number of dependents per family is large, the number of wage earners in each family can be increased, which makes the reduction in the wage rate easier to accept. Furthermore, such a policy brings about a reduction in the cost of labor to MNCs without shrinking their markets.

The most complex part of this policy concerns the process of fostering and steering income concentration. To obtain the desired result, the Brazilian government has been using various instruments, particularly credit, income and fiscal policies.

The first spurt of demand for durable consumers' goods originated from a rapid expansion of consumers' credit, benefiting the upper middle class. The resulting inflation reduced the real income of the mass of the population, freeing resources for a policy of public investments while helping to reduce production costs of private firms. The increase in the rate of profit of the firms producing durable consumers' goods was very rapid, creating leverage for an expansion of private investments. If we take into account the fact that the firms producing durable consumers' goods had been operating with a large margin of unused productive capacity, and that these enterprises reap substantial economies of scale during expansion, then we can easily understand the boom that took place.

The extremely high level of profit and the investment boom, particularly in the industrial sector producing for the rich minority, opened the door for an income distribution policy favoring the upper brackets of the salary scale, since the supply of professional cadres was rather inelastic. This situation, coinciding with a decline in the basic wage rate, engendered an extreme concentration of income not derived from property. A similar tendency can be observed within the public sector.

It is through fiscal policy, however, that the government has been pursuing the more ambitious objective of giving permanence to the new structures. Scores of "fiscal incentives" have been implemented, aimed at creating a sizable group of rentiers within the middle class. As a matter of fact, every person having to pay income tax (approximately 5 percent of the families) has been induced to compose an investment portfolio as an alternative to the payment of part of the tax due.* The poor, with a heavy burden of indirect taxes, are excluded from such privileges. The apparent objective of the government in adopting this policy is to link the purchas-

---

* A special provision of the tax law allows taxpayers to reduce their tax liability up to one-half if they invest that amount in government bonds or new issues of corporate securities.

ing power of the upper middle class to the most dynamic flow of income, the flow of profits. In this particular and important aspect, Brazil is engendering a new type of capitalism, heavily dependent upon the appropriation and utilization of profits to generate a certain type of consumption expenditure. This can only be obtained through decisive action on the part of the State to force the firms to open their capital (particularly difficult in the case of MNCs) and to pursue an adequate policy of distribution of dividends. An alternative to this would be the accumulation of an increasing public debt in the hands of the upper middle class, whose flow of interest would have to be fed with the proceeds of a tax on the profits of the corporations. Nowhere has a capitalist economy been so dependent upon the State to gear demand to supply.

The most significant feature of the Brazilian "model" is its structural tendency to exclude the mass of the population from the benefits of accumulation and technical progress. Thus, the durability of the system relies heavily on the capacity of the ruling groups to suppress all forms of opposition which its anti-social character tends to arouse.

23

Maoist Economic Development:
The New Man in the New China

John W. Gurley

While capitalist and Maoist processes of economic development have several elements in common, the differences between the two approaches are nevertheless many and profound. It is certainly not evident that one approach or the other is always superior, either in means or ends. What is evident, however, is that most studies by American economists of Chinese economic development are based on the assumption of capitalist superiority, and so China has been dealt with as though it were simply an underdeveloped United States—an economy that "should" develop along capitalist lines and that "should" forget all that foolishness about Marxism, Mao's thought, great leaps, and cultural revolutions, and get on with the job of investing its savings efficiently. This unthinking acceptance by American economists of the view that there is no development like capitalist development has resulted in studies of China that lack insight.

The practice of capitalism has not, of course, met the ideal specification for it as theorized by Adam Smith. In general, the theory holds that an economy can develop most rapidly if every person, whether as entrepreneur, worker, or consumer, is able to pursue his own self-interest in competitive markets without undue interference from government. Progress is best promoted not by government, but by entrepreneurs owning the material means of production, whose activities, guided by the profit motive, reflect consumers' demands for various goods and services. Labor productivity is enhanced by material incentives and the division of labor (specialization); economic progress is made within an environment of law and order, harmony of interests, and stability. It is by these means that economic development, according to the theory, can best be attained, and its attainment can best be measured by the national output.

In practice, many markets have been more monopolistic than competitive, government has interfered in numerous and extensive ways in competitive market processes in pursuit of greater equity in income distribution, higher employment of labor, and better allocation of economic resources. Capitalism of the individualist, competitive type has to some extent given way in most parts of the industrial capitalist world to a state welfare capitalism, in which government plays a larger role and private entrepreneurs and consumers somewhat smaller ones than envisaged by Adam Smith and his disciples. Despite these departures from the ideal model of capitalism,

Reprinted from *The Center Magazine*, Vol. III, No. 3 (May 1970), pp. 25–33, by permission of the Center for the Study of Democratic Institutions, Santa Barbara, California.

however, it is fair to say that the main driving force of the capitalist system remains private entrepreneurs who own the means of production, and that competition among them is still widespread and worldwide.

There is no doubt that capitalist development, whatever importance its departures from the Smithian model have had, has been highly successful in raising living standards for large numbers of people. It has been relatively efficient in using factors of production in ways best designed to provide all the goods that consumers by and large have demanded. It has also encouraged new ways of doing things—innovative activity and technological advances.

At the same time, however, there is a heavy emphasis in capitalist development—as there now is throughout most of the world—on raising the national output, on producing "things" in ever-increasing amounts. Implicit is the view that man is merely an input, a factor of production, a means to an end. Moreover, capitalist development has almost always been uneven in several crucial ways—in its alternating periods of boom and bust; in enriching some people thousands of times more than others; in developing production facilities with much more care than it has devoted to the welfare of human beings and their environment; in fostering lopsided development, both in terms of geographical location within a country and, especially in low-income countries, in terms of a narrow range of outputs, such as in one- or two-crop economies. The lopsided character of capitalist development has been evident historically in those nations that today have advanced industrial economies, but it is especially evident in the underdeveloped countries (with their mixture of feudal and capitalist features) that are tied in to the international capitalist system—those countries that, by being receptive to free enterprise and foreign capital, regardless of whether they are also receptive to freedom, are in the "free world."

This lopsidedness shows itself more markedly, of course, in the matter of trade. As satellites to the advanced capitalist countries, the underdeveloped regions supply raw materials, agricultural products, minerals, and oil, and receive in return manufactured and processed goods as well as basic food items. Much more trade takes place between the underdeveloped and the advanced capitalist countries than among the underdeveloped countries themselves. One consequence of this is the poor transportation within South America and Africa—while there are good highways or railroads running from mines, plantations, and oil fields to the seaports, it remains difficult to travel from one part of the continent to another.

The economic development of these poor capitalist countries is lopsided in many other ways, too. A few cities in each of these countries, with their airports, hotels, nightclubs, and light industries, are often built up to the point where they resemble the most modern metropolis in advanced industrial countries—but the rural areas, comprising most of the country and containing most of the people, are largely untouched by modernization. Industry, culture, entertainment, education, and wealth are highly concentrated in urban centers; a traveler to most of the poor "free world" countries, by flying to the main cities, can land in the middle of the twentieth century, but by going thirty miles out into the country in any direction he will find himself back in the Middle Ages. Education is usually for the elite and stresses the superiority of the educated over the uneducated, the superiority of urban over rural life, of mental over manual labor. The burden of economic development, which is essentially a restraint on consumption, is shared most inequitably among the people; the differences between rich and poor are staggering—they are nothing less than the differences between unbelievable luxury and starvation.

While some of these characteristics are not peculiar to the poor countries tied to the internationalist capitalist system (they can be found in the Soviet socialist bloc, too), and while some are related more to feudalism than to capitalism, much of the lopsided development is intimately connected with the profit motive. The key link between the two is the fact that it is almost always most profitable, from a private-business point of view, to build on the best. Thus a businessman locates a new factory in an urban center near existing ones, rather than out in the hinterlands, in order to gain access to supplies, a skilled labor force, and high-income consumers; to maximize profits, he hires the best, most qualified workers; a banker extends loans to those who are already successful; an educational system devotes its best efforts to the superior students, and universities, imbued with the private-business ethic of "efficiency," offer education to those best prepared and most able; promoters locate cultural centers for those best able to appreciate and afford them; in the interests of efficiency and comparative advantage, businessmen are induced to specialize (in cocoa or peanuts or coffee) —to build on what they have always done best.

This pursuit of efficiency and private profits through building on the best has led in some areas to impressive aggregate growth rates, but almost everywhere in the international capitalist world it has favored only a relative few at the expense of the many, and, in poor capitalist countries, it has left most in stagnant backwaters. Capitalist development, even when most successful, is always a trickle-down development.

The Maoists' disagreement with the capitalist view of economic development is profound. Their emphases, values, and aspirations are quite different from those of capitalist economists. Maoist economic development occurs within the context of central planning, public ownership of industries, and agricultural coöperatives or communes. While decision-making is decentralized to some extent, decisions regarding investment versus consumption, foreign trade, allocation of material inputs and the labor supply, prices of various commodities—these and more are essentially in the hands of the state. The profit motive is officially discouraged from assuming an important role in the allocation of resources, and material incentives, while still prevalent, are downgraded.

Perhaps the most striking difference between the capitalist and Maoist views concerns goals. Maoists believe that while a principal aim of nations should be to raise the level of material welfare of the population, this should be done only within the context of the development of human beings, encouraging them to realize fully their manifold creative powers. And it should be done only on an egalitarian basis—that is, on the basis that development is not worth much unless everyone rises together; no one is to be left behind, either economically or culturally. Indeed, Maoists believe that rapid economic development is not likely to occur *unless* everyone rises together. Development as a trickle-down process is therefore rejected by Maoists, and so they reject any strong emphasis on profit motives and efficiency criteria that lead to lopsided growth.

In Maoist eyes, economic development can best be attained by giving prominence to men rather than "things."

Recently, capitalist economists have begun to stress the importance for economic growth of "investment in human capital"—that is, investment in general education, job training, and better health. It has been claimed that expenditures in these directions have had a large "payoff" in terms of output growth. Although this might seem to represent a basic change in their concept of man in the development process, actually it does not. "Investment in human capital" means that economic resources are invested for the purpose of raising the skill and the educational and health levels of labor, not as an end in itself but as a means of increasing the productivity of labor. Thus economists are concerned with the "payoff" to investment in human capital, this payoff being the profit that can be made from such an expenditure. Indeed, the very term "human capital" indicates what these economists have in mind: man is another capital good, an input in the productive engine that grinds out commodities; if one invests in man, he may become more productive and return a handsome profit to the investor—whether the investor is the state, a private capitalist, or the laborer himself. Thus the preoccupation of capitalist economists is still with man as a means and not as an end.

The Maoists' emphasis, however, is quite different. First of all, while they recognize the role played by education and health in the production process, their emphasis is heavily placed on the transformation of ideas, the making of the communist man. Ideology, of course, may be considered as part of education in the broadest sense, but it is surely not the part that capitalist economists have in mind when they evaluate education's contribution to economic growth. Moreover, ideological training does not include the acquisition of particular skills or the training of specialists—as education and job training in capitalist countries tend to do. The Maoists believe that economic development can best be promoted by breaking down specialization, by dismantling bureaucracies, and by undermining the other centralizing and divisive tendencies that give rise to experts, technicians, authorities, and bureaucrats remote from or manipulating "the masses." Finally, Maoists seem perfectly willing to pursue the goal of transforming man even though it is temporarily at the expense of some economic growth. Indeed, it is clear that Maoists will not accept economic development, however rapid, if it is based on the capitalist principles of sharp division of labor and sharp (meaning unsavory or selfish) practices.

The proletarian world-view, which Maoists believe must replace that of the bourgeoisie, stresses that only through struggle can progress be made; that selflessness and unity of purpose will release a huge reservoir of enthusiasm, energy, and creativeness; that active participation by "the masses" in decision-making will provide them with the knowledge to channel their energy most productively; and that the elimination of specialization will not only increase workers' and peasants' willingness to work hard for the various goals of society but will also increase their ability to do this by adding to their knowledge and awareness of the world around them.

It is an essential part of Maoist thinking that progress is not made by peace and quietude, by letting things drift and playing safe, or, in the words of Mao Tse-tung, by standing for "unprincipled peace, thus giving rise to a decadent, philistine attitude. . . ." Progress is made through struggle, when new talents emerge and knowledge advances in leaps. Only through continuous struggle is the level of consciousness of people raised, and in the process they gain not only understanding but happiness.

Mao sees man engaged in a fierce class struggle—the bourgeoisie against the proletariat—the outcome of which, at least in the short run, is far from certain. The proletarian world outlook can win only if it enters tremendous ideological class struggles.

Maoists believe that each person should be devoted to "the masses" rather than to his own pots and pans, and should serve the world proletariat rather than, as the *Peking Review* has put it, reaching out with "grasping hands everywhere to seek fame, material gain, power, position, and limelight." They think that if a person is selfish he will resist criticisms and suggestions and is likely to become bureaucratic and elitist. He will not work as hard for community or national goals as he will for narrow, selfish ones. In any case, a selfish person is not an admirable person. Thus Maoists deëmphasize material incentives, for they are the very manifestation of a selfish, bourgeois society. While selflessness is necessary to imbue man with energy and the willingness to work hard, Maoists believe this is not sufficient; man must also have the ability as well. And such ability comes from active participation—from seeing and doing. To gain knowledge, people must be awakened from their half slumber, encouraged to mobilize themselves and to take conscious action to elevate and liberate themselves. When they actively participate in decision-making, when they take an interest in state affairs, when they dare to do new things, when they become good at presenting facts and reasoning things out, when they criticize and test and experiment scientifically—having discarded myths and superstitions—when they are aroused, then, says the *Peking Review*, "the socialist initiative latent in the masses [will] burst out with volcanic force and a rapid change [will take] place in production."

Finally, if men become "selfless," there will be discipline and unity of will, for these "cannot be achieved if relations among comrades stem from selfish interests and personal likes and dislikes." If men become "active," then along with extensive democracy they will gain true consciousness and ultimately freedom, in the Marxian sense of intelligent action. Together, selflessness and active participation will achieve ideal combinations of opposites: "a vigorous and lively political situation . . . is taking shape throughout our country, in which there is both centralism and democracy, both discipline and freedom, both unity of will and personal ease of mind."

It is important to note the "discipline" and "unity of will." As for the basic framework of Marxism-Leninism, Maoists believe that everyone should accept it, and they are quick to "work on" those who lag behind or step out of line. But, within this framework, the Maoists energetically and sincerely promote individual initiative, "reasoning things out and not depending on authorities or myths," "thinking for oneself," and so forth. Outside of this framework, an individual stands little chance; inside the framework, an individual is involved in a dynamic process of becoming "truly free," in the sense of being fully aware of the world around him and an active decision-maker in that world. Mao's thought is meant to lead to true freedom and to unity of will based on a proletarian viewpoint. So everyone must think alike—the Maoist way—to attain true freedom.

For Marx, specialization and bureaucratization were the very antithesis of communism. Man could not be free or truly human until these manifestations of alienation were eliminated, allowing him to become an all-around communist man. Maoists, too, have been intensely concerned with this goal, specifying it in terms of eliminating the distinction between town and countryside, mental and manual labor, and workers and peasants. The realization of the universal man is not automatically achieved by altering the forces of production, by the socialist revolution. Rather, it can be achieved only after the most intense and unrelenting ideological efforts to raise the consciousness of the masses through the creative study and creative use of Mao's thought. Old ideas, customs, and habits hang on long after the material base of the economy has been radically changed, and it takes one mighty effort after another to wipe out the bourgeois superstructure and replace it with the proletarian world outlook. This transformation of the "subjective world" will then have a tremendous impact on the "objective world."

In many ways Maoist ideology rejects the capitalist principle of building on the best, even though the principle cannot help but be followed to some extent in any effort at economic development. However, the Maoist departures from the principle are the important thing. While capitalism, in their view, strives one-sidedly for efficiency in producing goods, Maoism, while also seeking some high degree of efficiency, at the same time and in numerous ways builds on "the worst": experts are pushed aside in favor of decision-making by "the masses"; new industries are established in rural areas; the educational system favors the disadvantaged; expertise (and hence work proficiency in a narrow sense) is discouraged; new products are domestically produced rather than being imported "more efficiently"; the growth of cities as centers of industrial and cultural life is discouraged; steel, for a time, is made by "everyone" instead of by only the much more efficient steel industry.

Of course, Maoists build on "the worst" not because they take great delight in lowering economic efficiency; rather, their stated aims are to involve everyone in the development process, to pursue development without leaving a single person behind, to achieve a balanced growth rather than a lopsided one. Yet if Maoism were only that, we could simply state that, while Maoist development may be much more equitable than capitalist efforts, it is surely less efficient and thus less rapid; efficiency is being sacrificed to some extent for equity. But that would miss the more important aspects of Maoist ideology, which holds that the resources devoted to bringing everyone into the socialist development process—the effort spent on building on "the worst"—will eventually pay off not only in economic ways by enormously raising labor productivity but, more important, by creating a society of truly free men who respond intelligently to the world around them, and who are happy.

The sharp contrast between the economic development views of capitalist economists and those of the Chinese communists cannot be denied; their two worlds are quite different. The difference is not mainly between being Chinese and being American, although that is surely part of it but, rather, between Maoists in a Marxist-Leninist tradition and being present-day followers of the economics first fashioned by Adam Smith and later reformed by John Maynard Keynes. Whatever the ignorance and misunderstanding on the Chinese side regarding the doctrines of capitalist economics, it is clear that many Western economic experts on China have shown little interest in, and almost no understanding of, Maoist economic development. Most of the economic researchers have approached China as though it were little more than a series of tables in a yearbook which could be analyzed by Western economic methods and judged by capitalist values. The result has been a series of unilluminating studies, largely statistical or institutional in method, and lacking analysis of the really distinctive and interesting features of Maoist development.

Like seagulls following the wake of a ship, economists pursue numbers. The main concentration of numbers pertaining to the economy of Communist China is in *Ten Great Years*, which was published in September, 1959, by the State Statistical Bureau. This volume contains a wealth of data on almost all phases of economic activity, and so it has become one of the main sources for much of the empirical work on Chinese economic development. But throughout the nineteen-fifties economic data were published in hundreds of other sources—in official reports, statistical handbooks, economics books, and articles—so that altogether massive information, of varying degrees of reliability, became available on the first decade or so of China's development efforts. After 1958, however, the release of aggregate data just about came to a halt, so little research on the nineteen-sixties has been done by economists outside of China. The data of the nineteen-fifties continue to be worked over, adjusted, and refined, though there is no longer much more that can be said about them.

Much of this research has been concerned in one way or another with China's national output—its absolute size; its rates of growth; its components, like agriculture and industrial output, or consumption and investment goods; the extent to which national output has been affected by international trade and Soviet aid; and the planning methods utilized in its production.

There are, of course, scores of studies, though mostly of an empirical nature, on specialized aspects of the economic process. A few Western economists have actually visited China in recent years and have returned with much information, but mainly of a qualitative nature.

Economic research on China suffers from an ailment common to most of economics—a narrow empiricism. Thus most of the research studies of the Chinese economy deal with very small segments of the development process, and within these tiny areas the researchers busy themselves with data series—adding up the numbers, adjusting them in numerous ways, deflating them for price changes, and doing a lot of other fussy statistical

work. Each economist tills intensively his small plot, gaining highly specialized knowledge in the process, finally ending up an expert in his cramped
quarters. There are not many economists in the China field who try to see
Chinese economic development as a whole, as "the comprehensive totality
of the historical process." If the truth is the whole, as Hegel claimed, most
economic experts on China must be so far from the truth that it is hardly
worthwhile listening to them.

Moreover, it is often painful. Even a casual reader of the economic
research on Communist China cannot help but notice that many of the
researchers are not happy—to say the least—with the object of their investigation. This is immediately noticeable because it is so very unusual in
economics. Ordinarily, economists are utterly fascinated and almost infatu-
ated with their special areas of study—even with such an esoteric one as
"Game Theory Applied to Non-linear Development." But not so our China
experts. Indeed, it is quite apparent that many of them consider China to
be, not the Beloved, but the Enemy. And in dealing with the Enemy, their
research often reveals very strong, and undisguised, biases against China.

These biases show up in a variety of ways, from such trivial things as
changing Peking to Peiping (à la Dean Rusk), which reveals a wish that the
communists weren't there; to the frequent use of emotive words (the communists are not dedicated but "obsessed," leaders are "bosses," a decision
not to release data is described as "a sullen statistical silence," the extension of the statistical system becomes "an extension of its tentacles further
into the economy"); to the attribution of rather sinister motives to ordinary
economic and cultural policies (education and literacy are promoted for the
purpose of spreading evil Marxian doctrines, economic development is pursued for the principal purpose of gaining military strength for geographical
expansion—which is the theme of W. W. Rostow's book on *The Prospects
for Communist China*); to dire forecasts of imminent disaster based on
little more than wishful thinking; and on up to data manipulation of the
most questionable sort.

This strong propensity to treat China as the enemy has led to some
grossly distorted accounts of China's economic progress. The picture that
is presented by these studies as a whole is one in which China, while making some progress for a time in certain areas, is just barely holding on to
economic life. It is a picture of a China always close to famine, making little
headway while the rest of the world moves ahead, being involved in irrational economic policies, and offering little reason for hope that the lives of
her people will be improved. Our China experts, furthermore, know what
is wrong, and that, in a word, is communism. They seldom fail to pass
judgment on some aspect or other of Chinese economic development, and
this judgment is almost invariably capitalist-oriented. Thus national planning and government-controlled prices cannot be good because they do not
meet the criteria of consumer sovereignty and competitive markets; communes violate individualism and private property; ideological campaigns
upset order and harmony; the deëmphasis on material incentives violates
human nature and so reduces individual initiative and economic growth;
the breakdown of specialization lowers workers' productivity. This sort of
thing pervades much of the economic literature on China.

Given all this—the narrow specialized studies that are sometimes useful but not often enlightening, the distortions by omission or commission, the capitalist-oriented approaches and assessments, not to mention those evaluations of Communist China that are inspired by a strong allegiance to Chiang Kai-shek—given all this, it is little wonder that a fair picture of China's economic progress seldom gets presented. Seldom, not never: Barry Richman's book on *Industrial Society in Communist China*, Carl Riskin's work—for example, in *The Cultural Revolution 1967 in Review*—and several other research efforts are refreshingly objective, relatively free of capitalist cant, and approach Maoist ideology in a serious way.

The truth is that China over the past two decades has made very remarkable economic advances (though not steadily) on almost all fronts. The basic, overriding economic fact about China is that for twenty years she has fed, clothed, and housed everyone, has kept them healthy, and has educated most. Millions have not starved; sidewalks and streets have not been covered with multitudes of sleeping, begging, hungry, and illiterate human beings; millions are not disease-ridden. To find such deplorable conditions, one does not look to China these days but, rather, to India, Pakistan, and almost anywhere else in the underdeveloped world. These facts are so basic, so fundamentally important, that they completely dominate China's economic picture, even if one grants all of the erratic and irrational policies alleged by her numerous critics.

The Chinese—all of them—now have what is in effect an insurance policy against pestilence, famine, and other disasters. In this respect, China has outperformed every underdeveloped country in the world; and, even with respect to the richest one, it would not be farfetched to claim that there has been less malnutrition due to maldistribution of food in China over the past twenty years than there has been in the United States. If this comes close to the truth, the reason lies not in China's grain output far surpassing her population growth—for it has not—but, rather, in the development of institutions to distribute food evenly among the population. It is also true, however, that China has just had six consecutive bumper grain crops (wheat and rice) that have enabled her to reduce wheat imports and greatly increase rice exports. On top of this, there have been large gains in the supplies of eggs, vegetables, fruits, poultry, fish, and meat. In fact, China today exports more food than she imports. The Chinese are in a much better position now than ever before to ward off natural disasters, as there has been significant progress in irrigation, flood control, and water conservation. The use of chemical fertilizers is increasing rapidly, the volume now over ten times that of the early nineteen-fifties; there has been substantial gain in the output of tractors, pumps, and other farm implements; and much progress has been made in the control of plant disease and in crop breeding.

In education, there has been a major breakthrough. All urban children and a great majority of rural children have attended primary schools, and enrolments in secondary schools and in higher education are large, in proportion to the population, compared with pre-communist days. If "school" is extended to include as well all part-time, part-study education, spare-time education, and the study groups organized by the communes, factories, street organizations, and the army, then there are schools everywhere in China.

China's gains in the medical and public-health fields are perhaps the most impressive of all. The gains are attested to by many fairly recent visitors to China. For example, G. Leslie Wilcox, a Canadian doctor, a few years ago visited medical colleges, hospitals, and research institutes, and reported in "Observations on Medical Practices" (*Bulletin of the Atomic Scientists*, June, 1966) that everywhere he found good equipment, high medical standards, excellent medical care—almost all comparable to Canadian standards. As William Y. Chen, a member of the U.S. Public Health Service, wrote in "Medicine in Public Health" (*Sciences in Communist China*), "the prevention and control of many infectious and parasitic diseases which have ravaged [China] for generations" was a "most startling accomplishment." He noted, too, that "the improvement of general environmental sanitation and the practice of personal hygiene, both in the cities and in the rural areas, were also phenomenal."

While all these gains were being made, the Chinese were devoting an unusually large amount of resources to industrial output. China's industrial production has risen on the average by at least eleven per cent per year since 1950, which is an exceptionally high growth rate for an underdeveloped country. Furthermore, industrial progress is not likely to be retarded in the future by any lack of natural resources, for China is richly endowed and is right now one of the four top producers in the world of coal, iron ore, mercury, tin, tungsten, magnesite, salt, and antimony. In recent years, China has made large gains in the production of coal, iron, steel, chemical fertilizers, and oil. In fact, since the huge discoveries at the Tach'ing oilfield, China is now self-sufficient in oil and has offered to export some to Japan.

From the industrial, agricultural, and other gains, I would estimate that China's real G.N.P. has risen on the average by at least six per cent per year since 1949, or by at least four per cent on a per-capita basis. This may not seem high, but it is a little better than the Soviet Union did over a comparable period (1928–40), much better than England's record during her century of industrialization (1750–1850), when her income per capita grew at one half of one per cent per year, perhaps a bit better than Japan's performance from 1878 to 1936, certainly much superior to France's one per cent record from 1800 to 1870, far better than India's 1.3 per cent growth during 1950 to 1967; more important, it is much superior to the postwar record of almost all underdeveloped countries in the world.

This is a picture of an economy richly endowed in natural resources, but whose people are still very poor, making substantial gains in industrialization, moving ahead more slowly in agriculture, raising education and health levels dramatically, turning out increasing numbers of scientists and engineers, expanding the volume of foreign trade and the variety of products traded, and making startling progress in the development of nuclear weapons. This is a truer picture, I believe, than the bleak one drawn by some of our China experts.

The failure of many economic experts on China to tell the story of her economic development accurately and fully is bad enough. Even worse has been the general failure to deal with China on her own terms, within the framework of her own goals and methods for attaining those goals, or even to recognize the possible validity of those goals. Communist China is certainly not a paradise, but it is now engaged in perhaps the most interesting economic and social experiment ever attempted, in which tremendous efforts are being made to achieve an egalitarian development, an industrial development without dehumanization, one that involves everyone and affects everyone. All these efforts seem not to have affected Western economists, who have proceeded with their income accounts and slide rules, and their free-enterprise values, to measure and judge. One of the most revealing developments in the China field is the growing belief among the economic experts that further research is hardly worthwhile in view of the small amount of economic statistics that have come out of China since 1958. Apparently, it does not matter that seven hundred and seventy-five million people are involved in a gigantic endeavor to change their environment, their economic and social institutions, their standard of living, and themselves; that never before have such potentially important economic and social experiments been carried out; that voluminous discussions of these endeavors by the Maoists are easily available. No, if G.N.P. data are not forthcoming, if numbers can't be added up and adjusted, then the economy must be hardly worth bothering about.

What can be done? Probably not very much until a substantial number of younger economists become interested in China. It is a hopeful sign that many young economists are now breaking away from the stultifying atmosphere of present-day "neo-classical" economics and are trying to refashion the discipline into political economy, as it once was, so as to take account of the actual world and not the world of highly abstract models, scholastic debates, and artificial assumptions—all designed to justify the existing state of things and to accept without question the rather narrow, materialistic goals of capitalist society. This reformulation by the young will have to take place first, but once this task is well along, China is bound to be attractive to many of these "new" economists. Only then will we begin to get a substantial amount of research on China that makes sense.

The research that would make sense is any that takes Maoism seriously as a model of economic development, in terms both of its objectives and of the means employed to attain those objectives. A thoughtful consideration of Maoism means paying proper attention to Marxism-Leninism as well as to the Chinese past of the Maoists. The Marxist-Leninist goal of the communist man within a classless society in which each person works according to his ability and consumes according to his needs—this goal of the Maoists should be taken seriously in any economic analysis of what is now going on.

There is a core of development theory that would probably be accepted by both the capitalist and Maoist sides—that economic growth can be attained by increasing the amounts of labor, capital goods, and land used in production, by improving the quality of these factors of production, by combining them in more efficient ways and inspiring labor to greater efforts, and by taking advantage of economies of scale. Now, Maoism undoubtedly affects every one of these ingredients of economic growth, and often in ways quite different from the capitalist impact. For example, it is likely that Maoist ideology discourages consumption and encourages saving and investment, and so promotes the growth of the capital stock; it does this by preventing the rise of a high-consuming "middle class," by fostering the Maoist virtues of plain and simple living and devoting one's life to helping others rather than accumulating "pots and pans."

As another example, it is possible that Maoist economic development, by deëmphasizing labor specialization and reliance on experts and technicians, reduces the quality of the labor force and so slows the rate of economic growth. On the other hand, as Adam Smith once suggested, labor specialization, while increasing productivity in some narrow sense, is often at the expense of the worker's general intelligence and understanding. It was his view that "the man whose whole life is spent in performing a few simple operations . . . generally becomes as stupid and ignorant as it is possible for a human creature to become." The difference between the most dissimilar of human beings, according to Smith, is not so much the cause of division of labor as it is the effect of it. Consequently, while an economy might gain from the division of labor in some small sense, it could lose in the larger sense by creating men who are little more than passive and unreasoning robots. A major aim of the Maoists is to transform man from this alienated state to a fully aware and participating member of society. The emphasis on "Reds" rather than experts is just one part of this transformation which, it is felt, will release "an atom bomb" of talents and energy and enable labor productivity to take great leaps.

In addition to this argument, which is based on Maoists' interpretation of their own history and experience, it is also possible that the "universal man" in an underdeveloped economy would provide more flexibility to the economy. If most people could perform many jobs moderately well, manual and intellectual, urban and rural, the economy might be more able to cope with sudden and large changes; it could with little loss in efficiency mobilize its labor force for a variety of tasks. Further, since experience in one job carries over to others, a person may be almost as productive, in the job-proficiency sense, in any one of them as he would be if he specialized—a peasant who has spent some months in a factory can more easily repair farm equipment, and so on. Finally, a Maoist economy may generate more useful information than a specialist one and so lead to greater creativity and productivity. When each person is a narrow specialist, communication among such people is not highly meaningful. When, on the other hand, each person has basic knowledge about many lines of activity, the experiences of one person enrich the potentialities of many others.

The point is that this issue—which, I should stress, includes not only labor productivity (that is, the development of material things by human beings) but also the development of human beings themselves—this issue of generalists versus specialists, communist men versus experts, the masses versus bureaucrats, or whatever, is not to be laughed away, as it has been, in effect, by some China experts. How men, in an industrial society, should relate to machines and to each other in seeking happiness and real meaning in their lives has surely been one of the most important problems of the modern age. There is also another basic issue here: whether modern industrial society, capitalist or socialist, does in fact diminish man's essential powers, his capacity for growth in many dimensions, even though it does allocate them "efficiently" and increases his skills as a specialized input. Is man Lockean in nature—reactive to outside forces, adjusting passively to disequilibrium forces from without? Or is he essentially Leibnitzian —the source of acts, active, capable of growth, and having an inner being that is self-propelled? If the latter, how are these powers released?

The Maoists claim that the powers exist and can be released. If they are right, the implications for economic development are so important that it would take blind men on this side of the Pacific to ignore them.

part seven

The Human Cost of Development

econonic development is not a smooth evolutionary process of change. Rather, it is a painful process, which involves breaking up established ways of life and hurting many strongly entrenched vested interests. In the past, development, whether capitalist or socialist, has meant virtually a complete destruction of the old order and its values and institutions, and their replacement with a new ethic based on a belief in the efficacy of economic progress.

In the first reading, Charles Wilber examines the human costs of continued underdevelopment and compares them to the human costs of capitalist and socialist development experience. He also examines the pressures and forces that make the development process a painful one. Wilber concludes that rapid economic growth, while creating and intensifying a whole new set of human costs, is the fastest way to overcome the far worse human costs of continued underdevelopment. The article emphasizes E. H. Carr's observation that the cost of conservation falls just as heavily on the underprivileged as the cost of innovation on those who are deprived of their privileges.

In the second article of this part, Peter Berger argues that both the Brazilian and the Chinese development models are humanly unacceptable because they assume the sacrifice of at least a generation for the achievement of their respective goals. He argues that development policy should avoid the infliction of pain, and where that is impossible, a moral rather than a technical justification is required.

Continued underdevelopment is bringing untold suffering to millions of people. Unfortunately, both capitalist and socialist development have generated new suffering in the process of eliminating the old. The human costs of the development process in Brazil and China have been high indeed. In both the United States and the Soviet Union there has been high human cost accompanying development. The United States has been so interested in money-making and the Soviet Union in catching up that human values often have been sacrificed in the process: genocide of the American Indian, slavery, and sweatshops in the United States; and forced labor, purges, and dictatorship in the Soviet Union attest to this depressing conclusion.

In the final reading of this section, Denis Goulet argues that "liberation" must supplement "development" if the poor countries are not to escape the human costs of continued underdevelopment merely to succumb to the human

348

costs of the development process. The hope that Goulet holds out is that the poor countries, while eliminating the sufferings of underdevelopment as rapidly as possible, will draw upon the best from capitalist and socialist experience and combine it with their own uniqueness to produce a new liberated and humanistic civilization.

24

The Human Costs of Underdevelopment

Charles K. Wilber

THE COST OF UNDERDEVELOPMENT

It has sometimes been argued that, because of the tremendous social cost of economic development, industrialization should not be attempted. Rather, increased welfare through heightened agricultural efficiency should be aimed for; or industrialization, if followed, should proceed very slowly. Some would disagree that what is needed is *rapid* economic development. They ask why the hurry—why this "obsession" with economic growth?

While it is true that social change and industrialization have always entailed a high price, the price of underdevelopment is also very high. Professor E. H. Carr has remarked that "the cost of conservation falls just as heavily on the underprivileged as the cost of innovation on those who are deprived of their privileges."[1] The cost of underdevelopment is high indeed; chronic disease, hunger, famine, premature death, and degradation of the human spirit which lasts not for a few years, but century after century. For example, it is estimated that prior to 1949, 50 per cent of Chinese mortality was directly or indirectly caused by chronic malnutrition, and some 4 million persons died every year as a result of contamination by human excrement.[2] And the Chinese suffered 1,829 famines during the last 2,000 years—an average of almost a famine a year.[3] Famine in China extending from 1876 to 1879 is believed to have caused 9 million deaths, and a famine in China's Hunan Province in 1929 led to 2 million fatalities.[4] As another example, ten major famines in India between 1860 and 1900 resulted in 15 million deaths.[5] The 1918 influenza epidemic killed between 15 and 20 million Indians; as recently as the winter of 1942–43, the bodies of the famished littered the streets of Calcutta so profusely that their mere removal became impossible.[6] In the days of the Tsars, Russia was known throughout the world as the country of the great famines, and as late as the middle of the nineteenth century, Western Europe was still subject to frequent famines.[7] These are just a few examples of the cost of underdevelopment.

Table 1 brings together three indicators of the human cost of underdevelopment. As an example, of the estimated 22 million children born each year in the Group VI countries, approximately 4 million die before they reach their first birthday. If these countries had the infant mortality

Table 1 The Human Costs of Underdevelopment

Countries grouped by national income per capita	Infant mortality rate (average 1955–58)	Life expectancy (average 1955–58)	Caloric intake per capita (1960–62)
Group I: $1,000 and more	24.9	70.6	3,153
Group II: $575 to $1,000	41.9	67.7	2,944
Group III: $350 to $575	56.8	65.4	2,920
Group IV: $200 to $350	97.2	57.4	2,510
Group V: $100 to $200	131.1	50.0	2,240
Group VI: Less than $100	180.0	41.7	2,070

Source: United Nations, *The Economic Development of Latin America in the Post-War Period* (New York: United Nations, 1964), p. 62.

rate of Group 1 countries then the mortality of infants would be approximately 0.5 million. This means that because of underdevelopment, 3.5 million infants die *each year* in the Group VI countries.

The "mathematics of suffering" may be morbid, but it does give perspective to the human costs of economic underdevelopment. Professor Holzman faces the problem of human cost squarely. His consideration of the problem is worth quoting at length.

Let us turn now to the case of the nation caught in the "Malthusian trap," nations in which: (1) there has been no increase in the standard of living for centuries—perhaps there has even been a decline, (2) increases in output lead to a corresponding fall in the death rate so that no change in the standard of living occurs, i.e., those who live remain at subsistence, (3) the death rate is so high relative to the death rate in nations which have experienced secular economic progress that it is fair to say the inability to escape the "Malthusian trap" is responsible for the (premature) death of most of those born, and finally (4) escape from the "trap" requires a rate of investment so high that increases in productivity outrun increases in population. With such nations the case for a high rate of investment for a long period of time (one which enables the nation to escape the "trap") becomes much easier to justify and value judgments easier to make. The essential distinction between this case and that of the progressive economy is that loss of life can no longer be considered an "absolute," i.e., an infinite disutility. It was reasonable to consider it in this way in a progressive economy because loss of life is not comparable by any measure, with other changes in the level of individual welfare. In the case of the "Malthusian trap" nation, however, one is put in the position of having to compare losses of life between periods. That is to say, failure to attempt to escape the "trap" may be considered equivalent to condemning to death, needlessly, members of future generations. Under these circumstances, loss of life would seem to become a legitimate and measurable datum of the system. The question facing the planner is: shall we raise the rate of investment in the present to a point high enough to escape the "trap" even though this will involve a rise in the death rate of the present generation if we know that it will increase the life expectancy and raise the standard of

living of countless future generations? No matter what his decision, the
planner faced with such a question is responsible for imposing the death
sentence on someone. When life and death are compared on this plane,
escape from the trap might well seem to be the superior alternative since
by simple addition it becomes obvious that more lives would be saved than
lost in the process.[8]

Most of the peoples of the world exist in conditions of poverty which
are difficult for the affluent West to understand. And the effect on the dignity of the individual, the degradation of his very being, cannot be
measured.[9]

HUMAN COSTS AND ECONOMIC DEVELOPMENT PROGRAMS

There is no doubt that the human cost of economic development in the
past has been very high. However, the important question for the purposes
of this study is whether or not these costs are an inherent part of the
industrialization process. We might analyze the Soviet example in an attempt to answer this question. A good case can be made for the position
that not all of these costs are inherent, but instead are due to specific historical circumstances and mistakes.[10] Still others were due to the totalitarian nature of Stalinist communism and thus need not be repeated.[11]

A portion of the social cost in the Soviet Union can be attributed to the
extraordinary speed of industrialization which was necessitated by the fear
(real or imagined) of foreign attack. Professor Gerschenkron has pointed
out that:

> Much of what happened at the turn of the third and fourth decades of
> the century was the product of that specific historical moment. . . . It
> must not be forgotten that the smashing defeat of the country by Germany
> stood at the very cradle of the Soviet regime. Foreign intervention in the
> Civil War, however half-hearted, certainly left memories that were long in
> fading . . . after Hitler's advent to power . . . the threat of a military at-
> tack began to loom larger and larger each year. There is very little doubt
> that . . . Russian industrialization in the Soviet period was a function of
> the country's foreign and military policies.[12]

The adverse impact on the people of this rapid tempo of industrialization
was increased by the sharp decline in the international terms-of-trade
which required larger agricultural exports to obtain the same amount of
capital imports. In addition, Professor Gerschenkron points out that the
Soviets' willingness to push rapidly ahead in spite of the social costs
incurred was conditioned by the historical acceptance of force in Russia.

. . .

The major cause of the famine in the early 1930's was the massive destruction of livestock that occurred at the beginning of the collectivization
drive. This was caused by the attempt to collectivize all of the peasants'
livestock. Rather than acquiesce, the peasants slaughtered and ate their
livestock. The decision to collectivize livestock was probably the single
most important mistake made in the Soviet Union during the 1930's. The

communist countries that began collectivization later did not repeat this mistake. The eastern European countries collectivized at a much slower rate and even stopped temporarily when resistance became strong.[13] In China, "the principal domestic animal, the pig, was left in private hands . . . the Chinese were able to avoid mass slaughter of livestock and famine in carrying through full-scale collectivization."[14]

In conclusion, while the social costs incurred in the industrialization of the Soviet Union need not be repeated in the same degree by an underdeveloped country adopting the Soviet model or some part thereof, some social costs seem almost inevitable regardless of what development model is followed.

There are a number of reasons why the industrialization process is not a painless one. First, there is the need in many countries for a radical change in social structure. In many cases this can be brought about only by a more or less violent social revolution. The old order will fight to maintain its dominance and the new will defend itself against possible counterrevolution. And the period of revolution is not restricted to just the time of open civil war (if there is one) but extends until the inhibiting features of the old social structure are eradicated. The American Civil War officially ended in 1865 but the social revolution that engendered it goes on today in the battles of Little Rock, Birmingham, Watts, Detroit, and Washington, D.C. The collectivization battles of the 1930's were a continuation of the Russian Revolution of 1917.

Second, and closely allied to the first, is the need to develop new social institutions and to educate people to new habits and values. Peasants must be turned into factory workers. A new kind of discipline must be learned. People must be convinced that new ways of doing things can be good and beneficial. This is often not easy. The Luddites rose up and smashed the new machinery in the British Industrial Revolution. The Russian peasant tried to sabotage the introduction of the kolkhoz. The type of labor discipline that is required in an industrial society is alien to the habits of a pre-industrial society. It is difficult to convince people of the need for new habits and discipline exclusively by methods of persuasion. It is not so much that the need for discipline and change is not understood; but as often happens, what is understood is not yet sufficiently willed. Thus, the change-over from one set of habits and values to another is difficult, and some compulsion is often required. This compulsion took the form of the *explicit coercion* of the state police power to expedite the movement from individual to collective farms and to enforce factory discipline in the Soviet Union of the 1930's. In capitalist countries the implicit coercion of the market mechanism transferred labor from rural to urban areas and imposed discipline through the threat of starvation and unemployment.

Third is the need to increase the rate of capital accumulation. This involves widening the margin between consumption and total output. Despite the fact that consumption levels are already deplorably low in underdeveloped countries, it is most unlikely that they can be substantially raised in the early stages of development. "Often it is argued that (the) more human approach is what distinguished economic development under democratic conditions from what would take place under a Communist regime—in my opinion a rather dangerous assertion if, realistically, living standards will have to be kept low in order to allow development."[15] This need to restrain consumption in favor of capital accumulation can cause a rise in social discontent. The poorer classes will feel that after fighting for the recent revolution, and/or reforms, they are entitled to its fruits. The middle classes and the upper classes will resent the curtailment of their former privileges and "luxury" consumption. To keep this unrest from upsetting the development plans or from leading to counterrevolution a powerful, even ruthless, government policy of coercion may be needed. This, while enabling capital to be accumulated, will increase the social cost of doing so. It is wrong to envision economic development as a smooth evolutionary process of change since ". . . the happy picture of a quiet industrial revolution proceeding without undue stir and thrust has been . . . seldom reproduced in historical reality."[16] The changes necessary to initiate economic development are more likely to resemble a gigantic social and political earthquake.

. . .

CONCLUSION

From the discussion in this paper we can draw a number of conclusions. The social cost of development in the Soviet Union was high indeed—purges, Stalinist terror, forced labor, famine, and lack of freedom. The cost of capitalist development was high also—slavery, colonialism, genocide of native races, and lack of freedom. The extent of a cause and effect relationship is probably impossible to establish. It would seem, however, that particular historical circumstances, rather than the development process itself, account for the major share of the human costs. The human cost of either capitalist or communist development appears less than the cost of continued underdevelopment. Still, some social cost seems inevitable if economic development is to take place.

Given the inevitability of some social cost, how does one evaluate the acceptability of this cost relative to the potential benefits of economic development? Seeking refuge in some predetermined ideological position doesn't solve the problem because as Richard Ohmann has pointed out:

> A man who subscribes to a moral or social ideology runs the risk that someone will put it into practice and thereby burden it with a wretched freight of human error and venality. The guillotine becomes an argument against libertarianism, juvenile gang wars an argument against permissive parenthood, the carpetbaggers an argument against emancipation. When this happens, the ideologist may recant; or he may save his ideology by disowning the malpractice as irrelevant perversion. A third response is possible: to accept *la guillotine* along with *la liberte;* but in a man of good will, this requires a strong stomach and a certain obstinacy.[17]

None of these responses seems adequate to the problem. Possibly there is no adequate answer since our normal moral standards are so ambiguous.

However, the problem at least can be made clearer by briefly discussing two factors that affect moral judgments.

First, there are the "objective conditions controlling the environment in which behavior takes place."[18] An example of this would be a state of war. Restrictions of civil liberties, for example, are usually judged more acceptable in wartime than in time of peace. Economic development is also an objective condition. The prevailing objective conditions will help determine what is acceptable behavior on the part of the state and of individuals. This may be an ambiguous standard but it seems to be accepted by most people. For example, Professor Bowles has pointed out that ". . . the death of a political enemy on a battlefield is approved, the domestic execution of a political prisoner is disapproved."[19]

Second, there is the "ideology affecting the norms by which man evaluates such behavior."[20] In the example cited above, a state of war is an objective condition, while the historical tradition and system of beliefs which shape people's attitudes about civil liberties comprise the ideology or value system. Obviously the two factors interact. The objective conditions can alter the ideological commitments. For example, given the situation of ruthless guerrilla warfare in South Vietnam, many Americans become willing to view torture and napalm bombing of peasant villages as acceptable conduct. Even with roughly similar objective conditions, a value system can yield different judgments of identical actions. For example, in the aftermath of the Cuban revolution the execution of a few thousand Batista supporters was condemned by many Americans. The shooting of several hundred thousand Communists in the recent Indonesian revolution was received, if not with approval, at least with tolerance. Also, at least until recently, a government which did not allow white people to vote would be judged a dictatorship, while one that only disenfranchised colored people could be considered a democracy. In addition, of course, different value systems will judge the same actions or behavior differently. Raising the price of a good to take advantage of a temporary scarcity in its supply would have been condemned as a sin by Medieval Catholicism; in a capitalist society it would be considered good business practice.

The above discussion highlights the complexity of the problem of evaluating the social costs of economic development. Man seems to be faced with a dilemma. On the one hand, the failure to overcome underdevelopment *allows* untold human suffering to continue. On the other hand, the process of overcoming these human costs through speeding up development will most likely *generate* some new ones; and the faster the old human costs are overcome the more severe the new. Also, there is the danger that the centralized power needed to generate rapid development will be used, as with Stalin, to consolidate personal power and establish totalitarianism.

Let me close this discussion by quoting a comment received from a close colleague, Professor W. Michael Bailey, after he had read the paper.

> It seems most ironic that to be FREE (from want and privation) man must be made a SLAVE to some political and economic gyroscope that spins off goods in abundance while grinding away at moral freedom and the possibility of real human choices. In a sense your paper is the most immoral thing of all because it portrays so clearly the necessity for evil and provides

the perfect motive for doing for good reasons what so many want to do for the sheer pleasure of it and for the terrible beauty of the awesome power machine that man can make. False gods beckon on every side; only a few see God within the shadows, faint like a mist but more real than man's most titanic creations, as good is.

NOTES

1. E. H. Carr, *What is History?* (New York: Alfred A. Knopf, 1962), p. 102.
2. See Josué de Castro, *The Geography of Hunger* (Boston: Little, Brown and Co., 1952), pp. 29, 151.
3. *Ibid.*, p. 29.
4. *Colliers Encyclopedia*, 1962, Vol. 9, p. 552.
5. *Ibid.*
6. Castro, *op. cit.*, p. 177. Except for American grain shipments, there would probably have been famine in India during 1966–68.
7. *Ibid.*, p. 277. *Colliers Encyclopedia*, p. 552.
8. Franklyn Holzman, "Consumer Sovereignty and the Rate of Economic Development," *Economia Internazionale*, Vol. XI, No. 2 (1956), pp. 15–16.
9. For illuminating views on the effect of poverty on the human spirit see Carolina Maria de Jesus, *Child of the Dark* (New York: E. P. Dutton & Co., 1962), and Oscar Lewis, *The Children of Sanchez* (New York: Random House, 1961).
10. Professor Swianiewicz, however, argues that the rapid tempo of development adopted in the Soviet model necessarily causes a demand for labor that can be met at reasonable cost only through forced labor. See Swianiewicz, *Forced Labour and Economic Development* (London: Oxford University Press, 1965), pp. 189–207. However, this would be profitable only if the difference in consumption between free and forced labor exceeded the difference in output between the two kinds of labor. See Swianiewicz, pp. 25–40.
11. For an interesting discussion of this point see Alec Nove, "Was Stalin Really Necessary?" in his *Economic Rationality and Soviet Politics* (New York: Praeger, 1964), pp. 17–39.
12. Alexander Gerschenkron, *Economic Backwardness in Historical Perspective* (New York: Praeger, 1965), pp. 147–148.
13. The percentage of cows in the private sector in 1964 was 90 per cent in Poland, 47 per cent in East Germany, 22 per cent in Czechoslovakia, 57 per cent in Hungary, 62 per cent in Rumania, 35 per cent in Bulgaria, and 95 per cent in Yugoslavia. U.S. Department of Agriculture, *The U.S.S.R. and Eastern Europe Agricultural Situation* (Washington: Government Printing Office, 1966), p. 60.
14. Alec Nove, "Collectivization of Agriculture in Russia and China," *Symposium on Economic and Social Problems of the Far East*, ed. E. F. Szcpanik (Hong Kong: Hong Kong University Press, 1962), p. 19.
15. Gunnar Myrdal, *An International Economy* (New York: Harper & Brothers, 1956), p. 164.
16. Gerschenkron, *op. cit.*, p. 213.
17. Richard Ohmann, "GBS on the U.S.S.R." *The Commonweal* (July 24, 1964), p. 519.
18. Karl de Schweinitz, "Economic Growth, Coercion, and Freedom," *World Politics*, Vol. IX, No. 2 (January 1957), p. 168.
19. W. Donald Bowles, "Soviet Russia as a Model for Underdeveloped Areas," *World Politics*, Vol. XIV, No. 3 (April 1962), p. 502.
20. De Schweinitz, *op. cit.*, p. 168.

25

Policy and the Calculus of Pain

Peter L. Berger

The history of mankind is a history of pain. The pain inflicted by nature usually appears in the historical records only in its most spectacular manifestations, as in the most terrible famines, epidemics, or earthquakes. But the pain inflicted by men on each other is the indispensable raw material of the historian's reconstructions. Looking backward from the vantage point of the present, history appears as an endless series of massacres. The farther back these massacres lie in the past, the easier it is to overlook the human anguish they represent, especially if they are connected with what now appear to have been great turning points in history. Historians are very good at burying the trivia of individual suffering in the alleged magnalia (to borrow Cotton Mather's term) of the course of events. Philosophers of history have raised this trick of inattention to the level of an essential tool of their trade. When overlooking the pain becomes difficult, they provide its legitimations. The usual formula for the latter goes something like this: "Event X brought great suffering to many who had to live through it, but it was a good thing after all, because it led to event Y"—which event Y then usually turns out to be something from which the philosopher and his contemporaries now benefit. As Jacob Burckhardt pointed out (in his *Reflections on History*), this kind of philosophy of history has about the same logic as the farmer who sees proof of providence in the fact that a hailstorm destroyed his neighbor's field but not his own.

All men are vultures in that they live off the agonies of the past. At the foundations of every historical society there are vast piles of corpses, victims of the murderous acts that, directly or indirectly, led to the establishment of that society. There is no getting away from this fact, and there is nothing to be done about it. It is an inevitable burden of the human condition. But some men are vultures in a more active sense. They produce additional piles of corpses by their own actions. And they themselves, or more likely others in their service, produce the legitimations of the massacres even as the latter are taking place, and in some instances beforehand. It is this kind of thinking that is of interest here; it constitutes the ideological nexus between policy and pain.

Analysis of alternative policy options in terms of costs and benefits, of input and output, has become commonplace. Such analysis is typically very technical, and generally borrows its concepts and techniques from

Chapter 5, "Policy and the Calculus of Pain," in *Pyramids of Sacrifice: Political Ethics and Social Change*, by Peter L. Berger, © 1974 by Peter L. Berger, Basic Books, Inc., Publishers, New York. Reprinted by permission of Basic Books and Penguin Books Ltd.

economics, even where noneconomic phenomena are involved. To say that such analysis is technical is ipso facto to say that it is value-free. As was pointed out earlier, it is not the intention here to question the validity of this kind of analysis, or, in principle, its utility. It is of great importance, however, to see its limitations. There should be no objection, on methodological grounds, to the technical and value-free analysis of policy problems. But it must be clear at the same time that policy invariably *also* implies problems of values. Sooner or later, avowedly or covertly, all policy considerations involve choices between values, and all policy decisions are value-charged. What is proposed here, therefore, is a *non*-value-free expansion of costs/benefits analysis.

Most specifically, what is proposed is an input/output calculus of human suffering, aspects of which can be clarified in a technical way, without immediate value judgments. For example, it is possible to calculate quite objectively the relationship between a particular wage policy and the degree of deprivation it will entail for various groups. Or one may objectively describe the contribution of a campaign of terror to the attainment of particular political goals. But even if there is no moral intent in such analyses, any *application* of their results to policy making immediately and irrevocably takes place within a moral frame of reference. This is so even if, and perhaps especially if, the policy makers claim that their actions should be understood in purely technical terms. Therefore, it is proper that the value presuppositions of the following argument be made explicit. They are very simple: *It is presupposed that policy should seek to avoid the infliction of pain. It is further presupposed that, in those cases where policy does involve either the active infliction or the passive acceptance of pain, this fact requires a justification in terms of moral rather than technical necessity.*

Every mode of analysis "slices up" reality in a particular way. Thus a map of the world drawn by someone interested in the distribution of rainfall will look different from a map designed to show the spread of American investments. The calculus proposed here suggests a different way of "slicing up" the sociopolitical realities of the contemporary world, a different way of "mapping" them. In the dichotomy of capitalist and socialist models of development, Brazil and China regularly appear as polar opposites. This allocation, of course, is highly defensible in certain respects: Brazil is today the largest and most dynamic case of capitalist development in the Third World, as China is the most important case of the socialist alternative. What is more, each model has been deemed a success *in its own terms*. The analysis proposed here, though, is precisely geared to question these terms. It suggests that, whatever the dissimilarities, the two cases belong in the *same* category in one crucially important aspect: *Both the Brazilian and the Chinese models assume the sacrifice of at least a generation for the achievement of their respective goals.* A comparison of these two cases will therefore be very useful in elaborating what is meant by the proposed moral amplification of policy analysis.

When the military seized power in Brazil in 1964, it proclaimed the beginning of what it called (and still calls) the Brazilian Revolution.[1] The

immediate aims of the takeover were to prevent what the military per-
ceived as the communist direction of the Goulart government then in office,
to establish political order in the country, and to arrest the galloping rate
of inflation. The long-range goal was the transformation of Brazil from a
poor and backward into a rich and modern country. In 1971, as the military
regime proclaimed its First National Development Plan, it stated as its first
objective "to place Brazil, in a period of one generation, in the category of
developed nations."[2] To attain this objective, the regime has formulated in
considerable detail what is now widely called (by advocates as well as
critics) the "Brazilian model of development."

What are the key features of the model, as defined by those in charge
of it?

The model is explicitly and unabashedly capitalist. It presupposes that
development is best achieved by a capitalist market economy, and both its
economic and political policies are geared to providing a favorable environment for this type of development. Conversely, the model is not only explicitly antisocialist but is opposed to all forms of welfare policy deemed
to hinder capitalist development. The model is defined as avoiding both
"statism" and "denationalization." By "statism" is meant the control of central economic processes by the government; in the ideology of the regime,
"statism" is identified with socialism, and is considered as equivalent to
economic stagnation. By "denationalization" is meant the control of central
economic processes by foreign interests. The ideology of the regime is
emphatically nationalist, and in this respect if not in others it is fully in
accord (at least on the level of rhetoric) with the current polemic against
"dependency" in other Latin American countries. The capitalist development of Brazil is to be, in the long run, under the auspices of what is called
"national enterprise"—that is, it is to be a Brazilian capitalism, controlled
by Brazilians for Brazilian purposes. The opposition to "statism," however,
by no means implies a laissez-faire role played by government. The Brazilian government intervenes very powerfully in all areas of economic activity. Its interventions, however, are understood to be for the protection
and furtherance of a market economy. In addition, the opposition to "denationalization" does not imply a hostility to foreign capital. On the contrary, the regime has created unusually favorable conditions for foreign
investments, which since 1964 have flowed into Brazil in what may accurately be described as an avalanche. But this foreign capital is understood by the regime as an indispensable aid to the furtherance of "national
enterprise." Dependency on foreign economic interests is either denied by
advocates of the model or presented as a temporary phase in the development process.

The key emphasis is on economic growth, as measured in terms of
Gross National Product and per capita productivity. Indeed, the ideology
of the Brazilian model is a textbook instance of what its critics call "de-
velopmentalism" or "growthmanship." For all practical purposes, in the
rhetoric of the regime, economic growth *is* development. Both economic
and social policies are geared to "modernization," understood as the transformation of society in such a way as to facilitate rapid and enduring
economic growth. For example, there is a massive government program of

manpower training, PIPMO, which is viewed as the mobilization of "human resources" for economic growth. Even the educational programs of the government, such as MOBRAL, the vast literacy program, are defined in the same manner. The rationale of almost all government actions is explicitly economic, and the justifications are often stated in terms of technical economics. The "modernization" of the country is to be rapid and is to include the country as a whole. The latter goal is stated in terms of "national integration," meaning the overcoming of regional isolation and the economic rationalization of the continent-size expanse of Brazil. A potent symbol of "national integration" is the construction of the Transamazonic Highway, which, when completed, will link the impoverished Northeast with the pioneering areas of the Amazon Basin, and will link both with the more advanced regions of the south.

Conversely, there is a deemphasis of what may broadly be called the "distributionist" aspects of development. A less polite formulation would be that the model is "antiwelfare." One of the most-quoted dicta among advocates of the model is to the effect that "wealth must be created before it can be distributed." It is acknowledged that the short-term effects of the policies of the regime are increasing polarization of the population in terms of income distribution, and postponement in alleviation of the miseries of the most deprived groups. These effects are understood as being both necessary and temporary. In the long run, according to the ideology, all groups will benefit from the economic growth. An important aspect of this is the anti-inflation program of the government. Its economists concluded early that a rigorous policy of wage controls was essential to combat inflation, and this policy has been adhered to forcefully. The economic technicalities of the policy are complex (a key category is that of "monetary correction," which serves as a guideline to all government interventions in this area), but the practical consequences are quite simple: Severe limitations have been imposed on the economic advancement of large sectors of the population.

It is also acknowledged with considerable candor that such policies are difficult to pursue under conditions of representative democracy in the common Western sense. Brazil since 1964 has been a military dictatorship, only superficially adorned with some of the trappings of representative democracy. Apart from the actual practice of the government, even the new constitution formally gives near-dictatorial powers to the executive in all strategic areas of government. Apologists for the regime routinely deny its terroristic dimensions, but they generally admit its less than democratic character. The justification is the maintenance of political stability, which in turn is deemed essential for economic development. Democracy, like a more equitable distribution of economic benefits, will supposedly come later in the process of development.

The regime claims that it has gone a considerable way toward achievement of the goals set by the model. It has certainly succeeded in reversing the direction in which Brazil was moving under the Goulart administration (however one may wish to designate the same). It has also succeeded in imposing a condition that, in value-free terms, could be described as political stability. All organized opposition to the regime (with the possible exception of segments of the Catholic church) has either been suppressed or domesticated. All politically relevant media of communication are tightly controlled. Unlike the situation in some neighboring countries, there is virtually no guerrilla activity, rural or urban, in Brazil, and it is unlikely that any will develop. The country, in other words, continues to be firmly in the hands of the military government.

This political stability has indeed been utilized to provide a secure environment for the economic policies of the regime. The government claims that it has succeeded in bringing inflation down to a manageable rate. This claim is disputed by its critics (and, incidentally, it is only with regard to inflation that the critics charge that the government's statistics are fraudulent). Nobody disputes that in recent years Brazil has achieved remarkable economic growth. This achievement is what some enthusiastic commentators have called "the Brazilian miracle." In 1965, the year after the military took power, the GNP growth rate was 3.9 percent. The rate increased in an accelerated fashion from year to year. In 1972 it reached 11.3 percent. Between 1964 and 1970 (the year before the First National Development Plan was promulgated) the GNP increased by 52 percent; in the same period industrial production increased by 69 percent. To date there is no indication of a reversal in these trends. *In its own terms*, therefore, the model may be said to have succeeded in at least some of its short-run objectives, and to be well on the way to the long-run ones.

The terms of this assessment are put in question by asking about the costs of the model.[3] Even before such a critique gets to the matter of costs in human suffering, there are serious questions to be asked about the economic "distortions" of the model. The very first question will be: *What* is growing under the present policies? The answer is not clear in all details, but the general trend is clear enough: There has been a heavy expansion of capital-intensive (as against labor-intensive) industry, much of it producing durable consumer goods and much of it financed and/or controlled by foreign interests. The consumer goods produced (automobiles, television sets, refrigerators, and so on) remain unattainable luxuries for the bulk of Brazil's population. In other words, the priorities of production are geared to the consumption of a privileged minority. The role of foreign capital in this economic expansion has created a formidable national debt and has certainly promoted "dependency," at least in the economic sense. But the most important "distortions" have been brought about by the capital-intensive character of this type of industrialization.

If economic growth of such dimensions is tantamount to development, one may expect that its effects will be clearly noticeable in a decrease in unemployment. The opposite has been the case in Brazil. Unemployment has been growing, not decreasing. Thus between the census of 1960 and 1970 the percentage of the labor force in employment declined from 32.3 percent to 31.7 percent—not a dramatic decline, to be sure, but rather different from what one would expect during the unfolding of an economic "miracle." Even more ominously, the proportion of the labor force engaged in *industrial* employment also declined somewhat between the two census years. The import of these statistics may be captured by an image—that of, say, a Japanese-owned factory making sophisticated electronic equipment in the Northeast. Many such factories have been drawn there by a government policy of tax incentives to favor the poorer regions of the country. These incentives are unrelated to employment practices. Such a factory may even be fully automated—and it may import from Japan the few technicians needed to operate the automated plant. Quite apart from the question of whether Brazil really needs more sophisticated electronic equipment, and whether Japanese-owned factories should produce it, the impact of such a factory on its immediate social environment may be exactly zero. The image is that of a gleaming modern plant, with a few foreign technicians watching over an automated production process, turning out goods for which nobody in the area has the slightest use—and all this, very likely, in a community in which there is massive unemployment and unrelieved human misery.

The polarization of the population also appears quite clearly in the government's own statistics. Thus between the 1960 and 1970 censuses there has been a decrease in the share of the lowest strata of the population in total national income. Again, the decrease has not been dramatic; but, again, the notion of a development "miracle" would make one expect a change for the better rather than for the worse. In 1970 one-third of the total national income was in the hands of 5 percent of the population; in the same year, the poorest 40 percent received 10 percent of the income. But this is not yet the worst of the tale told by these statistics. The economic condition of the poor has not only declined relative to that of the more privileged strata (declined, that is, in "distributionist" terms), but it has declined *absolutely*. This result is attributable to a combination of inflation and the wage policy designed to combat inflation. Thus, between 1960 and 1970 the real minimum salary is estimated to have *declined* by about 30 percent. These are national figures; in some regions the decline may have been even greater. To understand the significance of a 30 percent decline in wage income, one must be aware of what these wages actually are. Thus, in 1968, 50 percent of the population had an annual per capita income of one hundred and twenty dollars—or thirty-five cents a day! Put simply: In populations living very close to the subsistence margin, even a slight decline in income may spell disaster; a decline of 30 percent, although drawn out over a ten-year period, may spell the difference between survival and starvation. And even if one allows every argument put forth by advocates of the model in justification of these facts (such as the argument that more recent statistics are more reliable and therefore not strictly comparable with earlier ones, so that the deterioration may be less than it seems, or the argument that wage income figures have little significance in certain rural settings), a clear conclusion emerges: For a large portion of the Brazilian people the alleged economic "miracle" has meant not less but more misery.

The overall picture that emerges is that of two nations, one relatively affluent, the other in various degrees of misery. Such a state of affairs, of course, exists in many countries of the Third World. The sheer size of Brazil, however, with its enormous territory and its population of about one hundred million, makes for a particular situation. Using reasonable criteria of differentiation, one may divide this population into about fifteen million in the sector of affluence and eighty-five million in the sector of misery. To see the economic import of these figures, one must focus on the fact that fifteen million is a very large number of people—indeed, it is the population of quite a few important countries with advanced industrial economies. As one commentator put it, Brazil is a Sweden superimposed upon an Indonesia. This "Sweden," though, can generate an intensive economic dynamic of its own, by and for itself—without having any great effect on the "Indonesia." More specifically, the "Sweden" constitutes a sizable domestic market for consumer goods such as automobiles, television sets, or even air-conditioning units, thus permitting economically profitable production of these commodities. This is a feature of the Brazilian situation that is absent in most Third World countries, where the domestic market is simply too small for this type of industrialization to be profitable. In this way, the very size of Brazil contributes an additional dimension to the process of polarization. It also contributes a seeming plausibility to the rhetoric of the regime: With a little luck, a visitor may travel all over the country and see nothing but "Sweden," with some bits of "Indonesia" either being absorbed into the former or serving as a colorful backdrop for it.

This is the dry stuff of economics. Behind it lies a world of human pain. For a very large segment of the population, life continues to be a grim daily struggle for physical survival. There are, of course, regional differences, with conditions in the Northeast being the worst in the country.[4] Millions of people in Brazil are severely undernourished, and some are literally starving to death. Millions of people in Brazil are afflicted with diseases directly related to malnutrition and lack of elementary public hygiene, and are abandoned to these diseases with little or no medical care. As always, it is the children among whom these conditions take their greatest toll. There are areas in the Northeast where about a third of all children die before they reach the age of three and in which life expectancy at birth is in the thirties (it is now in the seventies in Western industrial countries). It is on *these* realities that one must focus in relation to the economic data on unemployment, income distribution, and so on. The crucial fact is: *These are realities that kill human beings.* The word "kill" here does not have the metaphorical sense that it may have when people speak of underprivilege in the advanced societies—the sense of anomie, of wasted lives, of killing the spirit—but rather the most literal sense of *physical dying* and *physical death.* Needless to say, there is always the additional dimension of psychic suffering.

If only for reasons of comparison, it is tempting to try and arrive at a "body count" of all these victims. With some arithmetic on the demographic and economic data, it would be possible to arrive at a reasonable estimate. This is not the place for such an exercise. Suffice it to say that over, for example, a twenty-year period (as between the 1950 and 1970 Brazilian censuses) there would be a toll of several million human beings who, by the humane criteria of Western civilization, could be said to have died "prematurely" and "unnecessarily"—the first adverb referring to a comparison with even the poorest in an advanced industrial society, the second to a consideration of who could have been saved by various policies of public welfare. Put simply: Millions of human beings have died because Brazilian society is what it is. It is also useful to recall that a large percentage of these victims are children; the human costs of this situation are literally a "massacre of the innocent."

One point should be clarified in this connection: Opponents of the Brazilian model often couch their criticisms in terms of a comparison between the present situation and an ideal of egalitarian distribution. In other words, they criticize the status quo because of the large gap between the incomes of the higher and the lower strata. The question of just what is to be considered equity in income distribution is interesting, but it is *not* the burden of the present critique. It is not an abstract "lack of equality" that is at issue here, but the particular inequality between affluence and hunger. Put differently: The present critique of the Brazilian model is not that it is insufficiently egalitarian, but that it condones the starvation of children as an acceptable price for economic growth. The critique further assumes that a rejection of this price, through social policies that attack misery, is not necessarily tantamount to a program of radically egalitarian income redistribution.

When the Brazilian regime is discussed abroad, conversation usually centers on its terroristic character. There can be no question about the latter.[5] Since 1964, with varying periods of intensity, the Brazilian government has suppressed its opponents by terroristic means. The protection of civil rights and liberties has been inoperative in cases involving "national security," which has become an area of arbitrary force by the police apparatus of the regime. The independence and jurisdiction of the courts has been systematically undermined in this area. Large numbers of people have been illegally arrested and imprisoned for political offenses (real or suspected). There have been assassinations of political opponents of the regime by its security organs and by vigilante groups tolerated if not directly organized by the same organs (such as the "commandos to hunt communists"). Most loathsome of all, there has been systematic use of torture throughout the country, both as a means to extract information and as an instrument of intimidation. The direct application of terror has been linked to a nation-wide network on domestic espionage and censorship of all media of communication. In all of this, a vast police apparatus has been built up, centralized in the security division of the military police. Most of this terror has been directed against middle-class opponents of the regime. On a different level of society, and mostly under the auspices of local rather than national police organs, there has been brutal violence against various elements of the "marginal population" (that is, real or suspected criminal elements in the lower classes). The so-called "death squads" are the most notorious example of this.

There is a connection between the terror and the economic policies of the regime. Execution of the latter, with its aforementioned price of suffering, has certainly been facilitated by the silencing of criticism and the intimidation of all potential rebels. Nor should there be any question about the repulsiveness of these realities. The facts about torture alone (a torture that has been continuous and "systemic," and which cannot therefore be excused as an occasional aberration) would suffice for a moral condemnation of the regime. Nevertheless, in the preceding critique of the Brazilian model the emphasis has been placed elsewhere—namely, on the human costs of the economic policies of the model rather than on its political "support structure." The reason for this is simple: Victims of the former have been vastly more numerous than victims of the latter. It is estimated that between 1964 and 1972 (when Amnesty International published its report on the matter) about two thousand individuals were tortured. During the same period the number of assassinations by police organs and vigilante groups was probably in the hundreds. In 1973 it was estimated that there were about twenty thousand political prisoners in Brazil. These numbers in no way offer a moral justification of the terror, nor do they mitigate in the least the horror of any single instance. Nevertheless, in any assessment of the human costs of the Brazilian model it is the other realities of massive misery, involving millions of victims, that must take precedence.

How does the regime legitimate the human costs of its economic program? Needless to say, no advocate of the program would state its costs in the manner utilized here. However, unlike its position on the political terror (a position of simple denial), the regime's handling of the aforementioned economic realities has been remarkably candid. For a dictatorship, it has produced unusually honest economic statistics. Even the regime's critics have admitted this and indeed used official government statistics in their own arguments. Perhaps some of this can be explained by lack of efficiency in the censorship apparatus; the First National Development Plan proclaimed that its objectives were to be achieved "in accordance with the Brazilian natural character," and this at least potentially humanizing quality may have had certain influences even on the organs of oppression. All the same, the candor with which leading spokesmen and apologists of the regime have spoken about the inequities of the present situation is sometimes startling. Even the president, Emilio Médici, has been quoted as saying on one occasion that "the economy is doing very well; the people, not."

More than Latin insouciance or inefficiency lies behind this candor. There is a well-articulated legitimation, which essentially boils down to a single proposition: *The present inequities are a necessary and temporary stage in the process of development.* Both the necessity and the temporary character of the inequities are formulated in terms of economic theory. A term often heard in Brazil is that of "Gini's Coefficient," which refers to a measurement of income distribution produced decades ago by an Italian economist. Hardly heard outside technical discussions by economists in other countries, the term falls frequently from the lips of Brazilian bureaucrats and businessmen, who, one suspects, would not know a coefficient if they saw one. Whatever may have been Gini's own views, the way they are used in the ideology of the Brazilian regime is as follows: Economic growth inevitably produces sharp inequality in income distribution in the early stages. If this entails misery in the lower income groups, that too is inevitable. In the later stages of the process the misery will be alleviated and the distribution of economic benefits will also become more equitable. The important point is that all of this is understood to be the result of strictly economic mechanisms, functioning autonomously, without political interference. Indeed, any such interference with the strictly economic dynamic can only have deleterious results, inhibiting economic growth and thus postponing if not preventing the eventual alleviation of misery. The function of government in all of this is to facilitate economic growth, not to hinder it by misguided humanitarian interventions. European and North American economic history is supposed to illustrate the correctness of this view, but the stages of economic growth are assumed to be the same everywhere.

Delfim Neto, the economics professor who became minister of finance under the military regime and, for a while at least, virtual tsar of its economic policies, has taken this position frequently and forcefully. Assuming belief in this economic theory, a moral justification can be formulated quite readily: True, many people in Brazil today are suffering. True the government is doing less than it could to alleviate this suffering. But the government policies are designed to elevate Brazil to the status of a fully developed society by the end of this century. When this goal has been achieved, there will be a sharp and general alleviation of misery. In other words, the suffering of this generation will contribute directly to the happiness of the next. In elementary human terms, parents are made to sacrifice themselves for the future of their children.

The Brazilian regime has had a bad press in the Western world. Thus there are few intellectuals who accept this line of reasoning, except perhaps some hard-nosed economics professors whose opinions were unscathed by the turmoil of the 1960s. But the regime has its "fellow-travelers" in other groups, notably in business and government circles in the United States. Both in Brazil and outside it one may meet Americans from these groups who reiterate the preceding legitimations with unrestrained enthusiasm. Some of them will react with irritation and aggressiveness to any expression of doubt about the intellectual presuppositions of this point of view. "Everyone in Brazil is very happy with the regime, except for a handful of leftist agitators and terrorists," said a State Department official in Washington (who also denied that there was any "repression" by the Brazilian government—except against people who, he opined, fully deserved it). "The Brazilians have nothing to apologize for," replied a colleague of his in Brasilia when asked about the legitimations of the model (he misunderstood the term "legitimations," but his own feelings about the matter were clear enough). Indeed, among some American businessmen there has emerged what could be called a Brazilian "zionism": Brazil is now the Promised Land of capitalist development and perhaps even the last best hope of the Free World. As to the "marginals" who are not immediately sharing in the bonanza of the "Brazilian miracle"—well, those people have never had it any better, they are not like us, and in any case their children will be grateful for what is happening now. Who knows—perhaps it feels different to be hungry in Recife than it would in New York. As another American admirer of Brazil put it: "One must remember that these people have a different attitude to suffering than we do. They have been used to it all their lives."

China, like Brazil, is a country of continental vastness. China, like Brazil, is going through a process of national transformation that has been held up as a model for other countries. Unlike Brazil, what is taking place in China comes after a decades-long convulsion of bloody war with outside forces and internal civil war. Unlike Brazil (which is ruled by a dictatorship but which cannot be called totalitarian), the present Chinese regime has established what is probably the most pervasive totalitarianism of the twentieth century and perhaps of human history. While the Brazilian regime has engaged in terror against selected opponents, the Chinese regime has imposed upon its subject population a terroristic system of apocalyptic dimensions.

Since 1949, when the Communists achieved victory in the civil war on the mainland, this terror has swept across China in a series of cataclysms. Periodically, one wave of terror was followed by a period of relative relaxation, which in turn would be followed by a new terroristic campaign. This flood and ebb can be explained in part by the changing exigencies faced by the regime, and in part by Mao Tse-tung's belief in the necessity of "protracted struggle," a consciously anti-Confucian view of historical progress through conflict and disharmony. While the intensity of terror varied greatly at different times since the "liberation" of 1949, its availability and constant threat has remained a permanent feature of the regime. As the terror went through its periods of high and low tide, the numbers of its victims went through similar variations. In terms of physical destruction of human lives, the worst period came shortly after the establishment of the regime, from about 1950 to 1955.[6]

At least partly out of accordance with Maoist ideology, major new policy steps of the regime have been introduced in campaigns given the appearance of "movements." Some of these campaigns sought to mobilize the population for positive goals, others to destroy opposition and instill terror. Usually the two aims have been conjoined.

The first of these great campaigns was the Land Reform Movement, 1950–1952. It was inaugurated to redistribute land ownership to the poorer peasants and to liquidate the "landlord" class. Teams of party agitators appeared in virtually every village throughout China, "classifying" the population and then whipping up those groups classified as properly proletarian against those designated as "landlords" and "rich peasants." The culmination of most of these visitations were so-called "struggle meetings," at which selected members of the enemy class were accused of various crimes before large assemblies, condemned by "the masses," and executed either on the spot or soon thereafter. Reliable estimates give the total of two million executions during this two-year campaign. It seems plausible that this first phase of the terror had widespread support among the bulk of the peasantry, who had strong interests in the land redistribution provided by the reform law. There is every reason to believe that the peasants thought this redistribution to be the culmination of the revolution; the Communists, of course, only saw it as the first step in the revolutionary process of collectivization. Following the example of the Soviet Union, the Chinese regime expropriated the new owners in the second step of the process, transferring the redistributed land from private ownership to collectivist "cooperatives." The main difference from the Soviet model was the speed with which the regime passed from step one to step two. The first redistribution was completed in 1952; "cooperativization" took place in 1955. At this second point the regime encountered much broader peasant opposition, as it did again in 1958, when it tried to force the new cooperatives into gigantic communes during the Great Leap Forward.

Different campaigns had different target groups and policy implications. The Suppression of Counter-Revolutionaries Movement, 1951, was directed against all possible sources of political opposition, including old supporters of the Kuomintang and other "bourgeois elements." The standard operating procedure of "struggle teams" and "struggle meetings" was again followed here, as indeed it was in most subsequent campaigns. Compared with the Land Reform Movement there were fewer executions (probably about five hundred thousand throughout China), but there was a vast wave of arrests. In this campaign was inaugurated the "Reform through Labor" program, which has remained a constant feature of the regime ever since and which (again in an adaptation of the Soviet precedent via the Maoist ideological tenet of "learning from the masses" by physical labor) has provided the regime with a large manpower pool of forced labor. It is estimated that between three and four million people were sent to "Reform through Labor" camps by the Suppression of Counter-Revolutionaries Movement, some of them remaining in these camps for many years. There are few data on mortality rates in these camps.

The Resist-America Aid-Korea Movement of 1951, launched after China's entry into the Korean war, was directed against all vestiges of Western cultural influence, especially against Western missionaries and Chinese Christians. The Thought Reform Movement, 1951–1952, was directed against intellectuals. The Three-Anti and Five-Anti Movements, 1952, were directed, respectively, against insufficiently zealous or corrupt cadres in government and party, and against businessmen. They resulted in virtually total destruction of remaining private businesses. The Judicial Reform Movement, 1952, dealt with the legal system and, among other things, abolished lawyers. The Fulfillment of the Marriage Law Movement, 1953, was directed against "reactionary" patterns of family life. It featured bitter "struggle meetings" at which wives and daughters were encouraged to denounce their husbands and fathers, and was marked by a wave of suicides both of men thus denounced and of women who either refused to play their assigned part or regretted it afterward. The Anti-Hu Feng Movement, 1955, began with an official attack on a literary figure by that name, who as far back as 1941 (!) had allowed himself some criticisms of a speech by Mao on literature and the arts. Again, it was directed against intellectuals guilty of inadequate "thought reform." The Elimination of Counter-Revolutionaries Movement, 1955, was once more a broad campaign against all possible opposition elements, opened by a directive by Mao himself ordering that 5 percent of every organization should be purged. The purge was mainly by imprisonment rather than by physical liquidation, though there was still a large number of executions.

The year 1955 marked a certain watershed in the history of the regime's terror campaigns. The largest physical massacres took place before that date. Subsequent campaigns were characterized by at least relatively milder forms of terror—psychological pressures, public humiliations, beatings and occasional torture, and, most important, imprisonment, forced labor, and forced migration. This does not mean that there was no more physical liquidation, but it became less important as an instrument of coercion. The sheer magnitude of the massacres that had already taken place, and the "prophylactic" memory of these in the population at large, were undoubtedly major factors in this shift of emphasis. The Anti-Rightists Movement, 1957–1958, was directed against intellectuals who had been imprudent enough to make use of the brief period of relatively free expression permitted in 1956 after Mao's injunction of "letting a hundred flowers bloom." It was followed by a broader All-Nation Rectification Movement. The Great Leap Forward of 1958 was accompanied by relatively little terror, mainly because resistance to it was general and massive.[7] The dismal collapse of this effort, which resulted in a sharp decline in Mao's own power and the irrational policies of the most zealous Maoists within the regime, led to several years of relaxation.

This was interrupted by the cataclysm of the Great Proletarian Cultural Revolution, 1966–1968, which was unleashed by Mao to break the power of those who "followed the capitalist line" (that is, advocates of pragmatic, rational policies) and to revitalize the revolutionary spirit.[8] Unlike all the previous campaigns, this was a *genuine* struggle during which Mao's Red Guards encountered vigorous and finally successful resistance—first by the entrenched government and party bureaucrats, then by a growing mass of industrial workers, finally and decisively by the regional commands of the People's Liberation Army. As a result, while there was terror by the Red Guards, it involved relatively little physical liquidation of opponents. Most of the victims of the Cultural Revolution (probably somewhat over one hundred thousand) resulted from skirmishes between different factions of Red Guards and their antagonists. In 1969, after the reestablishment of government authority with a very strong military component, there was a measure of terror against "extreme leftists" among the Red Guards themselves, including executions. The demise of the Cultural Revolution, however, was accompanied by a gigantic Transfer to the Countryside Movement, in which millions (one estimate goes as high as twenty million!) of people were deported from the cities to "learn from the peasants," many of them former Red Guards and other "troublemakers." The effects of this continue to this day, as does the system of "May 7 Schools" for the "reeducation" of intellectuals and cadres. The peasant majority of the population was relatively untouched by these convulsions, and in the long run it probably benefited from them.

Western visitors reporting on China in the last few years have repeatedly commented on the differences in everyday social interactions as between today and the pre-1949 period. Whereas before the Communist takeover there was a tumultuous street life, with people pushing, fighting, and laughing, the scene today seems to be one of smooth, quiet cooperation. There is no dirt and there is no noise. Even Seymour Topping, one of the first American correspondents to enter China after the beginning of the current thaw, whose early reports were positively vibrating with awed admiration of everything he saw, remarked that street crowds in Canton seemed "strangely silent and ordered."[9] No wonder! After having lived through the holocausts outlined in the preceding paragraphs, any people would be inclined to cooperate quietly.

Anyone who looks at the record of the Communist regime since 1949 with even a modest intention of objectivity will be impressed by the enormous quantity of human pain directly traceable to the actions of the regime. It is a record of death, anguish, and fear, deliberately inflicted upon the most numerous people on earth. What is the actual number of victims? How many human beings were actually killed? There have been efforts to answer this question with numerical estimates.[10] This is a difficult undertaking, for both intrinsic and extrinsic reasons. It is intrinsically difficult because, in the nature of the case, only indirect evidence is available: The regime, obviously, does not publish yearly statistics on the number of people it killed. Estimates have to be put together by compiling information from the mainland press and from refugees' reports. The analyst of the Chinese terror is thus in the position of someone who tried to estimate the extent of Stalin's atrocities prior to the twentieth party congress or of the Nazis' persecution of the Jews prior to the end of World War II (in both instances, even the most anti-Stalinist and most anti-Nazi observers grossly underestimated the numbers of victims). The difficulty is compounded by the extrinsic fact of the pro-Chinese climate of opinion which, since President Nixon's visit to Peking, now stretches from Washington government circles, through the business community and the liberal news media, to the left-leaning intelligentsia. It appears that even a substantial number of China scholars have become very careful about making pejorative statements about the regime while they are waiting for their visas to the mainland. To ask about the number of Mao's victims in this atmosphere of Sinophile euphoria appears vulgar and inappropriate.

Morally significant questions have appeared vulgar since the days of the Hebrew prophets, and there is good moral reason for disturbing the current American mood about China (which, by the way, need not imply political opposition to the Nixon policy of detente between the two governments). All the same, as in the discussion of the human costs of the Brazilian model, this is not the place to attempt a "body count" of the Communist experiment in China. There can be no doubt, however, that the number of victims, even in the strictest sense of victims of physical liquidation, runs in the millions of human beings. One prominent American expert on China was asked recently to give his estimate of the number of outright executions during the worst period of terror, the years up to 1955. Assured that he would not be quoted by name, he replied: "No more than ten million, no less than five million." (It should be added that this individual is by no means identified as an enemy of the Communist regime and that, at any rate, his recent writing about China has been far from polemical.) Since 1955, there has been much less physical liquidation. But even leaving aside the monumental burden of psychic suffering—millionfold fear, anguish, and sorrow—there is the physical pain inflicted upon those who were hounded by the organized mobs of "enraged masses" in the various mobilization campaigns, and those who were imprisoned, sent to forced-labor camps and "May 7 Schools," or forcibly deported to the countryside. Millions of human beings were affected by these policies. There is no way of telling how many of them died in direct consequence. In this connection one should at least mention the policy of deliberate genocide carried out by the Chinese government in Tibet, after the suppression of the Tibetan revolt of 1959.[11]

Since the end of the Cultural Revolution, it appears that there has been a period of relaxation in China. There have been no mass campaigns of terror and executions. Western observers disagree on who is responsible for the moderations of the regime, even on who is presently in control, and what elements are likely to come to the fore in the future.[12] Yet there is no indication that the regime, despite its recent moderations, has dismantled its system of totalitarian controls (though it has given them new names and, to a degree, new organizational forms). Terror still lurks behind every corner of the road, in vivid memory and as an effective threat, and no one can predict the political vicissitudes that might once more unleash it with full force. Perhaps the weight of human pain to be accounted to Chinese Communism can be summarized as follows: *This regime has succeeded in making one of the liveliest peoples in the world walk the streets without noise and without laughter.*

If these have been the costs, what have been the achievements of the regime? Among Marxists there has been endless discussion as to whether China does or does not represent the purest form of socialism to date. This discussion has little meaning for non-Marxists. Among the latter, the discussion of achievements has centered on economic matters, and there is now a widespread consensus that the economic condition of most Chinese has greatly improved as against the pre-1949 period.

Evaluation of the economic achievements of the regime is also beset with considerable difficulties.[13] Unlike the Brazilian government, the Chinese authorities issue only sparse economic statistics, and issued almost none at all between 1959 and 1969. Much economic information is still regarded as a state secret and anyone who divulges it is severely punished. Outside observers have to compile a picture through the limited data released by Peking (often this involves "reading between the lines"), data on trade with China released by other governments, and the necessarily selective reports of tourists and refugees. There is one generally accepted proposition: The regime has succeeded in eliminating starvation (the last widespread famine was probably in 1959, following the economic fiasco of the Great Leap Forward). All recent reports on China agree that food appears to be plentiful and cheap. To what extent this is due to the socialist policies of the regime is another question: A crucial factor is that the Communists were the first in many decades to establish a strong central government with authority over the entire country, permitting them to take measures against famine that had been impossible for a long time (beginning with such simple things as the operation of a nationwide transportation system). Also, it is clear that a number of socialist policies, inspired by Maoist ideology, had severely detrimental economic effects, especially in the area of agricultural production. It could be logically argued that the economic gains were achieved by the immense diligence and productivity of the Chinese people *despite* the often surrealistic irrationalities of Maoist economic programs. Be this as it may, it is probably correct that most Chinese are better off today, in terms of nutrition and other basic necessities (housing and health are relevant categories), than they were before the Communist takeover. In aggregate amounts, these economic gains are modest. Once more, though, it is important to recall that in a population living close to the subsistence margin (this is so for a larger proportion of Chinese than of Brazilians) even small economic gains or losses can be of decisive importance.

It is virtually certain that the *distribution* of economic benefits is today much more egalitarian than it was before 1949. Except perhaps for the top political leadership secluded in the splendor of the Imperial City, there are few economically privileged groups, and the income gap between occupational categories is probably among the smallest in the world. Put differently, wage scales are highly egalitarian, despite the fact that the extreme egalitarian policies of the hard-line Maoists appear to have been quietly abandoned. Thus "material incentives," which were violently denounced during the Cultural Revolution, seem to have been restored in both industry and agriculture. Private plots, abolished in the communes in 1958, now seem to be generally tolerated and, according to some reports, account for an increasing proportion of agricultural production (in this way, quite possibly, reiterating the Soviet experience).

China is still a very poor country—as, indeed, its leaders keep saying in their desire to legitimate themselves as the vanguard of the Third World. By all conventional criteria China is still an underdeveloped society. Thus the *top* factory wage in 1971 was one hundred eight yuan (forty-two dollars) a month. While food and rents are very cheap, the limitations on consumption imposed by these wage levels become clear when one looks at some prices—for instance, of a wrist watch at one hundred twenty yuan, the cheapest transistor radio at thirty-one yuan, or a pair of leather shoes at seventeen yuan.[14] In view of this, the question of the likely future course of the Chinese economy is important. Again, there is widespread agreement that the future prospects are favorable if nondramatic. Economic growth rates since the early years of the regime have been very modest (since 1952, about 4 percent), but there seems to have been an acceleration since the end of the Cultural Revolution (1968–1971, 8.8 percent). The likelihood is that the Chinese economy will continue on a course of steady advance and that its benefits will be spread around fairly equitably, though no dramatic improvements are in prospect. In view of the fact that China is still overwhelmingly a country of peasants, it is especially important to look at the progress in agricultural production. This has been very modest indeed. It is thought-provoking that, in the period 1952–1967, the agricultural growth rate of China has been *precisely the same* as that of India, at 2.5 percent.[15] Need one recall that, during these years, there was no terror in India, no collectivization, and no "mobilization of the masses" in government-run campaigns? In 1973, at any rate, both China and India had to turn to foreign imports in order to feed their populations.

Whatever may have been the detrimental consequences of some Maoist economic policies, it seems plausible that (by contrast with the case of Brazil) the major human costs of this model must be accounted to the political rather than the economic policies of the Chinese regime, with the terror being the necessary focus of the accounting. How are these costs legitimated by advocates of the Maoist model? The most common response is a denial of the facts. Such denial is routine both with official representatives of the regime (in the now unlikely event that anyone raises the question with them) and with enthusiasts for Maoism (or what they perceive as such) outside China. The denial is commonly linked with a denunciation of all sources that affirm the facts being denied. This does not mean that all acts of official violence are denied, but the *dimensions* of the terror are enormously depreciated and contrary reports are invalidated as being the products of "imperialist propaganda." Whatever portion of the terror is admitted is then legitimated within the overall ideological frame of reference. Most basically: *The human costs exacted by the terror are interpreted as necessary and temporary aspects of the revolutionary process.*

The alleged necessity was continually reiterated during the Cultural Revolution in the following passage from the *Thought of Mao Tse-tung*, which Red Guards were in the habit of chanting in unison during acts of harassment or violence against "revisionists": "A revolution is not a dinner party, or writing an essay, or painting a picture, or doing embroidery; it cannot be so refined, so leisurely and gentle, so temperate, kind, courteous, restrained or magnanimous. A revolution is an insurrection, an act of violence by which one class overthrows another." In other words: To make an omelette, one must break eggs.

The alleged temporary character of these "not so refined" actions is legitimated by way of Marxist doctrine. The revolutionary process passes from establishment of the "dictatorship of the proletariat" through the "transition to socialism" to the millennial event of the "transition to communism." At the last the state will "wither away" and its coercive apparatus be dismantled. Different schools of Marxists disagree as to just where China is to be located on the road to the millennium. Except perhaps for the heady moment in 1958, when the Great Leap Forward was to be the beginning of the last "transition" (a claim, by the way, that impressed the Kremlin in about the same way as the Roman Curia would be impressed by the assertion that Jesus had just returned and was on his way to take over from the pope), even ardent Maoists have conceded that they were still operating this side of the coming of the kingdom. In this premillennial age, then, the coercive power of the state must continue to be used against counterrevolutionaries. The most prudent answer Maoists (as, indeed, other Marxists) can give, when asked when all this ugly business will come to an end, is the same answer given by the Revelation of St. John regarding the return of Jesus: "The Lord cometh *soon!*" So as not to confuse the moral issue, it should be pointed out that the earlier expectation legitimated martyrs while the more recent one legitimates the martyr makers. But in both cases an "adventist" propensity to fix precise dates in the near future has led to confusion and disappointments in the ranks of the faithful.

Unlike Brazil, China has had a very good press abroad, especially in recent years. As David Caute has shown, Western intellectuals have increasingly turned to China as they have become disillusioned with the Soviet Union.[16] These foreign sympathizers relate to the official legitimations of the regime in different ways. Some are self-consciously Maoist, imitating as best as they can, under unfavorable circumstances, the way of life enjoined by "the Great Helmsman" (Jean-Luc Godard has created a monument to this group in his film *La Chinoise*). These people, of course, replicate the official legitimations *in toto*, as their will to believe is total. There are other Western Marxists who do not identify themselves as Maoists but who look to China as an important socialist alternative to what they consider to be the failure of the Soviet exemplar (the Italian group known by the name of its publication, *Il Manifesto*, is a good example). Their legitimations are more complicated than those of the outright Maoists; indeed, it sometimes sounds as if they feel they know better what is *really* going on in China than do the Chinese themselves. Both the first and second groups of sympathizers move within the universe of discourse of Marxist ideology, and thus their interpretations of Chinese events often have a doctrinaire character that has little significance to outsiders (the question of whether China is already poised to make the "transition to communism," or is still laboring over the "transition to socialism," is a case in point). In both groups the legitimation of the human costs of the Chinese experiment ranges between denial of the fact of these costs and assurance that the costs are "necessary and temporary."

The most interesting legitimations come from people who are neither Maoists nor Marxists, but liberals (and, of late, even a few conservatives) who profess appreciation of the regime's alleged accomplishments while disavowing credence in its ideology. Among them are individuals renowned for their political independence and intellectual nonconformity. The recurring phenomenon of the sudden collapse of all critical faculties into a veritable orgy of gullibility, typically on the occasion of a very brief and thoroughly regimented visit to China, merits detailed analysis that cannot be undertaken here. Comments made by James Reston to Eric Sevareid after a trip to China in 1971 may serve as an example. One should read these words very slowly, while keeping in mind the record of blood and tears that was outlined earlier: "I'm a Scotch Calvinist. I believe in redemption of the human spirit and the improvement of man. Maybe it's because I believe that or I want to believe it that I was struck by the tremendous effort to bring out what is best in men, what makes them good, what makes them cooperate with one another and be considerate and not beastly to one another. They are trying that."[17]

Once more, the degree of simple denial of the facts of the Chinese Communist holocaust varies in the third group. Recent American writing on the regime has displayed a deafening silence on the earlier, most bloodthirsty period. Where the "repressive" features of the regime are mentioned, they are typically legitimated in terms of the economic achievements: All this ugly business is, of course, deplorable, and not in accordance with our own values. But the Chinese people have been freed from the threat of starvation, they are increasingly better off, and it seems that most of them are reasonably happy with the situation. Or, in the word used by Kenneth

Galbraith in writing about a visit to China, the present system "works."

Serious questions must be raised about this type of legitimation. As pointed out above, any assessment of the economic achievements of the regime is faced with formidable difficulties. Information is sparse and unreliable. It seems premature, to say the least, to maintain that the system "works," even in strictly economic terms. More weighty is the question of whether the extent to which it "works" can be attributed to the policies and ideology of the regime, or whether it is a case of the stupendous abilities of the Chinese people producing results as soon as they are given half a chance—as in the last few years, when the more grotesque follies of Maoism have been restrained in the economy. As to whether most Chinese are happy with the situation, there is no conceivable way of finding out, least of all by short-term visitors taken through selected places on guided tours. In terms of a *moral* assessment of the Chinese model, however, all the above considerations are off the mark: In order to provide even a rudimentary moral justification of the terror, it would be necessary to show that there is a direct causal relation between it and at least some of the alleged economic achievements. Put simply: Assuming that the Chinese people have more to eat today than they had before 1949, is this fact *in any way* due to the other fact that millions of their number were killed by the regime? Nowhere in the apologetic literature is the question posed in this way. The reason, no doubt, is because the answer is all too clear.

One more observation should be made on that aspect of the legitimation that emphasizes the differences between Western and Chinese values. Admittedly, this point is valid with regard to certain matters. For example, it is safe to say that the overwhelming majority of Chinese peasants have never had an interest in freedom of the press and that therefore they hardly feel deprived by its absence today. It is all the more important to understand the oppressiveness of the regime in terms of *their* values rather than those of Western intellectuals. In the center of the world of Chinese peasants were three values—the family as a social reality, the family as a religious reality (especially in connection with the ancestor cult), and the ownership (actual or aspired-to) of land. The Communists have, as far as they have been able, tried to smash the social reality of the traditional family; the most brutal aspects of this effort have been the alienation of children from their parents, deliberately fostered by agents of the regime, and the forcible separation of families in the policies of forced labor and "reeducation." The Communists have done their best to destroy visible manifestations of the religious life, not only in the Buddhist and other formal organizations, but on the level most important to the peasant, that of the ancestor cult; one of the most cruel measures in this respect has been the destruction of tombs, traditionally placed in the midst of cultivated fields. The treachery of the Communists' policy on land ownership has already been mentioned. From the peasants' point of view, they were first lured into support of the revolution by the promise of land, which was then given to them and taken away again within a span of five years. If, therefore, one has some doubts about the happiness of Chinese peasants in the semimilitarized communes in which they now live, these doubts have nothing to do with Western prejudices or "bourgeois liberties."

The most contemptible aspect of the legitimation that "the Chinese are different from us" pertains to the taking of life. Supposedly, "the Chinese put a different value on human life." The thesis is debatable in terms of historical generalization. The Confucian ethic was preeminently pacific, and the history of Western civilization is not exactly easy to interpret as a record of the respect for human life. The thesis is not debatable at all on the level of individual pain. It hurts as much to die, or to see ones loved ones die, in China as it does in America. Indeed, it hurts as much to be hungry in both of these places as well as in Brazil. Perhaps one should expand the critique of this type of legitimation by pointing out its inconsistency—if human life really means so little in China, why should one *praise* the regime for eliminating hunger? Is it only death by execution, but not death by starvation, that the Chinese "feel differently" about? Perhaps, though, it is enough to express contempt for those who justify the suffering of others by their own allegedly superior sensitivity.

The purpose of this [article] has not been to engage in a detailed discussion of the recent histories of Brazil and China. Rather it has been to highlight the moral calculus that ought to be employed in the assessment of the human costs of different models of social change. Nor has it been the intention to equate the cases of the two countries. In terms of direct "repression" by organs of the state, Brazil compares to China as Switzerland to the empire of Genghis Khan. In terms of the equitable spread of economic gains, on the other hand, China is to Brazil as a kibbutz utopia is to medieval Europe in the heyday of feudalism. If China today can still be understood under the Maoist slogan "Politics takes command," then Brazil should get the slogan "Economics takes command." The difference between the two phrases points to the difference between the two models as well as between the kinds of human costs they exact.

It is all the more interesting to perceive the similarity between official legitimations of these costs. In both cases, what is crucially involved is an alleged certainty about the future course of events, and thus about the consequences of one's own policies. What the alleged course of "Gini's Coefficient" performs in one legitimation, the concept of the "transition to communism" performs in the other. It is true that there are harsh realities to the process under way, the legitimators declare, but these are necessary stages as the process moves toward its goal and will disappear when the goal has been reached: No more misery and no more crass polarization when Brazil will have become a "fully developed society"—no more coercive use of state power when China will have "attained communism." But what if these articles of faith are put in question? For articles of faith they are; there is no way of arriving at them by way of the available empirical evidence. What if they are wrong? Or even, what if one cannot be certain about them? It is at this point that the postulate of ignorance, as elaborated in the preceding chapter, becomes relevant morally. As the postulate is seen as pertinent to both cases, their respective legitimations collapse. What remains is a mass of human pain, willfully inflicted without any justification.

The value presupposition of this [article] has been the avoidance of human pain in the making of development policy. The calculus of pain must be applied to every model of development, as indeed to every model of deliberate social change. Neither the Brazilian nor the Chinese model can stand up under this application. As one looks at the available information in terms of the calculus of pain, *neither* model is morally acceptable. Conversely, *neither* case can be cited either in defense of or as a final argument against, respectively, capitalism or socialism. Brazil does not exhaust the possibilities of capitalism, and there are socialist possibilities beyond Maoist China. It is the quest of such other possibilities that should preoccupy anyone concerned with the mitigation of human suffering in the course of social change.

NOTES

1. For an account of these events by an opponent, see Miguel Arraes, *Brazil—The People and the Power* (Harmondsworth, Middlesex: Penguin, 1972). For the events leading up to the military takeover, see Joseph Page, *The Revolution that Never Was* (New York: Grossman, 1972). For a more personal report of one who lived through the takeover, see Marcio Moreira Alves, *A Grain of Mustard Seed* (Garden City, N.Y.: Anchor, 1973).

2. *First National Development Plan, 1972/74*, published in English by the Brazilian government (Brasilia: 1971). The economic data on Brazil are taken from a variety of mostly periodical sources and are all based on Brazilian government statistics. It was not possible to refer to an overview in book form in English.

3. The most trenchant economic critique of the model is by the Brazilian economist Celso Furtado. His major book on this is not available to date in English; it was published in Spanish as *Análisis del modelo brasileño* (Buenos Aires: Centro Editor de América Latina, 1972). Furtado, while not a Marxist, is politically on the left. This type of critique, however, has now spread to some surprising quarters. Even Robert McNamara, in an official address as president of the World Bank, has recently associated himself with important aspects of the critique (notably the criticism of the anti-"distributionist" orientation of the Brazilian model).

4. For a graphic account, see Paul Gallet, *Freedom to Starve* (Harmondsworth, Middlesex: Penguin, 1972).

5. See Report on *Allegations of Torture in Brazil* (London: Amnesty International, 1972).

6. See Chow Ching-Wen, *Ten Years of Storm* (New York: Holt, Rinehart and Winston, 1960); Doak Barnett, *Communist China—the Early Years* (New York: Praeger, 1964). For a detailed account of these years in one area, see Ezra Vogel, *Canton under Communism* (New York: Harper Torchbooks, 1971), cc. 2–4.

7. For a brief but excellent report, see Stanley Karnow, *Mao and China* (New York: Viking, 1972), c. 5.

8. See Robert Elegant, *Mao's Great Revolution* (New York: World, 1971); Edward Rice, *Mao's Way* (Berkeley: University of California Press, 1972).

9. Tillman Durdin, James Reston, and Seymour Topping, *The New York Times Report from Red China* (New York: Quadrangle, 1971), p. 141.

10. The most comprehensive attempt is to be found in a report prepared by Richard Walker for a subcommittee of the U.S. Senate Committee on the Judiciary, *The Human Cost of Communism in China* (Washington, D.C.: U.S. Government Printing Office, 1971). The report is unimpressive in its use of sources and seems motivated by the bias to set the number of victims as high as possible. For an eyewitness account of conditions in Chinese prison camps ("Reform through Labor" camps, in which people are permanently confined, as against "Education through Labor" camps, in which confinement is for limited periods of time), see Bao Ruo-Wang and Rudolph Chelminski, *Prisoner of Mao* (New York: Coward, McCann & Geoghegan, 1973). The authors estimate a figure of sixteen million as reasonable for the inmates of these camps.

11. The term "genocide" is used deliberately. The charge of genocide was made in a careful report on the events in Tibet by the International Commission of Jurists, Geneva 1960. For a moving account of the same events, see the Dalai Lama's book, *My Land and My People* (New York: McGraw-Hill, 1962). The Tibetan record is particularly relevant to Peking's claim to lead the "anti-imperialist" forces of the Third World (as is China's more recent policy with regard to Bangladesh). Pro-Peking advocates have observed that Tibet was, after all, an integral part of China when these events took place. The statement is open to question juridically (in another report, Geneva 1959, the International Commission of Jurists concluded that Tibet was in fact and in law a sovereign state). More importantly, the moral persuasiveness of the observation is about that of, say, an assertion that the Nazis were justified in killing those Jews who were German citizens.

12. See, for example, Ching Ping and Dennis Bloodworth, *Heirs Apparent* (New York: Farrar, Straus and Giroux, 1973).

13. See the compendium prepared for the Joint Economic Committee of the U.S. Congress, *People's Republic of China—An Economic Assessment* (Washington, D.C.: U.S. Government Printing Office, 1972).

14. Data from Durdin et al., *The New York Times Report.*

15. Kuan-I Chen and J. S. Uppal, eds., *Comparative Development of India and China* (New York: Free Press, 1971), p. 46.

16. David Caute, *The Fellow-Travellers* (New York: Macmillan, 1973). For a comparison of earlier accounts of the Soviet Union with recent ones by visitors to China, see Paul Hollander, "The Ideological Pilgrim," *Encounter*, November 1973.

17. Durdin et al., *The New York Times Report*, pp. 354f.

26

"Development". . . or Liberation?

Denis Goulet

Latin Americans in growing numbers now denounce the lexicon of development experts as fraudulent. To illustrate, Gustavo Gutierrez, a Peruvian
theologian and social activist, concludes that "the term development con-
veys a pejorative connotation . . . (and) is gradually being replaced by the
term liberation . . . there will be a true development for Latin America only
through liberation from the domination by capitalist countries. That implies, of course, a showdown with their natural allies: our natural
oligarchies."[1]

Gutierrez is a major spokesman for "theology of liberation." Numerous
seminars and conferences have already been held on the theme in Colombia,
Mexico, Uruguay, Argentina, and elsewhere. For Gutierrez—as for Gustavo
Perez, René Garcia, Rubem Alves, Juan Segundo, Camilo Moncada, Emilio
Castro,[2] and others—"liberation" expresses better than "development" the
real aspirations of their people for more human living conditions. Gutierrez
does not attempt to review all the changes in the definition of development
since the Marshall Plan was launched in 1947. This task has already been
performed by others.[3] Instead he focuses his critical gaze on three perspectives with one of which most experts in "developed" countries identify.

THREE VIEWS OF DEVELOPMENT

For many economists development is synonymous with economic growth
measured in aggregate terms. A country is developed, they hold, when it
can sustain, by its own efforts and after having first reached a per capita
GNP (Gross National Product) level of $500 (for some observers) or $1000
(for others), an annual rate of growth ranging from 5% to 7%. According
to these criteria, certain countries are highly developed, while those on the
lowest rungs of the ladder are either underdeveloped or undeveloped. Similar comparisons can also be established between different regions and sectors within a single economy. Although this view is generally repudiated
today, it still retains some vestigial influence, thanks to the impact of works
like Walt Rostow's *The Stages of Economic Growth* and to the dominant
role still played by economists in planning. Even when they give lip-service

Reprinted from the *International Development Review*, Vol. XIII, No. 3 (September 1971), by permission of the publisher. Copyright 1971 © by the Society for International Development.

to other dimensions in development, many economists continue to sub-ordinate all non-economic factors to the practical requirements of their growth models.

The second outlook, far more prevalent today, was summarized at the start of the United Nations' First Development Decade in U Thant's phrase, "development = economic growth + social change." The trouble with this formula is that it either says too much or says too little since not any kind of growth will do, nor any kind of change.

Most social scientists adopt some variant of this conception as their own working definition of development; it is broad enough to embrace a variety of change processes emphasizing either economic, social, cultural or political factors. Nearly always, however, social scientists subordinate value judgments about human goals to the achievement of economic growth, to the creation of new social divisions of labor, to the quest for modern institutions, or to the spread of attitudes deemed compatible with efficient production. The last point is well illustrated by those who affirm that "modernity" is not the presence of factories, but the presence of a certain viewpoint on factories.

Behind an array of theories and special vocabularies, however, lingers the common assumption that "developed" societies ought to serve as models for others. Some observers, eager to minimize culture bias, reject the notion that all societies *ought* to follow patterns set by others. Nevertheless, they assert that modern patterns are inevitable, given the demonstration effects and technological penetration of modern societies throughout the world.

A third stream of development thinkers stresses ethical values. This group has always constituted, in some respects, a heretical minority. Its position centers on qualitative improvement in all societies, and in all groups and individuals within societies. Although all men must surely have enough goods in order to be more human, they say, development itself is simply a means to the human ascent. This perspective, at times called "the French school," is linked to such names as economist François Perroux, social planner Louis Lebret, theorist Jacques Austruy, and practicing politicians like Robert Buron and André Phillip. According to these men and their disciples, social change should be seen in the broadest possible historical context, within which all of humanity is viewed as receiving a summons to assume its own destiny. Their ideas have influenced United Nations agencies in some measure, but they have made their greatest inroads in religious writings on development: papal encyclicals, documents issued by the World Council of Churches and the Pontifical Commission on Justice and Peace, pastoral letters drafted by bishops in several countries. The single geographical area where the French school has achieved considerable penetration is Latin America.

This is why the conclusion reached by Gutierrez is particularly significant. According to Gutierrez, the French school, because of its historicity and its insistence on norms for social goals, is the least objectionable of the three perspectives he criticizes. Nevertheless, he argues, the realities barely hinted at by the French are better expressed by the term "liberation" than by "development." By using the latter term the French school does not dramatize its discontinuities with the other perspectives sharply enough. Worse still, its spokesmen employ such notions as foreign aid, technical cooperation, development planning, and modernization in ways which remain ambiguous at best. Consequently, in the eyes of many Latin Americans "development" has a pejorative connotation: it does not get to the roots of the problem and leads to frustration. Moreover, "development" does not evoke asymmetrical power relations operative in the world or the inability of evolutionary change models to lead, in many countries, to the desired objectives. Therefore, says Gutierrez, it is better to speak of liberation, a term which directly suggests domination, vulnerability in the face of world market forces, weak bargaining positions, the need for basic social changes domestically and for freer foreign policies.

THE LANGUAGE OF LIBERATION

To substitute for "development" the term "liberation" is to engage in what Brazilian educator Paulo Freire calls "cultural action for freedom."[4] Liberation implies the suppression of elitism by a populace which assumes control over its own change processes. Development, on the other hand, although frequently used to describe various change processes, stresses the benefits said to result from them: material prosperity, higher production and expanded consumption, better housing or medical services, wider educational opportunities and employment mobility, and so on. This emphasis, however, errs on two counts. First, it uncritically supports change strategies which value efficiency above all else, even if efficiency must be gained by vesting decisions in the hands of elites—trained managers, skilled technicians, high-level "manpower." A second failing, analyzed by Harvard historian Barrington Moore in *Social Origins of Dictatorship and Democracy,* is the dismissal of violence as unconstructive and the refusal to condemn the violence attendant upon legal change patterns.

Not theologians alone, but social scientists, planners, educators, and some political leaders in Latin America prefer the terminology of liberation to that of development. They unmask the hidden value assumptions of the conventional wisdom and replace them with a deliberate stress on self-development as opposed to aid, foreign investment, and technical assistance Since I have written a detailed critique of the Pearson, Peterson, Jackson and other development reports elsewhere,[5] there is no need to repeat here what is there said regarding the value assumptions and critical omissions of these reports. What is germane to the present discussion is the confirmation given these criticisms by Third World spokesmen in UNCTAD (United Nations Conference on Trade and Development) and GATT (General Agreement on Tariffs and Trade) meetings.[6] Not surprisingly, more and more leaders from underdeveloped areas are coming to regard "development" as the lexicon of palliatives. Their recourse to the vocabulary of liberation is a vigorous measure of self-defense, aimed at overcoming the structural vulnerability which denies them control over the economic, political, and cultural forces which impinge upon their societies. Even to speak of liberation, before achieving it, is a first conquest of cultural autonomy. Ultimately what is sought is to alter relationships between director and directed societies, between privileged elites and the populace at large within all societies. Ever more people are coming to understand that "to be underdeveloped" is to be relegated to a subordinate position in history, to be given the role of adjusting to, not of initiating, technological processes.

The language of liberation is being nurtured in societies where a new critical consciousness is being formed. For these societies, the models of genuine development are not those billed by U.S. aid agencies as success stories—South Korea, Greece, Taiwan, and Iran. Industrialization and economic growth have no doubt taken place in these lands, but no basic changes have occurred in class relationships and the distribution of wealth and power; the larger social system remains structurally exploitative. Moreover, economic gains have been won under the tutelage of repressive political regimes. Finally, as one European has observed, "U.S. aid seems to work best in countries which are lackeys of American foreign policy."

Revolutionary Latin Americans reject this kind of development. They look instead to China, Cuba, and Tanzania as examples of success. In China, mass starvation has been abolished and a feudal social system overthrown. Elitism in rulers is systematically uprooted whenever it reappears, and technological gains are subordinated to the cultural creation of a new man capable of autonomy. Cuba, notwithstanding its economic mistakes, freely admitted, has overcome its servile dependence on the United States and asserts itself increasingly in the face of the Soviet Union, upon whom it still relies heavily for financial, technical and military assistance. Moreover, Cuba has abolished illiteracy in sensational fashion, decentralized investment, and reduced the gap in living conditions between the countryside and the cities. And Tanzania is admired because it rejects mass-consumption as a model for society, practices self-reliance in its educational system (choosing to grant prestige to agricultural skills rather than to purely scientific ones geared to large-scale engineering projects), accepts foreign aid only when the overall impact of the projects financed will not create a new elite class within the nation itself, and in general subordinates economic gains to the creation of new African values founded on ancient communitarian practices.

For liberationists, therefore, success is not measured simply by the quantity of benefits gained, but above all by the way in which change processes take place. Visible benefits are no doubt sought, but the decisive test of success is that, in obtaining them, a society will have fostered greater popular autonomy in a non-elitist mode, social creativity instead of imitation, and control over forces of change instead of mere adjustment to them. The crucial question is: Will "underdeveloped" societies become mere consumers of technological civilization or agents of their own transformation? *At stake, therefore, is something more than a war over words; the battle lines are drawn between two conflicting interpretations of historical reality, two competing principles of social organization.* The first values efficiency and social control above all else, the second social justice and the creation of a new man.

Western development scholars are prone to question the validity of the new vocabulary of liberation. As trained social scientists, they doubt its analytical power, explanatory value, and predictive capacities. Yet their scepticism is misplaced inasmuch as empirical social science has itself proved unable to describe reality, let alone to help men change it in acceptable ways. Of late, however, a salutory modesty has begun to take hold of social scientists. Gunnar Myrdal (in *Asian Drama*) confesses the error of his early days as an "expert" on development, and challenges (in *Objectivity in Social Research*) the assumptions behind all value-free theories and research methods. More forcefully still, Alvin Gouldner, in *The Coming Crisis of Western Sociology*, argues the case for a new Utopian, value-centered radical sociology for the future. And economist Egbert de Vries[7] reaches the conclusion that no significant breakthroughs in development theory have been achieved in the last decade. Western development scholars, therefore, themselves lost in deep epistemological quagmire, are ill-advised to scorn the new theories.

One finds in truth great explanatory power, analytical merit, and predictive value in the writings of Latin American social scientists on development, dependence, and domination.[8] The new liberation vocabulary is valid, even empirically, because it lays bare structures of dependence and domination at all levels. Reaching behind the neutral "descriptive" words of developmental wisdom, it unmasks the intolerably high human cost to Latin Americans of economic development, social modernization, political institution-building and cultural westernization. The reality described by these writings is the pervasive impotence of vulnerable societies in the face of the impersonal stimuli which impinge upon them. Furthermore, their vocabulary enjoys high prescriptive value because it shows this powerlessness to be reversible: if domination is a human state of affairs caused and perpetuated by men, it can be overthrown by men. Finally, the highly charged political language of liberation has great predictive value to the extent that it can mobilize collective energies around a value which is the motor of all successful social revolutions—HOPE. Liberated hope is not the cold rational calculus of probability *à la* Herman Kahn or Henry Kissinger, but a daring calculus of *possibility* which reverses the past, shatters the present, and creates a new future.

"DEVELOPMENT" AS A HINGE WORD

In spite of its absolute superiority, however, the language of liberation remains, for many people in the "developed" world, tactically unmanageable. The historical connotations of the word sometimes lead them to resist mobilization around its theme, especially if these people are not themselves oppressors, but inert beneficiaries of impersonal oppressive systems. A second category of people may also find it difficult to respond, namely those insurgent professionals who can subvert "the system" only by mastering its tools and serving as a fifth column in alliance with revolutionary groups on the outside. Understandably, these persons will need to continue using the currently available "professional" terminology. It is considerations such as these which lie behind the question: Can "development" serve a useful hinge role in mobilization? The answer is affirmative if one agrees with political scientist Harvey Wheeler that

> . . . we don't possess a *revolutionary* social science to serve the utopian needs of the revolution. And those learned enough to create it are divorced from the activists who must prepare the way for the new utopianism. . . . Somehow, the radical activists and the radical scientists—the utopians—must come together.[9]

Desired changes within "developed" societies can ensue only in the wake of concerted (and much unconcerted) action emanating from a variety of change agents. There can be no objection on principle, therefore, to granting tentative validity to "development" as a hinge word.

For the benefit of those who have not yet been weaned from the sweet milk of palliative incrementalism,[10] "development" needs to be redefined, demystified, and thrust into the arena of moral debate. If critically used as a hinge word, it may open up new perspectives and render the leap into "liberation" possible for many people. Nevertheless, only from the third perspective on development summarized above can one find a suitable platform whence to make this leap of faith. The reason is that, of the three viewpoints, only this ethical, value-laden, humanist approach is rooted in history, and not in abstract theory. Before the language of liberation can sound convincing to the categories of people I have described, it must be shown that "development," as normally understood, alienates even its beneficiaries in compulsive consumption, technological determinisms of various sorts, ecological pathology and warlike policies. Worst of all, it makes those who benefit from development the structural accomplices of the underdevelopment of others. Surely this cannot be what authentic development is. As one reflects on its goals, he discovers that development, viewed as a human project, signifies total liberation. Such liberation aims at freeing men from nature's servitudes, from economic backwardness and oppressive technological institutions, from unjust class structures and political exploiters, from cultural and psychic alienation—in short, from all of life's inhuman agencies.

A new language, able to shatter imprisoning reality, must be born from the clash between vocabularies nurtured in different soils. The first will gestate in a Third World matrix and express the emerging consciousness of those who refuse to be objects, and declare their intent to become subjects, of history. The keys to this vocabulary are the conquest of autonomy and the will to create a new future. At the opposite pole, out of "developed" societies, must arise a subversive redefinition of development itself. Its function will be to destroy the First World's uncritical faith in the universal goodness of its notions of progress, achievement, social harmony, democracy, and modernization. Confrontation between the two is required because neither "development" alone nor "liberation" alone fully transcends both cultural domination and purely negative responses to oppression. Moreover, both terms can be used by symbol manipulators to mystify reality or rationalize palliative change strategies.

Nevertheless, it is clear that competing terminologies of development and liberation are not equally subject to distortion. On the scales of human justice, the interests which they express do not balance each other out. There is indeed, as Camus writes, universal meaning in the rebel's refusal to be treated as something less than a man. And as Marx put it, the oppressed masses are the latent historical carriers of universal human values. The battle to free men is not comparable to the struggle to maintain or expand privilege. Consequently, every trace of elitism and cultural manipulation must be purged from the development vocabulary and replaced with the symbols of liberation. Even then history will not give men any respite; rather, it will propel them into asking: Liberation for what? Ancient teleological questions reappear, concerning the good life, the good society, and men's final purposes. That they should keep arising is no sign of the weakness of men's words, but merely a clue to the grandeur of their historical task. That task is to strive endlessly to outstrip not only alienating material conditions but all particular images of the ideal society as well.

Intellectuals who discuss revolution and violence often utter irresponsible words which place bullets in other people's guns. As they debate development and liberation, the danger they face is less dramatic but no less destructive in the long run. For most of them resort to persuasive political definitions, thereby pre-empting all the intellectual ground upon which descriptive and evocative definitions might find their place. Such habits render genuine liberation impossible since true cultural emancipation admits of no sloganism, no sectarianism, no simplism. Revolutionary consciousness is critical of self no less than of others; and it brooks no verbal cheating even to achieve ideological gains. In final analysis, any liberation vocabulary must do two things. The first is to unmask the alienations disguised by the development lexicon: the alienation of the many in misery, of the few in irresponsible abundance. The second is to transform itself from the rallying cry of victims alone into the victory chant of all men as they empower themselves to enter history with no nostalgia for pre-history.

Success proves difficult because men have never fully learned the lesson implied in a statement by the Indian mystic Rabinadranath Tagore that, ultimately, only those values can be truly human which can be truly universal.

NOTES

1. Gustavo Gutierrez Merino, "Notes for a Theology of Liberation," *Theological Studies*, Vol. 31, No. 2 (June 1970), 243–261.
2. The writings of these men are found largely in papers circulated by documentary services such as LADOC (Latin American Bureau, U.S. Catholic Conference), ISAL (Iglesia y Sociedad en América Latina), and the THEOLOGY OF LIBERATION SYMPOSIUM (in Spanish), Bogota.
3. Cf. the excellent work by Jacques Freyssinet, *Le Concept de Sous-Développement*, Mouton, 1966. A brief review of the different meanings attached to the word "development" can be found in Denis Goulet, "That Third World," *The Center Magazine*, Vol. I, No. 6 (September 1968), 47–55.
4. Cf. Paulo Freire, *Cultural Action for Freedom*, Harvard Educational Review and Center for the Study of Development and Social Change, Monograph No. 1, 1970.

One may also consult the same author's *Pedagogy of the Oppressed*, Herder and Herder, 1970.

5. Cf. Denis Goulet and Michael Hudson, *The Myth of Aid: the Hidden Agenda of the Development Reports*, IDOC Books, 1970. This work contains two essays, one by Goulet entitled "Domesticating the Third World," and a second by Hudson on "The Political Economy of Foreign Aid."

6. On this cf., e.g., Guy F. Erb, "The Second Session of UNCTAD," *Journal of the World Trade Law*, Vol. 2, No. 3 (May/June 1968), 346–359. For a Latin American view, see the document entitled, "The Latin American Consensus of Viña del Mar," dated May 17, 1969.

7. Egbert de Vries, "A Review of Literature on Development Theory," *International Development Review*, Vol. X, No. 1 (March 1968), 43–49.

8. Cf., e.g., such works as F. Cardoso and E. Falleto, *Dependencia y Desarrollo on América Latina*, Santiago, 1967; Theotonio dos Santos, *El Nuevo caracter de la dependencia*, Santiago, 1968; Celso Furtado, *Dialéctica Do Desenvolvimento*, Rio de Janeiro, 1964; numerous essays by Alberto Guerreiro Ramos (a Brazilian now teaching at UCLA), *et al.*

9. Harvey Wheeler, "The Limits of Confrontation Politics," *The Center Magazine*, Vol. III, No. 4 (July 1970), 39.

10. The difference between palliative and creative incrementalism is explained in Denis Goulet, *Is Gradualism Dead?*, Council on Religion and International Affairs, 1970

part eight

What Is to Be Done?

In the most basic sense, most of the readings in this book address them-selves to the question, "What is to be done?"—either by analyzing the nature of underdevelopment or the process of development. The articles in Part Four, Agri-cultural Institutions and Strategy; Part Five, Industrial Institutions and Strategy; and Part Six, Comparative Models of Development, directly discuss the varied problems of promoting development.

The concluding part of this book deals with the problem of how to initiate a development program. That is, it deals with reforms and revolution. In the first reading, Frances Stewart and Paul Streeten set the stage for the subsequent ma-terial. They define and discuss four objectives of development: (a) elimination of poverty, (b) reduction of income inequality, (c) increased growth rate in incomes of the poorest sections of the population, and (d) optimization of GNP growth. They go on to discuss alternative strategies for achieving these objectives: (a) high growth/trickle-down and (b) three variants of redistribution (radical, in-cremental, and redistribution with growth).

In the second reading, Weaver, Jameson, and Blue provide a detailed descrip-tion of seven variants of redistribution with growth strategies. They then present a critique of those strategies labeled as "growth with equity." The traditional criti-cism of growth with equity is that the high growth/trickle-down approach is work-ing, but more time is needed before the final results can be assessed. The radical criticism questions whether such a strategy of development can be implemented under the present political and economic structures in the underdeveloped coun-tries. Whether the developing countries can manage such a change without violent revolution is a critical question of our time. It is conceivable that the ruling classes of an underdeveloped country will voluntarily give up their vested interests in the *status quo* to promote social and economic development. However, radicals doubt whether reform will succeed in transforming the social and political struc-tures of the underdeveloped countries. To them it seems more likely that change will not come about by completely peaceful, evolutionary means, but rather by social revolution that will destroy the power of the old ruling classes.

The third reading in this part focuses on a new international economic order. The 1975 Dag Hammarskjöld Report is primarily concerned with the multiplicity of elements and imperatives that bear upon the construction and implementation of a new international economic order. For the authors, a new development strategy aimed at liberated self-reliance can be successful only when complemented by a new international order. The essence of the new international order includes: (a) abolition of unequal economic relations, (b) better and larger flow of real resources, (c) international dialogue and cooperation, (d) management of the international commons, and (e) intercultural cooperation. The report concludes with an agenda for negotiation between Third World and industrialized countries. The areas of negotiation include: (a) transfer of basic foreign-owned assets to national control; (b) patterns of production and trade, with special reference to market and supply access, including both commodities and industry; (c) technology, knowledge and technical transfer and use arrangements; (d) transition toward a new industrial geography of the world; (e) financial transfers; and (f) access to food.

In the next reading, Ivan Illich argues that the underdeveloped countries must take charge of their own development. They must reject the meaning of development given by the rich countries if for no other reason than they will never have sufficient capital to pursue that type of development. Illich calls for a whole new program of research and policies. For example, because educational resources are so scarce underdeveloped countries can provide each citizen only between eight and thirty months of schooling. He asks: "Why not, instead, make one or two months a year obligatory for all citizens below the age of thirty?" Further, he argues that every dollar spent on doctors and not spent on purifying water costs lives of the poor. In effect, Illich is arguing that resources available for development now and over the next several generations will simply not be adequate to support a full-scale development program. Therefore, resources must be reallocated from serving the rich—private cars, organ transplant clinics, and so on—to aiding the poor—public transportation, water purification, and so on.

Illich further argues that revolutionaries in the underdeveloped world have succumbed to the same delusion. They claim that a change in political regime will permit them to expand the privileges of the rich to all. Illich's own program, however, also requires a revolution; if not of iron and blood, at least one of ideas and involving a radical shift in the pattern of power. It requires the kind of "liberation" that Denis Goulet discussed in the previous section of the book, and which is developed at greater length by Paulo Freire in "Pedagogy of the Oppressed," the last reading in the book. Freire argues that development worthy of humans will come about only when the mass of people recognize their oppression and consciously act to change it. That is, a revolution in ideas and values must accompany a transformation of structures.

27

New Strategies for Development: Poverty, Income Distribution, and Growth

Frances Stewart and Paul Streeten

It is now widely acknowledged that growth of GNP, conventionally measured, is unsatisfactory as the main target of development strategy and as the sole criterion of its success or failure. Among the many reasons why this is accepted, two have been singled out. First, many developing countries that have experienced rapid rates of growth of GNP have also and simultaneously generated increasing amounts of unemployment and underemployment. The growth rate of employment in the modern sector has been much slower than the growth rate of GNP, and much slower than the growth in numbers seeking modern sector jobs. Secondly, rapid growth in GNP has often been accompanied by a more unequal income distribution and increasing relative and, in some cases, absolute impoverishment of sections of the community. GNP has been "dethroned" mainly because it fails to incorporate any measure of a country's success in achieving fuller employment and a more even income distribution.

These two phenomena—growing unemployment and increasingly unequal income distribution—are connected, in that lower (relative and/or absolute) income levels are to be found mainly among those who fail to find modern sector employment, while the gains from growth of GNP have been concentrated on the employed. A measure of open unemployment is not a satisfactory proxy for poverty, because the openly unemployed are generally better off, since the really poor cannot afford to be unemployed. However, poverty (relative and absolute) may be a satisfactory proxy for at least part of the "employment" problem, since excess supply of people seeking modern sector jobs is reflected in low incomes arising from complete lack of employment (open unemployment), partial lack of work (few hours), or work of very low productivity (insufficient complementary resources or low productivity caused by low levels of living). It has therefore been suggested that the elimination of poverty and the achievement of greater equality in income distribution should at least supplement, if not replace, growth of GNP as a target of development. Indeed, in a formulation of policies that aim at meeting the basic needs of the poor people and at an appropriate inter-temporal allocation of these improvements, growth will turn out to be the *result*, not the *aim*, of economic policy. This paper aims at exploring the various meanings which

Frances Stewart and Paul Streeten, "New Strategies for Development: Poverty, Income Distribution, and Growth," *Oxford Economic Papers*, 28, 1976. Published by Oxford University Press.

may be attached to these new targets, and the strategies that have been proposed for their achievement.

DEFINING THE NEW TARGETS

We shall skate rapidly over those problems of definition and measurement that arise in the comparison of real income levels between different groups in the same society at the same time, different groups in different societies, and the same groups at different times, where the groups to be compared do not consume the same goods in the same proportions but spend differing proportions of their incomes on each of the goods. In such situations, a comparison of real income levels depends on the value attributed to each good. The market price is no guide since, apart from other difficulties, the use of price as a welfare weight is legitimate only if income distribution is considered optimal, and it is precisely income distribution that is in question. Where the bundle of commodities alters, as it does over time, there are further problems, which might make the purist give up altogether at this stage. But this is to be too finicky. Clearly income levels do differ in a way that is not simply in the eye of the beholder (i.e. the weight fixer); crude measures such as calorie consumption could be used as a start. Generally, money income (within a society at one time) is taken as the measure: if this is the measure adopted, then changes in the prices of the commodities consumed by the different groups must be included for a measure of changing income distribution over time. In fact this is rarely done.[1]

Most measures of income distribution over time do not include changes in relative prices of the goods consumed by different income groups. More specifically, money measures are used to prove points about real income distribution, without these adjustments.

Let us suppose we have a satisfactory measure of real income levels in different groups in society. This is a big supposition (i) because there are aggregation problems within groups, just as there are within societies, (ii) because theorists may be able to devise measures that are conceptually workable, but statisticians may not be able to provide the necessary data, and (iii) because, since the whole point of shifting from GNP to some new measure is to improve targets and achievement criteria, it is important that they should be consistent criteria. There remains the problem of defining more precisely the suggested targets of eliminating poverty and/or increasing the equality of income distribution. The first, most obvious point, is that there is a difference between these two suggested targets—elimination of poverty and reduced inequality. The first *appears* to be about the absolute income levels of certain (as yet undefined) sections of society; the second is unambiguously about the relative, not the absolute, level of income of the poor. The second might be achieved by reducing incomes throughout society, but reducing the incomes of those above the average most. Here the two targets would appear to be in conflict, since this sort of strategy would actually increase absolute poverty amongst the poorest.

An alternative strategy of raising all incomes, but raising those of the poor least, would contribute to achievement of the first target, elimination or reduction of poverty, but would actually worsen the situation *vis-à-vis* the second target. It is therefore important to be clear which of the two targets the revised strategy follows.

There are powerful arguments in favour of each. On the one hand, absolute poverty, malnutrition, poor health, bad housing would seem to be among the main evils of underdevelopment, and their eradication is what development should be about. On the other hand, people mind about their relative position in society; while it may be difficult to argue in over-developed societies that rising average income levels in fact improve anyone's welfare all that much, it remains true within those societies that relative improvements are strongly desired, and probably do increase the welfare of those who benefit from them.[2] By definition of course, relative improvements cannot be shared by all. Equality, for some at least, is an important end in itself, and some would be prepared to accept reductions in average levels, and even, up to a point, in all levels of income, to achieve greater equality. Concern with the employment problem, and the use of income distribution as a proxy for its measurement, also is mainly a matter of relative, not absolute, poverty: the problem arises because of vast *differences* between income-earning opportunities in different parts of society, as well as because of absolutely low income levels.

People mind not only about their *individual* relative position, but also about the average relative position *of a group* to which they belong: a class, region, or country. In comparing distribution between groups, some measure of the average income of the group is appropriate. Thus, when making international income comparisons, we usually compare income per head for different countries. Now it is possible for income distribution between groups to become more equal while distribution within groups becomes less equal, and vice versa. More particularly, policies that emphasize greater equality within low-income countries may widen the gap in incomes between rich and poor countries; while policies that aim at reducing the international gap often widen the domestic one.

The two objectives—poverty eradication and reduced inequality—may not be in as sharp opposition as might appear because the income level and size of the group singled out as below the absolute poverty line, the growth of whose incomes would be the prime target in a strategy for the eradication of absolute poverty, itself generally depends on their position *relative* to those in the rest of the population. What is to count as absolute poverty tends to be relative to average standards in the society in question. Con-trast, for example, the kind of income level Abel-Smith and Townsend[3] consider to be a minimum (below which people are in poverty) in the U.K. or in the U.S.A. (see Harrington [1962]), with the levels considered to be a minimum in India by Dandekar and Rath (1971). Interpreted in this way, the target poverty group depends on how the incomes of the poorest move, in relation to those of the society as a whole, and in this case much of the conflict between the two objectives is eliminated. However, to deal with it in this way, though convenient, conceals important differences in the way in which the objectives may be achieved. We shall therefore assume that the revised strategy may consist, in the short run at least, of two different objectives:

Revised strategy:
Objective A—elimination of poverty;
Objective B—reduced inequality in income distribution.

There are problems about both objectives. If for the objective of poverty elimination (as argued above) poverty is defined in relation to the average standard, it comes closer to the objective of reduced inequality. For the moment we assume it is not, but is independently identifiable. The objective of reduced inequality is subject to all the difficulties of defining what is to count as reduced inequality of income distribution.[4] It might be thought that a shift of the Lorenz curve entirely to the north-west can be described unambiguously as one of reduced inequality. Where the two Lorenz curves cross, as is the case with measures designed to help the poor which do so at the expense of middle-income groups but also redistribute something to the rich, the change is ambiguous. But even a non-crossing Lorenz curve gives an ambiguous result. By redistributing income from the richest man to anyone other than the poorest man, inequality between the poorest and the recipient is increased.[5] Only if everyone is moved nearer the average is the move unambiguously one towards greater equality.

In keeping with the spirit of the revised strategy, we may argue that the relative position of the poorest must improve, which rules out a situation where income is transferred from the rich and the poor to middle-income receivers. But ambiguity remains. The position of the poorest may improve in relation to some groups, and worsen in relation to others. Perhaps the best we can do is to require that the incomes of the poor increase in relation to the average. This is consistent with increasing disparities above the average. As far as the employment problem is concerned it is disparities in earning opportunities which are at the heart of the problem. It is arguable that for the unskilled and semi-skilled these would be largely captured by a measure of the relation of the incomes of the poor to the average.[6]

Quite apart from the possibility of intersecting Lorenz curves, the social significance of situations with the same index of inequality will vary, according to a number of considerations, often neglected.[7] The same income may not be described as equal to another income, for which the earner has worked longer or more disagreeable hours, if the choice was open to both and if equality is related to desert. Secondly, allowance might be made for time spent previously in acquiring skills and forgoing earnings during training. Thirdly, the same person's income may fluctuate between years and any one year's figure will then give a misleading impression of inequality. Fourthly, adjustments may have to be made for age and non-registered incomes. If the young have no or lower incomes than the old, though lifetime earnings are the same, apparent differences in income distribution may be simply due to different age structures. If the services of housewives are not included in national income calculations, apparent differences in distribution are due to this arbitrary convention. Fifthly, the social significance is difference according to the length of time persons remain in their income groups. Consider two societies. In one, the children of the rich become poor and those of the poor rich. In the other, subsequent generations stay in the same income group as their parents. We should describe the former as more egalitarian. Finally, one would want to know whether other dimensions of inequality coincide or cut across income inequalities: satisfaction from work, physical facilities, recognition, status, access to political power. A society in which inequalities are not only rigid and unchanging, but in which economic, social, and political inequalities coincide, is a more inegalitarian society than one in which the composition of the deciles is always changing and in which the different dimensions of inequality intersect, even though the Gini coefficients may be identical.

For both the objective of eradicating poverty and that of reducing inequality there remains, of course, the question of defining which groups at which income levels are to count as poor.

Ahluwalia and Chenery[8] have defined the revised strategy somewhat differently by focusing upon changes in income shares of different groups. They propose maximizing the weighted average of the *rate of growth* of the income of groups with different income levels—i.e. maximizing $G = w_1g_1 + w_2g_2 + w_3g_3 + w_4g_4$, where g_1, g_2, g_3, g_4 are the growth rates of incomes of different income groups in a society, and w_1, w_2, w_3, w_4 are the weights attributed to income growth at the different income levels. As they point out, GNP growth rate maximization consists of maximizing G, defining the w's as the initial share of each income group in the national income. An alternative strategy in which $w_1 = 0$, $w_2 = 0$, $w_3 = 0$, and w_4 (the weight of the poorest group) $= 1$ would amount to regarding only the incomes of the poorest group as an objective.[9] A third possibility is to weight each group equally, according to the number of people (or households, allowing for size and age composition) in it, so that a one per cent growth of the poorest 10 per cent has the same weight as a one per cent growth of the richest 10 per cent. Their approach is neat, as it enables one to continue to place some weight on income growth of sectors other than the poorest. In terms of our revised strategies, described above, in the special case where $w_4 = 1$, and $w_{1,2,3} = 0$, the Ahluwalia–Chenery strategy amounts to our objective A (poverty elimination). There is no way in which their approach can incorporate strictly distributional objectives— our objective B of reduced inequality.[10] We may thus distinguish a third possible objective of the revised strategy:

Objective C: the Ahluwalia–Chenery objective, or maximization of the weighted average of the growth rates of different income groups, with the stipulation that (a) $w_4 < 1$ (because where $w_4 = 1$ it becomes identical with our objective A of poverty elimination); and (b) the weights are not equal to the respective shares in the national income, but are less at above average, and more at below average income levels. This stipulation is necessary if more weight is to be attached to poverty elimination than under the old, unrevised strategy. This objective focuses on raising the *growth rate* of the income of the poor, instead of on B's *static* income inequality. However, the same weighted average growth rate has a different significance according to whether the initial situation is one of great or only mild inequality.

For completeness we define objective D as the unrevised strategy of

GNP growth optimization (i.e. weights are shares in national income).

In the discussion so far, we have avoided the important question of *time*. Appropriate policies to meet the various objectives may differ considerably according to the time-period to which the objective refers. At the most extreme, for example, if the time horizon were very short (say one year) then purely redistributive policies would be best for meeting any of the revised objectives. In the longer run, such policies could reduce the rate of growth of income of all groups including the poorest, and would thus be inappropriate as policies with longer time horizons. Alternatively, it might be possible to achieve *greater equality*, at a *higher level of living* for the bottom 10 per cent, after a period of time, only by increasing inequality for a limited period. If an economy consists of two sectors, one with high average incomes, the other with low average incomes, if there are not great inequalities within each sector, and if the high-income sector is initially small but absorbs an increasing number of workers from the low-income sector, until all are employed in the high-income sector, inequality is bound to increase in the transitional period, while everyone is becoming better off (absolutely) all the time. (The problem is more complicated if there are inequalities within the two sectors.) More generally, inter-temporal choices may have to be made with respect to degrees of equality at different times, and levels or growth rates of income of the poorest sections at different times. Some (but not all) of the conflicts between the various strategies turn out to be a question of differing time horizons. For each of the objectives, therefore, the time period and the inter-temporal value judgements have to be specified.

STRATEGIES

A number of different approaches have been proposed for meeting the revised objectives. Conflicts between these may partly (as argued above) be a question of inter-temporal value judgements, and judgements about inter-temporal trade-off opportunities, and partly of differences in objectives, since the objectives are rarely clearly defined, as between objectives A, B, and C above, but normally simply refer to giving more weight to distributional considerations. Here we need to define some of our terms. *Strategy* is often used to describe a set of policies towards development, but the term covers not only the policies but also the objectives they are intended to fulfil. Thus strategies differ because objectives differ as well as because proposed policies differ. We shall retain this meaning of strategy, using *objectives* to describe ends, and *programmes* to describe the *set of policies* designed to achieve the objectives.

In discussing strategies, there is a complex interaction between programmes and objectives.[11] As outside observers, we may be able to define our ultimate objectives (e.g. poverty elimination, reduced inequality, weighted growth and conventional growth) and maintain these (in theory), unaffected by the programmes. But in the actual economies under discussion, where the objectives are those of some group (or groups) within the society, the objectives are themselves a product of the situation of those defining the objectives, and this situation depends on past programmes. Let us assume the objectives in which we are interested are those of the official decision makers—government and civil servants: we are concerned with them, because they make decisions and therefore policy can be affected only by them. The objectives of the decision makers may be altered by past policies in four ways: first, they may change their objectives because their own *interests* alter as a result of past developments: for example, after a period of trade protection members of the Government may acquire an interest in continued, or increased, protection; secondly, the *results* of past policies may make them change their objectives. For example, growing unemployment and poverty have brought increasing attention to their elimination as objectives; thirdly, their *power* to bring different objectives about may alter, either through changes in the resistance to policies as a result of social, economic, and political factors (again a product in part of programmes), or through new techniques. Objectives respond to the possibility or impossibility of achievement. Putting a man on the moon was an objective of the 1960s, not the 1860s. Similarly, the political impossibility of achieving some end may rule it out as an objective. Fourthly, the social and political *composition* of the decision makers—the interests they represent and consequently their objectives—may alter as a result of past programmes. Of course, individual decision makers are continually changing. We are not concerned with that, but with changes in the social composition of the decision makers and the interests they represent. Similarly, when we talk of the interests of the decision makers we do not necessarily mean the actual interests of the individuals concerned (though this too is highly relevant) but the interests of the class (and region, tribe and race) from which they come, and whom (primarily) they represent.

It may be argued that though the day-to-day aims of decision makers may respond in this way to past developments, this is not true of ultimate objectives—these are forged out of deep political discussion, and reflect the ultimate aims of mankind—for, e.g., freedom and happiness. It is perfectly true that most National Plans lay down their objectives in this very general way; it is also true that, in a sense, all other objectives are only a means to achievement of these ultimate objectives. But the objectives that determine programmes are not of this kind; they are more of the A–D variety—derived objectives. There is a further distinction to be made. Many governments pay lip service to objectives which they have no real intention of implementing; we shall describe these as *nominal* objectives to distinguish them from real objectives. A real objective is one for which the decision makers will the means as well as the end. Indeed one can argue that real objectives by their nature are identified by revelation—by the policies adopted. Nominal objectives are to be identified by words: real, by deeds.[12]

We have defined programmes, and will be using the term in the discussion. But it is by no means clear that governments, as opposed to advisers, have programmes. Governments do have policies, but they are rarely undertaken as part of a coherent programme; *ex post*, it may be possible to identify the type of programme that a particular government's policies add up to; this does not mean that this was the *ex ante* intention of the government, nor indeed that, given the choice again, informed that it represents a particular programme, they would choose it again.

There are, then, a number of interacting elements that determine choice of strategy. Important among these are the initial situation, the nature of the decision makers and their power and power base, and the technical possibilities. These interactions help determine the possibility (technically and politically) of the various revised strategies. These interactions should become clearer in the discussion that follows. The strategies we shall discuss can be categorized as follows:

high growth and "trickle down"
redistribution: (i) radical,
                  (ii) incremental,
                  (iii) redistribution through growth.

RELATIONSHIP BETWEEN STRATEGIES AND OBJECTIVES

The four strategies named above need little elaboration, as their content is self-evident.

The strategy of high growth plus trickle down is, crudely, the strategy that was followed in the 1950s and 1960s, aimed at objective D (high growth with conventional weighting). The strategy was not based on the premiss that the only thing that matters is growth of GNP, but rather on the assumption that either (*a*) the elimination of poverty can be left to the government via redistribution of the fruits of growth; or (*b*) without any active intervention of the government, high growth of GNP would automatically raise the levels of living of the poor through a trickle-down mechanism. Dissatisfaction with the achievements in eliminating poverty during the period in which this was the strategy suggests that these assumptions were incorrect. It is clear that the two assumptions above, (*a*) and (*b*), are very different. Failure to achieve (*a*)—redistribution of the fruits of growth—may, in our view, somewhat naïvely, be regarded as a failure of will on the part of the government. (Here "will" includes the desire to implement a particular policy, and actual execution of the policy, given the apparent desire. The two cannot be distinguished completely since the reality of desires cannot be assessed independently of their execution.) In contrast, failure to fulfil assumption (*b*) is not a matter of will at all, but of misspecification of the mechanism of growth, the incorrect belief that rapid growth will be, broadly and after brief time lags, at least proportionate in all sectors and income levels. Failure in terms of assumption (*a*) may be due to belief in the validity of assumption (*b*)—i.e. the government feels no need to redistribute actively because it believes poverty will automatically be eliminated via trickle down, in the course of rapid growth. It is important to know what actually were the implicit assumptions during the past two decades, because the realism of much of the proposed revised strategies depends on it. If the failure was really a failure of will on the part of the government, then other policies which require similar acts of will may well fail too, unless we can find some distinguishing characteristic about them which makes this unlikely. It is therefore worth discussing the alternative assumptions and the nature of the failure more carefully.

It is obviously true that high growth was expected (at least initially) to increase incomes at all levels, which is one of the main reasons why the emphasis on GNP, a high savings rate, and a rapid growth rate were regarded as respectable. But it is also true (in many countries, and generalizing about the whole world there are always exceptions) that the combination of growing poverty and unemployment and growing GNP has been evident for some time; that most governments pay lip service to the need for redistributive policies, and that their policies continue to be predominantly protective of the haves and hostile to the have-nots. This is illustrated in tax policy, in public expenditure, government regulations and restrictions. Why is this? It seems to us three sets of reasons may be put forward, none of which really has much to do with *will*, which is why we reject the idea that failure of will is at the heart of the matter.

First, it is possible that governments lack the knowledge and/or the administrative power to redistribute effectively. It is true that public expenditure programmes benefiting the poor in the rural areas are far more difficult to administer than those for the urban élite. Similarly, tax systems are notoriously inefficient. There may therefore be something in this argument, but probably not very much since the governments often seem capable of administering complex programmes of import restrictions or investment licensing, where the protection of the privileged is in question. The administrative weakness of governments in this connection is at least in part a matter of lack of a political base which will enable the government to carry out the policy effectively. The élite, against whom redistributive measures must be aimed, form the personnel who administer the measures; they capture the machine and render it ineffective. Thus in India, despite enormously high marginal tax rates, few pay them. Contrast the apparently similar machinery for rural administration in India and China. In India the machinery is taken over by the landlords and worked to their advantage; in China, with no landlords, it is not. The difference is not a matter of machinery, or institutions, but of how they are run, who runs them, and what they want.

Secondly, the kind of growth strategy pursued may have required the kind of inequality generated, as necessary for its achievement. This · is partly (but only partly) the age-old question of incentives. It is also a matter of the requirements of modern technology. Modern technology requires— on the input side—labour and materials similar to those in the developed economies for which it was designed—i.e. a high proportion of highly skilled personnel, and high standards of literacy, discipline, and efficiency among the unskilled workers. For the required standards of efficiency, the workers must be fed, housed, educated more or less to Western standards; they need watches and bicycles to get to work on time; their clothes must be clean and neat. All these requirements mean that private and public expenditure must be disproportionately concentrated on the workers of modern industry, if it is to operate at all efficiently. So the uneven distribution of incomes (including public expenditure) is in part a necessary condition of a system which uses modern technology. In addition, the consumption goods produced by modern technology, also designed for the type of consumers typical of advanced countries, are suitable for consumers with much above average incomes in developing countries. To generate markets for these goods an unequal income distribution is needed. The high level of skills required by modern technology naturally leads to shortages of skilled workers and therefore tends to increase the quasi-rents of these workers; the opportunity of migration of these and higher level workers to advanced countries provides further upward pressure on their incomes. Hence the inequalities generated can be seen, in part, as a necessary consequence of the adoption of modern technology, while this itself is an intrinsic part of any strategy involving rapid growth, given the absence of efficient alternative technologies.

Transnational firms operating in developing countries contribute to this process. The excessive sophistication and over-elaboration of their products is, of course, partly the result of their having been developed in and initially for high-income, high-savings industrial countries. But this is not the whole story. Companies in search of profits should not find it difficult to invent and develop cheap, mass-produced consumer and producer products, appropriate for the lower incomes of the masses in the poor countries. But the *raison d'être* for transnational enterprise investment is a special monopolistic or oligopolistic advantage, enjoyed by the firm over actual or potential local rivals. If imitation is easy and this advantage soon lost, the incentive is lacking. Possibilities of imitation are avoided if production is geared to sophisticated, changing, technological processes and products in the advanced countries, to which the transnational companies have privileged access. It is therefore in the nature of the transnational enterprise that its products and processes should be excessively sophisticated in relation to the needs of a poor country and it therefore tends to reinforce inequalities.[13]

Thirdly, government policies are themselves in part determined by the strategy pursued and the consequent nature of development; they are not autonomously imposed on the strategy. The decision makers in government in developing countries are themselves part of the élite who have benefited, directly and indirectly, from the high-growing strategy, and rising incomes at upper levels. The policies become self-reinforcing. Thus, for example, protection establishes interests in its continuation and indeed extension, and these interests then see that the policy continues. Inequalities tend to beget policies which lead to accentuation of inequalities; the riches of the *nouveaux riches* bestow power and influence; this power and influence is then exerted to enforce policies which extend their power and wealth, and to thwart policies which threaten them. Government policies become a product of the strategy pursued. There is a reinforcing cycle: high growth leads to the adoption of Western technology, which tends (for technical reasons) to generate inequalities; those who benefit also gain power and set in motion further policies reinforcing the inequalities and the pattern of development which gave rise to it.

The high-growth policy thus tends not only to generate inequalities, but also to establish positions of power that make it extremely difficult to combat these inequalities by government redistributive policies, and indeed make it likely that anti-egalitarian policies will be adopted. Thus invalidity of assumption (*a*) on page 397 above itself leads to the invalidation of assumption (*b*).

The trickle-down strategy is one of pursuing objective D (high growth with conventional weighting)—in the earlier discussion—and aiming as a result also at achieving objective A—the elimination of poverty—as a consequence of rising absolute incomes throughout society, including the incomes of the poorest. It failed because in the event the poorest turned out in many cases (and, of course, there were exceptions) to receive a diminishing proportion of the growing income. This was partly because of the technical requirements of the high growth strategy which resulted, at least initially, in growing inequality (e.g. the Green Revolution); and partly because of the political consequences of the strategy, which created a newly enriched class, including most of the significant decision makers, who pursued policies which would preserve, and indeed increase, their privileges. It also failed because inequalities matter as well as income levels, which is not allowed for in objective D (high conventional growth).[14] Inequalities create the employment problem, not absolute poverty. And poverty is worse in a society in which others are getting richer—it is clearly worse psychologically, but it is also worse *materially*. This is because the type of services in a society changes in line with aggregate incomes, so that people with the same income, in terms of yesterday's goods, are worse off in terms of what is available today. For example, as societies grow richer, private cars replace buses, new buses replace old, cans and elaborate packages replace sacks, so that the poor become worse off because the products they once consumed are no longer available and their sophisticated substitutes are often more expensive. This changing composition of goods as average incomes rise refutes the belief—for developed countries as well as developing—that high growth is preferable to direct income redistribution, not only for the rich *but also for the poor*.

REDISTRIBUTION

The alternative to a "trickle-down" strategy in dealing with poverty is one of deliberate intervention to redistribute resources to the poorest sections of society, thus raising their relative position (the objective of reduced inequality). In the short run, any policy of redistribution should also have the effect of raising the absolute income levels, unless the immediate effect of the redistribution is a loss in aggregate output so great, that with a higher weight, *per capita* incomes of the poor none the less decline. In the longer run, the level of incomes of the poor, as compared with what it would have been under alternative non-redistributing strategies, depends on growth in aggregate incomes, and the changing share of the poor under the alternative strategies. If, as appears to have been the case with some high-growth strategies, a high growth rate is accompanied by

a falling share of income for the poorest categories of people, then redistribution can be accompanied by a reduction in the growth rate, without
reducing the absolute level of income of the poor below what this would
have been under the high-growth strategy. Given the relationship, discussed above, between the extent to which goods appropriate to the needs of
the poor are available and growth in aggregate incomes, a lower apparent
increase in low incomes may be consistent with a higher level of welfare in
a slow-growth situation than in a fast-growth one.

A number of alternative forms of redistribution have been proposed.

(i) Non-incremental redistribution. This is a policy of redistributing
existing assets. Redistribution of income without redistribution of assets—
e.g. by progressive taxation of income—has not been notably successful.
In countries as apparently dissimilar as the U.K. and Kenya the net effect
of an apparently progressive tax system has been to leave real incomes
much as they would be in a no-tax situation.[15] Redistribution of assets includes policies of land reform, and wider spread of ownership or nationalization of industrial property. It also includes radical reforms of institutions
to give to the poor greater access to educational and health services, to
credit and technology. Redistribution of income normally automatically
follows redistribution of assets. Where the assets being nationalized were
formerly in the hands of foreigners, nationalization does not necessarily
lead to greater equality *within* the nation, but it may do so *between* nations.
Substantial redistribution of assets within a nation involves such a break
with the past that it both requires and constitutes a revolution. This type
of redistribution is not therefore generally carried out by those who have
gained from past inequalities.

(ii) Incremental redistribution, or redistribution at the margin. Because
substantial and non-marginal redistribution, which we have described
above as *radical* redistribution, is a revolutionary requirement, it does not
normally form part of the advice given to existing governments and, from
the point of view of *realism*, cannot do so. For this reason, given the need
to alleviate poverty, incremental redistribution has been recommended.
Such incremental redistribution involves taxing the better off to redistribute
to the worse off. This has been the policy of democratic socialist regimes
for a long time, rarely having marked effects on the distribution of income,
precisely because the redistribution is marginal and if it threatens to become non-marginal, it is successfully resisted. Believing that resistance
stems from people's dislike of having their absolute income levels cut, the
latest version of incremental redistribution is (iii) *redistribution through
growth*.[16] This policy involves taking the extra income that would accrue
to the better off and redirecting it to the poor. As proposed the redistribution would take the form of providing *investment* resources to the poor, so
that the redistribution would give them a permanent source of income
rather than a temporary increase in consumption. If pursued over a long
period redistribution through growth would, though it started by being
incremental, end up by affecting the distribution of income and of assets
substantially. The policy corresponds to objective C (raising the growth
rate of the incomes of the poor) because it means a lower rate of growth

of incomes at the upper end, and a higher rate of growth at the lower end, without any absolute reduction of income, as in other forms of redistribution. The ILO report on Kenya (ILO, 1972) was the forerunner and inspiration of the approach, which was developed and sophisticated by Chenery *et al.* (1974). *Cognoscenti* will recognize that there are some differences between the two, including significant differences in nomenclature. The ILO Kenya strategy was *redistribution from growth*, while the Chenery approach was termed *redistribution with growth*.

To be successful the strategy requires that the policies will not significantly reduce the growth rate of GNP as conventionally measured. This is of obvious importance to the Kenya strategy since redistribution from growth can occur only so long as there is growth, unlike other forms of redistribution. The Chenery strategy redefines the target growth rate to give a higher weight to growth of incomes of the poorer groups. But if redistributive policies are to lead to a higher growth of this redefined target than the conventional non-redistributive trickle-down strategy, then it is clear that the new redistributive strategy must not too adversely affect the conventional GNP growth rate. Moreover, if redistribution is to occur from extra incomes—explicitly the Kenya strategy, implicitly the Chenery strategy—and not by cutting into existing standards, then the extent of possible redistribution will be limited by the growth in incomes.

There are two major problems about the strategy. The first concerns the required assumption that such redistribution could occur without seriously affecting the growth rate. Redistribution—once it became more than trivial—would involve redirecting additional incomes from consumption of high technology goods, and from production of such goods with advanced technology, to investment in small-scale activities, and production of investment and consumption goods for the worst off. But the bias of technological advance has been such that these latter areas have been almost entirely neglected. A policy which switched a substantial amount of resources to them would thus almost certainly reduce the rate of growth measured in conventional terms, at least for a time. While this would not matter at all as far as the objective of redistribution is concerned, it would matter as far as redistribution through growth is concerned because to the extent that the switch in resources was successful, the source of redistribution—the extra incomes generated by advanced technology among the élite—would dry up.

Secondly, the policy is probably as unrealistic politically as the earlier forms of redistribution. The trickle-down policy almost certainly failed because those who benefited from high growth did not wish to divert their gains to those who did not. The same applies to the redistribution through growth policy. The required restraint on incomes at the upper income end will be resisted just as previous redistribution was resisted—and resisted by the decision makers who form part of that group. This appears to be the evidence from Kenya: in 1972 the ILO[17] recommended redistribution through growth—and gave detailed requirements in terms of incomes and tax policy. Despite lip service paid to the Report at the time, there has been no serious attempt to put this part of the recommendations into effect.

Strategies towards poverty alleviation are easy to devise so long as the critical links between technology and income distribution, income distribution and decision makers, and decision makers and objectives, are ignored. Once made central, it seems difficult to avoid the conclusion that much wasted ingenuity has been put into devising *forms* of redistribution, when it is not lack of ingenious schemes but a basic political contradiction between the schemes and the real as opposed to nominal objectives of decision makers, that is critical. Viewed in this light, trickle down may offer a more realistic strategy for decision makers than recently developed forms of redistribution.

THE STEADY TRIPOD

One may distinguish, very broadly, between three schools of thought, each advocating a different strategy to eradicate poverty and reduce inequality.[18] They may be called, for want of better names, the Price Mechanists, the Radicals, and the Technologists.[19] The Price Mechanists argue that low production, low productivity, inequality and unemployment can be eliminated by setting the correct prices, which serve both as signals and as incentives.[20]

There is a powerful and vocal group of development economists who argue that many, if not all, of the disappointments with development efforts are due to faulty price policies. Governments have set the wrong price for capital (too low and often rationed, encouraging excessive scale and underutilization of capital, discriminating in favour of large firms and encouraging take-overs of local by foreign firms), for labour (too high, contributing to unemployment and underutilized capacity and discouraging exports), for the foreign exchange rate (overvalued, discouraging labour-intensive exports and encouraging high-cost import substitution), for the products and services of public enterprises (too low, subsidizing the private modern sector). If only governments were to set the right prices, economic growth, as well as jobs and justice, would triumph. Indeed, this group argues, many of the evils attributed to foreign investment, the multinational enterprise, the wrong technology, inappropriate products, the dominance of the developed country and the dependence of the underdeveloped country, the terms of trade, international inequality, etc., are *really* due to "distortions," to faulty pricing policies, which convey the wrong signals and provide wrong incentives.[21]

Most people would agree that "getting prices right" is not enough. Some would say it would go a long way towards combining more growth (and more efficient growth) with greater equality, others would say that the contribution would be only marginal, but all would agree that other things would have to be done as well, if only additional marketing efforts for the extra exports generated by the "right" price policies, or better facilities to improve the capital or labour markets. (But some would argue that the "right" prices themselves would provide sufficient incentives for the creation or improvement of these institutions.)

But to say "getting prices right is not enough" is open to two diametrically opposite interpretations. It might mean either that, by itself, it would make a contribution to the eradication of poverty and to greater equality, though this contribution would be greater if other things were done as well. But getting prices right is better than nothing. Alternatively, it might mean that while correct pricing policies *combined with* structural reforms, and in particular the redistribution of assets, would contribute to growth and equality, by themselves they might make matters worse or simply alter the manifestation of inequality.

No doubt, the "wrong" price policies can impede development, reduce employment, strengthen monopoly and aggravate inequality. But it does not follow that the "right" policies necessarily do the opposite. They might simply lead to *different* forms of the same evils. Let us assume that land and real capital equipment are scarce, while unskilled labour is plentiful. The supply of labour is growing faster than that of land and capital. We allow competition to prevail and factor rewards to be determined by marginal productivity. And we allow for a fair degree of substitution between labour and capital. Then rents per acre and real returns on capital will be high and rising (reflecting the growing relative scarcity of land and capital), while the wage rate will be low and falling (reflecting the growing abundance of labour). Producers will pay much to get hold of scarce resources of land and capital equipment and will offer little for the abundant supply of workers seeking jobs. Low wage costs will tend to expand employment and output, the extent depending on the elasticity of substitution. Processes, sectors, and products[22] that are labour-intensive will be encouraged and those requiring land and capital discouraged. Foreign capital will be attracted from higher-wage, lower-profit countries. High profits and low wages will tend to encourage domestic savings and hence increase the supply of capital inside the country. Moreover, there will be incentives to invent new methods and products that use labour and save land and capital. All this is fine and as it should be.

But these desirable incentives *depend upon* wages being low (and, if labour grows faster than land and capital, falling), while rents, interest and profits are high (and rising). If in such a society the distribution of land and capital were to be very equal (peasant proprietors or socialized ownership of means of production, though the latter would raise questions as to how the state determines wages and the disposition of the surplus and also about the unequal distribution of power), the functional differences would not matter because personal or household equality would still prevail. What a family loses on labour income, it gains on property income. But if property (land) distribution is unequal, if the ownership of assets, including access to educational opportunities, is highly concentrated, inequality might increase, even if the share of wages went up as a result of a fairly high elasticity of substitution. The difference between a high-wage, low-interest and a low-wage, high-interest policy is that in the first case the evil takes the form of unemployment, in the second of inequality between wage earners and property owners. "Getting prices right" may therefore transform inequality within the working class (between those with and without jobs) into inequality between workers and owners of assets.

To conclude: correct pricing is *certainly* not enough where ownership of assets is concentrated and, *by itself*, *may* make matters worse. This does not mean that correct pricing, combined with other policies, has not an important part to play.

This brings us to the second school of thought: the Radicals. This school believes that what matters is to redistribute assets, power, and access to income-earning opportunities. Only through such "structural" and institutional reforms, whether peacefully and gradually or through revolution and quickly, can growth and equality be achieved. To some (extreme) members of this school, there is only one road to salvation. The whole revolting, suffocating mess must be flushed away. What is to take its place is irrelevant. Even to ask that question reveals a desire to preserve the Establishment. To destroy is also to create.

> The fiery anarchist agitator Bakunin . . . was saying something of this kind: the entire rotten structure, the corrupt old world, must be razed to the ground, before something new can be built upon it; what this is to be is not for us to say; we are revolutionaries, our business is to demolish. The new men, purified from the infection of the world of idlers and exploiters and its bogus values—these men will know what to do. The French anarchist Georges Sorel once quoted Marx as saying "Anyone who makes plans for after the revolution is a reactionary."[23]

Those advocating this line are open to the criticism advanced by an examiner of the development paper in the Oxford Final Honour School: "Several candidates, having argued convincingly that a revolution would be a necessary condition of economic development, in a certain country, concluded that it would be a sufficient one." Even, or rather especially, revolutionary juntas must plan signals and incentives[24] for development in considerable detail.[25]

Other less extreme members of this school advocate expropriation with compensation, though unless the compensation falls short of the initial value of the expropriated asset, there will be no redistribution. Others again would confine redistribution to *additional* assets as they accumulate over time, and would bring about a more gradual redistribution, say by the transfer of a certain proportion of annual savings and investment to low-income groups. Whether as argued above such incremental redistribution is possible in the face of an unequal power structure is controversial.

Both revolutionary and evolutionary, both average and incremental redistributive reforms have tended to fail because of a failure to provide the signals and incentives to make the assets now owned by the poor at least as productive as they were when owned by the rich. Soviet Russia had a long struggle with its peasants. The Soviet hammer has been more successful than the sickle, largely because of a failure of agricultural price incentives. In Cuba,

> "Market anarchy" has been replaced . . . by the anarchy resulting from the interplay between chaotic decentralisation (chaotic because micro economic units, even if totally unselfish and devoted to collective welfare, have no accurate signals to guide their actions into socially optimal channels), and authoritarian centralization, which try as it may, is unable to coordinate and direct efficiently every decision involving resource allocation.[26]

Cuba's sugar estates and Chile's copper mines under Allende might have contributed more to the incomes of the poor had signals and incentives not been neglected.[27] Ironically some members of the Radical School commit the same error as the Price Mechanists: they mistake a necessary for a sufficient condition. In this way, they contribute to a redistribution of inequality, not to its reduction, to a perpetuation of poverty, not to its eradication.

Both the Price Mechanists and the Radicals are (often implicitly) optimistic about technology. They believe either that the technologies appropriate for the eradication of poverty and for the promotion of greater equality already exist, or that the "right" prices or the redistribution of assets will automatically provide the incentives to invent them. The third school, the Technologists, are not so optimistic.

They approach the solution of the problem of poverty, unemployment, inequality and low productivity like that of putting a man on the moon, or, nearer home, discovering new high-yielding varieties of wheat, maize, and rice. Industrial technology, public health, low-cost housing, birth control, nutrition, crops for small farmers, urbanization, require the concentration of brain power and research resources. The Technologists are right, in so far as neither prices and incentives nor "structural changes" can solve a problem where the appropriate technical solution just does not exist: where it has to be invented or discovered and where the incentives are too weak or too slow-working to produce "automatically" the right solution.

Consider, by way of illustration, the need for a capital-saving, efficient technology to provide jobs for all willing and able to work. With existing technology transferred from the West, fixed technical coefficients, unchanged composition of products and unchanged sectoral distribution of investment, only between 1 and 2 per cent of the additions to the labour force can be employed, if we assume that the labour force in developing countries grows at 3 per cent compared with 1 per cent in developed countries, and that income per head is one-twentieth. An appropriate technology to employ only the extra workers entering the labour market each year would have to be such that the investible resources per worker would be only one-sixtieth of what they are in developed countries. Even allowing for some substitution between labour and capital (by changing the product mix, the sectoral distribution or techniques), this is a large hole in the production function to fill.

Technological innovation, in this context, should be interpreted broadly. It includes innovation in institutions. Just as the appropriate hardware may be non-existent, so appropriate institutions may have to be invented. Management, administration, organization, like physical techniques, have been developed in the West to solve labour scarcity, to meet the demand of high incomes, in an environment of temperate climate. Rural institutions to meet the needs of a large, rapidly growing, poor rural labour force make quite different demands on the institutional imagination than those we have tended to transfer from the developed countries.

The technological solution would appear to be particularly appealing both to researchers in the developed countries and to policy-makers in the developing countries, because, on the face of it, it does not violate vested interests and therefore seems to escape political opposition. It appears to lie beyond ideology: ideologies of both the "right" Price Mechanists and the "left" Radicals. It seems to tackle problems in a scientific, practical, workmanlike manner. Technology has been called the opium of the intellectuals.

But technology is both result and cause of income, asset, and power distribution in the national and international system. As the "Green Revolution" has shown, if the distribution of assets like water, fertilizers, and credit is concentrated, it is the large farmers with controlled water supply who benefit, in some cases at the expense of the small farmers and landless labourers. A technology specifically invented to overcome food shortages for the growing number of poor people has reinforced and aggravated rural inequalities. Once again, the Technologists, like the Price Mechanists and the Radicals, may aggravate poverty and inequality or change its form.

Less than 2 per cent of total R.&D. is spent in the developing countries and only a fraction of this on the problems of poverty, even though the number of people is more than twice that in the developed countries. But even if a substantially larger proportion were spent, this would not mean that poverty would be eliminated, if the institutional arrangements and the power structure necessary for dissemination and application are weak or absent. And organized interests will oppose measures that hurt them.

The conclusion of the discussion is by now plain. We have an instance of the Theory of the Second Best, according to which $\alpha + \beta + \gamma$ yield the desired results, but α or β or γ by themselves, far from being "better than nothing," may move society away from the desired goal.[28] Only a three-pronged attack, combining signals and incentives, institutional reforms directed at the redistribution of assets (including access to education) and technical and institutional innovation, promise results. The precise combination of price policies, asset redistribution, and technological research will depend on a number of factors that will vary between countries: on the readiness of vested interests to yield, on the elasticity of substitution between factors, on the nature of the interdependence between sectors, on the degree of concentration of ownership, on the productivity of assets when redistributed, on the fiscal system, etc. But it is only on the three legs of this tripod that efficient redistribution can rest.

It may be objected that to demand a simultaneous attack on all three fronts is to ask for the impossible. This, it might be argued, is suggested by the frequent failure to meet any one of the three requirements. However, the relations between the three are such that failure to attempt change on one front only may prevent the change itself, or the desirable effects of the change. Hence the failure of one prong attacks may actually be due to confining attention to one aspect.

However, much may depend on the *order*[29] in which the policies are pursued. Taking one sequence may prevent the achievement of any or all of the targets. For example, price changes preceding income redistribution may establish patterns of production and consumption inimical to redistribution. Yet if redistribution precedes policy changes on technology and prices, it may establish pressures likely to bring them about. Irma Adelman concludes that the *sequence* of reform is critical to the relative success of some countries which have combined improvements in the incomes of the poor with accelerated growth.

Irma Adelman has argued that an "examination of the development process of those non-Communist countries which have recently successfully combined improvements in the incomes of the poor with accelerated growth (Israel, Japan, South Korea, Singapore and Taiwan) shows that they all followed a similar dynamic sequence of strategies . . ." (1975, pp. 307–8). Her strategies do not correspond precisely to ours, but the sequence is first, radical asset redistribution (sometimes accompanied by negative growth rates); secondly, massive accumulation of human capital and skill creation far in excess of current demand; and, thirdly, economic policies directed at rapid, labour-intensive economic growth, with the development of appropriate technologies for large countries and foreign trade for small countries. Historically, the "grow now, redistribute and educate later" strategy has been followed by some capitalist economies, but the "redistribute and educate now and grow later" strategy is the one followed by the economies studied by Irma Adelman. It is more consistent with current demographic trends and time scales.[30]

In considering the correct sequence one must pay attention to the pressures which reform on one front will have in inducing or preventing reform on the other two, and the likely impact of the one reform taken by itself. From this point of view, it seems that radical redistribution should come first, then the other steps may follow. This reverses the sequence in the now developed countries which was "grow first, redistribute later." This took many decades to make the poor better off and bring about greater equality; and it contrasts with the "redistribute marginally *and* grow" policy, or "redistribution with growth," which is likely to fail in one or both aims.

NOTES

1. I.e. if (Y'_{t10}/Y'_{b10}) is taken as our measure of income distribution at time t' $(Y'_{t10}, Y'_{b10}$ is the money income of the top tenth decile and the bottom tenth decile at time t'), then at time t'', the relevant ratio for comparison is

$$\left(\frac{Y''_{t10}}{1 + \Delta p_{t10}} \div \frac{Y''_{b10}}{1 + \Delta p_{b10}} \right)$$

where Δp_{t10}, Δp_{b10} measure the change in prices of the goods consumed between t' and t'' and not (Y''_{t10}/Y''_{b10}) for a comparison of income distribution between the two dates. Δp, the change in prices, itself depends upon which quantities are taken as weights. The two usual measures, Paasche and Laspeyres, use current and base period quantities respectively. But other quantities could be used as weights. In the light of the subsequent discussion on p. 397 the customary use of base period weights underestimates the impoverishment of the poor as average income grows.

2. Further, as discussed more fully below, the welfare associated with any given purchasing power tends to decline as average incomes rise because of the changing nature of the goods available for purchase.

3. Abel-Smith and Townsend (1965) defined poverty in Britain as occurring when people's standards fell below the level at which National Assistance became payable. This standard is relative as they explicitly recognize—"It must be recognised that any subsistence standard is inevitably influenced by current living standards, and

that we cannot define a poverty line in a vacuum but only in relation to the living standards of a particular society at a particular date" (p. 17). A similar definition is used by Atkinson (1969).

4. See Atkinson (1973) and Sen (1973a).

5. It could be argued that, although inequality between the poorest and the recipient is increased, that between the poorest and the richest diminishes by exactly the same amount, and in addition there is a reduction of the inequality between the recipient and the richest man. But this implies weighing increases and reductions in inequality against one another.

6. A measure of the relation of the incomes of the poor to the average is captured, corrected for inequality *among* the poor, in the measure suggested in equations 8 and 9 of A. K. Sen (1973b).

7. A good discussion is to be found in P. T. Bauer and A. R. Prest (1973).

8. M. Ahluwalia and H. Chenery, "The economic framework" in Chenery *et al.* (1974). See also Simon Kuznets (1972).

9. This might be described as the Rawls Strategy (see Rawls, 1972).

10. Distributional objectives mean that the *ratio* of measures of final to initial income distributions is an objective, not simply the absolute rates of growth of the incomes of different groups, as in the Ahluwalia–Chenery strategy.

11. See P. P. Streeten (1958).

12. If this position is taken to its extreme it becomes impossible to distinguish between objectives and policies and therefore to assess whether the right policies have been selected to meet a government's objectives, as Wilfred Beckerman has pointed out. However, it remains possible to assess policies in the light of declared or nominal objectives.

13. Langdon (1975) provides a fascinating case study of these effects for the soap industry in Kenya.

14. In some countries "trickle down" may have worked in raising incomes at most levels, but it was none the less *regarded* as a failure because of the *relative* impoverishment of some groups—in other words, whether it worked or not depended on whether our strategy of high growth and "trickle down" or redistribution was taken to be the objective. Possibly decision makers considered high growth the objective, while critics considered redistribution.

15. See Westlake (1973).

16. See ILO (1972) and Chenery *et al.* (1974).

17. ILO, *op. cit.* Chapter 20 on "The Cost of Inaction" does, however, discuss some of the points raised here.

18. In line with most current discussions, we focus on inequality in the distribution of income and assets. But these are only a small part of the problem. More important are inequalities of power and access to power, status, prestige, recognition, satisfaction from and facilities at work, conditions of work, degree of participation, freedom of choice, and many other dimensions.

19. See F. Stewart (1974).

20. The function of prices to serve as signals and as incentives can, of course, be separated.

21. Some members of the school believe that all this is due to lack of understanding of basic economic analysis, others that the "distortions" serve entrenched vested interests. Which of these views is correct makes, of course, a difference to the policy prescriptions.

22. Usually, more attention is paid to processes than to sectors and products. But it may be more rewarding to encourage labour-intensive sectors, like the non-organized sector, and appropriate products, than processes which are often dictated by the choice of product and sector. Cf. Frances Stewart, *loc. cit.* (1974).

23. Isaiah Berlin (1970, p. 26).

24. Signals and incentives need not be material ones; they may be moral ones. But many socialist economists have argued that the price system comes into its own under socialism.

25. The methodological similarity of the Price Mechanists and the Revolutionary Marxists reveals their common origin in nineteenth-century liberalism. The early Utopian socialists were more realistic and are more relevant today in their emphasis on detailed planning of institutions and incentives.

26. Carlos F. Díaz-Alejandro (1973, p. 92).

27. ". . . Chile's resource situation has worsened under the impact of a drastic decline in aid from the West and virtual elimination of private inflow of foreign capital—so that the economic regime is under severe stress, calling particularly for improved export performance, much the way we face this necessity. And yet Allende's advisers have given up the "sliding" exchange rate scheme of the earlier Frei government, which worked so well, and the balance of payments situation in consequence has continued to deteriorate disastrously. On a recent visit to Santiago I found that the system had broken down to a point where the divergence between the official and the unofficial parities was of the order of 1 to 10—thus resulting in a situation where selling foreign exchange at the official rate had become an act of honest idiocy that no one, including the distinguished members of the United Nations Secretariat in Santiago, was willing to perpetrate! Ironically, the resulting sabotage of the Allende regime's admirable efforts at socialist transformation has been far more effective than anything the ITT or the U.S. State Department could have planned or even implemented!"—Jagdish N. Bhagwati, "India in the international economy: a policy framework for a progressive society," Lal Bahadur Shastri Lecture, delivered before the fall of the Allende government.

28. The three schools clearly do not cover all relevant issues. In particular, we have left out the school that advocates using fiscal policy to redistribute *consumption* goods and services to the poor. Disregarding the difficulty of differentiating at very low income levels between unproductive and productive consumption, such redistribution as the sole measure of eradicating poverty and promoting equality has serious drawbacks. First, developing countries do not have an adequate fiscal machinery. Second, in order to maintain equality, redistribution of consumption goods and services would have to grow not only in absolute terms, but also as a proportion of national income. This would raise administrative, economic and political difficulties. Third, people may wish to earn their income rather than have it doled out. None of this implies that subsidizing consumption of the poor has not a supplementary part to play. It is by now well known how public services, like health and education, without other reforms, largely benefit the middle class. Another area that we have neglected in this section is the international impact on strategies for equality. Can countries pursue policies for equality, while remaining wide open to communications, foreign investment, the transnational enterprise, foreign technology and foreign products, and the whole structure of international relations with advanced industrial countries? Also left out of the discussion in this section are inter-temporal choices. By keeping the income of the lowest 40 per cent down for a number of years, a country (it has been argued) may be able to raise them to a higher level after a period than if it had raised them earlier. This is the proper formulation of the choice "growth versus equity." Formally, this can be solved by taking the net present value of the future flow of consumption of the bottom 40 per cent as the objective—though this would involve all the problems associated with the choice of the appropriate rate of discount. Nor have we discussed the important problem of how equality, once established, can be maintained in the presence of increasing returns, cumulative processes and unequal distribution of inherited characteristics. Finally, as Robert Cassen has reminded us, we have omitted the important problem of population policy. Redistributive and employment policies, through improved health and education, may reduce fertility and increase incomes per head, though reducing growth of total GNP. This is a powerful argument against the "grow now, redistribute later" strategy and strengthens our case.

29. A point made by Hirschman in correspondence, and Adelman (1975).

30. Irma Adelman concludes: "There is also evidence that the entire package—resource redistribution, massive education and labour-intensive growth policies—must be adopted in that sequence to achieve rapid success. Incomplete versions of this program, such as land reform alone or education without labour-intensive growth, have not worked. For the advanced countries which followed a grow-first pattern, economic development did eventually benefit the poor, but the time it took to do so was much longer (roughly two or more generations) than in our five successful cases (where it took only two decades)."

REFERENCES

1. ABEL-SMITH, B., and TOWNSEND, P., *The Poor and the Poorest*, Occasional Papers on Social Administration, No. 17, G. Bell and Sons, 1965.
2. ADELMAN, IRMA, "Development economics—a reassessment of goals," *The*

American Economic Review, Papers and Proceedings, May 1975, pp. 302–9.

3. ATKINSON, A. B., *Poverty in Britain and the Reform of Social Security*, Cambridge University Press, 1969.

4. ATKINSON, A. B., "On the measurement of inequality," in Atkinson, A. B. (ed.) *Wealth, Income and Inequality*, Harmondsworth, 1973.

5. BAUER, P. T., and PREST, A. R., "Income differences and inequalities," *Moorgate and Wall Street*, Autumn 1973.

6. BERLIN, I., *Fathers and Children*, The Romanes Lecture, Oxford, 1970.

7. CHENERY, H., *et al.*, *Redistribution with Growth*, Oxford University Press, 1974.

8. DANDEKAR, U. M., and RATH, N., "Poverty in India," *Economic and Political Weekly*, Vol. VI, No. 2, 1971.

9. DÍAZ-ALEJANDRO, C. F., review of Bernardo, R. M., *The Theory of Moral Incentives in Cuba*, *Journal of Economic Literature*, Vol. XI, No. 1, Mar. 1973.

10. HARRINGTON, M., *The Other America—Poverty in the United States*, Macmillan, New York, 1962.

11. ILO, *Employment, Incomes and Equality: A Strategy for Increasing Productive Employment in Kenya*, Geneva, 1972.

12. KUZNETS, SIMON, "Problems in comparing recent growth rates in developed and less-developed countries," *Economic Development and Cultural Change*, Vol. 20, No. 2, Jan. 1972, pp. 185–209, reprinted in *Population, Capital, and Growth*, Heinemann Educational Books, London, 1974.

13. LANGDON, S., "Multinational corporations, taste transfer and underdevelopment: a case study for Kenya," *Review of African Political Economy*, No. 2, Jan.–Apr. 1975.

14. MYRDAL, GUNNAR, *Asian Drama*, The Twentieth Century Fund and Pelican Books, 1968.

15. RAWLS, J., *A Theory of Justice*, London, 1972.

16. SEN, A. K. (a) *On Economic Inequality*, Oxford University Press, 1973. (b) "Poverty, inequality and unemployment: some conceptual issues in measurement," *The Economic and Political Weekly*, Vol. VIII, Special Number, 31–33, August 1973.

17. STEWART, F., "Technology and employment in LDCs," *World Development*, Mar. 1974.

18. STREETEN, P. P., Introduction to Gunnar Myrdal, *Value in Social Theory*, Routledge and Kegan Paul, 1958.

19. WESTLAKE, M. J., "Tax evasion, tax incidence and the distribution of income in Kenya," *East African Economic Review*, Vol. 5, No. 2, Dec. 1973.

28

A Critical Analysis of Approaches
to Growth and Equity

James H. Weaver, Kenneth P. Jameson, and Richard N. Blue

INTRODUCTION

For all of its success in raising growth rates of GNP, the postwar strategy
of economic development has come under criticism for its failures: continued unemployment, growth in income inequality within and across nations, increase in absolute poverty, etc. One common theme runs through
all of these critiques: the benefits of postwar development have not gone
to the poor of the world, and such a result offends any sense of justice
since it is the poor who face most directly the basic problems of survival.

In response, there is emerging an alternative strategy to achieve economic development in the Third World, one we will term "growth and
equity." It is not yet fully developed, and there are a number of variants
that have appeared. The next sections will specify the basic outlines of
seven such approaches. Since there are at least as many critiques of the
new models, the final sections will examine them, specifying those that
emanate from the defenders of the traditional, or "trickle down," strategy,
and then turning to those developed by proponents of a revolutionary
strategy for equitable growth.

The debate is far from settled as to which, if any, of the various models
will prove to be most viable. But the field of dispute is being clearly
delimited, and the goal of this article is to give its outlines.

COMMON CHARACTERISTICS OF THE SEVEN MODELS

All the "growth and equity" approaches have certain aspects in common.
All spring from a conviction that traditional reliance on growth of GNP
either will not benefit the poor in today's less developed countries or will
not benefit them quickly enough. They agree that in the near future social
revolution is not in the cards for most poor countries, and they are seeking
a way to achieve some degree of equity short of social revolution. Taiwan,

This paper was presented at the International Studies Association Convention, March 17–20, 1977. It
is published in *International Development Review* (1978/1), pp. 20–27. This paper reflects the authors'
views and does not reflect the views of the Agency for International Development.

Korea, Hong Kong, Israel, Japan, Singapore, and Sri Lanka are cited as examples of successful efforts.

These approaches also share a common assumption that peasants in less developed countries are responsive to economic opportunities. So the bottleneck in the poor countries is not the peasant; more likely it is the powerful elite residing in the capital city.

Finally, all give considerable emphasis to the social and political dimensions of growth and equity. They argue that one crucial limitation of past approaches was their narrow focus on simple economic factors—land, labor, and capital—to the exclusion of political, social, and cultural factors.

Let us turn now to an examination of each approach in turn.

i. Employment Generation

This approach resulted from the International Labor Organization (ILO) missions to Colombia, Kenya, Sri Lanka, etc., which found widespread and growing unemployment despite the growth of gross national product. Thus, it became apparent that growth policies must be reoriented to take into account the need to increase employment.

This perspective focused attention on the informal sector in these countries—retailers, petty traders, carpenters, and so on. A great deal of entrepreneurial talent exists among them, and the main barrier to a greater contribution on their part was access to capital on terms competitive with the formal sector. Thus, in developing their strategy, the ILO put primary emphasis on increasing the availability of capital to the informal sector and concentrating expenditures on employment-creating activities. Particular emphasis was also given to rural areas, especially to the use of labor-intensive production techniques in agriculture.

ii. Redirecting Investment

A second and similar approach has been formulated by Chenery and others at the World Bank, giving primary emphasis to the central role of capital formation. They argue that the poor must have greater capital to generate the incomes necessary to meet their needs. This suggests a reorientation of capital formation away from large-scale, centralized projects to investments that relate directly to the poor: education, health, credit, and so forth. Command over this type of wealth will increase the productivity of the poor and thereby increase their income. In the short run this may come at the expense of growth, but in the long run, the increased productivity and income of the poor will raise the incomes of all members of the society. Since even the well-off members of society will receive long-run benefits from this "trickle-up" strategy, they are unlikely to oppose it as they would a direct effort at asset redistribution.

iii. Meeting Basic Needs

Perhaps the first person to advocate a "basic needs" approach was Mahbub ul Haq of the World Bank. Ul Haq called it a direct attack on poverty. A second advocate was James Grant, president of the Overseas Development Council.

Sri Lanka is cited by Grant as an example of a poor country that has met basic needs with a low level of income. Sri Lanka had a per capita GNP of approximately $120 per annum in 1973, but had achieved levels of life expectancy, literacy, and infant mortality comparable to the United States in 1939. Life expectancy was 68 years; infant mortality was 45 per 1,000 births; the death rate was 6.4 per 1,000; the birth rate was 28.6 per 1,000; and 76 percent of the population was literate.

These impressive results were achieved through expansion of governmental services, one major component being a substantial price subsidy program for grain, which involved the distribution of two or three pounds of free grain per person per week. Low-cost education and health delivery systems were introduced. Sri Lanka has social service expenditures of 12–13 percent of GNP or 30–40 percent of total government expenditures, about $14–$15 per capita per year on social services.

Grant argues that the basic needs of the world's poorest billion could be met as in Sri Lanka for $14 or $15 billion per year of additional foreign aid. He proposes that the developed countries double their foreign aid flows, targeting them on the basic needs of those people living in absolute poverty.

Paul Streeten of the World Bank also favors a basic needs strategy. He advocates that the basic needs approach be seen as a principle around which to organize development thinking and efforts. The goal or target should be to meet the basic needs of all people everywhere. These needs include food, water, clothing, shelter, medical care, education, and participation in decision making. But these needs have to be viewed in their relation to an overall economic and social system of food and goods production, employment generation, education, health, and nutrition delivery.

Once the main elements of the system involved in meeting basic needs are identified, then *each* of these elements must be analyzed as a system and the interrelationships among the elements must be understood. Then alternative strategies for affecting these elements can be chosen for their effectiveness.

iv. Human Resource Development

The next three approaches assume redistribution of assets as a precondition. Irma Adelman argues that revolution is simply not likely for many poor countries, yet her studies have demonstrated that in absolute terms, the bottom 40–60 percent of the population in these countries are becoming worse off. She proposes a human resources development route to achieving growth with equity.

A precondition for its success is redistribution of productive assets—

land and physical capital—as occurred in Japan, Taiwan, and Korea. Also, provision must be made to ensure continued access to assets for the poor once the redistribution has taken place.

The next element of this strategy is a massive program to develop human resources, as in South Korea. In 1964, the educational level of the Korean population was three times that of an average underdeveloped country at Korea's level of per capita GNP.

This emphasis on human capital creation will inevitably be accompanied by a decade or so of slow growth of GNP, resulting in social tension, unrest, and political instability. Thus, the strategy calls for a strong government that can deal with these problems effectively.

Following the creation of human capital, the next step is a human resource intensive industrialization and growth strategy. Small countries will produce for the international market, while larger countries will produce labor and skill-intensive goods for their own domestic market. The high rate of employment generated by industrialization will provide the income that will lead to a demand for the goods produced and will ensure a wide distribution of benefits.

v. Agriculture First Development

John Mellor's approach to growth and equity resembles Adelman's in that it requires land reform before equitable growth can be achieved.

Agriculture plays two roles: first it must supply, at a stable price, the wage goods necessary for employment creation. Low-income people in LDC's spend the bulk of their income on agricultural goods. If their income increases, they will purchase more food, and if output does not increase, this will result in substantial price increases for agricultural products. Wages would thus have to rise and higher wages would slow efforts to employ more people. So increases in agricultural production are essential to the success of this approach.

The second role of agriculture is to supply employment, seemingly a difficult task if agricultural prices are stable and low. Mellor suggests that the manner of accomplishing this is through technical change in agriculture, primarily biological research: new seeds, new fertilizer practices, irrigation, and so on. Though the resulting increase in output won't directly raise employment, the increased spending of farmers will. For example, in India, Mellor found that rural spending of additional income is as follows: 12 percent for livestock, dairy products, meat, milk, and so on, and 18 percent for vegetables and fruit. A total of 30 percent goes to agricultural goods produced in labor-intensive fashion. These farmers also buy labor-intensive goods from the industrial sector, such as textiles, bicycles, transistor radios, and so on. These products are produced efficiently in small-scale firms that could be located in rural areas, close to their new markets. Workers in these plants then buy the grain produced in the rural sector, and the entire process generates employment and income.

Nonetheless, there will be substantial requirements for a capital-intensive infrastructure that must be provided from three sources: an increase in the domestic savings rate and in domestic production; an increase in foreign aid; an increase in foreign trade (that is, import capital-intensive intermediate goods and pay for them by exporting labor-intensive consumer goods—bicycles, textiles, shoes, for example).

vi. Integrated Rural Development

The rural economy approach has been most fully elaborated by Albert Waterston. Waterston argues that top-down approaches to development have not been successful in meeting the social needs of the rural poor, for strategies that focus on agriculture alone result in enrichment of the already rich farmers. Only those farmers who could afford the additional inputs could take advantage of new, high-yield varieties requiring water, fertilizer, pesticides, insecticides, and so on. Thus, the result of the Green Revolution has been to widen the already wide gap between the rich and the poor farmers.

But social service provision by government leads to a "welfare mentality," which Waterston sees in Tanzania and Sri Lanka. So there must be agricultural development along with social infrastructure and services.

From a review of hundreds of rural development efforts, Waterston has found six elements essential for success once land is equitably distributed: labor-intensive production, which is most likely to be adopted by small farmers; use of off-season labor surplus in building minor development works and infrastructure; labor-using light industry in processing of agricultural products, production of intermediate goods for agricultural production, and production of light consumer goods based on local raw materials; self-help or self-reliance; implementation by a government organization with power that cuts across ordinary ministry jurisdictions; and finally, "regional planning" with a hierarchy of development centers bridging the gap between villages and the capital city.

vii. The New International Economic Order

The above strategies concentrated on efforts within Third World countries. But given the degree of openness in most of them, such efforts cannot be abstracted from the international situation. Some analysts, such as Mahbub ul Haq, suggest that the international sphere must be altered before these strategies have any likelihood of success, since many of the required resources must come from the international sphere. Some of the most important elements in ul Haq's suggestions are as follows: a redistribution of international credit so that LDC's can command more capital resources; facility for the LDC's to diversify upstream into processing, transporting, and insuring their exports, and thereby gain a greater share of value added; reduction of developing countries' tariffs and quotas on labor-intensive goods produced in the LDC's; greater amounts of "foreign aid," but made automatic through international taxation on the seabeds or on nonrenewable resources; and finally, a restructuring of international institutions to allow a greater say by the LDC's.

With these changes, ul Haq sees the international sphere coming to play a more positive role in development—a role that may actually facilitate growth and equity development.

THE CRITIQUES OF GROWTH AND EQUITY

The proliferation of approaches to growth with equity is matched by a multiplicity of critiques emanating on the one hand from defenders of the traditional approach and on the other from exponents of revolutionary approaches. It will be useful to take them in turn.

i. Traditional Critique

There are three main components of the defense of the traditional approach. The first component directly disputes the validity of the data that purport to show the failure of traditional efforts. The data are simply not adequate and therefore conclusions cannot be reached. No incontrovertible data exist to prove absolute worsening of living standards of the poor. Also, unemployment data in the Third World are meaningless because many people have jobs that do not fit commonly accepted definitions but which provide them with a livelihood. Finally, even the observations of growing, relative inequality in countries such as Brazil are not unambiguous, and their interpretation is less so, since such changes may be short lived.

The second component of the traditional approach is the argument that attempts at rural development and at keeping people in rural areas are reactionary. History tells us that the source of dynamism and of hope for higher standards of living for the poor is urbanization and industrialization. It can also be shown that small-farmer agriculture is not an efficient way to increase food production. While small farmers may be more efficient on a per-acre basis, this overlooks the broader social cost of providing inputs and distribution facilities for them. It is clearly more costly to deliver fertilizer to 100 small farms than to a single large farm. Also, from the urban point of view, studies of urban migrants have shown that they feel they are better off in cities than in the countryside. In cities they have access to services, to health care, and to education. Hence the argument that people will not stay in rural areas, except through force and coercion, becomes more plausible.

The third and most important point is that the traditional approach to development is working, but it is simply being judged too soon. Western European development exhibited the identical problems that Brazil is being criticized for today—high unemployment rates, since there were large numbers of people to absorb as a result of mechanization, and a

temporary worsening of income distribution. But, in the long run, industrialization brought benefits to all the people in the society through jobs
and resulting higher incomes.

Brazil is the most cited example of the success, of the traditional approach. In the seven years from 1968 to 1974, Brazil's growth rate of 10
percent per year allowed it to double its GNP. Much of this growth came
about through industrial expansion, and much of it was engendered by an
active export promotion program. While such changes had their greatest
effect on the well-being of the owners of capital, those with technical skills,
or perhaps the military, the poor also benefited from the increase in the
number of jobs in the economy. Although real wages certainly did not rise,
and even fell in certain periods of the "miracle," the increase in the number of jobs is claimed to counterbalance this for the poor as a whole. The
same beneficial impact on family income is said to have occurred as more
members of the family joined the labor force.

The success is more general than just that in Brazil, for the benefits
are trickling down everywhere. One example of a pervasive benefit is health
care. Malaria and smallpox prevention programs have been widely effective in rural areas in underdeveloped countries. The falling infant mortality
rates in underdeveloped countries are prima facie evidence that health
benefits are reaching the people. For example, in Latin America there has
been a drop in infant mortality from 120 per 1,000 to 60 per 1,000 during
the last 30 years. That is obvious evidence that the poor are benefiting
from the development process.

Additional support comes from comparing a country like Costa Rica,
which followed the traditional growth strategy, with Cuba, which looked
to equity. Between 1960 and 1974, Costa Rica lowered infant mortality rates
more dramatically than did Cuba; in education it observed a greater percentage increase in enrollments at the primary level, similar increases at
the secondary level, and more than double the increase at the post-second-
ary level. In addition, GNP per capita in Cuba was almost constant throughout the period, and, though Costa Rica had a per capita income $150 below
that of Cuba in 1960, by 1974 it was $110 above Cuba's per capita income.

What is the answer to the problems of poverty and unemployment according to the traditionalists? The answer lies in more rapid growth of the
GNP, more use of multinational corporations and agribusiness, more reliance on export promotion, and finally and most importantly, the necessity
of "getting prices right." This last item includes slowing the growth of
wages, raising the cost of capital, allowing foreign exchange rates to be
market determined, and increasing prices paid to farmers.

Traditionalists cite Taiwan and Korea as examples of countries that
adopted this mix of policies and attained equitable growth using appropriate technologies once the market was allowed to operate.

ii. Revolutionary Critique

Turning now to the left, to the revolutionary critics of growth and equity,
we again find a healthy skepticism, but for very different reasons. As a

starting point, it is claimed that poverty groups in Third World countries will benefit little from a New International Economic Order. South Asia, where much of the world's poverty is concentrated, has a very low portion of its GNP related to foreign trade, in some cases as little as 5 percent. Thus, even with a new international economic order, there would be little impact on poverty. In addition, in the absence of changes in the class structure of countries, a new international economic order would not benefit the masses of people in the poor countries. It would be used to buy arms or to invest in the United States and Western Europe.

So, while a new international economic order is needed, that is not enough, for much of the problem is within the poor countries themselves. Those societies are integrated systems and thus changes in the economic conditions will not be decisive. They are integrated social, political, economic, historical units, with a certain power structure, which is benefiting from the existing system. Even in the very poorest countries in the world —Chad, Mali, or Bangladesh—there are very rich people; thus the minor technical changes that growth and equity strategists advocate do not deal with the basic problem. A slight change in agriculture or a slight change in rural development will have no effect in bringing about a change in society. Class structure cannot be ignored.

The growth and equity theory argues that governments in poor countries want to bring about development, but ignores the reality that elites find the present system to their liking; poverty serves a purpose. John Gurley has offered two explanations for continued poverty. One is that the poverty of the masses is a necessary cost of the privileges of the rich. Development requires awakening people, but if an elite wishes to keep its privileges, it is better that the people doze. The alternative explanation is that poverty is the carcass that is left behind from a strategy of development aimed at GNP growth, emphasizing efficiency, and building on the best. In either case, technical changes to raise growth rates will not have a meaningful impact on equity. Stronger reformist policies will also be ineffectual.

Regarding the models that require equitable land reform, it is highly unlikely that land reform will be carried out. Elites know that land reform will destroy their base of power and their positions of privilege and will establish new classes in the society, which will become the dominant groups. Threatening the elite with revolutions if they do not undertake land reform is like asking them to commit suicide lest they be killed. It would not work in underdeveloped countries any more than it would work internationally. Just as strong a case could be made for international land reform as for land reform in India. Yet no one expects that threats, arguments, or logic will convince the United States, the Soviet Union, or Australia, who dominate the world land mass despite their small populations, to bring about international land reform; they will not allow free migration to their lands. Neither will land reform be brought about in countries by appeals to the elite or by threats.

In addition, there are no really new formulations or new ideas in the growth and equity approaches. All of the ideas were encapsulated in the second five-year plan in India. New ways of putting old arguments will not change the way things are done either in poor countries or internationally. The elite will build loopholes into any plan proposed and they will hold on to their wealth and power.

For this same reason, it is not possible to use government taxation and expenditures to redistribute income. This will antagonize the capitalist class and will lead to a strike of capital, as happened in Chile. The results of a strike of capital will be economic chaos, stagnation in the economy, and ultimately, the overthrow of the reformist government.

In addition, development based on labor-intensive technologies will condemn the poor countries to be hewers of wood and drawers of water in perpetuity. Development must be based on the latest technology and the most dynamic industry (textiles in the case of the United Kingdom, chemicals in Germany, or electronics in Japan, for example).

The final point made is that virtually all of these new approaches have been proposed by Westerners, giving another example of intellectual imperialism to add to many previous ones.

What is the answer according to the Left? The answer is social revolution, and social revolution cannot be achieved through parliamentary means. It can only evolve over time as masses of people become aware of their situation, overthrow the government, and take power themselves. The best way to get land reform, it is argued, is to arm the peasants, who must take action themselves. The action cannot be taken for them by the Army, by the Communist party, or by anybody else. The people must realize that they are many, and the elite are few. For example, at the height of British rule in India, there were fewer than 10,000 British soldiers ruling hundreds of millions of people.

The system can only be maintained if the masses are immobilized, fatalistic, and apathetic. The elite cannot dominate and exploit an aroused and conscious people. So the job of development, according to the leftists, is not to preach nostrums about growth and equity to the rulers. The job, if development is the goal, is to mobilize the people in the poor countries and the progressive people in the United States, so that the United States government does not support repressive and reactionary regimes against the peoples' drive for liberation.

CONCLUSIONS

The dispute over growth and equity approaches to development occurs in two dimensions; first is the dispute among the various theories of growth and equity; second is the dispute between growth and equity and other approaches.

In terms of the first, several major points have become clear. First, it is apparent that asset redistribution is a key to the success of several of the theories, and differentiates them from the others. Thus, asset redistribution is an issue that must be faced. Second, there seems to be agreement that consumption levels of the poor must be maintained and improved— that some set of basic needs must be met. It is also apparent that much of the effort must occur in rural areas and that it must include a redirecting of investment resources to provide the poor with greater command over them. Beyond that there is no obvious agreement on the specific steps to be taken, nor on what trade-off exists or should exist between growth and equity. These will be issues of debate in the coming years.

In the other dimension, the conflict between growth and equity and either the traditionalist or the revolutionary approaches, the issues are less likely to be resolved. Perhaps of greatest use would be an indication of the intellectual role of the growth and equity approaches. Whether correct or not, there is a growing feeling among the intellectual elite in developed and underdeveloped capitalist countries that the traditional approach is simply not working, especially in terms of helping the poor.

Secondly, it is impossible for the intellectual elite in capitalist countries, such as the United States, to support leftist alternatives, such as socialist revolutions, despite their own revolutionary beginnings. However, recent victories have been on the socialist side (for example, Vietnam, Laos, Cambodia, and Mozambique). It was necessary that some new strategy be devised. Thus, growth and equity was inevitable as an alternative to the discredited traditional approach. The growth and equity strategy has become the only option for United States AID, the World Bank, and other donor agencies with capitalist backgrounds.

What we have before us today is the old "revolution versus evolution" controversy. The revolutionaries are quite convinced that there is no hope for the poor in less developed countries short of massive, sweeping social revolution. The evolutionists are not convinced that such revolutions would necessarily be the answer to the problems of the poor. The evidence on whether revolutions succeed in helping the poor, in guaranteeing human rights, and in expanding human development is certainly mixed, as any reading of the record of Russia, China, Cambodia, Mexico, Cuba, Bolivia, and Algeria would show.

It is also not clear whether capitalist development can bring growth and equity, nor whether the capitalist LDC's that seem to have achieved it (Taiwan and Korea, for example) can or should be emulated. The lack of human rights in those countries is all too apparent.

Thus, there are ambiguities in any of the approaches. But the basic needs of all the people must be met. There is something less than admirable about Western intellectuals who, writing in their book-lined studies, issue urgent calls for massive, sweeping revolution in less developed countries. There is even less to be admired in those Western intellectuals who insistently call for a continuation of the status quo that has been beneficial for them. There is, thus, a case for striking out and looking for an alternative that seeks growth and equity through new approaches to development.

REFERENCES

I. ADELMAN, "Growth, Income Distribution, and Equity Oriented Development Strategies," *World Development*, 3, Nos. 2–3 (February–March 1975).

H. CHENERY, *et al.*, *Redistribution with Growth* (Oxford, 1974).

J. GRANT, "A Fresh Approach to Meeting Basic Human Needs of the World's Poorest

Billion: Implications of the Chinese and Other 'Success Models'," presented at American Political Science Association Annual Meeting, Chicago, Illinois, September, 1976.

J. GURLEY, *China's Economy and the Maoist Strategy* (New York: Monthly Review, 1976).

M. UL HAQ, "Third World at the Crossroads. A Lingering Look at the Old Economic Order" (manuscript).

INTERNATIONAL LABOR ORGANIZATION, *Employment, Growth and Basic Needs: A One World Problem* (Geneva: ILO, 1976).

INTERNATIONAL LABOR ORGANIZATION, *Towards Full Employment: A Programme for Colombia* (Geneva: ILO, 1970).

DEEPAK, LAL, "Distribution and Development," *World Development*, 4, No. 9, 1976.

I. M. D. LITTLE, "Review of Adelman-Morris, Chenery, et al.," *Journal of Development Studies* (New York: North Holland Publishing Company, March 1976).

J. MELLOR, *The New Economics of Growth* (Ithaca: Cornell, 1976).

P. STREETEN and S. BURKI, "Basic Needs: An Issues Paper," World Bank, 1977.

A. WATERSTON, "A Viable Model for Rural Development," *Finance and Development* (December 1974 and March 1975).

29

Toward a New International Order

Transition toward a new international economic order will include joint dialogue and bargaining between Third World and industrialized countries. This can take place in global forums (e.g., UNCTAD), between Third World and industrial countries' regional groupings (e.g., ACP/EEC) or in a special *ad hoc* forum (e.g., the Paris OPEC-Third World/Western oil importer attempt at a dialogue in relations between the present Third World and industrialized economies).

If the forums are not global, they may run the risk of creating divisive tendencies among Third World countries. The fact that the ACP group membership was defined by the EEC illustrates this risk. Similarly, the attempt to divide OPEC and other Third World countries at the Paris talks was quite overt, especially on the issue of a dialogue on commodities other than oil. This is a reason for seeking global talks or a Third World definition of those Third World countries which should attend (for example by a constituency system, as discussed earlier). Vigilance to avoid being trapped by efforts to divide and rule must not lead to systematic insistence on mass global conferences as the sole appropriate forums, when alternatives give sufficient assurance that all interests will be considered.

The first step is the realization that systems, ways of thought and patterns of action previously viewed as fixed and unchangeable not only can but must be changed. The second is that entering into a dialogue leading to the preservation of the *status quo* is purposeless, mutually damaging, or both. The third step is to engage in negotiations on the measures and sequences of change. Areas in which positive negotiations could yield tangible short- to medium-term results include:

1. Transfer of basic foreign-owned assets to national control.
2. Patterns of production and trade, with special reference to market and supply access, including the cases of both commodities and industry.
3. Technology, knowledge and technical transfer and use arrangements.
4. Transition toward a new industrial geography of the world.
5. Financial transfers.
6. Access to food.

Reprinted from the 1975 Dag Hammarskjöld Report on Development and International Cooperation (*What Now: Another Development*), originally published in *Development Dialogue* (1975 1/2), the journal of the Dag Hammarskjöld Foundation, Uppsala, Sweden.

1. TRANSFER OF BASIC FOREIGN-OWNED
ASSETS TO NATIONAL CONTROL

The international community has long recognized the principle of national sovereignty over natural resources, but world power structures have not really accepted the meaningful exercise of this right. The right to national sovereignty over the economic processes is not of course limited to natural resources; it includes the whole of the productive sector.

There is, today, a widespread concern over foreign control of key sectors of the national economies in both industrialized and Third World countries. The reaction of industrialized countries to investment by petroleum producers in some of their enterprises contributes, ironically, to bringing to the fore the implications of foreign control. Conditions may thus have improved for the implementation of the rights that countries have but very often—if they are small or weak—cannot enforce without economically damaging confrontations they may be unable or unwilling to risk.

Third World countries need to own, manage, administer and market their own resources. Only to the extent that they are masters in their own houses can they be expected to participate fully in collective efforts at the international level. A resources policy of Third World countries managed, directly or indirectly, from industrialized countries will have no stability whatsoever. Negotiating power based on real control by Third World countries of their own economies is a precondition for meaningful international discussions. An orderly and effective transfer of foreign-owned resources to national control should be fostered and organized. This would avoid a long, drawn-out process of repetitive bickering and confrontation over the effective control of natural resources, leading to strains and tensions arising from nationalization and expropriations, actions which themselves generate retaliations. The sooner the process of effective national control is achieved, the better the conditions for international cooperation will be. This is an area in which the effectiveness of pure confrontation (e.g., Cuba and Iraq) and confrontation followed by negotiation (e.g., Tanzania, Peru and Algeria) have been demonstrated adequately enough to suggest that a real basis for a serious dialogue, free from the ghost of the "prompt, adequate, effective" compensation slogan, now exists.

Asset acquisition and compensation are operationally matters of parameters, practices and procedures. The problems lie in the ability to exercise the right involved, in what regard for damage to basic external economy interests means, and in how to settle differences in particular cases.

Under these circumstances continued debate on abstract principles is more often an exchange without communication than a dialogue aimed at establishing guidelines charting out broad parameters within which individual cases could be evaluated and negotiations conducted. The resulting situation produces uncertainty, increases risk, encourages unilateral action and retaliation, and impedes individual case negotiations. No one benefits from this, at least, not beyond the very short run.

A series of propositions which could form the basis for a more predictable, orderly and operationally acceptable framework is as follows:

National economic sovereignty includes the rights to produce, allocate production and determine who may produce.

These rights—and particularly the radical changes resulting from their exercise—carry a duty to take account of the basic needs (including access to supplies) of the people of other countries.

The rights to acquire and to regulate the use of assets within a country are an integral part of its economic sovereignty.

Exercise of the right to acquire entails a right to consider whether compensation should be paid, taking into account the total historic and economic context surrounding previous ownership of the acquired assets.

Contracts palpably based on coercion or radically unequal knowledge could be unilaterally abrogated or subject to compulsory renegotiation.

The definition of how to evaluate assets, the identification of relevant historical and economic circumstances (e.g. past profit remittances, tax treatment, transfer prices) and the use of clauses providing for automatic or contingent renegotiation of long-term agreements are among the areas in which technical work and negotiation would be needed to flesh out the five skeletal propositions into a workable set of guiding principles.

The control of TNCs is an area in which lines of action on a global level clearly beneficial to the Third World remain to be identified.

The capacity for autonomy and flexibility of the TNCs has put sovereignty to the test in rich as well as poor countries. New forms of management and control by states—individually, regionally and globally—are needed and can be in the interests of both industrial and Third World countries.

What global measures are appropriate requires thorough investigation. A weak international regulatory agency "checking" flimsy declarations on "desirable practices" would be a negative step, cosmetic at best, and at worst, a tool of those it purported to regulate. Two initial international actions should be on the international agenda for negotiation:

A *minimum code of conduct;* its violation would be recognized as giving a host state full right to take corrective and punitive actions with the support, or at least acquiescence, of other countries.

An *international data-collection, compilation-analysis and recording system* to make the workings of TNCs more available to national regulators and to the people whose lives are affected by TNC operations.

The code of conduct should be a floor—from which better terms can be negotiated—not a ceiling or goal. The data service should assist national or regional regulatory bodies. The development of these two international procedures should be possible [soon]. The dialogue leading to them and their initial operation should suggest further practicable steps.

2. NEW PATTERNS OF PRODUCTION AND TRADE

New patterns of production and international trade form the basis of a new international economic order. Self-reliance—nationally or regionally—is unlikely to require or in many cases even be consistent with absolutely declining levels of international trade. Changes in commodity terms of trade would allow an adequate increase to be achieved only if complemented by shifts in the composition of exports. Many areas of production development—nationally and regionally—are practicable only if effective access to industrial-economy, regional and Third World markets can be attained. In other fields such access would reduce costs and hasten the progress of primarily national-market and basic-need-oriented industrial projects. As already mentioned, commodities constitute the most critical area for the next few years. Action seems possible because:

> Not only is there a genuine joint interest of rich and poor countries in achieving more equitable and stable commodity arrangements, but the existence of this joint interest is perceived by many Third World and industrialized countries, governments and firms.
>
> A few initial steps and detailed, negotiable proposals exist— UNCTAD's Integrated Commodity Programme, for example.

The point is that if significant progress cannot be made on the commodity front [soon] then the prospects for a mutually destructive economic confrontation may be very real. Effective commodity action should comprise:

> Rapid achievement of parallel (not necessarily identical) agreements on fifteen to twenty key commodities, which provide for indexation, maximum and minimum price ranges and their adjustments, buffer stocks and intervention procedures, and access to supplies.
>
> International financing for the initial working capital of the schemes, which, if properly managed, would earn enough to meet interest and operating expenses.
>
> Back-up compensation agreements to mitigate falls in export proceeds (whether price- or quantity-related).
>
> Forward integration of Third World primary producers into marketing structures, market information generation and market management. This would reduce the role of the present, often destabilizing, terminal markets and of the brokerage firms. Probably, it would also involve wider use of multi-year, price- and quantity-defined contracts.
>
> Parallel integration of Third World primary exporters into processing and manufacturing stages prior to export. This measure would have to be backed by access development similar to that for non-traditional exports in general.

The above programme is a long way from being in itself a new international economic order. It is, however, equally far from the old model pursued with so little success over the past thirty years (one-commodity, fixed-money price range, primary-form-only). It is a practicable programme. For example, the package-of-commodity-agreements approach increases acceptability: European economies, like the Third World's, are concerned with grain supply assurances and ceiling prices; the USA, like West African states and Malaysia, has an interest in minimum, indexed oil-seed prices; Japan, like Algeria, is concerned with the cost and availability of sugar.

Assuming properly set and adjusted ranges and competent management, a buffer stock can turn a profit—as demonstrated by the International Tin Agreement. The maximum working capital likely to be needed at any one time is not by any means unobtainable in the context of a viable investment. Indexation of price ranges to some agreed world trade-price index would reduce the need for renegotiation of price ranges. It would be necessary only in cases in which their relationship to other commodities had to be changed to provide adequate supply or limit excess production.

National economic integration (including flexibility between domestically used and internationally traded products), economic balance, adjustment assistance, commodities (especially forward integration into marketing, processing and manufacturing) are interrelated. Progress on each front would smooth the way for progress on others. However, while action on commodities is important, effective access for non-traditional exports (including processed and manufactured stages of present primary product exports) to industrialized countries' markets will continue to be a critical factor in achieving more balanced, more equitable and more dynamic periphery–centre trade patterns. Similarly, in an alternative development based on self-reliant concentration or meeting basic needs, international trade is a supporting means not an end or the centre-piece of a material-growth-oriented dynamic. It is, however, a significant means qualitatively and usually quantitatively, and one whose proper utilization can be crucial to the success of national and collective self-reliance.

Effectiveness, certainty, freedom from discrimination, and growth are the most important features of access. Preferential treatment, while sometimes useful, is less critical, especially if "infant export-industry" promotion schemes are accepted *pari-passu* with "infant import-substitution industry" protection. For many manufactured goods the certainty that increasing volumes would be purchased if offered at competitive prices is far more important than minor tariff preferences against third-party producers.

The instruments to ensure access will probably undergo major changes in the coming years. Conventional measures, although useful, cannot by themselves ensure major changes in present trade patterns. They do not eliminate problems resulting from intra-TNC trade, foreign control of marketing channels or the "imitative" syndrome implicit in indirect commercial policy measures to stimulate trade. A mechanism that may emerge in the future is "negotiated planning," at governmental levels, of Third World countries' export growth. This will require institutional changes in market-economy industrialized countries. Planned expansion of trade implies governmental commitments to buy directly or to assure a certain level of imports by local enterprises. This could be coupled with agreed structural industrial transformation to avoid major disruptions. Also, facilitating direct market channels between Third World producers or exporters and industrialized wholesalers and users would broaden access, create alternatives to TNC extra-firm trade, invalidate in a number of products existing import monopolistic structures and permit the governments of industrialized countries to have a better overview of the types of commitments they could accept.

Systematic negotiation on the concrete conditions of effective access, backed by export promotion and marketing capacity build-up both by individual Third World countries and mutual cooperation for development centred on regions or products, could produce far greater results than wide-ranging exhortations for immediate, totally free access. These demands alarm industrial economies and—for most countries and products —cannot lead to major export gains until new capacity is installed. Given this need to build up production and marketing capacity on a product-by-product basis, there is every reason in the case of major products to negotiate rates of export growth and to cooperate in allowing transformation-adjustment schemes in rich countries to reduce human distress and economic loss. Thus, they would diminish resistance to major international economic reform.

In the case of centrally planned industrialized economies, the same principles apply, but in a somewhat different form. What is needed are medium- or long-term contracts for the purchase of processed and manufactured exports, whether as part of general trade agreements, linked to machinery export credits, or separately. With the exception of intra-CMEA agreements involving Cuba and Mongolia, and—to a lesser degree—Yugoslavia, socialist European countries have not given significant access to non-traditional exports of Third World countries. Given the planned nature of their consumption, production and trade patterns they are exceptionally well placed to provide assured access and negotiations aimed at achieving that end should be given high priority.

The link between borrowings (or more strictly repayments) and non-traditional export access is of relevance to market as well as centrally planned economies. There are examples of finance secured by and repaid through export contracts to the capital-exporting country. These should be sought both initially and by renegotiation. In respect of plant and machinery supply contract loans, guaranteed access for a portion of the products of the plant, preferably under contracts entered into in parallel with those for financing the plant, would often be the most advantageous way of guaranteeing that the loan could be serviced without heavy strains on the borrower's foreign-exchange earnings.

3. SOCIAL CONTROL OF TECHNOLOGY

Development of science and technology has become primarily a political and social issue, not a technical one. Producing technology, in the present international structure, means producing instruments of control and influence over other individuals, firms and nations. The capacity of technology to transform the nature, orientation and purpose of development is such that the question of who controls technology is central to who controls development. Technology can no longer be considered as a mere component of the production process; it is one of the principal factors of change. In such a context the private or national appropriation of technology and the proprietary orientation of research and development should give way to policies of strict social control of technological development and the concept of private property in knowledge must be changed. Technology must be considered as a social good whose administration and orientation must conform to social objectives.

The first step in this direction must be a reformulation of the patent and copyright systems. Work and some initiatives on the former are under way in UNCTAD but they are subject to formidable opposition from the dominant power structures. However, reform of patent and copyright regulations is far from adequate. Negotiation must involve effective transfer of related knowledge and experience and of training to allow its incorporation into the importer's body of usable and adaptable techniques. Requirements for locally based design, development and adaptation units in TNC subsidiaries in Third World countries might be a limited first step in this direction. The root of the problem lies not in the importation of knowledge and technology—the Japanese experience demonstrates that—but in a lack of selectivity, and above all, in paying for technology, without actually securing control over it, must less over its reproduction and adaptation.

Technological and technical knowledge transfer and use negotiations at the global level must be grounded on national and regional programmes of action, if they are to be meaningful. As with TNC regulation—of which knowledge transfer regulation is a part—the present capacity for international action is limited.

However, three areas for international action do exist:

> Support for technology development and adaptation in Third World countries should be made central (rather than marginal) to UN activities. The record of joint research in agriculture—however imperfect and limited—demonstrates the real potential that UNESCO, UNIDO, FAO and ILO have failed to tap.

> Reform and coordination of UN consultancy services in the technology transfer and development field should be pursued to make them more precise, operative and competent. This requires different, and fewer, permanent staff and more use of special-purpose, individual or firm, consultancy expertise.

> The draft UNCTAD code of conduct—if adopted as minimum provisions, the violation of which would be internationally accepted as justifying penalties—could be of some value in setting minimum standards for peripheral countries suffering from particularly onerous transfer terms and use restrictions, aggravated by inadequate knowledge on how to proceed. However, to adopt a watered-down version as long-term "ceiling" goals would be a counterproductive step, restricting present negotiation leaders, such as Mexico and the Andean Pact, more than it would help weaker countries.

4. TRANSITION TOWARD A NEW INDUSTRIAL GEOGRAPHY OF THE WORLD

Industrialization is a fundamental component of a need-oriented and self-reliant economy in Third World countries. Its three basic objectives are:

> To establish an industrial support base that would permit the highest degree of self-sufficiency in the satisfaction of basic needs. This

would diminish external vulnerability, an essential requirement of
self-reliance.

To develop a diversified industrial structure, which can sustain non-
imitative patterns of consumption appropriate to the resource-base,
environmental characteristics and socio-political choices of each
country. This would respond to the endogenous requirements of
another development.

To link parts of the industrial structure with the international economy so as to benefit from new patterns of trade relationships with
industrialized countries. This would foster the international dimension of self-reliance.

All three objectives imply a large degree of technological innovation and
industrial cooperation with other Third World countries at the subregional,
regional or interregional levels. In this context, the success of a new international economic order will be measured to a great extent by its ability
to achieve, in an orderly way, a radical change in the industrial geography
of the world, permitting a much more substantial participation of Third
World countries in total industrial output. Redeployment of new industrial
activities in Third World countries could become one of the most important
instruments for transferring real resources to them.

The rationale of redeployment emerges clearly from an assessment of
present trade and production patterns. Workers, specialized manpower,
energy, raw materials and even capital increasingly flow from Third World
countries toward industrialized centres where they are employed in intermediate and final industrial processing. Thus, the value added of the whole
productive process is internalized in industrial economies. A primary
objective of a new international economic order would be to reverse this
trend. Production should be located where a large number of the production
factors are found, rather than in the market centres where most are
now imported. These obvious advantages of Third World countries have not
been explored adequately—a fact which shows clearly that the present
patterns of world industrialization have little in common with even traditional textbook economic rationality and much more with power politics
and the imperatives of economic domination.

The "pull" factors drawing a more diversified economic activity
pattern to the Third World are accompanied by some "push" factors in the
over-industrialized parts of the world. Further concentration of factories
at the centre is likely to increase environmental problems. While pollution
can often be overcome, albeit at some real cost, the hazards involved in
the creation of extensive "heat islands" may ultimately limit the further
expansion of production. Overtaxing local ecosystems is likely to be self-
defeating for the population directly involved and detrimental to the collective ecological interest of mankind.

Industrial redeployment leading to a new geographical distribution
of production must be undertaken in the context of selective participation
by Third World countries in the international economic system. The
capacity to choose the type of new activities to be transferred is indispensable in maintaining a coherent development policy. Monitoring the

impact of new industries on local consumption patterns is required, to counteract undesired demonstration effects. This implies that many of the "new" industries would not necessarily be linked to national markets but could essentially be directed toward international markets, thus optimizing the income generation benefits of their relocation as a means to paying for imports in the service of basic needs while also minimizing the dangers of disrupting internal consumption styles.

It is clear that such changes will not come about easily. A number of problems and dangers, both for Third World and industrialized countries, seem evident. A planned process of transition is thus indispensable; if redeployment is to become a credible proposition it must help limit the inevitable transformation problems in industrialized countries.

Creating unemployment and disrupting human communities are not among the goals of another development, and the efficiency of the transition to another geography of production turns in large measure on identifying sequences which minimize these problems. The same is true regarding the possibilities of bringing about change largely by negotiation rather than by total confrontation. If trade unions in industrialized countries see another geography as meaning widespread unemployment and increasing social problems in their own countries they will become the most committed opponents of another development. It is imperative to demonstrate that the transition need not have these effects and that they can be averted. The level of absolute numbers involved in changes of employment, production patterns and location of economic activity is not excessively high. A 1 per cent annual shift in employment patterns in industrialized countries maintained over twenty-five years would certainly be adequate to allow the transition to another geography of production. Labour-force entry, departure and job-changes for other reasons are usually about ten times as high. Reconversion in the two years following the Second World War involved at least 25 per cent of most industrial-economy workers in job changes.

The pace and sequences of transformation require research, dialogue and negotiation. The efforts of the ILO regarding the 1976 World Employment Conference are a sign that increased attention is being paid to these issues. But much more priority should be given to them, especially in industrialized countries and international organizations. The Lima Charter of UNIDO will remain either a dead issue or a source of needlessly damaging discord until the road from 1975 to 1985 is mapped out to enable progress toward the Charter's generalized targets for the year 2000.

Within this context three points need to be stated:

Industrialized countries and their workers neither can nor will agree to a rapid pace of change—regardless of how well planned the transformation strategies are—unless large-scale human suffering is prevented.

Third World production capacity cannot be created immediately; it can be built up rapidly but only with assured market access.

Temporary problems of adjustment in industrialized countries will reveal a genuine need to adjust the pace of transition for specific countries, commodities and time periods.

These points do not lead to inevitable conflict. They do suggest that an agreed, globally regulated framework providing assured access but subject to limited, compensated adjustments in particular cases is necessary.

Regulation and joint planning of the transition period also stems from the need to avert a number of dangers confronting Third World countries. As stated above, a selective approach is necessary. It would:

Ensure that a new geography is not in fact planned and implemented by TNCs according to their own interests and objectives.

Choose types of production that will not result in a new, unequal structural relationship with industrialized countries at a higher, more sophisticated, but none the less dependent level.

Make certain that Third World countries do not become "pollution havens," by establishing adequate environmental safeguards.

Distribute the location of new industries along economically rational lines among Third World countries so that projects do not concentrate exclusively on larger, better endowed and relatively more industrialized countries.

Conduct negotiations toward linking the reduction of the temporary migration of unskilled workers with training and production transfers to the Third World.

Such negotiations might include:

Training programme requirements for all countries employing immigrant workers, related to their home-country skills and employment development needs.

Contracts with employing firms to stimulate phased transfer of production to Third World countries.

Enactment—as well as enforcement—of minimum-wage, incremental, social-security and housing provisions broadly comparable to those of national workers for all migrant workers, to assure the well-being of those who—for some years to come—will still need to work abroad. This would also make clear the true economic cost of migrant workers to industrialized countries and employers and thus encourage changes in the location of production.

5. FINANCIAL TRANSFERS

Financial transfers are a complementary instrument in a policy of redistribution of resources towards Third World countries. A new international economic order is centred on measures to put an end to the present drain of resources towards industrialized countries, to improve terms of exchange for Third World countries and to increase the resource-creating capacity by industrial redeployment. Financial transfers are necessary to complement and facilitate the attainment of these objectives, but they cannot take their place. In the same manner, they are complementary to national policies of change and must be oriented to support the objectives of another development.

Experience shows that reliance on purely financial transfers is unreal (real transfers in percentage terms of GNP are diminishing), inefficient ("aid" has not been primarily directed to countries or projects which make the needs of peoples their overriding concern), and politically dangerous (through action or abstention it is often used to control or impede economic policies of other countries).

To a large extent, financial transfers have been used as a political instrument to stimulate growth of those countries or projects which do not pose any threat to existing power structures, while withholding it from those which have embarked on the road of radical structural trans-formation. An odd correlation has emerged between "aid" and lack of respect for human rights, fostering large volumes of transfers to countries whose stability is based on torture, repression and disrespect for the dignity of man.

On a bilateral level, this practice—although reprehensible—reflects none the less the right of a country to choose the recipients of its transfers. This situation can only be changed from within those industrialized countries which pursue these policies, through a better control by parliaments, political parties and progressive pressure groups.

Worse still is the fact that public multilateral financial institutions, theoretically oriented by the values of the UN Charter, have often followed —under the cloak of "technical analysis"—very similar policies. There are signs of a positive evolution, at least at the conceptual level, but many constraints, both political (the decision-making structure) and financial (the sources of funds), remain and there is a long way to go before these institutions become real instruments of another development.

Changes appear easier to bring about in the UN institutions, whose voting system is more democratic; the creation of new funds, such as the Special Fund, the Human Settlements Foundation or the International Fund for Agricultural Development, underlines the need for clear policy guidelines (see Part Three for a discussion of the institutional problems). Finally, there are a few enlightened bilateral programmes, those of countries such as Sweden, the Netherlands, Canada and Norway which provide a *de facto* alternative to conservative policies.

Taken together, such bilateral sources and the UN resources already amount to US $2 to 3 billion per annum and are likely to increase rapidly. In addition, in such funds the proportion of real transfers is significantly higher than the world average, since they are more "recipient-oriented," less tied and offer softer conditions.

Financial transfers are by definition marginal in relation to the investment financed by Third World countries themselves. They must therefore be directed toward critical bottlenecks in such a manner as to become decisive. Decisions concerning resources transfer must be in tune with those of another development. Otherwise, they would only continue to contribute to maintaining the existing "order."

The following considerations should be . . . borne in mind . . . when reorienting financial transfers or confirming the positive orientations of some of them:

Bilateral financial transfers should not be offset by negative trade practices. They should on the contrary be a consistent element of a coherent national policy of international cooperation.

In order to support another development, financial transfers should be directed toward innovation aiming at solving the specific problems of Third World countries. They should in no circumstances be the vehicles for the exportation or indiscriminate transfer of irrelevant socio-economic models, technologies, etc. They should generously support autonomous research capacity and activities in the Third World.

Multilateral and bilateral financial transfers would be optimized if they were made systematically on a grant basis, or at least at no interest with long periods of reimbursement and adequate reimbursement holidays.

Financial transfers, whether supporting budgets or benefiting particular programmes or projects, should be effectively directed to meeting the requirements of another development in so far as they imply internal redistribution of resources: specifically, they should not merely replace savings which would have occurred in the absence of such transfers. In other words, they should accrue only to countries whose policies are seriously geared to the eradication of poverty and to the achievement of self-reliance, or to projects directly benefiting the poorest and most exploited or those whose situation is the most critical (young children, pregnant and nursing mothers).

Should transfers linked to projects continue to be deemed necessary, such projects should as a matter of principle be executed by host-country institutions, since foreign inputs, whether bilateral or multilateral, are of an ancillary nature.

Resource-transfers in the form of supply of technical assistance should draw consistently on the expertise available in the Third World itself.

Last but not least, the manner of transferring new international resources must be such as to overcome the present contradiction between the application of the principles of non-intervention and the respect for human rights; at the present time, in applying the former virtually no one questions the violation of the latter. This Report believes such policies cannot continue; they make a travesty of all that the United Nations should stand for. The international community has a right to decide what priorities should inform the resource-transfers that it finances. In such a framework respect for human rights must be an overriding criterion.

6. ACCESS TO FOOD

The main objective of a food policy for another development is to attain effective access to adequate food for all human beings. For poor countries this requires the highest attainable degree of self-sufficiency nationally or jointly with other Third World countries. This requires basic reforms in the land tenure and distribution structures together with income reallocation patterns which make food accessible to the poorer sectors of the people.

International action is needed to support the process of change and to provide for the food deficit which will continue to exist in the transitional period. International cooperation without internal changes would have no meaning; internal changes without international cooperation would not solve the immediate short-term food shortages.

Despite their limitations the conclusions of the World Food Conference and, more important, the OPEC initiatives which have led to the International Fund for Agricultural Development attaining its $1 billion initial funding target represent first steps. They should be followed up to ensure:

Adequate emergency supplies of food to poor countries facing crisis because of crop failures or sudden food and fertilizer price changes.

Support for Third World development of food-production capacity including research and input production capabilities.

Promotion of changes in socio-economic and technical-economic patterns which limit access to food even when it is physically available.

If IFAD and industrial-country programmes are to contribute to meeting these goals, a number of proposals and provisions need to be negotiated and implemented:

Providing adequate reserve stockpiles of basic foodstuffs to avoid starvation. This should be in an amount sufficient for at least two successive years of poor global harvests.

Financing of stockpiles by basic foodstuffs exporters and high-income importers and their location in or near major using regions.

Achieving agreed allocation procedures designed not simply to ration stocks but to operate two price systems to guarantee basic human needs globally and locally in years of scarcity by putting most or all the quantity shortfall and price pressure on luxury markets.

Moving towards reform of the industrial-economy agricultural protection policies which have systematically discouraged peripheral economies from aiming at surpluses. This has steadily eroded the world's food safety margin.

Providing effective access to supplies of and finance for agricultural inputs for Third World countries' agricultural build-up in respect both to physical availability and acceptable prices.

Substantially increasing finance for global, regional and national Third World agricultural research and development oriented to simple technology, more productive use of more labour, natural renewal of soils, control of the impact of drought, and forest and water management.

Relating the use of food and agricultural input supply transfers to the financing of land reform, rural public works of particular benefit to small farmers, and rural employment development programmes oriented to the needs for employment and for basic goods and services of rural workers and peasants.

30

Outwitting the "Developed" Countries

Ivan Illich

It is now common to demand that the rich nations convert their war machine into a program for the development of the Third World. The poorer four fifths of humanity multiply unchecked while their per capita consumption actually declines. This population expansion and decrease of consumption threaten the industrialized nations, who may still, as a result, convert their defense budgets to the economic pacification of poor nations. And this in turn could produce irreversible despair, because the plows of the rich can do as much harm as their swords. US trucks can do more lasting damage than US tanks. It is easier to create mass demand for the former than for the latter. Only a minority needs heavy weapons, while a majority can become dependent on unrealistic levels of supply for such productive machines as modern trucks. Once the Third World has become a mass market for the goods, products, and processes which are designed by the rich for themselves, the discrepancy between demand for these Western artifacts and the supply will increase indefinitely. The family car cannot drive the poor into the jet age, nor can a school system provide the poor with education, nor can the family icebox insure healthy food for them.

It is evident that only one man in a thousand in Latin America can afford a Cadillac, a heart operation, or a Ph.D. This restriction on the goals of development does not make us despair of the fate of the Third World, and the reason is simple. We have not yet come to conceive of a Cadillac as necessary for good transportation, or of a heart operation as normal health care, or of a Ph.D. as the prerequisite of an acceptable education. In fact, we recognize at once that the importation of Cadillacs should be heavily taxed in Peru, that an organ transplant clinic is a scandalous plaything to justify the concentration of more doctors in Bogotá, and that a Betatron is beyond the teaching facilities of the University of São Paolo.

Unfortunately, it is not held to be universally evident that the majority of Latin Americans—not only of our generation, but also of the next and the next again—cannot afford any kind of automobile, or any kind of hospitalization, or for that matter an elementary school education. We suppress our consciousness of this obvious reality because we hate to recognize the corner into which our imagination has been pushed. So persuasive is the power of the institutions we have created that they shape not only our preferences, but actually our sense of possibilities. We have forgotten how to speak about modern transportation that does not rely on automobiles and airplanes. Our conceptions of modern health care emphasize our ability to prolong the lives of the desperately ill. We have become unable to think of better education except in terms of more complex schools and of teachers trained for ever longer periods. Huge institutions producing costly services dominate the horizons of our inventiveness.

We have embodied our world view into our institutions and are now their prisoners. Factories, news media, hospitals, governments, and schools produce goods and services packaged to contain our view of the world. We —the rich—conceive of progress as the expansion of these establishments. We conceive of heightened mobility as luxury and safety packaged by General Motors or Boeing. We conceive of improving the general well-being as increasing the supply of doctors and hospitals, which package health along with protracted suffering. We have come to identify our need for further learning with the demand for ever longer confinement to classrooms. In other words, we have packaged education with custodial care, certification for jobs, and the right to vote, and wrapped them all together with indoctrination in the Christian, liberal, or communist virtues.

In less than a hundred years industrial society has molded patent solutions to basic human needs and converted us to the belief that man's needs were shaped by the Creator as demands for the products we have invented. This is as true for Russia and Japan as for the North Atlantic community. The consumer is trained for obsolescence, which means continuing loyalty toward the same producers who will give him the same basic packages in different quality or new wrappings.

Industrialized societies can provide such packages for personal consumption for most of their citizens, but this is no proof that these societies are sane, or economical, or that they promote life. The contrary is true. The more the citizen is trained in the consumption of packaged goods and services, the less effective he seems to become in shaping his environment. His energies and finances are consumed in procuring ever new models of his staples, and the environment becomes a by-product of his own consumption habits.

The design of the "package deals" of which I speak is the main cause of the high cost of satisfying basic needs. So long as every man "needs" his car, our cities must endure longer traffic jams and absurdly expensive remedies to relieve them. So long as health means maximum length of survival, our sick will get ever more extraordinary surgical interventions and the drugs required to deaden their consequent pain. So long as we want to use school to get children out of their parents' hair or to keep them off the street and out of the labor force, our young will be retained in endless schooling and will need ever-increasing incentives to endure the ordeal.

Rich nations now benevolently impose a straightjacket of traffic jams, hospital confinements, and classrooms on the poor nations, and by international agreement call this "development." The rich and schooled and old of the world try to share their dubious blessings by foisting their prepackaged solution onto the Third World. Traffic jams develop in São Paolo, while almost a million northeastern Brazilians flee the drought by walking 500 miles. Latin American doctors get training at the New York Hospital for Special Surgery, which they apply to only a few, while amoebic dysentery remains endemic in slums where 90 percent of the population live. A tiny minority gets advanced education in basic science in North America—not infrequently paid for by their own governments. If they return at all to Bolivia, they become second-rate teachers of pretentious subjects at La Paz or Cochabamba. The rich export outdated versions of their standard models.

The Alliance for Progress is a good example of benevolent production for underdevelopment. Contrary to its slogans, it did succeed—as an alliance for the progress of the consuming classes, and for the domestication of the Latin American masses. The Alliance has been a major step in modernizing the consumption patterns of the middle classes in South America by integrating them with the dominant culture of the North American metropolis. At the same time, the Alliance has modernized the aspirations of the majority of citizens and fixed their demands on unavailable products.

Each car which Brazil puts on the road denies fifty people good transportation by bus. Each merchandised refrigerator reduces the chance of building a community freezer. Every dollar spent in Latin America on doctors and hospitals costs a hundred lives, to adopt a phrase of Jorge de Ahumada, the brilliant Chilean economist. Had each dollar been spent on providing safe drinking water, a hundred lives could have been saved. Each dollar spent on schooling means more privileges for the few at the cost of the many; at best it increases the number of those who, before dropping out, have been taught that those who stay longer have earned the right to more power, wealth, and prestige. What such schooling does is to teach the schooled the superiority of the better schooled.

All Latin American countries are frantically intent on expanding their school systems. No country now spends less than the equivalent of 18 percent of tax-derived public income on education—which means schooling —and many countries spend almost double that. But even with these huge investments, no country yet succeeds in giving five full years of education to more than one third of its population; supply and demand for schooling grow geometrically apart. And what is true about schooling is equally true about the products of most institutions in the process of modernization in the Third World.

Continued technological refinements of products which are already established on the market frequently benefit the producer far more than the consumer. The more complex production processes tend to enable only the largest producer to continually replace outmoded models, and to focus the demand of the consumer on the marginal improvement of what he buys, no matter what the concomitant side effects: higher prices, diminished life span, less general usefulness, higher cost of repairs. Think of the multiple uses for a simple can opener, whereas an electric one, if it works at all, opens only some kinds of cans, and costs one hundred times as much.

This is equally true for a piece of agricultural machinery and for an academic degree. The midwestern farmer can become convinced of his need for a four-axle vehicle which can go 70 m.p.h. on the highway, has an electric windshield wiper and upholstered seats, and can be turned in for a new one within a year or two. Most of the world's farmers don't need such speed, nor have they ever met with such comfort, nor are they interested in obsolescence. They need low-priced transport, in a world where time is not money, where manual wipers suffice, and where a piece of heavy equipment should outlast a generation. Such a mechanical donkey requires entirely different engineering and design than one produced for the US market. This vehicle is not in production.

Most of South America needs paramedical workers who can function for indefinite periods without the supervision of an M.D. Instead of establishing a process to train midwives and visiting healers who know how to use a very limited arsenal of medicines while working independently, Latin American universities establish every year a new school of specialized nursing or nursing administration to prepare professionals who can function only in a hospital, and pharmacists who know how to sell increasingly more dangerous drugs.

The world is reaching an impasse where two processes converge: ever more men have fewer basic choices. The increase in population is widely publicized and creates panic. The decrease in fundamental choice causes anguish and is consistently overlooked. The population explosion overwhelms the imagination, but the progressive atrophy of social imagination is rationalized as an increase of choice between brands. The two processes converge in a dead end: the population explosion provides more consumers for everything from food to contraceptives, while our shrinking imagination can conceive of no other ways of satisfying their demands except through the packages now on sale in the admired societies.

I will focus successively on these two factors, since, in my opinion, they form the two coordinates which together permit us to define underdevelopment.

In most Third World countries, the population grows, and so does the middle class. Income, consumption, and the well-being of the middle class are all growing while the gap between this class and the mass of people widens. Even where per capita consumption is rising, the majority of men have less food now than in 1945, less actual care in sickness, less meaningful work, less protection. This is partly a consequence of polarized consumption and partly caused by the breakdown of traditional family and culture. More people suffer from hunger, pain, and exposure in 1969 than they did at the end of World War II, not only numerically, but also as a percentage of the world population.

These concrete consequences of underdevelopment are rampant; but underdevelopment is also a state of mind, and understanding it as a state of mind, or as a form of consciousness, is the critical problem. Underdevelopment as a state of mind occurs when mass needs are converted to the demand for new brands of packaged solutions which are forever beyond the reach of the majority. Underdevelopment in this sense is rising rapidly even in countries where the supply of classrooms, calories, cars, and clinics is also rising. The ruling groups in these countries build up services which have been designed for an affluent culture; once they have monopolized demand in this way, they can never satisfy majority needs.

Underdevelopment as a form of consciousness is an extreme result of what we can call in the language of both Marx and Freud *"Verdinglichung"* or reification. By reification I mean the hardening of the perception of real needs into the demand for mass manufactured products. I mean the translation of thirst into the need for a Coke. This kind of reification occurs in the manipulation of primary human needs by vast bureaucratic organizations which have succeeded in dominating the imagination of potential consumers.

Let me return to my example taken from the field of education. The intense promotion of schooling leads to so close an identification of school attendance and education that in everyday language the two terms are interchangeable. Once the imagination of an entire population has been "schooled," or indoctrinated to believe that school has a monopoly on formal education, then the illiterate can be taxed to provide free high school and university education for the children of the rich.

Underdevelopment is the result of rising levels of aspiration achieved through the intensive marketing of "patent" products. In this sense, the dynamic underdevelopment that is now taking place is the exact opposite of what I believe education to be: namely, the awakening awareness of new levels of human potential and the use of one's creative powers to foster human life. Underdevelopment, however, implies the surrender of social consciousness to pre-packaged solutions.

The process by which the marketing of "foreign" products increases underdevelopment is frequently understood in the most superficial ways. The same man who feels indignation at the sight of a Coca-Cola plant in a Latin American slum often feels pride at the sight of a new normal school growing up alongside. He resents the evidence of a foreign "license" attached to a soft drink which he would like to see replaced by "Cola-Mex." But the same man is willing to impose schooling—at all costs—on his fellow citizens, and is unaware of the invisible license by which this institution is deeply enmeshed in the world market.

Some years ago I watched workmen putting up a sixty-foot Coca-Cola sign on a desert plain in the Mexquital. A serious drought and famine had just swept over the Mexican highland. My host, a poor Indian in Ixmiquilpan, had just offered his visitors a tiny tequila glass of the costly black sugar-water. When I recall this scene I still feel anger; but I feel much more incensed when I remember UNESCO meetings at which well-meaning and well-paid bureaucrats seriously discussed Latin American school curricula, and when I think of the speeches of enthusiastic liberals advocating the need for more schools.

The fraud perpetrated by the salesmen of schools is less obvious but much more fundamental than the self-satisfied salesmanship of the Coca-Cola or Ford representative, because the schoolman hooks his people on a much more demanding drug. Elementary school attendance is not a harmless luxury, but more like the coca chewing of the Andean Indian, which harnesses the worker to the boss.

The higher the dose of schooling an individual has received, the more depressing his experience of withdrawal. The seventh-grade dropout feels his inferiority much more acutely than the dropout from the third grade.

The schools of the Third World administer their opium with much more effect than the churches of other epochs. As the mind of a society is progressively schooled, step by step its individuals lose their sense that it might be possible to live without being inferior to others. As the majority shifts from the land into the city, the hereditary inferiority of the peon is replaced by the inferiority of the school dropout who is held personally responsible for his failure. Schools rationalize the divine origin of social stratification with much more rigor than churches have ever done.

Until this day no Latin American country has declared youthful under-consumers of Coca-Cola or cars as lawbreakers, while all Latin American countries have passed laws which define the early dropout as a citizen who has not fulfilled his legal obligations. The Brazilian government recently almost doubled the number of years during which schooling is legally compulsory and free. From now on any Brazilian dropout under the age of sixteen will be faced during his lifetime with the reproach that he did not take advantage of a legally obligatory privilege. This law was passed in a country where not even the most optimistic could foresee the day when such levels of schooling would be provided for even 25 percent of the young. The adoption of international standards of schooling forever condemns most Latin Americans to marginality or exclusion from social life—in a word, underdevelopment.

The translation of social goals into levels of consumption is not limited to only a few countries. Across all frontiers of culture, ideology, and geography today, nations are moving toward the establishment of their own car factories, their own medical and normal schools—and most of these are, at best, poor imitations of foreign and largely North American models.

The Third World is in need of a profound revolution of its institutions. The revolutions of the last generation were overwhelmingly political. A new group of men with a new set of ideological justifications assumed power to administer fundamentally the same scholastic, medical, and market institutions in the interest of a new group of clients. Since the institutions have not radically changed, the new group of clients remains approximately the same size as that previously served. This appears clearly in the case of education. Per pupil costs of schooling are today comparable everywhere since the standards used to evaluate the quality of schooling tend to be internationally shared. Access to publicly financed education, considered as access to school, everywhere depends on per capita income. (Places like China and North Vietnam might be meaningful exceptions.)

Everywhere in the Third World modern institutions are grossly unproductive, with respect to the egalitarian purposes for which they are being reproduced. But so long as the social imagination of the majority has not been destroyed by its fixation on these institutions, there is more hope of planning an institutional revolution in the Third World than among the rich. Hence the urgency of the task of developing workable alternatives to "modern" solutions.

Underdevelopment is at the point of becoming chronic in many countries. The revolution of which I speak must begin to take place before this happens. Education again offers a good example: chronic educational underdevelopment occurs when the demand for schooling becomes so widespread that the total concentration of educational resources on the school system becomes a unanimous political demand. At this point the separation of education from schooling becomes impossible.

The only feasible answer to ever-increasing underdevelopment is a response to basic needs that is planned as a long-range goal for areas which will always have a different capital structure. It is easier to speak about alternatives to existing institutions, services, and products than to define them with precision. It is not my purpose either to paint a Utopia or to engage in scripting scenarios for an alternate future. We must be satisfied with examples indicating simple directions that research should take.

Some such examples have already been given. Buses are alternatives to a multitude of private cars. Vehicles designed for slow transportation on rough terrain are alternatives to standard trucks. Safe water is an alternative to high-priced surgery. Medical workers are an alternative to doctors and nurses. Community food storage is an alternative to expensive kitchen equipment. Other alternatives could be discussed by the dozen. Why not, for example, consider walking as a long-range alternative for locomotion by machine, and explore the demands which this would impose on the city planner? And why can't the building of shelters be standardized, elements be pre-cast, and each citizen be obliged to learn in a year of public service how to construct his own sanitary housing?

It is harder to speak about alternatives in education, partly because schools have recently so completely pre-empted the available educational resources of good will, imagination, and money. But even here we can indicate the direction in which research must be conducted.

At present, schooling is conceived as graded, curricular, class attendance by children, for about 1000 hours yearly during an uninterrupted succession of years. On the average, Latin American countries can provide each citizen with between eight and thirty months of this service. Why not, instead, make one or two months a year obligatory for all citizens below the age of thirty?

Money is now spent largely on children, but an adult can be taught to read in one tenth the time and for one tenth the cost it takes to teach a child. In the case of the adult there is an immediate return on the investment, whether the main importance of his learning is seen in his new insight, political awareness, and willingness to assume responsibility for his family's size and future, or whether the emphasis is placed on increased productivity. There is a double return in the case of the adult, because not only can he contribute to the education of his children, but to that of other adults as well. In spite of these advantages, basic literacy programs have little or no support in Latin America, where schools have a first call on all public resources. Worse, these programs are actually ruthlessly suppressed in Brazil and elsewhere, where military support of the feudal or industrial oligarchy has thrown off its former benevolent disguise.

Another possibility is harder to define, because there is as yet no example to point to. We must therefore imagine the use of public resources for education distributed in such a way as to give every citizen a minimum chance. Education will become a political concern of the majority of voters only when each individual has a precise sense of the educational resources that are owing to him—and some idea of how to sue for them. Something like a universal G.I. Bill of Rights could be imagined, dividing the public resources assigned to education by the number of children who are legally of school age, and making sure that a child who did not take advantage of his credit at the age of seven, eight, or nine would have the accumulated benefits at his disposal at age ten.

What could the pitiful education credit which a Latin American Republic could offer to its children provide? Almost all of the basic supply of books, pictures, blocks, games, and toys that are totally absent from the homes of the really poor, but enable a middle-class child to learn the alphabet, the colors, shapes, and other classes of objects and experiences which insure his educational progress. The choice between these things and schools is obvious. Unfortunately, the poor, for whom alone the choice is real, never get to exercise this choice.

Defining alternatives to the products and institutions which now preempt the field is difficult, not only, as I have been trying to show, because these products and institutions shape our conception of reality itself, but also because the construction of new possibilities requires a concentration of will and intelligence in a higher degree than ordinarily occurs by chance. This concentration of will and intelligence on the solution of particular problems regardless of their nature we have become accustomed over the last century to call research.

I must make clear, however, what kind of research I am talking about. I am not talking about basic research either in physics, engineering, genetics, medicine, or learning. The work of such men as Crick, Piaget, and Gell-Mann must continue to enlarge our horizons in other fields of science. The labs and libraries and specially trained collaborators these men need cause them to congregate in the few research capitals of the world. Their research can provide the basis for new work on practically any product.

I am not speaking here of the billions of dollars annually spent on applied research, for this money is largely spent by existing institutions on the perfection and marketing of their own products. Applied research is money spent on making planes faster and airports safer; on making medicines more specific and powerful and doctors capable of handling their deadly side-effects; on packaging more learning into classrooms; on methods to administer large bureaucracies. This is the kind of research for which some kind of counterfoil must somehow be developed if we are to have any chance to come up with basic alternatives to the automobile, the hospital, and the school, and any of the many other so-called "evidently necessary implements for modern life."

I have in mind a different, and peculiarly difficult, kind of research, which has been largely neglected up to now, for obvious reasons. I am calling for research on alternatives to the products which now dominate the market; to hospitals and the profession dedicated to keeping the sick alive; to schools and the packaging process which refuses education to those who are not of the right age, who have not gone through the right curriculum, who have not sat in a classroom a sufficient number of successive hours, who will not pay for their learning with submission to custodial care, screening, and certification or with indoctrination in the values of the dominant elite.

This counter-research on fundamental alternatives to current pre-packaged solutions is the element most critically needed if the poor nations are to have a livable future. Such counter-research is distinct from most of the work done in the name of the "year 2000," because most of that work seeks radical changes in social patterns through adjustments in the organization of an already advanced technology. The counter-research of which I speak must take as one of its assumptions the continued lack of capital in the Third World.

The difficulties of such research are obvious. The researcher must first of all doubt what is obvious to every eye. Second, he must persuade those who have the power of decision to act against their own short-run interests or bring pressure on them to do so. And, finally, he must survive as an individual in a world he is attempting to change fundamentally so that his fellows among the privileged minority see him as a destroyer of the very ground on which all of us stand. He knows that if he should succeed in the interest of the poor, technologically advanced societies still might envy the "poor" who adopt this vision.

There is a normal course for those who make development policies, whether they live in North or South America, in Russia or Israel. It is to define development and to set its goals in ways with which they are familiar, which they are accustomed to use in order to satisfy their own needs, and which permit them to work through the institutions over which they have power or control. This formula has failed, and must fail. There is not enough money in the world for development to succeed along these lines, not even in the combined arms and space budgets of the super-powers.

An analogous course is followed by those who are trying to make political revolutions, especially in the Third World. Usually they promise to make the familiar privileges of the present elites, such as schooling, hospital care, etc., accessible to all citizens; and they base this vain promise on the belief that a change in political regime will permit them to sufficiently enlarge the institutions which produce these privileges. The promise and appeal of the revolutionary are therefore just as threatened by the counter-research I propose as is the market of the now dominant producers.

In Vietnam a people on bicycles and armed with sharpened bamboo sticks have brought to a standstill the most advanced machinery for research and production ever devised. We must seek survival in a Third World in which human ingenuity can peacefully outwit machined might. The only way to reverse the disastrous trend to increasing underdevelopment, hard as it is, is to learn to laugh at accepted solutions in order to change the demands which make them necessary. Only free men can change their minds and be surprised; and while no men are completely free, some are freer than others.

31

Pedagogy of the Oppressed

Paulo Freire

While the problem of humanization has always, from an axiological point of view, been man's central problem, it now takes on the character of an inescapable concern.[1] Concern for humanization leads at once to the recognition of dehumanization, not only as an ontological possibility but as an historical reality. And as man perceives the extent of dehumanization, he asks himself if humanization is a viable possibility. Within history, in concrete, objective contexts, both humanization and dehumanization are possibilities for man as an uncompleted being conscious of his incompletion.

But while both humanization and dehumanization are real alternatives, only the first is man's vocation. This vocation is constantly negated, yet it is affirmed by that very negation. It is thwarted by injustice, exploitation, oppression, and the violence of the oppressors; it is affirmed by the yearning of the oppressed for freedom and justice, and by their struggle to recover their lost humanity.

Dehumanization, which marks not only those whose humanity has been stolen, but also (though in a different way) those who have stolen it, is a *distortion* of the vocation of becoming more fully human. This distortion occurs within history but it is not an historical vocation. Indeed, to admit of dehumanization as an historical vocation would lead either to cynicism or to total despair. The struggle for humanization, for the emancipation of labor, for the overcoming of alienation, for the affirmation of men as persons would be meaningless. This struggle is possible only because dehumanization, although a concrete historical fact, is *not* a given destiny but the result of an unjust order that engenders violence in the oppressors, which in turn dehumanizes the oppressed.

Because it is a distortion of being more fully human, sooner or later being less human leads the oppressed to struggle against those who made them so. In order for this struggle to have meaning, the oppressed must not, in seeking to regain their humanity (which is a way to create it), become in turn oppressors of the oppressors, but rather restorers of the humanity of both.

This, then, is the great humanistic and historical task of the oppressed: to liberate themselves and their oppressors as well. The oppressors, who oppress, exploit, and rape by virtue of their power, cannot find in this

Reprinted from the author's *Pedagogy of the Oppressed*, translated by Myra Bergman Ramos (New York: Herder and Herder, 1970), pp. 29–56, by permission of the author and The Seabury Press. Copyright 1970 by Paulo Freire.

power the strength to liberate either the oppressed or themselves. Only power that springs from the weakness of the oppressed will be sufficiently strong to free both. Any attempt to "soften" the power of the oppressor in deference to the weakness of the oppressed almost always manifests itself in the form of false generosity; indeed, the attempt never goes beyond this. In order to have the continued opportunity to express their "generosity," the oppressors must perpetuate injustice as well. An unjust social order is the permanent fount of this "generosity," which is nourished by death, despair, and poverty. This is why the dispensers of false generosity become desperate at the slightest threat to its source.

True generosity consists precisely in fighting to destroy the causes which nourish false charity. False charity constrains the fearful and sub- dued, the "rejects of life," to extend their trembling hands. True generosity lies in striving so that these hands—whether of individuals or entire peo- ples—need be extended less and less in supplication, so that more and more they become human hands which work and, working, transform the world.

This lesson and this apprenticeship must come, however, from the oppressed themselves and from those who are truly solidary with them. As individuals or as peoples, by fighting for the restoration of their humanity they will be attempting the restoration of true generosity. Who are better prepared than the oppressed to understand the terrible significance of an oppressive society? Who suffer the effects of oppression more than the oppressed? Who can better understand the necessity of liberation? They will not gain this liberation by chance but through the praxis of their quest for it, through their recognition of the necessity to fight for it. And this fight, because of the purpose given it by the oppressed, will actually constitute an act of love opposing the lovelessness which lies at the heart of the oppressors' violence, lovelessness even when clothed in false generosity.

But almost always, during the initial stage of the struggle, the op- pressed, instead of striving for liberation, tend themselves to become oppressors, or "sub-oppressors." The very structure of their thought has been conditioned by the contradictions of the concrete, existential situation by which they were shaped. Their ideal is to be men; but for them, to be men is to be oppressors. This is their model of humanity. This phenomenon derives from the fact that the oppressed, at a certain moment of their existential experience, adopt an attitude of "adhesion" to the oppressor. Under these circumstances they cannot "consider" him sufficiently clearly to objectivize him—to discover him "outside" themselves. This does not necessarily mean that the oppressed are unaware that they are down- trodden. But their perception of themselves as oppressed is impaired by their submersion in the reality of oppression. At this level, their perception of themselves as opposites of the oppressor does not yet signify engage- ment in a struggle to overcome the contradiction,[2] the one pole aspires not to liberation, but to identification with its opposite pole.

In this situation the oppressed do not see the "new man" as the man to be born from the resolution of this contradiction, as oppression gives way to liberation. For them, the new man is themselves become oppressors. Their vision of the new man is individualistic; because of their identification with the oppressor, they have no consciousness of themselves as persons or as members of an oppressed class. It is not to become free men that they want agrarian reform, but in order to acquire land and thus become landowners—or, more precisely, bosses over other workers. It is a rare peasant who, once "promoted" to overseer, does not become more of a tyrant towards his former comrades than the owner himself. This is because the context of the peasant's situation, that is, oppression, remains unchanged. In this example, the overseer, in order to make sure of his job, must be as tough as the owner—and more so. Thus is illustrated our previous assertion that during the initial stage of their struggle the oppressed find in the oppressor their model of "manhood."

Even revolution, which transforms a concrete situation of oppression by establishing the process of liberation, must confront this phenomenon. Many of the oppressed who directly or indirectly participate in revolution intend—conditioned by the myths of the old order—to make it their private revolution. The shadow of their former oppressor is still cast over them.

The "fear of freedom" which afflicts the oppressed,[3] a fear which may equally well lead them to desire the role of oppressor or bind them to the role of oppressed, should be examined. One of the basic elements of the relationship between oppressor and oppressed is *prescription*. Every prescription represents the imposition of one man's choice upon another, transforming the consciousness of the man prescribed to into one that conforms with the prescriber's consciousness. Thus, the behavior of the oppressed is a prescribed behavior, following as it does the guidelines of the oppressor.

The oppressed, having internalized the image of the oppressor and adopted his guidelines, are fearful of freedom. Freedom would require them to eject this image and replace it with autonomy and responsibility. Freedom is acquired by conquest, not by gift. It must be pursued constantly and responsibly. Freedom is not an ideal located outside of man; nor is it an idea which becomes myth. It is rather the indispensable condition for the quest for human completion.

To surmount the situation of oppression, men must first critically recognize its causes, so that through transforming action they can create a new situation, one which makes possible the pursuit of a fuller humanity. But the struggle to be more fully human has already begun in the authentic struggle to transform the situation. Although the situation of oppression is a dehumanized and dehumanizing totality affecting both the oppressors and those whom they oppress, it is the latter who must, from their stifled humanity, wage for both the struggle for a fuller humanity; the oppressor, who is himself dehumanized because he dehumanizes others, is unable to lead this struggle.

However, the oppressed, who have adapted to the structure of domination in which they are immersed, and have become resigned to it, are inhibited from waging the struggle for freedom so long as they feel incapable of running the risks it requires. Moreover, their struggle for freedom threatens not only the oppressor, but also their own oppressed comrades who are fearful of still greater repression. Whey they discover within themselves the yearning to be free, they perceive that this yearning can be transformed into reality only when the same yearning is aroused in their comrades. But while dominated by the fear of freedom they refuse to appeal to others, or to listen to the appeals of others, or even to the appeals of their own conscience. They prefer gregariousness to authentic comradeship; they prefer the security of conformity with their state of unfreedom to the creative communion produced by freedom and even the very pursuit of freedom.

The oppressed suffer from the duality which has established itself in their innermost being. They discover that without freedom they cannot exist authentically. Yet, although they desire authentic existence, they fear it. They are at one and the same time themselves and the oppressor whose consciousness they have internalized. The conflict lies in the choice between being wholly themselves or being divided; between ejecting the oppressor within or not ejecting him; between human solidarity or alienation; between following prescriptions or having choices; between being spectators or actors; between acting or having the illusion of acting through the action of the oppressors; between speaking out or being silent, castrated in their power to create and re-create, in their power to transform the world. This is the tragic dilemma of the oppressed which their education must take into account.

[This paper] will present some aspects of what the writer has termed the pedagogy of the oppressed, a pedagogy which must be forged *with*, not *for*, the oppressed (whether individuals or peoples) in the incessant struggle to regain their humanity. This pedagogy makes oppression and its causes objects of reflection by the oppressed, and from that reflection will come their necessary engagement in the struggle for their liberation. And in the struggle this pedagogy will be made and remade.

The central problem is this: How can the oppressed, as divided, unauthentic beings, participate in developing the pedagogy of their liberation? Only as they discover themselves to be "hosts" of the oppressor can they contribute to the midwifery of their liberating pedagogy. As long as they live in the duality in which *to be* is *to be like*, and *to be like* is *to be like the oppressor*, this contribution is impossible. The pedagogy of the oppressed is an instrument for their critical discovery that both they and their oppressors are manifestations of dehumanization.

Liberation is thus a childbirth, and a painful one. The man who emerges is a new man, viable only as the oppressor-oppressed contradiction is superseded by the humanization of all men. Or to put it another way, the solution of this contradiction is born in the labor which brings into the world this new man: no longer oppressor nor longer oppressed, but man in the process of achieving freedom.

This solution cannot be achieved in idealistic terms. In order for the oppressed to be able to wage the struggle for their liberation, they must perceive the reality of oppression not as a closed world from which there is no exit, but as a limiting situation which they can transform. This perception is a necessary but not a sufficient condition for liberation; it must become the motivating force for liberating action. Nor does the discovery by the oppressed that they exist in dialectical relationship to the oppressor, as his antithesis—that without them the oppressor could not exist[4]—in itself constitute liberation. The oppressed can overcome the contradiction in which they are caught only when this perception enlists them in the struggle to free themselves.

The same is true with respect to the individual oppressor as a person. Discovering himself to be an oppressor may cause considerable anguish, but it does not necessarily lead to solidarity with the oppressed. Rationalizing his guilt through paternalistic treatment of the oppressed, all the while holding them fast in a position of dependence, will not do. Solidarity requires that one enter into the situation of those with whom one is solidary; it is a radical posture. If what characterizes the oppressed is their subordination to the consciousness of the master, as Hegel affirms,[5] true solidarity with the oppressed means fighting at their side to transform the objective reality which has made them these "beings for another." The oppressor is solidary with the oppressed only when he stops regarding the oppressed as an abstract category and sees them as persons who have been unjustly dealt with, deprived of their voice, cheated in the sale of their labor—when he stops making pious, sentimental, and individualistic gestures and risks an act of love. True solidarity is found only in the plenitude of this act of love, in its existentiality, in its praxis. To affirm that men are persons and as persons should be free and yet to do nothing tangible to make this affirmation a reality is a farce.

Since it is in a concrete situation that the oppressor-oppressed contradiction is established, the resolution of this contradiction must be *objectively* verifiable. Hence, the radical requirement—both for the man who discovers himself to be an oppressor and for the oppressed—that the concrete situation which begets oppression must be transformed.

To present this radical demand for the objective transformation of reality, to combat subjectivist immobility which would divert the recognition of oppression into patient waiting for oppression to disappear by itself, is not to dismiss the role of subjectivity in the struggle to change structures. On the contrary, one cannot conceive of objectivity without subjectivity. Neither can exist without the other, nor can they be dichotomized. The separation of objectivity from subjectivity, the denial of the latter when analyzing reality or acting upon it, is objectivism. On the other hand, the denial of objectivity in analysis or action, resulting in a subjectivism which leads to solipsistic positions, denies action itself by denying objective reality. Neither objectivism nor subjectivism, nor yet psychologism is propounded here, but rather subjectivity and objectivity in constant dialectical relationship.

To deny the importance of subjectivity in the process of transforming the world and history is naïve and simplistic. It is to admit the impossible: a world without men. This objectivistic position is as ingenuous as that of subjectivism, which postulates men without a world. World and men do not exist apart from each other, they exist in constant interaction. Marx does not espouse such a dichotomy, nor does any other critical, realistic thinker. What Marx criticized and scientifically destroyed was not subjectivity, but subjectivism and psychologism. Just as objective social reality exists not by chance, but as the product of human action, so it is not transformed by chance. If men produce social reality (which in the "inversion of the praxis" turns back upon them and conditions them), then transforming that reality is an historical task, a task for men.

Reality which becomes oppressive results in the contradistinction of men as oppressors and oppressed. The latter, whose task it is to struggle for their liberation together with those who show true solidarity, must acquire a critical awareness of oppression through the praxis of this struggle. One of the gravest obstacles to the achievement of liberation is that oppressive reality absorbs those within it and thereby acts to submerge men's consciousness. Functionally, oppression is domesticating. To no longer be prey to its force, one must emerge from it and turn upon it. This can be done only by means of the praxis: reflection and action upon the world in order to transform it.

Making "real oppression more oppressive still by adding to it the realization of oppression" corresponds to the dialectical relation between the subjective and the objective. Only in this interdependence is an authentic praxis possible, without which it is impossible to resolve the oppressor-oppressed contradiction. To achieve this goal, the oppressed must confront reality critically, simultaneously objectifying and acting upon that reality. A mere perception of reality not followed by this critical intervention will not lead to a transformation of objective reality—precisely because it is not a true perception. This is the case of a purely subjectivist perception by someone who forsakes objective reality and creates a false substitute.

A different type of false perception occurs when a change in objective reality would threaten the individual or class interests of the perceiver. In the first instance, there is no critical intervention in reality because that reality is fictitious; there is none in the second instance because intervention would contradict the class interests of the perceiver. In the latter case the tendency of the perceiver is to behave "neurotically." The fact exists; but both the fact and what may result from it may be prejudicial to him. Thus it becomes necessary, not precisely to deny the fact, but to "see it differently." This rationalization as a defense mechanism coincides in the end with subjectivism. A fact which is not denied but whose truths are rationalized loses its objective base. It ceases to be concrete and becomes a myth created in defense of the class of the perceiver.

Herein lies one of the reasons for the prohibitions and the difficulties . . . designed to dissuade the people from critical intervention in reality. The oppressor knows full well that this intervention would not be to his interest. What *is* to his interest is for the people to continue in a state of submersion, impotent in the face of oppressive reality. . . . "To explain to the masses their own action" is to clarify and illuminate that action, both regarding its relationship of the objective facts by which it was prompted, and regarding its purposes. The more the people unveil this challenging reality which is to be the object of their transforming action, the more critically they enter that reality. In this way they are "consciously activating the subsequent development of their experiences." There would be no human action if there were no objective reality, no world to be the "not I" of man and to challenge him; just as there would be no human action if man were not a "project," if he were not able to transcend himself, to perceive his reality and understand it in order to transform it.

In dialectical thought, word and action are intimately interdependent. But action is human only when it is not merely an occupation but also a preoccupation, that is, when it is not dichotomized from reflection. Reflection, which is essential to action, is implicit in Lukács' requirement of "explaining to the masses their own action," just as it is implicit in the purpose he attributes to this explanation: that of "consciously activating the subsequent development of experience."

For us, however, the requirement is seen not in terms of explaining to, but rather dialoguing with the people about their actions. In any event, no reality transforms itself,[6] and the duty which Lukács ascribes to the revolutionary party of "explaining to the masses their own action" coincides with our affirmation of the need for the critical intervention of the people in reality through the praxis. The pedagogy of the oppressed, which is the pedagogy of men engaged in the fight for their own liberation, has its roots here. And those who recognize, or begin to recognize, themselves as oppressed must be among the developers of this pedagogy. No pedagogy which is truly liberating can remain distant from the oppressed by treating them as unfortunates and by presenting for their emulation models from among the oppressors. The oppressed must be their own example in the struggle for their redemption.

The pedagogy of the oppressed, animated by authentic, humanist (not humanitarian) generosity, presents itself as a pedagogy of man. Pedagogy which begins with the egoistic interests of the oppressors (an egoism cloaked in the false generosity of paternalism) and makes of the oppressed the objects of its humanitarianism, itself maintains and embodies oppression. It is an instrument of dehumanization. This is why, as we affirmed earlier, the pedagogy of the oppressed cannot be developed or practiced by the oppressors. It would be a contradiction in terms if the oppressors not only defended but actually implemented a liberating education.

. . . .

The pedagogy of the oppressed, as a humanist and libertarian pedagogy, has two distinct stages. In the first, the oppressed unveil the world of oppression and through the praxis commit themselves to its transformation. In the second stage, in which the reality of oppression has already been transformed, this pedagogy ceases to belong to the oppressed and becomes a pedagogy of all men in the process of permanent liberation. In both stages, it is always through action in depth that the culture of domination is culturally confronted.[7] In the first stage this confrontation occurs through the change in the way the oppressed perceive the world of oppression; in the second stage, through the expulsion of the myths created and developed in the old order, which like specters haunt the new structure emerging from the revolutionary transformation.

The pedagogy of the first stage must deal with the problem of the oppressed consciousness and the oppressor consciousness, the problem of men who oppress and men who suffer oppression. It must take into account their behavior, their view of the world, and their ethics. A particular problem is the duality of the oppressed: they are contradictory, divided beings, shaped by and existing in a concrete situation of oppression and violence.

Any situation in which "A" objectively exploits "B" or hinders his pursuit of self-affirmation as a responsible person is one of oppression. Such a situation in itself constitutes violence, even when sweetened by false generosity, because it interferes with man's ontological and historical vocation to be more fully human. With the establishment of a relationship of oppression, violence has *already* begun. Never in history has violence been initiated by the oppressed. How could they be the initiators, if they themselves are the result of violence? How could they be the sponsors of something whose objective inauguration called forth their existence as oppressed? There would be no oppressed had there been no prior situation of violence to establish their subjugation.

Violence is initiated by those who oppress, who exploit, who fail to recognize others as persons—not by those who are oppressed, exploited, and unrecognized. It is not the unloved who initiate disaffection, but those who cannot love because they love only themselves. It is not the helpless, subject to terror, who initiate terror, but the violent, who with their power create the concrete situation which begets the "rejects of life." It is not the tyrannized who initiate despotism, but the tyrants. It is not the despised who initiate hatred, but those who despise. It is not those whose humanity is denied them who negate man, but those who denied that humanity (thus negating their own as well). Force is used not by those who have become weak under the preponderance of the strong, but by the strong who have emasculated them.

For the oppressors, however, it is always the oppressed (whom they obviously never call "the oppressed" but—depending on whether they are fellow countrymen or not—"those people" or "the blind and envious masses" or "savages" or "natives" or "subversives") who are disaffected, who are "violent," "barbaric," "wicked," or "ferocious" when they react to the violence of the oppressors.

Yet it is—paradoxical though it may seem—precisely in the response of the oppressed to the violence of their oppressors that a gesture of love may be found. Consciously or unconsciously, the act of rebellion by the oppressed (an act which is always, or nearly always, as violent as the initial violence of the oppressors) can initiate love. Whereas the violence of the oppressors prevents the oppressed from being fully human, the response of the latter to this violence is grounded in the desire to pursue the right to be human. As the oppressors dehumanize others and violate their rights, they themselves also become dehumanized. As the oppressed, fighting to be human, take away the oppressors' power to dominate and suppress, they restore to the oppressors the humanity they had lost in the exercise of oppression.

It is only the oppressed who, by freeing themselves, can free their oppressors. The latter, as an oppressive class, can free neither others nor themselves. It is therefore essential that the oppressed wage the struggle to resolve the contradiction in which they are caught; and the contradiction will be resolved by the appearance of the new man: neither oppressor nor oppressed, but man in the process of liberation. If the goal of the oppressed is to become fully human, they will not achieve their goal by merely reversing the terms of the contradiction, by simply changing poles.

This may seem simplistic; it is not. Resolution of the oppressor-oppressed contradiction indeed implies the disappearance of the oppressors as a dominant class. However, the restraints imposed by the former oppressed on their oppressors, so that the latter cannot reassume their former position, do not constitute *oppression*. An act is oppressive only when it prevents men from being more fully human. Accordingly, these necessary restraints do not *in themselves* signify that yesterday's oppressed have become today's oppressors. Acts which prevent the restoration of the oppressive regime cannot be compared with those which create and maintain it, cannot be compared with those by which a few men deny the majority their right to be human.

However, the moment the new regime hardens into a dominating "bureaucracy"[8] the humanist dimension of the struggle is lost and it is no longer possible to speak of liberation. Hence our insistence that the authentic solution of the oppressor-oppressed contradiction does not lie in a mere reversal of position, in moving from one pole to the other. Nor does it lie in the replacement of the former oppressors with new ones who continue to subjugate the oppressed—all in the name of their liberation.

But even when the contradiction is resolved authentically by a new situation established by the liberated laborers, the former oppressors do not feel liberated. On the contrary, they genuinely consider themselves to be oppressed. Conditioned by the experience of oppressing others, any situation other than their former seems to them like oppression. Formerly, they could eat, dress, wear shoes, be educated, travel, and hear Beethoven; while millions did not eat, had no clothes or shoes, neither studied nor traveled, much less listened to Beethoven. Any restriction on this way of life, in the name of the rights of the community, appears to the former oppressors as a profound violation of their individual rights—although they had no respect for the millions who suffered and died of hunger, pain, sorrow, and despair. For the oppressors, "human beings" refer only to themselves; other people are "things." For the oppressors, there exists only one right: their right to live in peace, over against the right, not always even recognized, but simply conceded, of the oppressed to survival. And they make this concession only because the existence of the oppressed is necessary to their own existence.

This behavior, this way of understanding the world and men (which necessarily makes the oppressors resist the installation of a new regime) is explained by their experience as a dominant class. Once a situation of violence and oppression has been established, it engenders an entire way of life and behavior for those caught up in it—oppressors and oppressed alike. Both are submerged in this situation, and both bear the marks of oppression. Analysis of existential situations of oppression reveals that their inception lay in an act of violence—initiated by those with power. This violence, as a process, is perpetuated from generation to generation of oppressors, who become its heirs and are shaped in its climate. This climate creates in the oppressor a strongly possessive consciousness—possessive of the world and of men. Apart from direct, concrete, material possession of the world and of men, the oppressor consciousness could not understand itself—could not even exist. Fromm said of this consciousness that, without such possession, "it would lose contact with the world." The oppressor consciousness tends to transform everything surrounding it into an object of its domination. The earth, property, production, the creations of men, men themselves, time—everything is reduced to the status of objects at its disposal.

In their unrestrained eagerness to possess, the oppressors develop the conviction that it is possible for them to transform everything into objects of their purchasing power; hence their strictly materialistic concept of existence. Money is the measure of all things, and profit the primary goal. For the oppressors, what is worthwhile is to have more—always more— even at the cost of the oppressed having less or having nothing. For them, *to be* is *to have* and to be the class of the "haves."

As beneficiaries of a situation of oppression, the oppressors cannot perceive that if *having* is a condition of *being*, it is a necessary condition for all men. This is why their generosity is false. Humanity is a "thing," and they possess it as an exclusive right, as inherited property. To the oppressor consciousness, the humanization of the "others," of the people, appears not as the pursuit of full humanity, but as subversion.

The oppressors do not perceive their monopoly on *having more* as a privilege which dehumanizes others and themselves. They cannot see that, in the egoistic pursuit of *having* as a possessing class, they suffocate in their own possessions and no longer *are;* they merely *have.* For them, *having more* is an inalienable right, a right they acquired through their own "effort," with their "courage to take risks." If others do not have more, it is because they are incompetent and lazy, and worst of all is their unjustifiable ingratitude towards the "generous gestures" of the dominant class. Precisely because they are "ungrateful" and "envious," the oppressed are regarded as potential enemies who must be watched.

It could not be otherwise. If the humanization of the oppressed signifies subversion, so also does their freedom; hence the necessity for constant control. And the more the oppressors control the oppressed, the more they change them into apparently inanimate "things." This tendency of the oppressor consciousness to "in-animate" everything and everyone it encounters, in its eagerness to possess, unquestionably corresponds with a tendency to sadism.

> The pleasure in complete domination over another person (or other animate creature) is the very essence of the sadistic drive. Another way of formulating the same thought is to say that the aim of sadism is to transform a man into a thing, something animate into something inanimate, since by complete and absolute control the living loses one essential quality of life—freedom.[9]

Sadistic love is a perverted love—a love of death, not of life. One of the characteristics of the oppressor consciousness and its necrophilic view of the world is thus sadism. As the oppressor consciousness, in order to dominate, tries to deter the drive to search, the restlessness, and the creative power which characterize life, it kills life. More and more, the oppressors are using science and technology as unquestionably powerful instruments for their purpose: the maintenance of the oppressive order through manipulation and repression.[10] The oppressed, as objects, as "things," have no purposes except those their oppressors prescribe for them.

Given the preceding context, another issue of indubitable importance arises: the fact that certain members of the oppressor class join the oppressed in their struggle for liberation, thus moving from one pole of the contradiction to the other. Theirs is a fundamental role, and has been so throughout the history of this struggle. It happens, however, that as they cease to be exploiters or indifferent spectators or simply the heirs of exploitation and move to the side of the exploited, they almost always bring with them the marks of their origin: their prejudices and their deformations, which include a lack of confidence in the people's ability to think, to want, and to know. Accordingly, these adherents to the people's cause constantly run the risk of falling into a type of generosity as malefic as that of the oppressors. The generosity of the oppressors is nourished by an unjust order, which must be maintained in order to justify that generosity. Our converts, on the other hand, truly desire to transform the unjust order; but because of their background they believe that they must be the executors of the transformation. They talk about the people, but they do not trust them; and trusting the people is the indispensable precondition for revolutionary change. A real humanist can be identified more by his trust in the people, which engages him in their struggle, than by a thousand actions in their favor without that trust.

Those who authentically commit themselves to the people must reexamine themselves constantly. This conversion is so radical as not to allow of ambiguous behavior. To affirm this commitment but to consider oneself the proprietor of revolutionary wisdom—which must then be given to (or imposed on) the people—is to retain the old ways. The man who proclaims devotion to the cause of liberation yet is unable to enter into *communion* with the people, whom he continues to regard as totally ignorant, is grievously self-deceived. The convert who approaches the people but feels alarm at each step they take, each doubt they express, and each suggestion they offer, and attempts to impose his "status," remains nostalgic towards his origins.

Conversion to the people requires a profound rebirth. Those who undergo it must take on a new form of existence; they can no longer remain as they were. Only through comradeship with the oppressed can the converts understand their characteristic ways of living and behaving, which in diverse moments reflect the structure of domination. One of these characteristics is the previously mentioned existential duality of the oppressed, who are at the same time themselves and the oppressor whose image they have internalized. Accordingly, until they concretely "discover" their oppressor and in turn their own consciousness, they nearly always express fatalistic attitudes towards their situation.

> The peasant begins to get courage to overcome his dependence when he realizes that he is dependent. Until then, he goes along with the boss and says "What can I do? I'm only a peasant."[11]

When superficially analyzed, this fatalism is sometimes interpreted as a docility that is a trait of national character. Fatalism in the guise of docility is the fruit of an historical and sociological situation, not an essential characteristic of a people's behavior. It almost always is related to the power of destiny or fate or fortune—inevitable forces—or to a distorted view of God. Under the sway of magic and myth, the oppressed (especially the peasants, who are almost submerged in nature)[12] see their suffering, the fruit of exploitation, as the will of God—as if God were the creator of this "organized disorder."

Submerged in reality, the oppressed cannot perceive clearly the "order" which serves the interests of the oppressors whose image they have internalized. Chafing under the restrictions of this order, they often manifest a type of horizontal violence, striking out at their own comrades for the pettiest reasons.

> The colonized man will first manifest this aggressiveness which has been deposited in his bones against his own people. This is the period when the niggers beat each other up, and the police and magistrates do not know which way to turn when faced with the astonishing waves of crime in North Africa. . . . While the settler or the policeman has the right the livelong day to strike the native, to insult him and to make him crawl to them, you will see the native reaching for his knife at the slightest hostile or aggressive glance cast on him by another native; for the last resort of the native is to defend his personality vis-à-vis his brother.[13]

It is possible that in this behavior they are once more manifesting their duality. Because the oppressor exists within their oppressed comrades, when they attack those comrades they are indirectly attacking the oppressor as well.

On the other hand, at a certain point in their existential experience the oppressed feel an irresistible attraction towards the oppressor and his way of life. Sharing this way of life becomes an overpowering aspiration. In their alienation, the oppressed want at any cost to resemble the oppressor, to imitate him, to follow him. This phenomenon is especially prevalent in the middle-class oppressed, who yearn to be equal to the "eminent" men of the upper class. Albert Memmi, in an exceptional analysis of the "colonized mentality," refers to the contempt he felt towards the colonizer, mixed with "passionate" attraction towards him.

> How could the colonizer look after his workers while periodically gunning down a crowd of colonized? How could the colonized deny himself so cruelly yet make such excessive demands? How could he hate the colonizers and yet admire them so passionately? (I too felt this admiration in spite of myself.)[14]

Self-depreciation is another characteristic of the oppressed, which derives from their internalization of the opinion the oppressors hold of them. So often do they hear that they are good for nothing, know nothing and are incapable of learning anything—that they are sick, lazy, and unproductive—that in the end they become convinced of their own unfitness.

> The peasant feels inferior to the boss because the boss seems to be the only one who knows things and is able to run things.[15]

They call themselves ignorant and say the "professor" is the one who has knowledge and to whom they should listen. The criteria of knowledge imposed upon them are the conventional ones. "Why don't you," said a peasant participating in a culture circle, "explain the pictures first? That way it'll take less time and won't give us a headache."

Almost never do they realize that they, too, "know things" they have learned in their relations with the world and with other men. Given the circumstances which have produced their duality, it is only natural that they distrust themselves.

Not infrequently, peasants in educational projects begin to discuss a generative theme in a lively manner, then stop suddenly and say to the educator: "Excuse us, we ought to keep quiet and let you talk. You are the one who knows, we don't know anything." They often insist that there is no difference between them and the animals; when they do admit a difference, it favors the animals. "They are freer than we are."

It is striking, however, to observe how this self-depreciation changes with the first changes in the situation of oppression. I heard a peasant leader say in an *asentamiento*[16] meeting, "They used to say we were unproductive because we were lazy and drunkards. All lies. Now that we are respected as men, we're going to show everyone that we were never drunkards or lazy. We were exploited!"

As long as their ambiguity persists, the oppressed are reluctant to resist, and totally lack confidence in themselves. They have a diffuse, magical belief in the invulnerability and power of the oppressor.[17] The magical force of the landowner's power holds particular sway in the rural areas. A sociologist friend of mine tells of a group of armed peasants in a Latin American country who recently took over a latifundium. For tactical reasons, they planned to hold the landowner as a hostage. But not one peasant had the courage to guard him; his very presence was terrifying. It is also possible that the act of opposing the boss provoked guilt feelings. In truth, the boss was "inside" them.

The oppressed must see examples of the vulnerability of the oppressor so that a contrary conviction can begin to grow within them. Until this occurs, they will continue disheartened, fearful, and beaten.[18] As long as the oppressed remain unaware of the causes of their condition, they fatalistically "accept" their exploitation. Further, they are apt to react in a passive and alienated manner when confronted with the necessity to struggle for their freedom and self-affirmation. Little by little, however, they tend to try out forms of rebellious action. In working towards liberation, one must neither lose sight of this passivity nor overlook the moment of awakening.

Within their unauthentic view of the world and of themselves, the oppressed feel like "things" owned by the oppressor. For the latter, *to be* is *to have*, almost always at the expense of those who have nothing. For the oppressed, at a certain point in their existential experience, *to be* is not to resemble the oppressor, but *to be under* him, to depend on him. Accordingly, the oppressed are emotionally dependent.

The peasant is a dependent. He can't say what he wants. Before he discovers his dependence, he suffers. He lets off steam at home, where he

> shouts at his children, beats them, and despairs. He complains about his wife and thinks everything is dreadful. He doesn't let off steam with the boss because he thinks the boss is a superior being. Lots of times, the peasant gives vent to his sorrows by drinking.[19]

This total emotional dependence can lead the oppressed to what Fromm calls necrophilic behavior: the destruction of life—their own or that of their oppressed fellows.

It is only when the oppressed find the oppressor out and become involved in the organized struggle for their liberation that they begin to believe in themselves. This discovery cannot be purely intellectual but must involve action; nor can it be limited to mere activism, but must include serious reflection: only then will it be a praxis.

Critical and liberating dialogue, which presupposes action, must be carried on with the oppressed at whatever the stage of their struggle for liberation.[20] The content of that dialogue can and should vary in accordance with historical conditions and the level at which the oppressed perceive reality. But to substitute monologue, slogans, and communiqués for dialogue is to attempt to liberate the oppressed with the instruments of domestication. Attempting to liberate the oppressed without their reflective participation in the act of liberation is to treat them as objects which must be saved from a burning building; it is to lead them into the populist pitfall and transform them into masses which can be manipulated.

At all stages of their liberation, the oppressed must see themselves as men engaged in the ontological and historical vocation of becoming more fully human. Reflection and action become imperative when one does not erroneously attempt to dichotomize the content of humanity from its historical forms.

The insistence that the oppressed engage in reflection on their concrete situation is not a call to armchair revolution. On the contrary, reflection—true reflection—leads to action. On the other hand, when the situation calls for action, that action will constitute an authentic praxis only if its consequences become the object of critical reflection. In this sense, the praxis is the new *raison d'être* of the oppressed; and the revolution, which inaugurates the historical moment of this *raison d'être*, is not viable apart from their concomitant conscious involvement. Otherwise, action is pure activism.

To achieve this praxis, however, it is necessary to trust in the oppressed and in their ability to reason. Whoever lacks this trust will fail to initiate (or will abandon) dialogue, reflection, and communication, and will fall into using slogans, communiqués, monologues, and instructions. Superficial conversions to the cause of liberation carry this danger.

Political action on the side of the oppressed must be pedagogical action in the authentic sense of the word, and, therefore, action *with* the oppressed. Those who work for liberation must not take advantage of the emotional dependence of the oppressed—dependence that is the fruit of the concrete situation of domination which surrounds them and which engendered their unauthentic view of the world. Using their dependence to create still greater dependence is an oppressor tactic.

Libertarian action must recognize this dependence as a weak point and must attempt through reflection and action to transform it into independence. However, not even the best-intentioned leadership can bestow independence as a gift. The liberation of the oppressed is a liberation of men, not things. Accordingly, while no one liberates himself by his own efforts alone, neither is he liberated by others. Liberation, a human phenomenon, cannot be achieved by semihumans. Any attempt to treat men as semihumans only dehumanizes them. When men are already dehumanized, due to the oppression they suffer, the process of their liberation must not employ the methods of dehumanization.

The correct method for a revolutionary leadership to employ in the task of liberation is, therefore, *not* "libertarian propaganda." Nor can the leadership merely "implant" in the oppressed a belief in freedom, thus thinking to win their trust. The correct method lies in dialogue. The conviction of the oppressed that they must fight for their liberation is not a gift bestowed by the revolutionary leadership, but the result of their own *conscientização.**

The revolutionary leaders must realize that their own conviction of the necessity for struggle (an indispensable dimension of revolutionary wisdom) was not given to them by anyone else—if it is authentic. This conviction cannot be packaged and sold; it is reached, rather, by means of a totality of reflection and action. Only the leaders' own involvement in reality, within an historical situation, led them to criticize this situation and to wish to change it.

Likewise, the oppressed (who do not commit themselves to the struggle unless they are convinced, and who, if they do not make such a commitment, withhold the indispensable conditions for this struggle) must reach this conviction as Subjects, not as Objects. They also must intervene critically in the situation which surrounds them and whose mark they bear; propaganda cannot achieve this. While the conviction of the necessity for struggle (without which the struggle is unfeasible) is indispensable to the revolutionary leadership (indeed, it was this conviction which constituted that leadership), it is also necessary for the oppressed. It is necessary, that is, unless one intends to carry out the transformation *for* the oppressed rather than *with* them. It is my belief that only the latter form of transformation is valid.

The object in presenting these considerations is to defend the eminently pedagogical character of the revolution. The revolutionary leaders of every epoch who have affirmed that the oppressed must accept the struggle for their liberation—an obvious point—have also thereby implicitly recognized the pedagogical aspect of this struggle. Many of these leaders, however (perhaps due to natural and understandable biases against pedagogy), have ended up using the "educational" methods employed by the oppressor. They deny pedagogical action in the liberation process, but they use propaganda to convince.

It is essential for the oppressed to realize that when they accept the struggle for humanization they also accept, from that moment, their total

* The term *conscientização* refers to learning to perceive social, political, and economic contradictions, and to take action against the oppressive elements of reality.—Ed.

responsibility for the struggle. They must realize that they are fighting not merely for freedom from hunger, but for

> . . . freedom to create and to construct, to wonder and to venture. Such freedom requires that the individual be active and responsible, not a slave or a well-fed cog in the machine. . . . It is not enough that men are not slaves; if social conditions further the existence of automatons, the result will not be love of life, but love of death.[21]

The oppressed, who have been shaped by the death-affirming climate of oppression, must find through their struggle the way to life-affirming humanization, which does not lie *simply* in having more to eat (although it does involve having more to eat and cannot fail to include this aspect). The oppressed have been destroyed precisely because their situation has reduced them to things. In order to regain their humanity they must cease to be things and fight as men. This is a radical requirement. They cannot enter the struggle as objects in order *later* to become men.

The struggle begins with men's recognition that they have been destroyed. Propaganda, management, manipulation—all arms of domination —cannot be the instruments of their rehumanization. The only effective instrument is a humanizing pedagogy in which the revolutionary leadership establishes a permanent relationship of dialogue with the oppressed. In a humanizing pedagogy the method ceases to be an instrument by which the teachers (in this instance, the revolutionary leadership) can manipulate the students (in this instance, the oppressed), because it expresses the consciousness of the students themselves.

> The method is, in fact, the external form of consciousness manifest in acts, which takes on the fundamental property of consciousness—its intentionality. The essence of consciousness is being with the world, and this behavior is permanent and unavoidable. Accordingly, consciousness is in essence a "way towards" something apart from itself, outside itself, which surrounds it and which it apprehends by means of its ideational capacity. Consciousness is thus by definition a method, in the most general sense of the word.[22]

A revolutionary leadership must accordingly practice *co-intentional* education. Teachers and students (leadership and people), co-intent on reality, are both Subjects, not only in the task of unveiling that reality, and thereby coming to know it critically, but in the task of re-creating that knowledge. As they attain this knowledge of reality through common reflection and action, they discover themselves as its permanent re-creators. In this way, the presence of the oppressed in the struggle for their liberation will be what it should be: not pseudo-participation, but committed involvement.

NOTES

1. The current movements of rebellion, especially those of youth, while they necessarily reflect the peculiarities of their respective settings, manifest in their essence this preoccupation with man and men as beings in the world and with the world—pre-

occupation with *what* and *how* they are "being." As they place consumer civilization in judgment, denounce bureaucracies of all types, demand the transformation of the universities (changing the rigid nature of the teacher–student relationship and placing that relationship within the context of reality), propose the transformation of reality itself so that universities can be renewed, attack old orders and established institutions in the attempt to affirm men as the Subjects of decision, all these movements reflect the style of our age, which is more anthropological than anthropocentric.

2. As used throughout this paper, the term "contradiction" denotes the dialectical conflict between opposing social forces.—Translator's note.

3. This fear of freedom is also to be found in the oppressors, though, obviously, in a different form. The oppressed are afraid to embrace freedom; the oppressors are afraid of losing the "freedom" to oppress.

4. See Georg Hegel, *The Phenomenology of Mind* (New York, 1967), pp. 236–237.

5. Analyzing the dialectical relationship between the consciousness of the master and the consciousness of the oppressed, Hegel states: "The one is independent, and its essential nature is to be for itself; the other is dependent, and its essence is life or existence for another. The former is the Master, or Lord, the latter the Bondsman." *Ibid.*, p. 234.

6. "The materialist doctrine that men are products of circumstances and upbringing, and that, therefore, changed men are products of other circumstances and changed upbringing, forgets that it is men that change circumstances and that the educator himself needs educating." Karl Marx and Friedrich Engels, *Selected Works* (New York, 1968), p. 28.

7. This appears to be the fundamental aspect of Mao's Cultural Revolution.

8. This rigidity should not be identified with restraints that must be imposed on the former oppressors so they cannot restore the oppressive order. Rather, it refers to the revolution which becomes stagnant and turns against the people, using the old repressive, bureaucratic State apparatus (which should have been drastically suppressed, as Marx so often emphasized).

9. Eric Fromm, *The Heart of Man* (New York, 1966), p. 32.

10. Regarding the "dominant forms of social control," see Herbert Marcuse, *One-Dimensional Man* (Boston, 1964) and *Eros and Civilization* (Boston, 1955).

11. Words of a peasant during an interview with the author.

12. See Candido Mendes, *Memento dos vivos—A Esquerda católica no Brasil* (Rio, 1966).

13. Frantz Fanon, *The Wretched of the Earth* (New York, 1968), p. 52.

14. *The Colonizer and the Colonized* (Boston, 1967), p. x.

15. Words of a peasant during an interview with the author.

16. *Asentamiento* refers to a production unit of the Chilean agrarian reform experiment. —Translator's note.

17. "The peasant has an almost instinctive fear of the boss." Interview with a peasant.

18. See Regis Debray, *Revolution in the Revolution?* (New York, 1967).

19. Interview with a peasant.

20. Not in the open, of course; that would only provoke the fury of the oppressor and lead to still greater repression.

21. Fromm, *op. cit.*, pp. 52–53.

22. Alvaro Vieira Pinto, from a work in preparation on the philosophy of science. I consider the quoted portion of great importance for the understanding of a problem-posing pedagogy and wish to thank Professor Vieira Pinto for permission to cite his work prior to publication.

bibliography

PART ONE: Methodological Problems of Economic Development

BARAN, PAUL. "Economic Progress and Economic Surplus," *Science and Society*, 17, 4 (Fall 1953), pp. 289–317.

CHENERY, HOLLIS, et al. *Redistribution with Growth: An Approach to Policy.* Oxford: Oxford University Press, 1974.

DALTON, GEORGE. "Economics, Economic Development, and Economic Anthropology," *Journal of Economic Issues*, June 1968.

EMMANUEL, ARGHIRI. "Current Myths of Development," *New Left Review*, May–June 1974.

FEI, JOHN, C. H. and G. RANIS. *Development of the Labor Surplus Economy: Theory and Policy.* Homewood, Ill.: Irwin, 1964.

FRANK, ANDRE GUNDER. "Sociology of Development and Underdevelopment of Sociology." In *Latin America: Underdevelopment or Revolution?* New York: Monthly Review Press, 1969, pp. 21–94.

GOULET, DENIS. *The Cruel Choice.* New York: Atheneum, 1971.

———. "An Ethical Model for the Study of Values," *Harvard Educational Review*, 41, 2 (May 1971).

HEALEY, D. T. "Development Policy: New Thinking About an Interpretation," *Journal of Economic Literature*, September 1972.

HIRSCHMAN, ALBERT O. *The Strategy of Economic Development.* New Haven: Yale University Press, 1958.

MYRDAL, GUNNAR. *Asian Drama: An Inquiry into the Poverty of Nations.* New York: Pantheon, 1968.

———. *Economic Theory and Underdeveloped Regions.* New York: Harper & Row, 1971.

NURKSE, RAGNAR. *Problems of Capital Formation in Underdeveloped Countries.* Oxford: Basil Blackwell, 1958.

SEERS, DUDLEY. "The Limitations of the Special Case," *Bulletin of Oxford Institute of Economics and Statistics*, May 1963.

STREETEN, PAUL. "Economic Models and Their Usefulness for Planning in South Asia." In *Asian Drama: An Inquiry into the Poverty of Nations* by Gunnar Myrdal. New York: Pantheon, 1968.

TODARO, MICHAEL. *Economic Development in the Third World.* New York: Longmans, 1977.

UL HAQ, MAHBUB. *The Poverty Curtain: Choices for the Third World.* New York: Pantheon, 1968.

WEAVER, JAMES H. and KENNETH P. JAMESON. *Economic Development: Competing Paradigms—Competing Parables*, Occasional Paper No. 3, Development Studies Program, U.S. Agency for International Development, 1978.

PART TWO: Economic Development and Underdevelopment in Historical Perspective

BARAN, PAUL. "On the Roots of Backwardness." In *The Political Economy of Growth.* New York: Monthly Review Press, 1957, pp. 134–162.

BARRET-BROWN, MICHAEL. *The Economics of Imperialism.* Baltimore: Penguin, 1974.

DALTON, GEORGE. "History, Politics and Economic Development in Liberia," *Journal of Economic History*, 25, 4 (December 1965), pp. 569–591.

FURTADO, CELSO. *Development and Underdevelopment*. Berkeley: University of California Press, 1964.

——. *Obstacles to Development in Latin America*. New York: Doubleday, 1970.

GERSCHENKRON, ALEXANDER. *Economic Backwardness in Historical Perspective*. New York: Praeger, 1965.

GRIFFIN, K. B. *The Underdevelopment of Spanish America*. London: G. Allen, 1969.

HYMER, STEPHEN. "Robinson Crusoe and Primitive Accumulation," *Monthly Review*, 23 (September 1971), pp. 11–36.

POLANYI, KARL. *The Great Transformation: The Political and Economic Origins of Our Time*. Boston: Beacon Press, 1957.

RODNEY, WALTER. *How Europe Underdeveloped Africa*. Dar es Salaam: Tanzania Publishing House, 1972.

ROSTOW, W. W. *Stages of Economic Growth*, 2nd ed. New York: Cambridge University Press, 1971.

——, ed. *Economics of Take-off into Sustained Growth*. Proceedings of a conference held by the International Economic Association. New York: St. Martin's, 1963.

SUPPLE, BARRY E. *The Experience of Economic Growth: Case Studies in Economic History*. New York: Random House, 1963.

THOMAS, C. *Dependence and Transformation*. New York: Monthly Review Press, 1976.

PART THREE: Economic Development in a Revolutionary World: Trade and Dependency

AMIN, SAMIR. *Neo-Colonialism in West Africa*. New York: Monthly Review Press, 1973.

APTER, DAVID and LOUIS GOLDMAN, eds. *The Multinational Corporation and Social Change*. New York: Praeger, 1976.

EMMANUEL, ARGHIRI. *Unequal Exchange: A Study of the Imperialism of Trade*. New York: Monthly Review Press, 1972.

ERB, GUY F. and VALERIANA KALLAB, eds. *Beyond Dependency: The Developing World Speaks Out*. Washington, D.C.: Overseas Development Council, 1975.

FRANK, ANDRE GUNDER. *Capitalism and Underdevelopment in Latin America: Historical Studies of Chile and Brazil*. New York: Monthly Review Press, 1967.

GOULET, DENIS and MICHAEL HUDSON. *Myth of Aid*. Maryknoll, New York: Orbis Books, 1971.

GRIFFIN, KEITH and JOHN ENOS. "Foreign Assistance: Objectives and Consequences," *Economic Development and Cultural Change*, 18, 3 (April 1970), pp. 313–327.

HAYTER, TERESA. *Aid as Imperialism*. Middlesex: Pelican, 1971.

HYMER, STEPHEN and STEPHEN RESNICK. "International Trade and Uneven Development." In *Trade, Balance of Payments and Growth*, edited by Jagdish Bhagwati. New York: American Elsevier Publishing Co., 1971.

MAGDOFF, HARRY. *The Age of Imperialism*. New York: Monthly Review Press, 1969.

MUELLER, W. and R. NEWFARMER. *Multinational Corporations in Brazil and Mexico: Structural Sources of Economic and Non-economic Power*. Washington, D.C.: Government Printing Office, 1975.

PREBISCH, RAOUL. "The Role of Commercial Policy in Underdeveloped Countries," *American Economic Review*, 49, 2 (May 1959), pp. 251–273.

RADICE, HUGO, ed. *International Firms and Modern Imperialism*. Baltimore: Penguin, 1975.

RHODES, ROBERT I., ed. *Imperialism and Underdevelopment: A Reader*. New York: Monthly Review Press, 1970.

SINGER, H. W. "The Distribution of Gains Between Investing and Borrowing Countries," *American Economic Review*, 40, 2 (May 1950), pp. 473–485.

WACHTEL, HOWARD. *The New Gnomes: Multinational Banks in the Third World*. Washington, D.C.: Transnational Institute, 1977.

WEEKS, JOHN. "Employment, Growth and Foreign Domination in Underdeveloped Countries," *Review of Radical Political Economics*, 4, 1 (Spring 1972).

WEISSKOPF, THOMAS. "Capitalism, Underdevelopment and the Future of the Poor Countries," *Review of Radical Political Economics*, 4, 1 (Spring 1972).

——. "Dependence and Imperialism in India," *Review of Radical Political Economics*, 5, 1 (Spring 1973).

PART FOUR: Agricultural Institutions and Strategy

BARKIN, DAVID. "Cuban Agriculture: A Strategy of Economic Development," *Studies in Comparative International Development*, 7, 1 (Spring 1972), pp. 19–38.

BECKFORD, GEORGE L. *Persistent Poverty: Underdevelopment in Plantation Economies of the Third World*. New York: Oxford University Press, 1972.

CLEAVER, HARRY M., JR. "The Contradictions of the Green Revolution," *Monthly Review*, 24, 2 (June 1972), pp. 83–111.

DUMONT, RENE. *Lands Alive*. London: Merlin Press, 1965.

———. *Types of Rural Economy: Studies in World Agriculture*. New York: Praeger, 1957.

EICHER, CARL and LAURENCE WITT, eds. *Agriculture in Economic Development*. New York: McGraw-Hill, 1964.

GRIFFIN, KEITH. *The Political Economy of Agrarian Change*. London: Macmillan, 1974.

GURLEY, JOHN. "Rural Development in China 1949–72, and the Lessons To Be Learned from It," *World Development*, 3, 7–8 (July–August 1975), pp. 455–471.

JOHNSTON, BRUCE F. and SOREN T. NEILSON. "Agricultural and Structural Transformation in a Developing Economy," *Economic Development and Cultural Change*, 14, 3 (April 1966), pp. 279–301.

JOHNSTON, BRUCE F. and JOHN W. MELLOR. "The Role of Agriculture in Economic Development," *American Economic Review*, 51, 4 (September 1961), pp. 566–593.

LIEDHOLM, C.; D. BYERLEE; C. K. EICHER; and D. S. C. SPENCER. *Rural Employment in Tropical Africa: Summary of Findings*. East Lansing, Mich.: Michigan State University, 1977.

LIPTON, MICHAEL. *Why Poor People Stay Poor: A Study of Urban Bias in World Development*. Cambridge, Mass.: Harvard University Press, 1977.

MELLOR, JOHN. *The New Economics of Growth*. Ithaca, N.Y.: Cornell University Press, 1977.

NOVE, ALEC. "Collectivization of Agriculture in Russia and China." In *Symposium on Economic and Social Problems of the Far East*, edited by E. F. Szczpanik. Hong Kong: Hong Kong University Press, 1962, pp. 16–24.

STAVENHAGEN, RODOLFO, ed. *Agrarian Problems and Peasant Movements in Latin America*. New York: Doubleday, 1970.

PART FIVE: Industrial Institutions and Strategy

CULBERTSON, JOHN M. *Economic Development: An Ecological Approach*. New York: Knopf, 1971.

DOBB, MAURICE. *An Essay on Economic Growth and Planning*. London: Routledge & Kegan, 1960.

GOULET, DENIS. *The Uncertain Promise: Value Conflicts in Technology Transfer*. New York: IDOC North America, 1977.

HIRSCHMAN, ALBERT O. "The Political Economy of Import-Substituting Industrialization in Latin America," *Quarterly Journal of Economics*, 82, 1 (February 1968), pp. 1–32.

HORVAT, BRANKO. *Towards a Theory of Planned Economy*. Belgrade: Yugoslav Institute of Economic Research, 1964.

INTERNATIONAL LABOUR OFFICE. *Employment, Growth and Basic Needs: A One-World Problem*. New York: Praeger, 1977.

NOVE, ALEC. "The Problem of 'Success Indicators' in Soviet Industry," *Economics*, 15, 97 (February 1958), pp. 1–13.

RICHMAN, BARRY. "Capitalists and Managers in Communist China," *Harvard Business Review* (January–February 1967), pp. 57–78.

PART SIX: Comparative Models of Development

BELL, PETER F. and STEPHEN A. RESNICK. "The Contradictions of Post-War Development in Southeast Asia," *Review of Radical Political Economics*, 3, 1 (Spring 1972).

CLINE, HOWARD F. *Mexico: Revolution to Evolution, 1940–1960*. New York: Oxford University Press, 1963.

DESFOSSES, HELEN and JACQUES LEVESQUE, eds. *Socialism in the Third World*. New York: Praeger, 1975.

ECKSTEIN, ALEXANDER. *China's Economic Revolution.* Cambridge: Cambridge University Press, 1977.

GURLEY, JOHN G. *China's Economy and the Maoist Strategy.* New York: Monthly Review Press, 1976.

HORVAT, BRANKO. *An Essay on Yugoslav Society.* New York: International Arts and Sciences Press, 1969.

LOCKWOOD, W. W. *The Economic Development of Japan: Growth and Structural Change, 1868–1938.* Princeton, N.J.: Princeton University Press, 1954.

MACEWAN, A. "Contradictions in Capitalist Development: The Case of Pakistan," *Review of Radical Political Economics,* Spring 1971.

NOVE, ALEC. "The Soviet Model and Underdeveloped Countries," *International Affairs,* 37, 1 (January 1961), pp. 29–38.

SHIVJI, ISSA G. *Class Struggles in Tanzania.* Dar es Salaam: Tanzania Publishing House, 1973.

SPUBLER, NICOLAS. "Contrasting Economic Patterns: Chinese and Soviet Development Strategies," *Soviet Studies,* 15, 1 (July 1963), pp. 1–16.

THOMAS, C. "Bread and Justice: The Struggle for Socialism in Guyana," *Monthly Review,* 38, 4 (September 1976), pp. 23–26.

WHEELRIGHT, E. L. and BRUCE MCFARLANE. *The Chinese Road to Socialism.* New York: Monthly Review Press, 1970.

WILBER, CHARLES K. *The Soviet Model and Underdeveloped Countries.* Chapel Hill: The University of North Carolina Press, 1969.

PART SEVEN: The Human Cost of Development

ADELMAN, I. and C. T. MORRIS. *Economic Growth and Social Equity in Developing Countries.* Stanford, Calif.: Stanford University Press, 1973.

BERGER, PETER L. *Pyramids of Sacrifice: Political Ethics and Social Change.* New York: Basic Books, 1974.

CASTRO, JOSUE'DE. *The Geography of Hunger.* Boston: Little, Brown, 1952.

DE JESUS, MARIA CAROLINA. *Child of the Dark.* New York: Dutton, 1962.

"The Executive Life in Brazil." *Fortune* (December 1972), pp. 115–119.

HOLZMAN, FRANKLYN D. "Consumer Sovereignty and the Rate of Economic Development," *Economia Internazionale,* 11, 2 (1958), pp. 3–17.

LEWIS, W. ARTHUR. "Is Economic Growth Desirable?" In *The Theory of Economic Growth.* Homewood, Ill.: Irwin, 1955.

NAIR, KUSUM. *Blossoms in the Dust.* New York: Praeger, 1962.

SCHWEINITZ, KARL DE, JR. "Economic Growth, Coercion, and Freedom," *World Politics,* 9, 2 (January 1957), pp. 166–192.

PART EIGHT: What Is To Be Done?

CAIRNCROSS, FRANCES. "How Best to Help the Third World Industrialize," *Manchester Guardian Weekly,* September 20, 1975.

FRANK, ANDRE GUNDER. "Capitalist Underdevelopment or Socialist Revolution?" In *Latin America: Underdevelopment or Revolution?* New York: Monthly Review Press, 1969, pp. 371–409.

FREIRE, PAULO. *Pedagogy of the Oppressed.* New York: Herder and Herder, 1972.

GOULET, DENIS. "Political Will: The Key to Guinea-Bissau's Alternative Development Strategy," *International Development Review,* XIX, 4 (1977), pp. 2–8.

GUTIERREZ, GUSTAVO. *A Theology of Liberation.* Maryknoll, New York: Orbis Books, 1972.

HINTON, WILLIAM. *Fanshen: A Documentary of Revolution in a Chinese Village.* New York: Monthly Review Press, 1966.

HIRSCHMAN, ALBERT O. *A Basis for Hope.* New Haven, Conn.: Yale University Press, 1971.

LEONTIEF, WASSILY; ANNE P. CARTER; and PETER PETRI. *The Future of the World Economy.* New York: Oxford University Press, 1977.

MYRDAL, GUNNAR. *The Challenge of World Poverty.* Middlesex: Pelican, 1970.

NYERERE, JULIUS K. *Freedom and Development.* Oxford: Oxford University Press, 1974.

RANDALL, LAURA, ed. *Economic Development: Evolution or Revolution?* Boston: Heath, 1964.

SHAFFER, HARRY G. and JAN. S. PRYBYLA. *From Underdevelopment to Affluence: Western, Soviet and Chinese Views.* New York: Appleton-Century-Crofts, 1968.

TINBERGEN, JAN (coordinator). *Reshaping the International Order: A Report to the Club of Rome.* New York: Dutton, 1976.

ZEITLIN, MAURICE and JAMES PETRAS, eds. *Latin America: Reform or Revolution?* Greenwich, Conn.: Fawcett Publications, 1968.

——. *Revolutionary Politics and the Cuban Working Class.* Princeton, N.J.: Princeton University Press, 1970.

contributors

Irma Adelman is Professor of Economics, University of Maryland. She is the author of *Theories of Economic Growth and Development; Society, Politics and Economic Development: A Quantitative Approach;* and *Economic Growth and Social Equity in Developing Countries.*

Paul Baran was Professor of Economics at Stanford University before his death in 1964. His published works include *The Political Economy of Growth* (1957) and, with Paul M. Sweezy, *Monopoly Capital.* A collection of his articles has been published as *The Longer View: Essays Toward a Critique of Political Economy* (1970).

George L. Beckford is Professor of Economics, University of the West Indies, and author of *Persistent Poverty.*

Peter L. Berger is Professor of Sociology at Rutgers University and the author of *Invitation to Sociology; The Sacred Canopy;* and *The Homeless Mind* and coauthor of *Sociology: A Biographical Approach.* He is a former President of the Society for the Scientific Study of Religion.

R. C. Bhargava is with the Planning Department, Government of Uttar Pradesh, India.

Richard N. Blue is Director of the Development Studies Program, U. S. Agency for International Development. He is the author of *Political Change: A Film Guide.*

Harry M. Cleaver, Jr. is Assistant Professor of Economics, University of Texas, Austin.

Dudley Dillard is Professor of Economics, University of Maryland. He is the author of *The Economics of John Maynard Keynes* and *Economic Development of the North Atlantic Community.*

Peter Dorner is Director of the Land Tenure Center, University of Wisconsin, Madison, and Professor of Agricultural Economics. He is the author of *Land Reform and Economic Development* and *Land Reform in Latin America.*

Andre Gunder Frank has taught economics and social science at the University of Iowa, Michigan State University, Wayne State University, and Sir George Williams University in Montreal. He has also taught at the universities of Brasilia, Chile, and the National University of Mexico. He is the author of *Capitalism and Underdevelopment in Latin America* and *Latin America: Underdevelopment or Revolution?*

Paulo Freire was Professor of the History and Philosophy of Education in the University of Recife, Brazil, until exiled after the military coup in 1964. He then spent five years in Chile, working with UNESCO and the

Chilean Institute for Agrarian Reform in programs of adult education. He is presently serving as Educational Consultant to the office of Education of the World Council of Churches in Geneva.

Celso Furtado was formerly chief of the Development Division of the United Nations Economic Commission for Latin America, director of the Banco Nacional de Desenvolvimento Economico in Rio de Janeiro, executive head of the Agency for the Development of the Brazilian Northeast (SUDENE), and the Minister of Planning in the Brazilian Government. He was exiled after the military coup in 1964 and is now professeur associe at the Faculte de Droit et des Sciences Economiques at the University of Paris. He is the author of *Economic Growth of Brazil; Development and Underdevelopment; Diagnosis of the Brazilian Crisis;* and *Obstacles to Development in Latin America.*

Denis Goulet is a Senior Fellow, Overseas Development Council. Trained in philosophy and political science, he has been associated with both aid and research projects in Africa and Latin America and has taught in institutions in Europe and North America. He is the author of *The Cruel 'Choice; A New Moral Order; The Myth of Aid;* and *Value Conflicts in Technology Transfer.*

Keith Griffin is a Fellow of Magdalen College, Oxford University. He is the author of *Underdevelopment in Spanish America; Financing Development in Latin America;* and *Growth and Inequality in Pakistan.*

John W. Gurley is Professor of Economics, Stanford University. He is the coauthor (with E. S. Shaw) of *Money in a Theory of Finance* and *China's Economy and the Maoist Strategy.*

Mahbub ul Haq was Chief Economist of the Pakistan Planning Commission and was closely associated with the formulation of Pakistan's five-year development plans before joining the World Bank in April 1970, where he is presently serving as Director of the Policy Planning and Program Review Department. He is also the author of *The Poverty Curtain: Choices for the Third World.*

Peter Henriot has written extensively on population issues in underdeveloped countries. He is a Fellow at the Center for Concern, Washington, D.C.

W. F. Ilchman is Professor of Political Science at the University of California at Berkeley. He coauthored *The Political Economy of Change.*

Ivan Illich is one of the founders of the Center for Intercultural Documentation in Cuernavaca, Mexico. He was formerly Vice President of the Universidad Católica de Puerto Rico and worked for five years as a parish priest in a Puerto Rican and Irish neighborhood on the West side of Manhattan. He is the author of *Celebration of Awareness; Deschooling Society; Tools for Conviviality;* and *Medical Nemesis.*

Kenneth P. Jameson lived in Peru for three years, first as a Peace Corps volunteer in Huancayo and then as a Fulbright lecturer in Arequipa and in Lima. He is currently Associate Professor of Economics at the University of Notre Dame where he teaches Economic Development courses with an emphasis on Latin America. His most recent article, entitled "Growth and Equity: Can They Be Happy Together?" appeared in *International Development Review.*

Don Kanel is Professor of Agricultural Economics at the Land Tenure Center, University of Wisconsin, Madison.

Ronald Müller is Associate Professor of Economics, The American University, Washington, D.C. He is the coauthor (with Richard Barnet) of *Global Reach: The Power of the Multinational Corporation.*

Frances Stewart is Fellow of Queen Elizabeth House, Oxford University, and the author of many articles on economic development.

Paul Streeten is Warden of Queen Elizabeth House, Director of the Institute of Commonwealth Studies, and Fellow of Balliol College, Oxford University. He has also taught at the University of Sussex and has been Deputy Director-General of Economic Planning at the Ministry of Overseas Development. He is temporarily Senior Advisor, Policy Planning and Program Review Department, The World Bank. His publications include *Economic Integration; Value in Social Theory; Unfashionable Economics; The Frontiers of Development Studies;* and *Foreign Investment, Transnationals and Developing Countries.*

Albert Waterston is Director of the Governmental Affairs Institute and Professor of Economics, The American University, Washington, D.C. For many years he was involved in development planning for the World Bank. He is the author of *Planning in Pakistan; Planning in Yugoslavia;* and *Development Planning: Lessons of Experience.*

James H. Weaver is Professor of Economics, The American University, Washington, D.C. He is the author of *The International Development Association; University and Revolution;* and *Political Economy: Orthodox and Radical Views.*

Thomas E. Weisskopf is Associate Professor of Economics, University of Michigan. He is the author of *The Capitalist System* and many articles on development and underdevelopment.

Charles K. Wilber is Professor and Chairman of Economics, The University of Notre Dame. He is the author of *The Soviet Model and Underdeveloped Countries* and of articles in a variety of economics journals.

John Wong is Professor of Economics, University of Singapore.

About the Editor

Charles K. Wilber is Chairman and Professor of Economics at the University of Notre Dame. Previously he was Professor of Economics at The American University, Washington, D.C. He is also adjunct senior staff associate, George Meany Center for Labor Studies and a member of the board of directors, Association for Evolutionary Economics. In addition to numerous articles in journals, he has published *The Soviet Model and Underdeveloped Countries* and *The Political Economy of Development and Underdevelopment*. His subject matter ranges from Third World development through economic methodology to the economic history of industrialization in the Soviet Union.